1 MONTH OF
FREE
READING

at

www.ForgottenBooks.com

By purchasing this book you are eligible for one month membership to ForgottenBooks.com, giving you unlimited access to our entire collection of over 700,000 titles via our web site and mobile apps.

To claim your free month visit: www.forgottenbooks.com/free11446

Similar Books Are Available from
www.forgottenbooks.com

INDEX

CHOICE:
 domicil of, 56.
 essentials necessary to acquire a domicil of choice, 76-79.

CHOICE OF LAW:
 meaning of, 2, 3.
 to be determined by the court, 2.

CHOSES IN ACTION:
 when attached, 251-264.
 of wife, as affected by marriage, 352-361.

CITIZENS:
 laws that govern, while abroad, 46-53.
 by birth and by naturalization, 106-125.

CITIZENSHIP:
 by birth and by naturalization, 106-125.

CLERGYMEN:
 domicil of, 96.

COLLISION OF LAW:
 meaning of, 12-15.

COMITY:
 meaning of, 10, 11.
 defined, 11.
 as a matter of obligation, 10, 11.
 in bankruptcy, 200-214.
 in case of executors, administrators, trustees and receivers, 215-229.
 in case of foreign corporations, 265-282.

COMMERCIAL DOMICIL:
 person's character, as neutral or alien enemy, is determined by, 82-83.
 nature of, 83.
 resemblance of to civil domicil, 83, 84.
 difference between civil and commercial, 84.
 as to residence, 84, 85.
 as to intention, 85.
 as to abandonment, 86.
 as to doimcil by operation of law, 86, 87.
 special rules governing, 87.
 civil need not coincide with commercial, 87, 88.

COMMON CARRIER:
 contracts of, 500.

COMMON LAW:
 as to citizenship, 106-125.

COMPETENCY:
>to ehoose domicil, 76.
>of infants, 262-265.
>of married women, 262-265.
>to marry, 338-351.
>to make will, 553-567.

CONFLICT OF LAWS:
>nature of, 1-15.
>questions involved in, 1-3.
>foreign element necessary to have, 1-15.
>origin and growth of, 7-8.
>basis of, 8-11.
>rules of, 11, 12.
>names used instead of, 12-15.

CONSANGUINITY:
>as an impediment to marriage, 338-351.

CONSTRUCTION:
>of contracts, 439.
>of wills, 553-567.

CONSULS:
>jurisdiction of, in unchristian countries, 48.

CONTRACT:
>in uncivilized country, 103, 104.
>actions on, where brought, 126-149.
>marriage as a contract, 188, 338-351.
>capacity of infants to, 262-265.
>capacity of married women to, 262-265.
>in respect to personal property, 362-379.
>theory of the law of, 402.
>place where made, 403.
>validity of, 412.
>formalities of, 439.
>obligation of, 439.
>interpretation of, 439.
>performance of, 439.
>discharge of, 439.
>usurious, 470.
>within statute of frauds, 481.
>of married women, 493.
>contracts of carriers, 500.

CONVEYANCE:
>power of alien, to make, 124, 125.
>power to make, determined by what law, 262-265.
>of real estate, 401.

DEEDS:

capacity to make, 262-265.

DESCENT

of real estate, 547-553.

DIPLOMATIC AGENTS:

privileges of, 47.

DISABILITY:

of infants determined by what law, 262-265.
of married women determined by what law, 262-265.
to contract, 493.
to make will, governed by what law, 553-567.

DISCHARGE:

extra-territorial effect of, in bankruptcy, 200-214.
of contract, what law governs, 439.

DISTRIBUTION

of personal property is governed by law of domicil, 216, 547-553.

DIVORCE:

domicil as determining jurisdiction in case of divorce, 89-95, 184-200
power of states and federal government to regulate, 184-200.
extra-territorial effect of, 184-200.
service of process in cases of, 184-200.
law applied to divorce proceedings, 199.
domicil as determining jurisdiction in, 199.

DOMICIL:

defined, 56.
requisites of, 56.
intention as an element of, 56, 63-75, 77-79.
residence as an element of, 56, 63-75.
of origin, 56, 63-75.
of choice, 56, 63-75.
presumption in case of, 56.
importance of, 57.
distinguished from other terms, 57.
compared with "home," "residence," "habitancy" and "nationality,
57, 58.
how acquired or lost, 64, 65, 66, 67-75.
of origin, how acquired and lost, 57-68, 75.
of choice, how acquired and lost, 57-68, 75.
not governed by allegiance, 57-68.
reverter of, in case of domicil of origin, 57-68.
purpose of, 68.
a person cannot be without a domicil, 68, 69.

38

PROPERTY
  alien's right to acquire, 106-125.
  locality of actions, for injury to, 126-149.
  as affected by marriage, 352-361.
  transfers of personal, 362-379.
  conditional sales of personal, 380, 386, 392.
  gifts of personal, 397.
  mortgages of personal, 400.
  wills of, 553 567.

PUBLIC INTERNATIONAL LAW:
  defined and distinguished, 15.
  by what authority is it a part of the law of a country, 16-53.

REAL PROPERTY:
  taxes on is governed by what law, 99-101.
  conveyances of, 401.
  descent of, 547-553.
  will of, 553-567.

RECEIVER:
  powers of, 217-229.

REMEDY:
  is procedure, 573-580.

RESIDENCE:
  as an element in acquiring domicil, 56.
  meaning of, when used in a statute, 57, 58.
  actual residence as an element of domicil, 76-79.

REVERTER OF DOMICIL:
  in case of domicil of origin, 63-75, 79-82.
  when the rule applies, 79-82.

RIGHTS:
  of aliens, 106-125.
  of foreign assignees, in case of bankruptcy, 200-214.

SERVANTS:
  domicil of, 96, 97.

SERVICE·
  of process, 169-184.

SET-OFF:
  a part of procedure, 573-580.

SHIPS:
  are governed by what laws, 16-53.
  on the high seas, governed by what law, 52.

SITUS:
  of a debt, 254-261.

Floyd R. Mechem, Professor of Law in the University of Chicago. Second Edition. $2.00.

Agency—Mechem on Agency. A treatise by Floyd R. Mechem. $4.00 net.

American Law—Andrews' American Law. Second Edition by J. D. Andrews. 2 vols. $12.00. Same, 1 vol. ed., $5.00 net.

Bailments and Carriers—Goddard's Outlines, by Edwin C. Goddard, Professor of Law in the University of Michigan. $2.50 net.

Bailments and Carriers—Van Zile, by Philip T. Van Zile, Dean Detroit College of Law. Second Ed. $5.00.

Bankruptcy—Bays. A handbook on Debtor, Creditor and Bankruptcy, by A. W. Bays. $1.50.

Banks and Banking. A handbook by A. W. Bays. $1.50.

Blackstone's Commentaries—Cooley. 4th Edition Commentaries on the Laws of England by William Blackstone, with a translation of all foreign words and phrases appearing in the text and very full and copious notes by Thomas M. Cooley. Fourth Edition by J. D. Andrews. 2 volumes $9.00 net. Same, 3rd Edition $6.00 net.

Business Methods and Finance—By George L. Corlis, Dean Benton College of Law.

Carriers—Hutchinson. The Law of Carriers. Second Ed. by Floyd R. Mechem. $4.00.

Code Pleading—Phillips. Principles of Pleadings in Actions under the Codes of Civil Procedure by G. L. Phillips. $4.00 net.

Commercial Law—Bays. American Commercial Law Series. 9 vols. $12.00. Separately per volume $1.50.

Commercial Law—Corlis. By George L. Corlis, Dean Benton College of Law. 1 volume.

Common Law Pleading—Andrews' Stephen's Pleadings. By Henry John Stephen. Second Edition by J. D. Andrews. $3.50 net.

Contracts—Anson. Second American Edition, by Jerome C. Knowlton, Professor of Law in the University of Michigan. $3.50 net.

Contracts—Bays. A handbook, by A. W. Bays. $1.50.

Contracts—Hammon. The General Principles of Contracts, by Louis L. Hammon. $5.00 net.

Contracts—Willis. A treatise by Hugh E. Willis, Professor of Law, University of Minnesota Law School. $2.00 net.

Corporations—Municipal—Elliott. Second Edition, by John E. Macy, Professor in Boston University Law School. $4.00 net.

Corporations—Bays. A handbook by A. W. Bays. $1.50.

Corporations—Marshall—[Private]. A treatise. Second Edition by William L. Marshall and William L. Clark. $4.00 net.

Corporations—Abbott—[Public]. A treatise by Howard S. Abbott. 1 volume $4.00.

Criminal Law—Clark & Marshall—Crimes. Second Edition by Herschell B. Lazell. $5.00 net.

Criminal Law and Procedure Outlines—Washburn. By Emery Washburn. Third Ed. by M. D. Ewell. $2.50 net.

Damages—Willis. A concise treatise by Hugh E. Willis, Professor of Law, University of Minnesota. $2.00 net.

Dictionary—Cyclopedic Law Dictionary—Words, Phrases, Maxims, Definitions, Translations Thumb Index. 1 large volume $6.00.

Dictionary—Kinney's Dictionary and Glossary. $4.00.

by G. Fred Rush. $4.

Evidence—Hammon. A treatise mon. $5.00 net.

Evidence—Hughes. An illus Thomas W. Hughes, Profes University of Illinois. $4.00

Evidence—Kennedy. A pract Richard Lee Kennedy. $2.00

Evidence—Reynolds Theory of iam Reynolds. $3.00 net.

Evidence—Reynolds on Eviden and Cross Examination, Law

Insurance—Bays. A handbook,

Insurance—Kerr. $5.00.

International Law—Bordwell's W. P. Bordwell, Professor of Missouri. $3.50 net.

International Law—Taylor. of, by Hannis Taylor. $5.50

Jurisprudence—Pattee. The Law, by W. S. Pattee, Dea University of Minnesota. $

Legal Ethics—Warvelle. A fessional conduct by George

Negotiable Instruments—Bays Alfred W. Bays. $1.50.

Negotiable Instruments—B Bunker, Professor of Law Michigan Law School. $3.50

Negotiable Instruments—Ogde of the Indiana Law School.

Negotiable Instruments—Selov by Wm. H. Oppenheimer.

Partnership—Bays. A handbook

Partnership—Mechem. By Second edition, $2.50 net.

Partnership—Shumaker, by Second edition. $3.00 net.

Personal Property—Childs, by sometime Professor of La College of Law. $4.00 net.

Quizzers—Walsh. Students Q bers. Paper, each 50 cent

Real Property—Bays. A h Bays. $1.50.

Real Property—Tiffany, by 2 volumes. $10.00. Student's edition [2 volume

Real Property—Warvelle. E W. Warvelle. Second editi

Roman Law—Sandar's Justin American Ed. by W. E.

Sales—A handbook by Alfre

Suretyship—Spencer. A tre and Guaranty, by Edward Marquette Univ., College of

Torts—Cooley. A new Law John Lewis. $5.00 net.

Torts—Cooley's Elements, by $3.50 net.

Trusts—Pound, by Roscoe Pou

ISBN 978-1-330-04284-7
PIBN 10011446

Similar Books Are Available from
www.forgottenbooks.com

Legal Maxims, Vol. 1
With Observations and Cases, by George Frederick Wharton

Readings on the History and System of the Common Law
by Roscoe Pound

A Handbook of Bankruptcy Law
Embodying the Full Text of the Act of Congress, by Henry Campbell Black

The Principles of Pleading and Practice in Civil Actions in the High Court of Justice
by W. Blake Odgers

Real Estate Principles and Practices
by Philip A. Benson

The New Law-Dictionary
by Giles Jacob

On Foreign Jurisdiction and the Extradition of Criminals
by George Cornewall Lewis

Principles of the Law of Contract
by William Reynell Anson

A Treatise of the Law Relative to Merchant Ships and Seamen, Vol. 1 of 4
by Charles Abbott

A Manual of Constitutional History, Founded on the Works of Hallam, Creasy, May and Broom
by Forrest Fulton

Patent and Trade Mark Laws of the World
by B. Singer

Thomas Aquinas
Treatise on Law (Summa Theologica, Questions 90-97), by Thomas Aquinas

A Treatise on the Conflict of Laws, and the Limits of Their Operation in Respect of Place and Time
by Friedrich Carl von Savigny

A Summary of the Law of Lien
by Basil Montagu

Introduction to Roman Law
In Twelve Academical Lectures, by James Hadley

The Science of Law
by Sheldon Amos

The Oldest Laws in the World
Being an Account of the Hammurabi Code and the Sinaitic Legislation, by Chilperic Edwards

The Law of Torts
by Francis M. Burdick

Cases on Criminal Law
by Jerome C. Knowlton

Constitution and Laws of the Cherokee Nation
by Cherokee Nation

CHAPTER XIII.

CHAPTER XIV.

CHAPTER XV.

CHAPTER XVI.

CASES REPORTED

G.

H.

I

J.

L.

M.

N.

LEADING CASES

ON

PRIVATE INTERNATIONAL LAW.

CHAPTER I.

INTRODUCTION.

THE NATURE OF THE SUBJECT.

[Dicey Conflict of Laws, p. 1.*]

1. Questions Involved.
2. The Law of a Country.
3. Origin and Growth of Private International Law.
4. Basis of Private International Law.
5. Similarity of Rules as to the Choice of Law.
6. Various Names of the Subject.
7. Private International Law Defined and Distinguished.

Most of the cases which occupy an English Court are in every respect of a purely English character; the parties are Englishmen, and the cause of action arises wholly in England, as where *A*, a London tradesman, sues *X*, a citizen of London, for the price of goods sold and delivered in London. When this is so, every act done, or alleged to be done, by either of the parties clearly depends for its legal character on the ordinary rules of English law.

Cases, however, frequently come before our Courts which contain some foreign element; the parties, one or both of them, may be of foreign nationality, as where an Italian sues a Frenchman for the price of goods sold and delivered at Liverpool; the cause of action, or ground of defence, may depend upon transactions taking place wholly or in part in a foreign country; as where *A* sues *X* for an assault at Paris, or on a contract made in France and broken in England, or where *X* pleads in his defence a discharge under the French bankruptcy law; the transactions, lastly, in question, though taking place wholly in England, may, in some

*This extract is inserted by permission of the publishers of the American Edition of "Dicey on the Conflict of Laws."

way, have reference to the law or customs of a foreign country; this is so, for instance, when *A* wishes to enforce the trusts of a marriage settlement executed in England, but which on the face of it, or by implication, refers to French or Italian law.

Questions Involved.—Whenever a case containing any foreign element calls for decision, the judge before whom it is tried must, either expressly or tacitly, find an answer to, at least, two preliminary questions.

First Question.—Is the case before him one which any English Court has, according to the law of England, a right to determine?

The primary business of English tribunals is to adjudicate on transactions taking place in England between Englishmen, or at any rate between persons resident in England; or, briefly, to decide English disputes. There clearly may be matters taking place in a foreign country, or between foreigners, with which no English Court has, according to the law of England, any concern whatever; thus no Division of the High Court, and *a fortiori* no other English tribunal, will entertain an action for the recovery of land in any other country than England. When, therefore, a case coming before an English judge contains a foreign element, he must tacitly or expressly determine whether it is one on which he has a right to adjudicate. This first question is a question of jurisdiction (*forum*).

Second Question.—What (assuming the question of jurisdiction to be answered affirmatively) is the body of law with reference to which the rights of the parties are according to the principles of the law of England to be determined?

Is the judge, that is to say, to apply to the matter in dispute (*e. g.*, the right of *A* to obtain damages from *X* for an assault at Paris) the ordinary rules of English law applicable to like transactions taking place between Englishmen in England, or must he, because of the "foreign element" in the case, apply to its decision the rules of some foreign law, *e. g.*, the provisions of French law as to assaults?

This second question is an inquiry not as to jurisdiction, but as to the choice of law (*lex*).

Each of these inquiries, be it noted, must be answered by any judge, English or foreign, in accordance with definite principles, and, by an English judge, sitting in an English Court, in accordance with principles or rules to be found in the law of England. These rules make up that department of English law which deals with the conflict or laws, and may be provisionally described as principles of the law of England, governing the extra-territorial operation of law or recognition of rights. This branch of English law is as much part of the law of England as the Statute of Frauds, or the Statute of Distributions. The subject, however, with which we are dealing is, partly from ambiguity of language, and partly from other causes, involved in so much obscurity of its own that we may well examine somewhat further into the nature of our topic, and look at the matter from a somewhat different point of view from the side whence we have hitherto regarded it.

The Law of a Country.—The law of every country, as for example of England, consists of all the principles, rules, or maxims, enforced by the Courts of that country under the authority of the state.

It makes no difference for our present purpose, whether these principles be written or unwritten; whether they be expressed in Acts of Parliament, or exist as customs; whether they are the result of direct legislation, or are created by judicial decisions. Any rule or maxim whatsoever, which, when the proper occasion arises, will be enforced by the Courts of England under the authority of the state, is part of the law of England. Thus the rule that land descends to the heir, derived as it is from the Common Law; the rule that personal property goes to the next of kin, depending as it now does upon the Statute of Distributions; the principle that a simple contract is not valid without a consideration; or the doctrine, created as it is by judicial legislation, that the validity of a marriage ceremony, wherever made, depends on the law of the country where the marriage is celebrated, are each of them, however different in character and origin, rules enforced by English Courts, and therefore each of them both laws and part of the law of England.

The law of England, however, taken in its most extended and most proper sense, may, in common with the law of every civilized country, e. g., of Italy or of France, be divided into two branches.

The first branch of the law of England may be described, if not with absolute precision, yet with sufficient accuracy for our present object, as the body of rules which regulate the rights of the inhabitants of England and determine the legal effect of transactions taking place between Englishmen within the limits of England. Indirectly, indeed, these rules may, under certain circumstances, affect transactions taking place abroad; their direct and immediate effect, however, is to regulate the actions of men and women living in England. They may, therefore, for the sake of distinction from the other branch or portion of English law, be called the "territorial" or "local" law of England. This territorial law constitutes indeed so much the oldest and most important part of English law, that it has been constantly taken to be, and treated as, the whole of the law of the land. Blackstone's Commentaries, for example, though written with the avowed object of describing the whole of the "law of England," contain no mention of any rules which do not belong to the territorial or local law. With this branch of the law, important though it be, the writer on the conflict of laws has no direct concern.

The second branch of the law of England consists of rules which do not directly determine the rights or liabilities of particular persons, but which determine the limits of the jurisdiction to be exercised by the English Courts taken as a whole, and also the choice of the body of law, whether the territorial law of England or the law of any foreign country, by reference to which English Courts are to determine the different matters brought before them for decision.

These rules about jurisdiction and about the choice of law, which make up the second branch of the law of England, are directions for the guidance of the judges.

As to purely English transactions no such guidance can be needed. English Courts clearly have jurisdiction in respect of matters taking place within this country, for to determine the legal effect of such matters is the very object for which the Courts are constituted. The legal character, again, of acts done in England by Englishmen must obviously be determined by reference to the territorial law of England, since the very object for which this law is created is to regulate the actions of Englishmen in England.

The rules therefore in question, since they are inapplicable to purely English transactions, must have reference to cases which contain, or may contain, some foreign element. They are, in fact, directions for the guidance of the judges when called upon to deal with transactions which, either because of the foreign character of one, or of both, of the parties, or because something material to the case has been done, or is intended to be done, in a foreign country, or has been done with reference to some foreign law, may, possibly at least, require for their fair determination, reference to the provisions of some foreign law. If, for the sake of convenience, we dismiss for the moment from our attention all questions of jurisdiction, this second branch of the law of England nay be described in the following terms. It is that part of the aw of England which provides directions for the judges when alled upon to adjudicate upon any question in which the rights of oreigners, or the effect of acts done, or to be done, in a foreign :ountry, or with reference to a foreign law, require determination. These directions determine whether a given class of cases (*e. g.*, :ases as to contracts made in foreign countries) must be decided vholly by reference to the territorial law of England, or either vholly, or in part, by reference to the law of some foreign coun- ry, *e. g.*, France. Since these directions for the choice of law nay provide either that the territorial law of England shall, under :ertain circumstances, govern acts taking place abroad, *e. g.*, the >roper execution of a will made in France by a testator domiciled n England, or that foreign law shall, under certain circumstances, govern acts done in England, *e. g.*, the proper execution of a will nade in England by a testator domiciled in ·France, they may, is has been already intimated, be described as "rules for determin- ing the extra-territorial operation of law," or better, "the extra- territorial recognition of rights," and the branch of law with which we are concerned is, if we include within it both rules as :o jurisdiction and rules as to the choice of law, nothing else than :he subject generally treated of by English and American writers under the title of Conflict of Laws, and by Continental authors under the title of Private International Law.

A master of this twofold division of the law of England (or for that matter of any civilized country) puts a student on his guard against an ambiguity of language which, unless clearly per- :eived, introduces confusion into every discussion concerning the :onflict of laws.

The term "law of a given country," *e. g.*, law of England, or law of France, is an expression which, under different forms, nec- :ssarily recurs again and again in every treatise on private inter- national law. It is further an expression which appears to be per- fectly intelligible, and therefore not to demand any explanation. Yet, like many other current phrases, it is ambiguous. For the term "law of a given country" has, at least, two meanings. It may mean, and this is its most proper sense, every rule enforced by the Courts of that country. It may mean, on the other hand, and this is a very usual sense, that part of the rules enforced by the Courts of a given country which makes up the "local" or "ter- ritorial" law of a country. To express the same thing in a dif- ferent form, the term "law of a country" may be used as either

including the rules for the choice of law, or as excluding such
rules and including only those rules or laws which, as they refer
to transactions taking place among the inhabitants of a country
within the limits thereof, I have called local or territorial law.

This ambiguity may be best understood by following out its
application to the expression "law of England."

The term "law of England" may, on the one hand, mean
every rule or maxim enforced or recognized by the English
Courts, including the rules or directions followed by English
judges as to the limits of jurisdiction and as to the choice of law.
This is the sense in which the expression is used in the absolutely
true statement that "every case which comes before an English
Court must be decided in accordance with the law of England."
The term "law of England" may, on the other hand, mean, not
the whole of the law of England, but the local or territorial law
of England excluding the rules or directions followed by English
judges as to the limits of jurisdiction or as to the choice of law.
This is the sense in which the expression is used in the also absolutely true statements that "the validity of a will executed in England by a Frenchman domiciled in France is determined by English judges not in accordance with the law of England but in accordance with the law of France," or that "a will of freehold lands
in England, though executed by a foreigner abroad, will not be
valid unless executed in conformity with the law of England,".
i. e., with the provision of the Wills Act, 1837.

Hence the assertion that "while all cases which come for decision before an English Court must be decided in accordance
with the law of England, yet many such cases are, and must be,
decided in accordance, not with the law of England, but with the
law of a foreign country, e. g., France," though it sound paradox-
ical, or self-contradictory, is strictly true. The apparent contradiction is removed when we observe that in the two parts of the
foregoing statement the term law of England is used in two
different senses: in the earlier portion it means the whole law of
England, in the latter it means the territorial law of England.
This ambiguity is made plain to any one who weighs the meaning
of the well-known dictum of Lord Stowell with regard to the law
regulating the validity of a marriage celebrated in a foreign country. The question, it is therein laid down, "being entertained in
"an English Court, it must be adjudicated according to the prin-
"ciples of English law, applicable to such a case. But the only
"principle applicable to such a case by the laws of England is,

"that the validity of Miss Gordon's marriage rights must be tried "by reference to the law of the country, where, if they exist at all, "they had their origin. Having furnished this principle, the law "of England withdraws altogether, and leaves the legal question "to the exclusive judgment of the law of Scotland."

Let it be further borne in mind that the ambiguity affecting the term law of England affects the term law of France, law of Italy, and the like, and that with regard to statements where these terms are used, the reader should always carefully consider whether the expression is intended to include or to exclude the rules followed by the Courts of the given country, *e. g.*, France, as to the choice of law.

The general character of our subject being then understood, there remain several subordinate points which deserve consideration.

Origin and Growth of Private International Law.— *First.* The branch of law containing rules for the selection of law is in England, as elsewhere, of later growth than the territorial law of the land.

The development of rules about the conflict of law implies both the existence of different countries governed by different laws,—a condition of things which hardly existed when the law of Rome was the law of the civilized world,—and also the existence of peaceful and commercial intercourse between independent countries,—a condition of things which had no continuous existence during the ages of mediæval barbarism.

It was not, therefore, until the development of something like the state of society now existing in modern Europe that questions about the conflict of laws powerfully arrested the attention of lawyers. It is a fact of great significance that the countries where attention was first paid to this branch of law, and where it has been studied with the greatest care, have been countries such as Holland, Germany, Great Britain, or the United States, composed of communities, which, though governed under different laws, have been united by the force either of law or of sentiment into something like one state or confederacy. States of this description, such for example as the United Netherlands, both felt sooner than others the need for giving extra-territorial effect to local laws, and also found less difficulty than did other countries in meeting this necessity; since the local laws which the Courts applied were not in strictness foreign laws, but, from one point of view, laws prevailing in different parts of one state. In this mat-

ter the history of France supplies one of these instructive exceptions which prove the rule. France was never a confederacy, but
the provinces of the monarchy were governed by different laws.
Hence the call for determining the extra-provincial effect of customs raised judicial problems about the choice of law. It is also
noteworthy that few English decisions bearing on our subject are
of earlier date than the Union with Scotland. None are known
to me earlier than the accession of James I.

Basis of Private International Law.—*Secondly.* The
growth of rules for the choice of law is the necessary result of
the peaceful existence of independent nations combined with the
prevalence of commercial intercourse. From the moment that
these conditions are realized, the judges of every country are
compelled by considerations of the most obvious convenience to
exercise a choice of law, or, in other words, to apply foreign laws.
That this is so may be seen from an examination of the only
courses which, when a case involving any foreign element calls
for decision, are, even conceivably, open to the Courts of any
country forming part of the society of civilized nations.

The necessity for choosing between the application of
different laws might conceivably be avoided by rigid adherence
to one of two principles.

The Courts of any country, e. g., of England, might, on the
one hand, decline to give any decision on cases involving any foreign element, i. e., cases either to which a foreigner was a party,
or which were connected with any transaction taking place wholly,
or in part, beyond the limits of England.

No need for a choice of law would then arise, for the Courts
would in effect decline to decide any question not clearly governed
by the territorial law of England. This course of action would,
however, exclude Englishmen no less than foreigners from recourse to English tribunals. For an Englishman who had entered
into a contract with a Scotchman at Edinburgh, or with a Frenchman at Paris, would, if the principle suggested were rigidly carried out, be unable to bring an action in the English Courts for a
breach of the contract. To which it may be added that, were the
same principle adopted by the Courts of other countries, neither
party to such a contract would have any remedy anywhere for its
breach.

The English Courts might, on the other hand, determine to
decide every matter brought before them, whatever the cause of
action and wherever it arose, solely with reference to the local

law of England, and hence determine the effect of things done in Scotland or in France, exactly as they would do if the transactions had taken place between Englishmen in England.

Difficulties about the choice of law would, by the adoption of this principle, be undoubtedly removed, since the sole rule of selection would be, that the territorial law of England must in all cases be selected, or, in other words, that there must be no choice at all. Gross injustice would, however, inevitably result as well to Englishmen as to foreigners. The object of a legal decision or judgment is to enforce existing rights, or give compensation for the breach thereof, and it is not the object of a legal decision or judgment to create new rights, except in so far as such creation may be necessary for the enforcement or protection of rights already in existence. But to determine the legal effects of acts done in Scotland or in France, e. g., of a contract made between Scotchmen in Edinburgh, solely with reference to the local law of England, would be to confer upon one or other of the parties, or perhaps upon both, new rights quite different from those acquired under the agreement, or, in other words, to fail in the very object which it is sought to attain by means of a judgment. That this is so becomes even more manifest if we place before our minds a case of which the foreign element consists in the fact that two persons have intended in some transaction to regulate their rights by reference to a foreign law. *A* and *X*, Englishmen, living in England, agree in London that certain property shall be settled, as far as English law allows, in accordance with the rules of French law. If in interpreting the settlement an English judge were to decline to take any notice of the law of France, he would clearly fail in carrying out the intention of the parties, or, in other words, would fail in ensuring to either of them his rights under the settlement.

If, therefore, it is impossible for the Courts of any country, without injustice and damage to natives, no less than to foreigners, either to decline all jurisdiction in respect of foreign transactions, or to apply to such transactions no rules except those of the local law, a consequence follows which has hardly been sufficiently noted. It is this: that the Courts of every civilized country are constrained, not only by logical, but by practical necessity, to concern themselves with the choice of law, and must occasionally give extra-territorial effect now to their own local law, now to the law of some foreign state.

Is, or is not the enforcement of foreign law a matter of "com‐ity"? This is an inquiry which has greatly exercised the minds of jurists. We can now see that the disputes to which it has given rise are little better than examples of idle logomachy. If the assertion that the recognition or enforcement of foreign law depends upon comity means only that the law of no country can have effect as law beyond the territory of the sovereign by whom it was imposed, unless by permission of the state where it is allowed to operate, the statement expresses, though obscurely, a real and important fact. If, on the other hand, the assertion that the recognition or enforcement of foreign laws depends upon comity is meant to imply that, to take a concrete case, when Eng‐lish judges apply French law, they do so out of courtesy to the French Republic, then the term comity is used to cover a view which, if really held by any serious thinker, affords a singular specimen of confusion of thought produced by laxity of language. The application of foreign law is not a matter of caprice or option, it does not arise from the desire of the sovereign of England, or of any other sovereign, to show courtesy to other states. It flows from the impossibility of otherwise determining whole classes of cases without gross inconvenience and injustice to litigants, whether natives or foreigners.[1] It were well too in this matter to give heed to two observations. The first is that the Courts, *e. g.*, of England, never in strictness enforce foreign law; when they are said to do so, they enforce not foreign laws, but rights

---

[1] "In the silence of any positive rule, affirming, or denying, or restrain‐ing the operation of foreign laws, Courts of justice presume the tacit adoption of them by their own government, unless they are repugnant to its policy or prejudicial to its interests. It is not the comity of the Courts, but the comity of the nation [or state] which is administered, and ascer‐tained in the same way, and guided by the same reasoning by which all other principles of municipal law are ascertained and guided." *Bank of Augusta v. Earle*, 13 *Pet.* (*U. S.*) 589. (*1839*); *Story Conflict of Laws, 37.*

Mr. Justice Gray in the case of *Hilton v. Guyot*, 159 *U. S. 113*, 16 *S. C. R. 139*, held as follows: "No law has any effect, of its own force, beyond the limits of the sovereignty from which its authority is derived. The extent to which the law of one nation, as put in force within its territory, whether by executive order, by legislative act, or by judicial decree, shall be allowed to operate within the dominion of another nation, depends upon what our greatest jurists have been content to call "the comity of nations," although the phrase has been often criticised, no satisfactory substitute has been suggested.

"Comity," in the legal sense, is neither a matter of absolute obligation, on the one hand, nor of mere courtesy and good will, upon the other. But it is the recognition which one nation allows within its territory to the legislative, executive or judicial acts of another nation, having due regard both to international duty and convenience, and to the rights of its own citizens or of other persons who are under the protection of its laws."

acquired under foreign laws. The second observation is, that disputes about the effect of comity—and the remark applies to other controversies about the conflict of laws—have been confused by mixing together the question what, on a given subject, is the rule, or, in other words, the law which will be enforced by the judges, with the different inquiry, what are the motives which have led judges or legislators to adopt a particular rule as law. Assume, for the sake of argument, the truth of the doctrine that the enforcement of foreign laws depends upon comity. This dogma throws no light whatever on the nature of the rules upheld by English or other Courts as to the enforcement of foreign laws. To know, for example, that the Courts are influenced by considerations of comity is no guide to any one who attempts to answer the inquiry whether the tribunals of a given country accept "domicil," as do English Courts, or "nationality," as do Italian Courts, as determining the law which affects the validity of a will.

Similarity of Rules as to the Choice of Law.—*Thirdly.* Though the rules as to extra-territorial effect of law enforced by our Courts are part of the law of England, it should be noted that the law of every other civilized country, *e. g.,* of France, of Italy, or of Germany, contains rules for the choice of law, not indeed identical with, but very similar to, the rules for the same purpose to be found in the law of England.

That this should be so is natural. In any given case the laws among which a choice may rationally be made are limited in number. The selection of one or more of these laws is not a matter of caprice, but depends upon more or less definite reasons which are likely to influence all Courts and legislators. The grounds, for example, which induce the Courts of England to determine the formal validity of a contract, by the law of the place where it is made, are likely to weigh with the Courts of France or of Germany. There exists, moreover, a palpable convenience in the adoption by different countries of the same principle for the choice of law. Hence the mere fact that a particular rule for the selection of law has been followed by the French and American Courts is a valid though not absolutely decisive reason in favor of its being adopted by English Courts; and an appreciation of the advantages to be derived from uniformity has undoubtedly influenced both Courts and legislatures, when called upon to determine in a given class of cases what should be the rule as to the extra-territorial effect of law. Thus has come into existence a body of rules which, though in different countries they exist as laws only by virtue of the law of each particular country, and though they are by no means everywhere identical, exhibit wherever they exist marked features of similarity. This likeness is increased by the fact that the object aimed at by the Courts of different countries, in the adoption of rules as to the extra-territorial effect of law, is everywhere in substance one and the same. This aim is, in the main, to secure the extra-territorial effect of rights. All, or nearly all, the rules as to the choice of law, which are adopted by different civilized countries, are provisions for applying the principle that rights duly acquired under the law of one country shall be recognized in every country. Thus the law of England and the law of France seek in this respect the same object, viz., the securing that the rights which a man has attained by marriage, by purchase, or otherwise, *e. g.*, in Italy, shall be enforceable and enjoyable by him in England or France, and, conversely, that the rights which he has acquired in England may be enforceable and enjoyable by him in Italy. This community of the aim, pursued by the Courts and legislatures of different countries, lies at the very foundation of our subject. It is of itself almost enough to explain the great similarity between the rules as to the choice of law adopted by different countries.

Various Names of the Subject.—*Fourthly.* The department of law, whereof we have been considering the nature, has been called by various names, none of which are free from objection.

By many American writers, and notably by Story, it has been designated as the "conflict of laws." The apparent appropriateness of the name may be best seen from an example of the kind of case in which a "conflict" is supposed to arise. *H* and *W*, Portuguese subjects, are first cousins. By the law of Portugal they are legally incapable of intermarriage. They come to England and there marry each other in accordance with the formalities required by the English Marriage Acts. Our Courts are called upon to pronounce upon the validity of the marriage. If the law of England be the test the mariage is valid; if the law of Portugal be the test the marriage is invalid. The question at issue, it may be said, is, whether the law of England or the law of Portugal is to prevail. Here we have a conflict, and the branch of law which contains rules for determining it may be said to deal with the conflict of laws, and be for brevity's sake called by that title.

The defect, however, of the name is that the supposed "conflict" is fictitious and never really takes place. If English tribunals decide the matter in hand, with reference to the law of Portugal, they take this course not because Portuguese law vanquishes English law, but because it is a principle of the law of England that, under certain circumstances, marriages between Portuguese subjects shall depend for their validity on conformity with the law of Portugal. Any such expression, moreover, as "conflict," or "collision," of laws, has the further radical defect of concealing from view the circumstance that the question by the law of what country a given transaction shall be governed, is often a matter too plain to admit of doubt. No judge probably ever doubted that the validity of a contract for the purchase and sale of goods between French subjects made at Paris, and performed, or intended to be performed, in France, depends upon the rules of French law. The term conflict of laws has been defended on the ground of its applicability, not to any collision between the laws themselves, but to a conflict in the mind of a judge on the question which of two systems of law should govern a given case. This suggestion gives, however, a forced and new sense to a received expression. It also amounts simply to a plea that the term conflict of laws may be used as an inaccurate equivalent for the far less objectionable phrase choice of law.

Modern authors, and notably Mr. Westlake, have named our subject Private International Law.

This expression is handy and manageable. It brings into light the great and increasing harmony between the rules as to the application of foreign law which prevails in all civilized countries, such as England, France, and Italy. The tribunals of different countries, as already pointed out, follow similar principles in determining what is the law applicable to a given case, and aim at the same result, namely, the recognition in every civilized country of rights acquired under the law of any other country. Hence an action brought to enforce a right acquired under the law of one country, e. g., of France) will in general be decided in the same manner in whatever country it be maintained, whether, that is to say, it be brought in the Courts of England or of Germany. On this fact is based the defence of the name Private International Law. The rules, it may further be said, which the words designate, affect the rights of individuals as against one another, and therefore belong to the sphere of "private," not of public law; and these rules, as they constitute a body of principles common to all civilized countries, may be rightly termed "international."

The term, however, is at bottom inaccurate. The words private international law "should mean, in accordance with that use
"of the word 'international' which, besides being well established
"in ordinary language, is both scientifically convenient and ety-
"mologically correct, 'a private species of the body of rules which
"prevails between one nation and another.' Nothing of the sort
"is, however, intended; and the unfortunate employment of the
"phrase, as indicating the principles which govern the choice of
"the system of private law applicable to a given class of facts, has
"led to endless misconception of the true nature of this depart-
"ment of legal science." Nor does the inaccuracy of the term
end here. It confounds two classes of rules, which are generically
different from each other. The principles of international law,
properly so called, are truly "international" because they prevail
between or among nations; but they are not in the proper sense of
the term "laws," for they are not commands proceeding from any
sovereign. On the other hand, the principles of private international law are "laws" in the strictest sense of that term, for they
are commands proceeding from the sovereign of a given state,
e. g., England or Italy, in which they prevail; but they are not
"international," for they are laws which determine the private
rights of one individual as against another, and these individuals
may, or may not, belong to one and the same nation. Authors, in
short, who like Fœlix divide international law into public international law and private international law, use the words international and law in each of these expressions in a different sense.
Such ambiguity of language, unless fully acknowledged, must
lead, as it has led, to confusion of thought. Nor is much gained
by such an amendment of terminology as is achieved by a transpo-
sition of words. The expression "international private law" is no
doubt a slight improvement on private international law, as it
points out that the rules which the name denotes belong to the
domain of private law. But the name, improve it as you will, has
the insuperable fault of giving to the adjective international a
meaning different from the sense in which it is generally and correctly employed.

Other names for our subject, such as "comity," the "local
limits of law," "intermunicipal law," and the like, have not obtained sufficient currency to require elaborate criticism. Their
fault is, that either they are too vague for the designation of the
topic to which they are applied, or else they suggest notions which
are inaccurate. Thus the term "comity," as already pointed out,
is open to the charge of implying that a judge, when he applies

foreign law to a particular case, does so as a matter of caprice or favour, whilst the term "intermunicipal law" can be accurately used only by giving to each half of the word "intermunicipal" a sense which both is unusual and also demands elaborate explanation. A more accurate description of our topic is (it is submitted) "the extra-territorial effect of law," or better, Professor Holland's phrase "the extra-territorial recognition of rights." But such expressions are descriptions, not names. A writer, therefore, called upon to deal with our topic will act wisely in refusing to be tied down to any set form of words. He will, when convenient, use the admittedly inaccurate terms, conflict of laws, or private international law. But he will himself remember, and will attempt to impress upon his readers, that these names are nothing more than convenient marks by which to denote the rules maintained by the Courts of a given country, as to the selection of the system of law which is to be applied to the decision of cases that contain, or may contain, some foreign element, and also the rules maintained by the Courts of a given country, as to the limits of the jurisdiction to be exercised by its own Courts as a whole, or by foreign Courts.[2]

[2]**Private International Law Defined and Distinguished.**—"International law, in its widest and most comprehensive sense—including not only questions of right between nations, governed by what has been appropriately called the law of nations; but also questions arising under what is usually called *private international law,* or the *conflict of laws,* and concerning the rights of persons within the territory and dominion of one nation, by reason of acts, private or public, done within the dominions of another nation—is part of our law, and must be ascertained and administered by the Courts of justice, as often as such questions are presented in litigation between man and man, duly submitted to their determination." *Hilton v. Guyot, 159 U. S. 113, 16 S. C. Rep. 139.*

Private International Law differs from Public International Law in three particulars: First—*As to the persons on whom it operates.* As for instance, private individuals are the parties in this branch of the law, while public international law deals with nations. Second—*As to the transaction itself.* Private International law assumes control of transactions private in their nature, as for instance, a contract between two individuals, while public international law recognizes in general only those questions in which sovereign states are interested, as for instance, questions of peace, war, blockade, neutrality, right of search, etc. Third—*As to the remedy.* A question of private international law is decided by the Courts of the country or state in which the question comes up for adjudication. A question of public international law can be settled only through diplomatic channels or war. There is no independent judicial tribunal to decide questions of public international law. See *Minor Conflict of Laws, Sec. 2.*

Controversies between states of the Union come within the jurisdiction of the Supreme Court of the United States. *U. S. Const., Art. 3, Sec. 2.*

CHAPTER II.

TERRITORIAL JURISDICTION OF NATIONS.

REGINA v. KEYN, 1876.

[13 Cox C. C. 403; 2 Exch. Div. 63.]

COCKBURN, C. J.—The defendant has been convicted of the offence of manslaughter on the high seas, on a trial had at the Central Criminal Court, under the statute 4 and 5 Will. 4, c. 36, s. 22, which empowers the judges sitting there to hear and determine offences "committed on the high seas and other places within the jurisdiction of the Admiralty of England." The facts were admittedly such as to warrant the conviction, if there was jurisdiction to try the defendant as amenable to English law. Being in command of a steamship, the *Franconia,* and having occasion to pass the *Strathclyde,* a British ship, the defendant brough his ship unnecessarily close to the latter, and then, by negligence in steering, ran into the *Strathclyde,* and broke a hole in her, in consequence of which she filled with water and sank, when the deceased, whose death the accused is charged with having occasioned, being on board the *Strathclyde,* was drowned. That the negligence of which the accused was thus guilty, having resulted in the death of the deceased, amounts according to English law to manslaughter can admit of no doubt. The question is, whether the accused is amenable to our law, and whether there was jurisdiction to try him? The legality of the conviction is contested, on the ground that the accused is a foreigner; that the *Franconia,* the ship he commanded, was a foreign vessel, sailing from a foreign port, bound on a foreign voyage; that the alleged offence was committed on the high seas. Under these circumstances, it is contended, that the accused, though he may be amenable to the law of his own country, is not capable of being tried and punished by the law of England. The facts on which this defence is based are not capable of being disputed; but a twofold answer is given on the part of the prosecution:—1st. That, although the occurrence on which the charge is founded, took place on the high seas in this sense, that the place in which it happened was not within the body of a county, it occurred within three miles of the English coast; that, by the law of nations, the sea, for a space of three miles from the coast, is part of the territory of the country to which the coast belongs; that, consequently, the *Franconia,* at the time the offence was committed, was in English waters, and those on board were therefore subject to English law. 2ndly. That, although the negligence of which the accused was guilty occurred on board a foreign vessel, the death occasioned by such negligence took place on board a British vessel; and that as a British vessel is in point of law to be considered British territory, the offence having been consummated by the death of the deceased in a British ship, must be considered as having been committed on British territory. I reserve for future consideration the arguments thus advanced on the part of the Crown, and proceed, in the first instance, to consider the general question—how far, independently of them, the accused, having been at the time the offence was committed a foreign subject, in a foreign ship, on a foreign voyage, on the high seas, is amenable to the law of England. Now, no proposition of law can be more incontestable or more universally admitted than that, according to the general law of nations, a foreigner cannot be held criminally responsible to the law of a nation not his own, for acts done beyond the limits of its territory:—

No sovereignty (says Story, Conflict of Laws, s. 539) can extend its process beyond its own territorial limits, to subject either persons or property to its judicial decisions. Every exertion of authority of this sort beyond this limit is a mere nullity, and incapable of binding such persons or property in any other tribunals.

The power of this country (says Dr. Lushington, in the case of *The Zollverein,* 1 Sw. Adm. Rep. 96) is to legislate for its subjects all the world over, and as to foreigners within its jurisdiction, but no further.

This rule must, however, be taken subject to this qualification, namely, that if the legislature of a particular country should think fit by express enactment to render foreigners subject to its law with reference to offences committed beyond the limits of its territory, it would be incumbent on the Courts of such country to give effect to such enactment, leaving it to the state to settle the question of international law with the governments of other nations. The question of express legislation will be dealt with hereafter. For the present I am dealing with the subject with reference to the general law alone. To the general rule to which I have referred there is one exception—that of a foreigner on board the ship of another nation. But the exception is apparent rather than real; for by the received law of every nation a ship on the high seas carries its nationality and the law of its own nation with it, and in this respect has been likened to a floating portion of the national territory. All on board, therefore, whether subjects or foreigners, are bound to obey the law of the country to which the ship belongs, as though they were actually on its territory on land, and are liable to the penalties of that law for any offence committed against it. But they are liable to that law alone. On board a foreign ship on the high seas, the foreigner is liable to the law of the foreign ship only. It is **only** when a foreign ship comes into the ports or waters of another state that the ship and those on board become subject to the local law. These are the established rules of the law of nations. They have been adopted into our own municipal law, and must be taken to form part of it. According to the general law, therefore, a foreigner who is not residing permanently or temporarily in British territory, or on board a British ship, cannot be held responsible for an infraction of the law of this country. Unless, therefore, the accused Keyn, at the time the offence of which he has been convicted was committed, was on British territory, he could not be properly brought to trial under English law, in the absence of express legislation. Moreover, while the accused is thus on general principles exempt from being subject to our criminal law in respect of an offence committed on the high seas, if we proceed to look at the matter in a more technical point of view, with reference to jurisdiction, equal difficulties will be found to stand in the way of the prosecution. The indictment on which the defendant has been convicted alleges the offence to have been committed on the high seas, and it is admitted that the place at which it occurred cannot in any sense be said to have been within the body of a county. The case, therefore, if the indictment can be maintained, must necessarily fall within what would formerly have been the jurisdiction of the Admiral—a jurisdiction now transferred, but transferred unaltered, to the Common Law Courts. It becomes, therefore, necessary to inquire more particularly into the character and extent of the Admiralty jurisdiction. From the earliest period of our legal history, the cognizance of offences committed on the high seas had been left to the jurisdiction of the Admiral. And the reason is obvious. By the old common law of England, every offence was triable in the county only in which it had been committed, as from that county alone the "pais," as it was termed—in other words, the jurors by whom the fact was to be ascertained—could come. But only so much of the land of the outer coast as was uncovered by the sea was held to be within the body of the adjoining county. If an offence was committed on the high sea, in a bay, gulf, or estuary, *inter fauces terræ*, the common law could deal with it, because the parts of the sea so circumstanced were held to be within the body of the adjacent county or counties; but, along the coast, on the external sea, the jurisdiction of the common law extended no further than to low-water mark. As from time to time, when ships began to navigate the sea, offences would be committed on it which required to be repressed and punished, but the common law jurisdiction and procedure was inapplicable to such offences, as not having been committed within the boundary of any county, the authority of the Crown in the administration of justice in respect of such crimes was left to the Admiral, as exercising the authority of the sovereign upon the seas. Even the office of coroner could not, for the like reason, be executed by the coroner of a county in respect of matters arising on the sea. An inquest could not be held by one of these officers on a body found on the sea. Such jurisdiction could only be exercised by a coroner appointed by the Admiral. A similar difficulty existed as to wrongs done on the sea, and in respect of which the party wronged was entitled to redress by civil action, till the anomalous device of a fictitious venue, within the jurisdiction of the common-law courts, and which was not allowed to be disputed, was resorted to, and so the power of trying such actions was assumed.

Upon this footing the law has remained ever since. Whatever of the sea lies within the body of a county is within the jurisdiction of the common law. Whatever does not, belonged formerly to that of the Admiralty, and now belongs to the courts to which the jurisdiction of the admiral has been transferred by statute; while in the estuaries or mouths of great rivers, below the bridges, in the matter of murder and mayhem, the jurisdiction is concurrent. On the shore of the outer sea the body of the county extends so far as the land is uncovered by water. And so rigorous has been the line of demarcation between the two jurisdictions, that, as regards the shore between high and low-water mark, the jurisdiction has been divided between the Admiralty and the common law according to the state of the tide. Such was the law in the time of Lord Coke; and such it is still. We must, therefore, deal with this case as one which would have been under the ancient jurisdiction of the Admiral. But the jurisdiction of the Admiral, though largely asserted in theory, was never, so far as I am aware—except in the case of piracy, which, as the pirate was considered the *communis hostis* of mankind, was triable anywhere—exercised, or attempted to be exercised, over other than English ships. No instance of any such exercise, or attempted exercise, after every possible search has been made, has been brought to our notice. Nor, for the reason already given, could such jurisdiction be so exercised consistently with legal principle.

R. v. *Serva and others* (1 Den. C. C. 104; 1 Cox C. C. 292), R. v. *Lewis* (1 Dear. & Bell, 182; 7 Cox. C. C. 277).

In *Palmer's Case* (3 Wheat. 610); and in the cases of *United States* v. *Howard* (3 Wash. C. C. R. 334); *United States* v. *Klintock* (5 Wheat. 144); *United States* v. *Kessler* (1 Baldw. 15); and *United States* v. *Holmes*.

These decisions are conclusive in favour of the accused in the present case, unless the contention, on the part of the Crown, either that the place at which the occurrence out of which the present inquiry has arisen, was, though on the high seas, yet within British waters, by reason of its having been within three miles of the English shore; or that the death of the deceased having occurred in a British ship, the offence must be taken to have been there committed, so as in either case to give jurisdiction to the Admiralty, or the Courts substituted for it, shall prevail. These questions it becomes, therefore, necessary carefully to consider. On entering on the first of these questions it is material to have a clear conception of what the matter in controversy is. The jurisdiction of the Admiral, so largely asserted in theory in ancient times, being abandoned as untenable, it becomes necessary for the counsel for the Crown to have recourse to a doctrine of comparatively modern growth, namely, that a belt of sea, to a distance of three miles from the coast, though so far a portion of the high seas as to be still within the jurisdiction of the Admiral, is part of the territory of the realm, so as to make a foreigner in a foreign ship, within such belt, though on a voyage to a foreign port, subject to our law, though he would not be so on the high sea beyond such limit. It is necessary to keep the old assertion of jurisdiction and that of to-day essentially distinct, and it should be borne in mind that it is because all proof of the actual exercise of any jurisdiction by the Admiral over foreigners in the narrow seas totally fails, that it becomes necessary to give to the three-mile zone the character of territory in order to make good the assertion of jurisdiction over the foreigner therein. Now, it may be asserted without fear of contradiction that the position that the sea within a belt or zone of three miles from the shore, as distinguished from the rest of the open sea, forms part of the realm or territory of the Crown is a doctrine unknown to the ancient law of England, and which has never yet received the sanction of an English criminal court of justice. It is true that from an early period the kings of England, possessing more ships than their opposite neighbors, and being thence able to sweep the Channel, asserted the right of sovereignty over the narrow seas, as appears from the commissions issued in the fourteenth century, of which examples are given in the 4th Institute, in the chapter on the Court of Admiralty, and others are to be found in Selden's "Mare Clausum," book 2. At a later period, still more extravagant pretensions were advanced. Selden does not scruple to assert the sovereignty of the King of England over the sea as far as the shores of Norway, in which he is upheld by Lord Hale in his treatise "De jure maris": (Hargrave's Law Tracts, p. 10.)

But the claim to such sovereignty, at all times unfounded, has long since been abandoned. No one would now dream of asserting that the sovereign of these realms has any greater right over the surrounding seas than the sovereigns on the opposite shores; or that it is the especial duty and privilege of the Queen of Great Britain to keep the peace in these seas; or that the Court of Admiralty could try a foreigner committed in a foreign vessel in all parts of the channel. No writer of our day, except Mr. Chitty, in his treatise on the Prerogative, has asserted the ancient doctrine. Blackstone, in his chapter on the Prerogative in the Commentaries, while he asserts that the narrow seas are part of the realm, puts it only on the ground that the jurisdiction of the Admiralty extends over these seas. He is silent as to any jurisdiction over foreigners within them. The consensus of jurists which has been so much insisted on as authority, is perfectly unanimous as to the non-existence of any such jurisdiction. Indeed, it is because this claim of sovereignty is admitted to be untenable that it has been found necessary to resort to the theory of the three-miles zone. It is in vain, therefore, that the ancient assertion of sovereignty over the narrow seas is invoked to give countenance to the rule now sought to be established, of juris- diction over the three-miles zone. If this rule is to prevail, it must be on altogether different grounds. To invoke as its foundation, or in its support, an assertion of sovereignty which, for all prac- tical purposes, is, and always has been, idle and unfounded, and the invalidity of which renders it necessary to have recourse to the new doctrine, involves an inconsistency, on which it would be superfluous to dwell. I must confess myself unable to compre- hend how, when the ancient doctrine as to sovereignty over the narrow seas is adduced, its operation can be confined to the three- miles zone. If the argument is good for anything, it must apply to the whole of the surrounding seas. But the counsel for the Crown evidently shrank from applying it to this extent. Such a pretension would not be admitted or endured by foreign nations. That it is out of this extravagant assertion of sovereignty that the doctrine of the three-mile jurisdiction, asserted on the part of the Crown, and which, the older claim being necessarily abandoned, we are now called upon to consider, has sprung up, I readily admit. Let me endeavor to trace its origin and growth. With the celebrated work of Grotius, published in 1609, began the great contest of the jurists as to the freedom of the seas. The contro- versy ended, as controversies often do, in a species of compromise. While maintaining the freedom of the seas, Grotius, in his work "De Jure Belli et Pacis," had expressed an opinion that, while no right could be acquired to the exclusive possession of the ocean, an exclusive right or jurisdiction might be acquired in respect of particular portions of the sea adjoining the territory of individual States.

There can be no doubt that the suggestion of Bynkershoek, that the sea surrounding the coast to the extent of cannon-range should be treated as belonging to the state owning the coast, has with but very few exceptions, been accepted and adopted by the publicists who have followed him during the last two centuries. But it is equally clear that, in the practical application of the rule, in respect of the particular distance, as also in the still more essen- tial particular of the character and degree of sovereignty and dominion to be exercised, great difference of opinion and uncer- tainty have prevailed, and still continue to exist. As regards dis- tance, while the majority of authors have adhered to the three- mile zone, others, like Mr. Ortolan and Mr. Halleck, applying with greater consistency the principle on which the whole doctrine rests, insist on extending the distance to the modern range of cannon—in other words doubling it. This difference of opinion may be of little practical importance in the present instance, inasmuch as the place at which the offence occurred was within the lesser distance; but it is, nevertheless, not immaterial as showing how unsettled this doctrine still is. The question of sovereignty, on the other hand, is all-important. One set of writers, as, for instance, M. Hautefeuille, ascribes to the state territorial property and sovereignty over the three miles of sea, to the extent of the right of excluding the ships of all other nations, even for the purpose of passage—a doctrine flowing immediately from the principle of territorial property, but which is too monstrous to be admitted. Another set concedes territorial property and sovereignty, but makes it subject to the right of other nations to use these waters for the purpose of navigation. Others again, like M. Ortolan and M. Calvo, deny any right of territorial property, but concede "jurisdiction;" by which I understand the power of applying the law, applicable to persons on the land, to all who are within the territorial water, and the power of legislation in respect of it, so as to bind every one who comes within the jurisdiction, whether subjects or foreigners. Some, like M. Ortolan, would confine this jurisdiction to purposes of "safety and police" —by which I should be disposed to understand measures for the protection of the territory, and for the regulation of the navigation, and the use of harbours and roadsteads, and the maintenance of order among the shipping therein, rather than the general application of the criminal law. Other authors, for instance, Mr. Manning, would restrict the jurisdiction to certain specified purposes in which the local state has an immediate interest, namely, the protection of its revenue and fisheries, the exacting of harbour and light dues, and the protection of its coasts in time of war. Some of these authors, for instance, Professor Bluntschli, make a most important distinction between a commorant and a passing ship. According to this author, while the commorant ship is subject to the general law of the local State, the passing ship is liable to the local jurisdiction only in matters of "military and police regulations, made for the safety of the territory and population of the coast." None of these writers, it should be noted, discuss the question, or go the length of asserting that a foreigner in a foreign ship, using the waters in question for the purpose of navigation solely, on its way to another country, is liable to the crim-

inal law of the adjoining country for an offence committed on
board.

Now, when it is remembered that it is mainly on the statements and authorities of these writers, and to opinions founded on
them, that we are called upon to hold that foreigners on the so-
called territorial sea are subject to the general law of this country,
the discrepancy of opinion which I have been pointing out becomes
very material. Looking to this, we may properly ask those who
contend for the application of the existing law to the littoral sea
independently of legislation, to tell us the extent to which we are
to go in applying it. Are we to limit it to three miles, or to extend
it to six? Are we to treat the whole body of the criminal law
as applicable to it, or only so much as relates to "police and
safety"? Or are we to limit it, as one of these authors proposes,
to the protection of fisheries and customs, the exacting of harbour
and light dues, and the protection of our coasts in time of war?
Which of these writers are we to follow. What is there in these
conflicting views to guide us, in the total absence of precedent or
legal sanction, as to the extent to which we may subject foreigners
to our law? What is there in them which authorizes us to assume
not only that Parliament can of right deal with the three-mile
zone as forming part of our territory, but also that, by the mere
assent of other nations, the sea to this extent has become so completely a part of our territory as to be subject, without legislation,
to the whole body of our existing law, civil and criminal. But it
is said that, although the writers on international law are disagreed on so many essential points, they are all agreed as to the
power of a littoral state to deal with the three-mile zone as subject to its dominion, and that consequently we may treat it as
subject to our law. But this reasoning strikes me as unsatisfactory; for what does this unanimity in the general avail us when
we come to the practical application of the law in the particular
instance, if we are left wholly in the dark as to the degree to
which the law can be legitimately enforced? This unanimity of
opinion that the littoral sea is, at all events for some purposes,
subject to the dominion of the local state, may go far to show that,
by the concurrence of other nations, such a state may deal with
these waters as subject to its legislation. But it wholly fails to
show that, in the absence of such legislation, the ordinary law of
the local state will extend over the waters in question—which is
the point which we have to determine.

Not altogether uninfluenced, perhaps, by the diversity of

opinion to which I have called attention, the argument in support of the prosecution presents itself—not without some sacrifice of consistency—in more than one shape. At one time it is asserted that, for the space of three miles, not only the sea itself, but the bed on which it rests, forms part of the territory or realm of the country owning the coast, as though it were so much land; so that the right of passage and anchorage might be of right denied to the ships of other nations. At another time it is said that, while the right is of a territorial character, it is subject to a right of passage by the ships of other nations. Sometimes the sovereignty is asserted, not as based on territorial right, but simply as attaching to the sea, over which it is contended that the nation owning the coast may extend its law to the foreigner navigating within it. To those who assert that, to the extent of three miles from the coast, the sea forms part of the realm of England, the question might well be put, When did it become so? Was it so from the beginning? It certainly was not deemed to be so as to a three-mile zone, any more than as to the rest of the high seas, at the time the statutes of Richard II. were passed. For in those statutes a clear distinction is made between the realm and the sea, as also between the bodies of counties and the sea; the jurisdiction of the Admiral being (subject to the exception already stated as to murder and mayhem) confined strictly to the latter, and its exercise "within the realm" prohibited in terms. The language of the first of these statutes is especially remarkable ·

> The Admirals and their deputies shall not meddle from henceforth with anything done *within the realm of England, but only with things done upon the sea.*

It is impossible not to be struck by the distinction here taken between the realm of England and the sea; or, when the two statutes are taken together, not to see that the term "realm," used in the first statute, and "bodies of counties," the term used in the second statute, mean one and the same thing. In these statutes the jurisdiction of the Admiral is restricted to the high seas, and, in respect of murder and mayhem, to the great rivers below the bridges, while whatever is within the realm, in other words the body of a county, is left within the domain of the common law. But there is no distinction taken between one part of the high sea and another. The three-mile zone is no more dealt with as within the realm than the seas at large. The notion of a three-mile zone was in those days in the womb of time. When its origin is traced, it is found to be of comparatively modern growth. The first mention of it in any Court of this country was made by Lord Stowell, with reference to the rights of neutrality, in the first year of the present century, in the case of *The Twee Gebroeders* (3 C. Rob. 162). To this hour it has not, even in theory, yet settled into certainty. For centuries before it was thought of, the great landmarks of our judicial system had been set fast—the jurisdiction of the common law over the land and the inland waters contained within it, forming together the realm of England, that of the Admiral over English vessels on the seas, the common property or highway of mankind.

But I am met by an authority; and beyond question ancient authority may be found in abundance for the assertion that the bed of the sea is part of the realm of England, part of the territorial possessions of the Crown. Coke, commenting on sec. 439 of Littleton, says, in explaining the words "out of the realm:"

> If a man be upon the sea of England, he is within the kingdom or realme of England, and within the ligeance of the king of England, as of his crowne of England. And yet *altum mare* is out of the jurisdiction of the common law, and within the jurisdiction of the Lord Admiral.

Lord Hale, no doubt, in his work "De Jure Maris," speaks of the narraw seas, and the soil thereof, as "part of the King's waste, demesnes, and dominions, whether in the body of a county or not." But this was said, not with reference to the theory of the three-mile zone, which had not then been thought of, but (following Selden) to the wild notion of sovereignty over the whole of the narrow seas. This pretension failing, the rest of the doctrine, as it seems to me, fails with it. Moreover, Hale stops short of saying that the bed of the sea forms part of the realm of England, as a portion of its territory. He speaks of it under the vague terms of "waste," "demesnes," or "dominions." He carefully distinguishes between the parts of the sea which are within the body of a county and those which are not. It is true that, in his later work on the Pleas of the Crown, Lord Hale, speaking in the chapter on Treasons (vol. i, p. 154), of what is a levying of war against the King "within the realm," according to the required averment in an indictment for that offence, instances the hostile invasion of the King's ships ("which," he observes, "are so many royal castles"); and this, he says, "is a levying of war within the realm;" the reason he assigns being that "the narrow seas are of the ligeance of the Crown of England," for which he cites the authority of Selden. Here, again, we have Lord Hale blindly following "Master Selden," in asserting that the narrow seas owe allegiance to the Crown of England. A hostile attack by a subject on a ship of war on the narrow seas would be a levying of war against the sovereign, but it could not now be said to be high treason because done within the realm. Blackstone (Com. vol. i, p. 110) says that "the main or high seas" (which he afterwards described as beginning at low-water mark) "are part of the realm of England"—here Mr. Stephen, feeling that his author was going too far, interposes the words "in one sense"—"for thereon," adds Blackstone, "our Courts of Admiralty have jurisdiction; but they are not subject to the common law." This is, indeed, singular reasoning. Instead of saying that, because the seas are part of the realm of England, the Courts of Admiralty have jurisdiction over them, the writer reverses the position, and says, that because the Admiralty has jurisdiction these seas are part of the realm—which certainly does not follow. If it did, as the jurisdiction of the Admiralty extended as regards British ships, wherever the sea rolls, the entire ocean might be said to be within the realm.

But to what, after all, do these ancient authorities amount? Of what avail are they towards establishing that the soil in the three-mile zone is part of the territorial domain of the Crown? These assertions of sovereignty were manifestly based on the doctrine that the narrow seas are part of the realm of England. But that doctrine is now exploded. Who, at this day, would venture to affirm that the sovereignty asserted in those days now exists? What foreign jurist is there who would not deny—what English lawyer who would not shrink from maintaining—what foreign Government which would not repel such a pretension? I listened carefully to see whether any such assertion would be made; but none was made. No one has gone the length of suggesting, much less of openly asserting, that the jurisdiction still exists. It seems to me to follow that when the sovereignty and jurisdiction from which the property in the soil of the sea was inferred is gone, the territorial property which was supposed to be consequent upon it must necessarily go with it. But we are met here by a subtle and ingenious argument. It is said that although the doctrine of the jurisdiction of the Admiral over foreigners on the four seas has died out, and can no longer be upheld, yet that, as now, by the consent of other nations, sovereignty over this territorial sea is conceded to us, the jurisdiction formerly asserted may be revived, and made to attach to the newly-acquired domain. I am unable to adopt this reasoning. *Ex concessis*, the jurisdiction over foreigners in foreign ships never really existed; at all events, it has long been dead and buried. But it is evoked from its grave and brought to life for the purpose of applying it to a part of the sea which was included in the whole, as to which it is now practically admitted that it never existed. From the time the jurisdiction was asserted to the time when the pretension to it was dropped, it was asserted over this portion of the sea as part of the whole to which the jurisdiction was said to extend. If it was bad as to the whole indiscriminately, it was bad as to every part of that whole. But why was it bad as to the whole? Simply because the jurisdiction did not extend to foreigners in foreign ships on the high seas. The waters in question have always formed part of the high seas. They are alleged in this indictment to be so now. How, then, can the Admiral have the jurisdiction contended for over them if he had it not before? There having been no new statute conferring it, how has he acquired it? To come back to the subject of the realm, I cannot help thinking that some confusion arises from the term "realm" being used in more than one sense. Sometimes it is used, as in the statute of Richard II., to mean the land of England, and the internal sea within it, sometimes as meaning whatever the sovereignty of the Crown of England extended, or was supposed to extend, over. When it is used as synonymous to territory, I take the true meaning of the term "the realm of England" to be the territory to and over which the common law of England extends—in other words, all that is within the body of any county—to the exclusion of the high seas, which come under a different jurisdiction only because they are not within any of those territorial divisions, into which, among other things for the administration of the law, the kingdom is parceled out. At all events, I am prepared to abide by the distinction taken in the statutes of Richard II. between the realm and the sea. For centuries our judicial system in the administration of the criminal law has been divided into two distinct and independent branches, the one having jurisdiction over the land and any sea considered to be within the land; the other over the sea external to the land. No concurrent assent of nations, that a portion of what before was treated as the high seas, and as such common to all the world, shall now be treated as the territory of the local state, can of itself, without the authority of Parliament, convert that which before was in the eye of the law high seas into British territory, and so change the law, or give to the courts of this country, independently of legislation, a jurisdiction over the foreigner where they had it not before. The argument in support of the contrary appears to me, I must say, singularly inconsistent with itself. According to it the littoral sea is made to assume what I cannot help calling an amphibious character. At one time it is land, at another it is water. Is it desired to apply the law of the shore to it, so as to make the foreigner subject to that law—it becomes so much territory. Do you wish to keep it within the jurisdiction of the admiral—as you must do to uphold this indictment—it is made to resume its former character as part of the high seas. Unable to follow this vacillating reasoning, I must add that, to my mind, the contention that the littoral sea forms part of the realm or territory of Great Britain is fatal to the argument which it is intended to support. For, if the sea thus becomes part of the territory, as though it were actually *intra fauces terrœ*, it seems to follow that it must become annexed to the main land, and so become part of the adjoining county, in which case there would be an end to the Admiralty jurisdiction. The littoral sea cannot be land for one purpose and high sea for another. Nor is anything gained by substituting the term "territory" for land. The law of England knows but of one territory— that which is within the body of a county. All beyond it is the high sea, which is out of the province of English law, and to which it cannot be extended except by legislation. It does not appear to me that the argument for the prosecution is advanced by reference to encroachments on the sea, in the way of piers, breakwaters, harbours, and the like, even when projected into the open sea, or of forts erected in it, as is the case in the Solent. Where the sea or the bed on which it rests, can be physically occupied permanently, it may be made subject to occupation in the same manner as unoccupied territory. In point of fact, such encroachments are generally made for the benefit of the navigation ; and are therefore readily acquiesced in. Or they are for the purposes of defence, and come within the principle that a nation may do what is necessary for the protection of its own territory. Whether, if an encroachment on the sea were such as to obstruct the navigation of the ships of other nations, it would not amount to a just cause of complaint, as inconsistent with international rights, might, if the case arose, be deserving of serious consideration. That such encroachments are occasionally made seems to me to fall very far short of establishing such an exclusive property in the littoral sea as that it can be treated, to all intents and purposes, in the absence of legislation, as part of the realm. Again,

the fact, adverted to in the course of the discussion, that in the
west of England mines have been run out under the bed of the
sea to beyond low-water mark, seems to me to avail but little
towards the decision of the question of territorial property in the
littoral sea. But for the act of 21 & 22 Vict. c. 109, to which our
attention has been specially directed, I should have thought the
matter simple enough. Between high and low-water mark the
property in the soil is in the Crown, and it is to be assumed that it
is by grant or license from the Crown, or by prescription, which
presupposes a grant, that a mine is carried beneath it. Beyond
low-water mark the bed of the sea might be said to be unappropriated, and, if capable of being appropriated, would become the
property of the first occupier. I should not have thought that
the carrying one or two mines into the bed of the sea beyond low-
water mark could have any real bearing on a question of international law like the present.

It thus appearing, as it seems to me, that the littoral sea
beyond low-water mark did not, as distinguished from the rest
of the high seas, originally form part of the territory of the realm,
the question again presents itself, when and how did it become
so? Can a portion of the high seas have been converted into
British territory without any action on the part of the British
Government or Legislature—by the mere assertions of writers on
public law—or even by the assent of other nations? And when in
support of this position, or of the theory of the three-mile zone
in general, the statements of the writers on international law are
relied on, the question may well be asked, upon what authority are
these statements founded? When and in what manner have the
nations, who are to be affected by such a rule as these writers,
following one another, have laid down, signified their assent to
it? to say nothing of the difficulty which might be found in saying
to which of these conflicting opinions such assent had been given.
For, even if entire unanimity had existed in respect of the important particulars I have referred to, in place of so much discrepancy of opinion, the question would still remain, how far the law
as stated by the publicists had received the assent of the civilized
nations of the world. For writers on international law, however
valuable their labours may be in elucidating and ascertaining the
principles and rules of law, cannot make the law. To be binding,
the law must have received the assent of the nations who are to
be bound by it. This assent may be express, as by treaty or the
acknowledged concurrence of governments, or may be implied

from established usage—an instance of which is to be found in the fact that merchant vessels on the high seas are held to be subject only to the law of the nation under whose flag they sail, while in the ports of a foreign state they are subject to the local law as well as that of their own country. In the absence of proof of assent, as derived from one or other of these sources, no unanimity on the part of theoretical writers would warrant the judicial application of the law on the sole authority of their views or statements. Nor, in my opinion, would the clearest proof of unanimous assent on the part of other nations be sufficient to authorise the tribunals of this country to apply, without an Act of Parliament, what would practically amount to a new law. In so doing we should be unjustifiably usurping the province of the Legislature. The assent of nations is doubtless sufficient to give the power of parliamentary legislation in a matter otherwise within the sphere of international law; but it would be powerless to confer a jurisdiction beyond and unknown to the law, such as that now insisted on, a jurisdiction over foreigners in foreign ships on a portion of the high seas. When I am told that all other nations have assented to such an absolute dominion on the part of the littoral state, over this portion of the sea, as that their ships may be excluded from it, and that, without any open legislation, or notice to them or their subjects, the latter may be held liable to the local law, I ask, first, what proof there is of such assent as is asserted; and, secondly, to what extent has such assent been carried? a question of infinite importance, when, undirected by legislation, we are called upon to apply the law on the strength of such assent. It is said that we are to take the statements of the publicists as conclusive proof of the assent in question, and much eloquence has been expended in impressing on us the respect which is due to their authority, and that they are to be looked upon as witnesses of the fact, that those statements, or the foundation on which those statements rest, we are scarcely at liberty to question. I demur altogether to this position. I entertain a profound respect for the opinion of jurists when dealing with matters of juridical principle and opinion; but we are here dealing with a question not of opinion but of fact, and I must assert my entire liberty to examine the evidence, and see upon what foundation these statements are based. The question is not one of theoretical opinion, but of fact, and, fortunately, the writers upon whose statements we are called upon to act have afforded us the means of testing those statements by reference

to facts. They refer us to two things, and to these alone—
treaties and usage. Let us look a little more closely into both.
First, then, let us see how the matter stands as regards treaties.
It may be asserted, without fear of contradiction, that the rule
that the sea surrounding the coast is to be treated as a part of
the adjacent territory, so that the State shall have exclusive
dominion over it, and that the law of the latter shall be generally applicable to those passing over it in the ships of other
nations, has never been made the subject-matter of any treaty,
or, as matter of acknowledged right, or has formed the basis of
any treaty, or has even been the subject of diplomatic discussion.
It has been entirely the creation of the writers on international
law. It is true that the writers who have been cited constantly
refer to treaties in support of the doctrine they assert. But when
the treaties they refer to are looked at, they will be found to relate
to two subjects only—the observance of the rights and obligations
of neutrality, and the exclusive right of fishing. In fixing the
limits to which these rights should extend, nations have so far
followed the writers on international law as to adopt the principle
of the three-mile range as a convenient distance. There are several treaties by which nations have engaged, in the event of either
of them being at war with a third, to treat the sea within three
miles of each other's coasts as neutral territory, within which no
warlike opperations should be carried on; instances of which will
be found in the various treatises on international law. Thus, for
instance, in the treaties of commerce, between Great Britain and
France, of September, 1786; between France and Russia, of
January, 1787; between Great Britain and the United States, of
October, 1794, each contracting party engages, if at war with
any other nation, not to carry on hostilities within cannon-shot
of the coast of the other contracting party; or, if the other should
be at war, not to allow its vessels to be captured within the like
distance. There are many other treaties of the like tenor, a long
list of which is given by Azuni (vol. ii, p. 78) ; and various ordinances and laws have been made by the different states in order
to give effect to them. Again, nations possessing opposite or
neighbouring coasts, bordering on a common sea, have sometimes
found it expedient to agree that the subjects of each shall exercise
an exclusive right of fishing to a given distance from their own
shores, and also have accepted the three miles as a convenient
distance. Such, for instance, are the treaties made between this
country and the United States in relation to the fishery off the

coast of Newfoundland, and those between this country and France in relation to the fishery on their respective shores; and local laws have been passed to give effect to these engagements. But in all these treaties this distance is adopted, not as matter of existing right established by the general law of nations, but as matter of mutual concession and convention. Instead of upholding the doctrine contended for, the fact of these treaties having been entered into has rather the opposite tendency: for it is obvious that, if the territorial right of a nation bordering on the sea to this portion of the adjacent waters had been established by the common assent of nations, these treaty arrangements would have been wholly superfluous. Each nation would have been bound, independently of treaty engagement, to respect the neutrality of the other in these waters as much as in its inland waters. The foreigner invading the rights of the local fisherman would have been amenable, consistently with international law, to local legislation prohibiting such infringement, without any stipulation to that effect by treaty. For what object, then, have treaties been resorted to? Manifestly in order to obviate all questions as to concurrent or conflicting rights arising under the law of nations. Possibly, after these precedents and all that has been written on this subject, it may not be too much to say that, independently of treaty, the three-mile belt of sea might at this day be taken as belonging, for these purposes, to the local state. But it is scarcely logical to infer, from such treaties alone, that, because nations have agreed to treat the littoral sea as belonging to the country it adjoins, for certain specified objects, they have therefore assented to forego all other rights previously enjoyed in common, and have submitted themselves, even to the extent of the right of navigation on a portion of the high seas, and the liability of their subjects therein to the criminal law, to the will of the local sovereign, and the jurisdiction of the local state. Equally illogical is it, as it seems to me, from the adoption of the three-mile distance in these particular instances, to assume, independently of everything else, a recognition, by the common assent of nations, of the principle that the subjects of one state passing in ships within three miles of the coast of another shall be in all respects subject to the law of the latter. It may be that the maritime nations of the world are prepared to acquiesce in their appropriation of the littoral sea; but I cannot think that these treaties help us much towards arriving at such a conclusion. At all events, the question remains, whether judicially we can infer that the nations who have been

parties to them, and still further those who have not, have thereby
assented to the application of the criminal law of other nations to
their subjects on the waters in question, and on the strength of
such inference so apply the criminal law of this country. The
uncertainty in which we are left, so far as judicial knowledge
is concerned, as to the extent of such assent, presents, I think, a
very serious obstacle to our assuming the jurisdiction we are
called upon to exercise, independently of the, to my mind, still
more serious difficulty, that we should be assuming it without
legislative warrant. So much for treaties. Then how stands the
matter as to usage? When the matter is looked into, the only
usage found to exist is such as is connected with navigation, or
with revenue, local fisheries, or neutrality, and it is to these alone
that the usage relied on is confined. Usage as to the application
of the general law of local state to foreigners on the littoral sea,
notwithstanding reference to usage is frequently made by the
publicists in support of their doctrine, there is actually none. No
nation has arrogated to itself the right of excluding foreign vessels from the use of its external littoral waters for the purpose of
navigation, or has assumed the power of making foreigners in
foreign ships passing through these waters subject to its law,
otherwise than in respect of matters connected with the navigation, or with revenue, local fisheries, or neutrality. And it is to
these alone that the usage relied on is confined. Nor have the
tribunals of any nation held foreigners in these waters amenable
generally to the local criminal law in respect of offences. It is
for the first time in the annals of jurisprudence that a court is
now called upon to apply the criminal law of the country to such
a case as the present. It may well be, I say again, that, after all
that has been said and done in this respect—after the instances
which have been mentioned of the adoption of the three-mile
distance, and the repeated assertion of this doctrine by the writers
on public law—a nation which should now deal with this portion
of the sea as its own, so as to make foreigners within it subject
to its law, for the prevention and punishment of offences, would
not be considered as infringing the rights of other nations. But
I apprehend that as the ability so to deal with these waters would
result, not from any original or inherent right, but from the
acquiescence of other states, some outward manifestation of the
national will, in the shape of open practice or municipal legislation, so as to amount, at least constructively, to an occupation of
that which was before unappropriated, would be necessary to

render the foreigner, not previously amenable to our law, subject
to its general control. That such legislation, whether consistent
with the general law of nations or not, would be binding on the
tribunals of this country—leaving the question of its consistency
with international law to be determined between the governments
of the respective nations—can of course admit of no doubt. The
question is whether such legislation would not, at all events, be
necessary to justify our Courts in applying the law of this country
to foreigners under entirely novel circumstances in which it has
never been applied before. It is obviously one thing to say that
the Legislature of a nation may, from the common assent of other
nations, have acquired the full right to legislate over a part of
that which was before high sea, and as such common to the world;
another and a very different thing to say that the law of the local
state becomes thereby at once, without anything more, applicable
to foreigners within such part, or that, independently of legislation, the courts of the local state can *proprio vigore* so apply it.
The one position does not follow from the other; and it is essential
to keep the two things, the power of Parliament to legislate, and
the authority of our Courts, without such legislation, to apply
the criminal law where it could not have been applied before,
altogether distinct, which, it is evident, is not always done. It
is unnecessary to the defence, and equally so to the decision of
the case, to determine whether Parliament has the right to treat
the three-mile zone as part of the realm consistently with international law. That is a matter on which it is for Parliament itself
to decide. It is enough for us that it has the power to do so. The
question really is whether, acting judicially, we can treat the
power of Parliament to legislate as making up for the absence
of actual legislation. I am clearly of opinion that we cannot, and
that it is only in the instances in which foreigners on the seas have
been made specially liable to our law by statutory enactment that
that law can be applied to them. Let us, then, now see what has
been done herein in the way of legislation. The statutes relating
to the sea by which foreigners may be affected may be divided
into two classes, those which have no reference to the three-mile
zone, and those which have. The latter, again, may be divided
into those which expressly refer to the foreigner, and those which
are said to do so by implication only. It is desirable to dispose
of those first referred to before we come to the statutes which
have reference to the three-mile distance. First in order comes
the statute of the 28 Hen. 8, c. 15, upon which an argument has

been founded, resting on a broader basis than that of the modern doctrine, and which, if it could be upheld, would dispense with the necessity of resorting to the three-mile zone at all. It has been suggested that, independently of any legislation having special reference to the three-mile zone, the statute of Henry VIII., which transferred, as we have seen, the jurisdiction of the Admiral to the Courts of Common Law, had the effect of making foreigners subject to our law for offences committed on foreign ships within the narrow seas; the argument, if I apprehend it rightly, being, first, that the language of the statute, being general in its terms, must be taken to have included foreigners as well as subjects; secondly, that, inasmuch as, at the time when the statute of Henry VIII. was passed, the claim to dominion over the narrow seas was still asserted on the part of the Crown, the jurisdiction given to the Admiral by the prior Admiralty Commissions must be taken to have been co-extensive therewith, and such jurisdiction must therefore be considered as having been transferred by the statute. It is true that the language of the statute is quite general in its terms. After reciting the inconveniences arising from the existing jurisdiction, it enacts that "all treasons, felonies, robberies, murders, and confederacies committed in or upon the sea, or in any haven, river, creek, or place where the admiral or admirals have, or pretend to have"—which has been construed to mean rightfully assert—"jurisdiction, shall be inquired, tried, heard, and determined and judged in such shires and places in the realm as shall be limited by the King's commission, in like form and condition as if such offences had been committed on land." No doubt these words are large enough to include foreigners as well as subjects; but so they are to include the entire ocean as well as the narrow seas. And it cannot be supposed that anything so preposterous was contemplated as to make foreigners liable to the law of this country for offences committed on foreign ships all over the world. The statute must receive a reasonable construction, and the construction put upon it by the highest authorities has always been that all that it effected, or was intended to effect, was, as I have already stated, a transfer of jurisdiction only.

This being the true rule of construction, we have to consider whether the jurisdiction of the Admiral extended over foreigners on the high seas consistently with the rights of other nations, and I take it to be perfectly clear that it did not. Nor could it, consistently with the law of nations, be made to extend to them. For, if there is one proposition of international law more settled and

ndisputable than another, it is that the ships of each nation on the
high seas carry the law of their own nation with them, and that
those on board of them are amenable, in respect of offences committed in them (save and except in respect of piracy, which is an
offence against the law of all nations), to the law of such nation
alone: the only exception to this otherwise universal rule being
that the merchant ships of one nation, when in the ports and
waters of another, are subject to the law of the latter.   But this
liability is by all jurists treated as the exception to the general
rule.   To argue that, because merchant ships and those in them,
when in the waters of another state, are liable to the local law,
this liability can be extended to foreign ships all over the world,
is to make the exception swallow up the rule.   And this brings me
to the second branch of the argument, that the jurisdiction having
been asserted as to the narrow seas at the time the statute passed,
it must be taken to have been transferred by the statute.   The
answer to such a contention is that, no reference being made in
the statute to this now exploded claim of sovereignty, we must
read the statute as having transferred—as, indeed, it could alone
transfer—such jurisdiction only as actually existed.   Jurists are
now agreed that the claim to exclusive dominion over the narrow
seas, and consequent jurisdiction over foreigners for offences
committed thereon, was extravagant and unfounded, and the doctrine of the three-mile jurisdiction has taken the place of all such
pretensions.   In truth, though largely asserted in theory, the jurisdiction was never practically exercised in respect of foreigners.
The fallacy of such an argument as I have here referred to consists in supposing the jurisdiction to have had a real existence,
so as to be capable of being transferred without being first
expressly created by the statute.   And the position contended for
labours under this further difficulty, that it supposes a statutory
transfer, by implication, of a jurisdiction of one extent at the
time the statute was passed, and of another at the present
day.   One or two other statutes relating to the sea may be
disposed of in a few words, as having little or no bearing on the
question before us.   The Act of 5 Eliz. c. 5, an Act for the
protection of English shipping, after prohibiting, under penalties,
the importation of particular articles in foreign ships, provides
(s. 30) that such of the offences created by the Act as shall be
done on the main sea, or coasts of the sea, being no part of the
body of any county of this realm, and without the precincts,
jurisdiction, and liberty of the Cinque Ports, and out of any

haven or pier, shall be tried according to the statute of 28 Hen. 8. If done on the main sea, or coasts of the sea, within the jurisdiction of the Cinque Ports, such offence is to be tried before the Lord Warden, or his lieutenant or judge, or before judges of oyer and terminer, according to the statute of Hen. 8. It is obvious that this statute only affects the foreigner who is seeking our shores with the object of breaking the law. Coroners for counties, having under the old law no authority to inquire of matters arising on the sea unless within the body of the county, are now, by a recent Act of Parliament (6 Vict. c. 12) enabled, where there is no Admiralty coroner, to hold inquests on bodies found on the sea. That the Admiralty coroner or the county coroner is empowered to hold an inquest on a dead body found floating on the sea, though the body should prove to be that of a foreigner, can have no bearing on such a question as the present. Again, by the 7 Geo. 4, c. 38, justices of the peace are empowered to take any information upon oath touching any treason, piracy, felony, robbery, murder, conspiracy, or other offence, committed on the sea, or in any haven, river, creek, or place where the admiral has power are jurisdiction, and to commit or hold to bail. But this enactment, which is merely in furtherance of the administration of justice, has no special reference to foreigners, and would leave the question of jurisdiction to be disposed of by the Court before which the offence would afterwards come to be tried.

I pass on to the statutory enactments relating to foreigners within the three-mile zone. These enactments may be divided, first, into those which are intended to protect the interests of the state and those which are not; secondly, into those in which the foreigner is expressly named, and those in which he has been held to be included by implication only. Hitherto, legislation, so far as relates to foreigners in foreign ships in this part of the sea, has been confined to the maintenance of neutral rights and obligations, the prevention of breaches of the revenue and fishery laws, and, under particular circumstances, to cases of collision. In the two first the legislation is altogether irrespective of the three-mile distance, being founded on a totally different principle, namely, the right of a state to take all necessary measures for the protection of its territory and rights, and the prevention of any breach of its revenue laws.

The Legislature has omitted to adopt the alleged sovereignty over the littoral sea, to the extent of making our penal law applicable generally to foreigners passing through it for the purpose of navigation. Can a court of justice take upon itself, in such a matter, to do what the Legislature has not thought fit to do—that is, make the whole body of our penal law applicable to foreign vessels within three miles of our coasts? It is further apparent from these instances of specific legislation that, when asserting its power to legislate with reference to the foreigner within the three-mile zone, Parliament has deemed it necessary, wherever it was thought right to subject him to our law, expressly to enact that he should be so. We must take this, I think, as an exposition of the opinion of Parliament that specific legislation is here necessary, and consequently, that without it the foreigner in a foreign vessel will not come within the general law of this country in respect of matters arising on the sea. Legislation, in relation to foreign ships coming into British ports and waters, rests on a totally different principle, as was well explained by Dr. Lushington in the case of the *Annapolis* (1 Lush. Adm. 295).

Assuming everything, short of the ultimate conclusion, to be conceded to the prosecution—granting that the three-mile zone forms part of the territory or realm of England, and that without parliamentary interference the territorial sea has become part of the realm of England, so that jurisdiction has been acquired over it, the question arises—in whom is the jurisdiction? The indictment alleges that the offence was committed on the high seas. To support this averment the place in question must still remain part of the high sea. But if it is to be held to be the high sea, and so within the jurisdiction of the Admiral, the prosecution fails, because, *ex hypothesi*, the Admiral never had jurisdiction over foreigners in foreign ships: and no assent on the part of foreign nations to the exercise of dominion and jurisdiction over these waters can, without an Act of Parliament, confer on the Admiral or any other judge a larger jurisdiction than he possessed before. If the littoral sea is to be considered territory—in other words, no longer high sea—the present indictment fails, and this, whether the part in question has become part of a county or not. The only distinction known to the law of England, as regards the sea, is between such part of the sea as is within the body of a county and such as is not. In the first there is jurisdiction over the foreigner on a foreign ship; in the other, there is not. Such a thing as sea which shall be at one and the same time high sea and also part of the territory, is unknown to the present law, and never had an existence, except in the old and senseless

theory of a universal dominion over the narrow seas. To put this
shortly. To sustain this indictment the littoral sea must still be
considered as part of the high seas, and as such, under the jurisdiction of the Admiral. But the Admiral never had jurisdiction
over foreign ships on the high seas. How, when exercising the
functions of a British Judge, can he, or those acting in substitution for him, assume a jurisdiction which heretofore he did not
possess, except authorized by statute? In the result, looking to the
fact that all pretension to sovereignty or jurisdiction over foreign
ships in the narrow seas has long since been wholly abandoned—
to the uncertainty which attaches to the doctrine of the publicists
as to the degree of sovereignty and jurisdiction which may be
exercised on the so-called territorial sea—to the fact that the right
of absolute sovereignty therein, and of penal jurisdiction over the
subjects of other states, has never been expressly asserted or conceded among independent nations, or, in practice, exercised and
acquiesced in, except for violation of neutrality or breach of
revenue or fishery laws, which, as has been pointed out, stand on
a different footing,—as well as to the fact that, neither in legis-
lating with reference to shipping, nor in respect of the criminal
law, has Parliament thought proper to assume territorial sovereignty over the three-mile zone, so as to enact that all offences
committed upon it, by foreigners in foreign ships, should be
within the criminal law of this country, but, on the contrary,
wherever it was thought right to make the foreigner amenable to
our law, has done so by express and specific legislation, I cannot
think that, in the absence of all precedent, and of any judicial
decision or authority applicable to the present purpose, we should
be justified in holding an offence, committed under such circumstances, to be punishable by the law of England, especially as in
so holding we must declare the whole body of our penal law to be
applicable to the foreigner passing our shores in a foreign vessel
on his way to a foreign port. I am by no means insensible to the
argument *ab inconvenienti* pressed upon us by the Solicitor-Gen-
eral. It is, no doubt, desirable, looking to the frequency of col-
lisions in the neighborhood of our coasts, that the commanders
of foreign vessels, who, by unskilful navigation or gross want of
care, cause disaster or death, should be as much amenable to the
local law as those navigating our own vessels, instead of redress
having to be sought in the, perhaps, distant country of the
offender. But the remedy for the deficiency of the law, if it can
be made good consistently with international law—as to which

TERRITORIAL JURISDICTION OF NATIONS.

we are not called upon to pronounce an opinion—should be supplied by the action of the Legislature, with whom the responsibility for any imperfection of the law alone rests, not by a usurpation on our part of a jurisdiction which, without legislation, we do not judicially possess. This matter has been sometimes discussed upon the assumption that the alternative of the non-exercise of jurisdiction on our part must be the total impunity of foreigners in respect of collision arising from negligence in the vicinity of our coast. But this is a mistaken view. If by the assent of other nations the three-mile belt of sea has been brought under the dominion of this country, so that consistently with the right of other nations it may be treated as a portion of British territory, it follows, as a matter of course, that Parliament can legislate in respect of it. Parliament has only to do so, and the judges of the land will, as in duty bound, apply the law which Parliament shall so create. The question is, whether legislative action shall be applied to meet the exigency of the case, or judicial authority shall be strained and misapplied in order to overcome the difficulty. The responsibility is with the Legislature, and there it must rest.

Having arrived at this conclusion, it becomes necessary to consider the second point taken on the part of the Crown, namely, that though the negligence of which the accused was guilty occurred on board a foreign ship, yet, the death having taken place on board a British ship, the offence was committed within the jurisdiction of a British Court of Justice. This is the point insisted on by my Brothers Denman and Lindley, with the somewhat hesitating and reluctant assent of the Lord Chief Justice of the Common Pleas. I dissent altogether from their opinion. In considering this question it is necessary to bear in mind—which I am disposed to think has not always been done—that we must deal with this part of the case without any reference to the theory of the three-mile zone, and (as was very properly admitted by the Solicitor General) as though the two ships had met, and the occurrence had happened, on the ocean. The argument rests mainly on the authority of *Reg.* v. *Coombes* (1 Leach C. C. 388), in which, on a trial for a murder, under an Admiralty Commission it was held by all the judges that, where a shot had been fired from the shore at a person in a vessel on the sea, and had killed him, as the death took place on the sea, the offence was properly cognisable under an Admiralty Commission. The case of the *United States* v. *Davis* (2 Sumn. Rep. 482) is, in like manner, an

authority in favour of the view that where a person, firing a gun
from a ship lying in the waters of a foreign state, kills a person
on board another ship, lying in such waters, the offence is in
point of law committed on board the latter; and that, consequently, the person causing the death is amenable to the local
law, and not to that of the country to which his ship belongs.
The defendant was indicted before a Circuit Court of the United
States for manslaughter. He was the master of an American
ship, lying in the harbor of Raiatia, one of the Society Islands.
A disturbance having arisen on board the ship, the defendant
took his gun in hand, and the gun going off—whether fired
purposely or not was uncertain—a man on board another vessel
was unintentionally killed. The Court held, on the authority of
Coombes' case (1 Leach C. C. 388) that the offence, if any, had
been committed on a foreign vessel in the jurisdiction of a foreign
government, and that an American Court had, therefore, no jurisdiction to try him. The *ratio decidendi* in these cases does not
appear in the reports, and it becomes desirable, therefore, to see
by what principle the decision in such a case should be governed.
Now, homicide, whether it takes the form of murder or of manslaughter, necessarily involves two things essentially distinct—
the act of the party killing, as the cause of the death, and the
death of the party killed, as the effect of such act. Both are
necessary to constitute the crime. But it is obvious that the act
of the party killing may take place in one jurisdiction, the death
of the party killed in another. A person may be wounded on
the sea, and may die on the shore, or *vice versâ*. He may be
wounded in England; he may die in Scotland. In which is the
offence committed? As the blow was struck in the one, while
the death, without which the offence is not complete, took place
in the other, I answer, in neither; and the old authorities who
held at common law, before the difficulty arising from divided
jurisdictions had been got over by express legislation, that where
the wound was inflicted on the sea, and the person struck died
on the shore, or *vice versâ*—or where the wound was inflicted in
one county, and the death took place in another—the offender
could be tried in neither, because in neither had the entire offence
been committed—reasoned, in my opinion, logically, and, in
point of principle, rightly. These cases are not, however, in
point to the one before us, and, if I advert to them, it is only to
clear the way as I advance. We have, in this instance, not the
case of the blow or wound in one jurisdiction, and the death in

another; but as in *Reg.* v. *Coombes* (1 Leach C. C. 388), one in which the act causing the death begins in one jurisdiction and extends into another, in which it inflicts the blow or wound, from which, as its cause, death ensues. When a man strikes a blow with a club, or inflicts a wound by the thrust of a sword, or the stab of a knife, or blows out another's brains by putting a pistol to his head, the act takes effect immediately. If he hurls a stone or discharges a bullet from a gun or pistol at another person, at a distance, the instrument he uses passes from him; the stone or bullet, having left his hand, has to make its way through a given space before it strikes the blow it is intended to inflict. But the blow is as much the act of him who casts the stone, or fires the gun, as though it had taken effect immediately. In such a case the act, in lieu of taking effect immediately, is a continuing act till the end has been effected—that is, till the missile has struck the blow, the intention of the party using it accompanying it throughout its course. The act must be taken to be the act of the party in the effects it was intended to produce, till its agency has become exhausted and its operation has ceased. When, therefore, a person being in one jurisdiction fires a shot at a person who is in another, as was the case in *Reg.* v. *Coombes* (1 Leach C. C. 388), it may well be held that the blow struck by the bullet is an act done in the jurisdiction in which the bullet takes effect. *Reg.* v. *Coombes* (1 Leach C. C. 388) was therefore, in my opinion, rightly decided; and I think the same principle would apply where the master of a vessel purposely ran down another, and by so doing caused the death of a person on board. For, though his immediate act is confined to running his ship against the other, it is, nevertheless, his act which causes the ship run down to sink. It is as much his act which causes the death of the person drowned, as though he had actually thrown such person into the water. If, therefore, the defendant had purposely run into the *Strathclyde*, I should have been prepared to hold that the killing of the deceased was his act where the death took place, and, consequently, that the act—in other words, the offence of which he has been convicted—had been committed on board a British ship. Whether the same principle would apply to a case of manslaughter, arising from the running down of another ship through negligence, or to a case where death is occasioned by the careless discharge of a gun, may, indeed, admit of doubt. For, in such a case, there is no intention accompanying the act into its ulterior consequences. The negligence in running down a ship may be said to be confined to the improper navigation of the ship occasioning the mischief; the party guilty of such negligence is neither actually, nor in intention, and thus constructively, in the ship on which the death takes place. But let use assume the contrary: let us take the drowning of the deceased to have been the act of the defendant done on board a British vessel. Is this conclusive of the question? By no means. The subtle argument which would extend the negligence committed in one ship to another in which it produces its effect, finds its appropriate answer in reasoning, which, though perhaps also savouring of subtlety, is yet directly to the purpose, and must not be overlooked. For the question is—and this appears to me to have been lost sight of in the argument—not whether the death of the deceased, which no doubt took place in a British ship, was the act of the defendant in such ship, but whether the defendant, at the time the act was done, was himself within British jurisdiction. But, in point of fact, the defendant was, at the time of the occurrence, not on board the British ship, the *Strathclyde*, but on a foreign ship, the *Franconia*. And here we must remember that, *ex hypothesi*, we have to deal with the case on the assumption that both the vessels were on the high seas, and not in British waters. But, though, as we have just seen, an act, begun in one place or jurisdiction, may extend into another, it is obvious that the person doing such continuing act cannot himself be at the time in both. A man who, being in field A, throws a stone at another, who is in field B, does not thereby transfer himself to the latter. A man who fires a shot from the shore at one who is on the sea still remains on the shore, and *vice versâ*. One who, from the bank of a river dividing two territories, fires a rifle shot at a person on the opposite side, cannot be said to be in the territory where the shot strikes its object. One who from the deck of a vessel, by the discharge of a gun, either purposely or through negligence, kills or wounds another, is not thereby transported from the deck of his own vessel to that of the other. But, in order to render a foreigner liable to the local law, he must, at the time the offence was committed, have been within British territory if on land, or in a British ship if at sea. I cannot think that if two ships of different nations met on the ocean, and a person on board of one of them were killed or wounded by a shot fired from the other, the person firing it would be amenable to the law of the ship in which the shot took effect. According to the doctrine of Lord Coke in *Calvin's case* (4 Co. R. 1), protection and allegiance are co-relative; it is only where protection is afforded by the law that the obligation of allegiance to the law arises; or, as I prefer to put it, it is only for acts done when the person doing them is within the area over which the authority of British law extends, that the subject of a foreign state owes obedience to that law, or can be made amenable to its jurisdiction. But for the opinion expressed by Brother Denman, I should have thought it beyond all dispute that a foreign ship, when not in British waters, but on the high seas, was not subject to our law. Upon this point I had deemed all jurists unanimous, and could not have supposed that a doubt could exist. Upon what is the contrary opinion founded? Simply upon expediencey, which is to prevail over principle. What, it is asked, is to happen if one of your officers, enforcing your revenue laws, should be killed or injured by a foreigner on board a foreign ship? What is to happen if a British and foreign ship meeting on the ocean, a British subject should be killed by a shot fired from the foreign ship? In either of such cases would not the foreigner guilty of the offence be amenable to the English law? Could it be endured that he should escape with impunity? If brought within the reach of a British court of Justice, could he not be tried and punished for the offence, and ought he to be permitted to escape with impunity, or ought he not to be tried and punished for such offence? My first answer is, that the alternative is fallacious. He will not escape with impunity. He will be amenable to the law of his own country, and it is not to be presumed that the law of any civilised people will be such, or so administered, as that such an offence should escape without its adequate punishment. As regards the amenability of the offender under such circumstances to our own law, it will be time enough to determine the question when the case arises. If the conviction and punishment of the offender can only be obtained at the sacrifice of fundamental principles of established law, I, for one, should prefer that justice should fail in the individual case, than that established principles, according to which alone justice should be administered, should be wrested and strained to meet it. I think, therefore, that it is not enough that the running down of the *Strathclyde,* and so causing the death of the deceased, can be said to have been the act of the defendant on board the latter vessel, unless it can be made out that the defendant was also on board of it. But the defendant certainly was not actually, nor do I think—no intention on his part having accompanied the act—he can be said to have been,

in any sense, constructively, on board the *Strathclyde*. If, therefore, his own vessel was not within British Waters, but on the
high seas, he owed no obedience to the law of this country, and
cannot be punished for an infraction of it. In the case of *United
States* v. *Davis* (2 Sumn. Rep. 482), no such difficulty presented
itself. Both ships were in the harbour, and therefore in the water
of the local state, and the defendant was consequently amenable
to the local law. I am aware that this view is not in accordance
with the decision in the American case of *Adams* v. *The People* (1
Comstock's Rep. 173). In that case a fraud had been committed
at New York by the defendant, a citizen of the state of Ohio, and
residing in it, through an agent at New York, who was wholly
innocent and ignorant of the fraud. The accused set up as a
defence that he was a citizen of another state, and residing in it
when the alleged offence was committed, and therefore not subject
to the law of New York; but the objection was overruled, on the
ground that a criminal act done through the instrumentality of
an innocent agent is in law the act of the principal, who may,
therefore, be held to have committed the offence in the state in
which the act was done, and, being found in that state, will be
liable to be there tried and punished. Both exceptions taken
on the part of the Crown to the general rule that a foreigner,
committing an offence out of the jurisdiction of a country which
is not his own, cannot be brought to trial in the courts of the
former, thus failing, it appears to me that the general rule must
prevail, and that the defendant, having been a foreign subject, on
board a foreign ship, on a foreign voyage, and on the high seas at
the time the offence was committed, is not amenable to the law of
this country; that there was, therefore, no jurisdiction to try him,
and that, consequently, the conviction was illegal, and must be
quashed.

(In consequence of this decision, Parliament passed the St.
of 41 and 42 Vict. c. 73. By that act it was declared that, "for
the purpose of any offense declared by this act to be within the
jurisdiction of the Admiral, any part of the open sea within one
marine league of the coast measured from low-water mark shall
be deemed to be the open sea within the territorial waters of her
Majesty's dominions.")[3]

---

[3]**Territorial Limits of the United States.**—The territorial limits of the
United States, where it borders on the ocean, are determined by the law
of nations, and by that law it has been held to extend into the ocean the
distance of a marine league, or about three and a half English miles. The
distance is measured from low-water mark. Bays and other arms of the

sea wholly within the territory of a country, not exceeding two marine leagues in width at the mouth, are within the territorial limits. The Delaware and Chesapeake Bays are claimed to be within the jurisdiction of the United States. *Manchester v. Massachusetts, 139 U. S. 240, 35 Sup. Ct. Rep. 159.*

As a rule a nation has full jurisdiction and control over all persons and things within its boundaries, but by the comity of nations certain aliens bring their native laws with them. This privilege is conceded especially (1) to sovereigns traveling abroad with their trains; (2) to ambassadors, their suite, family, and servants; and (3) to the officers and crews of public vessels (not private vessels) in foreign ports, and to armies in their permitted transit through foreign territory. *Wools. Int. Law, Sec. 68.*

Diplomatic agents, such as ambassadors, legates, envoys, etc., represent their governments, and in order that they may exercise their diplomatic functions freely, they can neither be sued in the civil Courts nor arrested and tried for any breach of the criminal laws. They may be ordered to leave the country. *Hall Int. L. P. 169; Coppell v. Hall, 7 Wall. 542; Davis v. Packard, 7 Pet. 276; In re Baiz, 135 U. S. 403.*

State Limits.—The states bordering on the ocean extend out, as does the United States, the distance of a marine league from the shore Those states bordering on the Great Lakes extend to the boundary line between the United States and Canada. Where states are divided by rivers, the jurisdiction of each state extends to the middle of the stream. However, there are exceptions to this rule. The Hudson River, between New York and New Jersey, is wholly within the jurisdiction of New York. The Ohio River, between Ohio and Kentucky, is wholly in Kentucky. The states bordering on the Mississippi River which were formed out of the Northwest Territory have concurrent jurisdiction over the whole river. *Com. v. Peters, 12 Met. (Mass.) 387; Com. v. Manchester, 152 Mass. 230, 23 Am. St. Rep. 820; Booth v. Hubbard, 8 Ohio St. 244, State v. Babcock, 30 N. J. L. 29; Manchester v. Massachusetts, 139 U. S. 240, 35 Sup. Ct. Rep. 159.*

County Limits.—Counties bordering on the high seas did not at common law extend to the state limits, but ended at the water line. A state may extend the limits of its counties so as to coincide with its own limits; and this has been done in some states. *Manley v. People, 7 N. Y. 295; Biscoe v. State, 68 Md. 294; Com. v. Peters, 12 Met. 387; Manchester v. Mass., 139 U. S. 240, 35 Sup. Ct. Rep. 159.*

Ships on the High Seas.—The public and private vessels of every nation on the high seas, and out of the territorial limits of any other state, are subject to the jurisdiction of the state to which they belong. Such vessels are regarded as part of the territory of the nation under whose flag they sail. A foreign merchant vessel, while within state limits, is subject to the laws of the state, and is within the jurisdiction of its Courts, and crimes committed on such vessels, although between foreigners, are withing the control of the state unless a treaty provides otherwise. This is not true of a war ship; a war vessel carries its own nationality with it wherever it goes, and it is considered a part of the soil of the country to which it belongs. A war vessel, while in a foreign port, is not subject to the laws of that country.

Jurisdiction to punish for crimes committed on American ships on the high seas and in foreign ports is conferred by act of Congress on the Federal Courts. The state Courts can not take jurisdiction unless the crime was committed within state limits. If the vessel is a private one, and in a foreign port, it is also subject to the laws of the foreign country. *United*

States v. Holmes, 5 Wheat. 412; United States v. Palmer, 3 Wheat. 610; People v. Curtis, 50 N. Y. 321, 10 Am. Rep. 483.

By treaties with non-Christian countries, our consuls residing there have jurisdiction over our citizens who have committed offenses within the jurisdiction of such countries. The object is to withdraw citizens of the United States from the operation of crude and barbarous systems of justice there prevailing. *In re Ross, 140 U. S. 453, 35 Sup. Ct. Rep. 581.*

The *Trent case,* in 1862, illustrates the law as to a private vessel on the high seas. In this case, Commodore Wilkes, of the San Jacinto, a public vessels of the United States, removed Messrs. Mason and Slidell from a British private vessel on the high seas. England said her rights were violated, and insisted that Mason and Slidell should be returned. This was complied with by our government. Although Mason and Slidell were not British subjects, yet we had no authority to arrest them on a British private vessel on the high seas. If the British vessel was in an American port our authority would be unquestioned unless we had surrendered this right by treaty.

In the case of *Wildenhus, 120 U. S. 1,* one member of a foreign crew on a foreign ship killed a fellow sailor while the ship was in the port of Jersey City, New Jersey. The defendant was imprisoned by the authority of the laws of the state of New Jersey. The consul of Belgium applied for the release of *Wildenhus,* claiming that the law of his country should punish the offense, and not the laws of New Jersey. The Supreme Court of the United States in deciding the case held as follows: "It is part of the law of civilized nations that when a merchant vessel of one country enters the ports of another for the purposes of trade, it subjects itself to the laws of the place to which it goes, unless by treaty or otherwise the two countries have come to some different understanding or agreement. * * * Disorders which disturb only the peace of the ship or those on board, are to be dealt with exclusively by the sovereignty of the home of the ship, but those which disturb the public peace may be suppressed, and, if need be, the offenders punished by the proper authorities of the local jurisdiction. It may not be easy at all times to determine to which of the two jurisdictions a particular act of disorder belongs. Much will undoubtedly depend on the attending circumstances of the particular case, but all must concede that felonious homicide is a subject for the local jurisdiction, and that if the proper authorities are proceeding with the case in a regular way, the consul has no right to interfere to prevent it." The Court thus sustained the right of the state to punish this offender.

In the case of *United States v. Rodgers, 150 U. S. 249, (1893),* where a person was indicted in the United States District Court for assaulting with a dangerous weapon a man on board the steamer *Alaska,* an American boat, and then being on the Canadian side of the Detroit River, the Court decided that "the Great Lakes were high seas, and that the Courts of the United States have jurisdiction to try a person for such an offense when such vessel is in the Detroit River, out of the jurisdiction of any particular state, and within the territorial limits of the Dominion of Canada." The Canadian authorities would also have authority to punish such offense, and if the crime was committed on the Michigan side, the Michigan Courts would have jurisdiction.

As to jurisdiction over foreign ships in territorial waters, see article by *Charles W. Gregory, Michigan Law Review, February, 1904, Page 333.*

Criminal Prosecution for Acts Committed Without the State.—The states of the Union ceded to the United States all diplomatic authority, therefore they cannot be regarded as nations in the full sense of that term, yet they are sovereign as regards their own internal affairs. They retain all the rights incident to sovereignty which have not been ceded to the

Federal government. Have the states jurisdiction over crimes committed abroad? Some Courts have decided that they have, others that they have not.

In the case of *People v. Merrill, 2 Parker's Cr. Rep. (N. Y.) 590, (1855),* the Court held that "a state has no jurisdiction of crimes committed beyond its territorial limits." In this case Merrill and another took a free negro, an inhabitant of New York, into the District of Columbia and sold him as a slave. Merrill was indicted in New York for the sale made in the District of Columbia. Such a sale was lawful in the District of Columbia, but unlawful in the state of New York. "Every statute," the Court said, "is presumed to be enacted with reference to the local jurisdiction of the legislature of each state."

"To give it a broader construction, and make it applicable to a sale or transfer made in another state, would make it repugnant to the Constitution of the United States (*Amendment, Art. 6*), which declares that in criminal prosecutions the accused shall enjoy the right of a speedy and public trial by an impartial jury of the state and district wherein the crime shall have been committed; and also, Art. 4, Sec. 2, of the Constitution of the United States, which declares that the citizens of each state shall be entitled to all the immunities of the citizens of the several states; and provides that a person charged in any state with treason, or felony, or other crime, who shall flee from justice, or shall be found in another state, shall, on demand of the executive authority of the state from which he fled, be delivered up to be removed to the state having jurisdiction of the crime." [It will be noticed that the above case holds that the Sixth Amendment to the Constitution of the United States limits the powers of the states. The Supreme Court of the United States has decided that the first eight amendments are limitations upon the Federal government and not upon the states. See *Eilenbecker v. Plymouth County, 134 U. S. 31 (1890); Baron v. Baltimore, 7 Pet. (U. S.) 243 (1833); Twitchell v. Com., 7 Wall. 321 (1868); Fox v. Ohio, 5 Howard 410. Ed.*]

In the case of *State v. Main, 16 Wis. 422,* the Court said: "Although it is true as a general proposition, that the laws of a state have no force outside of its territorial limits, it is equally true that every state may, in the regulation of its own internal affairs, authorize certain acts to be done outside of its limits, and describe what effect they shall have within. Thus it pertains to every state to prescribe in what manner title to real estate within it shall be transferred."

The question here was whether the state law giving soldiers the privilege of voting when out of the state was valid. Court held it valid. And as to the state punishing those who were guilty of illegal voting under such circumstances, the Court said: "It seems to be well established that every nation has the right to punish its own citizens for the violation of its laws wherever committed. This right is based upon the duty of allegiance. The offender, of course, must be afterwards found within the state. It would not apply to citizens of other states."

Judge Bronson in *Adams v. People, 1 Coms. (N. Y.) 173,* said: "It does not occur to me that there are more than two cases where the question of allegiance can have anything to do with a criminal prosecution. *First,* when the accused is charged with a breach of the duty of allegiance, as in case of treason; and *Second,* when the government proposes to punish offenses committed by its own citizens beyond the territorial limits of the state.

"If the citizen could pass beyond the limits of his country and commit crimes against his country, and afterwards return into it and laugh to scorn its power of punishment, because the offense was committed outside

4

of it, the power of every nation to defend itself against treachery woul‹
be seriously impaired."

The case of *Hanks v. The State, 13 Texas Ct. of Appeals 289 (1882)*
is a later decision on this question. In this case Hanks and one P. F. Dill
man were jointly indicted in the District Court of Travis County for th
forgery of a transfer of a land certificate for a league and labor of land i¹
the state of Texas. It is alleged in the indictment that the acts consti
tuting the forgery were all committed in Caddo Parish, in the state o
Louisiana. No act or thing connected with the execution of the forger;
is charged to have been done in Texas; but the crime and injury, so fa
as this state is concerned, are averred to consist in the fact that the sai
forgery in Louisiana did then and there relate to and affect an interest ii
land in the state of Texas.

It was made a ground both in the motion to quash the indictmen
and in arrest of judgment, and is again urgently insisted upon in the abl
brief of counsel for appellant, that the facts alleged, if true, would con
stitute an offense against the sovereign state of Louisiana alone, and on
of which the Courts of this state would have no jurisdiction. In decidin;
the case, the Court said: "If the position thus assumed in behalf o
appellant be correct, then the legislature had no authority to pass the ac
quoted, and the same is an absolute nullity. Can this proposition b
maintained? It certainly cannot be found in any constitutional inhibition
state or Federal, depriving the legislature of the authority, and unless ther‹
is some authority of law superior to the right of a state legislature, whicl
could and should control the action of the latter within the scope of it
constitutional powers, we cannot well conceive how its enactments, i
reasonable and consistent with that power, could be hel   inoperative an‹
nugatory.

"Two authorities, which are to the effect that the legislature of on‹
state cannot define and punish crimes committed in another state, ar‹
mainly relied upon. The leading one is the case of *The State v. Knight*
taken from *2 Haywood*, and reported in *Taylor's North Carolina Reports
page 44.* The other is *People v. Merrill, 2 Parker's Criminal Reports (N
Y.) 590.* The defendant in the first case was indicted under a statute th‹
words of which were: 'And whereas there is reason to apprehend tha
wicked and ill-disposed persons resident in the neighboring states make ;
practice of counterfeiting the current bills of credit of this state, and b;
themselves or emissaries utter or vend the same, with an intention t‹
defraud the citizens of this state: Be it enacted, etc., that all such person
shall be subject to the same mode of trial, and on conviction liable to th‹
same pains and penalties as if the offense had been committed within th‹
limits of this state and prosecuted in the Superior Court of any district o
this state.' It was held that the jurisdiction to try in North Carolina wa
doubtful, and the prisoner was discharged.

"Mr. Wharton, in his work on the Conflict of Laws, says: 'The stur
diest advocates of the hypothesis that the *locus delicti* alone confers juris
diction have admitted that there are cases in which a person whose resi
dence is outside the territory may make himself, by conspiring extra
territorially to defeat its laws, infra-territorially responsible. If, fo
instance, a forger should establish on the Mexican side of the boundar;
between the United States and Mexico a manufactory for the forgery o
United States securities, for us to hold that when the mischief is don
he can take up his residence in the United States without even liability t
arrest, would not merely expose our government to spoliation, but brin‹
its authority into contempt. To say that in such a case the Mexican gov
ernment can be relied upon to punish is no answer; because, *first,* in coun
tries of such imperfect civilization, penal justice is uncertain; *secondl;*

in cases where, in such country, the local community gains greatly by the fraud and suffers by it no loss, the chances of conviction and punishment would be peculiarly slight; and, *thirdly*, because all that the offender would have to do to escape justice in such a case would be to walk over the boundary line into the United States, where on this hypothesis he would go free.' (*Wharton Conflict of Laws, Sec. 876*). Again he says: 'Thus it has been held that the originator of a nuisance to a stream in one country which affects such stream in another country is liable to prosecution in the latter country; that the author of a libel uttered by him in one country and published by others in another country, from which he is absent at the time, is liable in the latter country; that he who on one side of a boundary shoots a person on the other side is amenable in the country where the blow is received; that he who in one state employs an innocent agent to obtain goods by false pretenses in another state is amenable in the latter state; and that he who sells through agents, guilty or innocent, lottery tickets in another state is amenable in the state of the sale, though he was absent from such state personally. In England we have the same principle affirmed by the highest judicial authority,' and he quotes Lord Campbell as saying, 'that a person may, by the employment as well of a conscious as of an unconscious agent, render himself amenable to the law of England when he comes within the jurisdiction of our Courts;' and Sir R. Phillimore as saying, 'It is a monstrous thing that any technical rule of venue should prevent justice from being done in this country on a criminal for an offense which was perpetrated here, but the execution of which was concocted in another country.' (*Wharton Conflict of Laws, Sec. 877.* See also *Adams v. People, 1 Com.* (*N. Y.*) *173; Com. v. Macloon, 101 Mass. 1; Ham v. State, 4 Texas App. 645; Ex Parte Rogers, 10 Texas App. 655*).

Mr. Cooley, in his great work on Constitutional Limitations, treating of territorial limitation to legislative authority, says: 'The legislative authority of every state must spend its force within the territorial limits of the state. * * * It cannot provide for the punishment as crimes of acts committed beyond the state boundary, because such acts, if offenses at all, must be offenses against the sovereignty within whose limits they have been done.' But, after laying down this doctrine, in the very next sentence he says: 'But if the consequences of an unlawful act committed outside the state have reached their ultimate and injurious result within it, it seems that the perpetrator may be punished as an offender against such state.' (*Cooley's Const. Lim., 4 ed., pp. 154-5.*) If this latter rule be the law, then it is a solecism to say that the legislature cannot so declare it by express enactment.

Story, in his *Conflict of Laws*, says: "Although the penal laws of every country are in their nature local, yet an offense may be committed in one sovereignty in violation of the laws of another, and if the offender be afterwards found in the latter state, he may be punished according to the laws thereof, and the fact that he owes allegiance to another sovereignty is no bar to the indictment." *Story, Conflict of Laws, 4 ed., Sec. 625b.*

The court held that the state has authority to punish such an act, and that for forgery committed in Louisiana by parties there, against the state of Texas, such parties are criminally responsible to the state of Texas.

Civil Actions for Acts Without the State.—The case of *McDonald v. Mallory, 77 N. Y. 546 (1879)*, covers this phase of the question.

This action was brought by plaintiff as administratrix of Charles McDonald, deceased, to recover damages for his death.

The complaint alleged, in substance, the ownership of the steamer "City of Waco" by the defendants, and its employment as a freight and passenger vessel trading between the city of New York and the city of

Galveston, in the state of Texas; that defendants were citizens and r[
idents of the city of New York, and said steamer was registered a
belonged in the port of New York; that said Charles McDonald, a citiz
of the state of New York, and a resident in the city of Brooklyn, w
employed on the steamer as a fireman; that the steamer received on boa[
at New York, as freight to be carried to Galveston, 300 cases of petroleu[
that while the said steamer was lying at anchor on the high seas, outs[
the the harbor and bar of Galveston, Texas, a fire started on board of h
and by reason of the presence of said petroleum, which was reached
the fire, the said fire could not be extinguished, and the death of plaintif
intestate was caused by the violence of said fire, and by the culpa[
negligence of said defendents.

The complaint then alleges that said negligence and death occurr
within the territory of the state of New York, to wit: at the city of N[
York, and on board said steamer belonging to the state of New York, a[
being at first at the city of New York, and thereafter on the high se[
as above stated. The defendants demurred to the complaint, on t
ground that the court had no jurisdiction of the action.

The court held as follows: "Civil rights of action for matters occl
ring at sea, on board of a vessel belonging to one of the states, mr
depend upon the laws of that state, unless they arise out of some matt
over which jurisdiction has been vested in and exercised by the gover
ment of the United States. That under the statute of this state (Laws
New York) giving a right of action for causing death by a wrongful a
or neglect, an action was maintainable for causing the death of a citiz
of this state on the high seas, on board of a vessel hailing from and reg
tered in a port within the state; the vessel being at the time employed
the owners in their own business, and their negligence having caused t
death." *Judgment for plaintiff.*

It was decided in the case of *Crapo v. Kelly, 16 Wall. (U. S.) 6*
(1872), that the private vessel, "Arctic," while on the high seas was
portion of the territory of Massachusetts, and the assignment by t[
insolvent court of that state passed the title to her, in the same mann
and with the like effect as if she had been physically within the boun
of that state when the assignment was executed.

Laws of Newly Acquired Territory.—In *Blankard v. Galdy, 4 M[
222 (1693)*, the plaintiff was provost marshal of *Jamaica*, and by certa
articles made between him and the defendant, he granted a deputation
that office to the defendant for seven years and a half, under the yea[
rent of four hundred pounds; and the defendant gave bond for the p[
formance of the agreement. An action of debt was brought upon t
bond. The defendant pleaded the statute of 5 and 6 Edwd. 6, c. 16, ma
against buying and selling of offices, and averred that this office concern
the administration of justice in *Jamaica*, and that by virtue of that stat[
both the bond and articles were void. The plaintiff replied, that Jamai
was an island inhabited formerly by the Spaniard, and governed by th[
own laws ever since the conquest thereof by the English, and that t
execution of the said office only concerned the said island, and the inha
itants thereof, etc. The defendant rejoined, and confesses it to be a co
quered nation, but that ever since the conquest thereof it was parcel of tl
kingdom, and governed by the laws of England, and not by their o[
laws, etc. The plaintiff demurred to the rejoinder. The defendant join
in demurrer.

The only question was, whether the laws of England were in fo[
in *Jamaica*?

THE COURT. The laws by which the people were governed before t
conquest of the island, do bind them till new laws are given, and acts

parliament made here since the conquest do not bind them unless they are particularly named. The reason is, because though a conqueror may make new laws, yet there is a necessity that the former should be in force till new are obtained, and even then some of their old customs may remain. By the statute of 27 Hen. 8, c. 27, Wales was united to England, yet some of their customs still remain; it is so likewise in Ireland, which nation, though conquered, yet still retain their old customs, as in the case of Tanistry; so that there may be a part of the possessions of the crown of England (as the Isle of Man is) and yet not governed by our laws.

And therefore it was held, that Jamaica was not governed by the laws of England after the conquest thereof, till new laws were made; for they had neither sheriff or counties; they were only an assembly of people which are not bound by our laws, unless particularly mentioned. *Judgment for plaintiff.*

In the year 1722 it was determined by the privy council, upon an appeal to the king in council from the foreign plantations, *First,* that if there be a new and uninhabited country discovered by English subjects, such new found country is to be governed by the laws of England, but that after it becomes inhabited it shall not be bound by English statutes unless specially named. *Secondly,* that when the king of England conquers a country, he may impose upon the inhabitants what laws he pleases. But *Thirdly,* that until such laws be given by the conqueror, the laws and customs of the conquered country shall hold place, except where they are contrary to the established religion; or enact anything *malum in se;* or are silent; for that in all such cases the laws of the conquering country shall prevail. *2 Peere Wms. 75.*

In *Adv. Gen. of Bengal v. Ranee Surnomoye Dossee, 2 Moore's Privy Council (N. S.) 22,* the court stated the following rule: "Where Englishmen establish themselves in an uninhabited, or barbarous country, they carry with them not only the laws, but the sovereignty of their own state; and those who live among them and become members of their community, become partakers of and subject to the same laws." See *Story, Const. Law, Sec. 146-158; 1 Blackstone Com., 107.*

CHAPTER III.

DOMICIL.

PRICE v. PRICE, 1893.

[156 Pa. St. 617; 27 Atl. 291.]

1. Domicil Defined.
2. Requisites of Domicil.

3. Importance of Domicil.
4. Domicil Distinguished.

OPINION BY MR. CHIEF JUSTICE STERRET, Oct. 2, 1893:

In obedience to the precept of the orphans' court, this feigne issue was formed for the purpose of determining the dispute question of fact, whether, at the time of his decease in Augus 1890, Henry F. Price was a resident of and domiciled in Penr sylvania. The validity of the testamentary paper alleged to b his last will, as well as the jurisdiction of the register of wil in admitting the same to probate, depended upon the determir ation of that question. The proponent of said alleged will, th executor therein named, was made plaintiff in the issue, an decedent's only child was made defendant. In his declaration, th plaintiff "averred that said Henry F. Price, at the time of h decease, was a legal resident of Pennsylvania," etc. Defenc ant in her plea distinctly traversed that averment, and issu was joined thereon. It therefore follows that the burden c proof was on the plaintiff; and he recognized that fact by pro ing in the outset that decedent was born in West Chester, Pa that, about the time he attained his majority, he embarked i business and acquired a domicile of choice in the city of Phil delphia, and, after residing there for eight or ten years, he r moved to New York, many years ago, and there acquired an maintained his second domicile of choice. These facts were co ceded; but it was necessary for plaintiff to go further, and h accordingly introduced testimony tending to prove that sai decedent, less than two months before his decease, abandoned h New York domicile and resumed his domicile of origin in We Chester, Pa., and resided there until he died. This latter alleg tion, that he abandoned his New York domicile, etc., was co troverted by defendant, who introduced testimony tending ·

prove the contrary. It is not our purpose to review or discuss this conflicting testimony. It is sufficient to say that it bore directly on the issue formed by the pleadings and was clearly for the exclusive consideration of the jury, whose special province was to judge as to the credibility of the witnesses, weigh the evidence and determine for themselves whether it was true, as alleged by the plaintiff, that the decedent did abandon his New York residence and come to West Chester with the intention of thenceforth making his permanent home in this state. By their verdict in defendant's favor, the jury have by necessary implication declared that he did not; and unless the learned trial judge erred in one or more of the particulars complained of, their verdict should not be disturbed.

The question at issue, and the different phases thereof, as presented by the testimony, together with the law applicable thereto, were all clearly and accurately stated in the general charge and answers to defendant's points. In the language of her fourth, seventh and eighth points, which were affirmed and not excepted to, the following instructions were given: "4. If the jury find that the legal residence of Henry F. Price was, at the time of his decease, in the state of New York, the verdict must be for the defendant." "7. Acts alone are not sufficient to constitute residence, but it requires acts and intentions com bined." "8. The ownership of real estate in Chester county, not coupled with residence therein, is of no value with reference to domicile or residence." The first to seventh specifications, inclusive, are to the learned judge's answers to her remaining points, and the eighth and ninth are to portions of his charge recited therein respectively. In affirming the first and second points, he, in the language thereof, instructed the jury: "1. Henry F. Price having been a resident of the city of Brooklyn, in the state of New York, for more than fifteen years prior to June 30, 1890, the burden of proof is on the plaintiff in this cause to satisfy you that, at the time of his death, August 26, 1890, his legal residence was other than in the city of Brooklyn, aforesaid:" and "2. The plaintiffs having alleged that the legal residence of Henry F. Price, at the time of his decease, was in West Chester, said plaintiff must satisfy the jury of this fact, otherwise the verdict must be for the defendant."

There was certainly no error in affirming these points. It was proved by plaintiff and conceded by defendant that Brooklyn, New York, was decedent's chosen domicile for more than

fifteen years prior to June 30, 1890. In the absence of affirmative proof to the contrary, the presumption would be that Brooklyn continued to be the place of his legal residence until his
decease. The defendant was certainly not required to prove a
negative, especially in view of the pleadings, in which, as we have
seen, the plaintiff assumed the burden of proving the affirmative
fact upon which his whole case depended. Citation of authority
for a proposition so self-evident as that is surely not required.

In view of the evidence, we think there is no error in either
of the other answers to defendant's points. Neither of them
requires discussion. We find nothing in any of the instructions
complained of that is not substantially in harmony with the settled
principles of law, relating to the subject of domicile.

As generally defined, a person's domicile is the place where
he has his true, fixed and permanent home and principal establishment, and to which, whenever he is absent, he has the intention
of returning. Beginning life as an infant, every person is at first
necessarily dependent. When he becomes an independent person
he will find himself in possession of a domicile, which in most
cases will be the place of his birth, or domicile of origin as it is
termed. By his own act and will, he can then acquire for himself
a legal home or domicile different from that of origin, termed a
domicile of choice. This is acquired by *actual residence* coupled
with the *intention* to reside in a given place or country, and cannot be acquired in any other way. For that purpose, residence
need not be of long duration. If the intention of permanently
residing in a particular place exists, a residence in pursuance of
that intention, however short, will establish a domicile. The
requisite animus is the present intention of permanent or indefinite
residence in a given place or country, or, negatively expressed,
the absence of any present intention of not residing there permanently or indefinitely. (Domicile of origin must be presumed
to continue until another sole domicile has been acquired by actual
residence, coupled with the intention of abandoning the domicile
of origin.) This change must be animo et facto, and the burden
of proof is on the party who asserts the change: 5 Am. & Eng.
Enc. of Law, 857, 861 to 865, and cases there cited; Hood's Est.,
21 Pa. 106; Pfoutz v. Crawford, 36 Pa. 421; Reed's Ap., 71 Pa.
378, 383; Carey's Ap., 75 Pa. 201; Hindman's Ap., 85 Pa. 466,
469; Follweiler v. Lutz, 112 Pa. 107; Jacobs on Domicile. § 150;
Story's Confl. of Laws, § 55.

In those portions of the charge complained of in the last two

specifications the jury were rightly instructed "to recollect all the evidence, to pass upon the credibility of the witnesses, and then, after considering all the evidence, say whether or not Mr. Price had changed his residence, prior to his death, from the city of Brooklyn to the borough of West Chester. He did not change it to any other place. You cannot go astray on that point, for he never went to any other place, no matter what his intention may have been. His intention may have been to go to Birchrunville or Philadelphia, but an intention not carried out, not consummated by actual removal, amounts to nothing. It does not change his residence. His residence would remain where it was previous to any such thought or the existence of any such intention. .
If his residence was not changed to West Chester, it still remained in Brooklyn."

Again: "If the plaintiff has satisfied you that he changed his residence, in the way I have described to you, that the law requires it shall be changed, then your verdict will be for the plaintiff."

The case appears to have been carefully tried. We find no error in the instructions given to the jury. If they erred in not finding according to the weight of the evidence, the remedy was in the court below on the motion for new trial. That was considered and denied, presumably because the trial judge was satisfied with the verdict. We cannot review his action in that regard.

Judgment affirmed.[4]

[4]**Importance of Domicil.**—The fact of domicil is often one of the highest importance to a person; it determines his civil and political rights; it fixes his allegiance; it determines his belligerent or neutral character in time of war; it regulates his personal and social relations whilst he lives; and furnishes the rule for the disposal of his property, when he dies. *Abington v. N. Bridgewater, 23 Pick. (Mass.) 170.*

Domicil Distinguished from "Home," "Residence," "Habitancy," and "Nationality."—A person's permanent home or residence is his domicil. A temporary home or residence is not the same as domicil. *Gilman v. Gilman, 52 Me. 165, 83 Am. Dec. 502.* The term "resident" is often used in the sense of "domicil" as in case of insolvency statutes, testamentary matters, voting, eligibility for public office, attachments, and questions of jurisdiction. *People v. Platt, 50 Hun (N. Y.) 454; De Meli v. De Meli, 120 N. Y. 485; Ayer v. Weeks, 65 N. H. 248, 18 Atl. 1108.* The word "resident" in some statutes includes both a permanent and a temporary residence. *Van Matre v. Sankey, 148 Ill. 536, 36 N. E. 628.*

What the terms "residence," "inhabitant," "lives," and "resides" mean in any particular statute depends upon its purpose and the phraseology of the text. Each case must be decided upon the particular language of the statute, and the circumstances giving rise to the question. To fulfil the intention and requirements of some statutes, a commercial or business residence might be all the law required; whilst to gratify the intention of another statute, it may be necessary to hold residence to be more than a business residence, and to mean all that the word domicil means in its strictest and most technical application. *Tyler v. Murray, 57 Md. 418.* "Residence" when used in the statutes is generally construed to mean domicil, though not always. In *Long v. Ryan, 30 Gratt (Va.) 718,* a person was domiciled in Washington but went into Virginia intending to remain about nine months. His property was attached in Virginia under a statute permitting attachments against non-residents, but the court, notwithstanding his domicil in Washington, held him to be a resident of Virginia, and dismissed the attachment. See *Haggart v. Morgan, 5 N. Y. 422; Ludlow v. Szold, 90 Iowa 175; Wood v. Roeder, 45 Nebr. 311; 63 N. W. 853; Stratton v. Brigham, 2 Sneed 420; Ballinger v. Lautier, 15 Kan. 608; Clark v. Likens, 26 N. J. L. 207.*

In the case of *Burt v. Allen, 48 W. Va. 154, 86 Am. St. R. 29 (1900),* the court held: If a resident of a state, with a fixed intention to remove to another state, and in pursuance of such intention goes out of the state, he is, within the meaning of the attachment law or exemption law, a nonresident of the state, and he is a non-resident the moment he begins the removal of his person from the place of his residence, even before he gets outside the state, and to constitute him a non-resident, he need not acquire either a domicil or residence in another state.

The term "citizenship," in its ordinary sense of nationality, differs from the idea of domicil. A person may be a citizen or subject of one country, while domiciled in another. *Brown's Case, 5 Court of Claims, 571; Harral v. Harral, 39 N. J. Eq. 279, 51 Am. Rep. 17.* It is sometimes construed in the sense of domicil. *Firth v. Firth, 50 N. J. Eq. 137, 24 Atl. 916; Morris v. Gilmer, 129 U. S. 315.*

As between the states, under the 14th amendment to the Constitution of the United States, all persons born or naturalized in the United States, and subject to the jurisdiction thereof, are citizens of the United States, and of the state wherein they reside.

UDNY v. UDNY, 1869.

[1 H. L. Scotch & Div. App. Cs. 441.]

1. Domicil of Origin and of Choice.   3. Reverter of Domicil.
2. Domicil as Determining Status—   4. Commercial Domicil.
    Civil and Political.

THE late Colonel *John Robert Fullerton Udny,* of *Udny,* in the county of *Aberdeen,* though born at *Leghorn,* where his father was consul, had by paternity his domicil in *Scotland.* At the age of fifteen, in the year 1794, he was sent to *Edinburgh,* where he remained for three years. In 1797 he became an officer in the Guards. In 1802 he succeeded to the family estate. In 1812 he married Miss *Emily Fitzhugh,*—retired from the army,—and took upon lease a house in *London,* where he resided for thirty-two years, paying occasional visits to *Aberdeenshire.*

In 1844, having got into pecuniary difficulties, he broke up his establishment in **London** and repaired to *Boulogne,* where he remained for nine years, occasionally, as before, visiting *Scotland.* In 1846 his wife died, leaving the only child of her marriage, a son, who, in 1859, died a bachelor.

Some time after the death of his wife *Colonel Udny* formed at *Boulogne* a connection with Miss *Ann Allat,* which resulted in the birth at *Camberwell,* in *Surrey,* on the 9th of May, 1853, of a son, the above respondent, whose parents were undoubtedly unmarried when he came into the world. They were, however, united afterwards in holy matrimony at *Ormiston,* in *Scotland,* on the 2nd of January, 1854, and the question was whether the Respondent, under the circumstances of the case, had become legitimate *per subsequens matrimonium.*

The Court of Session (First Division) on the 14th of December, 1866 (3rd Series, vol. v. p. 164), decided that Colonel *Udny's* domicil of origin was Scotch, and that he had never altered or lost it, notwithstanding his long absence from *Scotland.* They therefore found that his son, the Respondent, "though illegitimate at his birth, was legitimated by the subsequent marriage of his parents." Hence this appeal, which the House regarded as involving questions of greatly more than ordinary importance.

The Appellant argued his own case.

Sir *Roundell Palmer,* Q. C., Mr. *Mellish,* Q. C., Mr. Fraser, and Mr. *Bristow,* appeared for the Respondent.

The following opinions of the Law Peers fully state the facts, the authorities, and the legal reasoning.

THE LORD CHANCELLOR:—

My Lords,—In this case the Appellant prays a judicial declaration that the Respondent is a bastard,—and is not entitled to succeed to the entailed estates of *Udny,* in *Aberdeenshire.*

The question depends upon what shall be determined to have been the domicil of the Respondent's father, the late Colonel *Udny,* at the time of his birth,—at the time of the Respondent's birth,—and at the time of the Colonel's marriage with the Respondent's mother.

The Appellant, who argued his case in person with very considerable ability, contended:—First: That the domicil of origin of Colonel *Udny* was English. Secondly: That even if that were not so, yet at the time of his first marriage, in 1812, he had abandoned *Scotland* for *England,* sold his commission in the army, took a house on lease for a long term in *London,* and resided there till he left *England* for *France* in 1844, for the purpose of avoiding his creditors; and that having thus acquired an English domicil he retained it, and never re-acquired his Scotch domicil. Thirdly: That, at all events, if he did recover his Scotch domicil, yet it was not recovered at the date of the Respondent's birth in May, 1853, nor even at the date of the intermarriage of the Respondent's parents in January, 1854.

As regards the first question, your Lordships did not hear the Respondents. You were satisfied that Colonel *Udny's* father, the consul, had never abandoned his Scotch domicil. Consequently you held that Colonel *Udny's* own domicil of origin was clearly Scotch, that having been the domicil of his father at the Colonel's birth.

A more difficult inquiry arose as to the domicil of Colonel Udny at the date of the Respondent's birth in May, 1853.

Colonel *Udny* appears to have left the army about the same time that he married his first wife, viz. in 1812, when he executed a contract and other instruments connected with his marriage, containing provisions referable to Scottish law, and describing himself as *of Udny, in the County of Aberdeen.* He, on his marriage, however, took a long lease of a house in *London,* in which he resided till 1844. He made frequent visits to *Scotland,* but had no residence there. He at one time contemplated restoring *Udny Castle*—and even three years after he had commenced his residence in *London* appears to have still thought it possible that he might complete the restoration—and plans were about that time submitted to him for that purpose. For many years, however, he seems to have abandoned all hope of so doing, owing to his means being insufficient. He was appointed a magistrate in *Scotland,* but appears not to have acted as such. When in *Scotland* he usually resided with friends, but occasionally at hotels in the neighborhood of his property, and he continually received detailed accounts of the estates, and took much interest in their management. His choice of *England* as a residence appears to have been considerably influenced by his taste for the sports of the turf. By his first marriage he had a son, *John Augustus Udny.*

The Judge Ordinary and the Court of Session concurred in opinion that the long and habitual residence in *England* was not sufficient to amount to an abandonment of the Colonel's Scottish domicil of origin. This point, I confess, appears to me to be one of great nicety. I am not prepared to say that I am satisfied with that conclusion; but neither should I be prepared, without further consideration, to recommend to your Lordships a reversal of the judgment appealed from on the ground that the opinions of the Court below upon this point were erroneous.

Owing to this action having been raised in the Colonel's lifetime, the Court below had the advantage of the testimony of Colonel *Udny* himself, a circumstance which does not often occur in questions of domicil. It appears to have been very candidly given, and (as was observed by the Lord Ordinary) by no means overstates the case in favor of the continuance of his Scottish domicil.

Several other witnesses were examined, who do not carry the case further. But, be this as it may, the events in the Colonel's life, subsequent to 1844, appear to me to be those upon which the question of his domicil at the birth of the Respondent really depend.

In 1844, the Colonel, after having been involved for some time in pecuniary difficulties (owing chiefly to his connection with the turf), was compelled to leave *England*, in order to avoid his creditors. He at first thought of taking some house "in the country," by which I think he meant in the rural parts of *England;* but afterwards the pressure of creditors became too great to admit of his so doing, and he appears, in the autumn, to have visited *Scotland*, where correspondence took place between himself and his agent as to arranging a trust deed by which Colonel *Udny* and his son, *John Augustus*, were to make provision, as far as possible, for the payment of their debts. On the 2nd of October, he writes to his agent, mentioning that a creditor is pressing for immediate payment of £1200—"So let there be no time lost." And by a letter of his son of the 4th of November, 1844, it appears that his father had left *England for Calais* on the previous day. He about this time sold the lease of the *London* house in which he had so long resided. He sold also (as he himself states in his evidence) all his furniture and "everything that was in the house, including what had belonged to his mother, his sister, and his first wife." He went from *Calais* to *Boulogne,* and there resided in a hired house till 1853. He says in his evidence:

When I went to *Boulogne* I had no further connection with *London.* I had a married sister living there, and various other relations. During the nine years when my headquarters were at *Boulogne* I never resided in *London.* The time that I came over for my wife's confinement in 1853 was the first time that I had visited *London* after leaving it for *Boulogne.* I remained there at that time only about a couple of days and returned to *Boulogne.* While I was at *Boulogne* I came over more than once to *Scotland* to visit my property. These were not long visits, but I did make them.

The wife alluded to in the above statement is the mother of the Respondent. The Colonel's first wife did not go with him to *Boulogne*, but she joined him for a short time in 1845, leaving him afterwards on account of ill-health, and residing with his brother in *London*. She died in 1846.

The Colonel at *Boulogne* formed an illicit connection with the mother of the Respondent, and in May, 1853, came to *England* in consequence of a wish that she should be attended in her confinement by an English accoucheur; and on the 9th of May, 1853, the Respondent was born at *Camberwell*. The Colonel appears to have returned almost immediately to *Boulogne*. He had been living on a very scanty allowance—his eldest son, too, was embarrassed—and at a very early period after the birth of the Respondent the father and son appear to have thought that the birth of this child might facilitate the barring of the entail of the Scotch estates; for in a letter of the 29th of May, 1853, the Colonel writes to his son: "I shall be glad to hear of your interview with Mr. *Skinner*" (their legal adviser). "I think the great difficulty will be the uncertainty of the child's life; however, you will talk over all these matters with him."

The Colonel was advised that by marrying tne Respondent's mother, he might, according to the laws of *Scotland,* render the Respondent legitimate, and that then the concurrence of the Appellant in barring the entail would not be requisite. The advice on this latter point was erroneous; but it is enough to say that the Colonel came over to *Scotland* in November, 1853, clearly with the intent to celebrate a marriage with the Respondent's mother, and with the hope of raising money for the benefit of his elder son and himself by getting rid of the entail. He was under an impression that his English creditors could not molest him whilst in *Scotland.* He was much mortified afterwards to find that this was not the case, and wrote several letters to his son and others expressive of his disgust at having been hurried away from *Boulogne,* and his dislike to residing in *Scotland.* But I cannot bring my mind to doubt that his intention in returning to *Scotland* was to do that which he accomplished, namely, to marry, in regular form, the Respondent's mother, and for that purpose to be domiciled there.

In his letter of the 9th of July, 1859, he expressly asserts it to have been his intention in 1853 to be permanently domiciled in *Scotland;* but that letter may be open to objection that it was written very shortly *ante litem motam*. I do not think that we can safely rely on the deed of disposition by his elder son of the 2nd of December, 1853, which recites "that the Colonel had made arrangements to return again to and to remain in *Scotland*," because the father was not a party to that instrument. But, on the other hand, though the recital itself may not be evidence, yet the Colonel took advantage of that instrument. And the whole course of the arrangements made shows that the Colonel's intent, for which alone he came to *Scotland*, was by his marriage to make the Respondent legitimate, and by means of that legitimation to deal with the estates. These objects required a Scottish domicil; and it would be singular to hold that he having, in fact, married on the 2nd of January, 1854, and resided in *Scotland* thenceforth to his death in 1861 (after the raising of the present action), the domicil must not be taken to have been Scottish, as it ought to be, for the purposes he had in view from the time of his return in 1853. It is true that the death of his elder son in the interval between the marriage and death of the Colonel, and the consequent falling in of the policies of insurance on his life, placed the Colonel to a certain degree in an easier position, and removed his apprehension of difficulty from his creditors; but I think his possible intention to leave *Scotland* (if molested by creditors) in no way disproves the existence of a resolution to remain, as he did, in that country (if allowed so to do) as his chosen and settled abode.

It seems therefore clear to me that the Colonel was, at the time of his marriage, domiciled in *Scotland;* but the question remains as to what was his domicil in Mav. 1853, at the time of the Respondent's birth.

If he were domiciled in *England* up to 1844, and retained an English domicil up to and after May, 1853, then the question would arise, which has not been determined in any case by the Scottish Courts, whether the child, being illegitimate at its birth, and its putative father not having at that time a power of legitimating him by means of a subsequent marriage with his mother, could be legitimated by his putative father subsequently *acquiring* a Scottish domicil before marriage with the mother.

I have myself held, and so have other judges in the English Courts, that according to the law of *England* a bastard child whose putative father was English at its birth could not be legitimated by the father afterwards acquiring a foreign domicil and marrying the mother in a country by the law of which a subsequent marriage would have legitimated the child. I see no reason to retract that opinion. The *status* of the child,—with respect to its capacity to be legitimated by the subsequent marriage of its parents,—depends wholly on the *status* of the putative father, not on that of the mother. If the putative father have an English domicil the English law does not, at the birth of the child, take notice of the putative father's existence. But if his domicil be Scottish, or of any other country allowing legitimation, though the mother be English at the birth, the putative father (as in *Munro* v. *Munro,* 7 Cl. & F. 842) is capable of legitimating the child. The foreign law, though deeming the child to be *filius nullius* at birth, yet recognizes the father as such at the moment of his acknowledging the child, either by marriage and formal recognition, as in *France,* or by marriage only, as in *Scotland.* I do not think that the English law can recognize a capacity in any Englishman, by change of domicil, to cause his paternity and consequent power of legitimation to be recognized. But however this may be, the question does not, in my judgment, here arise.

I am of opinion that the English domicil of Colonel *Udny,* if it were ever acquired, was formally and completely abandoned in 1844 when he sold his house and broke up his English establishment with the intention not to return. And, indeed, his return to that country was barred against him by the continued threat of process by his creditors. I think that on such abandoment his domicil of origin revived. It is clear that by our law a man must have some domicil, and must have a single domicil. It is clear, on the evidence, that the Colonel did not contemplate residing in *France*—and, indeed, that has scarcely been contended for by the Appellant. But the Appellant contends that when once a new domicil is acquired, the domicil of origin is obliterated, and cannot be re-acquired more readily or by any other means than those by which the first change of the original domicil is brought about, namely, *animo et facto.* He relied for this proposition on the decision in *Munroe* v. *Douglas* (5 Madd. 379) where Sir *John Leach* certainly held that a Scotsman, having acquired an Anglo-Indian domicil, and having finally quitted *India,* but not yet having settled elsewhere, did not re-acquire his original domicil; saying expressly, "I can find no difference in principle between an original domicil and an acquired domicil." That he acquired no new domicil may be conceded, but it appears to me that sufficient weight was not given to the effect of the domicil of origin, and that there is a very substantial difference in principle between an original and an acquired domicil. I shall not add to the many ineffectual attempts to define domicil. But the domicil of origin is a matter wholly irrespective of any animus on the part of its subject. He acquires a certain *status civilis,* as one of your Lordships has designated it, which subjects him and his property to the municipal jurisdiction of a country which he may never even have seen, and in which he may never reside during the whole course of his life, his domicil being simply determined by that of his father. A change of that domicil can only be effected *animo et facto*—that is to say, by the choice of another domicil, evidenced by residence within the territorial limits to which the jurisdiction of the new domicil extends. He, in making this change, does an act which is more nearly designated by the word "settling" than by any one word in our language. Thus we speak of a colonist settling in *Canada* or *Australia,* or of a Scotsman settling in *England,* and the word is frequently used as expressive of the act of change of domicil in the various judgments pronounced by our Courts. But this settlement *animo et facto* by which the new domicil is acquired is, of course, susceptible of abandonment if the intention be evidenced by facts as decisive as those which evidenced its acquirement.

It is said by Sir *John Leach,* that the change of the newly-acquired domicil can only be evidenced by an actual settling elsewhere or (which is, however, a remarkable qualification) by the subject of the change dying *in itinere* when about to settle himself elsewhere. But the dying *in itinere* to a wholly new domicil would not, I apprehend, change a domicil of origin if the intended new domicil were never reached. So that at once a distinction is admitted between what is necessary to re-acquire the original domicil and the acquiring of a third domicil. Indeed, the admission of Sir *John Leach* seems to have been founded on the actual decision in the case of *Colville* v. *Saunders,* cited in full in *Munroe* v. *Douglas,* from the Dictionary of Decisions. In that case, a person of Scottish origin became domiciled at *St. Vincent,* but left that island, writing to his father and saying that his health was injured, and he was going to *America;* and that if he did not succeed in *America* he would return to his native country. He was drowned in *Canada,* and some memoranda were found indicating an intention to return to *Scotland,* and it was held that his Scottish domicil had revived.

It seems reasonable to say that if the choice of a new abode and actual settlement there constitute a change of the original domicil, then the exact converse of such a procedure, viz., the intention to abandon the new domicil, and an actual abandonment of it, ought to be equally effective to destroy the new domicil. That which may be acquired may surely be abandoned, and though a man cannot, for civil reasons, be left without a domicil, no such difficulty arises if it be simply held that the original domicil revives. That original domicil depended not on choice but attached itself to its subject on his birth, and it seems to me consonant both to convenience and to the currency of the whole law of domicil to hold that the man born with a domicil may shift and vary it as often as he pleases, indicating each change by intention and act, whether in its acquisition or abandonment; and further, to hold that every acquired domicil is capable of simple abandonment *animo et facto* the process by which it was acquired, without its being necessary that a new one should be at the same time chosen, otherwise one is driven to the absurdity of asserting a person to be domiciled in a country which he has resolutely forsaken and cast off, simply because he may (perhaps for years) be deliberating before he settles himself elsewhere. Why should not the domicil of origin cast on him by no choice of his own, and changed for a time, be the state to which he naturally falls back when his first choice has been abandoned *animo et facto,* and whilst he is deliberating before he makes a second choice.

Lord *Cottenham* in *Munro* v. *Munro* (7 Cl. & F. 871) says, "So firmly indeed did the civil law consider the domicil of origin to adhere that it holds that if it be actually abandoned and a domicil acquired, but that again abandoned, and no new domicil acquired in its place, the domicil of origin revives." No authority is cited by his Lordship for this. He probably alluded to some observations which occur in the case of *La Virginie* (5 Rob. Adm. 99) where Sir *William Scott* said:

It is always to be remembered that the native character easily reverts, and that it requires fewer circumstances to constitute domicil in the case of a native subject than to impress the national character on one who is originally of another country.

In the case of *The Indian Chief* (3 Rob. Adm. 12) the question was whether the ship was the property of a British subject; for if so, her trading was illegal. The owner, Mr. *Johnson,* averred that he was an American. Sir *William Scott* held him to be an American by origin, but that having come to *England* in 1783 and remained till 1797, he had become an English merchant. But he quitted *England* before the capture of the vessel, and letters were produced shewing his intention to return to *America,* which he does not appear to have reached until after. And Sir *William Scott* says, "The ship arrives a few weeks after his departure, and taking it to be clear that the natural character of Mr. *Johnson* as a British merchant was founded on residence only, that it was acquired by residence, and rested on that circumstance alone, it must be held that from the moment he turned his back on the country where he had resided on his way to his own country he was in the act of resuming his original character, and is to be considered as an American. The character that is gained by residence ceases by residence. It is an adventitious character which no longer adheres to him from the moment that he puts himself in motion *bona fide* to quit the country *sine animo revertendi*."

Story, in his Conflict of Laws, sect. 47 (at the end), says: "If a man has acquired a new domicil different from that of his birth, and he removes from it with intention to resume his native domicil, the latter is re-acquired even while he is on his way, for it reverts from the moment the other is given up."

The qualification that he must abandon the new domicil with the special intent to resume that of origin is not, I think, a reasonable deduction from the rules already laid down by decision, because intent not followed by a definite act is not sufficient. The more consistent theory is, that the abandonment of the new domicil is complete *animo et facto,* because the *factum* is the abandonment, the *animus* is that of never returning.

I have stated my opinion more at length than I should have done were it not of great importance that some fixed common principles should guide the Courts in every country on international questions. In questions of international law we should not depart from any settled decisions, nor lay down any doctrine inconsistent with them. I think some of the expressions used in former cases as to the intent *"exuere patriam,"* or to become "a Frenchman instead of an Englishman," go beyond the question of domicil. The question of naturalization and of allegiance is distinct from that of domicil. A man may continue to be an Englishman, and yet his contracts and the succession to his estate may have to be determined by the law of the country in which he has chosen to settle himself. He cannot, at present at least, put off and resume at will obligations of obedience to the government of the country of which at his birth he is a subject, but he may many times change his domicil. It appears to me, however, that each acquired domicil may be also successively abandoned *simpliciter,* and that thereupon the original domicil *simpliciter* reverts.

For these reasons, my Lords, ⸱ propose to your Lordships the affirmation of the interlocutors complained of, and the dismissal of the appeal with costs.

LORD CHELMSFORDS :—

My Lords, at the opening of the argument of this appeal for the Respondent his learned counsel were informed that your Lordships were of opinion that the domicil of Colonel *Udny* down to the year 1812 was his Scotch domicil of origin, and that the case was therefore narrowed down to the questions raised by the Appellant,—whether that domicil had been superceded by the acquisition of another domicil in *England,* and whether such after acquired domicil was retained at the time of the birth of the Respondent, and continued down to the period of the marriage of the Respondent's parents in *Scotland.*

In considering these questions it will be necessary to ascertain the nature and effect of a domicil of origin ; whether it is like an after-acquired domicil, which when it is relinquished can be re acquired only in the same manner in which it was originally acquired, or whether, in the absence of any other domicil, the domicil of origin must not be had recourse to for the purpose of determining any question which may arise as to a party's personal rights and relations.

Story, in his Conflict of Laws (sect. 48), says, "The moment a foreign domicil is abandoned the native domicil is re-acquired." Great stress was laid by the Appellant in his reference to this passage upon the word "re-acquired," which is obviously an inaccurate expression. For, as was pointed out in the course of the argument, a domicil of origin is not an acquired domicil, but one which is attributed to every person by law. The meaning of *Story,* therefore, clearly is, that the abandonment of a subsequently-acquired domicil *ipso facto* restores the domicil of origin. And this doctrine appears to be founded upon principle, if not upon direct authority.

It is undoubted law that no one can be without a domicil. If, then, a person has left his native domicil and acquired a new one, which he afterwards abandons, what domicil must be resorted to to determine and regulate his personal *status* and rights? Sir *John Leach,* V. C., in *Munroe* v. *Douglas* (5 Madd. 405), held that in the case supposed the acquired domicil attaches to the person till the complete acquisition of a subsequent domicil, and (as to this point) he said there was no difference in principle between the original domicil and an acquired domicil. His Honour's words are: "A domicil cannot be lost by mere abandonment. It is not to be defeated *animo* merely, but *animo et facto,* and necessarily remains until a subsequent domicil be acquired, unless the party die *in itinere* towards an intended domicil." There is an apparent inconsistency in this passage, for the Vice-Chancellor having said that a domicil necessarily remains until a subsequent domicil be acquired *animo et facto,* added, "unless the party die *in itinere* towards an intended domicil;" that is, at a time when the acquisition of the subsequent domicil is incomplete and rests in intention only.

I cannot understand upon what ground it can be alleged that a person may not abandon an acquired domicil altogether and carry out his intention fully by removing *animo non revertendi;* and why such abandonment should not be complete until another domicil is acquired in lieu of the one thus relinquished.

Sir *William Scott,* in the case of *The Indian Chief* (3 Rob. Adm. 20), said: "The character that is gained by residence ceases by residence. It is an adventitious character which no longer adheres to a person from the moment he puts himself in motion *bona fide* to quit the country *sine animo revertendi,*" and he mentions the case of a British-born subject, who had been resident in *Surinam* and *St. Eustatius,* and had left those settlements with an intention of returning to this country, but had got no farther than *Holland,* the mother country of those settlements, when the war broke out; and it was determined by the Lords of Appeal that he was *in itinere,* that he had put himself in motion, and was in pursuit of his native British character.

Sir *John Leach* seems to me to be incorrect also in saying that in the case of the abandonment of an acquired domicil there is no difference in principle between the acquisition of an entirely new domicil and the revival of the domicil of origin. It is said by *Story,* in sect. 47 of his Conflict of Laws, that "If a man has acquired a new domicil different from that of his birth, and he removes from it with an intention to resume his native domicil, the latter is re-acquired even while he is on his way *in itinere;* for it reverts from the moment the other is given up." This certainly cannot be predicated of a person journeying towards a new domicil which it is his intention to acquire.

I do not think that the circumstances mentioned by *Story* in the above passage, viz., that the person has removed from his acquired domicil with an intention to resume his native domicil, and that he is *in itinere* for the purpose, are at all necessary to restore

the domicil of origin. The true doctrine appears to me to be expressed in the last words of the passage: "It" (the domicil of
origin) "reverts from the moment the other is given up."

This is a necessary conclusion if it be true that an acquired
domicil ceases entirely whenever it is intentionally abandoned, and
that a man can never be without a domicil. The domicil of origin
always remains, as it were, in reserve, to be resorted to in case no
other domicil is found to exist. This appears to me to be the true
principle upon this subject, and it will govern my opinion upon the
present appeal.

Upon the question whether Colonel *Udny* ever acquired an
English domicil which superseded his domicil of origin, there can
be no doubt that his long residence in *Grosvenor Street* for the
space of thirty-two years from 1812 to 1844, is calculated to produce a strong impression in favor of the acquisition of such a
domicil. Time is always a material element in questions of domicil; and if there is nothing to counteract its effect, it may be conclusive upon the subject. But in a competition between a domicil
of origin and an alleged subsequently-acquired domicil there may
be circumstances to shew that however long a residence may have
continued no intention of acquiring a domicil may have existed at
any one moment during the whole of the continuance of such residence. The question in such a case is not, whether there is evidence of an intention to retain the domicil of origin, but whether
it is proved that there was an intention to acquire another domicil.
As already shewn, the domicil of origin remains till a new one is
acquired *animo et facto*. Therefore, a wish or a desire expressed
from time to time to return to the place of the first domicil, or any
looking to it as the ultimate home, although wholly insufficient for
the retention of the domicil of origin, may yet amount to material
evidence to rebut the presumption of an intention to acquire a new
domicil arising from length of residence elsewhere. In this view
it would be a fair answer to the question, Did Colonel *Udny* intend
to make *England* his permanent home? to point to all his acts and
declarations with respect to *Scotland* and his estates there, to the
offices which he held, to the institutions to which he belonged, and
to his subscriptions to local objects, shewing, that though his pursuits drew him to *England* and kept him there, and his circumstances prevented his making *Udny Castle* fit for his residence, he
always entertained a hope, if not an expectation, that a change in
his fortunes might eventually enable him to appear in his country

of origin, and to assume his proper position there as a Scotch proprietor.

If the residence in *England* began under circumstances which indicate no intention that it was to be permanent, when did it assume the character of permanence by proof that the Colonel had intentionally given up his Scotch domicil and adopted a different one? It appears to me upon this question of fact, that throughout the whole of the Colonel's residence in *London* there was always absent the intention to make it his permanent home which is essential to constitute a domicil; residence alone, however long, being immaterial unless coupled with such intention. But even if it should be considered that Colonel *Udny's* residence in *England,* though not originally intended to be his permanent home, after a certain length of time ripened into a domicil, yet in 1844 he gave up the house in *Grosvenor Street* and returned to *Boulogne,* where he remained for nine years without any apparent intention of again taking up his residence in *England.* This abandonment of the English residence, both in will and deed, although accompanied with no immediate intention of resuming the Scotch domicil, put an end at once to the English domicil, and the domicil of origin *ipso facto* became the domicil by which the personal rights of Colonel *Udny* were thenceforth to be regulated.

This makes it unnecessary to consider what would have been the condition of the Respondent if his birth had taken place in *England* before the resumption of the Scotch domicil by Colonel *Udny,* and the subsequent marriage of his parents in *Scotland* after that domicil had been resumed. Because the domicil being Scotch, the place of the birth of the Respondent is wholly immaterial, and the case is completely governed by the authority of the cases of *Dalhousie* v. *McDouall* (7 Cl. & F. 817) and *Munro* v. *Munro* (Ibid. 842), in each of which the birth of the illegitimate child, and also the subsequent marriage of the parents, took place in *England,* but the domicil being Scotch it was held that neither the place of the marriage nor the place of the birth affected the *status* of the child.

The existence of the Scotch domicil renders it also unnecessary to consider whether the parents of the Respondent went to *Scotland* for the purpose merely of legitimating the Respondent by their marriage there, and deprives the case of *Rose* v. *Ross* (4 Wils. & Shaw, 289), which was insisted upon by the Appellant, of all application. For in that case, as stated by the Lord Chancellor, "the parties were domiciled in *England,* the child was born in

England, the parties went to *Scotland* for the purpose expressly of being married, and having been married they returned to *England* to the place of their former domicil."

I agree with my noble and learned friend that the interlocutors appealed from ought to be affirmed.

LORD WESTBURY :—

The law of *England,* and of almost all civilized countries, ascribes to each individual at his birth two distinct legal states or conditions; one by virtue of which he becomes the subject of some particular country, binding him by the tie of natural allegiance, and which may be called his political *status;* another, by virtue of which he has ascribed to him the character of a citizen of some particular country, and as such is possessed of certain municipal rights, and subject to certain obligations, which latter character is the civil *status* or condition of the individual, and may be quite different from his political *status.* The political *status* may depend on different laws in different countries; whereas the civil *status* is governed universally by one single principle, namely, that of domicil, which is the criterion established by law for the purpose of determining civil *status.* For it is on this basis that the personal rights of the party, that is to say, the law which determines his majority or minority, his marriage, succession, testacy, or intestacy, must depend. International law depends on rules which, being in great measure derived from the Roman law, are common to the jurisprudence of all civilized nations. It is a settled principle that no man shall be without a domicil, and to secure this result the law attributes to every individual as soon as he is born the domicil of his father, if the child be legitimate, and the domicil of the mother if illegitimate. This has been called the domicil of origin, and is involuntary. Other domicils, including domicil by operation of law, as on marriage, are domicils of choice. For as soon as an individual is *sui juris* it is competent to him to elect and assume another domicil, the continuance of which depends upon his will and act. When another domicil is put on, the domicil of origin is for that purpose relinquished, and remains in abeyance during the continuance of the domicil of choice; but as the domicil of origin is the creature of law, and independent of the will of the party, it would be inconsistent with the principles on which it is by law created and ascribed, to suppose that it is capable of being by the act of the party entirely obliterated and extinguished. It revives and exists whenever there is no other domicil, and it does not require to be regained or reconstituted *animo et facto,* in the manner which is necessary for the acquisition of a domicil of choice.

Domicil of choice is a conclusion or inference which the law derives from the fact of a man fixing voluntarily his sole or chief residence in a particular place, with an intention of continuing to reside there for an unlimited time. This is a description of the circumstances which create or constitute a domicil, and not a definition of the term. There must be a residence freely chosen, and not prescribed or dictated by any external necessity, such as the duties of office, the demands of creditors, or the relief from illness; and it must be residence fixed not for a limited period of particular purpose, but general and indefinite in its future contemplation. It is true that residence originally temporary, or intended for a limited period, may afterwards become general and unlimited, and in such a case so soon as the change of purpose, or *animus manendi,* can be inferred the fact of domicil is established.

The domicil of origin may be extinguished by act of law, as, for example, by sentence of death or exile for life, which puts an end to the *status civilis* of the criminal; but it cannot be destroyed by the will and act of the party.

Domicil of choice, as it is gained *animo et facto,* so it may be put an end to in the same manner. Expressions are found in some books, and in one or two cases, that the first or existing domicil remains until another is acquired. This is true if applied to the domicil of origin, but cannot be true if such general words were intended (which is not probable) to convey the conclusion that a domicil of choice, though unequivocally relinquished and abandoned, clings, in despite of his will and acts, to the party, until another domicil has *animo et facto* been acquired. The cases to which I have referred are, in my opinion, met and controlled by other decisions. A natural-born Englishman may, if he domiciles himself in *Holland,* acquire and have the *status civilis* of a Dutchman, which is of course ascribed to him in respect of his settled abode in the land, but if he breaks up his establishment, sells his house and furniture, discharges his servants, and quits *Holland,* declaring that he will never return to it again, and taking with him his wife and children, for the purpose of traveling in *France* or *Italy* in search of another place of residence, is it meant to be said that he carries his Dutch domicil, that is, his Dutch citizenship, at his back, and that it clings to him pertinaciously until he has finally set up his tabernacle in another country? Such a conclusion would be absurd; but there is no absurdity and, on the contrary, much reason, in holding that an acquired domicil may be effectually abandoned by unequivocal intention and act; and that when it is so determined the domicil of origin revives until a new domicil of choice be acquired. According to the *dicta* in the books and cases referred to, if the Englishman whose case we have been supposing lived for twenty years after he had finally quitted *Holland,* without acquiring a new domicil, and afterwards died intestate, his personal estate would be administered according to the law of *Holland,* and not according to that of his native country. This is an irrational consequence of the supposed rule. But when a proposition supposed to be authorized by one or more decisions involves absurd results, there is great reason for believing that no such rule was intended to be laid down.

In Mr. Justice *Story's* Conflict of Laws (the last edition) it is stated that "the moment the foreign domicil (that is, the domicil of choice) is abandoned. the native domicil or domicil of origin is re-acquired."

And such appears to be the just conclusion from several decided cases, as well as from the principles of the law of domicil.

In adverting to Mr. Justice *Story's* work, I am obliged to dissent from a conclusion stated in the last edition of that useful book, and which is thus expressed, "The result of the more recent English cases seems to be, that for a change of national domicil there must be a definite and effectual change of nationality." In support of this proposition the editor refers to some words which appear to have fallen from a noble and learned lord in addressing this House in the case of *Moorehouse* v. *Lord* (10 H. L. C. 272) when in speaking of the acquisition of a French domicil, Lord *Kingsdown* says, "A man must intend to become a Frenchman instead of an Englishman."

These words are likely to mislead, if they were intended to signify that for a change of domicil there must be a change of nationality, that is, of natural allegiance.

That would be to confound the political and civil states of an individual, and to destroy the difference between *patria* and *domicilium.*

The application of these general rules to the circumstances of the present case is very simple. I concur with my noble and learned friend that the father of Colonel *Udny,* the consul at *Leghorn,* and afterwards at *Venice,* and again at *Leghorn,* did not by his residence there in that capacity lose his Scotch domicil. Colonel *Udny* was, therefore, a Scotchman by birth. But I am certainly inclined to think that when Colonel *Udny* married, and (to use the ordinary phrase) settled in life and took a long lease of a house in *Grosvenor Street,* and made that a place of abode of himself and his wife and children, becoming, in point of fact, subject to the municipal duties of a resident in that locality ; and when he had remained there for a period, I think, of thirty-two years, there being no obstacle in point of fortune, occupation, or duty, to his going to reside in his native country; under these circumstances, I should come to the conclusion, if it were necessary to decide the point, that Colonel *Udny* deliberately chose and acquired an English domicil. But if he did so, he as certainly relinquished that English domicil in the most effectual way by selling or surrendering the lease of his house, selling his furniture, discharging his servants, and leaving *London* in a manner which removes all doubt of his ever intending to return there for the purpose of residence. If, therefore, he acquired an English domicil he abandoned it absolutely *animo et facto.* Its acquisition being a thing of choice, it was equally put an end to by choice. He lost it the moment he set foot on the steamer to go to *Boulogne,* and at the same time his domicil or origin revived. The rest is plain. The marriage and the consequences of that marriage must be determined by the law of *Scotland,* the country of his domicil.

LORD COLONSAY :—

I regard this case as one of very considerable importance, inasmuch as it has afforded an opportunity for bringing out, more clearly than has been done in any of the former cases, the radical distinction between domicil of origin and domicil of choice. The principles of that distinction and the facts have been so clearly put before the House that I need do no more than express my concurrence.

JUDGMENT :—Ordered and Adjudged, that the said interlocutor of the Lords of Session in *Scotland,* of the Second Division, of the 14th of December, 1866, complained of in the said appeal, be varied by substituting for the words "that he never lost his said domicil of origin" these words, "and that if such domicil of origin was ever changed, yet by leaving *England* in 1844 his domicil of origin reverted;" and that, with this variation, the said interlocutor be, and the same is, hereby affirmed, and that the said petition and appeal be, and the same is, hereby dismissed this House.[5] Solicitors for the Appellant : *Coverdale, Lee, Bristow & Withers.* Solicitors for the Respondent : *White, Broughton & White.*

Domicil of Origin. Legitimate Child.—The domicil of origin of a legitimate child is the domicil of the father at the time of the birth of the child. *Price v. Price, 156 Pa. St. 617, 27 Atl. 291; Dalhousie v. McDowail, 7 Cl. & F. 817.*

Illegitimate or Posthumous Child.—The domicil of origin of an illegitimate or posthumous child is the domicil of the mother at the time of the child's birth. *Blythe v. Ayres, 96 Cal. 532, 31 Pac. Rep. 915, 19 L. R. A. 40; Houlton v. Loubec, 35 Me. 411; Udny v. Udny, L. R. 1 Scotch App. Cas. 441.*

Foundling.—The domicil of origin of a foundling is the place where the child was born or found. *Washington v. Beaver, 3 W. & S. (Pa.) 548; Dicey Conflict of Laws, page 101.*

Legitimated Child.—The domicil of origin of a legitimated child is the domicil of the father at the time of the child's birth. *Dicey Conflict of Laws, page 104; Munro v. Munro, 7 Cl. & F. 817.* The rule seems to be that one born illegitimate but afterwards legitimated stands in the position he would have occupied if he had been born legitimate, and that his domicil of origin is the state or country where his father was domiciled at the time of the illegitimate's birth.

Minor on Conflict of Laws disagrees with this statement of the rule. He says: "The subsequent acknowledgment by the father, or his intermarriage with the mother, which by the law of many countries renders the bastard legitimate, may, as we shall presently see, cause the infant's domicil *thereafter* to be governed by that of the father. But the bastard's domicil in such case would cease to be the domicil of origin, and would become a constructive domicil. His first and original domicil was that of the mother, and hence when he *afterwards* acquires the domicil of the father by reason of the legitimation, it cannot be referred back to the time of his birth, even though the legitimation itself be referred to that date. The domicil of origin is assigned at the moment of birth; whatever is *then* the condition of the child will determine the locality of that domicil. If he be then illegitimate, and the mother's domicil is once assigned him legally as his domicil of origin, no other domicil of *origin* can be assigned him. That would be to give him two domicils at the same time." *Minor Conflict of Laws, Sec. 33; Blythe v. Ayres, 96 Cal. 532, Ives v. McNicoll, 59 Ohio St. 402, 43 L. R. A. 772.*

Domicil of Choice.—A person on reaching the age of majority, if free from other disabilities, may choose a permanent home for himself, which is called in the law a domicil of choice.

Essentials Necessary to Domicil of Choice.—The essentials necessary to choose a new domicil are: (1) Capacity to choose, (2) Intention to take up the new home permanently or for an indefinite time, (3) Actual physical presence in the place chosen. *Price v. Price, 156 Pa. St. 617, 27 Atl. 291; Mitchell v. U. S., 21 Wall. 350; Hartford v. Champion, 58 Conn. 268, 20 Atl. 471; Wilkins v. Marshall, 80 Ill. 74.*

Capacity to Choose.—A person *sui juris* may change his domicil as often as he pleases. To effect such a change, naturalization in the country he adopts as his domicil is not essential. He need not do all that is necessary to divest himself of his original nationality. There must be a voluntary change of residence; the residence at the place chosen for the domicil must be actual; to the *factum* of residence there must be added the *animus manendi;* and that place is the domicil of a person in which he has voluntarily fixed his habitation, not for a mere temporary or special purpose, but with a present intention of making it his home, unless or until something which is uncertain or unexpected shall happen to induce him to adopt some other permanent home. *Harral v. Harral, 39 N. J. Eq. 279; Firth v. Firth, 50 N. J. Eq. 137, 24 Atl. 916.*

Intention.—In *Bell v. Kennedy, L. R. 1 Scotch & Div. App. 320, Beale's Cases Conflict of Laws, p. 140*, Bell, the deceased, was born in Jamaica, settled and married there, and all his property was there. Finally he determined to leave the island, and he did so, and bought property in Scotland, but he never determined upon any place as a permanent home. The question was whether Scotch law or English (Jamaica) applied as to a certain part of his estate. And it was held that he had not lost his domicil in Jamaica by his residence elsewhere. He was resident in Scotland, but without the intention of remaining, and therefore he still retained his domicil of origin.

Domicil is largely a question of intention. *Matzenbaugh v. People, 194 Ill. 108; Hascall v. Hafford, 107 Tenn. 355.* Intention alone does not control. If a person removes to another place with an intention of remaining there for an indefinite time, it becomes his domicil, notwithstanding he may have a floating intention of returning to his old residence at some future time. *Ringgold v. Bailey, 5 Md. 186, 59 Am. Dec. 107; Berry v. Wilcox, 44 Nebr. 82; Contra In Re Capdevielle, 2 H. & C. 985.*

One who lets his house in the town of his domicil for several successive years, and establishes himself with his family in what appears to be a permanent residence in another town, and intends to go on living in the same way, cannot retain his former domicil merely by desiring to do so and continuing to vote there, without any actual intention of living there again. *Dickinson v. Brookline, 181 Mass. 195.*

An inhabitant of one state does not acquire a domicil in another state by merely going there to seek employment, with the intention of residing there if he shall find it, or living there permanently if the place suits him, and the contingency never happens. *Ross v. Ross, 103 Mass. 575.*

Two things must concur to establish domicil,—the fact of residence, and the intention of remaining. These two must exist, or must have existed, in combination.

Where a person entirely abandons his former residence in one state with no intention of returning, and goes with his family to another residence in another state with the intention of making the latter his residence for an indefinite time, the latter state is his domicil notwithstanding the fact that, after he and his family arrive at the new residence, which is only about a half mile from the state line, they go on the same day on a visit to spend the night with a neighbor in the former state intending to return in the morning of the next day, but he is detained there by sickness, until he dies, and never does in fact return to his new home. *White v. Tennant, 31 West Va. 790, 8 S. E. 596.*

If the residence and the intention to stay indefinitely concur, a domicil is acquired at once, however short a time the residence or the intent continues. Absence, however long, for pleasure or travel, or business, will not change domicil. *Dupuy v. Wurtz, 53 N. Y. 556; Cadwalader v. Howell, 18 N. J. L. 138.*

P. was born in Scotland, in 1792, of Scotch parents. In 1810 he obtained a commission in the army, and immediately proceeded with his regiment on foreign service, and served abroad till 1860, when he retired from the army. From 1860 till his death he resided in lodgings, hotels, and boarding houses in various parts of England, dying in 1882, intestate and a bachelor, in a private hotel in London, leaving no real estate in England, and no property whatsoever in Scotland. From the year 1810 till his death he never revisited Scotland, and for the last twenty years of his life never left the territorial limits of England. Held that the domicil of the intestate at his death was Scotch. The facts did not show intention to throw off his Scotch domicil. *In Re Patience, 29 Ch. Div. 976 (1885).*

Actual Presence.—The mere intent to acquire a new domicil without physical presence at the new place will not change the domicil. *In Re Raffeuel, 3 Sw. & Tr. 49; In re Marrett, 36 Ch. Div. 400; Talmadge v. Talmadge, 66 Ala. 199.*

There must be *actual residence* in the place chosen as a new domicil. *Ennis v. Smith, 14 How. 399.*

In *Borland v. Boston, 132 Mass. 89, 42 Am. Rep. 424,* a person having his domicil in Boston, left that city in 1876 with his family to reside in Europe for an indefinite time, with the fixed purpose never to return to Boston as a place of residence, and to make some place other than Boston his residence when he should return; and, while in Europe, before May 1, 1877, fixed upon a place of residence in another state, but remained in Europe till 1879. Held, that he retained his domicil in Boston for the purposes of taxation on May 1, 1877.

A man may be domiciled in a country without having a fixed habitation in some particular spot in that country. *In re Craignish, 3 Chancery 180 (1892).*

In *Lowry v. Bradley, 1 Speer's Eq. 1; 39 Am. Dec. 142,* Lowry was domiciled in South Carolina. He separated from his wife, and proceeded to Alabama, declaring that he would never return to South Carolina. He boarded at a house near the town of Blakely, in Alabama. He did not buy a plantation, neither did he open a house of his own. The court held he was domiciled in Alabama. The mode of living is not material; whether on rent, at lodgings, or in the house of a friend. He left South Carolina with the intention of never returning; he reached Alabama with the intent to remain there, these together constituted a new domicil.

In *Cooper v. Beers, 143 Ill. 25, 33 N. E. Rep. 61,* Cooper and wife were domiciled in Missouri, which they afterwards abandoned, intending to ultimately become residents of either Bloomington or Salem, Illinois, but before they had determined which place, or had adopted any home at either, she died intestate. Her domicil of origin was Illinois. The husband's domicil of origin was Ohio. Counsel contended that Mrs. Cooper's domicil at her death was Illinois. Court held that the proof fails to show with certainty a fixed and unalterable intention to make Illinois presently her home. No time was ever fixed when residence should begin, and no act intended as an act of removal or in aid of removal to Illinois is proved. Mrs. Cooper, so long as the relations between herself and her husband were not adverse, his domicil was her domicil, and changed with his throughout their married life. There is no pretence in argument, and no evidence in the record tending in any degree to prove that Mrs. Cooper's husband was ever domiciled in Illinois.

The wife cannot change the domicil of the husband. *Porterfield v. Augusta, 67 Me. 556; Scloles v. Murray, 44 Iowa 190.*

Where the boundary line between the towns of R. and N. B. passed through a dwelling house in such a direction as that that portion of the house which was in N. B. was sufficient in itself to constitute a habitation, while the portion in R. was not sufficient for that purpose, it was held, that a person, by occupying such house, acquired a domicil in N. B.

It seems that if, in such case, the line had divided the house more equally, the fact that the occupant had habitually slept in that part, which was in N. B., would be a preponderating circumstance to show that he was domiciled in that town, and, in the absence of other evidence, would be decisive of the question. *Abington v. North Bridgewater, 23 Pick. (Mass.) 177.*

Motive.—Men change their domiciles with very varying purposes or motives. The desire to live in a healthier region, to have better social or educational advantages, to enjoy better church privileges, to be near one's relatives, to live in a new and growing country, to avoid or escape arrest under a criminal charge, and sometimes to be relieved of disagreeable surroundings,—these and many more may be classed among the purposes —sole purposes, if you please—with which men change their residence. Yet, if the change be in fact made with the intent to acquire a new residence, either permanent or of an indefinite duration, this is a change of domicil. The intent that the new habitation shall, or shall not be, permanent, or of indefinite duration, and not the purpose in making the change, is the pivot on which the inquiry turns. *Young v. Pollak, 85 Ala. 439, 5 So. Rep. 279; McConnell v. Kelley, 138 Mass. 372 (1885).*

Domicil While in Transit.—A domicil once acquired continues till a new one is gained. While in transit the old domicil remains. *Littlefield v. Inhabitants of Brooks, 50 Me. 475; Shaw v. Shaw, 98 Mass. 158.*

While a person is in transit three might claim him: the one he has left, the one he is in, and the one to which he is proceeding. In such case the home would not be changed, either to the place of his actually bodily presence, or of his destination, because in neither would the fact of actual presence and the intent to reside concur. *Otis v. Boston, 12 Cush. 44.*

Can the husband by sending his wife and household goods to the new home acquire a domicile there before he actually arrives there in person? In *Hart v. Horn, 4 Kan. 232,* the court said no. Actual physical presence of the husband is necessary to the acquisition of a new domicil.

In *Bangs v. Brewster, 111 Mass. 382,* the decision was the other way. In this case, a shipmaster who was domiciled at Brewster sent his wife to Orleans, where they expected to live thereafter. The wife arrived at Orleans about six months before her husband. The court said that by sending his wife to Orleans with the intent to make it his home, he thereby changed his domicil.

The weight of authority in this country is with the Kansas decision.

BANK v. BALCOM, 1868.

[35 Conn. 351.]

PARK, J. The principal question in this case is in regard to the domicil of Mrs. Lewin at the time of her death. She died in the state of New York, and the administrator of her estate claims that her domicil at the time was in Connecticut; while the administrator of the estate of her husband claims that it was in the state of New York.

It appears by the finding of the court that her husband was a native of the state of New York; that he married Mrs. Lewin while temporarily residing in Connecticut; that immediately after their marriage they went to the state of Missouri, and resided there till the spring of 1862, when they returned to Connecticut, and after residing at various places in the state, became permanently located in the town of Branford. While their domicil continued there, Mrs. Lewin received a bequest that had been left her by her brother. Sometime in the spring of 1866 Mr. Lewin and his wife left Branford with the intent to abandon his residence there, and went to Geneseo in the state of New York, where he remained till the death of his wife, which occurred in the month of July of the same year.

The character of Mr. Lewin's residence at Geneseo is thus described in the report of the committee. "He did not go to Geneseo with the intent to adopt that place as a place of permanent residence. He and his wife, being in feeble health, went to Geneseo for the purpose of spending the summer there in the house of his brother-in-law, in the hope that the health of himself and wife might be benefited by the change of air, and by the use of the water of certain mineral springs near Geneseo. From the time he left Branford until the death of his wife he had no definite intentions in regard to the selection of any place as the place of his future residence. So far as he had any intention on the subject it was, during the whole period of time, an intention conditional and uncertain, whereby all decision in his mind upon the question was left in abeyance, to be determined in the future by the turn which his wife's disease might take, and by other circumstances which might or might not arise."

In the month of August of the same year he left Geneseo and returned to Connecticut, and not long afterwards became permanently settled in the town of Windham. These facts render it apparently clear that Mr. Lewin was not domiciled in the state of New York at the time his wife died.

But it is claimed that, inasmuch as he was a native of the state of New York, and inasmuch as he left Branford with no intention of returning to that place to reside, and went to the state of New York, and remained there, in fact, for a time, no matter what the character of his abiding may have been, he became domiciled there, on the principle that a native domicil easily reverts. Would it be claimed that if Mr. Lewin had left Branford with the intent to take up his residence in the state of Ohio, and on his way sojourned a few days in the state of New York, that would be sufficient? And what real difference is there between that case and the present? In both cases Mr. Lewin had no intention of permanently remaining in the state of New York. All the difference there is consists in the fact, that in one case his mind is made up in regard to his future residence and in the other it is not. His abiding in both cases is temporary. We said in another case upon the present circuit, that a temporary residence did not change its character by mere lapse of time. Whether it is longer or shorter it is temporary still. But the principle that a native domicil easily reverts applies only to cases where a native citizen of one country goes to reside in a foreign country, and there acquires a domicil by residence without renouncing his original allegiance. In such cases his native domicil reverts as soon as he begins to execute an intention of returning; that is, from the time he puts himself in motion *bona fide* to quit the country *sine animo revertendi*, because the foreign domicil was merely adventitious, and *de facto*, and prevails only while actual and complete. The Indian Chief, 3 *Rob. Adm. R.*, 17, 24; The Venus, 8 *Cranch*, 253, 280, 301; The State *v.* Hallett, 8 *Ala.*, 159; Case of Miller's Estate, 3 *Rawle*, 312, 319; The Ann Green, 1 *Gall.*, 275, 286; Catlin *v.* Gladding, 4 *Mason*, 308; Matter of Wrigly, 8 *Wend.*, 134, 140.

This principle has reference to a national domicil in its enlarged sense, and grows out of native allegiance or citizenship. It has no application when the question is between a native and acquired domicil, where both are under the same national jurisdiction. It was so held in the case of Monroe *v.* Douglas, 5 *Maddock*, 379. In that case the question was between the native domicil of a party in Scotland, and a domicil of residence acquired by the same party in India, and the Vice Chancellor said he could find no difference in principle between the original domicil of the party and the acquired one in India. See also 1 *American Leading Cases*, 742.

If this principle does not apply to the case in question, then it follows from this finding that Mr. Lewin had no domicil in the state of New York when his wife died, but his domicil at that time remained in the town of Branford, in accordance with the maxims that universally prevail in relation to this subject, that every person must have a domicil somewhere, that he can have but one domicil for one and the same purpose, and that a domicil once acquired continues until another is established. Abington *v.* North Bridgewater, 23 *Pick.*, 170; Thorndike *v.* City of Boston, 1 *Met.*, 242; Crawford *v.* Wilson, 4 *Barb.*, 504; Rue High, Appellant, 2 *Doug.* (*Mich.*) 515; Somerville *v.* Lord Somerville, 5 *Vesey*, 750; Greene *v.* Greene, 11 *Pick.*, 410; Walker *v.* Bank of Circleville, 15 *Ohio*, 288.

It is claimed further, that the bonds in question became the property of Mr. Lewin by *donatio causa mortis*. But it is clear that no gift was intended by Mrs. Lewin, as plainly appears by her letter to the officers of the bank, and besides, a gift of this nature must be made in contemplation of the approach of death and must be given to take effect only in case the donor dies. Ray-

6

mond *v.* Sellick, 10 *Conn.*, 480. Nothing of this kind appears in the case.

Again, it is claimed that the court of probate for the district of New Haven granted letters of administration on the estate of Mr. Lewin as domiciled in the state of New York; and it is insisted that this is conclusive on the subject. But the judgment of a court of limited jurisdiction is never conclusive of a jurisdictional question. Its jurisdiction may always be controverted. Sears *v.* Terry, 26 *Conn.*, 273; Jochumsen *v.* Suffolk Savings Bank, 3 *Allen*, 87; 2 *Redfield on Wills*, 49.

We advise the Superior Court that the administrator of the estate of Mrs. Lewin is entitled to the property.

In this opinion the other judges concurred.[6]

[6] A domicil once acquired remains until a new one is acquired actually, *facto et animo;* the fact and intention must concur; *Story Confl. Laws, Sec. 47.* There is one recognized exception to this rule, which is that the domicil of birth easily reverts, and therefore if a man has acquired a new domicil different from that of his birth, and he removes from it with an intention to resume his native domicile, the latter is reacquired, even while he is on his way, *in itinere;* for the native domicil reverts the moment the acquired domicil is given up with the intention of resuming the former; *Story Confl. Laws, Sec. 47.* In this, as in other cases, *exceptio probat regulam. Reed's Appeal, 71 Pa. St. 378.*

COMMERCIAL DOMICIL.

[Dicey Conflict of Laws, Appendix, Note 4.*]

1. Person's Character Determined by Domicil.— In time of war the answer to the question whether a person is or is not to be considered an alien enemy is, in most cases at any rate, to be determined by reference, not to his nationality or allegiance, but to his trading residence or commercial domicil. Every person domiciled in a state engaged in hostilities with our own, whether he is a born subject of that state or not, is to be regarded as an alien enemy; and, speaking generally, a person domiciled in a neutral country is to be regarded as for commercial purposes a neutral, even though he be in fact a British subject, or a subject of a state at war with England. "The position is a clear one, that "if a person goes into a foreign country, and engages in trade "there, he is, by the law of nations, to be considered a merchant of

*This "note" is inserted by permission of the American Publisher of "Dicey on the Conflict of Laws."

"that country, and a subject for all civil purposes, whether that
"country be hostile or neutral; and he cannot be permitted to
"retain the privileges of a neutral character during his residence
"and occupation in an enemy's country." A person's character,
in short, as a friend or enemy, is in time of war to be determined
by what is termed his commercial domicil. Persons who are com-
mercially domiciled in a neutral country are, as far as belligerents
are concerned, neutrals; whilst, on the other hand, persons com-
mercially domiciled in a hostile country are, whatever their
nationality or allegiance, to be considered enemies, for "persons
"resident in a country carrying on trade, by which both they and
"the country were benefited, were to be considered as the subjects
"of that country, and were considered so by the law of nations, at
"least so far as by that law to subject their property to capture by
"a country at war with that in which they lived." Thus, if there
be a war between England and France, a British subject residing
and trading in France is an alien enemy; whilst a British subject
or a French citizen who resides and carries on business in Portugal is, even though he may trade with France, a neutral.

II. Nature of Commercial Domicil.—The nature of
the trading residence or commercial domicil, which determines a
person's friendly or hostile character in time of war, may be made
clear by comparing such commercial domicil with the domicil
properly so called, which is referred to in the body of this treatise,
and is, in this Note, termed, for the sake of distinction, a civil
domicil. Each domicil is a kind of residence, each bears a close
resemblance to the other, but they are distinguished by marked
differences.

(A) RESEMBLANCE OF COMMERCIAL DOMICIL TO CIVIL DOMI-
CIL.—A trading or commercial domicil bears so close a resemblance to a civil domicil that it is often described in language
which appears to identify the two kinds of domicil. Thus
Arnould writes of the domicil which determines a person's character in time of war: "That is properly the domicil of a person
"where he has his true, fixed, permanent home and principal
"establishment, in which, when present, he has the intention of
"remaining (*animus manendi*), and from which he is never
"absent without the intention of returning (*animus revertendi*)
"directly he shall have accomplished the purpose for which he
"left it;" whilst Duer states with regard to the national character
of a merchant: "It is determined solely by the place of his per-
"manent residence. In the language of the law, it is fixed by his

"domicil. He is a political member of the country into which by
"his residence and business he is incorporated—a subject of the
"government that protects him in his pursuits—that his industry
"contributes to support, and of whose national resources his own
"means are a constituent part." Nor are the points in which the
two kinds of domicil resemble each other hard to discern. They
are each kinds or modes of residence. The constituent elements
of each are, first, "residence;" secondly, a "purpose or intention"
(on the part of the person whose domicil is in question) "with
regard to residence." In spite, however, of the terms used by
high authorities, and of the undoubted likeness between the two
kinds of domicil, they are different in essential particulars.

(B) DIFFERENCES BETWEEN CIVIL AND COMMERCIAL
DOMICIL.—The fundamental distinction between a civil domicil
and a commercial domicil is this: A civil domicil is such a permanent residence in a country as makes that country a person's
home, and renders it, therefore, reasonable that his civil rights
should in many instances be determined by the laws thereof. A
commercial domicil, on the other hand, is such a residence in a
country for the purpose of trading there as makes a person's
trade or business contribute to or form part of the resources of
such country, and renders it, therefore, reasonable that his hostile,
friendly, or neutral character should be determined by reference
to the character of such country. When a person's civil domicil
is in question, the matter to be determined is whether he has or
has not so settled in a given country as to have made it his home.
When a person's commercial domicil is in question, the matter to
be determined is whether he is or is not residing in a given
country with the intention of continuing trade there. From this
fundamental distinction arise the following differences:—

(1) *As to residence.*—Residence in a country is in general
Prima facie evidence of a person having there his civil domicil,
but it is only *prima facie* evidence, the effect of which may be
quite got rid of by proof that a person has never lived in the country with the intention of making it his permanent home. But
residence is far more than *prima facie* evidence of a person's commercial domicil. In time of war a man is taken to be domiciled
for commercial purposes in the country where he in fact resides,
and, if he is to escape the effect of such presumption, he must
prove affirmatively that he has the intention of not continuing to
reside in such country. A long period further of residence,
which, as regards civil rights, is merely evidence of domicil,

might, it would seem, be absolutely conclusive in determining national character in time of war.

(2) *As to intention.*—The intention, or *animus*, which, in combination with residence, constitutes a civil domicil, is different from the intention or *animus* which, together with residence, makes up a commercial domicil.

The intention which goes to make up the existence of a civil domicil is the present intention of residing permanently, or for an indefinite period, in a given country. The intention which goes to make up the existence of a commercial domicil is the intention to continue residing and trading in a given country for the present. The former is an intention to be settled in a country and make it one's home, the latter is an intention to continue residing and trading there. Hence, on the one hand, a person does not acquire a civil domicil by residence in a country for a definite purpose or period, and cannot by residence in one country, *e. g.,* France, get rid of a domicil in another, *e. g.,* England, if he retains the purpose of ultimately returning to England, as his home; while, on the other hand, the intention "which the law attributes to a person "residing in a hostile country, is not disproved by evidence that he "contemplated a return to his own country at some future period. "If the period of his return is wholly uncertain—if it remains in "doubt at what time, if at all, he will be able to accomplish the "design,—the design, however seriously entertained, will not avail "to refute the legal presumption. A residence for an indefinite "period is, in the judgment of law, not transitory, but permanent. "Even when the party has a fixed intention to return to his own "country at a certain period, yet if a long interval of time—an "interval not of months, but of years—is to elapse before his plan "of removal can be effected, no regard will be had to an intention "of which the execution is so long deferred."

D, domiciled in England, goes to British India with the full intention of residing there till he has made his fortune in trade, and of then returning to England, where he has his domicil of origin. He resides in India for twenty years. He retains his English civil domicil. Suppose, however, that *D,* under exactly similar circumstances in every other respect, takes up his residence not in British India, but in the Portuguese settlement in India, and after war has broken out between England and Portugal, continues to reside and trade in the Portuguese settlement, though still retaining his intention of ultimately returning to England. *D* thereupon acquires a Portuguese commercial domicil.

(3) *As to abandonment.*—The rules as to abandonment are different. A civil domicil once acquired can be changed only by complete abandonment in fact of the country where a person is domiciled. The intention to change, even if accompanied by steps for carrying out a change, will not, it would seem, produce a change as long as the person whose domicil is in question continues in fact to reside in the country where he has been domiciled.

A commercial domicil in time of war can, it would seem, be cnanged, under some circumstances, by the intention to change it, accompanied by steps taken for the purpose of effecting a change. "The native national character, that has been lost, or partially sus- "pended, by a foreign domicil, easily reverts. The circumstances, "by which it may be restored, are much fewer and slighter than "those that were originally necessary to effect its change. The "adventitious character, that a domicil imposes, ceases with the "residence from which it arose. It adheres to the party no longer "than he consents to bear it. It is true, his mere intention to "remove—an intention not manifested by overt acts, but existing "secretly in his own breast, . is not sufficient to efface the "character that his domicil impressed; something more than mere "verbal declarations, some solid fact, showing that the party is in "the act of withdrawing, is always necessary to be proved; *still,* "*neither his actual return to his own country, nor even his actual* "*departure from the territories of that in which he resided, is* "*indispensable.*"

(4) *As to domicil by operation of law.*—It may fairly be doubted whether the rules as to domicil by operation of law, *e. g.,* in the case of persons who have in fact no home, or of dependent persons, which play so large a part in the law of civil domicil, can be without considerable limitations applied to the ascertainment of commercial domicil. *D,* for example, is a French subject, whose domicil of origin is English. He has an acquired domicil in France. Both France and America declare war against England. *D* thereupon leaves France, intending to settle in New York. He resumes during the transit from one country to another his domicil of origin; but it can hardly be supposed that he is not during such transit an alien enemy. *D,* again, is an infant, or a married woman, carrying on a commercial business on his or her own account in France during a war with England. It can hardly be maintained that the fact of the father in the one case, or the husband in the other, having an English domicil and

being resident in England will free *D* from the character of an alien enemy.

(5) *As to special rules.*—There are one or two rules as to commercial domicil which can have no application to an ordinary civil domicil. Thus, according to American decisions at least, an American citizen (and the same principle would perhaps be applied by English Courts to British subjects) cannot, by emigration from his own country during the existence of hostilities, acquire such a foreign domicil as to protect his trade during the war against the belligerent claims either of his own country or of a hostile power. So, again, a neutral merchant may, at any time, withdraw his property and funds from a hostile country, and such a withdrawal may restore him to his neutral domicil. But whether the subject of a belligerent state can, after the outbreak of hostilities, withdraw from a hostile state so as to escape the imputation of trade with the enemy is doubtful. If the withdrawal can be effected at all, either it must be done within a short period after the outbreak of war, or any delay in effecting it must be shown to have arisen from necessity or from compulsion.

III. Person's Civil Need Not Coincide With His Commercial Domicil.—From the distinctions between a civil and a commercial domicil, the conclusion follows that a person may have a civil domicil in one country, and, at the same time, a commercial domicil or residence in another. Thus, suppose that *D's* domicil of origin is English, and that he goes to France and sets up in trade there without any purpose of making France his permanent home, but with the distinct intention of returning to England within ten years. He clearly retains his English domicil of origin; and the outbreak of a war between France and England does not of itself affect *D's* civil domicil.

If *D* continues to reside and trade in France after the outbreak of hostilities, though without any change of intention as to the time of his stay in France, he will acquire a French commercial domicil. In other words, he will have a civil domicil in England and a commercial domicil in France.

Nor is this fact really inconsistent with Rule 3, that no person can, at the same time, have more than one domicil. It only illustrates the fact constantly dwelt upon in this treatise, that residence is different from domicil, and that a person while domiciled in one country may, in fact, reside in another.[7]

[7] A Chinaman who resides in the United States, and who is doing business here, has a commercial domicil here, and does not forfeit such

domicil by a temporary absence at his domicil of origin. *Law Ow Bew v. United States, 144 U. S. 47; United States v. Chin Quong Look, 52 Fed. Rep. 203; Fong Yue Ting v. United States, 149 U. S. 698.*

An English company with a permanent general agency in New York was held as to business done through such agency to have, in time of war, a commercial domicil in New York. *Martine v. Int. Life Ins. Co., 53 N. Y. 359.*

CHAPTER IV.

DOMICIL OF PARTICULAR PERSONS.

WATERTOWN v. GREAVES, 1901.

[50 C. C. App. 172, 112 Fed. Rep. 183.]

1. Domicil of Particular Persons.
2. Domicil and Taxation.
3. Domicil and Acts in Uncivilized Countries.

Married Women.

In Error to the Circuit Court of the United States for the District of Massachusetts.

BROWN, District Judge. This writ of error is brought to review the rulings of the Circuit Court of the District of Massachusetts in an action of tort for the recovery of damages for injuries caused by a defective sidewalk.

The first question to be considered is that of jurisdiction. The plaintiff below sued as a citizen of Rhode Island. It is contended for the town that upon the evidence the plaintiff below was not a citizen of Rhode Island, and that the Court erred in the instructions to the jury as to the right of a married woman, deserted by her husband, to establish an independent domicil.

That the plaintiff went to Rhode Island before the date of the writ, April 3, 1900, with the intention of living there permanently, must be taken as a fact established by a special finding of the jury. Other relevant facts are that the plaintiff and her husband resided together in Lowell, Mass., and were citizens of that state until some time in 1892 or 1893, when her husband deserted her, and has never since lived in Lowell or contributed to her support; that she has not seen or heard from him since, and that at the date of trial she did not know whether he was alive or dead; that she never had procured a divorce, and, so far as she knew, her husband had never made application for a divorce. The record contains no evidence of the circumstances under which the husband of the plaintiff below deserted her; but, inasmuch as it is the ordinary duty of the husband to abide with the family, there is, in the present case, a sufficient presumption that the wife was guilty of no fault, in the absence of any suggestion to the contrary based on the evidence. The evidence was insufficient to establish a presumption of death. Neither was there any evidence that the husband had left the state of Massachusetts, or had changed the citizenship which he had at the date of desertion. It appeared that the plaintiff was obliged to support herself by her own exertions.

The third assignment of error is as follows:

"The court erred in instructing the jury that, while the general rule of law is that the domicil and citizenship of a wife follow that of her husband, still, if a husband deserts his wife, as there is evidence tending to show was the fact in this case, the wife's domicil would not necessarily follow that of her husband; that plaintiff might acquire a domicil and citizenship in Rhode Island, independent of that of her husband, if he were living; that if the husband deserted his wife and abandoned his residence, and went to parts unknown, and there remained for years without having any communication with his wife, and without making any contribution to her support, the wife had the right to acquire a domicil and citizenship, if she choose so to do, in a place different from that of the domicil and citizenship of her husband at the time he deserted her, or from the place of the domicil or citizenship of the husband after such desertion."

It is well settled that each state has the right to determine the civil status and capacities of its inhabitants. *Pennoyer* v. *Neff,* 95 U. S. 714. 722, 24 L. Ed. 565; *Hekking* v. *Pfaff* (C. C.) 82 Fed. 403.

An examination of the decisions of the Supreme Court of Rhode Island upon the question of the right of a deserted wife to establish for herself an independent domicil satisfies us that there was no error in the instructions above set forth.

In *Ditson* v. *Ditson*, 4 R. I. 87 (a leading case in this country; see *Atherton* v. *Atherton*, 181 U. S. 166, 21 Sup. Ct. 544, 45 L. Ed. 794), Chief Justice Ames said. on page 107:

"Although, as a general doctrine, the domicil of the husband is, by law, that of the wife, yet when he commits an offense, or is guilty of such dereliction of duty in the relation as entitles her to have it either partially or totally dissolved, she not only may, but must, to avoid condonation, establish a separate domicil of her own. This she may establish—nay, when deserted or compelled to leave her husband, necessity frequently compels her to establish—in a different judicial or state jurisdiction than that of her husband, according to the residence of her family or friends. Under such circumstances she gains, and is entitled to gain, for the purposes of jurisdiction, a domicil of her own, and, especially if a native of the state to which she flies for refuge, is, upon familiar principles. readily redintegrated in her old domicil."

The Court says also:

"Whatever was the former domicil of the petitioner, we are satisfied that she is, and has, for upwards of the last three years, been a domiciled citizen of Rhode Island, her only home, in the house of her father, and that as such citizen, and upon such notice, we have power and jurisdiction over her case, and to change her condition from that of a married to that of a single woman, granting to her the relief which, under like circumstancs, the law and policy of Rhode Island accords to all its citizens."

From this decision it would appear to be the law of Rhode Island that a married woman, unlawfully deserted by her husband, may establish an independent domicil, and thus become a citizen of the state of Rhode Island.

It is contended that this decision is merely to the effect that she may establish a domicil for the purposes of divorce. We regard it, however, as a clear and learned statement of limitations, upon the general rule that the domicil of the husband is that of the wife.

The learned Chief Justice, after stating the general doctrine, proceeds:

"A more proper case for the application in favor of a petitioner for divorce of the foregoing principles relating to the jurisdiction of the court over her case, and to the question of her domicil in this state, can hardly be imagined."

From this decision, it is apparent that the Court did not consider a judicial decree essential as a condition precedent to the establishment of citizenship, since it is in express terms stated that the petitioner, for upwards of three years, had been a domiciled citizen of Rhode Island.

For the town it is contended that the right of a married woman is limited to a quasi domicil for the purpose of divorce, and that this decision goes no farther. But the question of citizenship was directly passed upon, and citizenship was held to exist upon a state of facts showing unjustifiable desertion.

Moreover, the case of *Howland* v. *Granger, 22* R. I. *2*, 45 Atl. 740, contains a statement by the Supreme Court of Rhode Island which seems to us satisfactory evidence that the domicil which the wife may acquire upon desertion is not merely a quasi domicil for the purpose of divorce, leaving her general rights as a citizen of the state in abeyance until the pronouncement of a decree of divorce, a vinculo or a mensa et thoro, but a full and independent domicil for all purposes. This case was an action brought by a married woman to recover the amount of a personal property tax paid under protest. The husband, on the day of the assessment, was a domiciled inhabitant of the state of Rhode Island. The wife was at that time living in Asheville, N. C., for her health, with the intention of making said place her permanent home, and contended that she was a citizen of North Carolina, and therefore not liable to a personal tax in Rhode Island. There was no abandonment. The persons were living apart, but the unity of the marriage relation existed undisturbed. No question of divorce was involved. The Court said:

"After a careful examination of the authorities, however, we have come to the conclusion that though a wife may acquire a domicil distinct from that of her husband whenever it is necessary or proper for her to do so, as, for instance, where the husband and wife are living apart by mutual consent (In re Florance, 54 Hun. 328, 7 N. Y. Supp. 578) ; or where the wife has been abandoned by the husband (Schute v. Sargent, 67 N. H. 305, 36 Atl. 282) ; or for purpose of divorce (Ditson v. Ditson, 4 R. I. 87) ; or, in short, whenever the wife has adversary interests to those of her husband,—she cannot acquire such a domicil so long as the unity of the marriage relation continues, notwithstanding that from consideration of health, as in the present case, or of expediency, one of the parties, with the consent of the other, is actually living in a different place from the other."

See, also, *White* v. *White,* 18 R. I. 292, 27 Atl. 506.

The defendant, now plaintiff in error, contends that "the proposition that the exception made in divorce cases to the common-law rule, as to the domicil of the wife following that of the husband, does not extend to proceedings other than a suit for divorce, was expressly declared by the Supreme Court in *Barber* v. *Barber,* 21 How. 582, 16 L. Ed. 226."

We do not so read this opinion. The point there involved was whether a woman who had been divorced a mensa et thoro might establish an independent domicil. It was decided that she could. It was neither decided nor intimated in the opinion that an independent domicil could not be established without a judicial decree. The Court, seems, however, to have recognized the following prinicples:

The rule that the domicil of the wife is that of the husband is probably found to rest upon the legal duty of the wife to follow and dwell with the husband wherever he goes.

That, upon the commission of an offense which entitles her to have the marriage dissolved, she is discharged thereby immediately, and without a judicial determination of the question, from her duty to follow and dwell with him.

That if the husband abandons their domicil and his wife, and relinquishes altogether his marital control and protection, he yields up that power and authority over her which alone make his domicil hers.

Upon page 594, 21 How., and page 230, 16 L. Ed., of the opinion, in a quotation from Bishop. appears this language :

"Courts, however, may decline to recognize such domicil in a collateral proceeding; that is, a proceeding other than a suit for divorce."

It may be considered, in some jurisdictions, that the appropriate proceeding for establishing the wrongs which entitle a wife to an independent domicil is a proceeding for divorce a vinculo or a mensa et thoro, and that, in consequence of the difficulties of establishing these wrongs in a collateral inquiry, the Courts should require an adjudication by a divorce court which determines finally and for all purposes the status of the wife. See Minor, Conf. Laws, § 47. But this is rather a rule of procedure or of evidence than a rule of right, and is analogous to the rule of equity that a creditor shall establish his right by a judgment of law, before attacking in equity a fraudulent conveyance.

There seems to be no conflict of authority as to the point that, by the delictum of the husband, the wife is immediately absolved from her duty to follow and dwell with him, and that she is thereafter entitled, as a matter of right, to choose her own domicil.

We are of the opinion that the question whether, in order to assert or establish this right in a collateral proceeding, she must first procure a judicial decree establishing her status, as against her husband and all the world, is a distinct question.

If a plea in abatement had raised the question of the wife's domicil, and, before a hearing on the plea, she had applied to the divorce courts of Rhode Island and procured a decree of divorce, that decree, so far as the question of citizenship was concerned, would give her no new rights, but would furnish her with judicial evidence that before the bringing of action she was a citizen of Rhode Island.

The rulings of the Circuit Court as to the legal rights of a deserted wife, in the case at bar, were in accordance with the law as stated in *Cheever* v. *Wilson*, 9 Wall. 108, 124, 19 L. Ed. 604, 609 :

"The rule is that she may acquire a separate domicil whenever it is necessary or proper that she should do so. The right springs from the necessity for its exercise, and endures as long as the necessity continues. The proceeding for a divorce may be instituted where the wife has her domicil."

This implies that the domicil may be acquired prior to and independently of proceedings for divorce. And this implication is in agreement with the express decision of the Rhode Island court.

Moreover, various expressions of the Supreme Court seem to recognize that, if the wife is living apart by the fault of the husband, the rule that his domicil is her domicil is inapplicable. Thus, in *Atherton* v. *Atherton*, 181 U. S. 155, 21 Sup Ct. 544. 45 L. Ed. 794, are repeated the expressions of the Court in *Cheely* v. *Clayton*, 110 U. S. 701, 705, 709, 4 Sup. Ct. 328, 330, 28 L. Ed. 298, 299:

"If a wife is living apart from her husband without sufficient cause, his ᴗomicil is in law her domicil"; and "it is hard to see how, if she unjustifiably refuses to live with her husband, * * * she could lawfully acquire in his lifetime a separate domicil in another state," etc.

The question whether the wife, in order to bring suit as a citizen of another state from that in which her husband is domiciled, must establish her right to acquire a separate domicil by the judgment of a proper tribunal in a direct proceeding for that ᴑurpose, is one that presents difficulties.

It may be said that there are practical difficulties in trying collaterally the relations of husband and wife, and in determining whether or not the husband has been guilty of such a delictum as justifies a separate domicil. But similar difficulties do not preclude a husband from asserting, in defense of an action for supplies furnished to a wife, the adultery or other misconduct of the wife. Such cases involve a collateral inquiry into the rights of husband and wife arising from a breach of the obligations of marriage, yet it has never been held that the husband must establish the fact of the wife's delictum in a direct proceeding for that purpose. *Gill* v. *Read*, 5 R. I. 343, 73 Am. Dec. 73.

The wife may not desire a divorce a vinculo or a mensa et thoro; she may be ready to condone the fault of the husband in case he shall return; she may desire, for her own sake or that of her family, to avoid publicity; or she may die before she has established her rights by a judicial decree.

The difficulties that might arise from adopting a rigid rule that the wife's domicil shall be presumed to be her husband's until she overcomes this presumption by a judicial decree seem more serious than those that would arise from trying the question of domestic relations collaterally.

We should hesitate long before deciding that the only exception to the rule that the domicil of the wife follows that of her husband is in judicial proceedings whose express object is to show that the relation itself ought to be dissolved or modified, since there is grave danger that serious injustice might arise. See *Le Sueur* v. *Le Sueur*, 1 Prob. Div. 139-142; Eversley, Dom. Rel. (1896) p. 167.

2 Bish. Mar. & Div. §§ 114, 115, upon which counsel for the town relies, seems to recognize that the rule should not always prevail in non-divorce cases.

Furthermore, upon principle, it is difficult to see why a wife who is completely abandoned by her husband, even in consequence of her own fault, should be precluded from establishing an independent domicil. If the husband, justifiably or unjustifiably, renders it impossible for her to dwell with him, and voluntarily relinquishes altogether his marital control and protection, so that the abandonment is a completed fact, it cannot be said, in strictness, that her dwelling apart from him is her continuous fault. Her original fault may have justified the abandonment, but his renunciation of his former obligations keeps her from his home, and if she must find for herself another home, and from necessity or convenience goes to another state, it is difficult to see why she should be precluded from the ordinary rights of a citizen of that state. The expressions of the Supreme Court in *Atherton* v. *Atherton*, 181 U. S. 155, 21 Sup. Ct. 544, 45 L. Ed. 794, which relate to a wife living apart without sufficient cause, or through an unjustifiable refusal to live with the husband, do not cover a case in which the living apart is caused by the husband's total abandonment of the wife.

In the present case, however, we are relieved from a consideration of this question by the presumption that the wife was guilty of no fault which justified either the original desertion or its long continuance.

We are of opinion especially that in the present case, and upon the present assignments of error, the defendant is not entitled to make the objection that the proper evidence of the right of the wife to an independent domicil is a judicial decree.

No objection was made to the introduction of evidence of facts upon which, according to the general law as well as the law of Rhode Island, the wife became entitled, as a matter of legal right, to establish an independent domicil.

The judgment of the Circuit Court is affirmed.[8]

---

[8]**Minors.**—The domicil of a minor follows that of its parents. If both parents be dead, the domicil of the child will be that of origin, or, if that has been changed by the parents, that of its last surviving parent. The infant, of its own volition, cannot change its domicil. *Van Matre* v.

Sankey, 148, Ill. 536, 36 W. E. 628. Infants having a domicil in one state, who after the death of both their parents take up their residence at the home of their paternal grandmother and next of kin in another state, acquire her domicil. *La Mar v. Micou, 114; U. S. 218; In re Vance, 92 Cal. 195.* If a minor is emancipated, he may choose a domicil for himself. *Lowell v. Newport, 66 Me. 78; Wheeler v. Burrow, 18 Ind. 14.*

Adopted Child.—The domicil of a minor orphan child, who has been adopted is that of the adoptive parent with whom it resides. *Woodward v. Woodward, 87 Tenn. 644, 11 S. W. 892; Washburn v. White, 140 Mass. 568; Ross v. Ross, 129 Mass. 243, 37 Am. Rep. 321.*

Ward.—A guardian appointed in the state of the domicil of the ward (not being the natural guardian or a testamentary guardian) cannot remove the ward's domicil beyond the limits of the state in which the guardian is appointed and to which his legal authority is confined. He may, however, change the ward's domicil from one county to another within the same state and under the same law. The widowed mother, being the natural guardian, may change the domicil of her child. But when the widow, by marrying again, acquires the domicil of a second husband, she does not, by taking her children by the first husband to live with her there, make the domicil which she derives from her second husband their domicil; and they retain the domicil which they had, before her second marriage, acquired from her or from their father. *La Mar v. Micou, 112 U. S 452; Louisville v. Sherley, 80 Ky. 71.*

Clergymen.—The domicil of a clergyman is presumed to be at the place where he has charge of a parish. A missionary does not thereby forfeit his domicil, nor acquire a new one in the place to which he is sent. *Allgood v. Williams, 92 Ala. 551, 8 So. Rep. 722.*

In the case of *Hayes v. Hayes, 74 Ill. 312*, it was decided that a clergyman who was domiciled in Illinois, and who left the state to take charge of a congregation in Iowa, and had lived there for two years, acquired property there, and voted there, was still domiciled in Illinois.

Students.—A student does not acquire a residence at the seat of learning unless he goes there with an intention of always remaining. *Vanderpoel v. O'Hanlon, 53 Iowa 246; 36 Am. Rep. 216; Opinion of the Judges, 5 Met. 587; Fry's Election Case, 71 Pa. St. 302.* A residence at a college or other seminary for the purpose of instruction, would not confer a right to vote in the town where such an institution exists, if the student had not severed himself from his father's control, but resorted to his house as a home, and continued under his direction and management. *Dale v. Irwin, 78 Ill. 170; Sanders v. Getchell, 76 Me. 158.* The fact that one is a student in a university does not of itself entitle him to vote where the university is situated, nor does it prevent his voting there. It all depends upon the kind of residence required by the state law. *Putnam v. Johnson, 10 Mass. 488; Berry v. Wilcox, 44 Nebr. 82 (1895); Stewart v. Kyser, 105 Cal. 459.*

Officers.—Officers may or may not acquire a domicil at the place of their duties. It will depend upon the intent. However, an officer who has not changed his domicil may lose his vote by not complying with the registration laws of his domicil. *Sterling v. Horner, 74 Md. 573 (1891); Venable v. Paulding, 19 Minn. 488; Hannon v. Grizzard, 89 N. C. 115.*

Soldiers.—A soldier retains the domicil which he had on entering the service. *Brewer v. Linnaeus, 36 Me. 428.* Such persons may change their domicil in the ordinary way. *Mooar v. Harvey, 128 Mass. 219; Remey v. Board, 80 Iowa 470; Wood v. Fitzgerald, 3 Oreg. 568; Stewart v. Kyser, 105 Cal. 459.*

Servants.—A servant may, or may not, take the domicil of the master. It depends upon the combination of fact and intention. *Moreland v. Davidson, 71 Pa. St. 371; Cerro Gordo Co. v. Hancock Co., 58 Iowa 114.* An apprentice, or minor bound out to service, takes the domicil of the master. *Maddox v. State, 32 Ind. 14; Oldtown v. Falmouth, 40 Me. 106.*

A man laboring in one town with no other intention as to residence except to have a home wherever he works, may well be deemed to live there with the purpose of remaining for an indefinite period of time, and thus to have there all the home he has anywhere, as much of a domicil as such a wanderer can have. *Wilbraham v. Ludlow, 99 Mass. 587.*

Prisoners.—An imprisonment for years in the state prison, pursuant to a legal sentence, does not, of itself, change domicil. *Topsham v. Lewiston, 74 Me. 236 (1882).* Imprisonment in a state prison in this country does not work civil death. The strict civil death, at common law, seems to have been confined to the cases of persons professed, or abjured, or banished the realm as in cases of monks, and cases of crimes attended with forfeiture of the estate and corruption of blood. By statute in some states a life sentence operates as the natural death of a person, especially as to marriage or the settlement of his estate. *Baltimore v. Chester, 53 Vt. 315 (1881).*

Fugitives.—One who leaves his home through fear of criminal prosecution does not lose his domicil, but, if he goes to a new place with the intention to remain permanently, he acquires a domicil there. *Cobb v. Rice, 130 Mass. 231; Ayers v. Weeks, 65 N. H. 248, 18 Atl. 1108; Young v. Pollak, 85 Ala. 439, 5 So. Rep. 279; Ennis v. Smith, 14 How. 400; Chitty v. Chitty, 118 N. C. 647, 24 S. E. 517, 32 L. R. A. 394.*

Insane Persons.—Persons totally insane cannot change domicil. *Pittsfield v. Detroit, 53 Me. 442.* But a person under guardianship as a weakminded person may have sufficient mental capacity to choose a domicil for himself. *Talbot v. Chamberlain, 149 Mass. 57 (1889).* A person insane from birth, living with his parents till he reaches majority, retains the father's domicil. *Monroe v. Jackson, 55 Me. 55; Upton v. Northbridge, 15 Mass. 237; Holyoke v. Haskins, 5 Pick. 20; Jackson v. Polk, 19 Ohio St. 28; Anderson v. Anderson, 42 Vt. 350.*

Paupers.—A pauper remaining at the county poor house does not acquire a domicil in the township in which the poor house is located. *Clark v. Robinson, 88 Ill. 498.* Such pauper, however, is not under such legal restraint as to prevent his acquiring a domicil there. *Sturgeon v. Korte, 34 Ohio St. 525.* Such persons may acquire a domicil at a veterans' home, infirmary, if it is their intention to do so. *Stewart v. Kyser, 105 Cal. 459; Phillips v. Boston, 183 Mass. 344 (1903).*

Corporations.—As regards domicil, a corporation does not differ from a natural person. If any person, natural or artificial, as a result of choice or on technical grounds of birth or creation, has a domicil in one place, it cannot have one elsewhere, because what the law means by domicil is the one technically pre-eminent headquarters, which as a result either of fact or of fiction, every person is compelled to have in order that by aid of it certain rights and duties which have been attached to it by the law may be determined. It is settled that a corporation has its domicil in the jurisdiction of the state which created it, and as a consequence that it has not a domicil anywhere else. *Bergner v. Dreyfus, 172 Mass. 154, 70 Am. St. Rep. 251; Boston Investment Co. v. Boston, 158 Mass. 461; Shaw v. Quincy Mining Co., 145 U. S. 444; In re Hohorst, 150 U. S. 653.* If a corporation is chartered in several states, it is domiciled in each state. *Memphis Ry. Co. v. Alabama, 107 U. S. 581; Railroad v. Barnhill, 91 Tenn. 395, 19 S. W. Rep. 21; St. Louis Ry. Co. v. James, 161 U. S. 545; Ala. and Ga. Manf. Co. v. Riverdale. 127 Fed. Rep. 497 (1904).*

7

DOMICIL AND TAXATION.

FROTHINGHAM v. SHAW, 1899.

[175 Mass. 59, 78 Am. St. Rep. 475.]

PETITION, to the Probate Court, by the executor of the will of Joseph Frothingham, for instructions as to the payment of a collateral inheritance tax on the residuary legacies. The case was heard on agreed facts, and came here by successive appeals from decrees of the Probate Court and of a single justice of this court finding that the tax was payable, and directing the executor to pay the same. The facts appear in the opinion.

MORTON, J. At the time of his death the testator was domiciled at Salem, in this Commonwealth, and his estate, except certain real estate situated here and appraised at $2,100, and cash in a savings bank in Salem amounting to $993, was, and for many years had been, in the hands of his agents in New York, and consisted of bonds and stock of foreign corporations, a certificate of indebtedness of a foreign corporation, bonds secured by mortgage on real estate in New Hampshire, the makers living in New York, and of cash on deposit with a savings bank and with individuals in Brooklyn;—the total being upwards of $40,000.

There has been no administration in New York, and the petitioners have taken possession of all the property except the real estate, and have paid all of the debts and legacies except the residuary legacies. None of the legacies are entitled to exemption if otherwise liable to the tax.

The petitioners contend that the stocks, bonds, etc., were not "property within the jurisdiction of the Commonwealth," within the meaning of St. 1891, c. 425, § 1, and that, if they were, the succession took place by virtue of the law of New York and not of this state.

It is clear that if the question of the liability of the testator to be taxed in Salem for the property had arisen during his lifetime he would have been taxable for it under Pub. St. c. 11, §§ 4, 20, notwithstanding the certificates, etc., were in New York; *Kirtland* v. *Hotchkiss*, 100 U. S. 491; *State Tax on Foreign-Held Bonds*, 15 Wall. 300; Cooley, Taxation, (2d ed.) 371; and the liability would have extended to and included the bonds secured by mortgage. *Kirtland* v. *Hotchkiss* and *State Tax on Foreign-Held Bonds, ubi supra.* *Hale* v. *County Commissioners*, 137

Mass. 111. It is true that the Public Statutes provide that personal property wherever situated, whether within or without the Commonwealth, shall be taxed to the owner in the place where he is an inhabitant. But it is obvious that the Legislature cannot authorize the taxation of property over which it has no control, and the principle underlying the provision is that personal property follows the person of the owner, and properly may be regarded, therefore, for the purpose of taxation, as having a situs at his domicil, and as being taxable there. After the testator's death the property would have been taxable to his executors for three years or until distributed and paid over to those entitled to it, and notice thereof to the assessors; showing that the fiction, if it is one, is continued for the purpose of taxation after the owner's death. Pub. St. c. 11, § 20, cl. 7. *Hardy* v. *Yarmouth,* 6 Allen, 277. In the present case the tax is not upon property as such, but upon the privilege of disposing of it by will, and of succeeding to it on the death of the testator or intestate, and it "has some of the characteristics of a duty on the administration of the estates of deceased persons." *Minot* v. *Winthrop,* 162 Mass. 113, 124. *Callahan* v. *Woodbridge,* 171 Mass. 595. *Greves* v. *Shaw,* 173 Mass. 205. *Moody* v. *Shaw,* 173 Mass. 375. In arriving at the amount of the tax the property within the jurisdiction of the Commonwealth is considered, and we see no reason for supposing that the Legislature intended to depart from the principle heretofore adopted, which regards personal property for the purposes of taxation as having a situs at the domicil of its owner. This is the general rule, Cooley on Taxation, (2d ed.) 372; and though it may and does lead to double taxation, that has not been accounted a sufficient objection to taxing personal property to the owner during his life at the place of his domicil, and we do not see that it is a sufficient objection to the imposition of succession taxes or administration duties under like circumstances after his death.

In regard to the mortgage bonds it is to be noted, in addition to what has been said, that this case differs from *Callahan* v. *Woodbridge.* In that case the testator's domicil was in New York, and it does not appear from the opinion that the note and mortgage deed were in this State. In this case the domicil was in this Commonwealth, and we think that for the purpose of taxation the mortgage debt may be regarded as having a situs here. This is the view taken in Hanson's Death Duties, (4th ed.) 239, 240, which is cited apparently with approval by Mr. Dicey, though he calls attention to cases which may tend in another direction. See Dicey, Confl. of Laws, 319, note 1.

It seems to us, therefore, that for the purposes of the tax in question the property in the hands of the executor must be regarded as having been within the jurisdiction of this Commonwealth at the time of the testator's death. See *In re Swift*, 137 N. Y. 77; *Miller's estate*, 182 Penn. St. 157.

The petitioners further contend that the succession took place by virtue of the law of New York. But it is settled that the succession to movable property is governed by the law of the owner's domicil at the time of his death. This, it has been often said, is the universal rule, and applies to movables wherever situated. *Stevens* v. *Gaylord*, 11 Mass. 256, *Dawes* v. *Head*, 3 Pick. 128, 144, 145. *Fay* v. *Haven*, 3 Met. 109. *Wilkins* v. *Ellett*, 9 Wall. 740; *S. C.* 108 U. S. 256. *Freke* v. *Carbery*, L. R. 16 Eq. 461. *Attorney General* v. *Campbell*, L. R. 5 H. L. 524. *Duncan* v. *Lawson*, 41 Ch. D. 394. *Sill* v. *Worswick*, 1 H. Bl. 665, 690. Dicey, Confl. of Laws, 683. Story, Confl. of Laws, (7th ed.) §§ 380, 481.

If there are movables in a foreign country, the law of the domicil is given an extraterritorial effect by the courts of that country, and in a just and proper sense the succession is said to take place by force of and to be governed by the law of the domicil. Accordingly, it has been held that legacy and succession duties as such were payable at the place of domicil in respect to movable property wherever situated, because in such cases the succession or legacy took effect by virtue of the law of domicil. *Wallace* v. *Attorney General*, L. R. 1. Ch. 1. Dicey, Confl. of Laws, 785. Hanson's Death Duties, 423, 526.

With probate or estate or administration duties as such it is different. They are levied in respect of the control which every government has over the property actually situated within its jurisdiction irrespective of the place of domicil. *Laidlay* v. *Lord Advocate*, 15 App. Cas. 468, 483. Hanson's Death Duties, (4th ed.) 2, 63.

Of course any State or country may impose a tax and give it such name or no name as it chooses, which shall embrace, if so intended, the various grounds upon which taxes are or may be levied in respect of the devolution of estates of deceased persons, and which shall be leviable according as the facts in each particular case warrant. In England, for instance, the estate duty, as it is termed, under the Finance Act of 1894 (57 & 58 Vict. c.

30) has largely superseded the probate duty, and under some circumstances takes the place of the legacy and succession duty also.. Hanson's Death Duties, (4th ed.) 62, 63, 81.

But whatever the form of the tax, the succession takes place and is governed by the law of the domicil; and, if the actual situs is in a foreign country, the courts of that country cannot annul the succession established by the law of the domicil. *Dammert. v. Osborn,* 141 N. Y. 564. In further illustration of the extent to which the law of the domicil operates, it is to be noted that the domicil is regarded as the place of principal administrattion, and any other administration is ancillary to that granted there. Payment by a foreign debtor to the domiciliary administrator will be a bar to a suit brought by an ancillary administrator subsequently appointed. *Wilkins* v. *Ellett* and *Stevens* v. *Gaylord, ubi supra. Hutchins* v. *State Bank,* 12 Met. 421. *Martin* v. *Gage,* 147 Mass. 204. And the domiciliary administrator has sufficient standing in the courts of another State to appeal from a decree appointing an ancillary administrator. *Smith* v. *Sherman,* 4 Cush. 408. Moreover, it is to be observed, if that is material, that there has been no administration in New York, that the executor was appointed here, and has taken possession of the property by virtue of such appointment and must distribute it and account for it according to the decrees of the courts of this Commonwealth. To say, therefore, that the succession has taken place by virtue of the law of New York would be no less a fiction than the petitioners insist that the maxim *mobilia sequuntur personam* is when applied to matters.of taxation.

The petitioners contend that in *Callahan* v. *Woodbridge* it was held that the succession to the personal property in this State took place by virtue of the law of this State, although the testator was domiciled in New York. We do not so understand that case. That case and *Greves* v. *Shaw* and *Moody* v. *Shaw, ubi supra,* rest on the right of a State to impose a tax or duty in respect to the passing on the death of a non-resident of personal property belonging to him and situated within its jurisdiction. We think that the decree should be affirmed.[9]

So ordered.

---

[9]The old rule by which personal property was regarded as subject to the law of the owner's domicil, grew up in the Middle Ages, when movable property consisted chiefly of gold and jewels, which could be easily carried by the owner from place to place, or secreted in spots known only to himself. In modern times, since the great increase in amount and variety of

DOMICIL, AND ACTS IN UNCIVILIZED COUNTRIES.

DICEY CONFLICT OF LAWS, APPENDIX, NOTE I.*

THE Rules in this Digest apply only to rights acquired under the law of a civilized country. What, however, is the law, if any, which in the opinion of English Courts governs transactions taking place in an uncivilized country, e. g., in the Soudan, or in some part of the world not under the sovereignty of any ruler recognized by European law?

The question is one which may at times come before an English Court; it is also one to which, in the absence of decisions, nothing like a final answer can be given; all that can be done is to note a few points, as to the matter before us, on which it is possible to conjecture, at any rate, what would be the view taken by English Courts.

We may assume that the legal effect of a transaction taking place, e. g., a contract made, in an uncivilized country could not come before an English Court unless one of the parties at least were the subject of some civilized state.

(1) *As to domicil.*—An Englishman—and probably the citizen of any civilized country—does not, it would seem, by fixing his permanent residence, or settling in an uncivilized country, acquire, for legal purposes, a domicil in such country. A domiciled Englishman who settles in China, and *a fortiori* who settles in a strictly barbarous country, retains his English domicil. *A,* an Englishman, was settled in Shanghai. "In these circumstances it "was admitted by the petitioner's counsel [in a case as to liability "to legacy duty] that they could not contend that the testator's "domicil was Chinese. This admission was rightly made. The

----

that rule has yielded more and more to the *lex situs,* the law of the place where the property is kept and used.

For purposes of taxation, personal property may be separated from its owner, and he may be taxed, on its account, at the place where it is, although not the place of his domicil, and even if he is not a citizen or a resident of the state which imposes the tax. *Pullman Car Co. v. Pa., 141 U. S. 18,* and case cited; *Buck v. Miller, 147 Ind. 586, 45 N. E. 647, 62 Am. St. Rep. 452.*

See*McKeen v. County of Northampton, 49 Pa. St. 519, 88 Am. Dec. 515; New Orleans v. Stempel, 175 U. S. 309; Hunt v. Perry 165 Mass. 287, 43 N. E. 103; 129 Pa. St. 338, 18 Atl. 132; In re Bronson, 150 N. Y. 1; Dicey Conflict of Laws. P. 781.*

*This "note" is inserted by permission of the American publishers of "Dicey on the Conflict of Laws."

"difference between the religion, laws, manners, and customs of
"the Chinese and of Englishmen is so great as to raise every
"presumption against such a domicil, and brings the case within
"the principles laid down by Lord Stowell in his celebrated judg-
"ment in *The Indian Chief* [1801, 3 Rob. Ad. Cas. 29], and by
"Dr. Lushington in *Maltass v Maltass*" [1844, 1 Rob. Ecc. Cas.
67, 80, 81]. (*In re Tootal's Trusts*, 1883, 23 Ch. D. 532, 534,
judgment of *Chitty*, J. Semble, however, that the cases do not
show that an Englishman might not for legal purposes acquire a
domicil in such a country as China. All they actually establish
is the strength of the presumption against his intending to acquire
a domicil in China, or rather to subject himself to Chinese law.)

The principle laid down or suggested in these words by Mr.
Justice Chitty—namely, that settlement in an uncivilized country
does not change the domicil of the citizen of a civilized country, or
at any rate of a domiciled Englishman—goes (if it can be maintained) some way towards solving one or two difficult questions,
e. g., What is the law governing the validity of a will made in an
uncivilized country by an Englishman domiciled in in England?

(2) *As to marriage.*—A marriage made in a strictly barbarous country between British subjects, or between a British
subject and a citizen of a civilized country, *e. g.*, an Italian, and
it would seem even between a British subject and a native of such
uncivilized country, will, it is submitted, be held valid as regards
forms, if made in accordance with the requirements of the English common law; and it is extremely probable that, with regard
to such a marriage, the common law might now be interpreted as
allowing the celebration of a marriage *per verba de præsenti* without the presence of a minister in orders. A local form, also, if
such there be, would seem to be sufficient, at any rate where one
of the parties is a native. It is, however, essential that the intention of the parties should be an intention to contract a "marriage"
in the sense in which that term is known in Christian countries,
i. e., the union of one man to one woman for life to the exclusion
of all others. Capacity to marry would apparently depend upon
the law of the domicil of the parties, or perhaps more strictly of
the husband.

(3) *As to contract.*—Capacity to contract must, it would
seem, depend upon the law of the domicil of the parties to the
agreement. If either of the parties were under an incapacity by
the law of his domicil to enter into a contract, an agreement made
by him in an uncivilised country would probably not be enforceable

against him in England. This we may be pretty certain would be the case were the party under an incapacity an English infant domiciled in England.

The formalities of a contract probably, and its effect almost certainly, would, under the circumstances supposed, be governed by the proper law of the contract, *i. e.*, by the law contemplated by the parties. Suppose X and A enter into a contract in the Soudan. If the contract is to be performed in England, the incidents would be governed by English law; whilst, if it is to be performed in Germany, its incidents would be governed by German law.

(4) *As to alienation of movables.*—If the movables are at the time of the alienation situate in the barbarous country, probably English Courts might hold that the alienation must, in order to be valid, be one which, if made in England, would be valid according to the English common law. There is little doubt that if, though the alienation takes place in an uncivilised country, the movables alienated are situated in a civilised country, the validity of the alienation would depend on the law of that country (*lex situs*).

(5) *Torts.*—When an act which damages A or his property is done by X in a barbarous country, the character of the act cannot depend on the law of the country where it is done. If both X and A are domiciled in England, the act is probably wrongful and actionable in England, if it would have been tortious if done in England. If the two parties are domiciled, the one in England and the other, *e. g.*, in Germany, then the act is probably actionable in England, if it be one which is wrongful both according to the law of England and according to the law of Germany. But we can here be guided by nothing but analogy, and all we can do is to consider how far the rules which govern the possibility of bringing an action in England for a tort committed in a foreign and civilised country can by analogy be made applicable to an action for a tort committed in an uncivilised country. An action cannot be maintained in England for a trespass to land in an uncivilised country.

(6) *Procedure.*—An action in England in respect of any transaction taking place in an uncivilised country is clearly, as regards all matters of procedure, governed by English law.

On most of the points, however, considered in this Note, and many others which might suggest themselves, we must trust wholly to conjecture, and must admit that what is the law, if any, governing transactions taking place in an uncivilised country, is in many instances a matter of absolute uncertainty. If, for example, X, an Englishman domiciled in England, whilst in an uncivilised country promises A, a Scotchman domiciled in Scotland, out of gratitude for some past service, to pay A £10 on their return home, is the promise governed by English law, and therefore invalid for want of a consideration, or by Scotch law, under which, apparently, it may be valid? How, again, if the position of the parties had been reversed, and the promise had been made by A, the Scotchman domiciled in Scotland, to X, the Englishman domiciled in England? To these and similar inquiries no certain reply is, it is conceived, possible.

CHAPTER V.

NATIONALITY.

UNITED STATES v. WONG KIM ARK, 1898.

[169 U. S. 649, 42 Sup. Ct. Rep. 890.]

In this case, the question presented by the record is whether a child born in the United States, of parents of Chinese descent, who, at the time of his birth, are subjects of the Emperor of China, but have a permanent domicil and residence in the United States, and are there carrying on business, and are not employed in any diplomatic or official capacity under the Emperor of China, becomes at the time of his birth a citizen of the United States, by virtue of the first clause of the Fourteenth Amendment of the Constitution, "All persons born or naturalized in the United States, and subject to the jurisdiction thereof, are citizens of the United States and of the state wherein they reside."

Mr. Justice Gray, in delivering the opinion of the court, said: In construing any act of legislation, whether a statute enacted by the legislature, or a constitution established by the people as the supreme law of the land, regard is to be had, not only to all parts of the act itself, and of any former act of the same law-making power, of which the act in question is an amendment; but also to the condition, and to the history, of the law as previously existing, and in the light of which the new act must be read and interpreted.

The Fourteenth Article of Amendment of the Constitution declares that "all persons born or naturalized in the United States, and subject to the jurisdiction thereof, are citizens of the United States and of the state wherein they reside." The Constitution nowhere defines the meaning of these words, either by way of inclusion or of exclusion, except in so far as this is done by the affirmative declaration that "all persons born or naturalized in the United States, and subject to the jurisdiction thereof, are citizens of the United States." In this, as in other respects, it must be interpreted in the light of the common law, the principles and history of which were familiarly known to the framers of the Constitution. *Minor v. Happersett,* 21 Wall, 162; *Ex parte Wilson,* 114 U. S. 417; *Boyd v. United States,* 116 U. S. 616; *Smith v. Alabama,* 124 U. S. 465. The language of the Constitution, as has been well said, could not be understood without reference to the common law. 1 Kent Com. 336; *Moore v. United States,* 91 U. S. 270. The interpretation of the Constitution of the United States is necessarily influenced by the fact that its provisions are framed in the language of the English common law, and are to be read in the light of its history. *Smith v. Alabama,* 124 U. S. 465.

The fundamental principle of the common law with regard to English nationality was birth within the allegiance, also called "ligealty," "obedience," "faith" or "power," of the King. The principle embraced all persons born within the King's allegiance and subject to his protection. Such allegiance and protection were mutual and were not restricted to natural-born subjects and naturalized subjects, or to those who had taken an oath of allegiance; but were predicable of aliens in amity, so long as they were within the kingdom. Children, born in England, of such aliens, were therefore natural-born subjects. But the children, born within the realm, of foreign ambassadors, or the children of alien enemies, born during and within their hostile occupation of part of the King's dominions, were not natural-born subjects, because not born within the allegiance, the obedience, or the power, or, as would be said at this day, within the jurisdiction of the King. *Calvin's Case,* 7 Rep. 1; *Doe v. Jones,* 4 T. R. 300; Dicey Conflict of Laws, pp. 173-177, 741.

Mr. Dicey, in his careful and thoughtful Digest of the Law of England with reference to the Conflict of Laws, published in 1896, states the following propositions, his principal rules being printed below in italics: "*British subject means any person who owes permanent allegiance to the crown.* 'Permanent' allegiance is used to distinguish the allegiance of a British subject from the allegiance of an alien who, because he is within the British dominions, owes 'temporary' allegiance to the Crown. *'Natural born British subject' means a British subject who has become a British subject at the moment of his birth.*" "*Subject to the exceptions hereinafter mentioned, any person who (whatever the nationality of his parents) is born within the British dominions is a natural born British subject.* This rule contains the leading principle of English law on the subject of British nationality." The exceptions afterwards mentioned by Mr. Dicey are only these two: "1· Any person who (his father being an alien enemy) is born in a part of the British dominions, which at the time of such person's birth is in hostile occupation, is an alien " "2· Any person whose father (being an alien) is at the time of such person's birth an ambassador or other diplomatic agent accredited to the Crown by the sovereign of a foreign state is (though born within the British dominions) an alien."

It thus clearly appears that by the law of England for the last three centuries, beginning before the settlement of this country, and continuing to the present day, aliens while residing in the dominions possessed by the Crown of England, were within the allegiance, the obedience, the faith or loyalty, the protection, the power, the jurisdiction, of the English sovereign; and therefore every child born in England of alien parents was a natural-born subject, unless the child of an ambassador or other diplomatic agent of a foreign state, or of an alien enemy in hostile occupation of the place where the child was born.

The same rule was in force in all the English colonies upon this continent down to the time of the Declaration of Independence, and in the United States afterwards, and continued to prevail under the Constitution as originally established. *The Charming Betsy*, 2 Crauch 64, 119; *Inglis v. Sailors' Snug Harbor*, 3 Pet. 99; *Shanks v. Dupont*, 3 Pet. 242; *Dred Scott v. Sandford*, 19 How. 393; *United States v. Rhodes*, 1 Abbott (U. S.) 28

The Supreme Court of North Carolina, speaking by Mr. Justice Gaston, said: "Before our Revolution, all free persons born within the dominions of the King of Great Britain, whatever their color or complexion, were native-born British subjects; those born out of his allegiance were aliens." "Upon the Revolution, no other change took place in the law of North Carolina, than was consequent upon the transition from a colony dependent on an European King to a free and sovereign state;" "British subjects in North Carolina became North Carolina freemen;" and all free persons born within the state are born citizens of the state." "The term 'citizen,' as understood in our law, is precisely analogous to the term 'subject' in the common law, and the change of phrase has entirely resulted from the change of government. The sovereignty has been transferred from one man to the collective body of the people; and he who before was a 'subject of the King' is now 'a citizen of the state '" *State v. Manuel*, 4 Dev. & Bat. 20, 24-26.

It was contended by one of the learned counsel for the United States that the rule of the Roman law, by which the citizenship of the child followed that of the parent, was the true rule of international law, as now recognized in most civilized countries, and had superseded the rule of the common law, depending on birth within the realm, originally founded on feudal considerations.

There is little ground for the theory that, at the time of the adoption of the Fourteenth Amendment of the Constitution of the United States, there was any settled and definite rule of international law, generally recognized by civilized nations, inconsistent with the ancient rule of citizenship by birth within the dominion.

Both in England and in the United States, indeed, statutes have been passed, at various times, enacting that certain issue born abroad of English subjects, or of American citizens, respectively, should inherit, to some extent at least, the rights of their parents. But those statutes applied only to cases coming within their purport; and they have never been considered, in either country, as affecting the citizenship of persons born within its dominion.

By the Constitution of the United States, Congress was empowered "to establish an uniform rule of naturalization." In the exercise of this power, Congress, by successive acts, beginning with the act entitled "An act to establish an uniform rule of naturalization," passed at the second session of the First Congress under the Constitution, has made provision for the admission to citizenship of three principal classes of persons: First. Aliens, having resided for a certain time within the limits and under the jurisdiction of the United States," and naturalized individually by proceedings in a court of record. Second. Children of persons so naturalized, "dwelling within the United States, and being under the age of twenty-one years at the time of such naturalization." Third. Foreign-born children of American citizens, coming within the definitions prescribed by Congress. Acts of March 26, 1790, c. 3; January 29, 1795, c. 20; June 18, 1798, c. 54; 1 Stat. 103, 414, 566, April 14, 1802, c. 28; March 26, 1804, c. 47; 2 Stat. 153, 292; February 10, 1855, c. 71; 10 Stat. 604; Rev. Stat. §§ 2165, 2172, 1993

In the act of 1790, the provision as to foreign-born children of American citizens was as follows: "The children of citizens of the United States, that may be born beyond sea, or out of the limits of the United States, shall be considered as natural-born citizens: Provided, that the right of citizenship shall not descend to persons whose fathers have never been resident in the United States." 1 Stat. 104. In 1795, this was reënacted, in the same words, except in substituting, for the words "beyond sea, or out of the limits of the United States," the words "out of the limits and jurisdiction of the United States." 1 Stat. 415.

In 1802, all former acts were repealed, and the provisions concerning children of citizens were reënacted in this form ˙ "The children of persons duly naturalized under any of the laws of the United States, or who, previous to the passing of any law on that subject by the Government of the United States, may have become citizens of any one of the said States under the laws thereof, being under the age of twenty-one years at the time of their parents being so naturalized or admitted to the rights of citizenship, shall, if dwelling in the United States, be considered as citizens of the United States; and the children of persons who now are, or have been citizens of the United States shall, though born out of the limits and jurisdiction of the United States, be considered as citizens of the United States: Provided, that the right of citizenship shall not descend to persons whose fathers have never resided within the United States." Act of April 14, 1802. c. 28, § 4; 2 Stat. 155.

The provision of that act, concerning "the children of persons duly naturalized under any of the laws of the United States," not being restricted to the children of persons already naturalized, might well be held to include children of persons thereafter to be naturalized. 2 Kent Com. 51, 52; *West* v. *West*, 8 Paige, 433; *United States* v. *Kellar*, 11 Bissell, 314; *Boyd* v. *Thayer*, 143 U. S. 135, 177.

But the provision concerning foreign-born children, being expressly limited to the children of persons who then were or had been citizens, clearly did not include foreign-born children of any person who became a citizen since its enactment. 2 Kent Com. 52, 53; Binney on Alienigenæ, 20, 25; 2 Amer. Law Reg. 203, 205. Mr. Binney's paper, as he states in his preface, was printed by him in the hope that Congress might supply this defect in our law.

In accordance with his suggestions, it was enacted by the statute of February 10, 1855, c. 71, that "persons heretofore born, or hereafter to be born, out of the limits and jurisdiction of the United States, whose fathers were or shall be at the time of their birth citizens of the United States, shall be deemed and considered and are hereby declared to be citizens of the United

States: Provided, however, that the rights of citizenship shall not descend to persons whose fathers never resided in the United States." 10 Stat. 604; Rev. Stat. § 1993.

It thus clearly appears that, during the half century intervening between 1802 and 1855, there was no legislation whatever for the citizenship of children born abroad, during that period, of American parents who had not become citizens of the United States before the act of 1802; and that the act of 1855, like every other act of Congress upon the subject, has, by express proviso, restricted the right of citizenship, thereby conferred upon foreign-born children of American citizens, to those children themselves, unless they became residents of the United States. Here is nothing to countenance the theory that a general rule of citizenship by blood or descent has displaced in this country the fundamental rule of citizenship by birth within its sovereignty.

So far as we are informed, there is no authority, legislative, executive or judicial, in England or America, which maintains or intimates that the statutes (whether considered as declaratory, or as merely prospective,) conferring citizenship on foreign-born children of citizens, have superseded or restricted, in any respect, the established rule of citizenship by birth within the dominion. Even those authorities in this country, which have gone farthest towards holding such statutes to be but declaratory of the common law, have distinctly recognized and emphatically asserted the citizenship of native-born children of foreign parents. 2 Kent Com. 39, 50, 53, 258 note; *Lynch* v. *Clarke*, 1 Sandf. Ch. 583, 659; *Ludlam* v. *Ludlam*, 26 N. Y. 356, 371.

Passing by questions once earnestly controverted, but finally put at rest by the Fourteenth Amendment of the Constitution, it is beyond doubt that, before the enactment of the Civil Rights Act of 1866 or the adoption of the Constitutional Amendment, all white persons, at least, born within the sovereignty of the United States, whether children of citizens or of foreigneers, excepting only children of ambassadors or public ministers of a foreign government, were native-born citizens of the United States.

In the fore front, both of the Fourteenth Amendment of the Constitution, and of the Civil Rights Act of 1866, the fundamental principle of citizenship by birth within the dominion was reaffirmed in the most explicit and comprehensive terms.

The Civil Rights Act, passed at the first session of the Thirty-ninth Congress, began by enacting that "all persons born in the United States, and not subject to any foreign power, excluding Indians not taxed, are hereby declared to be citizens of the United States; and such citizens, of every race and color, without regard to any previous condition of slavery or involuntary servitude, except as a punishment for crime whereof the party shall have been duly convicted, shall have the same right, in every State and Territory in the United States, to make and enforce contracts, to sue, be parties and give evidence, to inherit, purchase, lease, sell, hold and convey real and personal property, and to full and equal benefit of all laws and proceedings for the security of person and property, as is enjoyed by white citizens, and shall be subject to like punishment, pains and penalties, and to none other, any law, statute, ordinance, regulation or custom, to the contrary notwithstanding." Act of April 9, 1866 c. 31, § 1 ; 14 Stat. 27.

The same Congress, shortly afterwards, evidently thinking it unwise, and perhaps unsafe, to leave so important a declaration of rights to depend upon an ordinary act of legislation, which might be repealed by any subsequent Congress, framed the Fourteenth Amendment of the Constitution, and on June 16, 1866, by joint resolution proposed it to the legislatures of the several States; and on July 28, 1868, the Secretary of State issued a proclamation showing it to have been ratified by the legislatures of the requisite number of States.   14 Stat. 358; 15 Stat. 708.

The first section of the Fourteenth Amendment of the Constitution begins with the words, "All persons born or naturalized in the United States, and subject to the jurisdiction thereof, are citizens of the United States and of the State wherein they reside." As appears upon the face of the amendment, as well as from the history of the times, this was not intended to impose any new restrictions upon citizenship, or to prevent any persons from becoming citizens by the fact of birth within the United States, who would thereby have become citizens according to the law existing before its adoption. It is declaratory in form, and enabling and extending in effect. Its main purpose doubtless was, as has been often recognized by this court, to establish the citizenship of free negroes, which had been denied in the opinion delivered by Chief Justice Taney in *Dred Scott* v. *Sandford*, (1857) 19 How. 393; and to put it beyond doubt that all blacks, as well as whites, born or naturalized within the jurisdiction of the United State, are citizens of the United States. *The Slaughterhouse Cases*, (1873) 16 Wall. 36, 73; *Strauder* v. *West Vir-*

ginia, (1879) 100 U. S. 303, 306; *Ex parte Virginia,* (1879) 100 U. S. 339, 345; *Neal* v. *Delaware,* (1880) 103 U. S. 370, 386; *Elk v. Wilkins,* (1884) 112 U. S. 94, 101. But the opening words, "all persons born," are general, not to say universal, restricted only by place and jurisdiction, and not by color or race—as was clearly recognized in all the opinions delivered in *The Slaughter-house Cases,* above cited.

In those cases, the point adjudged was that a statute of Louisiana, granting to a particular corporation the exclusive right for twenty-five years to have and maintain slaughterhouses within a certain district including the city of New Orleans, requiring all cattle intended for sale or slaughter in that district to be brought to the yards and slaughterhouses of the grantee, authorizing all butchers to slaughter their cattle there, and empowering the grantee to exact a reasonable fee for each animal slaughtered, was within the police powers of the State, and not in conflict with the Thirteenth Amendment of the Constitution as creating an involuntary servitude, nor with the Fourteenth Amendment as abridging the privileges or immunities of citizens of the United States, or as depriving persons of their liberty or property without due process of law, or as denying to them the equal protection of the laws.

Mr. Justice Miller, delivering the opinion of the majority of the court, after observing that the Thirteenth, Fourteenth and Fifteenth Articles of Amendment of the Constitution were all addressed to the grievances of the negro race, and were designed to remedy them, continued as follows: "We do not say that no one else but the negro can share in this protection. Both the language and spirit of these Articles are to have their fair and just weight in any question of construction. Undoubtedly, while negro slavery alone was in the mind of the Congress which proposed the Thirteenth Article, it forbids any other kind of slavery, now or hereafter. If Mexican peonage or the Chinese coolie labor system shall develop slavery of the Mexican or Chinese race within our territory, this Amendment may safely be trusted to make it void. *Peonage Cases,* 123 Fed. Rep. 671; *United States* v. *McClellan,* 127 Fed. Rep. 971. And so if other rights are assailed by the States, which properly and necessarily fall within the protection of these Articles, that protection will apply, though the party interested may not be of African descent." 16 Wall. 72. And in treating of the first clause of the Fourteenth Amendment, he said: "The distinction

8

between citizenship of the United States and citizenship of a State is clearly recognized and established. Not only may a man be a citizen of the United States without being a citizen of a State, but an important element is necessary to convert the former into the latter. He must reside within the State to make him a citizen of it, but it is only necessary that he should be born or naturalized in the United States to be   citizen of the Union." 16 Wall. 73, 74.

Mr. ‚ustice Field, in a dissenting opinion, in which Chief Justice Chase and Justices Swayne and Bradley concurred, said of the same clause : "It recognizes in express terms, if it does not create,. citizens of the United States, and it makes their citizenship dependent upon the place of their birth, or the fact of their adoption, and not upon the constitution or laws of any State or the condition of their ancestry." 16 Wall. 95, 111. Mr. Justice Bradley also said : "The question is now settled by the Fourteenth Amendment itself, that citizenship of the United States is the primary citizenship in this country ; and that state citizenship is secondary and derivative, depending upon citizenship of the United States and the citizen's place of residence. The States have not now, if they ever had, any power to restrict their citizenship to any classes or persons." 16 Wall. 112. And Mr. Justice Swayne added: "The language employed is unqualified in its scope. There is no exception in its terms, and there can be properly none in their application. By the language 'citizens of the United States' was meant all such citizens; and by 'any person' was meant all persons within the jurisdiction of the State. No distinction is intimated on account of race or color. This court has no authority to interpolate a limitation that is neither expressed nor implied. Our duty is to execute the law, not to make it. The protection provided was not intended to be confined to those of any particular race or class, but to embrace equally all races, classes and conditions of men." 16 Wall. 128, 129.

Mr. Justice Miller, indeed, while discussing the causes which led to the adoption of the Fourteenth Amendment, made this remark: "The phrase, 'subject to its jurisdiction,' was intended to exclude from its operation children of ministers, consuls, and citizens or subjects of foreign States. born within the United States." 16 Wall. 73. This was wholly aside from the question in judgment, and from the course of reasoning bearing upon that question. It was unsupported by any argument, or by any reference to authorities; and that it was not formulated with the same care and exactness, as if the case before the court had called for an exact definition of the phrase, is apparent from its classing foreign ministers and consuls together—whereas it was then well settled law, as has since been recognized in a judgment of this co..rt in which Mr. Justice Miller concurred, that consuls, as such, and unless expressly invested with a diplomatic character in addition to their ordinary powers, are not considered as entrusted with authority to represent their sovereign in his intercourse with foreign States or to vindicate his prerogatives, or entitled by the law of nations to the privileges and immunities of ambassadors or public ministers, but are subject to the jurisdiction, civil and criminal, of the courts of the country in which they reside. 1 Kent Com. 44; Story Conflict of Laws, § 48; Wheaton International Law, (8th ed.) § 249; *The Anne*, (1818) 3 Wheat, 435, 445, 446; *Gittings* v. *Crawford*, (1838) Taney, 1, 10; *In re Baiz*, (1890) 135 U. S. 403, 424.

In weighing a remark uttered under such circumstances, it is well to bear in mind the often quoted words of Chief Justice Marshall: "It is a maxim not to be disregarded, that general expressions, in every opinion, are to be taken in connection with the case in which those expressions are used. If they go beyond the case, they may be respected, but ought not to control the judgment in a subsequent suit when the very point is presented for decision. The reason of this maxim is obvious. The question actually before the court is investigated with care, and considered in its full extent. Other principles which may serve to illustrate it are considered in their relation to the case decided, but their possible bearing on all other cases is seldom completely investigated." *Cohens* v. *Virginia*, (1821) 6 Wheat. 264, 399.

That neither Mr. Justice Miller, nor any of the justices who took part in the decision of *The Slaughterhouse Cases*, understood the court to be committed to the view that all children born in the United States of citizens or subjects of foreign States were excluded from the operation of the first sentence of the Fourteenth Amendment, is manifest from a unanimous judgment of the court, delivered but two years later, while all those judges but Chief Justice Chase were still on the bench, in which Chief Justice Waite said: "Allegiance and protection are, in this connection," (that is, in relation to citizenship,) "reciprocal obligations. The one is a compensation for the other: allegiance for protection, and protection for allegiance." "At common law,

with the nomenclature of which the framers of the Constitution
were familiar, it was never doubted that all children, born in a
country, of parents who were its citizens, became themselves,
upon their birth, citizens also. These were natives, or natural-
born citizens, as distinguished from aliens or foreigners. Some
authorities go further and include as citizens children born within
the jurisdiction, without reference to the citizenship of their
parents. As to this class there have been doubts, but never as to
the first. For the purposes of this case it is not necessary to
solve these doubts. It is sufficient, for everything we have now
to consider, that all children, born of citizen parents within the
jurisdiction, are themselves citizens." *Minor* v. *Happersett*,
(1874) 21 Wall. 162, 166–168. The decision in that case was
that a woman born of citizen parents within the United States
was a citizen of the United States, although not entitled to vote,
the right to the elective franchise not being essential to citizenship.

The only adjudication that has been made by this court upon
the meaning of the clause, "and subject to the jurisdiction
thereof," in the leading provision of the Fourteenth Amendment,
is *Elk* v. *Wilkins*, 112 U. S. 94, in which it was decided that an
Indian born a member of one of the Indian tribes within the
United States, which still existed and was recognized as an
Indian tribe by the United States, who had voluntarily separated
himself from his tribe, and taken up his residence among the
white citizens of a State, but who did not appear to have been
naturalized, or taxed, or in any way recognized or treated as a
citizen, either by the United States or by the State, was not a
citizen of the United States, as a person born in the United States,
"and subject to the jurisdiction thereof," within the meaning of
the clause in question.

That decision was placed upon the grounds, that the meaning
of those words was, "not merely subject in some respect or
degree to the jurisdiction of the United States, but completely
subject to their political jurisdiction, and owing them direct and
immediate allegiance;" that by the Constitution, as originally
established, "Indians not taxed" were excluded from the persons
according to whose numbers representatives in Congress and
direct taxes were apportioned among the several States, and
Congress was empowered to regulate commerce, not only "with
foreign nations," and among the several States, but "with the
Indian tribes;" that the Indian tribes, being within the territorial
limits of the United States, were not, strictly speaking, foreign

States, but were alien nations, distinct political communities, the members of which owed immediate allegiance to their several tribes, and were not part of the people of the United States; that the alien and dependent condition of the members of one of those tribes could not be put off at their own will, without the action or assent of the United States; and that they were never deemed citizens, except when naturalized, collectively or individually, under explicit provisions of a treaty, or of an act of Congress; and, therefore, that "Indians born within the territorial limits of the United States, members of, and owing immediate allegiance to, one of the Indian tribes (an alien, though dependent, power), although in a geographical sense born in the United States, are no more 'born in the United States, and subject to the jurisdiction thereof,' within the meaning of the first section of the Fourteenth Amendment, than the children of subjects of any foreign government born within the domain of that government, or the children born within the United States of ambassadors or other public ministers of foreign nations." And it was observed that the language used, in defining citizenship, in the first section of the Civil Rights Act of 1866, by the very Congress which framed the Fourteenth Amendment, was "all persons born in the United States, and not subject to any foreign power, excluding Indians not taxed." 112 U. S. 99–103.

Mr. Justice Harlan and Mr. Justice Woods, dissenting, were of opinion that the Indian in question, having severed himself from his tribe and become a *bona fide* resident of a State, had thereby become subject to the jurisdiction of the United States, within the meaning of the Fourteenth Amendment; and, in reference to the Civil Rights Act of 1866, said: "Beyond question, by that act, national citizenship was conferred directly upon all persons in this country, of whatever race (excluding only 'Indians not taxed'), who were born within the territorial limits of the United States, and were not subject to any foreign power." And that view was supported by reference to the debates in the Senate upon that act, and to the ineffectual veto thereof by President Johnson, in which he said: "By the first section of the bill, all persons born in the United States, and not subject to any foreign power, excluding Indians not taxed, are declared to be citizens of the United States. This provision comprehends the Chinese of the Pacific States, Indians subject to taxation, the people called Gypsies, as well as the entire race designated as blacks, persons of color, negroes, mulattoes, and persons of African blood. Every individual of those races, born in the United States, is, by the bill, made a citizen of the United States." 112 U. S. 112–114.

The decision in *Elk* v. *Wilkins* concerned only members of the Indian tribes within the United States, and had no tendency to deny citizenship to children born in the United States of foreign parents of Caucasian, African or Mongolian descent, not in the diplomatic service of a foreign country.

The real object of the Fourteenth Amendment of the Constitution, in qualifying the words, "All persons born in the United States," by the addition, "and subject to the jurisdiction thereof," would appear to have been to exclude, by the fewest and fittest words, (besides children of members of the Indian tribes, standing in a peculiar relation to the National Government, unknown to the common law,) the two classes of cases—children born of alien enemies in hostile occupation, and children of diplomatic representatives of a foreign State—both of which, as has already been shown, by the law of England, and by our own law, from the time of the first settlement of the English colonies in America, had been recognized exceptions to the fundamental rule of citizenship by birth within the country. *Calvin's Case*, 7 Rep. 1, 18*b*; Cockburn on Nationality, 7; Dicey Conflict of Laws, 177; *Inglis* v. *Sailors' Snug Harbor*, 3 Pet. 99, 155; 2 Kent Com. 39, 42.

The foregoing considerations and authorities irresistibly lead us to these conclusions: The Fourteenth Amendment affirms the ancient and fundamental rule of citizenship by birth within the territory, in the allegiance and under the protection of the country, including all children here born of resident aliens, with the exceptions or qualifications (as old as the rule itself) of children of foreign sovereigns or their ministers, or born on foreign public ships, or of enemies within and during a hostile occupation of part of our territory, and with the single additional exception of children of members of the Indian tribes owing direct allegiance to their several tribes. The Amendment, in clear words and in manifest intent, includes the children born, within the territory of the United States, of all other persons, of whatever race or color, domiciled within the United States. Every citizen or subject of another country, while domiciled here, is within the allegiance and the protection, and consequently subject to the jurisdiction, of the United States. His allegiance to the United States is direct and immediate, and, although but local and temporary, continuing only so long as he remains within our territory, is yet, in the words of Lord Coke, in *Calvin's Case*, 7

Rep. 6a, "strong enough to make a natural subject, for if he hath issue here, that issue is a natural-born subject;" and his child, as said by Mr. Binney in his essay before quoted, "if born in the country, is as much a citizen as the natural-born child of a citizen, and by operation of the same principle." It can hardly be denied that an alien is completely subject to the political jurisdiction of the country in which he resides—seeing that, as said by Mr. Webster, when Secretary of State, in his Report to the President on *Thrasher's Case* in 1851, and since repeated by this court, "independently of a residence with intention to continue such residence; independently of any domiciliation; independently of the taking of any oath of allegiance or of renouncing any former allegiance, it is well known that, by the public law, an alien, or a stranger born, for so long a time as he continues within the dominions of a foreign government, owes obedience to the laws of that government, and may be punished for treason, or other crimes, as a native-born subject might be, unless his case is varied by some treaty stipulations." Ex. Doc. H. R. No. 10, 1st sess. 32d Congress, p. 4; 6 Webster's Works, 526; *United States* v. *Carlisle*, 16 Wall. 147, 155; *Calvin's Case*, 7 Rep. 6a; Ellesmere on Postnati, 63; 1 Hale P. C. 62; 4 Bl. Com. 74, 92.

To hold that the Fourteenth Amendment of the Constitution excludes from citizenship the children, born in the United States, of citizens or subjects of other countries, would be to deny citizenship to thousands of persons of English, Scotch, Irish, German or other European parentage, who have always been considered and treated as citizens of the United States.

Whatever considerations, in the absence of a controlling provision of the Constitution, might influence the legislative or executive branch of the Government to decline to admit persons of the Chinese race to the status of citizens of the United States, there are none that can constrain or permit the judiciary to refuse to give full effect to the peremptory and explicit language of the Fourteenth Amendment, which declares and ordains that "All persons born or naturalized in the United States, and subject to the jurisdiction thereof, are citizens of the United States."

Chinese persons, born out of the United States, remaining subjects of the emperor of China, and not having become citizens of the United States, are entitled to the protection of and owe allegiance to the United States, so long as they are permitted by the United States to reside here; and are "subject to the jurisdiction thereof," in the same sense as all other aliens residing in the

United States. *Yick Wo* v. *Hopkins*, (1886) 118 U. S. 356; *Law Ow Bew* v. *United States*, (1892) 144 U. S. 47, 61, 62; *Fong Yue Ting* v. *United States*, (1893) 149 U. S. 698, 724; *Lem Moon Sing* v. *United States*, (1895) 158 U. S. 538, 547; *Wong Wing* v. *United States*, (1896) 163 U. S. 228, 238.

It is true that Chinese persons born in China cannot be naturalized, like other aliens, by proceedings under the naturalization laws. But this is for want of any statute or treaty authorizing or permitting such naturalization, as will appear by tracing the history of the statutes, treaties and decisions upon that subject—always bearing in mind that statutes enacted by Congress, as well as treaties made by the President and Senate, must yield to the paramount and supreme law of the Constitution.

The power, granted to Congress by the Constitution, "to establish an uniform rule of naturalization," was long ago adjudged by this court to be vested exclusively in Congress. *Chirac* v. *Chirac*, (1817) 2 Wheat. 259. For many years after the establishment of the original Constitution, and until two years after the adoption of the Fourteenth Amendment, Congress never authorized the naturalization of any but "free white persons." Acts of March 26, 1790, c. 3, and January 29, 1795, c. 20; 1 Stat. 103, 414; April 14, 1802, c. 28, and March 26, 1804, c. 47; 2 Stat. 153, 292; March 22, 1816, c. 32; 3 Stat. 258; May 26, 1824, c. 186, and May 24, 1828, c. 116; 4 Stat. 69, 310. By the treaty between the United States and China, made July 28, 1868, and promulgated February 5, 1870, it was provided that "nothing herein contained shall be held to confer naturalization upon citizens of the United States in China, nor upon the subjects of China in the United States." 16 Stat. 740. By the act of July 14, 1870, c. 254, § 7, for the first time, the naturalization laws were "extended to aliens of African nativity and to persons of African descent." 16 Stat. 256. This extension, as embodied in the Revised Statutes, took the form of providing that those laws should "apply to aliens [being free white persons, and to aliens] of African nativity and to persons of African descent;" and it was amended by the act of February 18, 1875, c. 80, by inserting the words above printed in brackets. Rev. Stat. (2d ed.) § 2169; 18 Stat. 318. Those statutes were held, by the Circuit Court of the United States in California, not to embrace Chinese aliens. *In re Ah Yup*, (1878) 5 Sawyer, 155. And by the act of May 6, 1882, c. 126, § 14, it was expressly enacted that "hereafter no state court or court of the United States shall admit Chinese to citizenship." 22 Stat. 61.

In *Fong Yue Ting* v. *United States*, (1893) above cited, this court said: "Chinese persons not born in this country have never been recognized as citizens of the United States, nor authorized to become such under the naturalization laws." 149 U. S. 716.

The convention between the United States and China of 1894 provided that "Chinese laborers or Chinese of any other class, either permanently or temporarily residing in the United States, shall have for the protection of their persons and property all rights that are given by the laws of the United States to citzens of the most favored nation, excepting the right to become naturalized citizens." 28 Stat. 1211. And it has since been decided, by the same judge who held this appellee to be a citizen of the United States by virtue of his birth therein, that a native of China of the Mongolian race could not be admitted to citizenship under the naturalization laws. *In re Gee Hop*, (1895) 71 Fed. Rep. 274.

The Fourteenth Amendment of the Constitution, in the declaration that "all persons born or naturalized in the United States, and subject to the jurisdiction thereof, are citizens of the United States and of the State wherein they reside," contemplates two sources of citizenship, and two only: birth and naturalization. Citizenship by naturalization can only be acquired by naturalization under the authority and in the forms of law. But citizenship by birth is established by the mere fact of birth under the circumstances defined in the Constitution. Every person born in the United States, and subject to the jurisdiction thereof, becomes at once a citizen of the United States, and needs no naturalization. A person born out of the jurisdiction of the United States can only become a citizen by being naturalized, either by treaty, as in the case of the annexation of foreign territory; or by authority of Congress, exercised either by declaring certain classes of persons to be citizens, as in the enactments conferring citizenship upon foreign-born children of citizens, or by enabling foreigners individually to become citizens by proceedings in the judicial tri bunals, as in the ordinary provisions of the naturalization acts.

The power of naturalization, vested in Congress by the Constitution, is a power to confer citizenship, not a power to take it away. "A naturalized citizen," said Chief Justice Marshall, "becomes a member of the society, possessing all the rights of a native citizen, and standing, in the view of the Constitution, on the footing of a native. The Constitution does not authorize Congress to enlarge or abridge those rights. The simple power of the National Legislature is to prescribe a uniform rule of naturalization, and the exercise of this power exhausts it, so far as respects the individual. The Constitution then takes him up, and, among other rights, extends to him the capacity of suing in the courts of the United States, precisely under the same circumstances under which a native might sue." *Osborn v. United States Bank,* 9 Wheat. 738, 827. Congress having no power to abridge the rights conferred by the Constitution upon those who have become naturalized citizens by virtue of acts of Congress, *a fortiori* no act or omission of Congress, as to providing for the naturalization of parents or children of a particular race, can affect citizenship acquired as a birthright, by virtue of the Constitution itself, without any aid of legislation. The Fourteenth Amendment, while it leaves the power, where it was before, in Congress, to regulate naturalization, has conferred no authority upon Congress to restrict the effect of birth, declared by the Constitution to constitute a sufficient and complete right to citizenship.

No one doubts that the Amendment, as soon as it was promulgated, applied to persons of African descent born in the United States, wherever the birthplace of their parents might have been; and yet, for two years afterwards, there was no statute authorizing persons of that race to be naturalized. If the omission or the refusal of Congress to permit certain classes of persons to be made citizens by naturalization could be allowed the effect of correspondingly restricting the classes of persons who should become citizens by birth, it would be in the power of Congress, at any time, by striking negroes out of the naturalization laws, and limiting those laws, as they were formerly limited, to white persons only, to defeat the main purpose of the Constitutional Amendment.

The fact, therefore, that acts of Congress or treaties have not permitted Chinese persons born out of this country to become citizens by naturalization, cannot exclude Chinese persons born in this country from the operation of the broad and clear words of the Constitution, "All persons born in the United States, and subject to the jurisdiction thereof, are citizens of the United States."

Upon the facts agreed in this case, the American citizenship which Wong Kim Ark acquired by birth within the United States has not been lost or taken away by anything happening since his birth. No doubt he might himself, after coming of age, renounce this citizenship, and become a citizen of the country of his parents, or of any other country; for by our law, as solemnly declared by Congress, "the right of expatriation is a natural and inherent right of all people," and "any declaration, instruction, opinion, order or direction of any officer of the United States, which denies, restricts, impairs or questions the right of expatriation, is declared inconsistent with the fundamental principles of the Republic." Rev. Stat. § 1999, reënacting act of July 27, 1868, c. 249, § 1; 15 Stat. 223, 224. Whether any act of himself, or of his parents, during his minority, could have the same effect, is at least doubtful. But it would be out of place to pursue that inquiry; inasmuch as it is expressly agreed that his residence has always been in the United States, and not elsewhere; that each of his temporary visits to China, the one for some months when he was about seventeen years old, and the other for something like a year about the time of his coming of age, was made with the intention of returning, and was followed by his actual return, to the United States; and "that said Wong Kim Ark has not, either by himself or his parents acting for him, ever renounced his allegiance to the United States, and that he has never done or committed any act or thing to exclude him therefrom."

The evident intention, and the necessary effect, of the submission of this case to the decision of the court upon the facts agreed by the parties, were to present for determination the single question, stated at the beginning of this opinion, namely, whether a child born in the United States, of parents of Chinese descent, who, at the time of his birth, are subjects of the Emperor of China, but have a permanent domicil and residence in the United States, and are there carrying on business, and are not employed in any diplomatic or official capacity under the Emperor of China, becomes at the time of his birth a citizen of the United States. For the reasons above stated this court is of opinion that the question must be answered in the affirmative.

Order affirmed.[10]

———

[10]**Who May be Naturalized.**—The statute of the United States applies only to "aliens being free white persons and to aliens of African nativity and to persons of African descent." The word "white" includes only members of the Caucasian race. The Japanese, Chinese, and Hawaiians have been refused naturalization. The Caucasian, Ethiopian, and American Indian are the only races permitted, under the present law, to become citizens by naturalization. The Malays and Mongolians are excluded, and naturalization papers granted to such aliens are void. *In re Takuji Yamashita, 30 Wash. Rep. 234, 70 Pac. Rep. 482; In re Camille, 6 Fed. Rep. 256; In re Po, 28 N. Y. Supp. 383; In re Kanaka Niau, 6 Utah 659, 21 Pac. Rep. 993, 4 L. R. A. 726; In re Saito, 62 Fed. Rep. 126; In re Rodriguez, 81 Fed.*

Rep. 337. Females may take out naturalization papers as well as males. *Pequignot v. City of Detroit, 16 Fed. Rep. 211.*

Methods of Naturalization.—Naturalization may be effected in the following ways: *First.* By general naturalization laws; *Second.* By marriage of an alien woman to a citizen of the United States; *Third.* By the acquisition of foreign territory; *Fourth.* By admission of a territory to statehood; *Fifth.* By grant of the privilege to certain named individuals. *Boyd v. Thayer, 143 U. S. 135, 36 Sup. Ct. Rep. 103.*

The wife and minor children of an alien who takes out naturalization papers are citizens of the United States, and if any alien has declared his intention of becoming a citizen, and dies before he is actually naturalized, his widow and children shall be considered as citizens, upon taking the oath of allegiance. An alien woman who marries a citizen shall herself be deemed a citizen. *Pequignot v. City of Detroit, 16 Fed. Rep. 211.*

On the acquisition of foreign territory it may be provided that the inhabitants of such territory shall become citizens, if no such provision, such inhabitants are not citizens, and can only become citizens under the regulations of Congress. As to the status of the inhabitants of Porto Rico and the Philippine Islands see *De Lima v. Bidwell, 182 U. S. 1; Huns v. N. Y., 182 U. S. 392; Gonzales v. Williams, (Jan. 4. 1904). 24 Sup. Ct. Rep. 177; In re Gonzalez, 118 Fed. Rep. 941.*

Conditions Necessary to Naturalization Under General Law.—An alien may be admitted to become a citizen (under the general law) of the United States in the following manner: *First.* Make a declaration of intention to become a citizen, made before the clerk of a state or Federal Court, and this declaration (or first papers) may be made at any time after the alien arrives, but it must be made at least two years before the oath of allegiance (last papers). *Second.* He must have resided within the United States for a period of five years, and within the state or territory where the court is held one year. *Third.* He must be a moral and law-abiding person. *Fourth.* Renounce his allegiance to his foreign sovereignty. *Fifth.* Take the oath of allegiance. This completes the naturalization, and until the oath is taken the person is an alien. The declaration of intention does not confer citizenship.

The making of a declaration of intention two years before the oath of allegiance is not necessary if an alien has continuously resided in the United States for a period of five years, three of which immediately preceded his arriving at majority. In such cases the declaration of intention and oath of allegiance may be made at the same time. *City of Minneapolis v. Reum, 56 Fed. Rep. 576.*

Alien Friends and Alien Enemies.—*Alien Friends* are subjects or citizens of foreign countries with which we are at peace. Alien enemies are those who are subject to some foreign country with which the United States is at war. Alien enemies are of two kinds—alien enemies in fact and alien enemies by operation of law. Alien enemies in fact are subjects or citizens of the country with which we are at war, alien enemies by operation of law are cases of our own citizens residing in the enemy's country or carrying on business there after the breaking out of war. *The Venus, 8 Cranch 253.*

Rights of Aliens.—An alien may acquire, hold, or dispose of personal property, or he may make contracts, sue and be sued, the same as a citizen. He is liable for tort and may sue for tort. An alien who is residing in this country, though his sovereign be at war with us, and is allowed to remain after the breaking out of hostilities, has capacity to sue and be sued. But aliens who reside in the enemy's country would not be allowed to sue in our courts during the continuance of war. *Clark v. Morey, 10 Johns (N. Y.) 69.*

At the common law, aliens are incapable of taking by descent or inheritance, for they are not allowed to have any inheritable blood in them. But they may take by grant or devise though not by descent. In other words, they may take by the act of a party, but not by operation of law; and they may convey or devise to another, but such a title is always liable to be divested at the pleasure of the sovereign by *office-found.* In such cases the sovereign, until entitled by *office-found* or its equivalent, cannot pass the title to a grantee. In these respects there is no difference between an alien friend and an alien enemy. *Hauenstein v. Lynham, 100 U. S. 483.*

In most states the common law disabilities of aliens are modified and they are allowed to acquire and hold real estate to the same extent as citizens, but in some states non-resident aliens are not allowed to hold or acquire real estate. *Wunderle v. Wunderle, 144 Ill. 40; Furenes v. Nickelson, 86 Iowa 508; Microsi v. Phillipi, 91 Ala. 299; State v. Smith, 70 Cal. 153.*

CHAPTER VI.

LOCALITY OF ACTIONS.

BRITISH SO. AFRICA CO. v. COMPANHIA DE MOCAMBIQUE, 1893.

[18 L. R. App. Cas. 602.]

1. Local and Transitory Actions   2. Actions for Injuries to Land in a
    Distinguished.   Foreign Jurisdiction.

Appeal from an order of the Court of Appeal.

In an action by the respondents against the appellants the plaintiffs by their statement of claim alleged (inter alia) that the plaintiff company was in possession and occupation of large tracts of land and mines and mining rights in South Africa; and that the defendant company by its agents wrongfully broke and entered and took possession of the said lands, mines and mining rights, and ejected the plaintiff company, its servants, agents and tenants therefrom; and also took possession of some of the plaintiff's personal property and assaulted and imprisoned some of the plaintiffs.

Alternatively the plaintiffs alleged in paragraph 16 that the defendants did the above acts maliciously and without any just cause or excuse and with intent to injure and destroy the plaintiffs' trade and to deprive the plaintiffs of their lands, mines and mining rights and to put an end to their existence as a trading company in South Africa.

The plaintiffs claimed (Inter alia) (1.) a declaration that the plaintiff company were lawfully in possession and occupation of the lands, mines and mining rights and other property; (2.) an injunction restraining the defendant company from continuing to occupy or from asserting any title to the said lands, mines and mining rights, and from withholding and keeping possession of the said other property; (3.) £250,000 damages.

The statement of defence in paragraph 1—as to so much of the statement of claim as alleged a title in the plaintiff company to the lands, mines and mining rights, and alleged that the defendants by their agents wrongfully broke and entered the same, and claimed a declaration of title and an injunction—

whilst denying the alleged title and the alleged wrongful acts, said that the lands, mines and mining rights were situate abroad, to wit in South Africa, and submitted that the Court had no jurisdiction to adjudicate upon the plaintiff's claim; and in paragraph 2 submitted that as matter of law paragraph 16 of the statement of claim disclosed no valid cause of action. The allegations in paragraph 9 of the defence are sufficiently stated at the close of the judgment of Lord Herschell L.C.

In paragraph 2 of the reply the plaintiffs objected that paragraphs 1 and 9 of the defence were bad in law, and alleged that paragraph 1 did not shew that there was any Court other than that in which this action was brought having jurisdiction to adjudicate on the plaintiffs' said claim; and the plaintiffs further alleged that there was no competent tribunal having jurisdiction to adjudicate on the said claims in the country where the acts complained of were committed; and that the acts complained of were illegal according to the laws of the country where the same were committed.

An order having been made for the disposal of the points of law thus raised by the pleadings, the Queen's Bench Division (Lawrence and Wright JJ.) made an order that judgment be entered for the defendants dismissing the action so far as it claimed a declaration of title to land, and also so far as it claimed damages or an injunction in relation to trespass to land, and also as to such portion of paragraph 16 of the statement of claim as referred to trespass to land; the objections raised by paragraph 2 of the reply being overruled.

The Court of Appeal (Fry and Lopes L.JJ., Lord Esher M.R. dissenting) made an order which—after reciting that the plaintiffs by their counsel had abandoned their appeal so far as it related to a declaration that the plaintiff company were lawfully in possession and occupation of the lands, mines and mining rights and other property in the statement of claim mentioned, and also so far as it related to an injunction restraining the defendant company from continuing to occupy or from asserting any title to the said lands, mines and mining rights and from withholding and keeping possession of the said other property—ordered that the order of the Queen's Bench Division do stand affirmed as regards so much of the relief sought by the statement of claim as aforesaid; but as to the residue of the relief sought by the statement of claim declared that Her Majesty's Supreme Court has jurisdiction to entertain the same; and ordered that the

question as to the plaintiffs' demurrer to the 9th paragraph of
the defence do stand over until the trial of the action, to be dealt
with by the judge at the trial.

LORD HERSCHELL L.C. :—

My Lords, the principal question raised by this appeal is
whether the Supreme Court of Judicature has jurisdiction to try
an action to recover damages for a trespass to lands situate in a
foreign country.

It is not in controversy that prior to the Judicature Acts no
such jurisdiction could have been exercised; but it is asserted on
behalf of the respondents that the only barrier to its exercise was
the technical one, that the venue in such a case must be local, and
that the rules made under the Judicature Acts which have abolished local venues have removed the sole impediment which prevented the Courts entertaining and adjudicating on cases of this
description.   This contention has been sustained by a majority
of the Court of Appeal, reversing the judgment of the Queen's
Bench Division, with which, however, the Master of the Rolls
agreed.

The nature of the controversy between the parties renders it
necessary to consider the origin of the distinction between local
and transitory actions, and the development of the law which
determined the venue or place of trial of issues of fact.

It was necessary originally to state truly the venue—that is,
the place in which it arose—of every fact in issue, whether those
on which the plaintiff relied, or any matter stated by way of
defence; and if the places were different, each issue would be
tried by a jury summoned from the place in which the facts in
dispute were stated to have arisen.   After the statute 17 Car. 2,
c. 8, which provided that "after verdict judgment should not be
stayed or reversed for that there was no right venue, so as the
cause were tried by a jury of the proper county or place where
the action was laid," the practice arose, which ultimately became
regular and uniform, of trying all the issues by a jury of the
venue laid in the action, even though some of the facts were laid
elsewhere.   When juries ceased to be drawn from the particular
town, parish, or hamlet where the fact took place, that is, from
amongst those who were supposed to be cognisant of the circumstances, and came to be drawn from the body of the county generally, and to be bound to determine the issues judicially after

hearing witnesses, the law began to discriminate between cases in which the truth of the venue was material and those in which it was not so. This gave rise to the distinction between transitory and local actions, that is, between those in which the facts relied on as the foundation of the plaintiff's case have no necessary connection with a particular locality and those in which there is such a connection. In the latter class of actions the plaintiff was bound to lay the venue truly; in the former he might lay it in any county he pleased. It was, however, still necessary to lay every local fact with its true venue on peril of a variance if it should be brought in issue. Where a local matter occurred out of the realm, a difficulty arose, inasmuch as it was supposed that the issue could not be tried, as no jury could be summoned from the place, and it was by the general rule essential that a jury should be summoned from the venue laid to the fact in issue. It was, however, early decided that, notwithstanding the general rule, such matters might be tried by a jury from the venue in the action, and thus the difficulty was removed and the form was introduced of adding after the statement of the foreign place the words, "To wit at Westminster in the county of Middlesex," or whatever else might happen to be the venue in the action.

The point arose in 30 & 31 Eliz., in an action of assumpsit on a policy of assurance. Cited in *Dowdale's Case*, 6 Rep. 47 b. The plaintiff declared that the defendant at London "did assume that such a ship should sail from Melcomb Regis, in the county of Dorset, to Abvile in France safely, and that the said ship in sailing towards Abvile, scilicet in the river of Soame in the realm of France, was arrested by the King of France." The parties came to issue whether the ship was so arrested or not, and this issue was tried before the Chief Justice in London, and found for the plaintiff. It was moved in arrest of judgment, that this issue, arising from a place without the realm, could not be tried; and, if it could, it was contended the jury should come from Melcomb, "for bv common intendment they may have best knowledge of the arrest." But it was resolved that the issue should be tried where the action was brought. "Here," it was said, "the promise was made here in London, which is the ground and foundation of the action; and therefore there is in this case of necessity it shall be tried, or otherwise it should not be tried at all."

It is, I think, important to observe that the distinction between local and transitory actions depended on the nature of the matters involved and not on the place at which the trial had to take place.

9

It was not called a local action because the venue was local, or a transitory action because the venue might be laid in any county, but the venue was local or transitory according as the action was local or transitory. It will be seen that this distinction is material when the Judicature Rule upon which so much turns comes to be examined.

My Lords, I cannot but lay great stress upon the fact that whilst lawyers made an exception from the ordinary rule in the case of a local matter occurring outside the realm for which there was no proper place of trial in this country, and invented a fiction which enabled the Courts to exercise jurisdiction, they did not make an exception where the cause of action was a local matter arising abroad, and did not extend the fiction to such cases. The rule that in local actions the venue must be local did not, where the cause of action arose in this country, touch the jurisdiction of the Courts, but only determined the particular manner in which the jurisdiction should be exercised; but where the matter complained of was local and arose outside the realm, the refusal to adjudicate upon it was in fact a refusal to exercise jurisdiction, and I cannot think that the Courts would have failed to find a remedy if they had regarded the matter as one within their jurisdiction, and which it was proper for them to adjudicate upon.

The earliest authority of importance is *Skinner* v. *East India Company*, 6 State Trials, 710, 719. The House of Lords in that case referred it to the judges to report whether relief could be obtained in respect of the matter mentioned in the petition, either at law or in equity, and if so in what manner. The judges answered, "that the matters touching the taking away of the petitioner's ship and goods and assaulting of his person, notwithstanding the same were done beyond the seas, might be determined upon by His Majesty's ordinary Courts at Westminster. And as to the dispossessing him of his house and island, that he was not relievable in any ordinary Court of Law."

Notwithstanding the opinion thus expressed, Lord Mansfield entertained and acted on the view that where damages only were sought in respect of a trespass committed abroad, and action might be maintained in this country, although it was one which would here be a local action. See *Mostyn* v. *Fabrigas*, 1 Cowp. 161, 180. He referred to two cases which had come before him. One was an action against Captain Gambier for pulling down the houses of some sutlers. Objection was taken to the action founded on the case just referred to of *Skinner* v. *East India Company*, 6

State Trials, 710, 719. Lord Mansfield overruled the objection, on this principle, that the reparation was personal and for damages and that otherwise there would be a failure of justice, for it was on the coast of Nova Scotia, where there were no regular Courts of Judicature, and if there had been, Captain Gambier might never go there again, and therefore the reason of locality in such an action in England did not hold. The other case was that of Admiral Palliser, who was sued for destroying fishing huts on the Labrador Coast, where, it was said, there were no local courts, and therefore whatever injury had been done there by any of the King's officers would have been altogether without redress if the objection of locality would have held. The consequence of that circumstance shewed (said Lord Mansfield) that "where the reason fails, even in actions which in England would be local actions, yet it does not hold to places beyond the seas within the King's dominions." It does not appear clear from the language used by Lord Mansfield that he would have regarded a trespass to land committed beyond the seas and outside the King's dominions as within the cognizance of our Courts.

The view acted on by Lord Mansfield in the two cases referred to has not been followed. It came before the Court of Queen's Bench for consideration in *Doulson* v. *Matthews*, 4 T. R. 503, which was an action of trespass for entering the plaintiff's house in Canada and expelling him therefrom. The decisions of Lord Mansfield were relied on by the plaintiff, but the action was held not to lie. Buller J. in delivering judgment said: "It is now too late for us to inquire whether it were wise or politic to make a distinction between transitory and local actions; it is sufficient for the Courts that the law has settled the distinction, and that an action quare calusum fregit is local. We may try actions here which are in their nature transitory, though arising out of a transaction abroad; but not such as are in their nature local."

In saving that we may not try actions here arising out of transactions abroad which are in their nature local, I do not think that the learned judge was referring to the mere technical difficulty of there being no venue in this country in which these transactions could be laid, but to the fact that our Courts did not exercise jurisdiction in matters arising abroad "which were in their nature local." The case of *Doulson* v. *Matthews*, 4 T. R. 503, has ever since been regarded as law, and I do not think it has been considered as founded merely on the technical difficulty that in this country a local venue was requisite in a local action.

In the case of *Mayor of London* v. *Cox*, Law Rep. 2 H. L. at p. 261, that very learned judge, Willes J., said: "And even in superior Courts themselves, where the subject-matter is such as to imply a local limit of jurisdiction, the exception is peremptory; there is no necessity for a dilatory plea, nor is the objection waived by pleading in chief. Thus, if an action of trespass to land situate abroad were brought in the Queen's Bench, the defendant need not plead a dilatory plea shewing what Court has jurisdiction; but if the foreign locality appeared upon the count he might demur, and if it did not appear, he might plead in chief or bar a denial of the trespass (which would be assumed as alleged within the jurisdiction), and at the trial the plaintiff would be non-suited or lose the verdict; and whether upon demurrer or plea the ordinary judgment would be given for the defendant (*Doulson* v. *Matthews*)."

It is clear that Willes J. regarded an action of trespass to land situate abroad as outside the local limit of jurisdiction of the Court of Queen's Bench. The same learned judge, in *Phillips* v. *Eyre*, Law Rep. 6 Q. B. at p. 28, said: "Our Courts are said to be more open to admit actions founded upon foreign transactions than those of any other European country; but there are restrictions in respect of locality which exclude some foreign causes of action altogether, namely, those which would be local if they arose in England, such as trespass to land; and even with respect to those not falling within that description, our Courts do not undertake universal jurisdiction."

In the case of *The M. Moxham*, 1 P. D. 107, where injury had been caused to a pier belonging to an English company, but situated in a Spanish port, the ship, by the alleged negligent navigation of which the damage had been caused, was arrested in Spain, but was released on an agreement with the owners that their liability should be determined by proceedings in the English Courts. James L. J. said, that but for the agreement come to between the parties "very grave difficulties indeed might have arisen as to the jurisdiction of this Court to entertain any jurisdiction or proceedings whatever with respect to injury done to foreign soil."

The distinction between matters which are transitory or personal and those which are local in their nature, and the refusal to exercise jurisdiction as regards the latter where they occur outside territorial limits, is not confined to the jurisprudence of this country. Story, in his work on the Conflict of Laws (s. 551), after stating that by the Roman law a suit might in many cases be brought, either where property was situate or where the party sued had his domicil, proceeds to say that "even in countries acknowledging the Roman law it has become a very general principle that suits in rem should be brought where the property is situate; and this principle is applied with almost universal approbation in regard to immovable property. The same rule is applied to mixed actions, and to all suits which touch the realty."

In section 553, Story quotes the following language of Vattel · "The defendant's judge" (that is, the competent judge) says he, "is the judge of the place where the defendant has his settled abode, or the judge of the place where the defendant is when any sudden difficulty arises, provided it does not relate to an estate in land, or to a right annexed to such an estate. In such a case, as property of this kind is to be held according to the laws of the country where it is situated, and as the right of granting it is vested in the ruler of the country, controversies relating to such property can only be decided in the state in which it depends." He adds, in the next section: "It will be perceived that in many respects the doctrine here laid down coincides with that of the common law. It has been already stated by the common law personal actions, being transitory, may be brought in any place where the party defendant can be found; that real actions must be brought in the forum rei sitæ; and that mixed actions are properly referable to the same juris diction. Among the latter are actions for trespasses and injuries to real property which are deemed local; so that they will not lie elsewhere than in the place rei sitæ."

The doctrine laid down by foreign jurists, which is said by Story to coincide in many respects with that of our common law, obviously had relation to the question of jurisdiction, and not to any technical rules determining in what part of a country a cause was to be tried. Story was indeed regarded by one of the learned judges in the Court below (Lopes, L.J., [1892] 2 Q. B. 420) as sanctioning the view that our rules in regard to venue in the case of local actions offered the only obstacle to the exercise of jurisdiction in actions of trespass to real property. The passage relied on is as follows (s. 554): "Lord Mansfield and Lord Chief Justice Eyre held at one time a different doctrine, and allowed suits to be maintained in England for injuries done by pulling down houses in foreign unsettled regions, namely, in the desert coasts of Nova Scotia and Labrador. But this doctrine has been since overruled as untenable according to the actual jurisprudence of England, however maintainable it might be upon general principles of international law, if the suit were for personal damages only."

By the words "untenable according to the actual jurisprudence of England," I do not think Story was referring to the rule which in this country regulated the place of trial in the case of local actions. Nor am I satisfied that either Lord Mansfield or Story would have regarded an action of trespass to land as a suit for personal damages only, if the title to the land were in issue, and in order to determine whether there was a right to damages it was necessary for the Court to adjudicate upon the conflicting claims of the parties to real estate. In both the cases before Lord Mansfield, as I understand them, no question of title to real property was in issue. The sole controversy was,. whether the British officers sued were, under the circumstances, justified in interfering with the plaintiffs in their enjoyment of it.

The question what jurisdiction can be exercised by the Courts of any country according to its municipal law cannot, I think, be conclusively determined by a reference to principles of international law. No nation can execute its judgments, whether against persons or movables or real property, in the country of another. On the other hand, if the Courts of a country were to claim, as against a person resident there, jurisdiction to adjudicate upon the title to land in a foreign country, and to enforce its adjudication in personam, it is by no means certain that any rule of international law would be violated. But in considering what jurisdiction our Courts possess, and have claimed to exercise in relation to matters arising out of the country, the principles which have found general acceptance amongst civilized nations as defining the limits of jurisdiction are of great weight.

It was admitted in the present case, on behalf of the respondents, that the Court could not make a declaration of title, or grant an injunction to restrain trespasses, the respondents having in relation to these matters abandoned their appeal in the Court below. But it is said that the Court may inquire into the title, and, if the plaintiffs and not the defendants are found to have the better title, may award damages for the trespass committed. My Lords, I find it difficult to see why this distinction should be drawn. It is said, because the Courts have no power to enforce their judgment by any dealing with the land itself, where it is outside their territorial jurisdiction. But if they can determine the title to it and compel the payment of damages founded upon such determination, why should not they equally proceed in personam against a person who, in spite of that determination, insists on disturbing one who has been found by the Court to be the owner of the property?

It is argued that if an action of trespass cannot be maintained in this country where the land is situate abroad a wrong-doer by coming to this country might leave the person wronged without any remedy. It might be a sufficient answer to this argument to say that this is a state of things which has undoubtedly existed for centuries without any evidence of serious mischief or any intervention of the legislature; for even if the Judicature Rules have the effect contended for, I do not think it can be denied that this was a result neither foreseen nor intended. But there appear to me, I confess, to be solid reasons why the Courts of this country should, in common with those of most other nations, have refused to adjudicate upon claims of title to foreign land in proceedings founded on an alleged invasion of the proprietary rights attached to it, and to award damages founded on that adjudication.

The inconveniences which might arise from such a course are obvious, and it is by no means clear to my mind that if the Courts were to exercise jurisdiction in such cases the ends of justice would in the long run, and looking at the matter broadly, be promoted. Supposing a foreigner to sue in this country for trespass to his lands situate abroad, and for taking possession of and expelling him from them, what is to be the measure of damages? There being no legal process here by which he could obtain possession of the lands, the plaintiff might, I suppose, in certain circumstances, obtain damages equal in amount to their value. But what would there be to prevent his leaving this country after obtaining these damages and re-possessing himself of the lands? What remedy would the defendant have in such a case where the lands are in an unsettled country, with no laws or regular system of government, but where, to use a familiar expression, the only right is might? Such an occurrence is not an impossible, or even an improbable, hypothesis. It is quite true that in the exercise of the undoubted jurisdiction of the Courts it may become necessary incidentally to investigate and determine the title to foreign land; but it does not seem to me to follow that because such a question may incidentally arise and fall to be adjudicated upon, the Courts possess, or that it is expedient that they should exercise, jurisdiction to try an action founded on a disputed claim of title to foreign lands.

Reliance was placed on the decisions of Courts of Equity, as shewing that our Courts were ready, when no technical difficulty of venue stood in the way, to adjudicate on the title to lands situate abroad. If the refusal of the Common Law Courts to exercise jurisdiction in cases of the nature now under consideration had been regarded as the result of a mere technical difficulty, I cannot help thinking that the Courts of Equity, which were, in early days, at all events, keen to supplement the deficiencies of the Common Law, when the requirements of justice were impeded by technical difficulties, would have found some means of affording a remedy. Lord Mansfield, in his judgment in *Mostyn* v. *Fabrigas* (1 Cowp. 161, 180), refers to a case of an injury in the East Indies similar to that with which he had to deal in the case of Captain Gambier, in which Lord Hardwicke in a Court of Equity had directed satisfaction to be made in damages. But in this exercise of jurisdiction he has not been followed by any judge of the Court of Chancery.

Whilst Courts of Equity have never claimed to act directly upon land situate abroad, they have purported to act upon the conscience of persons living here. In *Lord Crawstown* v. *Johnston* (3 Ves. 170, 182), Sir R. P. Arden, Master of the Rolls, said: "*Archer* v. *Preston, Lord Arglasse* v. *Muschamp*, and *Lord Kildare* v. *Eustace*, clearly shew that with regard to any contract made, or equity between persons in this country, respecting lands in a foreign country, particularly in the British dominions, this Court will hold the same jurisdiction as if they were situate in England."

Story, in his Conflict of Laws, ss. 544, 545, although he says that to the extent of the decision in *Crawstown* v. *Johnston*, (3 Ves. 170), there may, perhaps, not be any well-founded objection, nevertheless expresses the view that the doctrine of the English Courts of Chancery on this head of jurisdiction seems carried to an extent which may perhaps in some cases not find a perfect warrant in the general principles of international public law, and therefore it must have a very uncertain basis as to its recognition in foreign countries so far as it may be supposed to be founded upon the comity of nations. My Lords, the decisions of the Courts of Equity do not, to my mind, afford any substantial support to the view that the ground upon which the Courts of Common Law abstained from exercising jurisdiction in relation to trespasses to real property abroad was only the technical difficulty of venue.

In the case of *Whitaker* v. *Forbes* (Law Rep. 10 C. P. 583)—where the action was begun before but the demurrer was heard in the Court of Appeal after the Judicature Acts came into operation—the question arose whether the plaintiff could recover against a defendant resident in this country the arrears of rent-charge issuing out of lands in Australia. The opinion expressed by Lord Blackburn in the course of the appeal in that case was much relied on by the respondents: "I do not think that this case" (said the learned judge) "raises any question as to jurisdiction, though in some respects it has been argued as if it did. The case turns on the technical distinction between local actions where the trial must be local, and transitory actions, and the question is one of venue only." It is unnecessary to consider whether in circumstances such as gave rise to the action of *Whitaker* v. *Forbes* an action might, since the Judicature Rules came into force, be maintained in the Courts of this country. I do not think the dictum of the learned judge in that case can be regarded as of any great weight in determining the question with which your Lordships have to deal.

The terms of rule 1 of Order XXXVI., which are relied on by the plaintiffs, are as follows: "There shall be no local venue for the trial of any action except where otherwise provided by statute." The language used appears to me important. The rule does not purport to touch the distinction between local and transitory actions—between matters which have no necessary local connection, and those which are local in their nature. It deals only with the place of trial, and enables actions, whatever their nature, to be tried in any county. But it is, in my opinion, a mere rule of procedure, and applies only to those cases in which the courts at that time exercised jurisdiction. It has been more than once held that the rules under the Judicature Acts are rules of procedure only, and were not intended to affect, and did not affect, the rights of parties. Thus in *Kendall* v. *Hamilton* (4 App. Cas. 503, 516), it was suggested that the law laid down in *King* v. *Hoare* (13 M. & W. 494), had been altered by the Judicature Acts owing to the abolition of a plea in abatement. Lord Cairns said: "I am unable to agree to this suggestion. I cannot think that the Judicature Acts have changed what was formerly a joint right of action into a right of bringing several and separate actions. And although the form of objecting, by means of a plea

in abatement to the non-joinder of a defendant, who ought to be
included in the action, is abolished, yet I conceive that the application to have the person so omitted included as a defendant ought to
be granted or refused on the same principles on which a plea in
abatement would have succeeded or failed."

Again, in *Britain* v. *Rossiter* (11 Q. B. D. at p. 1229), Lord
Esher M.R. said: "I think that the true construction of the
Judicature Acts is that they confer no new rights; they only con-
firm the rights which previously were found to be existing in the
Courts either of Law or Equity."

According to the contention of the respondents in this case
the rule under consideration had the effect of conferring upon
them a right of action in this country which they would not
otherwise have possessed. As I have already pointed out, a
person whose lands, situate in this country, were trespassed
upon always had a right of action in respect of the trespass. The
rules relating to venue did no more than regulate the manner
in which the right was to be enforced. But in respect of a trespass to land situate abroad there was no right of action, for an
alleged right which the Courts would neither recognize nor
enforce did not constitute any right at all in point of law.

My Lords, I have come to the conclusion that the grounds
upon which the Courts have hitherto refused to exercise jurisdiction in actions of trespass to lands situate abroad were substantial and not technical, and that the rules of procedure under
the Judicature Acts have not conferred a jurisdiction which did
not exist before. If this conclusion be well founded, I do not
think that the allegation contained in paragraph 16 of the statement of claim, "that the defendant company did and committed
the acts above mentioned and complained of with intent to injure
and destroy the trade of the plaintiff company, and to deprive
it of its aforesaid lands, territories, mines, minerals, and mining
rights and property," disclosed a cause of action cognizable by
our Courts any more than the paragraph complaining of trespass.

The 9th paragraph of the statement of defence alleged that
the lands in question were in the possession of a certain native
chief named Umtasa, who exercised sovereignty over the same,
and that by a concession or treaty granted by Umtasa and his
indunas or council to the defendants, they acquired the right to
possession and occupation of the lands, and that the plaintiffs
were wrongfully attempting to take possession of the lands, and
that the defendants did the acts complained of in order to prevent

the plaintiffs from so wrongfully taking possession of them. This defence was demurred to bv the 2d paragraph of the reply. The Queen's Bench Division overruled the demurrer; but the Court of Appeal varied this judgment by ordering the demurrer to stand over until the trial of the action, to be dealt with by the judge at the trial. The Master of the Rolls thought the decision of the Divisional Court on this point correct. And I do not understand that either of the learned judges who concurred in varying the order doubted that, if proved, the paragraph in dispute disclosed a valid defence in point of law. The case of *Thompson* v. *Barclay*, 6 L. J. (O.S.) Ch. 93; 9 L. J. (O.S.) Ch. 215, and others of the same description, in which it is said the Courts have refused to recognize the sovereign rights of provinces which had revolted from a State at amity with Great Britain, and whose independence was not shewn to have been recognized by the proper authorities in this country, appear to me to have no application to the circumstances of the present case. I do not see any sufficient ground for disturbing the judgment of the Queen's Bench Division on this point. Whether the plea can be proved, and whether the determination of any question raised by it will be for the judge and not the jury, is a question which does not arise at the present time.

For the reasons with which I have troubled your Lordships at some length, I think the judgment appealed from should be reversed and the judgment of the Divisional Court restored, and that the respondents should pay the costs here and in the Court below and I move your Lordships accordingly.

LITTLE v. CHICAGO & ST. PAUL RY. CO., 1896.

[65 Minn. 48, 33 L. R. A. 423.]

MITCHELL, J. This action was brought to recover damages for injuries to real estate situated in Wisconsin, caused by the negligence of the defendant. The question presented is, can the courts of this state take cognizance of actions to recover damages to real estate lying without the state; in other words, is such an action local or transitory in its nature?

The history of the progress of the English common law respecting the locality of actions will aid in determining how this question ought to be decided on principle. Originally, all actions were local. This arose out of the constitution of the old jury, who were but witnesses to prove or disprove the allegations of the parties, and hence every case had to be tried by a jury of the vicinage, who were presumed to have personal knowledge of the parties as well as of the facts. But, as circumstances and conditions changed, the courts modified the rule in fact, although not in form. For that purpose they invented a fiction by which a party was permitted to allege, under a videlicet, that the place where the contract was made or the transaction occurred was in any county in England. The courts took upon themselves to determine when this fictitious averment should and when it should not be traversable. They would hold it not traversable for the purpose of defeating an action it was invented to sustain, but always traversable for the purpose of contesting a jurisdiction not intended to be protected by the fiction. Those actions in which it was held not traversable came to be known as transitory, and those in which it was held traversable as local, actions. Actions for personal torts, wherever committed, and upon contracts (including those respecting lands), wherever executed, were deemed transitory, and might be brought wherever the defendant could be found.

As respects actions for injuries to real property, we cannot discover that it was definitely settled in England to which class they belonged prior to the American Revolution. As late as 1774, in the leading case of Mostyn v. Fabrigas, 1 Cowp. 161, 2 Smith, Lead. Cas. (9th Ed.) 916, Lord Mansfield, who did more than any other jurist to brush away those mere technicalities which had so long obstructed the course of justice, referred to two cases in which he had held that actions would lie in England for injuries to real estate situated abroad. In that same case he said: "Can it be doubted that actions may be maintained here, not only upon contracts, which follow the persons, but for injuries done by subject to subject, especially for injuries where the whole that is prayed is a reparation in damages or satisfaction to be made by process against the person or his effects within the jurisdiction of the court? While all that is there said as to actions for injuries to real property is obiter, yet it clearly indicates the views of that great jurist on the subject. And we cannot discover that it was fully settled in England that actions for injuries to lands were local until the decision of Doulson v. Matthews, 4 Term R. 503, in 1792,—16 years after the declaration of American independence. The courts of England seem to have finally settled down upon the rule that an action is transitory where the transaction on which it is founded might have taken place anywhere; but is local when the transaction is necessarily local,—that is, could only have happened in a particular place. As an injury to land can only be committed where the land lies, it followed that, according to this test, actions for such injuries were held to be local. As the distinction between local and transitory venues was abolished by the judicature act of 1873, we infer that actions for injuries to lands lying abroad may now be maintained in England.

It is somewhat surprising that the American courts have generally given more weight to the English decisions on the subject rendered after the Revolution than to those rendered before, and hence have almost universally held that actions for injuries to lands are local. In the leading case of Livingston v. Jefferson, 1 Brock. 203, Fed. Cas. No. 8,411, which has done more than any other to mold the law on the subject in this country, Chief Justice Marshall argued against the rule, showing that it was merely technical, founded on no sound principle, and often defeated justice; but concluded that it was so thoroughly established by authority that he was not at liberty to disregard it. But so unsatisfactory and unreasonable is the rule that since that time it has, in a number of states, been changed by statute, and in others the courts have frequently evaded it by metaphysical distinctions in order to prevent a miscarriage of justice. Chief Justice Marshall's own state of Virginia changed the rule by statute as early as 1819. Some courts have made a subtle distinction between faults of omission and of commission. Thus in Titus v. Inhabitants of Frankfort, 15 Me. 89, which was an action against a town for damages sustained by reason of defects in a highway, it was held that, while highways must be local, the neglect of the defendant to do its duty, being a mere nonfeasance, was transitory. It has also been held that where trespass upon land is followed by the asportation of timber severed from the land, if the plaintiff waives the original trespass, and sues simply for the conversion of the property so carried away, the action would become transitory. American U. Tel. Co. v. Middleton, 80 N. Y. 408; Whidden v. Seelye, 40 Me. 247. Again, it has been sometimes held that an action for injury to real estate is transitory where the gravamen of the action is negligence,—as for negligently setting fire to the plaintiff's premises. Home Ins. Co. v. Pennslyvania R. Co., 11 Hun. 182; Barney v. Burstenbinder, 7 Lans. 210. In Ohio the rule has been repudiated,

at least as to causes of action arising within the state, as being
wholly unsuited to their condition, because under their judicial
system it would result in many cases in a total denial of justice.
Genin v. Grier, 10 Ohio, 209.

Almost every court or judge who has ever discussed the
question has criticised or condemned the rule as technical, wrong
on principle, and often resulting in a total denial of justice, and yet
has considered himself bound to adhere to it under the doctrine
of stare decisis.

An action for damages for injuries to real property is on
principle just as transitory in its nature as one on contract or for
a tort committed on the person or personal property. The reparation is purely personal, and for damages. Such an action is
purely personal and in no sense real. Every argument founded
on practical considerations against entertaining jurisdiction of
actions for injuries to lands lying in another state could be
urged as to actions on contracts executed, or for personal torts
committed, out of the state, at least where the subject-matter of
the transaction is not within the state. Take, for example, personal actions on contracts respecting lands which are conceded
to be transitory. An investigation of title of boundaries, etc., may
be desirable, and often would be essential to the determination
of the case, yet such considerations have never been held to render
the actions local. Another serious objection to the rule is that
under it a party may have a clear, legal right without a remedy
where the wrongdoer cannot be found, and has no property
within the state where the land is situated. As suggested by
plaintiff's counsel, if the rule be adhered to, all that the one who
commits an injury to land, whether negligently or willfully, has
to do in order to escape liability, is to depart from the state
where the tort was committed, and refrain from returning. In
such case the owner of the land is absolutely remediless.

We recognize the respect due to judicial precedents, and the
authority of the doctrine of stare decisis; but, inasmuch as this
rule is in no sense a rule of property, and as it is purely technical,
wrong in principle, and in practice often results in a total denial
of justice, and has been so generally criticised by eminent jurists,
we do not feel bound to adhere to it, notwithstanding the great
array of judicial decisions in its favor. If the courts of England,
generations ago, were at liberty to invent a fiction in order to
change the ancient rule that all actions were local, and then fix
their own limitations to the application of the fiction we cannot

see why the courts of the present day shouɪɑ deem themselves slavishly bound by those limitations.

It is ssuggested that the statutes of this state, in conformity to the old rule, make actions for injuries to real property local. G. S. 1894, §§ 5182, 5183. This is true, and strangely enough, in 1885 the legislature went so far as to provide that, if the county designated in the complaint is not the proper one, the court should have no jurisdiction of the action. But this statute has no application to causes of action arising out of the state. While it settles the rule, and indicates the policy of this state as to actions for injuries to real property within the state, we do not think it ought to have any weight in determining what the rule should be as to causes of action arising out of the state, which can have no local venue here under the provisions of the statute. It does not appear whether the plaintiff lives in this state or in Wisconsin, but this is immaterial, for the place of his residence cannot affect the nature of the action. It is also true that in this particular case jurisdiction of the defendant could be obtained in Wisconsin, but this fact is likewise immaterial, and for the same reason.

Order reversed.

BUCK, J. I dissent. The doctrine laid down in the foregoing opinion is conceded to be against the great weight of judicial authority, and, according to my view, is unsound in principle, and contrary to a wise public policy. The plaintiff is a citizen of the state of Wisconsin, and the defendant a railroad corporation organized under the laws of that state with its line constructed therein and extending into this state. The action is brought in Minnesota to recover for damages done by the defendant to plaintiff's real estate situate in the state of Wisconsin. In my opinion, the action is one clearly local in its nature, and not transitory, and the courts of this state have no jurisdiction over the subject matter.

In Cooley on Torts (page 471) it is said that:

"The distinction between transitory and local actions is this· If the cause of action is one that might have arisen anywhere, then it is transitory: but if it could only have arisen in one place, then it is local. Therefore, while an action of trespass to the person or for the conversion of goods is transitory, action for flowing lands is local, because they can be flooded only where they are. For the most part, the actions which are local are those brought for the recovery of real estate, or for injuries thereto or to easements.

[Here the injury allegeo consisted in burning the grass, roots, vegetable mold, and other material forming part of the plaintiff's land.] * * * That actions for trespasses on lands in a foreign country cannot be sustained is the settled law in England and in this country."

I am not able to state whether it has been changed by statutory enactment, and the majority opinion merely infers that it has been so changed. Blackstone, whose Commentaries were written and delivered in the form of lectures before the students of Oxford University in 1758, says, that: "All over the world actions transitory follow the person of the defendant, while territorial suits must be discusssed in the territorial tribunal. I may sue a Frenchman here for a debt contracted abroad; but lands lying in France must be sued for there, and English lands must be sued for in the kingdom of England."

The case of *Mostyn v. Fabrigas,* 1 Cowp. 161, decided in 1774, is referred to as a leading case, yet the question here involved was not before the court in that case. There the plaintiff, Fabrigas, brought an action against Mostyn for assault and false imprisonment committeed on the Island of Minorca, and it was held that the court had jurisdiction of the subject-matter. This was a transitory action, within the rules of all the courts. That a jurist as great as Lord Mansfield should inject into his opinion in that case a remark that was entirely without any relevancy to the question under consideration, adds but little force to its weight. And its force is still further lessened by the fact that ever since that decision the law of England has been setted by other eminent jurists as otherwise, and contrary to the majority opinion in this case. It seems to me misleading to call the case of *Mostyn v. Fabrigas* a leading one, and cite it as such upon an important legal question, when the point here involved was not there in issue. While the great weight of authority is manifestly against the doctrine laid down by the majority opinion, it may be well to refer to some of them more in detail.

In the case of *Allin v. Connecticut R. L. Co.,* 150 Mass. 560, 23 N. E. 581, it was held that an action of tort for breaking and entering the plaintiff's close, situated in another state, could not be brought in the commonwealth of Massachusetts; and the court, in commenting upon the statute of that state which required actions for trespass quare clausum to be brought in the county where the land lies, said: "There seems to be no reason for holding that the statute renders an action for trespass to lands outside the state transitory which does not apply to an action for trespass to lands within the state." The statute has been in existence nearly 100 years, and we have not been referred to any authority or dictum to sustain the position of the plaintiff. On the contrary, the action of trespass quare clausum has always been treated as a local action. In the case of *Niles v. Howe*, 57 Vt. 388, it was held that trespass on the freehold would not lie in that state for a trespass committed on lands situated in the state of Massachusetts.

In *Du Breuil v. Pennsylvania Co.*, 130 Ind. 137, 29 N. E. 909, the court say an action cannot be maintained in this state for an injury to land lying in another state, caused by a railway company having a line of railroad running through this and such other state. That court also applied the same doctrine to an action for injury to land caused by fire escaping from a locomotive, in the case of *Indiana, B & W. Ry. Co. v. Foster*, 107 Ind. 430, 8 N. E. 264. In the first Indiana case above cited Chief Justice Elliott says: "The case before us is one in which the land-lies within the territory of another sovereignty, and there can be no doubt upon principle or authority that our courts have no jurisdiction." In *Eachus v. Trustees*, 17 Ill. 534, it was held that the courts of Illinois had no jurisdiction in an action to recover for injuries to land situate in Lake county, in the state of Indiana. In *Bettys v. Milwaukee & St. P. Ry. Co.*, 37 Wis. 323, it was held that an action for injury to realty situated in Iowa could not be maintained in the courts of the state of Wisconsin. Chief Justice Ryan, delivering the opinion of the court, said that it was plainly a local action under all of the authorities, which could not be maintained in the state of Wisconsin; and he cited Co. Litt. 282a; Bac. Abr. "Action" A (p. 799); Comyn, Dig. "Action" N, 4, 5 (p. 251); *Doulson v. Matthews*, 4 Term R. 503.

In the state of New York the doctrine is well settled by numerous decisions of its highest court that suits cannot be there maintained for injuries to lands situated in other states. See *American U. Tel. Co. v. Middleton*, 80 N. Y. 408; *Cragin v. Lovel*, 88 N. Y. 258; *Sentenis v. Ladew*, 140 N. Y. 463, 35 N. E. 650; *Dodge v. Colby*, 108 N. Y. 445, 15 N. E. 703. In the last case Chief Justice Ruger, in delivering the opinion, says:

"The doctrine that the courts of this state have no jurisdiction of actions for trespass upon lands situated in other states is too well settled to admit of discussion or dispute. * * *

The claim urged by the plaintiff, that, if not permitted to maintain this action, he is without remedy for a most serious injury, is quite groundless, and affords no reason for the assumption of a jurisdiction by this court which it does not possess. The plaintiff would seem to have the same remedy for the trespasses alleged that all other parties have for similar injuries. His lands cannot be intruded upon without the presence in the state of the wrong-doer, and no reason is suggested why he could not seek his remedy against the actual wrongdoers in the courts having jurisdiction. His remedy is ample, and it is no excuse for assuming a jurisdiction which we do not have that the plaintiff desires a remedy against a particular person, rather than one against the real perpetrators of the injury, who were exposed to prosecution in the place where the wrong was committed."

This language would apply to the plaintiff in this case. The defendant is a resident of the state of Wisconsin, subject to its laws, and service of summons can there be readily and easily made upon it. The gravamen of the complaint is injury to the freehold, and the records of title to that freehold, whether in or out of the plaintiff, are accessible without trouble, and witnesses, doubtless, are obtainable without extra expense. The plaintiff is not without redress otherwise than in the courts of Minnesota. In fact it is not claimed that the courts of Wisconsin have no jurisdiction to try this action, and it is plain that they have such jurisdiction.

As a matter of policy, citizens of other states should not be permitted the use of our courts to redress wrongs and injuries to real property committed within their own territory. That is not what our courts were created or organized for. Nonresidents should not be invited to bring to our courts litigation arising over injuries to real property outside of our territorial limits. Certainly there is nothing in our constitution or laws which justifies them in imposing the burden of maintaining courts at our expense for their use and benefit. Protection of our own citizens is the primary object and duty of our own courts, and it is, to say the least, a very generous and liberal interpretation of the law which accords to suitors residing in other states the right to litigate in our courts questions of injury to real estate there situate, while the courts of those states reject the claim of our own citizens to litigate there injury to real estate situate here; notably the adjoining state of Wisconsin, which adjoins our state, and where the subject-matter of this litigation is situated.

It is clearly against our interests that those living in the state of Wisconsin near the division line should be encouraged in this class of litigation because our laws may be more favorable as to the rules of evidence, or for any other cause, and thus necessitate taxation of our people that nonresidents may have a forum to litigate that which ought to be and is a local action in the state of Wisconsin. Our citizens have no such right in the courts of Wisconsin. Comity should be reciprocal, and this can be more properly obtained by legislative enactments of the respective states than by an interpretation in direct conflict with the almost universal judicial decisions elsewhere. But I should seriously doubt the wisdom of any such enactment. It might, perhaps, prevent the miscarriage of justice in some cases, but it would aid such miscarriage in many instances.

The defendant, like many other railroad corporations, extends its line from other states to this, and owns a vast amount of lands here. It may allege that citizens of our state are committing injuries to its real property here, and if such a person owns land in Wisconsin, or shall be found there, it could, under such a law, commence a suit in the courts of Wisconsin, and thus put our citizens to the trouble and expense of going to that state for trial of a case which in all fairness should be tried here. Railroad companies thus situated have great facilities for transporting their witnesses over their own lines without expense to themselves, while a poor man, charged, perhaps unjustly, with a trespass, must travel hundreds of miles into another state to meet his accusers, or suffer judgment by default. The majority opinion means defeat for the railroad company in this case, but it would mean victory for them hereafter if an alleged trespasser upon their lands in Minnesota is caught in Wisconsin and made to answer in its courts, if such a law should prevail there. Now citizens of Wisconsin will have an unjust advantage over citizens of Minnesota. Again, suppose the courts of California should adopt the doctrine of the majority opinion, and one of our citizens should visit that state for pleasure, health, or business, and is there sued by some one claiming that lands belonging to him situate here have been damaged by such citizen of Minnesota, would it not seem a miscarriage of justice that the trial in such case must take place thousands of miles away from the man's home, and from the situs of the property alleged to have been injured? The hardship of such a proceeding would seem to be intolerable, and I cannot give my assent to any such doctrine, whatever may be the rule as to the trial of actions upon voluntary contracts between parties; and I prefer that the rule should be that for injuries to real property the jurisdiction of our courts should only be co-extensive with its territorial sovereignty.

This doctrine, which is so strongly imbedded in the common law and judicial authorities of the country, is further adhered to by our own statute, which provides that actions for injuries to real property shall be brought in the county where the subject of the action is situated, and prohibits the court from having jurisdiction if brought in any other county. G. S. 1894, § 5183. Thus we have a legislative recognition of the doctrine that actions for injuries to real estate are local. If there is any implication arising from legislative enactments as to the jurisdiction of courts to try actions for injury to real estate elsewhere, it would be against the contention of the plaintiff. The statute makes no distinction between trespass to lands within and without the state. It does not make the action for trespass to lands outside the state transitory. There is no warrant in the language of the constitution or statute which justifies the majority opinion, and, if sound, it must rest upon some other foundation than is to be found in the letter of the law. It is a rule which is more favorable to the plaintiff than the defendant. The former can select his own forum; the latter is helpless. No change of venue can be granted, because none is authorized.

In criminal cases the doctrine of local venue applies. One of the specifications of complaint in the immortal Declaration of Independence against Great Britain was, "For transporting us beyond seas to be tried for pretended offenses." Our constitution (article 1, § 6) provides that: "In all criminal prosecutions the accused shall enjoy the right to a speedy and public trial by an impartial jury of the county or district wherein the crime shall have been committed, which county or district shall have been previously ascertained by law." No one pretends but that this is a sound and reasonable principle of law, and I have never known of its being assailed as tending to a miscarriage of justice. This constitutional guaranty applies to petty offenses wherever a small fine might be imposed, and yet where, perhaps, all the property which a man owns might be at stake, he can, if found in another state, perhaps thousands of miles away from home and witnesses and the location of the alleged injured property, be tried civilly in a foreign sovereignty. Why could he not also in a civil action be tried in China, Russia, England, Spain, Cuba, or Mexico, if found there, and there served with process, if the doctrine of the majority opinion is to prevail? In the case of *Niles v. Howe*, 57 Vt. 388, the court sav: "It would hardly be claimed that our courts had jurisdiction over a crime committed in another state. And yet the same reasoning that supports the doctrine of local venue applies equally to crimes and real actions."

I think that the order should be affirmed.[11]

---

[11]In the case of *Matthaei v. Galitzin, 18 Eq. L. R. 340*, where one foreigner sued another foreigner on a contract relating to real property situate in a foreign country, the court said: "A foreigner resident abroad cannot bring another foreigner into this court respecting property with which this court has nothing to do. This court is not to be made a vehicle for settling disputes arising between parties resident abroad." Actions for damages for injuries to land must be brought in the state where the land is situated. *Howard v. Ingersoll, 23 Ala. 673; Cofrode v. Circuit Judge, 79 Mich. 332*.

In an action for the recovery of damages for a personal injury, the court, in *Burdick v. Freeman, 120 N. Y. 420*, (*1890*) said: "The courts of this state may, in their discretion, entertain jurisdiction of such an action between citizens of an other state actually domiciled therein when the action was begun and tried, though the injury was committed in the state of their residence and domicil."

A personal action for battery committed in a foreign country, where the parties afterwards came into this jurisdiction, may be maintained in our courts. *Dewitt v. Buchanan, 54 Barb. (N. Y.) 31; Roberts v. Dunsmuir, 75 Cal. 203*.

The courts of Texas follow the doctrine that they will not undertake to adjudicate rights which originated in another state or country, under statutes materially different from the law of Texas in relation to the same subject. Especially is this true if the parties have access to their state or country. *Mexican Natl. Ry. v. Jackson, 89 Texas 107 (1896)*.

In *Gardner v. Thomas, 14 Johnson 134*, the question was whether the court would take cognizance of a tort committed on the high seas, on board of a foreign vessel, both the parties being subjects or citizens of the country to which the vessel belonged. The court said: "It must be conceded that the law of nations gives complete and entire jurisdiction to the courts of the country to which the vessel belongs, but not exclusively. It is exclusive only as it respects the public injury, but concurrent with the tribunals of other nations, as to the private remedy."

It is discretionary with the court whether it will take jurisdiction, and if to take jurisdiction will break up the voyage of the vessel and cause loss to the owners, the court will refuse to take jurisdiction and leave the parties to seek redress in their own country as was done in this case.

PENAL LAWS.

HUNTINGTON v. ATTRILL, 1892.

[146 U. S. 657.]

1. Penal Law Defined.
2. Distinguished From Accumulative Damages.
3. Extra-territorial Effect of Laws.
4. What Personal Disabilities Imposed by the Law of a State are Considered Penal.

5. Rule of Construction Applied to Penal Laws.
6. Purpose and Scope of the 'Full Faith and Credit Clause" of the Constitution of the United States.
7. Effect of the "Full Faith and Credit Clause."

In this case a New York statute made the officers of a corporation, who signed and recorded false certificates of the amount of its captital stock, liable for all its debts. The statute was violated by an officer of a certain New York corporation, and a judgment was recovered in New York against him thereunder. Action being brought upon the judgment in Maryland, its courts held that the New York statute was a penal statute, and refused to enforce the judgment. On appeal to the Supreme Court of the United States, under the "full faith and credit" clause of the federal constitution, Mr. Justice Gray said:

The question whether due faith and credit were thereby denied to the judgment rendered in another State is a Federal question, of which this court has jurisdiction on this writ of error. *Green v. Van Buskirk,* 5 Wall. 307, 311; *Crapo v. Kelly,* 16 Wall. 610, 619; *Dupasseur v. Rochereau,* 21 Wall. 130, 134; *Crescent City Co. v. Butchers' Union,* 120 U. S. 146, 147; *Cole v. Cunningham,* 133 U. S. 107; *Carpenter v. Strange,* 141 U. S. 87, 103.

In order to determine this question, it will be necessary, in the first place, to consider the true scope ana meaning of the fundamental maxim of international law, stated by Chief Justice Marshall in the fewest possible words: "The courts of no country execute the penal laws of another." *The Antelope,* 10 Wheat. 66, 123. In interpreting this maxim, there is danger of being misled by the different shades of meaning allowed to the word "penal" in our language.

In the municipal law of England and America, the words "penal" and "penalty" have been used in various senses. Strictly and primarily, they denote punishment, whether corporal or pecuniary, imposed and enforced by the State, for a crime or offense against its laws. *United States v. Reisinger,* 128 U. S. 398, 402;

United States v. Chouteau, 102 U. S. 603, 611. But they are also commonly used as including any extraordinary liability to which the law subjects a wrongdoer in favor of the person wronged, not limited to the damages suffered. They are so elastic in meaning as even to be familiarly applied to cases of private contracts, wholly independent of statutes, as when we speak of the "penal sum" or "penalty" of a bond. In the words of Chief Justice Marshall: "In general, a sum of money in gross, to be paid for the non-performance of an agreement, is considered as a penalty, the legal operation of which is to cover the damages which the party, in whose favor the stipulation is made, may have sustained from the breach of contract by the opposite party." *Taylor v. Sandiford,* 7 Wheat. 13, 17.

Penal laws, strictly and properly, are those imposing punishment for an offence committed against the State, and which, by the English and American constitutions, the executive of the State has the power to pardon. Statutes giving a private action against the wrongdoer are sometimes spoken of as penal in their nature, but in such cases it has been pointed out that neither the liability imposed nor the remedy given is strictly penal.

The action of an owner of property against the hundred to recover damages caused by a mob was said by Justices Willes and Buller to be "penal against the hundred, but certainly remedial as to the sufferer." *Hyde v. Cogan,* 2 Doug. 699, 705, 706. A statute giving the right to recover back money lost at gaming, and, if the loser does not sue within a certain time, authorizing a *qui tam* action to be brought by any other person for threefold the amount, has been held to be remedial as to the loser though penal as regards the suit by a common informer. *Bones v. Booth,* 2 W. Bl. 1226 *Brandon v. Pate,* 2 H. Bl. 308; *Grace v. M'Elroy,* 1 Allen, 563; *Read v. Stewart,* 129 Mass. 407, 410; *Cole v. Groves,* 134 Mass. 471. As said by Mr. Justice Ashhurst in the King's Bench, and repeated by Mr. Justice Wilde in the Supreme Judicial Court of Massachusetts, "it has been held, in many instances, that where a statute gives accumulative damages to the party grieved, it is not a penal action." *Woodgate v. Knatchbull,* 2 T. R. 148, 154; *Read v. Chelmsford,* 16 Pick. 128, 132. Thus a statute giving to a tenant, ousted without notice, double the yearly value of the premises against the landlord, has been held to be "not like a penal law where a punishment is imposed for a crime," but "rather as a remedial than a penal law," because "the act indeed does give a penalty, but it is to the party grieved." *Lake v. Smith,* 1 Bos.

& Pul. (N. R.) 174, 179, 180, 181 ; *Wilkinson v. Colley,* 5 Burrow, 2694, 2698.   So in an action given by a statute to a traveller injured through a defect in a highway, for double damages against the town, it was held unnecessary to aver that the facts constituted an offence, or to conclude against the form of the statute, because, as Chief Justice Shaw said: "The action is purely remedial, and has none of the characteristics of a penal prosecution. All damages for neglect or breach of duty operate to a certain extent as punishment; but the distinction is that it is prosecuted for the purpose of punishment, and to deter others from offending in like manner. Here the plaintiff sets out the liability of the town to repair, and an injury to himself from a failure to perform that duty. The law gives him enhanced damages; but still they are recoverable to his own use, and in form and substance the suit calls for indemnity." *Reed v. Northfield,* 13 Pick. 94, 100, 101.

The test whether a law is penal, in the strict and primary sense, is whether the wrong sought to be redressed is a wrong to the public, or a wrong to the individual, according to the familiar classification of Blackstone: "Wrongs are divisible into two sorts or species: *private wrongs and public wrongs.* The former are an infringement or privation of the private or civil rights belonging to individuals, considered as individuals; and are thereupon frequently termed *civil injuries;* the latter are a breach and violation of public rights and duties, which affect the whole community, considered as a community; and are distinguished by the harsher appellation of *crimes and misdemeanors."* 3 Bl. Com. 2.

Laws have no force of themselves beyond the jurisdiction of the State which enacts them, and can have extra-territorial effect only by the comity of other States. The general rules of international comity upon this subject were well summed up, before the American Revolution, by Chief Justice De Grey, as reported by Sir William Blackstone: "Crimes are in their nature local, and the jurisdiction of crimes is local. And so as to the rights of real property, the subject being fixed and immovable. But personal injuries are of a transitory nature, and *sequuntur forum rei."* *Rafael v. Verelst,* 2 W. B. 1055, 1058.

Crimes and offences against the laws of any State can only be defined, prosecuted and pardoned by the sovereign authority of that State; and the authorities, legislative, executive or judicial, of other States take no action with regard to them, except by way of extradition to surrender offenders to the State whose laws they have violated, and whose peace they have broken.

Proceedings *in rem* to determine the title to land must necessarily be brought in the State within whose borders the land is situated, and whose courts and officers alone can put the party in possession. Whether actions to recover pecuniary damages for trespasses to real estate, "of which the causes," as observed by Mr. Westlake (Private International Law, 3d ed. p. 213), "could not have occurred elsewhere than where they did occur," are purely local, or may be brought abroad, depends upon the question whether they are viewed as relating to the real estate, or only as affording a personal remedy. By the common law of England, adopted in most of the States of the Union, such actions are regarded as local, and can be brought only where the land is situated. *Doulson v. Matthews*, 4 T. R. 503; *McKenna v. Fisk*, 1 How. 241, 248. But in some States and countries they are regarded as transitory, like other personal actions; and whether an action for trespass to land in one State can be brought in another State depends on the view which the latter State takes of the nature of the action. For instance, Chief Justice Marshall held that an action could not be maintained in Virginia, by whose law it was local, for a trespass to land in New Orleans. *Livingston v. Jefferson*, 1 Brock. 203. On the other hand, an action for a trespass to land in Illinois, where the rule of the common law prevailed, was maintained in Louisiana, Chief Justice Eustis saying: "The present action is, under our laws, a personal action, and is not distinguished from any ordinary civil action as to the place or tribunal in which it may be brought." *Holmes v. Barclay*, 4 La. Ann. 63. And in a very recent English case, in which the judges differed in opinion upon the question whether, since local venue has been abolished in England, and action can be maintained there for a trespass to land in a foreign country, all agreed that this question depended on the law of England. *Companhia de Mocambique v. British South Africa Co.* (1892) 2 Q. B. 358. See also *Cragin v. Lovell*, 88 N. Y. 258; *Allin v. Connecticut River Lumber Co.*, 150 Mass. 560.

In order to maintain an action for an injury to the person or to movable property, some courts have held that the wrong must be one which would be actionable by the law of the place where the redress is sought, as well as by the law of the place where the wrong was done. See, for example, *TheHalley*, L. R. 2 P. C. 193, 204; *Phillips v. Eyre*, L. R. 6 Q. B. 1, 28, 29; *The M. Moxham*, 1 P. D. 107, 111; *Wooden v. Western New York & Pennsylvania Railroad*, 126 N. Y. 10; *Ash v. Baltimore & Ohio Rail-*

road, 72 Maryland 144. But such is not the law of this court. By our law, a private action may be maintained in one State, if not contrary to its own policy, for such a wrong done in another and actionable there, although a like wrong would not be action-able in the State where the suit is brought. *Smith v. Condry*, 1 How. 28; *The China*, 7 Wall. 53, 64; *The Scotland*, 105 U. S. 24, 29, *Dennick v. Railroad Co.*, 103 U. S. 11; *Texas & Pacific Railway v. Co.r*, 145 U. S. 593.

Upon the question what are to be considered penal laws of one country, within the international rule which forbids such laws to be enforced in any other country, so much reliance was placed by each party in argument upon the opinion of this court in *Wisconsin v. Pelican Ins. Co.*, 127 U. S. 265, that it will be convenient to quote from that opinion the principal proposition there affirmed:

"The rule that the courts of no country execute the penal laws of another applies not only to prosecutions and sentences for crimes and misdemeanors, but to all suits in favor of the State for the recovery of pecuniary penalties for any violation of stat-utes for the protection of its revenues, or other municipal laws, and to all judgments for such penalties." p. 290.

"The application of the rule to the courts of the several States and of the United States is not affected by the provisions of the Constitution and of the act of Congress, by which the judgments of the courts of any State are to have such faith and credit given to them in every court within the United States as they have by law or usage in the State in which they were rendered." p. 291.

"The essential nature and real foundation of a cause of action are not changed by recovering judgment upon it; and the technical rules, which regard the original claim as merged in the judgment, and the judgment as implying a promise by the de-fendant to pay it, do not preclude a court, to which a judgment is presented for affirmative action, (while it cannot go behind the judgment for the purpose of examining into the validity of the claim,) from ascertaining whether the claim is really one of such a nature that the court is authorized to enforce it." pp. 292, 293.

"The statute of Wisconsin, under which the State recovered in one of her own courts the judgment now and here sued on, was in the strictest sense a penal statute, imposing a penalty upon any insurance company of another State, doing business in the State of Wisconsin without having deposited with the proper officer of the State a full statement of its property and business during the previous year. The cause of action was not any private injury, but solely the offence committed against the State by violating her law. The prosecution was in the name of the State, and the whole penalty, when recovered, would accrue to the State." p. 299.

Such were the grounds upon which it was adjudged in that case that this court, under the provision of the Constitution giving it original jurisdiction of actions between a State and citizens of another State, had no jurisdiction of an action by a State upon a judgment recovered by it in one of its own courts against a citi zen or a corporation of another State for a pecuniary penalty for a violation of its municipal law.

Upon similar grounds, the courts of a State cannot be compelled to take jurisdiction of a suit to recover a like penalty for a violation of a law of the United States. *Martin v. Hunter,* 1 Wheat. 304, 330, 337; *United States* v. *Lathrop,* 17 Johns. 4, 265; *Dalefield v. Illinois,* 2 Hill (N. Y.) 159, 169; *Jackson v. Rose,* 2 Virg. Cas. 34; *Ely* v. *Peck,* 7 Conn. 239; *Davison* v. *Champlin,* 7 Conn. 244; *Haney v. Sharp,* 1 Dana, 442; *State v. Pike,* 15 N. H. 83, 85; *Ward v. Jenkins,* 10 Met. 583, 587; 1 Kent Com. 402-404. The only ground ever suggested for maintaining such suits in a State court is that the laws of the United States are in effect laws of each State. *Claflin v. Houseman,* 98 U. S. 130, 137; Platt, J., in *United States v. Lathrop,* 17 Johns. 22; *Ordway v. Central Bank,* 47 Maryland, 217. But in *Claflin v. Houseman* the point adjudged was that an assignee under the bankrupt law of the United States could assert in a state court the title vested in him by the assignment in bankruptcy; and Mr. Justice Bradley, who delivered the opinion in that case, said the year before, when sitting in the Circuit Court, and speaking of a prosecution in a court of the State of Georgia for perjury committed in that State in testifying before a commissioner of the Circuit Court of the United States, "It would be a manifest incongruity for one sovereignty to punish a person for an offence committed against the laws of another sovereignty." *Ex parte Bridges,* 2 Woods, 428, 430. See also *Loney's case,* 134 U. S. 372.

Beyond doubt, (except in cases removed from the state court in obedience to an express act of Congress in order to protect rights under the Constitution and laws of the United States), a Circuit Court of the United States cannot entertain jurisdiction of a suit in behalf of the State, or of the people thereof, to recover a penalty imposed by way of punishment for a violation of a stat-

ute of the State, "the courts of the United States," as observed by
Mr. Justice Catron, delivering a judgment of this court, "having
no power to execute the penal laws of the individual States."
Gwin v. Breedlove, 2 How. 29, 36, 37; *Gwin v. Barton*, 6 How. 7;
Iowa v. Chicago &c. Railway, 37 Fed. Rep. 407; *Ferguson v.
Ross*, 38 Fed. Rep. 161; *Texas v. Day Land & Cattle Co.*, 41 Fed.
Rep. 228; *Dey v. Chicago &c. Railway*, 45 Fed. Rep. 82.

For the purpose of extra-territorial jurisdiction, it may well
be that actions by a common informer, called, as Blackstone says,
"popular actions, because they are given to the people in general,"
to recover a penalty imposed by statute for an offence against the
law, and which may be barred by a pardon granted before action
brought, may stand on the same ground as suits brought for such
a penalty in the name of the State or of its officers, because they
are equally brought to enforce the criminal law of the State.   3 Bl.
Com. 161, 162; 2 Bl. Com. 437, 438; *Adams v. Woods*, 2 Cranch,
336; *Gwin v. Breedlove*, above cited; *United States v. Connor*,
138 U. S. 61, 66; *Bryant v. Ela, Smith* (N. H.) 396.   And personal disabilities imposed by the law of a State, as an incident or
consequence of a judicial sentence or decree, by way of punishment of an offender, and not for the benefit of any other person
—such as attainder, or infamy, or incompetency of a convict to
testify, or disqualification of the guilty party to a cause of divorce
for adultery to marry again—are doubtless strictly penal, and
therefore have no extra-territorial operation.   Story on Conflict
of Laws, §§ 91, 92; Dicey on Domicil, 162; *Folliott v. Ogden*, 1 H.
Bl. 123, and 3 T. R. 726; *Logan v. United States*, 144 U. S. 263,
303; *Dickson v. Dickson*, 1 Yerger, 110; *Ponsford v. Johnson*,
2 Blatchford, 15; *Commonwealth v. Lane*, 113 Mass. 458, 471;
Van Voorhis v. Brintnall, 86 N. Y. 18, 28, 29.

The question whether a statute of one State, which in some
aspects may be called penal, is a penal law in the international
sense, so that it cannot be enforced in the courts of another State,
depends upon the question whether its purpose is to punish an
offence against the public justice of the State, or to afford a private remedy to a person injured by the wrongful act.   There
could be no better illustration of this than the decision of this
court in *Dennick v. Railroad Co.*, 103 U. S. 11.

In that case, it was held that, by virtue of a statute of New
Jersey making a person or corporation, whose wrongful act, neglect or default should cause the death of any person, liable to an
action by his administrator, for the benefit of his widow and next

of kin, to recover damages for the pecuniary injury resulting to them from his death, such an action, where the neglect and the death took place in New Jersey, might, upon general principles of law, be maintained in a Circuit Court of the United States held in the State of New York by an administrator of the deceased, appointed in that State.

Mr. Justice Miller, in delivering judgment, said: "It can scarcely be contended that the act belongs to the class of criminal laws which can only be enforced by the courts of the State where the offence was committed, for it is, though a statutory remedy, a civil action to recover damages for a civil injury. It is, indeed, a right dependent solely on the statute of the State; but *when the* act is done for which the law says the person shall be liable, and the action by which the remedy is to be enforced is a personal and not a real action, and is of that character which the law recognizes as transitory and not local, we cannot see why the defendant may not be held liable in any court to whose jurisdiction he can be subjected by personal process or by voluntary appearance, as was the case here. It is difficult to understand how the nature of the remedy, or the jurisdiction of the courts to enforce it, is in any manner dependent on the question whether it is a statutory right or a common law right. Wherever, by either the common law or the statute law of a State, a right of action has become fixed and a legal liability incurred, that liability may be enforced and the right of action pursued in any court which has jurisdiction of such matters and can obtain jurisdiction of the parties." 103 U. S. 17, 18.

That decision is important as establishing two points: 1st. The court considered "criminal laws," that is to say, laws punishing crimes, as constituting the whole class of penal laws which cannot be enforced extra-territorially. 2d. A statute of a State, manifestly intended to protect life, and to impose a new and extraordinary civil liability upon those causing death, by subjecting them to a private action for the pecuniary damages thereby resulting to the family of the deceased, might be enforced in a Circuit Court of the United States held in another State, without regard to the question whether a similar liability would have attached for a similar cause in that State. The decision was approved and followed at the last term in *Texas & Pacific Railway* v. *Cox*, 145 U. S. 593, 605, where the Chief Justice, speaking for the whole court, after alluding to cases recognizing the rule where the laws of both jurisdictions are similar, said: "The question, however, is one of general law, and we regard it as settled in *Dennick* v. *Railroad Co."*

That decision has been also followed in the courts of several States. *Herrick* v. *Minneapolis & St. Louis Railway,* 31 Minnesota, 11; *Chicago &c. Railroad* v. *Doyle,* 60 Mississippi, 977; *Knight* v. *Wets Jersey Railroad,* 108 Penn. St. 250; *Morris* v. *Chicago &c. Railway,* 65 Iowa, 727; *Missouri Pacific Railway* v. *Lewis,* 24 Nebraska, 848; *Higgins* v. *Central New England Railroad,* 155 Mass., 176.

In the case last cited, a statute of Connecticut having provided that all actions for injuries to the person, including those resulting instantaneously or otherwise in death, should survive; and that for an injury resulting in death from negligence the executor or administrator of the deceased might maintain an action to recover damages not exceeding $5000, to be distributed among his widow and heirs in certain proportions; it was held that such an action was not a penal action, and might be maintained under that statute in Massachusetts by an administrator, appointed there, of a citizen thereof, who had been instantly killed in Connecticut by the negligence of a railroad corporation; and the general principles applicable to the case were carefully stated as follows: "These principles require that, in cases of other than penal actions, the foreign law, if not contrary to our public policy, or to abstract justice or pure morals, or calculated to injure the State or its citizens, shall be recognized and enforced here, if we have jurisdiction of all necessary parties, and if we can see that, consistently with our own forms of procedure and law of trials, we can do substantial justice between the parties. If the foreign law is a penal statute, or if it offends our own policy, or is repugnant to justice or to good morals, or is calculated to injure this State or its citizens, or if we have not jurisdiction of parties who must be brought in to enable us to give a satisfactory remedy, or if under our forms of procedure an action here cannot give a substantial remedy, we are at liberty to decline jurisdiction." 155 Mass. 180.

The provision of the statute of New York, now in question, making the officers of a corporation, who sign and record a false certificate of the amount of its capital stock, liable for all its debts, is in no sense a criminal or *quasi* criminal law. The statute, while it enables persons complying with its provisions to do business as a corporation, without being subject to the liability of general partners, takes pains to secure and maintain a proper corporate fund for the payment of the corporate debts. With this aim, it makes the stockholders individually liable for the debts of the corporation until the capital stock is paid in and a certificate of the payment made by the officers; and makes the officers liable for any false and material representation in that certificate. The individual liability of the stockholders takes the place of a corporate fund, until that fund has been duly created; and the individual liability of the officers takes the place of the fund, in case their statement that it has been duly created is false. If the officers do not truly state and record the facts which exempt them from liability, they are made liable directly to every creditor of the company, who by reason of their wrongful acts has not the security, for the payment of his debt out of the corporate property, on which he had a right to rely. As the statute imposes a burdensome liability on the officers for their wrongful act, it may well be considered penal, in the sense that it should be strictly construed. But as it gives a civil remedy, at the private suit of the creditor only, and measured by the amount of his debt, it is as to him clearly remedial. To maintain such a suit is not to administer a punishment imposed upon an offender against the State, but simply to enforce a private right secured under its laws to an individual. We can see no just ground, on principle, for holding such a statute to be a penal law, in the sense that it cannot be enforced in a foreign state or country.

The decisions of the Court of Appeals of New York, so far as they have been brought to our notice, fall short of holding that the liability imposed upon the officers of the corporation by such statute is a punishment or penalty which cannot be enforced in another State.

In *Garrison* v. *Howe*, the court held that the statute was so far penal that it must be construed strictly, and therefore the officers could not be charged with a debt of the corporation, which was neither contracted nor existing during a default in making the report required by the statute; and Chief Justice Denio, in delivering judgment, said: "If the statute were simply a remedial one, it might be said that the plaintiff's case was within its equity; for the general object of the law doubtless was, beside enforcing the duty of making reports for the benefit of all concerned, to enable parties proposing to deal with the corporation to see whether they could safely do so." "But the provision is highly penal, and the rules of law do not permit us to extend it

by construction to cases not fairly within the language." 17 N.
Y. 458, 465, 466.

In *Jones* v. *Barlow*, it was accordingly held that officers were
only liable for debts actually due, and for which a present right
of action exists against the corporation; and the court said:
"Although the obligation is wholly statutory, and adjudged to be a
penalty, it is in substance, as it is in form, a remedy for the collection of the corporate debts. The act is penal as against the defaulting trustees, but is remedial in favor of creditors. The liability of defaulting trustees is measured by the obligation of the
company, and a discharge of the obligations of the company, or a
release of the debt, bars the action against the trustees." 62 N. Y.
202, 205, 206.

The other cases in that court, cited in the opinion of the Court
of Appeals of Maryland in the present case, adjudged only the
following points: Within the meaning of a statute of limitations
applicable to private actions only, the action against an officer is
not "upon a liability created by statute, other than a penalty or
forfeiture," which would be barred in six years, but is barred in
three years as "an action upon a statute for a penalty or forfeiture
where action is given to the party aggrieved," because the provisions in question, said the court, "impose a penalty, or a liability
in that nature." *Merchants' Bank* v. *Bliss*, 35 N. Y. 412, 417.
A count against a person as an officer for not filing a report cannot be joined with one against him as a stockholder for debts contracted before a report is filed, that being "an action on contract."
Wiles v. *Suydam*, 64 N. Y. 173, 176. The action against an officer
is an action *ex delicto*, and therefore does not survive against
his personal representatives. *Stokes* v. *Stickney*, 96 N. Y. 323.

In a later case than any of these, the court, in affirming the
very judgment now sued on, and adjudging the statute of 1875
to be constitutional and valid, said that "while liability within the
provision in question is in some sense penal in its character, it
may have been intended for the protection of creditors of corporations created pursuant to that statute." *Huntington* v. *Attrill*,
118 N. Y. 365, 378. And where such an action against an officer
went to judgment before the death of either party, it was decided
that "the original wrong was merged in the judgment, and that
thus became property with all the attributes of a judgment in an
action *ex contractu*," and that if, after a reversal of judgment for
the plaintiff, both parties died, the plaintiff's representatives
might maintain an appeal from the judgment of reversal, and

have the defendant's representatives summoned in. *Carr* v. *Rischer*, 119 N. Y. 117, 124.

We do not refer to these decisions as evidence in this case of the law of New York, because in the courts of Maryland that law could only be proved as a fact, and was hardly open to proof on the demurrer, and, if not proved in those courts, could not be taken judicial notice of by this court on this writ of error. *Hanley* v. *Donoghue*, 116 U. S. 1 ; *Chicago & Alton Railroad* v. *Wiggins Ferry*, 119 U. S. 615; *Wernwag* v. *Pawling*, 5 Gill & Johns. 500, 508; *Coates* v. *Mackey*, 56 Maryland, 416, 419. Nor, for reasons to be stated presently, could those decisions, in any view, be regarded as concluding the courts of Maryland, or this court upon the question whether this statute is a penal law in the inter national sense. But they are entitled to great consideration, because made by a court of high authority, construing the terms of a statute with which it was peculiarly familiar; and it is satisfactory to find no adjudication of that court inconsistent with the views which we take of the liability in question.

That court and some others, indeed, have held that the liability of officers under such a statute is so far in the nature of a penalty, that the creditors of the corporation have no vested right therein, which cannot be taken away by a repeal of the statute before judgment in an action brought thereon. *Victory Co.* v. *Beecher*, 97 N. Y. 651, and 26 Hun, 48; *Union Iron Co.* v. *Pierce*, 4 Bissell, 327; *Breitung* v. *Lindauer*, 37 Michigan, 217, 230; *Gregory* v. *German Bank*, 3 Colorado, 332. But whether that is so, or whether, within the decision of this court *Hawthrone* v. *Calef*, 2 Wall. 10, 23, such a repeal so affects the security which the creditor had when his debt was contracted, as to impair the obligation of his contract with the corporation, is aside from the question now before us.

It is true that the courts of some States, including Maryland, have declined to enforce a similar liability imposed by the statute of another State. But, in each of those cases, it appears to have been assumed to be a sufficient ground for that conclusion, that the liability was not founded in contract, but was in the nature of a penalty imposed by statute; and no reasons were given for considering the statute a penal law in the strict, primary and international sense. *Derrickson* v. *Smith*, 3 Dutcher, (27 N. J. Law), 166; *Halsey* v. *McLean*, 12 Allen, 438; *First National Bank* v. *Price*, 33 Maryland, 487.

It is also true that in *Steam Engine Co.* v. *Hubbard*, 101 U.

11

S. 188, 192, Mr. Justice Clifford referred to those cases by way of argument. But in that case, as well as in *Chase v. Curtis*, 113 U. S. 452, the only point adjudged was that such statutes were so far penal that they must be construed strictly; and in both cases jurisdiction was assumed by the Circuit Court of the United States, and not doubted by this court, which could hardly have been if the statute had been deemed penal within the maxim of international law. In *Flash v. Conn*, 109 U. S. 371, the liability sought to be enforced under the statute of New York was the liability of a stockholder arising upon contract; and no question was presented as to the nature of the liability of officers.

But in *Hornor v. Henning*, 93 U. S. 228, this court declined to consider a similar liability of officers of a corporation in the District of Columbia as a penalty. See also *Neal v. Moultrie*, 12 Georgia, 104; *Cady v. Sanford*, 53 Vermont, 632, 639, 640; *Nickerson v. Wheeler*, 118 Mass. 295, 298; *Post v. Toledo &c. Railroad*, 144 Mass. 341, 345; *Woolverton v. Taylor*, 132 Illinois, 197; Morawetz on Corporations (2d ed.) § 908.

The case of *Missouri Pacific Railway v. Humes*, 115 U. S. 512, on which the defendant much relied, related only to the authority of the legislature of a State to compel railroad corporations, neglecting to provide fences and cattle-guards on the lines of their roads, to pay double damages to the owners of cattle injured by reason of the neglect; and no question of the jurisdiction of the courts of another State to maintain an action for such damages was involved in the case, suggested by counsel, or in the mind of the court.

The true limits of the international rule are well stated in the decision of the Judicial Committee of the Privy Council of England, upon an appeal from Canada, in an action brought by the present plaintiff against Attrill in the Province of Ontario upon the judgment to enforce which the present suit was brought. The Canadian judges, having in evidence before them some of the cases in the Court of Appeals of New York, above referred to, as well as the testimony of a well-known lawyer of New York that such statutes were, and had been held by that court to be, strictly penal and punitive, differed in opinion upon the question whether the statute of New York was a penal law which could not be enforced in another country, as well as upon the question whether the view taken by the courts of New York should be conclusive upon foreign courts, and finally gave judgment for the defendant. *Huntington v. Attrill*, 17 Ontario, 245, and 18 Ontario App. 136.

In the Privy Council, Lord Watson, speaking for Lord Chancellor Halsbury and other judges, as well as for himself, delivered an opinion in favor of reversing the judgment below, and entering a decree for the appellant, upon the ground that the action "was not, in the sense of international law, penal, or, in other words, an action on behalf of the government or community of the State of New York for punishment of an offence against their municipal law." The fact that that opinion has not been found in any series of reports readily accessible in this country, but only in 8 Times Law Reports, 341, affords special reasons for quoting some passages.

"The rule" of international law, said Lord Watson, "had its foundation in the well recognized principle that crimes, including in that term all breaches of public law punishable by pecuniary mulct or otherwise, at the instance of the state government, or of some one representing the public, were local in this sense, that they were only cognizable and punishable in the country where they were committed. Accordingly no proceeding, even in the shape of a civil suit, which had for its object the enforcement by the State, whether directly or indirectly, of punishment imposed for such breaches by the *lex loci*, ought to be admitted in the courts of any other country. In its ordinary acceptation, the word 'penal' might embrace penalties for infractions of general law, which did not constitute offences against the State; it might, for many legal purposes, be applied with perfect propriety to penalties created by contract; and it, therefore, when taken by itself, failed to mark that distinction between civil rights and criminal wrongs, which was the very essence of the international rule."

After observing that, in the opinion of the Judicial Committee, the first passage above quoted from *Wisconsin* v. *Pelican Ins. Co.,* 127 U. S. 265, 290, "disclosed the proper test for ascertaining whether an action was penal within the meaning of the rule," he added: "A proceeding, in order to come within the scope of the rule, must be in the nature of a suit in favor of the State whose law had been infringed. All the provisions of municipal statutes for the regulation of trade and trading companies were presumably enacted in the interest and for the benefit of the community at large; and persons who violated those provisions were, in a certain sense, offenders against the state law as well as against individuals who might be injured by their misconduct. But foreign tribunals did not regard those violations of statute law as offences against the State, unless their vindication rested

with the State itself or with the Community which it represented.
Penalties might be attached to them, but that circumstance would
not bring them within the rule, except in cases where those penalties were recoverable at the instance of the State, or of an official duly authorized to prosecute on its behalf, or of a member of
the public in the character of a common informer. An action by
the latter was regarded as an *actio popularis* pursued, not in his
individual interest, but in the interest of the whole community."

He had already, in an earlier part of the opinion, observed:
"Their lordships could not assent to the proposition that in considering whether the present action was penal in such sense as to
oust their jurisdiction, the courts of Ontario were bound to pay
absolute deference to any interpretation which might have been
put upon the statute of 1875 in the State of New York. They
had to construe and apply an international rule, which was a matter of law entirely within the cognizance of the foreign court
whose jurisdiction was invoked. Judicial decisions in the State
where the cause of action arose were not precedents which must
be followed, although the reasoning upon which they were
founded must always receive careful consideration and might be
conclusive. The court appealed to must determine for itself, in
the first place, the substance of the right sought to be enforced,
and, in the second place, whether its enforcement would, either
directly or indirectly, involve the execution of the penal law of
another State. Were any other principle to guide its decision, a
court might find itself in the position of giving effect in one case,
and denying effect in another, to suits of the same character, in
consequence of the causes of action having arisen in different
countries; or in the predicament or being constrained to give
effect to laws which were, in its own judgment, strictly penal."

In this view that the question is not one of local, but of international law, we fully concur. The test is not by what name the
statute is called by the legislature or the courts of the State in
which it was passed, but whether it appears to the tribunal which
is called upon to enforce it to be, in its essential character and
effect, a punishment of an offence against the public, or a grant
of a civil right to a private person.

In this country, the question of international law must be determined in the first instance by the court, state or national, in
which the suit is brought. If the suit is brought in a Circuit
Court of the United States, it is one of those questions of general
jurisprudence which that court must decide for itself, uncon-

trolled by local decisions. *Burgess* v. *Seligman*, 107 U. S. 20, 33; *Texas & Pacific Railway* v. *Cox*, 145 U. S. 593, 605, above cited. If a suit on the original liability under the statute of one State is brought in a court of another State, the Constitution and laws of the United States have not authorized its decision upon such a question to be reviewed by this court. *New York Ins. Co.* v. *Hendren*, 92 U. S. 286; *Roth* v. *Ehman*, 107 U. S. 319. But if the original liability has passed into judgment in one State, the courts of another State, when asked to enforce it, are bound by the Constitution and laws of the United States to give full faith and credit to that judgment, and if they do not, their decision, as said at the outset of this opinion, may be reviewed and reversed by this court on writ of error. The essential nature and real foundation of a cause of action, indeed, are not changed by recovering judgment upon it. This was directly adjudged in *Wisconsin* v. *Pelican Ins. Co.*, above cited. The difference is only in the appellate jurisdiction of this court in the one case or in the other.

If a suit to enforce judgment rendered in one State, and which has not changed the essential nature of the liability, is brought in the courts of another State, this court, in order to determine, on writ of error, whether the highest court of the latter State has given full faith and credit to the judgment, must determine for itself whether the original cause of action is penal in the international sense. The case, in this regard, is analogous to one arising under the clause of the Constitution which forbids a State to pass any law impairing the obligation of contracts, in which, if the highest court of a state decides nothing but the original construction and obligation of a contract, this court has no jurisdiction to review its decision; but if the state court gives effect to a subsequent law, which is impugned as impairing the obligation of a contract, this court has power, in order to determine whether any contract has been impaired, to decide for itself what the true construction of the contract is. *New Orleans Waterworks* v. *Louisiana Sugar Co.*, 125 U. S. 18, 38. So if the state court, in an action to enforce the original liability under the law of another State, passes upon the nature of that liability and nothing else, this court cannot review its decision; but if the state court declines to give full faith and credit to a judgment of another State, because of its opinion as to the nature of the cause of action on which the judgment was recovered, this court, in determining whether full faith and credit have been given to that judgment, must decide for itself the nature of the original liability.

Whether the Court of Appeals of Maryland gave full faith and credit to the judgment recovered by this plaintiff in New York depends upon the true construction of the provisions of the Constitution and of the act of Congress upon that subject.

The provision of the Constitution is as follows: "Full faith and credit shall be given in each State to the public acts, records and judicial proceedings of every other State. And the Congress may by general laws prescribe the manner in which such acts, records and proceedings shall be proved, and the effect thereof." Art. 4, sect. 1.

This clause of the Constitution, like the less perfect provision on the subject in the Articles of Confederation, as observed by Mr. Justice Story, "was intended to give the same conclusive effect to judgments of all the States, so as to promote uniformity, as well as certainty, in the rule among them;" and had three distinct objects: first, to declare, and by its own force establish, that full faith and credit should be given to the judgment of every other State; second, to authorize Congress to prescribe the manner of authenticating them; and third, to authorize Congress to prescribe their effect when so authenticated. Story on the Constitution, §§ 1307, 1308.

Congress, in the exercise of the power so conferred, besides prescribing the manner in which the records and judicial proceedings of any State may be authenticated, has defined the effect thereof, by enacting that "the said records and judicial proceedings, so authenticated, shall have such faith and credit given to them in every court within the United States, as they have by law or usage in the courts of the State from which they are taken." Rev. Stat. § 905, re-enacting Act of May 26, 1790, c. 11, 1 Stat. 122.

These provisions of the Constitution and laws of the United States are necessarily to be read in the light of some established principles, which they were not intended to overthrow. They give no effect to judgments of a court which had no jurisdiction of the subject-matter or of the parties. *D'Arcy* v. *Ketchum,* 11 How. 165; *Thompson* v. *Whitman,* 18 Wall. 457. And they confer no new jurisdiction on the courts of any State; and therefore do not authorize them to take jurisdiction of a suit or prosecution of such a penal nature, that it cannot, on settled rules of public and international law, be entertained by the judiciary of any other

State than that in which the penalty was incurred. *Wisconsin* v. *Pelican Ins. Co.*, above cited.

Nor do these provisions put the judgments of other States upon the footing of domestic judgments, to be enforced by execution; but they leave the manner in which they may be enforced to the law of the State in which they are sued on, pleaded, or offered in evidence. *McElmovle* v. *Cohen*, 13 Pet. 312, 325. But when duly pleaded and proved in a court of that State, they have the effect of being not merely *prima facie* evidence, but conclusive proof, of the rights thereby adjudicated; and a refusal to give them the force and effect, in this respect, which they had in the State in which they were rendered, denies to the party a right secured to him by the Constitution and laws of the United States. *Christmas* v. *Russell*, 5 Wall. 290; *Green* v. *Van Buskirk*, 5 Wall. 307, and 7 Wall. 139; *Insurance Co.* v. *Harris*, 97 U. S. 331, 336; *Crescent City Co.* v. *Butchers' Union*, 120 U. S. 141. 146, 147; *Carpenter* v. *Strange*, 141 U. S. 87.

The judgment rendered by a court of the State of New York, now in question, is not impugned for any want of jurisdiction in that court. The statute under which that judgment was recovered was not, for the reasons already stated at length, a penal law in the international sense. The faith and credit, force and effect, which that judgment had by law and usage in New York was to be conclusive evidence of a direct civil liability from the individual defendant to the individual plaintiff for a certain sum of money, and a debt of record, on which an action would lie, as on any other civil judgment *inter partes*. The Court of Appeals of Maryland, therefore, in deciding this case against the plaintiff, upon the ground that the judgment was not one which it was bound in any manner to enforce, denied to the judgment the full faith, credit and effect to which it was entitled under the Constitution and laws of the United States.

Judgment reversed, and case remanded to the Court of Appeals of the State of Maryland for further proceedings not inconsistent with the opinion of this court.[12]

---

[12]**Penal Laws.**—Whether a liability is penal or not must be determined by the state in which enforcement is sought. The courts differ as to the meaning of penal law. In the case of *Adams v. Ry. Co., 67 Vt. 76, (1894)*, an action brought in Vermont to recover for a death caused in Massachusetts, under the statute of that state which provided for a recovery of damages not exceeding $5,000 nor less than $500 to be assessed with reference to the degree of culpability of the corporation, the court said: "A statute giving a right of recovery is often penal as to one party and

remedial as to the other. It is said that in such cases the true test is
whether the main purpose of the statute is the giving of compensation for
an injury sustained, or the infliction of a punishment upon the wrongdoer.
We think an application of this test to the provision in question shows it
to be penal. The foundation of the action is the loss of a life by reason
of the defendant's negligence. There was no right of action at common
law. This statute gives a right of action to the personal representative of
the deceased, for the benefit of the widow and children, or widow, or next
of kin. If the right of recovery is established, the damages are to be five
hundred dollars in any event. Any recovery beyond this is to be assessed
with reference to the degree of the defendant's culpability. It appears,
then, that whatever the damages may be, or whomsoever the person for
whose benefit they are recovered, they are not given with reference to the
loss sustained. If the recovery could be had only for the benefit of widow
and children the statute might perhaps more easily be looked upon as
remedial. But the recovery may be for the benefit of distant relatives who
had no claim upon the deceased for support. * * * The wrongdoer is
to be punished whether the person receiving the amount of the recovery
has sustained a substantial injury or not." This decision was approved
by the Supreme Court of Kansas in the case of *Dale v. Ry. Co., 57 Kans.
601, (1897)*.

In *Commonwealth v. Green, 17 Mass. 575, (1822)*, the court held that a
person rendered infamous in one state is not infamous in another state
and may testify as a witness in the latter state. It is a rule, quotes the
court, that a sentence which attacks the *honor, rights,* or *property* of a
criminal, cannot extend beyond the limits of the territory of the sovereign
who pronounced it. To enforce such a foreign law would be to punish the
second time for the offense, and, in some measure, to carry it into execution. See *Sims v. Sims, 75 N. Y. 466, (1878)*; *Contra. State v. Foley, 15
Nev. 64, (1880)*.

Foreign obligation to support a bastard child not enforced, *Graham v.
Monsergh, 22 Vt. 543, (1850)*. To forfeit treble damages for usury not
enforced, *Blaine v. Curtis, 59, Vt. 120, (1887)*. Foreign obligation to support a son-in-law not enforced, *De Brimont v. Penniman, 10 Blatch.
(U. S.) 436, (1873)*. The foreign liabilities of directors of a corporation
may be either contractual or penal. If contractual it may be enforced in
any state; but a liability imposed which bears no proportion to the amount
of harm done is penal, and cannot be enforced in another state. *Farr v.
Briggs, 72 Vt. 225 (1900)*.

The case of *Taylor v. W. U. Tel. Co., 95 Iowa 740, (1895)*, held: A
statute of South Dakota which allows the recovery of fifty dollars in
addition to actual damages where a telegram is negligently delayed, provides a statute penalty and will not be enforced in an Iowa suit, and it
matters not whether the penalty provided is given to the public or to
individuals. *Carnahan v. W. U. T. Co., 89 Ind. 526, (1883)*; *American
Co. v. Ellis, 156 Ind. 212, (1901)*. Contra, *Brady v. Daly, 175 U. S. 148,
(1899)*. As to corporations, see *Erickson v. Nesmith, 4 Allen (Mass.)
233*; *Bank v. Rindge, 154 Mass. 203*; *Hancock Bank v. Ellis, 172 Mass. 39*.

CHAPTER VII.

PROCEEDINGS IN PERSONAM AND IN REM.

PENNOYER v. NEFF, 1877.

[95 U. S. 714.]

MR. JUSTICE FIELD delivered the opinion of the court.

This is an action to recover the possession of a tract of land, of the alleged value of $15,000, situated in the State of Oregon. The plaintiff asserts title to the premises by a patent of the United States issued to him in 1866, under the act of Congress of Sept. 27, 1850, usually known as the Donation Law of Oregon. The defendant claims to have acquired the premises under a sheriff's deed, made upon a sale of the property on execution issued upon a judgment recovered against the plaintiff in one of the circuit courts of the State. The case turns upon the validity of this judgment.

It appears from the record that the judgment was rendered in February, 1866, in favor of J. H. Mitchell, for less than $300, including costs, in an action brought by him upon a demand for services as an attorney; that, at the time the action was commenced and the judgment rendered, the defendant therein, the plaintiff here, was a non-resident of the State; that he was not personally served with process, and did not appear therein; and that the judgment was entered upon his default in not answering the complaint upon a constructive service of summons by publication.

The Code of Oregon provides for such service when an action is brought against a non-resident and absent defendant, who has property within the State. It also provides, where the action is for the recovery of money or damages, for the attachment of the property of the non-resident. And it also declares that no natural person is subject to the jurisdiction of a court of the State, "unless he appear in the court, or be found within the State, or be a resident thereof, or have property therein; and, in the last case, only to the extent of such property at the time the jurisdiction attached." Construing this latter provision to mean, that, in an action for money or damages where a defendant does not appear in the court, and is not found within the State, and is not a resident thereof, but has property therein, the jurisdiction of the court extends only over such property, the declaration expresses a principle of general, if not universal, law. The authority of every tribunal is necessarily restricted by the territorial limits of the State in which it is established. Any attempt to exercise authority beyond those limits would be deemed in every other forum, as has been said by this court, an illegitimate assumption of power, and be resisted as mere abuse. *D'Arcy* v. *Ketchum et al.*, 11 How. 165. In the case against the plaintiff, the property here in controversy sold under the judgment rendered was not attached, nor in any way brought under the jurisdiction of the court. Its first connection with the case was caused by a levy of the execution. It was not, thereore, disposed of pursuant to any adjudication, but only in enforcement of a personal judgment, having no relation to the property, rendered against a non-resident without service of process upon him in the action, or his appearance therein. The court below did not consider that an attachment of the property was essential to its jurisdiction or to the validity of the sale, but held that the judgment was invalid from defects in the affidavit upon which the order of publication was obtained, and in the affidavit by which the publication was proved.

There is some difference of opinion among the members of this court as to the rulings upon these alleged defects. The majority are of opinion that inasmuch as the statute requires, for an order of publication, that certain facts shall appear by affidavit *to the satisfaction of the court or judge*, defects in such affidavit can only be taken advantage of on appeal, or by some other direct proceeding, and cannot be urged to impeach the judgment collaterally. The majority of the court are also of opinion that the provision of the statute requiring proof of the publication in a newspaper to be made by the "affidavit of the printer, or his foreman, or his principal clerk," is satisfied when the affidavit is made by the editor of the paper. The term "printer," in their judgment, is there used not to indicate the person who sets up the type,—he does not usually have a foreman or clerks,—it is rather used as synonymous with publisher. The Supreme Court of New York so held in one case; observing that, for the purpose of making the required proof, publishers were "within the spirit of the statute." *Bunce* v. *Reed,* 16 Barb. (N. Y.) 350. And, following this ruling, the Supreme Court of California held that an affidavit made by a "publisher and proprietor" was sufficient. *Sharp* v. *Daugney,* 33 Cal. 512. The term "editor," as used when the statute of New York was passed, from which the Oregon law is borrowed, usually included not only the person who wrote or selected the articles for publication, but the person who published the paper and put it into circulation. Webster, in an early edition of his Dictionary, gives as one of the definitions of an editor, a person "who superintends the publication of a newspaper." It is principally since that time that the business of an editor has been separated from that of a publisher and printer, and has become an independent profession.

If, therefore, we were confined to the rulings of the court below upon the defects in the affidavits mentioned, we should be unable to uphold its decision. But it was also contended in that court, and is insisted upon here, that the judgment in the State court against the plaintiff was void for want of personal service of process on him, or of his appearance in the action in which it was rendered, and that the premises in controversy could not be subjected to the payment of the demand of a resident creditor except by a proceeding *in rem;* that is, by a direct proceeding against the property for that purpose. If these positions are sound, the ruling of the Circuit Court as to the invalidity of that judgment must be sustained, notwithstanding our dissent from the reasons upon which it was made. And that they are sound would seem to follow from two well-established principles of public law respecting the jurisdiction of an independent State over persons and property. The several States of the Union are not, it is true, in every respect independent, many of the rights and powers which originally belonged to them being now vested in the government created by the Constitution. But, except as restrained and limited by that instrument, they possess and exercise the authority of independent States, and the principles of public law to which we have referred are applicable to them. One of these principles is, that every State possesses exclusive jurisdiction and sovereignty over persons and property within its territory. As a consequence, every State has the power to determine for itself the civil *status* and capacities of its inhabitants, to pre-

scribe the subjects upon which they may contract, the forms and
solemnities with which their contracts shall be executed, the rights
and obligations arising from them, and the mode in which their
validity shall be determined and their obligations enforced; and
also to regulate the manner and conditions upon which property
situated within such territory, both personal and real, may be
acquired, enjoyed, and transferred. The other principle of public
law referred to follows from the one mentioned; that is, that no
State can exercise direct jurisdiction and authority over persons
or property without its territory. Story, Confl. Laws, c. 2;
Wheat. Int. Law, pt. 2, c. 2. The several States are of equal
dignity and authority, and the independence of one implies the
exclusion of power from all others. And so it is laid down by
jurists, as an elementary principle, that the laws of one State
have no operation outside of its territory, except so far as is
allowed by comity; and that no tribunal established by it can
extend its process beyond that territory so as to subject either
persons or property to its decisions. "Any exertion of authority
of this sort beyond this limit," says Story, "is a mere nullity, and
incapable of binding such persons or property in any other tribunals." Story, Confl. Laws, sect. 539.

But as contracts made in one State may be enforceable only
in another State, and property may be held by non-residents,
the exercise of the jurisdiction which every State is admitted to
possess over persons and property within its own territory will
often affect persons and property without it. To any influence
exerted in this way by a State affecting persons resident or property situated elsewhere, no objection can be justly taken; whilst
any direct exertion of authority upon them, in an attempt to give
ex-territorial operation to its laws, or to enforce an ex-territorial
jurisdiction by its tribunals, would be deemed an encroachment
upon the independence of the State in which the persons are
domiciled or the property is situated, and be resisted as usurpation.

Thus the State, through its tribunals, may compel persons
domiciled within its limits to execute, in pursuance of their contracts respecting property elsewhere situated, instruments in such
form and with such solemnities as to transfer the title, so far as
such formalities can be complied with; and the exercise of this
jurisdiction in no manner interferes with the supreme control
over the property by the State within which it is situated. *Penn
v. Lord Baltimore*, 1 Ves. 444; *Massie v. Watts*, 6 Cranch, 148;
Watkins v. Holman, 16 Pet. 25; *Corbett v. Nutt*, 10 Wall. 464.

So the State, through its tribunals, may subject property situated within its limits owned by non-residents to the payment of the demand of its own citizens against them; and the exercise of this jurisdiction in no respect infringes upon the sovereignty of the State where the owners are domiciled. Every State owes protection to its own citizens; and, when non-residents deal with them, it is a legitimate and just exercise of authority to hold and appropriate any property owned by such non-residents to satisfy the claims of its citizens. It is in virtue of the State's jurisdiction over the property of the non-resident situated within its limits that its tribunals can inquire into that non-resident's obligations to its own citizens, and the inquiry can then be carried only to the extent necessary to control the disposition of the property. If the non-resident have no property in the State, there is nothing upon which the tribunals can adjudicate.

These views are not new. They have been frequently expressed, with more or less distinctness, in opinions of eminent judges, and have been carried into adjudications in numerous cases. Thus, in *Picquet* v. *Swan*, 5 Mas. 35, Mr. Justice Story said:—

"Where a party is within a territory, he may justly be subjected to its process, and bound personally by the judgment pronounced on such process against him. Where he is not within such territory, and is not personally subject to its laws, if, on account of his supposed or actual property being within the territory, process by the local laws may, by attachment, go to compel his appearance, and for his default to appear judgment may be pronounced against him, such a judgment must, upon general principles, be deemed only to bind him to the extent of such property, and cannot have the effect of a conclusive judgment *in personam*, for the plain reason, that, except so far as the property is concerned, it is a judgment *coram non judice.*"

And in *Boswell's Lessee* v. *Otis*, 9 How. 336, where the title of the plaintiff in ejectment was acquired on a sheriff's sale, under a money decree rendered upon publication of notice against non-residents, in a suit brought to enforce a contract relating to land, Mr. Justice McLean said:—

"Jurisdiction is acquired in one of two modes: first, as against the person of the defendant by the service of process; or, secondly, by a procedure against the property of the defendant within the jurisdiction of the court. In the latter case, the defendant is not personally bound by the judgment beyond the property in question. And it is immaterial whether the proceeding against the property be by an attachment or bill in chancery. It must be substantially a proceeding *in rem."*

These citations are not made as authoritative expositions of the law; for the language was perhaps not essential to the decision of the cases in which it was used, but as expressions of the opinion of eminent jurists. But in *Cooper* v. *Reynolds,* reported in the 10th of Wallace, it was essential to the disposition of the case to declare the effect of a personal action against an absent party, without the jurisdiction of the court, not served with process or voluntarily submitting to the tribunal, when it was sought to subject his property to the payment of a demand of a resident complainant; and in the opinion there delivered we have a clear statement of the law as to the efficacy of such actions, and the jurisdiction of the court over them. In that case, the action was for damages for alleged false imprisonment of the plaintiff; and, upon his affidavit that the defendants had fled from the State, or had absconded or concealed themselves so that the ordinary process of law could not reach them, a writ of attachment was sued out against their property. Publication was ordered by the court, giving notice to them to appear and plead, answer or demur, or that the action would be taken as confessed and proceeded in *ex parte* as to them. Publication was had; but they made default, and judgment was entered against them, and the attached property was sold under it. The purchaser having been put into possession of the property, the original owner brought ejectment for its recovery. In considering the character of the proceeding, the court, speaking through Mr. Justice Miller, said:—

"Its essential purpose or nature is to establish, by the judgment of the court, a demand or claim against the defendant, and subject his property lying within the territorial jurisdiction of the court to the payment of that demand. But the plaintiff is met at the commencement of his proceedings by the fact that the defendant is not within the territorial jurisdiction, and cannot be served with any process by which he can be brought personally within the power of the court. For this difficulty the statute has provided a remedy. It says that, upon affidavit being made of that fact, a writ of attachment may be issued and levied on any of the defendant's property, and a publication may be made warning him to appear; and that thereafter the court may proceed in the case, whether he appears or not. If the defendant appears, the cause becomes mainly a suit *in personam*, with the added incident, that the property attached remains liable, under the control of the court, to answer to any demand which may be established against the defendant by the final judgment of the court. But if there is no appearance of the defendant, and no service of process on him, the case becomes in its essential nature a proceeding *in rem*, the only effect of which is to subject the property attached to the payment of the demand which the court may find to be due to the plaintiff. That such is the nature of this proceeding in this latter class of cases is clearly evinced by two well-established propositions: first, the judgment of the court, though in form a personal judgment against the defendant, has no effect beyond the property attached in that suit. No general execution can be issued for any balance unpaid after the attached property is exhausted. No suit can be maintained on such a judgment in the same court, or in any other; nor can it be used as evidence in any other proceeding not affecting the attached property; nor could the costs in that proceeding be collected of defendant out of any other property than that attached in the suit. Second, the court, in such a suit, cannot proceed, unless the officer finds some property of defendant on which to levy the writ of attachment. A return that none can be found is the end of the case, and deprives the court of further jurisdiction, though the publication may have been duly made and proven in court."

The fact that the defendants in that case had fled from the State, or had concealed themselves, so as not to be reached by the ordinary process of the court, and were not non-residents, was not made a point in the decision. The opinion treated them as being without the territorial jurisdiction of the court; and the grounds and extent of its authority over persons and property thus situated were considered, when they were not brought within its jurisdiction by personal service or voluntary appearance.

The writer of the present opinion considered that some of the objections to the preliminary proceedings in the attachment suit were well taken, and therefore dissented from the judgment of the court; but to the doctrine declared in the above citation he agreed, and he may add, that it received the approval of all the

judges. It is the only doctrine consistent with proper protection
to citizens of other States. If, without personal service, judgments *in personam,* obtained *ex parte* against non-residents and
absent parties, upon mere publication of process, which, in the
great majority of cases, would never be seen by the parties interested, could be upheld and enforced, they would be the constant
instruments of fraud and oppression. Judgments for all sorts of
claims upon contracts and for torts, real or pretended, would be
thus obtained, under which property would be seized, when the
evidence of the transactions upon which they were founded, if
they ever had any existence, had perished.

Substituted service by publication, or in any other authorized
form, may be sufficient to inform parties of the object of proceedings taken where property is once brought under the control
of the court by seizure or some equivalent act. The law assumes
that property is always in possession of its owner, in person
or by agent; and it proceeds upon the theory that its seizure will
inform him, not only that it is taken into the custody of the court,
but that he must look to any proceedings authorized by law upon
such seizure for its condemnation and sale. Such service may
also be sufficient in cases where the object of the action is to
reach and dispose of property in the State, or of some interest
therein, by enforcing a contract or a lien respecting the same,
or to partition it among different owners, or, when the public is
a party, to condemn and appropriate it for a public purpose. In
other words, such service may answer in all actions which are
substantially proceedings *in rem.* But where the entire object of
the action is to determine the personal rights and obligations of
the defendants, that is, where the suit is merely *in personam,*
constructive service in this form upon a non-resident is ineffectual
for any purpose. Process from the tribunals of one State cannot run into another State, and summon parties there domiciled
to leave its territory and respond to proceedings against them.
Publication of process or notice within the State where the
tribunal sits cannot create any greater obligation upon the non-
resident to appear. Process sent to him out of the State, and
process published within it, are equally unavailing in proceedings
to establish his personal liability.

The want of authority of the tribunals of a State to adjudicate upon the obligations of non-residents, where they have no
property within its limits, is not denied by the court below; but
the position is assumed, that, where they have property within

the State, it is immaterial whether the property is in tne first
instance brought under the control of the court by attachment or
some other equivalent act, and afterwards applied by its judgment to the satisfaction of demands against its owner; or such
demands be first established in a personal action, and the property
of the non-resident be afterwards seized and sold on execution.
But the answer to this position has already been given in the
statement, that the jurisdiction of the court to inquire into and
determine his obligations at all is only incidental to its jurisdiction over the property. Its jurisdiction in that respect cannot be
made to depend upon facts to be ascertained after it has tried
the cause and rendered the judgment. If the judgment be previously void, it will not become valid by the subsequent discovery
of property of the defendant, or by his subesquent acquisition of it.
The judgment, if void when rendered, will always remain void;
it cannot occupy the doubtful position of being valid if property
be found, and void if there be none. Even if the position assumed
were confined to cases where the non-resident defendant possessed property in the State at the commencement of the action,
it would still make the validity of the proceedings and judgment
depend upon the question whether, before the levy of the execution, the defendant had or had not disposed of the property. If
before the levy the property should be sold, then, according to this
position, the judgment would not be binding. This doctrine
would introduce a new element of uncertainty in judicial proceedings. The contrary is the law: the validity of every judgment depends upon the jurisdiction of the court before it is rendered, not upon what may occur subsequently. In *Webster* v.
Reid, reported in 11th of Howard, the plaintiff claimed title to
land sold under judgments recovered in suits brought in a territorial court of Iowa, upon publication of notice under a law of
the territory, without service of process; and the court said:—

"These suits were not a proceeding *in rem* against the land,
but were *in personam* against the owners of it. Whether they
all resided within the territory or not does not appear, nor is
it a matter of any importance. No person is required to answer
in a suit on whom process has not been served, or whose property has not been attached. In this case, there was no personal
notice, nor an attachment or other proceeding against the land,
until after the judgments. The judgments, therefore, are nullities,
and did not authorize the executions on which the land was sold."

12

The force and effect of judgments rendered against non-residents without personal service of process upon them, or their voluntary appearance, have been the subject of frequent consideration in the courts of the United States and of the several States, as attempts have been made to enforce such judgments in States other than those in which they were rendered, under the provision of the Constitution requiring that "full faith and credit shall be given in each State to the public acts, records, and judicial proceedings of every other State;" and the act of Congress providing for the mode of authenticating such acts, records, and proceedings, and declaring that, when thus authenticated, "they shall have such faith and credit given to them in every court within the United States as they have by law or usage in the courts of the State from which they are or shall be taken." In the earlier cases, it was supposed that the act gave to all judgments the same effect in other States which they had by law in the State where rendered. But this view was afterwards qualified so as to make the act applicable only when the court rendering the judgment had jurisdiction of the parties and of the subject-matter, and not to preclude an inquiry into the jurisdiction of the court in which the judgment was rendered, or the right of the State itself to exercise authority over the person or the subject-matter. *M'Elmoyle* v. *Cohen,* 13 Pet. 312. In the case of *D'Arcy* v. *Ketchem,* reported in the 11th of Howard, this view is stated with great clearness. That was an action in the Circuit Court of the United States for Louisiana, brought upon a judgment rendered in New York under a State statute, against two joint debtors, only one of whom had been served with process, the other being a non-resident of the State. The Circuit Court held the judgment conclusive and binding upon the non-resident not served with process; but this court reversed its decision, observing, that it was a familiar rule that countries foreign to our own disregarded a judgment merely against the person, where the defendant had not been served with process nor had a day in court; that national comity was never thus extended; that the proceeding was deemed an illegitimate assumption of power, and resisted as mere abuse; that no faith and credit or force and effect had been given to such judgments by any State of the Union, so far as known, and that the State courts had uniformly, and in many instances, held them to be void. "The international law," said the court, "as it existed among the States in 1790, was that judgment rendered in one State, assuming to bind the person of a citizen of another, was void within the foreign State, when the defendant had not been served with process or voluntarily made defence; because neither the legislative jurisdiction nor that of courts of justice had binding force." And the court held that the act of Congress did not intend to declare a new rule, or to embrace judicial records of this description. As was stated in a subsequent case, the doctrine of this court is, that the act "was not designed to displace that principle of natural justice which requires a person to have notice of a suit before he can be conclusively bound bv its result, nor those rules of public law which protect persons and property within one State from the exercise of jurisdiction over them by another." *The Lafayette Insurance Co.* v. *French et al.,* 18 How. 404.

This whole subject has been very fully and learnedly considered in the recent case of *Thompson* v. *Whitman*, 18 Wall. 457, where all the authorities are carefully reviewed and distinguished, and the conclusion above stated is not only reaffirmed, but the doctrine is asserted, that the record of a judgment rendered in another State may be contradicted as to the facts necessary to give the court jurisdiction against its recital of their existence. In all the cases brought in the State and Federal courts, where attempts have been made under the act of Congress to give effect in one State to personal judgments rendered in another State against non-residents, without service upon them, or upon substituted service by publication, or in some other form, it has been held, without an exception, so far as we are aware, that such judgments were without any binding force, except as to property, or interest in property, within the State, to reach and affect which was the object of the action in which the judgment was rendered, and which property was brought under control of the court in connection with the process against the person. The proceeding in such cases, though in the form of a personal action, has been uniformly treated, where service was not obtained, and the party did not voluntarily appear, as effectual and binding merely as a proceeding *in rem,* and as having no operation beyond the disposition of the property, or some interest therein. And the reason assigned for this conclusion has been that which we have already stated, that the tribunals of one State have no jurisdiction over persons beyond its limits, and can inquire only into their obligations to its citizens when exercising its conceded jurisdiction over their property within its limits. In *Bissell* v. *Briggs*, decided by the Supreme Court of Massachusetts

as early as 1813, the law is stated substantially in conformity with
these views. In that case, the court considered at length the effect
of the constitutional provision, and the act of Congress mentioned,
and after stating that, in order to entitle the judgment rendered
in any court of the United States to the full faith and credit
mentioned in the Constitution, the court must have had jurisdiction not only of the cause, but of the parties, it proceeded to
illustrate its position by observing, that, where a debtor living in
one State has goods, effects, and credits in another, his creditor
living in the other State may have the property attached pursuant
to its laws, and, on recovering judgment, have the property applied
to its satisfaction; and that the party in whose hands the property
was would be protected by the judgment in the State of the
debtor against a suit for it, because the court rendering the judgment had jurisdiction to that extent; but that if the property
attached were insufficient to satisfy the judgment, and the creditor
should sue on the judgment in the State of the debtor, he would
fail, because the defendant was not amenable to the court rendering the judgment. In other words, it was held that over the
property within the State the court had jurisdiction by the attachment, but had none over his person; and that any determination
of his liability, except so far as was necessary for the disposition
of the property, was invalid.

In *Kilbourn* v. *Woodworth,* 5 Johns. (N. Y.) 37, an action of
debt was brought in New York upon a personal judgment
recovered in Massachusetts. The defendant in that judgment
was not served with process; and the suit was commenced by
the attachment of a bedstead belonging to the defendant, accompanied with a summons to appear, served on his wife after she
had left her place in Massachusetts. The court held that the
attachment bound only the property attached as a proceeding
in rem, and that it could not bind the defendant, observing, that
to bind a defendant personally, when he was never personally
summoned or had notice of the proceeding, would be contrary
to the first principles of justice, repeating the language in that
respect of Chief Justice DeGrey, used in the case of *Fisher* v.
Lane, 3 Wils. 297, in 1772. See also *Borden* v. *Fitch,* 15 Johns.
(N. Y.) 121, and the cases there cited, and *Harris* v. *Hardeman
et al.,* 14 How. 334. To the same purport decisions are found in
all the State courts. In several of the cases, the decision has been
accompanied with the observation that a personal judgment thus
recovered has no binding force without the State in which it is

rendered, implying that in such State it may be valid and binding. But if the court has no jurisdiction over the person of the defendant by reason of his non-residence, and, consequently, no authority to pass upon his personal rights and obligations; if the whole proceeding, without service upon him or his appearance, is *coram non judice* and void; if to hold a defendant bound by such a judgment is contrary to the first principles of justice,—it is difficult to see how the judgment can legitimately have any force within the State. The language used can be justified only on the ground that there was no mode of directly reviewing such judgment or impeaching its validity within the State where rendered; and that, therefore, it could be called in question only when its enforcement was elsewhere attempted. In later cases, this language is repeated with less frequency than formerly, it beginning to be considered, as it always ought to have been, that a judgment which can be treated in any State of this Union as contrary to the first principles of justice, and as an absolute nullity, because rendered without any jurisdiction of the tribunal over the party, is not entitled to any respect in the State where rendered. *Smith* v. *McCutchen,* 38 Mo. 415; *Darrance* v. *Preston,* 18 Iowa, 396; *Hakes* v. *Shupe,* 27 id. 465; *Mitchell's Administrator* v. *Gray,* 18 Ind. 123.

Be that as it may, the courts of the United States are not required to give effect to judgments of this character when any right is claimed under them. Whilst they are not foreign tribunals in their relations to the State courts, they are tribunals of a different sovereignty exercising a distinct and independent jurisdiction, and are bound to give to the judgments of the State courts only the same faith and credit which the courts of another State are bound to give to them.

Since the adoption of the Fourteenth Amendment to the Federal Constitution, the validity of such judgments may be directly questioned, and their enforcement in the State resisted on the ground that proceedings in a court of justice to determine the personal rights and obligations of parties over whom that court has no jurisdiction do not constitute due process of law. Whatever difficulty may be experienced in giving to those terms a definition which will embrace every permissible exertion of power affecting private rights, and exclude such as is forbidden, there can be no doubt of their meaning when applied to judicial proceedings. They then mean a course of legal proceedings according to those rules and principles which have been established in our systems of jurisprudence for the protection and enforcement of private rights. To give such proceedings any validity, there must be a tribunal competent by its constitution—that is, by the law of its creation—to pass upon the subject-matter of the suit; and, if that involves merely a determination of the personal liability of the defendant, he must be brought within its jurisdiction by service of process within the State, or his voluntary appearance.

Except in cases affecting the personal *status* of the plaintiff, and cases in which that mode of service may be considered to have been assented to in advance, as hereinafter mentioned, the substituted service of process by publication, allowed by the law of Oregon and by similar laws in other States, where actions are brought against non-residents, is effectual only where, in connection with process against the person for commencing the action, property in the State is brought under the control of the court, and subjected to its disposition by process adapted to that purpose, or where the judgment is sought as a means of reaching such property or affecting some interest therein; in other words, where the action is in the nature of a proceeding *in rem*. As stated by Cooley in his Treatise on Constitutional Limitations, 405, for any other purpose than to subject the property of a non-resident to valid claims against him in the State, "due process of law would require appearance or personal service before the defendant could be personally bound by any judgment rendered."

It is true that, in a strict sense, a proceeding *in rem* is one taken directly against property, and has for its object the disposition of the property, without reference to the title of individual claimants; but, in a larger and more general sense, the terms are applied to actions between parties, where the direct object is to reach and dispose of property owned by them, or of some interest therein. Such are cases commenced by attachment against the property of debtors, or instituted to partition real estate, foreclose a mortgage, or enforce a lien. So far as they affect property in the State, they are substantially proceedings *in rem* in the broader sense which we have mentioned.

It is hardly necessary to observe, that in all we have said we have had reference to proceedings in courts of first instance, and to their jurisdiction, and not to proceedings in an appellate tribunal to review the action of such courts. The latter may be taken upon such notice, personal or constructive, as the State creating the tribunal may provide. They are considered as rather a continuation of the original litigation than the commencement of a new action. *Nations et al.* v. *Johnson et al.*, 24 How. 195.

It follows from the views expressed that the personal judgment recovered in the State court of Oregon against the plaintiff herein, then a non-resident of the State, was without any validity, and did not authorize a sale of the property in controversy.

To prevent any misapplication of the views expressed in this opinion, it is proper to observe that we do not mean to assert, by any thing we have said, that a State may not authorize proceedings to determine the *status* of one of its citizens towards a non-resident, which would be binding within the State, though made without service of process or personal notice to the non-resident. The jurisdiction which every State possesses to determine the civil *status* and capacities of all its inhabitants involves authority to prescribe the conditions on which proceedings affecting them may be commenced and carried on within its territory. The State, for example, has absolute right to prescribe the conditions upon which the marriage relations between its own citizens shall be created, and the causes for which it may be dissolved. One of the parties guilty of acts for which, by the law of the State, a dissolution may be granted, may have removed to a State where no dissolution is permitted. The complaining party would, therefore, fail if a divorce were sought in the State of the defendant; and if application could not be made to the tribunals of the complainant's domicile in such case, and proceedings be there instituted without personal service of process or personal notice to the offending party, the injured citizen would be without redress. Bish. Marr. and Div., sect. 156.

Neither do we mean to assert that a State may not require a non-resident entering into a partnership or association within its limits, or making contracts enforceable there, to appoint an agent or representative in the State to receive service of process and notice in legal proceedings instituted with respect to such partnership, association, or contracts, or to designate a place where such service may be made and notice given, and provide, upon their failure, to make such appointment or to designate such place that service may be made upon a public officer designated for that purpose, or in some other prescribed way, and that judgments rendered upon such service may not be binding upon the non-residents both within and without the State. As was said by the Court of Exchequer in *Vallee* v. *Dumergue*, 4 Exch. 290, "It is not contrary to natural justice that a man who has agreed to receive a particular mode of notification of legal proceedings should be bound by a judgment in which that particular mode of notification has been followed, even though he may not have actual notice of them." See also *The Lafayette Insurance Co.* v. *French et al.,* 18 How. 404, and *Gillespie* v. *Commercial Mutual Marine Insurance Co.,* 12 Gray (Mass.), 201. Nor do we doubt that a State, on creating corporations or other institutions for pecuniary or charitable purposes, may provide a mode in which their conduct may be investigated, their obligations enforced, or their charters revoked, which shall require other than personal service upon their officers or members. Parties becoming members of such corporations or institutions would hold their interest subject to the conditions prescribed by law. *Copin* v. *Adamson,* Law Rep. 9 Ex. 345.

In the present case, there is no feature of this kind, and, consequently, no consideration of what would be the effect of such legislation in enforcing the contract of a non-resident can arise. The question here respects only the validity of a money judgment rendered in one State, in an action upon a simple contract against the resident of another, without service of process upon him, or his appearance therein.

Judgment affirmed.[13]

_____

[13]*McEwen v. Zimmer, 38 Mich. 765; Arndt v. Griggs, 134 U. S. 316; Rand v. Hanson, 154 Mass. 87; Tyler v. Court of Registration, 175 Mass. 71.*

DIVORCE.

ANDREWS v. ANDREWS, 1903.

[188 U. S. 14.]

1. Nature of the Marriage Contract.
2. Powers of State and Federal Governments to Regulate Marriage and Divorce.
3. Full Faith and Credit Clause.
4. Extra-territorial Effect of Judgment of Divorce.
5. Domicil as Determining Jurisdiction in Cases of Divorce.
6. The Law Applied to Divorce Proceedings.
7. Service of Process Upon Defendant.

THE plaintiff and the defendant in error, each claiming to be the lawful widow of Charles S. Andrews, petitioned to be appointed administratrix of his estate. The facts were found as follows:

Charles S. and Kate H. Andrews married in Boston in April, 1887, and they lived together at their matrimonial domicil in the

State of Massachusetts. In April, 1890, the wife began a suit for separate maintenance, which was dismissed in December, 1890, because of a settlement between the parties, adjusting their property relations.

In the summer of 1891, Charles S. Andrews, to quote from the findings, "being then a citizen of Massachusetts and domiciled in Boston, went to South Dakota to obtain a divorce for a cause which occurred here while the parties resided here, and which would not authorize a divorce by the laws of this Commonwealth; he remained personally in that State a period of time longer than is necessary by the laws of said State to gain a domicil there, and on November 19, 1891, filed a petition for divorce in the proper court of that State."

Concerning the conduct of Charles S. Andrews and his purpose to obtain a divorce in South Dakota, whilst retaining his domicil in Massachusetts, the facts were found as follows:

"The husband went to South Dakota and took up his residence there to get this divorce, and that he intended to return to this State when the business was finished. He boarded at a hotel in Sioux Falls all the time, and had no other business there than the prosecution of this divorce suit. I find, however, that he voted there at a state election in the fall of 1891, claiming the right to do so as a *bona fide* resident under the laws of that State. His intention was to become a resident of that State for the purpose of getting his divorce, and to that end to do all that was needful to make him such a resident, and I find he became a resident if, as a matter of law, such finding is warranted in the facts above stated."

And further, that—

"The parties had never lived together as husband and wife in South Dakota, nor was it claimed that either one of them was ever in that State except as above stated."

With reference to the divorce proceedings in South Dakota it was found as follows:

"The wife received notice, and appeared by counsel and filed an answer, denying that the libellant was then or ever had been a *bona fide* resident of South Dakota, or that she had deserted him, and setting up cruelty on his part toward her. This case was settled, so far as the parties were concerned, in accordance with the terms of the agreement of April 22, 1892, signed by the wife and consented to by the husband, and, for the purpose of carrying out her agreement 'to consent to the granting of divorce for desertion in South Dakota,' she requested her counsel there to withdraw her appearance in that suit, which they did, and thereafterwards, namely, on May 6, 1892, a decree granting the divorce was passed, and within a day or two afterwards the said Charles, having attained the object of his sojourn in that State, returned to this Commonwealth, where he resided and was domiciled until his death, which occurred in October, 1897."

By the agreement of April 22, 1892, to which reference is made in the finding just quoted, it was stipulated that a payment of a sum of money should be made by Charles S. Andrews to his wife, and she authorized her attorney on the receipt of the money to execute certain papers, and it was then provided as follows:

"Fourth. Upon the execution of such papers M. F. Dickinson, Jr., is authorized in my name to consent to the granting of divorce for desertion in the South Dakota court."

Respecting the claim of Annie Andrews to be the wife of Charles S. Andrews, it was found as follows:

"Upon his return to this State he soon met the petitioner, and on January 11, 1893, they were married in Boston, and ever after that lived as husband and wife in Boston, and were recognized as such by all until his death. The issue of this marriage are two children, still living."

It was additionally found that Annie Andrews married Charles S. Andrews in good faith and in ignorance of any illegality in the South Dakota divorce, and that Kate H. Andrews, as far as she had the power to do so, had connived at and acquiesced in the South Dakota divorce, had preferred no claim thereafter to be the wife of Charles S. Andrews until his death when in this case she asserted her right to administer his estate as his lawful widow

From the evidence above stated the ultimate facts were found to be that Andrews had always retained his domicil in Massachusetts, had gone to Dakota for the purpose of obtaining a divorce, in fraud of the laws of Massachusetts, and with the intention of returning to that State when the divorce was procured, and hence that he had never acquired a *bona fide* domicil in South Dakota. Applying a statute of the State of Massachusetts forbidding the enforcement in that State of a divorce obtained under the circumstances stated, it was decided that the decree rendered in South Dakota was void in the State of Massachusetts, and hence that Kate H. Andrews was the widow of

Charles S. Andrews and entitled to administer his estate. 176 Massachusetts, 92.

MR. JUSTICE WHITE, after making the foregoing statement, delivered the opinion of the court.

It was suggested at bar that this court was without jurisdiction. But it is unquestionable that rights under the Constitution of the United States were expressly and in due time asserted and that the effect of the judgment was to deny these rights. Indeed, when the argument is analyzed we think it is apparent that it but asserts that, as the court below committed no error in deciding the Federal controversy, therefore there is no Federal question for review. But the power to decide whether the Federal issue was rightly disposed of involves the exercise of jurisdiction. *Penn Mutual Life Insurance Company* v. *Austin*, (1897) 168 U. S. 685. As the Federal question was not unsubstantial and frivolous, we pass to a consideration of the merits of the case.

The statute of the State of Massachusetts, in virtue of which the court refused to give effect to the judgment of divorce, is as follows:

"SEC. 35. A divorce decreed in another State or country according to the laws thereof by a court having jurisdiction of the cause and of both the parties, shall be valid and effectual in this Commonwealth; but if an inhabitant of this Commonwealth goes into another State or country to obtain a divorce for a cause which occurred here, while the parties resided here, or for a cause which would not authorize a divorce by the laws of this Commonwealth, a divorce so obtained shall be of no force or effect in this Commonwealth." 2 Rev. Laws Mass. 1902, ch. 152, p. 1357; Pub. Stat. 1882, c. 146, § 41.

It is clear that this statute, as a general rule, directs the courts of Massachusetts to give effect to decrees of divorce rendered in another State or country by a court having jurisdiction. It is equally clear that the statute prohibits an inhabitant of Massachusetts from going into another State to obtain a divorce, for a cause which occurred in Massachusetts whilst the parties were domiciled there, or for a cause which would not have authorized a divorce by the law of Massachusetts, and that the statute forbids the courts of Massachusetts from giving effect to a judgment of divorce obtained in violation of these prohibitions. That the statute establishes a rule of public policy is undeniable. Did the court fail to give effect to Federal rights when it applied the provisions of the statute to this case, and, therefore, refused to enforce the South Dakota decree? In other words, the question for decision is, does the statute conflict with the Constitution of the United States? In coming to the solution of this question it is essential, we repeat, to bear always in mind that the prohibitions of the statute are directed solely to citizens of Massachusetts domiciled therein, and that it only forbids the enforcement in Massachusetts of a divorce obtained in another State by a citizen of Massachusetts who, in fraud of the laws of the State of Massachusetts, whilst retaining his domicil, goes into another State for the purpose of there procuring a decree of divorce.

We shall test the constitutionality of the statute, first by a consideration of the nature of the contract of marriage and the authority which government possesses over the subject; and, secondly, by the application of the principles thus to be developed to the case in hand.

1. That marriage, viewed solely as a civil relation, possesses elements of contract is obvious. But it is also elementary that marriage, even considering it as only a civil contract, is so interwoven with the very fabric of society that it cannot be entered into except as authorized by law, and that it may not, when once entered into, be dissolved by the mere consent of the parties. It would be superfluous to cite the many authorities establishing these truisms, and we therefore are content to excerpt a statement of the doctrine on the subject contained in the opinion of this court delivered by Mr. Justice Field, in *Maynard* v. *Hill*, (1888) 125 U. S. 190:

"Marriage, as creating the most important relation in life, as having more to do with the morals and civilization of the people than any other institution, has always been subject to the control of the legislature. That body prescribes the age at which parties may contract to marry, the procedure or form essential to constitute marriage, the duties and obligations it creates, its effects upon the property rights of both, present and prospective, and the acts which may constitute grounds for its dissolution." (p. 205.)

　　*　　*　　*　　*　　*　　*　　*　　*　　*

"It is also to be observed that, whilst marriage is often termed by text writers and in decisions of courts a civil contract—generally to indicate that it must be founded upon the agreement of the parties, and does not require any religious ceremony for its solemnization—it is something more than a mere contract.

The consent of the parties is of course essential to its existence, but when the contract to marry is executed by the marriage, a relation between the parties is created which they cannot change. Other contracts may be modified, restricted, or enlarged, or entirely released upon the consent of the parties. Not so with marriage. The relation once formed, the law steps in and holds the parties to various obligations and liabilities. It is an institution, in the maintenance of which in its purity the public is deeply interested, or it is the foundation of the family and of society, without which there would be neither civilization nor progress." (p. 210.)

It follows that the statute in question was but the exercise of an essential attribute of government, to dispute the possession of which would be to deny the authority of the State of Massachusetts to legislate over a subject inherently domestic in its nature and upon which the existence of civilized society depends. True, it is asserted that the result just above indicated will not necessarily flow from the conclusion that the statute is repugnant to the Constitution of the United States. The decision that the Constitution compels the State of Massachusetts to give effect to the decree of divorce rendered in South Dakota cannot, it is insisted, in the nature of things be an abridgment of the authority of the State of Massachusetts over a subject within its legislative power, since such ruling would only direct the enforcement of a decree rendered in another State and therefore without the territory of Massachusetts. In reason it cannot, it is argued, be held to the contrary without disregarding the distinction between acts which are done within and those which are performed without the territory of a particular State. But this disregards the fact that the prohibitions of the statute, so far as necessary to be considered for the purposes of this case, are directed, not against the enforcement of divorces obtained in other States as to persons domiciled in such States, but against the execution in Massachusetts of decrees of divorce obtained in other States by persons who are domiciled in Massachusetts and who go into such other States with the purpose of practicing a fraud upon the laws of the State of their domicil; that is, to procure a divorce without obtaining a *bona fide* domicil in such other State. This being the scope of the statute, it is evident, as we shall hereafter have occasion to show, that the argument, whilst apparently conceding the power of the State to regulate the dissolution of marriage among its own citizens, yet, in substance, necessarily denies the possession of such power by the State. But, it is further argued, as the Constitution of the United States is the paramount law, and as, by that instrument, the State of Massachusetts is compelled to give effect to the decree, it follows that the Constitution of the United States must prevail, whatever may be the result of enforcing it.

Before coming to consider the clause of the Constitution of the United States upon which the proposition is rested, let us more precisely weigh the consequences which must come from upholding the contention, not only as it may abridge the authority of the State of Massachusetts, but as it may concern the powers of government existing under the Constitution, whether state or Federal.

It cannot be doubted that if a State may not forbid the enforcement within its borders of a decree of divorce procured by its own citizens who, whilst retaining their domicil in the prohibiting State, have gone into another State to procure a divorce in fraud of the laws of the domicil, that the existence of all efficacious power on the subject of divorce will be at an end. This must follow if it be conceded that one who is domiciled in a State may whenever he chooses go into another State and, without acquiring a bona fide domicil therein, obtain a divorce, and then compel the State of the domicil to give full effect to the divorce thus fraudulently procured. Of course, the destruction of all substantial legislative power over the subject of the dissolution of the marriage tie which would result would be equally applicable to every State in the Union. Now, as it is certain that the Constitution of the United States confers no power whatever upon the government of the United States to regulate marriage in the States or its dissolution, the result would be that the Constitution of the United States has not only deprived the States of power on the subject, but whilst doing so has delegated no authority in the premises to the government of the United States. It would thus come to pass that the governments, state and Federal, are bereft by the operation of the Constitution of the United States of a power which must belong to and somewhere reside in every civilized government. This would be but to declare that, in a necessary aspect, government had been destroyed by the adoption of the Constitution. And such result would be reached by holding that a power of local government vested in the States when the Constitution was adopted had been lost to the States, though not delegated to the Federal government, because each State was endowed as a consequence of the adoption of the Constitution with the means of destroying the authority with respect to the dissolution of the marriage tie as to every other State, whilst having no right to save its own power in the premises from annihilation.

But let us consider the particular clause of the Constitution of the United States which is relied upon, in order to ascertain whether such an abnormal and disastrous result can possibly arise from its correct application.

The provision of the Constitution of the United States in question is section 1 of article IV, providing that "full faith and credit shall be given in each State to the public acts, records, and judicial proceedings of every other State." The argument is that, even although the Massachusetts statute but announces a rule of public policy, in a matter purely local, nevertheless it violates this clause of the Constitution. The decree of the court of another State, it is insisted, and not the relation of the parties to the State of Massachusetts and their subjection to its lawful authority, is what the Constitution of the United States considers in requiring the State of Massachusetts to give due faith and credit to the judicial proceedings of the courts of other States. This proposition, however, must rest on the assumption that the Constitution has destroyed those rights of local self-government which it was its purpose to preserve. It, moreover, presupposes that the determination of what powers are reserved and what delegated by the Constitution is to be ascertained by a blind adherence to mere form in disregard of the substance of things. But the settled rule is directly to the contrary. Reasoning from analogy, the unsoundness of the proposition is demonstrated. Thus, in enforcing the clause of the Constitution forbidding a State from impairing the obligations of a contract, it is settled by the decisions of this court, although a State, for adequate consideration, may have executed a contract sanctioning the carrying on of a lottery for a stated term, no contract protected from impairment under the Constitution results, because, disregarding the mere form and looking at substance, a State may not, by the application of the contract clause of the Constitution, be shorn of an ever inherent authority to preserve the public morals by suppressing lotteries. *Stone* v. *Mississippi*, 101 U. S. 814; *Douglas* v. *Kentucky*, 168 U. S. 488. In other words, the doctrine is, that although a particular provision of the Constitution may seemingly be applicable, its controlling effect is limited by the essential nature of the powers of government reserved to the States when the Constitution was adopted. In view of the rule thus applied to the contract clause of the Constitution, we could not maintain the claim now made as to the effect of the due faith and credit clause, without saying that the States must, in the nature of things, always possess the power to legislate for the preservation of the morals of society, but that they need not have the continued authority to save society from destruction.

Resort to reasoning by analogy, however, is not required, since the principle which has been applied to the contract clause has been likewise enforced as to the due faith and credit clause.

In *Thompson* v. *Whitman,* (1874) 18 Wall. 457, the action in the court below was trespass for the conversion of a sloop, her tackle, furniture, etc., upon a seizure for an alleged violation of a statute of the State of New Jersey. By special plea in bar the defendant set up that the seizure was made within the limits of a named county in the State of New Jersey, and by answer to this plea the plaintiff took issue as to the place of seizure, thus challenging the jurisdiction of the justices who had tried the information and decreed the forfeiture and sale of the property. The precise point involved in the case, as presented in this court, was whether or not error had been committed by the trial court in receiving evidence to contradict the record of the New Jersey judgment as to jurisdictional facts asserted therein, and especially as to facts stated to have been passed upon by the court which had rendered the judgment. It was contended that to permit the jurisdictional facts, which were foreclosed by the judgment, to be reëxamined would be a violation of the due faith and credit clause of the Constitution. This court, however, decided to the contrary, saying:

"We think it clear that the jurisdiction of the court by which a judgment is rendered in any State may be questioned in a collateral proceeding in another State, notwithstanding the provision of the fourth article of the Constitution and the law of 1790, and notwithstanding the averments contained in the record of the judgment itself."

The ground upon which this conclusion was predicated is thus embodied in an excerpt made from the opinion delivered by Mr. Chief Justice Marshall, speaking for the court, in *Rose* v. *Himely,* 4 Cranch, 241, 269, where it was said:

"Upon principle, it would seem, that the operation of every judgment must depend on the power of the court to render that judgment; or, in other words, on its jurisdiction over the subject-matter which it has determined. In some cases, that jurisdiction, unquestionably, depends as well on the state of the thing, as on the constitution of the court. If, by any means whatever, a prize court should be induced, to condemn, as prize of war, a vessel which was never captured, it could not be contended that this condemnation operated a change of property. Upon principle, then, it would seem, that, to a certain extent, the capacity of the court to act upon the thing condemned, arising from its being within, or without their jurisdiction, as well as the constitution of the court, may be considered by that tribunal which is to decide on the effect of the sentence."

And the same principle, in a different aspect, was applied in *Wisconsin v. Pelican Insurance Co.*, (1888) 127 U. S. 265. In that case the State of Wisconsin had obtained a money judgment in its own courts against the Pelican Insurance Company, a Louisiana corporation. Availing itself of the original jurisdiction of this court, the State of Wisconsin brought in this court an action of debt upon the judgment in question. The answer of the defendant was to the effect that the judgment was not entitled to extra-territorial enforcement, because the claim upon which it was based was a penalty imposed upon the corporation for an alleged violation of the insurance laws of the State of Wisconsin. The answer having been demurred to, it was, of course, conceded that the claim which was merged in the judgment was such a penalty. This court, having concluded that ordinarily a penalty imposed by the laws of one State could have no extra-territorial operation, came then to consider whether, under the due faith and credit clause of the Constitution of the United States, a judgment rendered upon a penal statute was entitled to recognition outside of the State in which it had been rendered, because the character of the cause of action had been merged in the judgment as such. In declining to enforce the Wisconsin judgment and in deciding that, notwithstanding the judgment and the due faith and credit clause of the Constitution, the power existed to look back of the judgment and ascertain whether the claim which had entered into it was one susceptible of being enforced in another State, the court, speaking through Mr. Justice Gray, said (p. 291) :

"The application of the rule to the courts of the several States and of the United States is not affected by the provisions of the Constitution and of the act of Congress, by which the judgments of the courts of any State are to have such faith and

13

credit given to them in every court within the United States as they have by law or usage in the State in which they were ren- dered. Constitution, art. 4, sec. 1; act of May 26, 1790, chap. 11, 1 Stat. 122; Rev. Stat. § 905.

"Those provisions establish a rule of evidence, rather than of jurisdiction. While they make the record of a judgment, rendered after due notice in one State, conclusive evidence in the courts of another State, or of the United States, of the matter adjudged, they do not affect the jurisdiction, either of the court in which the judgment is rendered, or of the court in which it is offered in evidence. Judgments recovered in one State, of the Union, when proved in the courts of another government, whether state or national, within the United States, differ from judg- ments recovered in a foreign country in no other respect than in not being reëxaminable on their merits, nor impeachable for fraud in obtaining them, if rendered by a court having jurisdiction of the cause and of the parties. *Hanley v. Donoghue*, 116 U. S. 1, 4.

"In the words of Mr. Justice Story, cited and approved by Mr. Justice Bradley speaking for this court, 'The Constitution did not mean to confer any new power upon the States, but sim- ply to regulate the effect of their acknowledged jurisdiction over persons and things within their territory. It did not make the judgments of other States domestic judgments to all intents and purposes, but only gave a general validity, faith and credit to them as evidence. No execution can issue upon such judgments without a new suit in the tribunals of other States. And they enjoy not the right of priority or lien which they have in the State where they are pronounced, but that only which the *lex fori* gives to them by its own laws in their character of foreign judg- ments.' Story's Conflict of Laws, § 609; *Thompson v. Whitman*, 18 Wall. 457, 462, 463.

"A judgment recovered in one State, as was said by Mr. Jus- tice Wayne, delivering an earlier judgment of this court, 'does not carry with it, into another State, the efficacy of a judgment upon property or persons, to be enforced by execution. To give it the force of a judgment in another State, it must be made a judg- ment there; and can only be executed in the latter as its laws may permit.' *McElmoyle v. Cohen*, 13 Pet. 312, 325.

"The essential nature and real foundation of a cause of action are not changed by recovering judgment upon it; and the tech- nical rules, which regard the original claim as merged in the judgment, and the judgment as implying a promise by the defendant to pay it, do not preclude a court, to which a judgment is presented for affirmative action (while it cannot go behind the judgment for the purpose of examining into the validity of the claim), from ascertaining whether the claim is really one of such a nature that the court is authorized to enforce it."

2. When the principles which we have above demonstrated by reason and authority are applied to the question in hand, its solution is free from difficulty. As the State of Massachusetts had exclusive jurisdiction over its citizens concerning the marriage tie and its dissolution, and consequently the authority to prohibit them from perpetrating a fraud upon the law of their domicil by temporarily sojourning in another State, and there, without acquiring a *bona fide* domicil, procuring a decree of divorce, it follows that the South Dakota decree relied upon was rendered by a court without jurisdiction, and hence the due faith and credit clause of the Constitution of the United States did not require the enforcement of such decree in the State of Massachusetts against the public policy of that State as expressed in its statutes. Indeed, this application of the general principle is not open to dispute, since it has been directly sustained by decisions of this court. *Bell* v. *Bell*, 181 U. S. 175; *Streitwolf* v. *Streitwolf*, 181 U. S. 179. In each of these cases it was sought in one State to enforce a decree of divorce rendered in another State, and the authority of the due faith and credit clause of the Constitution was invoked for that purpose. It having been established in each case that at the time the divorce proceedings were commenced, the plaintiff in the proceedings had no *bona fide* domicil within the State where the decree of divorce was rendered, it was held, applying the principle announced in *Thompson* v. *Whitman*, 18 Wall. 457, *supra*, that the question of jurisdiction was open for consideration, and that as in any event domicil was essential to confer jurisdiction, the due faith and credit clause did not require recognition of such decree outside of the State in which it had been rendered. A like rule, by inverse reasoning, was also applied in the case of *Atherton* v. *Atherton*, 181 U. S. 155. There a decree of divorce was rendered in Kentucky in favor of a husband who had commenced proceedings in Kentucky against his wife, then a resident of the State of New York. The courts of the latter State having in substance refused to give effect to the Kentucky divorce, the question whether such refusal constituted a violation of the due faith and

credit clause of the Constitution was brought to this court for decision. It having been established that Kentucky was the domicil of the husband and had ever been the matrimonial domicil, and, therefore, that the courts of Kentucky had jurisdiction over the subject-matter, it was held that the due faith and credit clause of the Constitution of the United States imposed upon the courts of New York the duty of giving effect to the decree of divorce which had been rendered in Kentucky.

But it is said that the decrees of divorce which were under consideration in *Bell* v. *Bell* and *Streitwolf* v. *Streitwolf* were renderd in *ex parte* proceedings,ˈ the defendants having been summoned bv substituted service, and making no appearance; hence, the case now under consideration is taken out of the rule announced in those cases, since here the defendant appeared and consequently became subject to the jurisdiction of the court by which the decree of divorce was rendered. But this disregards the fact that the rulings in the cases referred to were predicated upon the proposition that jurisdiction over the subject-matter depended upon domicil, and without such domicil there was no authority to decree a divorce. This becomes apparent when it is considered that the cases referred to were directly rested upon the authority of *Thompson* v. *Whitman, supra,* where the jurisdiction was assailed, not because there was no power in the court to operate, by *ex parte* proceedings, on the *res*, if jurisdiction existed, but solely because the *res* was not at the time of its seizure within the territorial sway of the court, and hence was not a subject-matter over which the court could exercise jurisdiction by *ex parte* or other proceedings. And this view is emphasized bv a consideration of the ruling in *Wisconsin* v. *Pelican Insurance Company, supra,* where the judgment was one *inter partes*, and yet it was held that, in so far as the extra territorial effect of the judgment was concerned, the jurisdiction over the subject-matter of the State and its courts was open to inquiry, and if jurisdiction did not exist the enforcement of the judgment was not compelled by reason of the due faith and credit clause of the Constitution.

Indeed, the argument by which it is sought to take this case out of the rule laid down in the cases just referred to and which was applied to decrees of divorce in the *Bell* and *Streitwolf* cases practically invokes the overruling of those cases, and in effect, also, the overthrow of the decision of the *Atherton* case, since, in reason, it but insists that the rule announced in those cases should not be applied merely because of a distinction without a difference.

This is demonstrated as to *Thompson* v. *Whitman* and *Wisconsin* v. *Pelican Insurance Co.*, by the considerations already adverted to. It becomes clear, also, that such is the result of the argument as to *Bell* v. *Bell* and *Streitwolf* v. *Streitwolf*, when it is considered that in both those cases it was conceded, *arguendo*, that the power to decree the divorce in *ex parte* proceedings by substituted service would have obtained if there had been *bona fide* domicil. The rulings made in the case referred to hence rested not at all upon the fact that the proceedings were *ex parte*, but on the premise that there being no domicil there could be no jurisdiction. True it is, that in *Bell* v. *Bell* and *Streitwolf* v. *Streitwolf* the question was reserved whether jurisdiction to render a divorce having extra-territorial effect could be acquired by a mere domicil in the State of the party plaintiff, where there had been no matrimonial domicil in such State—a question also reserved here. But the fact that this question was reserved does not affect the issue now involved, since those cases proceeded, as does this, upon the hypothesis conceded, *arguendo*, that if there had been domicil there would have been jurisdiction, whether the proceedings were *ex parte* or not, and therefore the ruling on both cases was that at least domicil was in any event the inherent element upon which the jurisdiction must rest, whether the proceedings were *ex parte* or *inter partes*. And these conclusions are rendered certain when the decision in *Atherton* v. *Atherton* is taken into view, for there, although the proceeding was *ex parte*, as it was found that *bona fide* domicil, both personal and matrimonial, existed in Kentucky, jurisdiction over the subject-matter was held to obtain, and the duty to enforce the decree of divorce was consequently declared. Nor is there force in the suggestion that because in the case before us the wife appeared, hence the South Dakota court had jurisdiction to decree the divorce. The contention stated must rest on the premise that the authority of the court depended on the appearance of the parties and not on its jurisdiction over the subject-matter—that is, *bona fide* domicil, irrespective of the appearance of the parties. Here again the argument, if sustained, would involve the overruling of *Bell* v. *Bell* and *Streitwolf* v. *Streitwolf*. As in each of the cases jurisdiction was conferred, as far as it could be given, by the appearance of the plaintiff who brought the suit, it follows that the decision that

there was no jurisdiction because of the want of *bona fide* domicil
was a ruling that in its absence there could be no jurisdiction
over the subject-matter irrespective of the appearance of the
party by whom the suit was brought.   But it is obvious that the
inadequacy of the appearance or consent of one person to confer
jurisdiction over a subject-matter not resting on consent includes
necessarily the want of power of both parties to endow the court
with jurisdiction over a subject-matter, which appearance or
consent could not give.   Indeed, the argument but ignores the
nature of the marriage contract and the legislative control over its
dissolution which was pointed out at the outset.   The principle
dominating the subject is that the marriage relation is so interwoven with public policy that the consent of the parties is impotent to dissolve it contrary to the law of the domicil.   The
proposition relied upon, if maintained, would involve this contradiction in terms: that marriage may not be dissolved by the
consent of the parties, but that they can, by their consent, accomplish the dissolution of the marriage tie by appearing in a court
foreign to their domicil and wholly wanting in jurisdiction, and
may subsequently compel the courts of the domicil to give effect
to such judgment despite the prohibitions of the law of the
domicil and the rule of public policy by which it is enforced.

Although it is not essential to the question before us, which
calls upon us only to determine whether the decree of divorce
rendered in South Dakota was entitled to extra-territorial effect,
we observe, in passing, that the statute of South Dakota made
domicil, and not mere residence, the basis of divorce proceedings in that State.   As without reference to the statute of South
Dakota and in any event domicil in that State was essential to
give jurisdiction to the courts of such State to render a decree of
divorce which would have extra-territorial effect, and as the
appearance of one or both of the parties to a divorce proceeding could not suffice to confer jurisdiction over the subject-matter where it was wanting because of the absence of domicil
within the State, we conclude that no violation of the due faith
and credit clause of the Constitution of the United States arose
from the action of the Supreme Judicial Court of Massachusetts
in obeying the command of the state statute and refusing to give
effect to the decree of divorce in question.

Affirmed.

MR. JUSTICE BREWER, MR. JUSTICE SHIRAS and MR. JUSTICE
PECKHAM dissent.

MR. JUSTICE HOLMES, not being a member of the court when the case was argued, takes no part.[14]

"**Law Applied to Divorce Proceedings.**—Whether or not a particular act or omission is a ground for divorce depends upon the law of the forum. The law of the forum is the law of the place where the party is domiciled at the time of divorce proceedings. *Hunt v. Hunt, 72 N. Y. 217, 28 Am. Rep. 129; Colburn v. Colburn, 70 Mich. 647, 38 N. W. 607.* See *Minor Conflict of Laws, 183.* A divorce is granted only for a cause recognized by the law of the forum. *Dorsey v. Dorsey, 7 Watts 349, 32 Am. Dec. 767.* See *Succession of Benton, 59 L. R. A. 135,* and notes.

It is well established that the mere fact that the marital offense did not occur at the forum does not defeat jurisdiction. The state has the power to determine for what causes divorce will be granted, and in this way the court may or may not grant a divorce for an offense that occurred in another state or country. *Cheever v. Wilson, 9 Wall. 108, 19 L. Ed. 604; Cheely v. Clayton, 110 U. S. 701, 28 L. Ed. 298; Thompson v. State, 28 Ala. 12; Shaw v. Shaw, 98 Mass. 158; Ditson v. Ditson, 4 R. I. 87; Dunham v. Dunham, 162 Ill. 589, 35 L. R. A. 70.*

Domicil of the Parties.—To give the court jurisdiction to grant divorce, at least one of the parties must be domiciled within the state. *De Meli v. De Meli, 120 N. Y. 485, 24 N. E. 996; Watkins v. Watkins, 135 Mass. 83; Colburn v. Colburn, 70 Mich. 647; Van Fossen v. State, 37 Ohio St. 317; 41 Am. Rep. 507.*

By the weight of authority, whenever it is proper or necessary, a wife may acquire a separate domicil for the purposes of a suit by her for divorce. *Cheever v. Wilson, 9 Wall. 108, 19 L. Ed. 604; Chapman v. Chapman, 129 Ill. 386, 21 N. E. 806; Dunham v. Dunham, 162 Ill. 589, 35 L. R. A. 70; Ditson v. Ditson, 4 R. I. 87; Hill v. Hill, 166 Ill. 54, 46 N. E. 751.*

According to international law, the domicil for the time being of the married pair affords the only true test of jurisdiction to dissolve their marriage. *Le Mesurier v. Le Mesurier, —— Appeal Cases 517.* (1895). But to grant a qualified divorce, the court may take jurisdiction though the husband is domiciled in another country. *Armytage v. Armytage, Probate 178.* (1898).

A divorce granted to parties not domiciled within the state is not entitled to extra-territorial recognition, and as to other states, the decree is a nullity, and the divorced persons who marry again may be prosecuted for polygamy. *State v. Armington, 25 Minn. 29.*

The jurisdiction of the court to grant divorce is not affected by—(1) the residence of the parties, or (2) the allegiance of the parties, or (3) the domicil of the parties at the time of the marriage, or (4) the place of the marriage, or (5) the place where the offence in respect of which divorce is sought, is committed. *Dicey Conflict of Laws, P. 269. Franklin v. Franklin, 154 Mass. 515, 28 N. E. 681; Firth v. Firth, 50 N. J. Eq. 137; Ditson v. Ditson, 4 R. I. 87; Jones v. Jones, 67 Miss. 195; Succession of Benton, 106 La. 494, 59 L. R. A. 135, and notes.*

Service of Process Upon Defendant.—Where the defendant is absent from the state, the statutes of most of the states provide for extra-territorial service, either actual or constructive. *Cheely v. Clayton, 110 U. S. 701; Ditson v. Ditson, 4 R. I. 87; Prettyman v. Prettyman, 125 Ind. 149, 25 N. E. 179;* Some states have refused to recognize divorces granted where only one of the parties was before the court. *People v. Baker, 76 N. Y. 78; Atherton v. Atherton, 155 N. Y. 129, 49 N. E. 933; Harris v.*

Harris, 115 N. C. 587, 20 S. E. 187; Doerr v. Forsythe, 50 Ohio St. 726, 35 N. E. 1055; Dunham v. Dunham, 162 Ill. 589, 44 N. E. 841; Cummington v. Belchertown, 149 Mass. 223.

If the defendant is a non-resident, and has not been served with process within the state, and has not appeared, the decree must be confined to a severance of the marrital relation, and the court cannot decree alimony, nor decree custody of children if the children are beyond the jurisdiction of the state, nor impose upon the defendant a disability to marry again. *Cooper v. Reynolds, 10 Wall. 308; Garner v. Garner, 56 Mo. 127; De La Montanya v. De La Montanya, 112 Cal. 101, 32 L. R. A. 82; Rodgers v. Rodgers, 56 Kan. 483, 43 Pac. Rep. 779; Dow v. Blake, 148 Ill. 76, 35 N. E. 761; Bullock v. Bullock, 51 N. J. Eq. 444, 27 Atl. 435; Thurston v. Thurston, 58 Minn. 279, 59 N. W. 1017; Kline v. Kline, 57 Iowa 386, 10 N. W. 825.*

BANKRUPTCY.

IN RE WAITE, 1885.

[99 N. Y. 433.]

1. Title of Foreign Assignees in Bankruptcy.
2. Extra-territorial Effect of Bankrupt and Insolvent Laws.
3. Involuntary Assignments in Bankruptcy.
4. Voluntary Assignments in Bankruptcy.
5. Rights of Creditors.
6. Administration in Bankruptcy.

EARL, J. On the 15th day of October, 1881, Haynes & Sanger, a firm doing business in the city of New York, having become insolvent, made a general assignment, for the benefit of their creditors, to Charles Waite, who was a member of the firm of Pendle & Waite, and in their assignment preferred that firm as creditors for a large amount. Pendle & Waite did business in New York and London, Waite being a citizen of this country residing in the city of New York and having charge of the business of his firm there, and Pendle being a citizen of England and having charge of the firm business there. That firm became insolvent and suspended business in England in February, 1882, and Waite then went to England, and there he and Pendle filed a petition in the London Court of Bankruptcy, in which they recited their inability to pay their debts in full, and that they were "desirous of instituting proceedings for the liquidation of their affairs by arrangement or composition with their creditors, and hereby submit to the jurisdiction of this court in the matter of such proceeding." Waite signed the petition in person, and through his counsel at once secured the appointment of Schofield as receiver, in bankruptcy, of the firm property.

Liquidation by arrangement or composition is a proceeding under the English Bankruptcy Act which provides that the filing of such a petition is an act of bankruptcy; that a compromise proposition may be made by a debtor, and that if such proposition shall be accepted by the creditors at a general meeting, and then confirmed at a second general meeting, and registered by the court, it becomes binding and may be carried out under the supervision of the court; that if it appears to the court on satisfactory evidence that a composition cannot in consequence of legal difficulties, or for any other sufficient cause, proceed without injustice or undue delay to the creditors, or the debtor, the court may adjudge the debtor a bankrupt and proceedings may be had accordingly, and that the title of the trustee in bankruptcy, when appointed, relates back to the time of the commission of the act of bankruptcy.

For reasons which it is unnecessary now to consider or relate, the composition failed, and then upon the application of creditors, which was opposed by Waite, Pendle & Waite were adjudged bankrupts, and Schofield was appointed trustee of the firm property. By the English law, the due appointment of a trustee in bankruptcy, under the English Bankruptcy Act, transfers to the trustee all the personal property of the bankrupt wherever situated, whether in Great Britain or elsewhere.

Notwithstanding his bankruptcy, Waite continued to act as assignee of Haynes & Sanger and converted the assets of that firm into money, and under the preference given to his firm paid himself for the firm of Pendle & Waite the sum of $14,333.70 He paid no portion of that sum to Pendle or to the creditors of his firm, the American creditors of such firm having been fully paid from other assets of the firm.

After all this, Waite filed his petition in the Court of Common Pleas of the city of New York for a settlement of his accounts as assignee, and citations were issued, served and published for that purpose, and a referee was appointed to take and state his accounts. In his accounts he entered and claimed a credit for the sum paid to himself as above stated. Schofield, through his attorney, appeared upon the accounting and as trustee objected to the credit and claimed that sum should be paid to him. The referee ruled that the law of this State does not recognize the validity of foreign bankruptcy proceedings to transfer title to property of the bankrupt situated here, and for that reason held that the payment by Waite, as assignee, to himself as a member of the firm of Pendel & Waite, was valid, and that he was entitled to the credit claimed. The same view of the law was taken at the Special and General Terms of the Common Pleas, and then Schofield appealed to this court.

We have stated the facts as found by the referee, and as the respondent did not and could not except to the findings, and is therefore in no condition to complain of them, we must assume that they were based upon sufficient evidence.

The transfer of the property of Pendle & Waite to Schofield as trustee was *in invitum,* solely by operation of the English Bankrupt Law. While the proceeding first instituted by the bankrupts to arrange a composition with their creditors was voluntary, the final proceeding through which the adjudication in bankruptcy was had, and the trustee appointed was adversary and against their will, having no basis of voluntary consent to rest on. (*Willitts* v. *Waite,* 25 N. Y. 577.)

If the transfer effected by the bankruptcy proceedings is to have the same effect here as in England, then the title to the money due to the bankrupts from Haynes & Sanger was vested in the trustee. Schofield was appointed receiver of the property of the bankrupts in March, 1882, and then the title passed out of them. That title continued in him as receiver until he was appointed trustee. After he was appointed receiver and before or after he was appointed trustee (which does not appear), Waite as assignee paid himself as a member of the firm of Pendle & Waite the sum of money in controversy. He had notice of the bankruptcy proceedings and knew that the title to the money due from Haynes & Sanger and from himself as their assignee had passed out of the bankrupts to Schofield, and hence he had no right to make payment to them. Schofield became substituted in their place, and Waite was bound to make payment to him, and cannot, therefore, have credit for a payment wrongfully made. And Schofield, standing in the place of the original creditors of Haynes & Sanger, had the right to appear upon the accounting and object to the erroneous payment made in disregard of his rights. But the alleged payment was merely formal, not real. Waite, the assignee, still has the money and is accountable for it to the proper party. It is not perceived how it can be claimed that Schofield was bound at any time before the accounting to make any demand upon the assignee. He was a creditor holding the claim originally due to Pendle & Waite, and as such he could appear upon the accounting, with all the rights of any other creditor, to protect his interests, and he could not be prejudiced by a payment alleged to have been made by the assignee to himself. All this is upon the assumption that the transfer to Schofield as trustee is to have the same force and effect here as against the bankrupts as in England; and whether it must have, is the important and interesting question to be determined upon this appeal.

It matters not that Waite was a citizen of this country, domiciled here. He went to England and invoked and submitted to the jurisdiction of the Bankruptcy Court there and is bound by its adjudication to the same extent as if he had been domiciled there. The adjudication estopped him just as every party is estopped by the adjudication of a court which has jurisdiction of his person and of the subject-matter.

We have not a case here where there is a conflict between the foreign trustee and domestic creditors. So far as appears, no injustice whatever will be done to any of our own citizens, or to any one else, by allowing the transfer to have full effect here. Indeed justice seems to require that this money should be paid to the foreign trustee for distribution among the foreign creditor of the bankrupts.

The effect to be given in any country to statutory *in invitum* transfers of property through bankruptcy proceedings in a foreign country has been a subject of much discussion among publicists and judges, and unanimity of opinion has not and probably never will be reached. We shall not enter much into the discussion of the subject and thus travel over ground so much marked by the foot-steps of learned jurists. Our main endeavor will be to ascertain what, by the decisions of the courts of this State, has become the law here.

In *Bird* v. *Caritat* (2 Johns. 342), it was held that a suit could be brought in this State in the name of a foreign bankrupt by his assignees for their benefit as such, the name of the bankrupt being used, because by the common-law rule, now abrogated, a *chose in action* was not assignable so as to entitle the assignee to sue thereon in his own name. In writing the opinion Chancellor KENT, then chief justice, said: "The demurrer to the second plea raises the question whether the assignees under a commission of bankruptcy sued out in England can maintain a suit at law here in their own names. This is more a question concerning form than substance, for there can be no doubt of the right of the assignees to collect the debts due to the

bankrupt either by a suit directly in their own names or as trustees
using the name of the bankrupt.   It is a principle of general practice among nations to admit and give effect to the title of foreign
assignees.   This is done on the ground that the conveyance under
the bankrupt laws of the country where the owner is domiciled
is equivalent to a voluntary conveyance by the bankrupt."   In
Raymond v. Johnson (11 Johns. 488), it was held that although
the court will recognize and protect the right of an assignee under
the insolvent law of another State, yet an action brought in this
State must be in the name of the insolvent.   In *Holmes* v. *Remsen*
(4 Johns. Ch. 460), Chancellor KENT wrote an elaborate opinion
holding that foreign assignees in bankruptcy took title to all the
property of the bankrupt, wherever situated, with the same force
and effect as if the bankrupt had made a voluntary assignment
of his property, and that such a title was good even against subsequent attaching creditors in a country other than that where
the bankruptcy adjudication was had and the statutory transfer
was made, and he said: "It is admitted in every case that foreign assignees duly appointed under foreign ordinances are
entitled as such to sue for debts due to the bankrupt's estate."
In *Holmes* v. *Remsen* (20 Johns. 229), the suit was between the
same parties and involved the same questions, and the effect of
the foreign bankruptcy proceeding was again elaborately considered by PLATT, J., and he gave expression to views in reference
thereto differing from those of Chancellor KENT which have
been followed in most of the subsequent cases in this State upon
the same subject.   He held that a statutory assignment of a
debtor's property under the laws of a foreign country is not
equivalent to a voluntary assignment by the debtor, and that
such an assignment will not hold good here to the prejudice of
the rights of domestic creditors pursuing their remedy by attachment under our laws.   But he admitted that foreign assignees
appointed in bankruptcy proceedings could by the rules of international courtesy and comity come here and institute suits in our
courts to recover the property of the bankrupt when the interest
of creditors pursuing their remedy under the local laws were
not brought in question or prejudiced.   He adopted in substance
the views of Mr. Caines, the learned lawyer who, arguing for
the attaching creditors in both cases between the same parties,
said: "We admit that the bankrupt assignment passes all the
property of the bankrupt, here and everywhere, provided always
that there are no creditors here having claims on that property.

We admit the right of the assignees of the bankrupt to collect his property here and take it to England, if there are no creditors of the bankrupt here; but not otherwise. If there are creditors attaching here there is a *conflictus legum* and the foreign law must yield." The other judges declined to express any opinion upon the questions mainly considered by Judge PLATT, but concurred with him upon a minor point not involved here, and upon that point the case was decided. In *Plestoro* v. *Abraham* (1 Paige, 236), the facts were these: Abraham, a British subject domiciled in England, in July, 1828, left that country for the United States, bringing with him certain personal property, and arrived in New York about the 1st of September when the goods were deposited in the public store under the charge of the defendant Thompson as collector of the port Shortly after Abraham left England a commission in bankruptcy was taken out against him there by virtue of which he was duly declared a bankrupt; and on the 8th day of August, Johnson, one of the complainants, was appointed by the commissioners provisional assignee. On the 24th day of September, 1828, the complainants, the provisional assignee and the creditors of Abraham, all of whom were British subjects and residents of England, filed their bill and obtained an injunction restraining the collector from delivering the goods to Abraham, and restraining the latter from receiving or prosecuting for the same. Abraham put in his answer neither admitting nor denying the proceedings under the commission, but alleging that he left England in the lawful pursuit of his business with a *bona fide* intention of returning, and denying that he was insolvent or had committed any act of bankruptcy. Chancellor WALWORTH denied a motion to dissolve the injunction, and held that the assignee could have maintained the action alone without joining the creditors; and in his opinion, referring to the decision of Chancellor KENT in *Holmes* v. *Remsen,* he said that it was "doubtful whether that decision to its full extent can be sustained," that "it was strongly questioned and ably opposed by PLATT, J.," in the subsequent case between the same parties, and that it stood opposed to the opinions of the State courts in various cases cited; but he held that the case before him steered clear of all the decisions cited, because in those cases the contest was between foreign assignors and domestic creditors, claiming under the laws of the country where the property was situated, and the suits were brought, while in that case the controversy was between the bankrupt and his assignee and creditors,

all residing in the country under whose laws the assignment was
made, and the property itself, at the time of the assignment, was
constructively within the jurisdiction of that country, being on
the high seas in the actual possession of a British subject. That
case was taken by appeal to the Court of Errors (3 Wend. 538),
where the order of the chancellor was reversed. It is claimed
by the counsel for the respondent and was so held by the court
below in this case, that the Court of Errors held in that case
that the statutory assignment in England was wholly inoperative
here, and that the foreign assignee, therefore, was not vested
with the title to the property here even as against the bankrupt.
We are of opinion that it was not so held, and that the point was
left undecided by that case. MARCY, J., writing an opinion for
affirmance in which SUTHERLAND, J., concurred, expressed views
similar to those announced by PLATT, J., in *Holmes* v. *Remsen,*
and held that the foreign assignee could sue in our courts, and
that his title to the property was good as against the bankrupt.
Senator ALLEN, writing an opinion, held that the order should
be reversed on the ground that an injunction was not the proper
remedy, and we cannot discover that he intimated any opinion as
to the important question discussed by MARCY, J., and in *Holmes*
v. *Remsen* by Chancellor KENT and PLATT, J.; and no definite
views upon the same question were expressed by Senator MAY-
NARD in the opinion read by him. He said: "The cases, therefore, in which it has been held that an assignment did not transfer
the property of a bankrupt in a foreign country appear to me not
applicable to the case now under consideration." And further:
"If the assignment in this case did operate a transfer of the
property in question, what need is there of the aid of a Court of
Chancery to enable the assignee to obtain possession of it? If
by virtue of the assignment the assignee acquired a *legal title* to
the property, the courts of law are abundantly competent to afford
equitable relief." Senator OLIVER, also writing for reversal, said:
"The question is not whether a foreign assignee shall be permitted to sue in our courts; in relation to that there can be but
one opinion. Had the proceedings in bankruptcy in this case
been perfected the bankrupt asquiescing in their justice and
propriety, and the assignee substituted in his place, and a question
had arisen between him and a debtor of the estate, no one would
have doubted or questioned the right of the assignee to sue in
our courts." But he held that the title of the foreign assignee
was not good here as against the bankrupt himself unless he

chose to acquiesce in it, and he also reached the conclusion that even if the title of the assignee were good here, an injunction was not a proper remedy. Senator STEBBINS writing for reversal held that the statutory transfer in England could have no operation here, and that, therefore, the foreign assignee did not have title to the property, and that even if he did have title an injunction was not the proper remedy. Senator THROOP wrote for affirmance holding that the title of the foreign assignee was good as against the bankrupt, and that an injunction was a proper remedy. No other opinions were written. Justices MARCY and SUTHERLAND and Senators THROOP and WOODWARD voted for affirmance, and seventeen senators for reversal. It does not appear, and cannot be ascertained upon what ground the fourteen senators who voted for reversal, writing no opinions, based their votes. Some may have concurred in the result upon one ground and some upon another. The most obvious ground, in which all who voted for reversal seemed to concur, was that an injunction was not a proper remedy. That case has been much criticized by judges and text-writers, and the impossibility of determining what was adjudicated by it has frequently been recognized. In *Johnson* v. *Hunt* (23 Wend. 87), one Hollis and Johnson and Miller were residents of Chenango county in this State. Hollis absconded, and a warrant of attachment was issued against him as an absconding debtor. After notice of the attachment had been published Johnson and Miller, being creditors of Hollis, having separate demands against him, went in pursuit of and overtook him in Pennsylvania, where they respectively obtained process, from a justice's court and recovered judgments against him, on which executions were issued, by virtue of which he was arrested and taken into custody. To obtain his liberty he paid Johnson the amount of his judgment and turned out certain personal property to Miller in satisfaction of his judgment. The property thus turned out belonged to Hollis in Chenango county when he absconded, and it was brought back into that county where it was demanded of him by the plaintiffs in that action, who had been appointed trustees of the estate of Hollis. The demand not having been complied with, the action was commenced to recover the value of the property. Upon the trial of the action the court charged the jury that if the property was removed from this State, and the defendants knew that Hollis was an absconding debtor at the time when they received it from him in Pennsylvania, he and they being citizens of this State, and the property being received after the publication of the notice of the issuing of the attachment, they were liable for it, whether it was removed from this State before or after publication of the notice, and that the legal proceedings had in Pennsylvania were no protection to the defendants. The jury found a verdict for the plaintiffs, and the defendants took the case by writ of error to the Supreme Court, where the judgment was reversed, COWEN, J., writing the opinion. He held that the act under which the attachment against Hollis was issued was in the nature of a bankrupt law, and that the assignment of Hollis' property to trustees was *in invitum*, and therefore inoperative outside of this State; and he claimed that it was decided in the case of *Abraham* v. *Plestoro* that an assignment *in invitum* under the law of one State or nation has no operation in another, even with respect to its own citizens; that the bankrupt, a subject of the very country under whose laws he was proceeded against, may, on crossing the territorial limits of such country, dispose of the property which he has brought with him, and may withhold it entirely from the creditors who are proceeding against him in the foreign jurisdiction. We think we have already shown, that, at least, it cannot be known that such was the decision in *Abraham* v. *Plestoro*. As neither he nor either of his associates was a member of the court which rendered that decision, he had no better means of knowing what was decided thereby than we have, and we cannot concur in his views in reference thereto. But we are left by his opinion at a loss to determine whether he meant to deny all force and effect to the title of statutory trustees or assignees appointed in a foreign country, or merely as against creditors pursuing their debtor for the collection of their debts. From the fact that he cited, as authorities, Kent's Commentaries and Story on the Conflict of Laws, and from certain expressions and qualifications contained in his opinion we are inclined to think that he did not mean to lay down an unqualified and universal rule that an *in invitum* title under bankruptcy proceedings in one country can have no force and operation whatever in another country. It was not necessary for the decision of that case to lay down such a rule, as the defendants there simply did what was lawful in the State of Pennsylvania, under its laws, to procure payment of their debts. The point decided is properly stated in the head-note as follows: "The property of an absconding debtor taken by him from this State and transferred by him in another State in satisfaction of a judgment there rendered against him was not subject to the control of the trustees of his estate after the property was brought back to this State, although he and the creditor to whom the transfer was made were at the time residents of this State, and the transfer was made after the publication of the notice that an attachment had issued." The question we are now considering, therefore, still remained undecided, and again came under elaborate discussion in *Hoyt* v. *Thompson* (5 N. Y. 320), where effect was given in this State to the title of an assignee from statutory trustees appointed in another State, and Judges RUGGLES and PAIGE approved the rules of law announced by PLATT, J., in *Holmes* v. *Remsen*. RUGGLES, J., said that until the decision of *Abraham* v. *Plestoro*, "it had been uniformly held in this State, that in virtue of comity, the assignees of a foreign bankrupt were entitled to sue for, and recover debts due to the bankrupt within this State, except where the claim of the assignee came in conflict with creditors in this State claiming under attachments against the bankrupt's property, "and that it is a mistake to suppose that that case established in its strictest sense, and without qualification, the doctrine that a foreign assignment in bankruptcy is absolutely inoperative and void in this State, and that it was impossible to say that that case was decided on grounds affecting the question we are now considering, and he dissented from the decision in *Johnson* v. *Hunt* so far as it was founded upon a different view of the case of *Abraham* v. *Plestoro*. Judge PAIGE, while expressing some views seemingly in accordance with those expressed by Judge COWEN in *Johnson* v. *Hunt*, yet said: "Where neither the rights of domestic creditors or of foreign creditors proceeding against the property under our laws are involved, the foreign assignees may be permitted to sue in our courts for the benefit of all the creditors on principles of national comity without a surrender of the principle that a foreign statutory assignment does not operate a transfer of the property in this State. Allowing foreign assignees to sue in our courts when neither the rights of our own creditors, nor the rights of foreign citizens pursuing the remedies afforded by our laws will be prejudiced, may be regarded as a mere manifestation of respect for a foreign nation accorded upon principles of national courtesy, and not as a concession that the assignment under which the assignees claim has under our laws any force or validity in this State." But the question as to the effect in this State of a foreign statutory assignment and the rights of the assignee here was again left undecided, the judges who did not write expressing no opinion in reference thereto. A motion for a reargument was made in that case (19 N. Y. 207), and upon that motion, Comstock, J., wrote an opinion in which he said that "the comity which is due to a sister State may require that the assignee of an insolvent person or corporation in that State should be allowed to sue a debtor here; but neither justice nor comity demands that the foreign law should be recognized to the extent of divesting the titles of our own citizens fairly acquired." In *Willitts* v. *Waite* (25 N. Y. 577), it was held that statutory receivers appointed in Ohio could not enforce their title to the property of the insolvent in this State against creditors subsequently attaching it here, under our laws. In that case, while Sutherland, J., was of opinion that from comity the courts of this State should recognize and allow some effect to a foreign involuntary bankrupt proceeding, yet he erroneously said that he understood that a title under such proceedings "would not be recognized by the courts of this State, even when the question arises entirely between the bankrupt and his assignees and creditors all residing in the country under whose laws the assignment was made." Allen, J., writing in the same case, said: "A *quasi* effect may be given to the law (of a foreign State) as a matter of comity, and interstate or international courtesy, when the rights of creditors or *bona fide* purchasers, or the interests of the State do not interfere, by allowing the foreign statutory or legal transferee to sue for it in the courts of the State in which the property is;" and that "the State will do justice to its own citizens so far as it can be done by administering upon property within its jurisdiction, and will yield to comity in giving effect to foreign statutory assignments, only so far as may be done without impairing the remedies or lessening the securities which our laws have provided for our citizens." The rule, as stated by Judges Platt, Ruggles, Allen, and other eminent jurists, whose opinions we have quoted, were also fully recognized in the following cases: (*Petersen* v. *Chemical Bk.*, 32 N. Y. 21; *Kelly* v. *Crapo*, 45 id. 86; *Osgood* v. *Maguire*, 61 id. 524; *Hibernia Bk.* v. *Lacombc*, 84 id. 367; *Matter of Bristol*, 16 Abb. Pr. 184; *Runk* v. *St. John*, 29 Barb. 585; *Barclay* v. *Quicksilver Mining Co.*, 6 Lans. 25; *Hooper* v. *Tuckerman*, 3 Sandf. 311; *Olyphant* v. *Atwood*, 4 Bosw. 459; *Hunt* v. *Jackson*, 5 Blatchf. 349.)

From all these cases the following rules are to be deemed thoroughly recognized and established in this State: (1) The statutes of foreign States can in no case have any force or effect in this State *ex proprio vigore,* and hence the statutory title of foreign assignees in bankruptcy can have no recognition here solely by virtue of the foreign statute. (2) But the comity of nations which Judge DENIO in *Petersen* v. *Chemical Bank (supra)* said is a part of the common law, allows a certain effect here to titles derived under, and powers created by the laws of other countries, and from such comity the titles of foreign statutory assignees are recognized and enforced here, when they can be, without injustice to our own citizens, and without prejudice to the rights of creditors pursuing their remedies here under our statutes; provided also, that such titles are not in conflict with the laws or the public policy of our State. (3) Such foreign assignees can appear and, subject to the conditions above mentioned, maintain suits in our courts against debtors of the bankrupt whom they represent, and against others who have interfered with, or withhold the property of the bankrupt.

If it be admitted, as it must be under the authorities cited, that Schofield can, as assignee of Pendle & Waite, have a standing in our courts and that his title will be so far recognized here that he can sue the debtors of that firm to recover the amount owing to the firm, why may he not sue the bankrupts? If the assignee could sue Haynes & Sanger to recover what they owed the bankrupts, why can he not be permitted to sue the bankrupts for money or property placed in their hands to pay the debt? If he could sue Haynes & Sanger, why could he not sue their assignee, although a member of the bankrupt firm, to recover the money placed in his hands to pay their debt? No principle of justice, no public policy requires the courts of this State to ignore the title of this assignee at the instance of one of the bankrupts. No injustice will be done to Waite if this money be taken to pay his creditors, and public policy does not require that the courts of this State should protect him in his efforts either to cheat his creditors or his partner. If it be conceded, as it must be, that the title of a foreign statutory assignee is good in this State for any purpose against anybody, it seems to us that it ought to be held good against the bankrupt against whom an adjudication in bankruptcy has been pronounced which is binding upon him.

Before such an adjudication can be held to be efficacious in a foreign country to transfer title to property, the bankrupt court must have had jurisdiction of the bankrupt either because made in the country of his domicile or because he, although domiciled elsewhere, submitted to the jurisdiction or in some other way came under the jurisdiction of the bankrupt court. Here Pendle & Waite did most of their business in England. Most of their assets and of their creditors were there, and while Pendle alone was domiciled there, Waite went there and submitted to the jurisdiction of the Bankrupt Court and exposed himself to the operation of the English law. He is therefore bound by the adjudication of the court as he would have been if domiciled there, and the judgment had been in a common-law court upon any personal cause of action.

The decisions in the Federal courts, and in most of the other States, are in harmony with the views we have expressed; and so are the doctrines of all the great jurists who have written upon the subject of private international law. (2 Bell's Comm. 681, 687; Wheaton's Int. L. [8th ed., by Dana], §§ 89, 90, 91, 144 and note; 2 Kent's Comm. 405; Wharton's Confl. of Laws, §§ 353, 368, 391, 735, 736; Story's Confl. of Laws, §§ 403, 410, 412, 414, 420, 421.)

There are but two cases in this State which really hold any thing in conflict with these views, and they are *Mosselman v. Caen,* (34 Barb. 66; N. Y. Sup. Ct. [4 T. & C.] 171). In the first case the action was by foreign trustees, appointed in bankruptcy proceedings, to recover goods in the possession of the defendant in this country, and the plaintiffs recovered. The defendant appealed, and sought to reverse the judgment, upon the ground that the plaintiffs did not, as trustees, have any title to the property. The judgment was affirmed, on the ground that the defendant did not raise the question of title at the trial. But the judges writing were of opinion that the plaintiffs did not have any title to the bankrupt's property located here, and one of them (SUTHERLAND, J.) stated that the case of *Abraham v. Plestoro* (3 Wend. 538), confirmed by *Johnson v. Hunt,* "would seem to be conclusive upon the question, whether our courts will recognize or enforce a right or title acquired under a foreign bankrupt law or foreign bankruptcy judicial proceedings. The case of *Abraham v. Plestoro* was certainly very broad in its repudiation of foreign bankruptcy proceedings, and went much further than the case of *Holmes v. Remsen* (20 Johns. 229); but I think it must be deemed conclusive authority for saying, that had the defendant raised the question by demurrer, or on the trial, it must have been held that the plaintiffs could not maintain this action." In the second case DAVIS, P. J., writing the opinion of the court, said: "It seems to be the settled law of this State that our courts will not recognize or enforce a right or title acquired under a foreign bankrupt law, or foreign bankrupt proceedings, so far as affects property within their jurisdiction, or demands against residents of the State." These two cases are unsupported by authority, and are, we think, opposed to sound principles, and are in conflict with the current of authority in this State.

We are, therefore, of opinion that Schofield was competent to appear upon the accounting to protect the interests of the bankrupt estate which he represented, and that, upon the facts as they appear in this record, his objection to the allowance of the payment made by the assignee to himself ought to have prevailed, and that he should be recognized as a creditor for the amount of such payment.

It follows that the orders of the General and Special Terms should be reversed, and, as the facts may be varied or more fully presented upon a new hearing, the matter should be remitted to the Special Term for further proceedings upon the same or new evidence, in accordance with the rules of law herein laid down, and that the appellant should recover from the respondent costs of the appeals to the General Term and to this court.

All concur.

Ordered accordingly.[15]

---

[15]The English Court of Bankruptcy has no jurisdiction to make an adjudication of bankruptcy against a foreigner, domiciled and resident abroad, who has never been in England, even though he is a member of an English firm which has traded and contracted debts in England. *Exparte Blain 12 Chan. Div. 522 (1879).* Bankruptcy is a very serious matter. It alters the status of the bankrupt. This cannot be overlooked or forgotten when we are dealing with foreigners, who are not subject to our jurisdiction. *In re A. B. & Co., 1 Q. B. 541; In re Pearson, 2 Q. B. 263.*

It is the settled law of England that an assignment under the bankrupt law of a foreign country passes all the personal property of the bankrupt situate, and all debts owing in England, and that the attachment of such property by an English creditor, after bankruptcy, with or without notice to him, is invalid to overreach the assignment. And the same doctrine holds there under English assignment as to personal property and debts of the bankrupt in foreign countries. The same doctrine obtains in France and Holland, *Armani v. Castrique, 13 M. & W. 443; Story Conflict of Laws, Sections 409, 417.* But the ubiquity of the operation of assignments under foreign bankrupt laws has always been denied in this country, and such assignments are not permitted to prevail against a subsequent attachment of the bankrupt's effects found here. The Law of Germany is the same. *Whart. Conf. Laws, Sec. 844; McDougall v. Page, 55 Vt. 187.*

There is no doubt that a debt or liability arising in any country may be discharged by the laws of that country; and that such a discharge, if it releases the debt or liability, and does not merely interfere with the remedy, or course of procedure to enforce it, will be an effectual answer to the claim, not only in the courts of that country, but in every other country. This is the law of England, and is a principle of private international law adopted in other countries. *Peck v. Hibbard, 26 Vt. 698; Story Conflict of Laws, Sections 335, 338; Ellis v. McHenry, L. R. 6, C. P. 228.*

A discharge in insolvency by a court of insolvency having jurisdiction of the debtor and creditor, will bar a suit in any other jurisdiction to recover a debt that was provable in the insolvency court. *Bank v. Hall, 86 Me. 107* (1893).

As a general proposition, it is also true that a discharge under a foreign bankrupt law is no bar to an action in the courts of another country on a contract made and to be performed there. *McMillan v. McNeill, 4 Wheat. 209; Smith v. Buchanan, 1 East 6.* A debt contracted by a resident of Vermont to a resident of Canada, and payable in Canada, is not barred by a discharge under the United States Bankrupt Act, where the creditor was not a party to and had no personal notice of the proceedings. *McDaugall v. Page, 55 Vt. 187, 45 Am. Rep. 602.*

The English courts hold that a commission in bankruptcy passes the title to personal property of the bankrupt wherever it is situated. *Batcheller v. National Bank, 157 Mass. 33.* The court of the domicil has the right to pronounce a universally valid judgment with regard to the personal property of the bankrupt. *In re Artola Hermanos, 24 Queen's Bench Div. 640* (1890).

Bankrupt laws in the United States do not operate extra-territorially. *Guillander v. Howell, 35 N. Y. 657; Bank v. Hall, 86 Me. 107.* Involuntary transfers of property, such as work by operation of law, as foreign bankrupt and insolvent laws, have no legal operation out of the state in which the law was passed. *Barnett v. Kinney, 147 U. S. 476.* A *voluntary* transfer, if valid where made, is valid everywhere, being the exercise of the personal right of the owner to dispose of his own. *Cole v. Cunningham, 133 U. S. 107.*

The operation of voluntary or common law assignments upon property situated in other states will be respected, except so far as they come in conflict with the rights of local creditors, or with the laws or public policy of the state in which the assignment is sought to be enforced. But the rule with respect to statutory assignments is somewhat different. The prevailing American doctrine is that a conveyance under a state insolvent law operates only upon property within the territory of that state, and that with respect to property in other states it is given only such effect as the laws of such state permit; and that, in general, it must give way to claims of creditors pursuing their remedies there. It passes no title to real estate situated in another state. *Security Trust Co. v. Dodd, Mead & Co., 173 U. S. 624.* An insolvent assignment will not pass title to foreign real estate. *Watson v. Holden, 58 Kan. 666.* Title to real estate is exclusively governed by the law of the country where the real estate is situated. *Osborn v. Adams, 18 Pick. 245; McCormick v. Sullivant, 10 Wheat. 202.* A bankrupt assignment does not vest in the assignee title to real estate in a foreign country. *Oakey v. Bennett, 11 How. 33; Harvey v. Edens, 69 Tex. 420.*

The administration in bankruptcy of the property of a bankrupt which has passed to the trustee is governed by the law of the country where the bankruptcy proceedings take place (*lex fori*). *Dicey Conflict of Laws, p. 671.*

For history and constitutionality of national bankruptcy law in the United States, see *Hanover Nat. Bank v. Moyses, 186 U. S. 181 (1902).* Also, see *Jaquith v. Rowley, 188 U. S. 620; Earling v. Seymour Lumber Co., 113 Fed. Rep. 483; Singer v. Nat. Bedstead Co., 11 Am. B. R. 276.*

CHAPTER VIII.

FOREIGN EXECUTORS, ADMINISTRATORS, TRUSTEES, AND RECEIVERS.

WILKINS v. ELLETT, 1883.

[108 U. S. 256.]

1. Extra-territorial Powers of Such Officers.
2. Relation Between Principal and Ancillary Administration.

MR. JUSTICE GRAY delivered the opinion of the court.

This is an action of assumpsit on the common counts, brought in the Circuit Court of the United States for the Western District of Tennessee. The plaintiff is a citizen of Virginia, and sues as administrator, appointed in Tennessee, of the estate of Thomas N. Quarles. The defendant is a citizen of Tennessee, and surviving partner of the firm of F. H. Clark & Company. The answer sets up that Quarles was a citizen of Alabama at the time of his death; that the sum sued for has been paid to William Goodloe, appointed his administrator in that State, and has been inventoried and accounted for by him upon a final settlement of his administration; and that there are no creditors of Quarles in Tennessee. The undisputed facts, appearing by the bill of exceptions, are as follows:

Quarles was born at Richmond, Virginia, in 1835. In 1839 his mother, a widow, removed with him, her only child, to Courtland, Alabama. They lived there together until 1856, and she made her home there until her death in 1864. In 1856 he went to Memphis, Tennessee, and there entered the employment of F. H. Clark & Company, and continued in their employ as a clerk, making no investments himself, but leaving his surplus earnings on interest in their hands, until January, 1866, when he went to the house of a cousin in Courtland, Alabama, and while there died by an accident, leaving personal estate in Alabama. On the 27th of January, 1866, Goodloe took out letters of administration in Alabama, and in February, 1866, went to Memphis, and there, upon exhibiting his letters of administration, received from the defendant the sum of money due to Quarles, amounting to $3,-

455.22 (which is the same for which this suit is brought), and included it in his inventory, and in his final account, which was allowed by the probate court in Alabama. There were no debts due from Quarles in Tennessee. All his next of kin resided in Virginia or in Alabama; and no administration was taken out on his estate in Tennessee until June, 1866, when letters of administration were there issued to the plaintiff.

There was conflicting evidence upon the question whether the domicil of Quarles at the time of his death was in Alabama or in Tennessee. The jury found that it was in Tennessee, under instructions, the correctness of which we are not prepared to affirm, but need not consider, because assuming them to be correct, we are of opinion that the court erred in instructing the jury that, if the domicil was in Tennessee, they must find for the plaintiff; and in refusing to instruct them, as requested by the defendant, that the payment to the Alabama administrator before the appointment of one in Tennessee, and there being no Tennessee creditors, was a valid discharge of the defendant, without reference to the domicil.

There is no doubt that the succession to the personal estate of a deceased person is governed by the law of his domicil at the time of his death; that the proper place for the principal administrator of his estate is that domicil; that administration may also be taken out in any place in which he leaves personal property; and that no suit for the recovery of a debt due to him at the time of his death can be brought by an administrator as such in any State in which he has not taken out administration.

But the reason for this last rule is the protection of the rights of citizens of the State in which the suit is brought; and the objection does not rest upon any defect of the administrator's title in the property, but upon his personal incapacity to sue as administrator beyond the jurisdiction which appointed him.

If a debtor, residing in another State, comes into the State in which the administrator has been appointed, and there pays him, the payment is a valid discharge everywhere. If the debtor, being in that State, is there sued by the administrator, and judgment recovered against him, the administrator may bring suit in his own name upon that judgment in the State where the debtor resides. *Talmage* v. *Chapel*, 16 Mass. 71; *Biddle* v. *Wilkins*, 1 Pet. 686.

The administrator, by virtue of his appointment and authority as such, obtains the title in promissory notes or other written evidences of debt, held by the intestate at the time of his death, and coming to the possession of the administrator; and may sell, transfer and indorse the same; and the purchasers or indorsees may maintain actions in their own names against the debtors in another State, if the debts are negotiable promissory notes, or if the law of the State in which the action is brought permits the assignee of a chose in action to sue in his own name. *Harper* v. *Butler,* 2 Pet. 239; Shaw, C. J., in *Rand* v. *Hubbard,* 4 Met. 252, 258-260; *Petersen* v. *Chemical Bank,* 32 N. Y. 21. And on a note made to the intestate, payable to bearer, an administrator appointed in one State may sue in his own name in another State. *Barrett* v. *Barrett,* 8 Greenl. 353; *Robinson* v. *Crandall,* 9 Wend. 425.

In accordance with these views, it was held by this court when this case was before it after a former trial, at which the domicil of the intestate appeared to have been in Alabama, that the payment in Tennessee to the Alabama administrator was good as against the administrator afterwards appointed in Tennessee. *Wilkins* v. *Ellett,* 9 Wall. 740.

The fact that the domicil of the intestate has now been found by the jury to be in Tennessee does not appear to us to make any difference. There are neither creditors nor next of kin in Tennessee. The Alabama administrator has inventoried and accounted for the amount of this debt in Alabama. The distribution among the next of kin, whether made in Alabama or in Tennessee, must be according to the law of the domicil; and it has not been suggested that there is any difference between the laws of the two States in that regard.

The judgment must therefore be reversed, and the case remanded with directions to set aside the verdict and to order a

New trial.[16]

---

[16]The powers of executors, administrators, receivers, and trustees in foreign jurisdictions are about the same. Comity recognizes that such officers appointed in one jurisdiction may protect interests and enforce claims elsewhere, when to do so does not interfere with the rights of local creditors, pursuing their remedies in the local courts. *Gilman* v. *Ketcham,* *84 Wis. 60, 54 N. W. 395; Chicago Ry. Co. v. Packet, 108 Ill. 317, 48 Am. Rep. 557; Whitman v. Mast, 11 Wash. 318, 48 Am. St. Rep. 874; Parker v. Mill Co., 91 Wis. 174, 64 N. W. 751; Comstock v. Frederickson, 51 Minn. 350; Wilson v. Keels, 54 S. C. 545, 32 S. E. 702.*

The weight of authority seems to be that trustees have no extra-territorial power of official action. *Booth* v. *Clark, 17 How. 164; Hale v. Harris, 112 Iowa 372, 83 N. W. 1046; Ayres v. Seibel, 82 Iowa 347, 47 N. W. 989.* In the case of *Fidelity Ins., Safe and Deposit Co. v. Nelson, 30 Wash. 340, 70 Pac. Rep. 961,* the court held that a foreign trustee could maintain an action respecting the trust property when no local creditor is affected.

Voluntary payments by debtors to a foreign executor or administrator discharge the debts. *Vroom v. Van Horne, 10 Paige (N. Y. Chan.) 549, 42 Am. Dec. 94; Schluter v. Bank, 117 N. Y. 125, 22 N. E. 572, 5 L. R. A. 541, 15 Am. St. Rep. 494; Dexter v. Berge, 76 Minn. 216, 78 N. W. 1111.*

This is the rule only where there is no domestic administrator, or he is appointed after the debt is paid, or at least after suit is brought by the domiciliary administrator. *Bull v. Fuller, 78 Iowa 20, 42 N. W. 572, 16 Am. St. Rep. 419; National Bank v. Sharp, 53 Md. 521; Greenwalt v. Bastian, 10 Kan. App. 101.*

It has been held that where there is a domestic administrator payment to a foreign administrator is no discharge. *Equitable Life Ass. v. Vogel, 76 Ala. 441, 52 Am. Rep. 344; Walker v. Welker, 55 Ill. App. 118; Amsden v. Danielson, 18 R. I. 787, 35 Am. Rep. 70; Murphy v. Crouse, 135 Cal. 14, 66 Pac. Rep. 971.*

In *Maas v. Savings Bank, 176 N. Y. 377, 68 N. E. 658*, the court decided that payment to the foreign domiciliary administrator in good faith, without knowledge that another administrator had been appointed in the state, and it does not appear that the decedent had any creditors in the state, operated as a discharge of the indebtedness. See *Stone v. Scripture, 4 Lans. (N. Y.) 186.*

JOHNSON v. POWERS, 1891.

[139 U. S. 156.]

MR. JUSTICE GRAY delivered the opinion of the court.

This is a bill in equity, filed in the Circuit Court of the United States for the Northern District of New York, by George K. Johnson, a citizen of Michigan, in behalf of himself and of all other persons interested in the administration of the assets of Nelson P. Stewart, late of Detroit in the county of Wayne and State of Michigan, against several persons, citizens of New York, alleged to hold real estate in New York under conveyances made by Stewart in fraud of his creditors.

The bill is founded upon the jurisdiction in equity of the Circuit Court of the United States, independent of statutes or practice in any State, to administer, as between citizens of different States, any deceased person's assets within its jurisdiction. *Payne v. Hook, 7 Wall. 425; Kennedy v. Creswell, 101 U. S. 641.*

At the threshold of the case, we are met by the question whether the plaintiff shows such an interest in Stewart's estate as to be entitled to invoke the exercise of this jurisdiction.

He seeks to maintain his bill, both as administrator, and as a creditor, in behalf of himself and all other creditors of Stewart.

The only evidence that he was either administrator or creditor is a duly certified copy of a record of the probate court of the county of Wayne and State of Michigan, showing his appointment by that court as administrator of Stewart's estate; the subsequent appointment by that court, pursuant to the statutes of Michigan, of commissioners to receive, examine and adjust all claims of creditors against the estate; and the report of those commissioners, allowing several claims, including one to this plaintiff, "George K. Johnson, for judgments against claimant in Wayne Circuit Court as endorser," and naming him as administrator as the party objecting to the allowance of all the claims.

The plaintiff certainly cannot maintain this bill as administrator of Stewart, even if the bill can be construed as framed in that aspect; because he admits that he has never taken out letters of administration in New York; and the letters of administration granted to him in Michigan confer no power beyond the limits of that State, and cannot authorize him to maintain any suit in the courts, either State or national, held in any other State. *Stacy* v. *Thrasher*, 6 How. 44, 58; *Noonan* v. *Bradley*, 9 Wall. 394.

The question remains whether, as against these defendants, the plaintiff has proved himself to be a creditor of Stewart. The only evidence on this point, as already observed, is the record of the proceedings before commissioners appointed by the probate court in Michigan. It becomes necessary therefore to consider the nature and the effect of those proceedings.

They were had under the provisions of the General Statutes of Michigan, (2 Howell's Statutes, §§ 5888-5906,) "the general idea" of which, as stated by Judge Cooley, "is that all claims against the estates of deceased persons shall be duly proved before commissioners appointed to hear them, or before the probate court when no commissioners are appointed. The commissioners act judicially in the allowance of claims, and the administrator cannot bind the estate by admitting their correctness, but must leave them to be proved in the usual mode." *Clark* v. *Davis*, 32 Michigan, 154, 157. The commissioners, when once appointed, become a special tribunal, which, for most purposes, is independent of the probate court, and from which either party may appeal to the circuit court of the county; and, as against an adverse claimant, the administrator, general or special, represents the estate, both before the commissioners and upon the appeal. 2 Howell's Statutes, §§ 5907-5917; *Lothrop* v. *Conely*, 39 Michigan, 757. The decision of the commissioners, or of the circuit court on appeal, should properly be only an allowance or disallowance of the claim, and not in the form of a judgment at common law.

La Roe v. *Freeland,* 8 Michigan, 530. But, as between the parties to the controversy, and as to the payment of the claim out of the estate in the control of the probate court, it has the effect of a judgment, and cannot be collaterally impeached by either of those parties. *Shurbun v. Hooper,* 40 Michigan, 503.

Those statutes provide that, when the administrator declines to appeal from a decision of the commissioners, any person interested in the estate may appeal from that decision to the circuit court; and that, when a claim of the administrator against the estate is disallowed by the commissioners and he appeals, he shall give notice of his appeal to all concerned by personal service or by publication. 2 Howell's Statutes, §§ 5916, 5917. It may well be doubted whether, within the spirit and intent of these provisions, the administrator, when he is also the claimant, is not bound to give notice to other persons interested in the estate, in order that they may have an opportunity to contest his claim before the commissioners, and whether an allowance of his claim, as in this case, in the absence of any impartial representative of the estate, and of other persons interested therein, can be of any binding effect, even in Michigan. See *Lothrop* v. *Conely,* above cited.

But we need not decide that point, because upon broader grounds it is quite clear that those proceedings are incompetent evidence, in this suit and against these defendants, that the plaintiff is a creditor of Stewart or of his estate.

A judgment *in rem* binds only the property within the control of the court which rendered it; and a judgment *in personam* binds only the parties to that judgment and those in privity with them.

A judgment recovered against the administrator of a deceased person in one State is no evidence of debt, in a subsequent suit by the same plaintiff in another State, either against an administrator, whether the same or a different person, appointed there, or against any other person having assets of the deceased. *Aspden* v. *Nixon,* 4 How. 467; *Stacy* v. *Thrasher,* 6 How. 44; *McLean* v. *Meek,* 18 How. 16; *Low* v. *Bartlett,* 8 Allen, 259

In *Stacy* v. *Thrasher,* in which a judgment, recovered in one State against an administrator appointed in that State, upon an alleged debt of the intestate, was held to be incompetent evidence of the debt in a suit brought by the same plaintiff in the Circuit Court of the United States held within another State against an administrator there appointed of the same intestate, the reasons given by Mr. Justice Grier have so strong a bearing on the case before us, and on the argument of the appellant, as to be worth quoting from:

"The administrator receives his authority from the ordinary, or other officer of the government where the goods of the intestate are situate. But coming into such possession by succession to the intestate, and encumbered with the duty to pay his debts, he is considered in law as in privity with him, and therefore bound or estopped by a judgment against him. Yet his representation of his intestate is a qualified one, and extends not beyond the assets of which the ordinary had jurisdiction." 6 How. 58.

In answering the objection that to apply these principles to a judgment obtained in another State of the Union would be to deny it the faith and credit, and the effect, to which it was entitled by the Constitution and laws of the United States, he observed that it was evidence, and conclusive by way of estoppel, only between the same parties, or their privies, or on the same subject matter when the proceeding was *in rem;* and that the parties to the judgments in question were not the same; neither were they privies, in blood, in law or by estate; and proceeded as follows:

"An administrator under grant of administration in one State stands in none of these relations to an administrator in another. Each is privy to the testator, and would be estopped by a judgment against him; but they have no privity with each other, in law or in estate. They receive their authority from different sovereignties, and over different property. The authority of each is paramount to the other. Each is accountable to the ordinary from whom he receives his authority. Nor does the one come by succession to the other into the trust of the same property, encumbered by the same debts." 6 How. 59, 60.

"It is for those who assert this privity to show wherein it lies, and the argument for it seems to be this: That the judgment against the administrator is against the estate of the intestate, and that his estate, wheresoever situate, is liable to pay his debts; therefore the plaintiff, having once established his claim against the estate by the judgment of a court, should not be called on to make proof of it again. This argument assumes that the judgment is *in rem*, and not *in personam,* or that the estate has a sort of corporate entity and unity. But this is not true, either in fact or in legal construction. The judgment is against the person of the administrator, that he shall pay the debt of the intestate out of the funds committed to his care. If there be another admin-

istrator in another State. liable to pay the same debt, he may be
subjected to a like judgment upon the same demand, but the
assets in his hands cannot be affected by a judgment to which he
is personally a stranger." "The laws and courts of a State can
only affect persons and things within their jurisdiction. Consequently, both as to the administrator and the property confided
to him, a judgment in another State is *res inter alios acta*. It
cannot be even *prima facie* evidence of a debt; for if it have any
effect at all, it must be as a judgment, and operate by way of
estoppel." 6 How. 60, 61.

In *Low* v. *Bartlett*, above cited, following the decisions of
this court, it was held that a judgment allowing a claim against
the estate of a deceased person in Vermont, under statutes similar to those of Michigan, was not competent evidence of debt in
a suit in equity brought in Massachusetts by the same plaintiff
against an executor appointed there, and against legatees who had
received money from him; the court saying: "The judgment in
Vermont was in no sense a judgment against them, nor against
the property which they had received from the executor." 8
Allen, 266.

In the case at bar, the allowance of Johnson's claim by the
commissioners appointed by the probate court in Michigan, giving it the utmost possible effect, faith and credit, yet, if considered as a judgment *in rem*, bound only the assets within the jurisdiction of that court, and, considered as a judgment *inter partes*,
bound only the parties to it and their privies. It was not a judgment against Stewart in his lifetime, nor against his estate wherever it might be: but only against his assets and his administrator
in Michigan. The only parties to the decision of the commissioners were Johnson, in his personal capactiy, as claimant, and
Johnson, in his representative capacity, as administrator of those
assets, as defendant. The present defendants were not parties to
that judgment, nor in privity with Johnson in either capacity. If
any other claimant in those proceedings had been the plaintiff
here, the allowance of his claim in Michigan would have been no
evidence of any debt due to him from the deceased, in this suit
brought in New York to recover alleged property of the deceased
in New York from third persons, none of whom were parties to
those proceedings, or in privity with either party to them. The
fact that this plaintiff was himself the only party on both sides of
those proceedings cannot, to say the least, give the decision
therein any greater effect against these defendants.

The objection is not that the plaintiff cannot maintain this bill without first recovering judgment on his debt in New York, but that there is no evidence whatever of his debt except the judgment in Michigan, and that that judgment, being *res inter alios acta,* is not competent evidence against these defendants.

This objection being fatal to the maintenance of this bill, there is no occasion to consider the other questions, of law or of fact, mentioned in the opinion of the Circuit Court and discussed at the bar.[17]

Decree affirmed.

[17]The rule that a foreign executor cannot sue or be sued in this state applies only to claims and liabilities resting wholly upon the representative character, i. e., suits brought upon debts due to or by the testator in his lifetime or based upon some transaction with him; it does not prevent such executor from suing or being sued upon a contract made with him as executor. *Johnson v. Wallis, 112 N. Y. 230 (1889).*

A foreign executor or administrator cannot be sued as such. *Hedenberg v. Hedenberg, 46 Conn. 30; Jackson v. Johnson, 34 Ga. 511; Strauss v. Phillips, 189 Ill. 1, 59 N. E. 560; Durie v. Blauvelt, 49 N. J. L. 114; Fairchild v. Hagel, 54 Ark. 61; Elting v. First Natl. Bnk, 173 Ill. 368, 50 N. E. 1095.*

In some states, under some circumstances, they may be sued, for instance if he comes to reside within the foreign state he may be sued there. *Colbert v. Daniel, 32 Ala. 314.* Or if he is in a foreign state with assets. *Laughlin v. Solomon, 180 Pa. 181, 36 Atl. 704.*

If an administrator sues and gets judgment against a party, he may sue on this judgment in another state. *Green v. Heritage, 63 N. J. L. 455, 43 Atl. 698.*

A successor or representative of the deceased who succeeds to the rights and liabilities of the deceased may sue and be sued in a foreign jurisdiction. *King v. Martin, 67 Ala. 177; Perkins v. Stone, 18 Conn. 270.*

Property once coming under the control of the executor or administrator remains under such control. *Clark v. Holt, 16 Ark. 257; Petersen v. Chemical Bank, 32 N. Y. 21.*

The transfer of real estate is governed by the law of the place where the real estate is situated, and usually the foreign executor or administrator cannot transfer, but if he is given power in the will, he may validly convey. *Thurber v. Carpenter, 18 R. I. 782; Green v. Alden, 92 Me. 177, 42 Atl. 359; Babcock v. Collins, 60 Minn. 73, 61 N. W. 1020.* If made trustee he may sell foreign lands. *Hoysradt v. Tionesta Gas Co., 194 Pa. 251, 45 Atl. 62.*

In *Reynolds v. McMullen, 55 Mich. 568,* the court held that where a mortgage upon real property in Michigan belongs to a person who dies in another state and whose estate is in course of regular and valid administration under a local administrator in Michigan, no foreign administrator can sell the mortgage claim to strangers; the title thereto is in the local administrator for purposes of administration, and only he can sue on it or assign or discharge it of record.

A power given to an executor may not be exercised by an administrator who succeeds the executor. *Conklin v. Egerton, 21 Wend. (N. Y.) 430.*

Administration may be granted upon chattels brought into the state, whether rightfully or wrongfully, after the death of the owner. *Stevins v. Wright, 51 N. H. 600; In re Hughes, 95 N. Y. 55; Merefield v. Harris, 126 N. C. 626, 36 S. E. 125.* Property taken into another state by the domiciliary administrator or agent, for temporary purpose, the state into which it is taken can exercise no control over it. *Crescent Ins. Co. v. Stafford, 3 Woods 94; Wells v. Miller, 45 Ill. 382; Christy v. Vest, 36 Iowa 285; Martin v. Sage, 147 Mass. 204, 17 N. E. 310.* If a foreign administrator is refused payment, the claim may be turned over to the domestic administrator, who may sue and recover the claim. *McCully v. Cooper, 114 Cal. 258, 46 Pac. 82.*

Where administrations are granted to different persons in different states, they are so far regarded as independent of each other, that a judgment obtained against one will furnish no right of action against the other, to affect assets receievd by the latter in virtue of his own administration; for in contemplation of law, there is no privity between him and the other administrator. *Judy v. Kelley, 11 Ill. 211.*

CHICAGO, M. & ST. P. RY. v. KEOKUK, 1883.

[108 Ill. 317.]

This was an attachment suit brought by the Chicago, Milwaukee and St. Paul Railway Company, against the Keokuk Northern Line Packet Company, in the circuit court of Adams county, in this State. The writ of attachment was, on the 21st day of April, 1881, levied upon the barge "G. W. Duncan," lying at Quincy, in said county, as the property of the defendant. Samuel C. Clubb, under the provision of section 29 of our Attachment act, "that any person other than the defendant claiming the property attached may interplead," etc., interpleaded in the case, claiming the property so attached, under an appointment as receiver of the property and effects of said packet company, by the circuit court of St. Louis, in the State of Missouri, in a certain cause in said court wherein said packet company was defendant. There was judgment in favor of the interpleader, Clubb, which, on appeal, was affirmed by the Appellate Court for the Third District, and the railway company appealed to this court.

The plaintiff in the attachment suit had first filed a replication to the pleas of the interpleader, traversing the same, but afterward, on its motion granted by the court, it withdrew the replication, as having been filed by mistake, and then moved the court to file its plea in abatement, which had been intended to be filed instead of the replication, denying the right to interplead as receiver under the appointment of a foreign court, which motion the court overruled, whereupon said plaintiff company filed the plea in abatement, which plea the court, on motion of said Clubb, ordered to be stricken from the files. The plaintiff company then refiled its said replication, upon which issue was joined and the trial had. The interpleader's first plea alleges the barge was his own property at the time of the attachment of it; the second, that it was his property as receiver; the third, that at such time it was in his possession as receiver.

The facts of the case shown by the evidence are, that at the October term, 1880, of the circuit court of the city of St. Louis, in the State of Missouri, Samuel C. Clubb was duly appointed receiver of the Keokuk Northern Line Packet Company, an insolvent corporation of that State, with power and authority to take possession of all the business and property of the corporation, and to manage the affairs thereof, under the orders of the court, the receiver giving bond in the sum of $200,000 for the faithful discharge of his duties. At the time of such appointment the barge "G. W. Duncan," in question, was lying at the landing at St. Louis, within the State of Missouri, and within the jurisdiction of said court. The receiver immediately took possession of the barge, and afterward, on the 6th day of November, 1880, he chartered the barge to the steamer, "E. W. Cole," for a trip up the Mississippi river and return. The barge was taken, under the charter, up the river as far as Quincy, Illinois, where it was detained by the ice, and remained until the levy of the writ of attachment in this case upon it on the 21st day of April, 1881. At the request of the captain of the steamer "E. W. Cole," the receiver released him from the charter, and took possession of the barge at Quincy, and ever since, until the levy of the attachment, retained such possession, having a watchman over and guarding the barge against danger. The receiver made an effort to have the barge removed to St. Louis as soon as the river was clear of ice, having made a contract with a steamboat line for the purpose, but did not succeed in having the removal made before the attachment. The court which appointed the receiver, at its April term, 1881, made an order authorizing the receiver to intervene in the attachment suit, and take the necessary steps to secure possession of the barge.

MR CHIEF JUSTICE SHELDON delivered the opinion of the Court:

We will consider the case as properly presenting by the pleadings the question of the right to interplead in the suit in the capacity of receiver.

The general doctrine that the powers of a receiver are coëxtensive only with the jurisdiction of the court making the

appointment, and particularly that a foreign receiver should not
be permitted, as against the claims of creditors resident in another
State, to remove from such State the assets of the debtor, it being
the policy of every government to retain in its own hands the
property of a debtor until all domestic claims against it have been
satisfied, we fully concede; and were this the case of property
situate in this State, never having been within the jurisdiction
of the court that appointed the receiver, and never having been in
the possession of the receiver, it would be covered by the above
principles, which would be decisive against the claim of the
appellee. But the facts that the property at the time of the
appointment of the receiver was within the jurisdiction of the
court making the appointment, and was there taken into the actual
possession of the receiver, and continued in his possession until
it was attached, take the case, as we conceive, out of the range
of the foregoing principles. We are of the opinion that by the
receiver's taking possession of the barge in question within the
jurisdiction of the court that appointed him, he became vested
with a special property in the barge, like that which a sheriff
acquires by the seizure of goods in execution, and that he was
entitled to protect this special property while it continued, by
action, in like manner as if he had been the absolute owner.
Having taken the property in his possession, he was responsible
for it to the court that appointed him, and had given a bond in a
large sum to cover his responsibility as receiver, and to meet
such liability he might maintain any appropriate proceeding to
regain possession of the barge which had been taken from him.
(*Boyle* v. *Townes,* 9 Leigh, 158; *Singerly* v. *Fox,* 75 Pa. 114.)
It is well settled that a sheriff does, by the seizure of goods in
execution, acquire a special property in them, and that he may
maintain trespass, trover or replevin for them.

It is claimed that there was here an abandonment of the barge
by leasing it and suffering it to be taken out of the State,—that
the purpose in so doing was an unlawful one, and a gross violation of official duty. We do not so view it. The receiver was,
by his appointment, authorized to manage the affairs of the corporation under the orders of the court. The business of the corporation was running boats on the Mississippi river, and chartering the barge for a trip up that river was but continuing the
employ of the barge in the business of the corporation, and
therefrom making an increase of the assets to be distributed
among the creditors. *Brownell* v. *Manchester,* 1 Pick. 233,

decides that a sheriff in the State of Massachusetts, who had
attached property in that State, did not lose his special property
by removing the attached property into the State of Rhode
Island for a lawful purpose. *Dick* v. *Bailey et al.* 2 La. Ann.
974, holds otherwise in respect to property attached in Mississippi, and sent by the sheriff into Louisiana for an illegal purpose. It is laid down in Drake on Attachment, (5th ed.) sec.
292, that the mere fact of removal by an officer of attached property beyond his bailiwick into a foreign jurisdiction, without
regard to the circumstances attending it, will not dissolve the
attachment; that if the purpose was lawful, and the possession
continued, the attachment would not be dissolved; but if the
purpose was unlawful, though the officer's possession remained,
or if lawful and he lost his possession, his special property in
the goods would be divested,—citing the two cases above named.
We do not consider that there was any unlawful purpose here in
the chartering and employing of the barge, as was done.

It is insisted the possession of the barge was lost. There
was certainly evidence tending to show possession by the receiver
up to the time of the attachment, and in support of the judgment
of the Appellate Court we must presume that it found the existence of all the facts necessary to sustain the judgment, where
there was evidence tending to show their existence, and that
court's finding of fact is conclusive upon us. By taking the
barge into his possession within the jurisdiction of the court that
appointed him, a special property in the barge became vested in
the receiver, and it is the established rule that where a legal title
to personal property has once passed and become vested in
accordance with the law of the State where it is situated, the
validity of such title will be recognized everywhere. *Cantwell*
v. *Sewell*, 5 Hurl. & N. 728; *Clark* v. *Connecticut Peat Co.* 35
Conn. 303; *Taylor* v. *Boardman*, 25 Vt. 581; *Crapo* v. *Kelly*, 16
Wall. 610; *Waters* v. *Barton*, 1 Cold. (Tenn.) 450.

Under this rule we hold that where a receiver has once
obtained rightful possession of personal property situated within
the jurisdiction of his appointment, which he was appointed to
take charge of, he will not be deprived of its possession, though he
take it, in the performance of his duty, into a foreign jurisdiction; that while there it can not be taken from his possession by
creditors of the insolvent debtor who reside within that jurisdiction. Where a receiver of an insolvent manufacturing corporation, appointed by a court in New Jersey, took possession of

its assets, and for the purpose of completing a bridge which it
had contracted to build in Connecticut, purchased iron with the
funds of the estate and sent it to that State, it was decided that
the iron was not open to attachment in Connecticut by a creditor
residing there. (*Pond* v. *Cooke*, 45 Conn. 126.) And where C.
was appointed, by a court in Arkansas, receiver of property of
T., a defendant in a suit, and ordered to ship it to Memphis for
sale, and to hold the proceeds subject to the order of the court,
and did so ship it to Memphis, where it was attached by creditors
of T., it was held that C. could maintain an action of replevin for
the property in Tennessee. (*Cagill* v. *Wooldridge*, 8 Baxter,
580.) *Kilmer* v. *Hobart*, 58 How. Pr. 452, decides that receivers
appointed in another State, and operating a railway as such, but
having property in their hands as receivers in New York, can not
there be sued,—that an attachment issued in such suit will be
vacated.

This is not the case of the officer of a foreign court seeking,
as against the claims of creditors resident here, to remove from
this State assets of the debtor situate here at the time of the
officer's appointment, and ever since, and of which he had had no
previous possession. It is to such a case as that, as we understand, that the authorities cited by appellant's counsel apply, and
not to a case like the present, where the property was, at the time
of the appointment of the foreign receiver, within the jurisdiction
of the appointing court, and there taken into the receiver's possession, and subsequently suffered by him to be brought into this
State in the performance of his duty, and his possession here
wrongfully invaded, and he seeking but redress for such invasion.

The judgment of the Appellate Court must be affirmed.

Judgment affirmed.[18]

---

[18]Receivers, as a general rule, have no extra-territorial powers. *Booth
v. Clark*, 17 How. 164; *Fitzgerald* v. *Fitzgerald*, 41 Nebr. 374; *Wyman v.
Eaton*, 107 Iowa 214, 43 L. R. A. 695; *Catlin* v. *Wilcox*, etc., 123 Ind. 447.

A receiver is distinguishable from the executor or administrator in
that the receiver is a successor. *Relfe* v. *Rundle*, 103 U. S. 225.

A federal court will not appoint a receiver and take property out of
the possession of a receiver appointed by a state court. *Shields* v. *Cole-
man*, 157 U. S. 168. An ancillary receiver may be appointed to take charge
of assets within the state, and his power is limited to that jurisdiction.
Holbrook v. *Ford*, 153 Ill. 633, 39 N. E. 1091; *Reynolds* v. *Stockton*, 140
U. S. 254.

If no domestic creditors, the court will not appoint an ancillary
receiver. *Mabon* v. *Ougley*, 156 N. Y. 196, 50 N. E. 805. Assets collected
within the state may be applied to domestic creditors by the ancillary
receiver, or the court may order the assets transmitted to the principal

receiver to be distributed along with the principal estate. *Fawcett v. Order of Iron Hall, 64 Conn. 170, 29 Atl. 614; Failey v. Fee, 83 Md. 83, 34 Atl. 839; Buswell v. Iron Hall, 161 Mass. 224, 36 N. E. 1065; Baldwin v. Hosmer, 101 Mich. 119, 59 N. W. 432; People v. Granite Association, 161 N. Y. 492 (1900); Robertson v. Stead, 135 Mo. 135, 36 S. W. 610; Osgood v. Maguire, 61 N. Y. 524.*

A receiver may sue upon his individual right, in any jurisdiction, for property bought by him, or contract made by him, or in all cases where the right accrues to the receiver. *Cooke v. Orange, 48 Conn. 401; Merchants Nat. Bank v. Pa. Steel Co., 57 N. J. L. 336, 30 Atl. 545; Wilkinson v. Culver, 25 Fed. 639.*

CHAPTER IX.

FOREIGN JUDGMENTS.

HILTON v. GUYOT, 1895.

[159 U. S. 113.]

1. Extra-territorial Recognition of Judgments.

2. Conclusiveness of Foreign Judgments.

The first of these two cases was an action at law, brought December 18, 1885, in the Circuit Court of the United States for the Southern District of New York, by Gustave Bertin Guyot, as official liquidator of the firm of Charles Fortin & Co., and by the surviving members of that firm, all aliens and citizens of the Republic of France, against Henry Hilton and William Libbey, citizens of the United States and the State of New York, and trading as copartners, in the cities of New York and Paris and elsewhere, under the firm name of A. T. Stewart & Co. The action was upon a judgment recovered in a French court at Paris in the Republic of France by the firm of Charles Fortin & Co., all whose members were French citizens, against Hilton and Libbey, trading as copartners as aforesaid, and citizens of the United States and of the State of New York.

The complaint alleged that the judgment of the French court remains in full force and effect; that the French court had jurisdiction of the subject matter, and of the parties; that the plaintiffs have been unable to collect the said judgment or any part thereof, by reason of the absence of the said defendants, they having given up their business in Paris prior to the recovery of the said judgment on appeal, and having left no property within the jurisdiction of the Republic of France, out of which the said judgment might be made; and that there is still justly due and owing from the defendants to the plaintiffs the sum of $195,122.47.

The defendants in their answer alleged that the plaintiffs had no just claim against the defendants; that the defendants were not present at Paris at the time of the suit; and that the defendants appeared by attorney solely for the purpose of protecting their property which was within the jurisdiction of the French court. The answer further alleged that there was not a full and fair trial in the lower French court, and consequently the judgment is void.

The answer further alleged that it would be against natural justice to enforce this judgment without an examination of the merits thereof. The defendants claim also, that judgments rendered in the United States may be examined anew in the French courts, that our judgments are not conclusive in France.

The plaintiffs filed a replication to the answer denying its allegations, and setting up in bar thereof the judgment sued on.

The circuit court directed a verdict for the plaintiffs in the sum of $277,775.44, being the amount of the French judgment and interest. The defendants, having duly excepted to the rulings and direction of the court, sued out a writ of error.

The writ of error in the action at law and the appeal in the suit in equity were argued together in this court January 19, 22, and 23, 1894; and, by direction of the court, were reargued in April, 1894, before a full bench.

Mr. James C. Carter and *Mr. Elihu Root* for plaintiffs in error and appellants. *Mr. Horace Russell* was on their briefs.

Mr. William G. Choate, (with whom was *Mr. William D. Shipman* on the brief,) for defendants in error and appellees.

GRAY, J. In order to appreciate the weight of the various authorities cited at the bar, it is important to distinguish different kinds of judgments. Every foreign judgment, of whatever nature, in order to be entitled to any effect, must have been rendered by a court having jurisdiction of the cause, and upon regular proceedings and due notice. In alluding to different kinds of judgments, therefore, such jurisdiction, proceedings, and notice will be assumed. It will also be assumed that they are untainted by fraud the effect of which will be considered later.

A judgment *in rem,* adjudicating the title to a ship or other movable property within the custody of the court, is treated as valid everywhere. As said by Chief Justice Marshall: "The sentence of a competent court, proceeding *in rem,* is conclusive with respect to the thing itself, and operates as an absolute change of the property. By such sentence, the right of the former owner is lost, and a complete title given to the person who claims under the decree. No court of coördinate jurisdiction can examine the sentence. The question, therefore, respecting its conformity to general or municipal law can never arise, for no coördinate tribunal is capable of making the inquiry." Williams *v.* Armroyd, 7

Cranch, 423, 432. The most common illustrations of this are decrees of courts of admiralty and prize, which proceed upon principles of international law. Croudson v. Leonard, 4 Cranch, 434; Williams v. Armroyd, above cited; Ludlow v. Dale, 1 Johns. Cas. 16. But the same rule applies to judgments *in rem* under municipal law. Hudson v. Guestier, 4 Cranch, 293; Ennis v. Smith, 14 How. 400, 430; Wisconsin v. Pelican Ins. Co., 127 U. S. 265, 291; Scott v. McNeal, 154 U. S. 34, 46; Castrique v. Imrie, L. R. 4 H. L. 414; Monroe v. Douglas, 4 Sandf, Ch. 126.

A judgment affecting the status of persons, such as a degree confirming or dissolving a marriage, is recognized as valid in every country, unless contrary to the policy of its own law. Cottington's case, 2 Swans. 326; Roach v. Garvan, 1 Ves. Sen. 157; Harvey v. Farnie, 8 App. Cas. 43; Cheely v. Clayton, 110 U. S. 701. It was of a foreign sentence of divorce, that Lord Chancellor Nottingham, in the House of Lords, in 1688, in Cottington's case, above cited, said: "It is against the law of nations not to give credit to the judgments and sentences of foreign countries, till they be reversed by the law, and according to the form, of those countries wherein they were given. For what right hath one kingdom to reverse the judgment of another? And how can we refuse to let a sentence take place till it be reversed? And what confusion would follow in Christendom, if they should serve us so abroad, and give no credit to our sentences."

Other judgments, not strictly *in rem*, under which a person has been compelled to pay money, are so far conclusive that the justice of the payment cannot be impeached in another country, so as to compel him to pay it again. For instance a judgment in foreign attachment is conclusive, as between the parties, of the right to the property or money attached. Story on Conflict of Laws (2d ed.), § 592a. And if, on the dissolution of a partnership, one partner promises to indemnify the other against the debts of the partnership, a judgment for such a debt, under which the latter has been compelled to pay it, is conclusive evidence of the debt in a suit by him to recover the amount upon the promise of indemnity. It was of such a judgment, and in such a suit, that Lord Nottingham said: "Let the plaintiff receive back so much of the money brought into court as may be adequate to the sum paid on the sentence for custom, the justice whereof is not examinable here." Gold v. Canham (1689), 2 Swans. 325; s. c. 1 Cas. in Ch. 311. See also Tarleton v. Tarleton, 4 M. & S. 20; Konitzky v. Meyer, 49 N. Y. 571.

Other foreign judgments which have been held conclusive of the matter adjudged were judgments discharging obligations contracted in the foreign country between citizens or residents thereof. Story's Conflict of Laws, §§ 330–341 ; May v. Breed, 7 Cush. 15. Such was the case, cited at the bar, of Burroughs or Burrows v. Jamineau or Jemino, Mos. 1 ; s. c. 2 Stra. 733 ; 2 Eq. Cas. Ab. 525, pl. 7 ; 12 Vin. Ab. 87, pl. 9 ; Sel. Cas. in Ch. 69 ; 1 Dick. 48.

In that case, bills of exchange, drawn in London, were negotiated, indorsed, and accepted at Leghorn in Italy, by the law of which an acceptance became void if the drawer failed without leaving effects in the acceptor's hands. The acceptor, accordingly, having received advices that the drawer had failed before the acceptances, brought a suit at Leghorn against the last indorsees, to be discharged of his acceptances, paid the money into court and obtained a sentence there, by which the acceptances were vacated as against those indorsees and all the indorsers and negotiators of the bills, and the money deposited was returned to him. Being afterwards sued at law in England by subsequent holders of the bills, he applied to the Court of Chancery and obtained a perpetual injunction. Lord Chancellor King, as reported by Strange, "was clearly of opinion that this cause was to be determined according to the local laws of the place where the bill was negotiated, and the plaintiff's acceptance of the bill having been vacated and declared void by a court of competent jurisdiction, he thought that sentence was conclusive and bound the Court of Chancery here;" as reported in Viner, that "the court at Leghorn had jurisdiction of the thing, and of the persons;" and, as reported by Mosely, that, though "the last indorsees had the sole property of the bills, and were therefore made the only parties to the suit at Leghorn, yet the sentence made the acceptance void against the now defendants and all others." It is doubtful, at the least, whether such a sentence was entitled to the effect given to it by Lord Chancellor King. See Novelli v. Rossi, 2 B. & Ad. 757; Castrique v. Imrie, L. R. 4 H. L. 414, 435; 2 Smith's Lead. Cas. (2d ed.) 450.

The remark of Lord Hardwicke, *arguendo*, as Chief Justice, in Boucher v. Lawson (1734), that "the reason gone upon by Lord Chancellor King, in the case of Borroughs v. Jamineau, was certainly right, that where any court, whether foreign or domestic, that has the proper jurisdiction of the case, makes a determination, it is conclusive to all other courts," evidently had reference, as the context shows, to judgments of a court having jurisdiction

of the thing; and did no*t* touch the effect of an executory judgment for a debt. Cas. temp. Hardw. 85, 89; s. c. Cunningham,
144, 148.

In former times, foreign degrees in admiralty *in personam*
were executed, even by imprisonment of the defendant, by the
Court of Admiralty in England, upon letters rogatory from the
foreign sovereign, without a new suit.   Its right to do so was
recognized by the Court of King's Bench in 1607 in a case of
habeas corpus, cited by the plaintiffs, and reported as follows: "If
a man of Frizeland sues an Englishman in Frizeland before the
Governor there, and there recovers against him a certain sum;
upon which the Englishman, not having sufficient to satisfy it,
comes into England, upon which the Governor sends his letters
massive into England, *omnes magistratus infra regnum Angliæ
rogans*, to make execution of the said judgment.   The Judge of
the Admiralty may execute this judgment by imprisonment of the
party, and he shall not be delivered by the common law; for this
is by the law of nations, that the justice of one nation should be
aiding to the justice of another nation, and for one to execute the
judgment of the other; and the law of England takes notice of
this law, and the Judge of the Admiralty is the proper magistrate
for this purpose; for he only hath the execution of the civil law
within the realm.   Pasch. 5 Jac. B. R. Weir's case, resolved upon
an *habeas corpus*, and remanded." 1 Rol. Ab. 530, pl. 12; 6 Vin.
Ab. 512, pl. 12.   But the only question there raised or decided
was of the power of the English Court of Admiralty, and not of
the conclusiveness of the foreign sentence; and in later times the
mode of enforcing a foreign decree in admiralty is by a new libel.
See the City of Mecca, 5 P. D. 28, and 6 P. D. 106.

The extraterritorial effect of judgments *in personam*, at law
or in equity, may differ, according to the parties to the cause.   A
judgment of that kind between two citizens or residents of the
country, and thereby subject to the jurisdiction, in which it is rendered, may be held conclusive as between them everywhere.   So,
if a foreigner invokes the jurisdiction by bringing an action
against a citizen, both may be held bound by a judgment in favor
of either.   And if a citizen sues a foreigner, and judgment is rendered in favor of the latter, both may be held equally bound.
Ricardo *v.* Garcias, 12 Cl. & Fin. 368; The Griefswald, Swabey,
430, 435; Barber *v.* Lamb, 8 C. B. (N. S.) 95; Lea *v.* Deakin, 11
Biss. 23.

The effect to which a judgment, purely executory, rendered

in favor of a citizen or resident of the country, in a suit there brought by him against a foreigner, may be entitled in an action thereon against the latter in his own country—as is the case now before us—presents a more difficult question, upon which there has been some diversity of opinion.

Early in the last century, it was settled in England that a foreign judgment on a debt was considered not, like a judgment of a domestic court of record, as a record or a specialty, a lawful consideration for which was conclusively presumed; but as a simple contract only.

In recent times, foreign judgments rendered within the dominions of the English Crown, and under the law of England, after a trial on the merits, and no want of jurisdiction, and no fraud or mistake, being shown or offered to be shown, have been treated as conclusive by the highest courts of New York, Maine, and Illinois. Lazier v. Wescott (1862), 26 N. Y. 146, 150; Dunstan v. Higgins (1893), 138 N. Y. 70, 74; Rankin v. Goddard (1866), 54 Me. 28, and (1868) 55 Me. 389; Baker v. Palmer (1876), 83 Ill. 568. In two early cases in Ohio, it was said that foreign judgments were conclusive, unless shown to have been obtained by fraud. Silver Lake Bank v. Harding (1832), 5 Ohio, 545, 547; Anderson v. Anderson (1837), 8 Ohio, 108, 110. But in a later case in that State it was said that they were only *prima facie* evidence of indebtedness. Pelton v. Platner (1844), 13 Ohio, 209, 217. In Jones v. Jamison (1860), 15 La. Ann. 35, the decision was only that, by virtue of the statutes of Louisiana, a foreign judgment merged the original cause of action as against the plaintiff.

In view of all the authorities upon the subject, and of the trend of judicial opinion in this country and in England, following the lead of Kent and Story, we are satisfied that, where there has been opportunity for a full and fair trial abroad before a court of competent jurisdiction, conducting the trial upon regular proceedings, after due citation or voluntary appearance of the defendant, and under a system of jurisprudence likely to secure an impartial administration of justice between the citizens of its own country and those of other countries, and there is nothing to show either prejudice in the court, or in the system of laws under which it was sitting, or fraud in procuring the judgment, or any other special reason why the comity of this nation should not allow its full effect, the merits of the case should not, in an action brought in this country upon the judgment, be tried afresh, as on a new trial or an appeal, upon the mere assertion of the party that the judgment was erroneous in law or in fact. The defendants, therefore, cannot be permitted, upon that general ground, to contest the validity or the effect of the judgment sued on.

But they have sought to impeach that judgment upon several other grounds, which require separate consideration.

It is objected that the appearance and litigation of the defendants in the French tribunals were not voluntary, but by legal compulsion, and therefore the French courts never acquired such jurisdiction over the defendants, that they should be held bound by the judgment.

Upon the question what should be considered such a voluntary appearance, as to amount to a submission to the jurisdiction of a foreign court, there has been some difference of opinion in England.

But it is now settled in England that, while an appearance by the defendant in a court of a foreign country, for the purpose of protecting his property already in the possession of that court, may not be deemed a voluntary appearance, yet an appearance solely for the purpose of protecting other property in that country from seizure is considered as a voluntary appearance. De Crosse Brissac v. Rathbone (1860), 6 H. & N. 301; s. c. 20 Law Journal (N. S.), Exch. 238; Schibsby v. Westenholz (1870), L. R. 6 Q. B. 155, 162; Voinet v. Barrett (1885), 1 Cab. & El. 554; s. c. 54 Law Journal (N. S.), Q. B. 521, and 55 Law Journal (N. S.), Q. B. 39.

The present case is not one of a person travelling through or casually found in a foreign country. The defendants, although they were not citizens or residents of France, but were citizens and residents of the State of New York, and their principal place of business was in the city of New York, yet had a storehouse and an agent in Paris, and were accustomed to purchase large quantities of goods there, although they did not make sales in France. Under such circumstances, evidence that their sole object in appearing and carrying on the litigation in the French courts was to prevent property, in their storehouse at Paris, belonging to them, and within the jurisdiction, but not in the custody, of those courts, from being taken in satisfaction of any judgment that might be recovered against them, would not, according to our law, show that those courts did not acquire jurisdiction of the persons of the defendants.

It is now established in England by well considered and

strongly reasoned decisions of the Court of Appeal, that foreign judgments may be impeached, if procured by false and fraudulent representations and testimony of the plaintiff, even if the same question of fraud was presented to and decided by the foreign court.

But whether these decisions can be followed in regard to foreign judgments, consistently with our own decisions as to impeaching domestic judgments for fraud, it is unnecessary in this case to determine, because there is a distinct and independent ground upon which we are satisfied that the comity of our nation does not require us to give conclusive effect to the judgments of the courts of France; and that ground is, the want of reciprocity, on the part of France, as to the effect to be given to the judgments of this and other foreign countries.

There is hardly a civilized nation on either continent, which, by its general law, allows conclusive effect to an executory foreign judgment for the recovery of money. In France, and in a few smaller States,—Norway, Portugal, Greece, Monaco, and Hayti, —the merits of the controversy are reviewed, as of course, allowing to the foreign judgment, at the most, no more effect than of being *prima facie* evidence of the justice of the claim. In the great majority of the countries on the continent of Europe,—in Belgium, Holland, Denmark, Sweden, Germany, in many cantons of Switzerland, in Russia and Poland, in Roumania, in Austria and Hungary (perhaps in Italy), and in Spain,—as well as in Egypt, in Mexico, and in a great part of South America, the judgment rendered in a foreign country is allowed the same effect only as the courts of that country allow to the judgments of the country in which the judgment in question is sought to be executed.

The prediction of Mr. Justice Story (in section 618 of his Commentaries on the Conflict of Laws, already cited) has thus been fulfilled, and the rule of reciprocity has worked itself firmly into the structure of international jurisprudence.

The reasonable, if not the necessary, conclusion appears to us to be that judgments rendered in France, or in any other foreign country, by the laws of which our own judgments are reviewable upon the merits, are not entitled to full credit and conclusive effect when sued upon in this country, but are *prima facie* evidence only of the justice of the plaintiff's claim.

In holding such a judgment, for want of reciprocity, not to be conclusive evidence of the merits of the claim, we do not pro-

ceed upon any theory of retaliation upon one person by reason
of injustice done to another; but upon the broad ground that
international law is founded upon mutuality and reciprocity, and
that by the principles of international law recognized in most
civilized nations, and by the comity of our own country, which it
is our judicial duty to know and to declare, the judgment is not
entitled to be considered conclusive.

By our law, at the time of the adoption of the Constitution,
a foreign judgment was considered as *prima facie* evidence, and
not conclusive. There is no statute of the United States, and
no treaty of the United States with France, or with any other
nation, which has changed that law, or has made any provision
upon the subject. It is not to be supposed that, if any statute or
treaty had been or should be made, it would recognize as conclusive the judgments of any country, which did not give like
effect to our own judgments. In the absence of statute or treaty,
it appears to us equally unwarrantable to assume that the comity
of the United States requires anything more.

If we should hold this judgment to be conclusive, we should
allow it an effect to which, supposing the defendants' offer to be
sustained by actual proof, it would, in the absence of a special
treaty, be entitled in hardly any other country in Christendom,
except the country in which it was rendered. If the judgment had
been rendered in this country, or in any other outside of the jurisdiction of France, the French courts would not have executed or
enforced it, except after examining into its merits. The very
judgment now sued on would be held inconclusive in almost any
other country than France. In England, and in the Colonies
subject to the law of England, the fraud alleged in its procure-
ment would be a sufficient ground for disregarding it. In the
courts of nearly every other nation, it would be subject to re-
examination, either merely because it was a foreign judgment,
or because judgments of that nation would be re-examinable in
the courts of France.

For these reasons, in the action at law, the

> *Judgment is reversed, and the cause remanded to the Circuit
> Court with directions to set aside the verdict and to order
> a new trial.*

For the same reasons, in the suit in equity between these
parties, the foreign judgment is not a bar, and, therefore, the

> *Decree dismissing the bill is reversed, the plea adjudged bad,
> and the cause remanded to the Circuit Court for further
> proceedings not inconsistent with this opinion.*

Mr. Chief Justice FULLER, with whom concurred Mr. Justice HARLAND, Mr. Justice BREWER, and Mr. Justice JACKSON, dissenting.

Plaintiffs brought their action on a judgment recovered by them against the defendants in the courts of France, which courts had jurisdiction over person and subject-matter, and in respect of which judgment no fraud was alleged, except in particulars contested in and considered by the French courts. The question is whether under these circumstances, and in the absence of a treaty or act of Congress, the judgment is re-examinable upon the merits. This question I regard as one to be determined by the ordinary and settled rule in respect of allowing a party, who has had an opportunity to prove his case in a competent court, to retry it on the merits, and it seems to me that the doctrine of *res judicata* applicable to domestic judgments should be applied to foreign judgments as well, and rests on the same general ground of public policy that there should be an end of litigation.

This application of the doctrine is in accordance with our own jurisprudence, and it is not necessary that we should hold it to be required by some rule of international law. The fundamental principle concerning judgments is that disputes are finally determined by them, and I am unable to perceive why a judgment *in personam* which is not open to question on the ground of want of jurisdiction, either intrinsically or over the parties, or of fraud, or on any other recognized ground of impeachment, should not be held *inter partes*, though recovered abroad, conclusive on the merits.

Judgments are executory while unpaid, but in this country execution is not given upon a foreign judgment as such, it being enforced through a new judgment obtained in an action brought for that purpose.

The principle that requires litigation to be treated as terminated by final judgment properly rendered, is as applicable to a judgment proceeded on in such an action, as to any other, and forbids the allowance to the judgment debtor of a retrial of the original cause of action, as of right, in disregard of the obligation to pay arising on the judgment and of the rights acquired by the judgment creditor thereby.

That any other conclusion is inadmissible is forcibly illustrated by the case in hand. Plaintiffs in error were trading copartners in Paris as well as in New York, and had a place of business in Paris at the time of these transactions and of the commencement of the suit against them in France. The subjects of the suit were commercial transactions, having their origin, and partly performed, in France under a contract there made, and alleged to be modified by the dealings of the parties there; and one of the claims against them was for goods sold to them there. They appeared generally in the case, without protest, and by counterclaims relating to the same general course of business, a part of them only connected with the claims against them, became actors in the suit and submitted to the courts their own claims for affirmative relief, as well as the claims against them. The courts were competent, and they took the chances of a decision in their favor. As traders in France they were under the protection of its laws and were bound by its laws, its commercial usages, and its rules of procedure. The fact that they were Americans and the opposite parties were citizens of France is immaterial, and there is no suggestion on the record that those courts proceeded on any other ground than that all litigants, whatever their nationality, were entitled to equal justice therein. If plaintiffs in error had succeeded in their cross suit and recovered judgment against defendants in error, and had sued them here on that judgment, defendants in error would not have been permitted to say that the judgment in France was not conclusive against them. As it was, defendants in error recovered, and I think plaintiffs in error are not entitled to try their fortune anew before the courts of this country on the same matters voluntarily submitted by them to the decision of the foreign tribunal. We are dealing with the judgment of a court of a civilized country, whose laws and system of justice recognized the general rules in respect to property and rights between man and man prevailing among all civilized peoples. Obviously the last persons who should be heard to complain are those who identified themselves with the business of that country, knowing that all their transactions there would be subject to the local laws and modes of doing business. The French courts appear to have acted "judically, honestly, and with the intention to arrive at the right conclusion;" and a result thus reached ought not to be disturbed.

[The learned Chief Justice here recited extracts from the opinions in Nouvion v. Freeman, 15 App. Cas. 1, and Godard v. Gray, L. R. 6 Q. B. 139, and continued:]

In any aspect, it is difficult to see why rights acquired under foreign judgments do not belong to the category of private rights acquired under foreign laws. Now the rule is universal in this country that private rights acquired under the laws of foreign States will be respected and enforced in our courts unless contrary to the policy or prejudicial to the interests of the State where this is sought to be done; and although the source of this rule may have been the comity characterizing the intercourse between nations, it prevails to-day by its own strength, and the right to the application of the law to which the particular transaction is subject is a juridical right.

And, without going into the refinements of the publicists on the subject, it appears to me that that law finds authoritative expression in the judgments of courts of competent jurisdiction over parties and subject-matter.

It is held by the majority of the court that defendants cannot be permitted to contest the validity and effect of this judgment on the general ground that it was erroneous in law or in fact; and the special grounds relied on are *seriatim* rejected. In respect of the last of these, that of fraud, it is said that it is unnecessary in this case to decide whether certain decisions cited in regard to impeaching foreign judgments for fraud could be followed consistently with our own decisions as to impeaching domestic judgments for that reason, "because there is a distinct and independent ground upon which we are satisfied that the comity of our nation does not require us to give conclusive effect to the judgments of the courts of France, and that ground is the want of reciprocity on the part of France as to the effect to be given to the judgments of this and other foreign countries." And the conclusion is announced to be "that judgments rendered in France or in any other foreign country, by the laws of which our own judgments are reviewable upon the merits, are not entitled to full credit and conclusive effect when sued upon in this country, but are *prima facie* evidence only of the justice of the plaintiff's claim." In other words, that although no special ground exists for impeaching the original justice of a judgment, such as want of jurisdiction or fraud, the right to retry the merits of the original cause at large, defendant being put upon proving those merits, should be accorded in every suit on judgments recovered in countries where our own judgments are not given full effect, on that ground merely.

I cannot yield my assent to the proposition that because by legislation and judicial decision in France that effect is not there given to judgments recovered in this country which, according to our jurisprudence, we think should be given to judgments

wherever recovered, (subject, of course, to the recognized exceptions,) therefore we should pursue the same line of conduct
as respects the judgments of French tribunals. The application
of the doctrine of *res judicata* does not rest in discretion; and
it is for the government, and not for its courts, to adopt the
principle of retorsion, if deemed under any circumstances desirable or necessary.

As the court expressly abstains from deciding whether the
judgment is impeachable on the ground of fraud, I refrain from
any observations on that branch of the case.

Mr. Justice HARLAN, Mr. Justice BREWER, and Mr. Justice
JACKSON concur in this dissent.

FERGUSON v. CRAWFORD, 1877.

[70 N. Y. 253.]

RAPALLO, J. This action was brought to foreclose a mortgage, held by the plaintiff, on certain real estate in the county of
Westchester. One of the defences was, that the rights of the
plaintiff, as mortgagee, had been barred by a judgment of foreclosure of a mortgage prior to his, in favor of one McFarquahar,
covering the same premises, under which judgment the premises
had been sold to the defendant Horton. It was alleged in the
answer that the plaintiff was a defendant in the McFarquahar
action, in which the judgment had been rendered, and appeared
therein, by John W. Mills, as his attorney, but did not put in any
answer.

On the trial of the present action, the defendants, in support
of this defence, put in evidence the judgment-roll in the last-mentioned action, which roll contained a notice of appearance for the
present plaintiff, and a consent that judgment be entered, purporting to be signed by Mills. The judgment was entered by default
for want of an answer, and on this consent, and recited that the
summons had been served on the defendants therein, and that none
of them had appeared, except the present plaintiff, by John W.
Mills, his attorney, and some others named in the judgment.

Thereupon the plaintiff called Mills as a witness, and offered
to prove by him, 1st. That the signature to the notice of appearance and consent was a forgery; 2d. That Mills was never authorized to appear for the plaintiff; and 3d. That he never did appear
for him.

No proof of service of the summons on the plaintiff is attached to or contained in that judgment-roll, and it appears to be conceded on the present argument, as matter of fact, that no such service was made. The defendants rely wholly upon the effect of the recital in the judgment and the notice of appearance contained in the judgment-roll, and claim that in a collateral action these import absolute verity and cannot be contradicted by extrinsic evidence.

They also claim that the case of *Brown* v. *Nichols* (42 N. Y., 26) is decisive of this case. There a judgment had been recovered against a defendant who had not been served with process, but for whom an attorney had appeared without authority, and it was held by this court that the judgment could not be attacked on that ground for want of jurisdiction in a collateral proceeding.

That decision does not reach the present case. It is not founded upon any doctrine which precludes a party from showing, as matter of fact, that he was never brought before the court, or appeared in it, but is based upon a long line of authority, which holds that when an attorney of the court appears for a party his appearance is recognized and his authority will be presumed to the extent, at least, of giving validity to the proceeding. That he is an officer of the court, amenable to it for misconduct, and to any party for whom he assumes to act without authority, for all damages occasioned by such action, and for reasons of public policy the court holds the appearance good, leaving the aggrieved party to his action for damages against the attorney, granting relief against the judgment, only in a direct application, and in case the attorney is shown to be irresponsible. (*Denton* v. *Noyes*, 6 Johns., 296.) This, however, is an entirely different case. The offer was not merely to show that the attorney was not authorized to appear, but that he did not in fact appear, and that the pretended appearance was a forgery.

None of the principles upon which the decisions in *Denton* v. *Noyes*, and *Brown* v. *Nichols* rest, can be applied to such a case. There is no act of any officer of the court which public policy requires should be recognized. There is no party against whom the innocent defendant can have redress. He is sought to be held bound by a judgment when he was never personally summoned or had notice of the proceeding, which result has been frequently declared to be contrary to the first principles of justice, and this is sought to be accomplished by means of a judgment entered upon forged papers. No principle of public policy requires or sanctions sustaining such a judgment. The only difficulty in the case arises upon the objection that the evidence offered tends to contradict the record, and from the adjudications which attach to the judgment of a court of general jurisdiction, a conclusive presumption of jurisdiction over the parties, which cannot be contradicted except by matter appearing on the face of the record itself.

It is an elementary principle recognized in all the cases that, to give binding effect to a judgment of any court, whether of general or limited jurisdiction, it is essential that the court should have jurisdiction of the person as well as the subject-matter, and that the want of jurisdiction over either may always be set up against a judgment when sought to be enforced, or any benefit is claimed under it. There is no difference of opinion as to this general rule, but the point of difficulty is as to the manner in which this want of jurisdiction must be made to appear, in the case of a judgment of a domestic court of general jurisdiction, acting in the exercise of its general powers, when it comes in question in a collateral action: Whether, when the record is silent as to the steps taken to bring the parties into court, it may be proved by evidence that they were not legally summoned and did not appear; or whether, when the record recites that they were summoned or appeared, such recitals may be contradicted by extrinsic evidence; or whether the jurisdiction over the person and subject-matter is a presumption of law, which cannot be contradicted, unless it appears on the face of the record itself that there was a want of such jurisdiction, as in cases where the record shows that the service of process was by publication or some other method than personal.

On these points there has been as much diversity of opinion, especially between the courts of this State and those of other States, as upon any general question which can be mentioned, although there has yet been no authoritative adjudication in this State on the subject. It is well settled by our own decisions, that in the case of a judgment of a court of general jurisdiction of a sister State, although it is entitled to the benefit of the presumption of jurisdiction which exists in favor of a judgment of one of our own courts, yet the want of jurisdiction may be shown by extrinsic evidence, and that even a recital in the judgment record that the defendant was served with process, or appeared by attorney, or of any other jurisdictional fact, is not conclusive, but may be contradicted by extrinsic evidence. (*Borden* v. *Fitch*, 15 John., 121; *Starbuck* v. *Murray*, 5 Wen., 148; *Shumway* v.

Stillman, 6 Wen., 447; *Kerr* v. *Kerr*, 41 N. Y., 272; *Hoffman* v. *Hoffman*, 46 N. Y., 30.)

And the same rule prevails in some of the other States in regard to the judgments of courts of sister States. Although some have held, even in regard to such a judgment, that if the record contains recitals showing jurisdiction, they cannot be contradicted. (*Field* v. *Gibbs*, 1 Peters, C. C. R., 155; *Roberts* v. *Caldwell*, 5 Dana, 512; *Ewer* v. *Coffin*, 1 Cushing, 23; 1 R. I., 73; *Shelton* v. *Tiffin*, 6 How. [U. S.], 186.)

After considerable research I have been unable to find a single authoritative adjudication, in this or any other State, deciding that in the case of a domestic judgment of a court of general jurisdiction, want of jurisdiction over the person may be shown by extrinsic evidence, while there are a great number of adjudications in neighboring States, holding that in the case of such judgments, parties and privies are estopped in collateral actions to deny the jurisdiction of the court over the person as well as the subject-matter, unless it appear on the face of the record that the court had not acquired jurisdiction; and that in such cases there is a conclusive presumption of law that jurisdiction was acquired by service of process or the appearance of the party. The cases are very numerous, but the citation of a few of them will suffice.

In *Cook* v. *Darling* (18 Pick., 393), in an action of debt on a domestic judgment, the defendant pleaded that, at the time of the supposed service upon him of the writ in the original action, he was not an inhabitant of the State of Massachusetts; that he had no notice of the action, and did not appear therein.

This plea was held bad on demurrer, on the ground that the judgment could not be impeached colaterally. In *Granger* v. *Clarke* (22 Maine, 128), also an action on a judgment, the plea was the same, with the addition that the judgment had been obtained by fraud; but it was held to constitute no defence. *Coit* v. *Haven* (30 Conn., 190) was a *scire facias* on a judgment, and the defendant pleaded that the writ in the original action was never served upon him, etc.; and the court held, in an elaborate opinion, that a judgment of a domestic court of general jurisdiction could not be attacked collaterally, unless the want of jurisdiction appeared upon the face of the record, and that jurisdictional facts, such as the service of the writ and the like, were conclusively presumed in favor of such a judgment, unless the record showed the contrary, although this rule did not apply to foreign judgments, or judgments of the courts of sister States, or to domestic judgments of inferior courts, and that the only remedy in such a case was by writ of error, or application to a court of equity.

The same rule is held in *Penobscot R. R. Co.* v. *Weeks* (52 Maine, 456; *Wingate* v. *Haywood*, (40 N. H., 437; *Clark* v. *Bryan* (16 Md., 171); *Callen* v. *Ellison* (13 Ohio St. R., 446); *Horner* v. *Doe* (1 Ind., 131); *Wright* v. *Marsh* (2 Iowa, 94), and *Pierce* v. *Griffin* (16 Iowa, 552), and in numerous other cases which are referred to in the case of *Hahn* v. *Kelly* (34 Cal., 391), which adopts the same rule and contains a full and instructive discussion of the question.

There are many cases in other States, and in the courts of the United States, containing expressions general in their char acter, which would seem to sanction the doctrine that a want of jurisdiction over the person or subject-matter may in all cases be shown by extrinsic evidence, and they are sometimes cited as authorities to that effect. (*Elliott* v. *Piersol*, 1 Peters, 340; *Hollingsworth* v. *Barbour*, 4 Peters, 466; *Hickey* v. *Stewart*, 3 How. [U. S.], 750; *Shriver* v. *Lynn*, 2 How. [U S.], 43; *Williamson* v. *Berry*, 8 How., 495; *Same* v. *Ball*, 8 How., 495; *Girvin* v. *McCowell*, 8 Sm. & M., 351; *Enos* v. *Smith*, 7 Sm. & M., 85; *Campbell* v. *Brown*, 6 How. [Miss.], 106; *Schafer* v. *Gates*, 2 B. Monroe, 453; *Wilcox* v. *Jackson*, 13 Peters, 498; *Miller* v. *Ewing*, 8 Sm. & M., 421, and numerous other cases not cited.) But an examination of these cases discloses that they all relate either to judgments of inferior courts, or courts of limited jurisdiction, or courts of general jurisdiction acting in the exercise of special statutory powers, which proceedings stand on the same footing with those of courts of limited and inferior jurisdiction (3 N. Y., 511) or courts of sister States, or to cases where the want of jurisdiction appeared on the face of the record, or to cases of direct proceedings to reverse or set aside the judgment. I have not found one which adjudicated the point now under consideration, otherwise than those to which I have referred. There are some cases which hold that the want of authority of an attorney to appear may be shown by extrinsic evidence, although the record states that an attorney appeared for the party, but those are placed expressly on the ground that such evidence does not contradict the record. (*Bodurtha* v. *Goodrich*, 3 Gray, 508; *Shelton* v. *Tiffin*, 6 How. [U. S.], 186; 14 How., 340). Those cases are, however, in conflict with the decision of this court, in *Brown* v. *Nichols* (42 N. Y., 26), and in many other cases.

The learned annotators of Smith's Leading Cases, *Hare &* *Wallace* (1 Sm. L. Cases, vol. 1, p. 842 [marg.]) sum the matter up by saying: "Whatever the rule may be where the record is silent, it would seem clearly and conclusively established by a weight of authority too great for opposition, unless on the ground of local and peculiar law, that no one can contradict that which the record actually avers, and that a recital of notice or appearance, or a return of service by the sheriff in the record of a domestic court of general jurisdiction, is absolutely conclusive and cannot be disproved by extrinsic evidence."

It is quite remarkable, however, that notwithstanding the formidable array of authority in its favor, the courts of this State have never sustained this doctrine by any adjudication, but on the contrary the great weight of judicial opinion, and the views of some of our most distinguished jurists, are directly opposed to it.

As has been already stated, our courts have settled by adjudication in regard to judgments of sister States, that the question of jurisdiction may be inquired into, and a want of jurisdiction over the person shown by evidence, and have further decided (in opposition to the holding of courts of some of the other States) that this may be done, even if it involves the contradiction of a recital in the judgment record. In stating the reasons for this conclusion, our courts have founded it on general principles, quite as applicable to domestic judgments as to others, and save in one case (*Kerr* v. *Kerr*, 41 N. Y., 272), have in their opinions made no discrimination between them. (*Borden* v. *Fitch,* 15 Johns., 121; *Starbuck* v. *Murray,* 5 Wend., 148; *Noyes* v. *Butler,* 6 Barb., 613, and cases cited.)

When we come to consider the effect of these authorities, it is difficult to find any solid ground upon which to rest a distinction between domestic judgments and judgments of sister States in regard to this question, for under the provisions of the Constitution of the United States, which requires that full faith and credit shall be given in each State to the public acts, records and judicial proceedings of every other State, it is now well settled that when a judgment of a court of a sister State is duly proved in a court of this State, it is entitled here to all the effect to which it is entitled in the courts of the State where rendered. If conclusive there it is equally conclusive in all the States of the Union; and whatever pleas would be good to a suit therein in the State where rendered, and none others can be pleaded in any court in the United States. (*Hampton* v. *McConnel,* 3 Wheaton,

234; Story Com. on Cons., § 183; *Mills* v. *Duryee*, 7 Cranch, 481.)

In holding, therefore, that a defense that the party was not served and did not appear, although the record stated that he did, was good, our courts must have held that such is the law of this State and the common law, and consequently, that in the absence of proof of any special law to the contrary in the State where the judgment was rendered, it must be presumed to be also the law of that State. The judgments of our courts can stand on no other logical basis. The distinction which is made in almost all the other States of the Union between the effect of domestic judgments and judgments of sister States, in regard to the conclusiveness of the presumption of jurisdiction over the person, is sought to be explained, by saying that in regard to domestic judgments the party aggrieved can obtain relief by application to the court in which the judgment was rendered, or by writ of error, whereas in the case of a judgment rendered against him in another State he would be obliged to go into a foreign jurisdiction for redress, which would be a manifestly inadequate protection; and therefore the Constitution may be construed so as to apply only where the persons affected by the judgment were within the operation of the proceeding. This explanation, however, does not remove the difficulty in making the distinction, for if there is a conclusive presumption that there was jurisdiction, that presumption must exist in one case as well as in the other. The question whether or not the party is estopped, cannot be made to depend upon the greater inconvenience of getting rid of the estoppel in one case than in another.

But aside from this observation as to the effect of the authorities, an examination of them shows that our courts did in fact proceed upon a ground common to both classes of judgments. The reasons are fully stated in the case of *Starbuck* v. *Murray* (5 Wend., 148). In that case, which was an action upon a Massachusetts judgment, the defendant pleaded that no process was served on him in the suit in which the judgment sued on was rendered, and that he never appeared therein in person or by attorney, and this plea was held good, notwithstanding that the record of the judgment stated that the defendant appeared to the suit. MARCY, J., in delivering the opinion of the court, and referring to the argument that the defendant was estopped from asserting anything against the allegation of his appearance contained in the record, says: "It appears to me that this proposition assumes the very fact to be established, which is the only question in issue. For what purpose does the defendant question the jurisdiction of the court? Solely to show that its proceedings and judgments are void, and therefore the supposed record is not in truth a record. If the defendant had not proper notice of, and did not appear to, the original action, all the State courts, with one exception, agree in opinion that the paper introduced, as to him, is no record. But if he cannot show even against the pretended record that fact, on the alleged ground of the uncontrollable verity of the record, he is deprived of his defence by a process of reasoning that is to my mind little less than sophistry. The plaintiff in effect declares to the defendant—the paper declared on, is a record, because it says you appeared; and you appeared, because the paper is a record. This is reasoning in a circle. The appearance makes the record uncontrollable verity, and the record makes the appearance an unimpeachable fact." And again, at p. 160, he says: "To say that the defendant may show the supposed record to be a nullity, by showing a want of jurisdiction in the court which made it, and at the same time to estop him from doing so because the court has inserted in the record an allegation which he offers to prove untrue, does not seem to me to be very consistent."

This is but an amplification of what is sometimes more briefly expressed in the books, that where the defence goes to defeat the record, there is no estoppel. That the reasoning of MARCY, J., is applicable to domestic judgments, is also the opinion of the learned annotators to Phillip's Evidence. (Cowen and Hill's notes [1st Ed.], p. 801, note 551.) Referring to the opinion of MARCY, J., before cited, they say: "The same may be said respecting any judgment, sentence or decree. A want of jurisdiction in the court pronouncing it may always be set up when it is sought to be enforced, or when any benefit is claimed under it; and the principle which ordinarily forbids the impeachment or contradiction of a record has no sort of application to the case." The dicta of our judges are all to the same effect, although the precise case does not seem to have arisen. In *Bigelow* v. *Stearns* (19 Johns., 41), SPENCER, Ch. J., laid down the broad rule that if a court, whether of limited jurisdiction or not, undertakes to hold cognizance of a cause without having gained jurisdiction of the person by having him before them in the manner required by law, the proceedings are void. In *Latham* v. *Edgerton* (9 Cow., 227), SUTHERLAND, J., in regard to a judgment of a court of

common pleas, says: "The principle that a record cannot be impeached by pleading, is not applicable to a case like this. The
want of jurisdiction is a matter that may always be set up against
a judgment when sought to be enforced or where any benefit is
claimed under it." Citing *Mills* v. *Martin* (19 Johns., 33), he
also says (p. 229): "The plaintiff below might have applied to
the court to set aside their proceedings, but he was not bound
to do so. He had a right to lie by until the judgment was set up
against him, and then to show that the proceedings were void for
want of jurisdiction. In *Davis* v. *Packard* (6 Wend., 327, 332),
in the Court of Errors, the Chancellor, speaking of domestic
judgments, says: "If the jurisdiction of the court is general or
unlimited both as to parties and subject-matter, it will be presumed to have had jurisdiction of the cause unless it appears
affirmatively from the record, *or by the showing of the party
denying the jurisdiction of the court,* that some special circumstances existed to oust the court of its jurisdiction in that particular case." In *Bloom* v. *Burdick* (1 Hill, 130), BRONSON, J.,
says: "The distinction between superior and inferior courts, is not
of much importance in this particular case, for whenever it
appears that there was a want of jurisdiction, the judgment will
be void in whatever court it was rendered;" and in *People* v.
Cassels (5 Hill, 164, 168), the same learned judge makes the
remark, that no court or officer can acquire jurisdiction by the
mere assertion of it, or by falsely alleging the existence of facts
upon which jurisdiction depends. In *Harrington* v. *The People*
(6 Barb., 607, 610), PAIGE, J., expresses the opinion that the
jurisdiction of a court, whether of general or limited jurisdiction,
may be inquired into, although the record of the judgment states
facts giving it jurisdiction. He repeats the same view in *Noyes*
v. *Butler* (6 Barb., 613, 617), and in *Hard* v. *Shipman* (6
Barb., 621, 623, 624), where he says of superior as well as inferior
courts, that the record is never conclusive as to the recital of a
jurisdictional fact, and the defendant is always at liberty to show
a want of jurisdiction, although the record avers the contrary.
If the court had no jurisdiction, it had no power to make a record,
and the supposed record is not in truth a record. (Citing *Starbuck* v. *Murray*, 5 Wend., 158.) The language of GRIDLEY, J.,
in *Wright* v. *Douglass* (10 Barb., 97, 111), is still more in point.
He observes: "It is denied by counsel for the plaintiff, that want
of jurisdiction can be shown collaterally to defeat a judgment of
a court of general jurisdiction. The true rule, however, is that

laid down in the opinion just cited (op. of BRONSON, J., in *Bloom v. Burdick*, 1 Hill, 138 to 143), that in a court of general jurisdiction, it is to be presumed that the court has jurisdiction till the contrary appears, but the want of jurisdiction may always be shown *by evidence*, except in one solitary case," viz: "When jurisdiction depends on a fact that is litigated in a suit, and is adjudged in favor of the party who avers jurisdiction, then the question of jurisdiction is judicially decided, and the judgment record is conclusive evidence of jurisdiction until set aside or reversed by a direct proceeding."

The General Term, in that case, held that a judgment of the Supreme Court was void for want of service of an attachment, notwithstanding that the record averred that the attachment had been duly served and returned, according to law. The judgment in the case cited was reversed (7 N. Y., 564), but not upon the point referred to here. It cannot, however, be held to be an adjudication upon that point, because the judgment was not rendered in the exercise of the general powers of the court, but in pursuance of a special statutory authority.

In the *Chemung Canal Bank* v. *Judson* (8 N. Y., 254), the general principle is recognized, that the jurisdiction of any court exercising authority over a subject may be inquired into, and in *Adams* v. *The Saratoga & Washington R. R. Co.* (10 N. Y., 328, 333), GRIDLEY, J., maintains as to the judgments of all courts, that jurisdiction may be inquired into, and disproved by evidence, nothwithstanding recitals in the record, and says that such is the doctrine of the courts of this State, although it may be different in some of the other States, and perhaps also in England; and he says the idea is not to be tolerated, that the attorney could make up a record or decree, reciting that due notice was given to the defendant of a proceeding, when he never heard of it, and the decree held conclusive against an offer to show this vital allegation false. That was a case of a special proceeding, and, therefore, not an authority on the point. In *Pendleton* v. *Weed* (17 N. Y., 75), where a judgment of the Supreme Court was sought to be attacked collaterally, it is said by STRONG, J.: "It is undoubtedly true that the want of jurisdiction of the person is a good defence in answer to a judgment when set up for any purpose, *and that such jurisdiction is open for inquiry;*" and by COMSTOCK, J., at p. 77: "I assent to the doctrine that where there is no suit or process, appearance or confession, no valid judgment can be rendered in any court; that in such a case *the*

recital in the record of jurisdictional facts is not conclusive."
(Citing *Starbuck* v. *Murray.*) "I think it is always the right of
a party against whom a record is set up, to show that no jurisdiction of his person was acquired, and consequently that there
was no right or authority to make up the record against him."
SELDEN and PRATT, JJ., concurred in these views, but the case
was disposed of on a different point.

In *Porter* v. *Bronson* (29 How. Pr., 292, and S. C., 19, Abb.
Pr., 236), the Court of Common Pleas of the City of New York
held, at General Term, that assuming the Marine Court to be
a court of record, a defendant in an action on a judgment of that
court might set up that he was not served with process and did
not appear, notwithstanding recitals in the record showing jurisdiction; and in *Bolton* v. *Jacks* (6 Rob., 198), JONES, J., says that
it is now conceded, at least in this State, that want of jurisdiction
will render void the judgment of any court, whether it be of
superior or inferior, of general, limited or local jurisdiction, or of
record or not, and that the bare recital of jurisdictional facts in
the record of a judgment of any court, whether superior or
inferior, of general or limited jurisdiction, is not conclusive, but
only *prima facie* evidence of the truth of the fact recited, and the
party against whom a judgment is offered, is not by the bare
fact of such recitals estopped from showing by affirmative proof,
that they were untrue and thus rendering the judgment void
for want of jurisdiction. He cites in support of this opinion, several of the cases which I have referred to, and *Dobson* v. *Pearce*
(12 N. Y., 164), and *Hatcher* v. *Rocheleau* (18 N. Y., 92).

It thus appears that the current of judicial opinion in this
State is very strong and uniform in favor of the proposition stated
by JONES J., in 6 Rob., 198, and if adopted here, is decisive of
the present case. It has not as yet, however, been directly adjudicated, and if sustained, it must rest upon the local law of this
State, as it finds no support in adjudications elsewhere. There
are reasons, however, founded upon our system of practice, which
would warrant us in so holding. The powers of a court of equity
being vested in our courts of law, and equitable defences being
allowable, there is no reason why, to an action upon a judgment,
the defendant should not be permitted to set up, by way of
defence, any matter which would be ground or relief in equity
against the judgment; and it is conceded in those States where
the record is held conclusive, that when the judgment has been
obtained by fraud, or without bringing the defendant into court,

and the want of jurisdiction does not appear upon the face of the record, relief may be obtained in equity.

The technical difficulty arising from the conclusiveness of the record is thus obviated. In the present case, the judgment is set up by the defendants as a bar to the plaintiff's action. But it must be borne in mind, that this is an equitable action, being for the foreclosure of a mortgage. The defendants set up the fore-closure in the McFarquahar case as a bar, but being in a court of equity, the plaintiff had a right to set up any matter showing that the defendants ought not in equity to avail themselves of that judgment. They offered to show that it was entered *ex parte* on forged papers. It does not appear that the plaintiff ever had any knowledge of it, and it is not pretended that he was legally summoned. Such a judgment would never be upheld in equity, even in favor of one ignorant of the fraud and claiming *bona fide* under it. He stands in no better position than any other party claiming *bona fide* under a forged instrument.

The case is analogous in principle to that of the *Bridgeport Savings Bank* v. *Eldredge* (28 Conn., 557). That was a bill filed by a second mortgagee to redeem mortgaged premises from a first mortgagee. The first mortgagee had obtained a decree of fore-closure against the second mortgagee, and the time limited for redemption had expired. The record of the decree found the fact that legal service of the bill in the first suit had been made on the second mortgagee, but in fact none had been made, and he had no actual knowledge of the pendency of the suit until after the time limited for redemption had expired; and he would have redeemed if he had known of the decree.

It was held, 1. That the decree was not in any proper sense a bar to the present suit, as a judgment at law would be a bar to a suit at law; but that, without impugning the decree, the court could, for equitable reasons shown, allow a further time for redemption.

2. That, therefore, the question whether the plaintiff could contradict the record by showing that no service of the bill was, in fact, made upon him, did not present itself as a technical one, to be determined by the rules with regard to the verity of judicial records, but only in its relation to the plaintiff's rights to equit-able relief, and therefore that evidence of want of notice was admissible.

The bill to redeem was not framed to open the former decree, and contained no allegations adapted to or praying for such relief, but was in the ordinary form of a bill for redemption, taking no notice of the previous decree. The decree was set up in the answer, and it was averred that it was rendered on legal notice to the plaintiff. The court, however, held that this defence might be rebutted by evidence of facts which should preclude defendants from taking advantage of a decree of which they could not conscientiously avail themselves.

Under the system of practice in this State, no reply to an answer setting up new matter is required, but the plaintiff is allowed to rebut it by evidence. Neither is it necessary to anticipate a defence arising upon a deed or record by inserting matter in the complaint in avoidance of it. The defence may never be set up, and the plaintiff is not bound to suppose that it will be. The state of the pleadings, therefore, presents no difficulty. The only question which might be raised is, that McFarquahar, in whose name the decree was obtained, should be before the court, but no such objection was made at the trial, and if it had been, I do not see that he has any interest in the question. All the parties claiming under the decree and sale are parties to this action, and I see no reason why the validity of the McFarquahar foreclosure cannot be tried herein as well as upon a motion or in a separate suit to set aside the decree.

The judgment should be reversed, and a new trial ordered with costs to abide the event.

All concur; ANDREWS, J., in result.

Judgment reversed.[19]

---

[19]See *Grover and Baker Sewing Machine Co. v. Radcliffe, 137 U. S. 287; Price v. Schaeffer, 161 Pa. St. 530; Thompson v. Whitman, 18 Wall. 457; Keyser v. Lowell, 117 Fed. Rep. 400.*

SITUS OF A DEBT.

CHICAGO R. I. RY. v. STURM, 1899.

[174 U. S. 710.]

THE defendant in error brought an anction against the plaintiff in error in a justices' court of Belleville, Republic County, Kansas, for the sum of $140, for wages due. Judgment was rendered for him in the sum of $140 and interest and costs.

The plaintiff in error appealed from the judgment to the district court of the county, to which court all the papers were transmitted, and the case docketed for trial.

On the 10th of October, 1894, the case was called for trial, when plaintiff in error filed a motion for continuance, supported by an affidavit affirming that on the 13th day of December, 1893, in the county of Pottawattomie and State of Iowa, one A. H. Willard commenced an action against E. H. Sturm in justices' court before Oride Vien, a justice of the peace for said county, to recover the sum of $78.63, with interest at the rate of ten per cent per annum, and at the same time sued out a writ of attachment and garnishment, and duly garnisheed the plaintiff in error, and at that time plaintiff in error was indebted to defendant in error in the sum of $77.17 for wages, being the same wages sought to be recovered in this action;

That plaintiff in error filed its answer, admitting such indebtedness;

That at the time of the commencement of said action in Pottawattomie County the defendant was a non-resident of the State of Iowa, and that service upon him was duly made by publication, and that afterwards judgment was rendered against him and plaintiff in error as garnishee for the sum of $76.16, and costs of suit amounting to $19, and from such judgment appealed to the district court of said county, where said action was then pending undetermined;

That the moneys sought to be recovered in this action are the same moneys sought to be recovered in the garnishment proceedings, and that under the laws of Iowa its courts had jurisdiction thereof, and that the said moneys were not at the time of the garnishment exempt from attachment, execution or garnishment; that the justice of the peace at all of the times of the proceedings was a duly qualified and acting justice, and that all the proceedings were commenced prior to the commencement of the present action, and that if the case be continued until the next term of the court the action in Iowa will be determined and the rights of plaintiff in error protected.

The motion was denied, and the plaintiff in error pleaded in answer the same matters alleged in the affidavit for continuance, and attached to the answer a certified copy of the proceedings in the Iowa courts. It also alleged that it was a corporation duly organized under the laws of the States of Illinois and Iowa, doing business in the State of Kansas.

The defendant in error replied to the answer, and alleged that the amount due from plaintiff in error was for wages due for services rendered within three months next prior to the commencement of the action; that he was a resident, head of a family, and that the wages were exempt under the laws of Kansas, and not subject to garnishment proceedings; that plaintiff in error knew these facts, and that the Iowa court had no jurisdiction of his property or person.

Evidence was introduced in support of the issues, including certain sections of the laws of Iowa relating to service by publication, and to attachment and garnishment, and judgment was rendered for the defendant in error in the amount sued for.

A new trial was moved, on the ground, among others, that the "decision is contrary to and in conflict with section 1, article IV, of the Constitution of the United States."

The motion was denied.

On error to the Court of Appeals, and from thence to the Supreme Court, the judgment was affirmed, and the case was then brought here.

The defendant in error was notified of the suit against him in Iowa and of the proceedings in garnishment in time to have protected his rights.

The errors assigned present in various ways the contention that the Supreme Court of Kansas refused to give full faith and credit to the records and judicial proceedings of the courts of the State of Iowa, in violation of section 1, article IV, of the Constitution of the United States, and of the act of Congress entitled "An act to prescribe the mode in which the public acts, records and judicial proceedings in each State shall be authenticated so as to take effect in every other State," approved May 26, 1790.

No appearance for defendant in error

Mr. Justice McKENNA, after making the foregoing statement, delivered the opinion of the court.

How proceedings in garnishment may be availed of in defence—whether in abatement or bar of the suit on the debt attached or for a continuance of it or suspension of execution—the practice of the States of the Union is not uniform. But it is obvious and necessary justice that such proceedings should be allowed as a defence in some way.

In the pending suit plaintiff in error moved for a continuance, and not securing it pleaded the proceedings in garnishment in answer. Judgment, however, was rendered against it, and sustained by the Supreme Court, on the authority of *Missouri Pacific*

Railway Co. v. *Sharitt,* 43 Kansas, 375, and "for the reasons stated by Mr. Justice Valentine in that case."

The facts of that case were as follows: The Missouri Pacific Railway Company was indebted to Sharitt for services performed in Kansas. Sharitt was indebted to one J. P. Stewart, a resident of Missouri. Stewart sued him in Missouri, and attached his wages in the hands of the railway company, and the latter answered in the suit in accordance with the order of garnishment on the 28th of July, 1887, admitting indebtedness, and on the 29th of September was ordered to pay its amount into court. On the 27th of July Sharitt brought an action in Kansas against the railway company to recover for his services, and the company in defence pleaded the garnishment and order of the Missouri court. The amount due Sharitt having been for wages, was exempt from attachment in Kansas. It was held that the garnishment was not a defence. The facts were similar therefore to those of the case at bar.

The ground of the opinion of Mr. Justice Valentine was that the Missouri court had no jurisdiction because the *situs* of the debt was in Kansas. In other words, and to quote the language of the learned justice, "the *situs* of a debt is either with the owner thereof, or at his domicil; or where the debt is to be paid; and it cannot be subjected to a proceeding in garnishment anywhere else. . . It is not the debtor who can carry or trans fer or transport the property in a debt from one State or jurisdiction into another. The *situs* of the property in a debt can be changed only by the change of location of the creditor who is the owner thereof, or with his consent."

The primary proposition is that the *situs* of a debt is at the domicil of a creditor, or, to state it negatively, it is not at the domicil of the debtor.

The proposition is supported by some cases; it is opposed by others. Its error proceeds, as we conceive, from confounding debt and credit, rights and remedies. The right of a creditor and the obligation of a debtor are correlative but different things, and the law in adapting its remedies for or against either must regard that difference. Of this there are many illustrations, and a proper and accurate attention to it avoids misunderstanding. This court said by Mr. Justice Gray in *Wyman* v. *Halstead,* 109 U. S. 654, 656: "The general rule of law is well settled, that for the purpose of founding administration all simple contract debts are assets at the domicil of the debtor." And this is not because of defective

17

title in the creditor or in his administrator, but because the policy of the State of the debtor requires it to protect home creditors. *Wilkins* v. *Ellett,* 9 Wall. 740; 108 U. S. 256. Debts cannot be assets at the domicil of the debtor if their locality is fixed at the domicil of the creditor, and if the policy of the State of the debtor can protect home creditors through administration proceedings, the same policy can protect home creditors through attachment proceedings.

For illustrations in matters of taxation, see *Kirtland* v. *Hotchkiss,* 100 U. S. 491; *Pullman's Car Co.* v. *Pennsylvania,* 141 U. S. 18; *Savings and Loan Society* v. *Multnomah County,* 169 U. S. 421.

Our attachment laws had their origin in the custom of London. Drake, § 1. Under it a debt was regarded as being where the debtor was, and questions of jurisdiction were settled on that regard. In *Andrews* v. *Clerke,* 1 Carth. 25, Lord Chief Justice Holt summarily decided such a question, and stated the practice under the custom of London. The report of the case is brief, and is as follows:

"Andrews levied a plaint in the Sheriff's Court in London and, upon the usual suggestion that one T. S. (the garnishee) was debtor to the defendant, a foreign attachment was awarded to attach that debt in the hands of T. S., which was accordingly done; and then a diletur was entered, which is in nature of an imparlance in that court.

"Afterwards T. S. (the garnishee) pleaded to the jurisdiction setting forth that the cause of debt due from him to the defendant Sir Robert Clerke, and the contract on which it was founded, did arise, and was made at H. in the county of Middlesex, *extra jurisdictionem curiæ;* and this plea being overruled, it was now moved (in behalf of T. S., the garnishee,) for a prohibition to the sheriff's court aforesaid, suggesting the said matter, (viz.) that the cause of action did arise *extra jurisdictionem,* etc., but the prohibition was denied because the debt always follows the person of the debtor, and it is not material where it was contracted, especially as to this purpose of foreign attachments; for it was always the custom in London to attach debts upon bills of exchange, and goldsmith's notes, etc., if the goldsmith who gave the note on the person to whom the bill is directed, liveth within the city without any respect had to the place where the debt was contracted."

The idea of locality of things which may be said to be intangible is somewhat confusing, but if it be kept up the right of the creditor and the obligation of the debtor cannot have the same, unless debtor and creditor live in the same place. But we do not think it is necessary to resort to the idea at all or to give it important distinction. The essential service of foreign attachment laws is to reach and arrest the payment of what is due and might be paid to a non-resident to the defeat of his creditors. To do it he must go to the domicil of his debtor, and can only do it under the laws and procedure in force there. This is a legal necessity, and considerations of *situs* are somewhat artificial. If not artificial, whatever of substance there is must be with the debtor. *He and he only has something in his hands.* That something is the *res,* and gives character to the action as one in the nature of a proceeding *in rem. Mooney* v. *Buford & George Mfg. Co.,* 72 Fed. Rep. 32; Conflict of Laws, § 549, and notes.

To ignore this is to give immunity to debts owed to non-resident creditors from attachment by their creditors, and to deny necessary remedies. A debt may be as valuable as tangible things. It is not capable of manual seizure, as they are, but no more than they can it be appropriated by attachment without process and the power to execute the process. A notice to the debtor must be given, and can only be given and enforced where he is. This, as we have already said, is a necessity, and it cannot be evaded by the insistence upon fictions or refinements about *situs* or the rights of the creditor. Of course, the debt is the property of the creditor, and because it is, the law seeks to subject it, as it does other property, to the payment of *his* creditors. If it can be done in any other way than by process against and jurisdiction of his debtor, that way does not occur to us.

Besides the proposition which we have discussed there are involved in the decision of the *Sheritt case* the propositions that a debt may have a *situs* where it is payable, and that it cannot be made migratory by the debtor. The latter was probably expressed as a consequence of the primary proposition and does not require separate consideration. Besides there is no fact of change of domicil in the case. The plaintiff in error was not temporarily in Iowa. It was an Iowa corporation and a resident of the State, and was such at the time the debt sued on was contracted, and we are not concerned to inquire whether the cases which decide that a debtor temporarily in a State cannot be garnisheed there, are or are not justified by principle.

The proposition that the *situs* of a debt is where it is to be

paid, is indefinite. "All debts are payable everywhere, unless there
be some special limitation or provision in respect to the payment;
the rule being that debts as such have no *locus* or *situs,* but accompany the creditor everywhere, and authorize a demand upon the
debtor everywhere." 2 Parsons on Contracts, 8th edition, 702.
The debt involved in the pending case had no "special limitation
or provision in respect to payment." It was payable generally
and could have been sued on in Iowa, and therefore was attachable in Iowa. This is the principle and effect of the best considered cases—the inevitable effect from the nature and transitory
actions and the purpose of foreign attachment laws if we would
enforce that purpose. *Embree* v. *Hanna,* 5 Johns. 101; *Hull* v.
Blake, 13 Mass. 153; *Blake* v. *Williams,* 6 Pick. 286; *Harwell* v.
Sharp, 85 Georgia, 124; *Harvey* v. *Great Northern Railway Co.,*
50 Minnesota, 405; *Mahany* v. *Kephart,* 15 W. Va. 609; *Leiber*
v. *Railroad Co.,* 49 Iowa, 688; *National Fire Ins. Co.* v. *Chambers,*
53 N. J. Eq. 468; *Holland* v. *Mobile & Ohio Railroad,* 84 Tenn.
414; *Pomeroy* v. *Rand, McNally & Co.,* 157 Illinois, 176; *Berry
Bros.* v. *Nelson, Davis & Co.,* 77 Texas, 191; *Weyth Hardware
Co.* v. *Lang,* 127 Missouri, 242; *Howland* v. *Chicago, Rock Island
&c. Railway,* 134 Missouri, 474.

Mr Justice Valentine also expressed the view that "if a debt
is exempt from a judicial process in the State where it is created,
the exemption will follow the debt as an incident thereto into any
other State or jurisdiction into which the debt may be supposed
to be carried." For this he cites some cases.

It is not clear whether the learned justice considered that the
doctrine affected the jurisdiction of the Iowa courts or was but
an incident of the law of *situs* as expressed by him. If the latter,
it has been answered by what we have already said. If the former,
it cannot be sustained. It may have been error for the Iowa court
to have ruled against the doctrine, but the error did not destroy
jurisdiction. 134 Missouri, 474.

But we do not assent to the proposition. Exemption laws
are not a part of the contract; they are part of the remedy and
subject to the law of the forum. Freeman on Executions, sec.
209, and cases cited; also *Mineral Point Railroad* v. *Barron,* 83
Illinois, 365; *Carson* v. *Railway Co.,* 88 Tennessee, 646; *Couley*
v. *Chilcote,* 25 Ohio St. 320; *Albrecht* v. *Treitschke,* 17 Nebraska,
205; *O'Connor* v. *Walter,* 37 Nebraska, 267; *Chicago, Burling-
ton &c. Railroad* v. *Moore,* 31 Nebraska, 629; *Moore* v. *Chicago,
Rock Island &c. Railroad,* 43 Iowa, 385; *Broadstreet* v. *Clark,*

D. & C. M & St. Paul Railroad, Garnishee, 65 Iowa, 670; *Stevens* v. *Brown,* 5 West Virginia, 450.   See also *Bank of United States* v. *Donnally,* 8 Pet. 361; *Wilcox* v. *Hunt,* 13 Pet. 378; *Townsend* v. *Jemison,* 9 How. 407; *Walworth* v. *Harris,* 129 U. S. 365; *Penfield* v. *Chesapeake, Ohio &c. Railroad,* 134 U. S. 351.   As to the extent to which *lex fori* governs, see Conflict of Laws, 571, *ct. seq.*

There are cases for and cases against the proposition that it is the duty of the garnishee to notify the defendant, his creditor, of the pendency of the proceedings, and also to make the defence of exemption, or he will be precluded from claiming the proceedings in defence of an action against himself.   We need not comment on the cases or reconcile them, as such notice was given and the defence was made.   The plaintiff in error did all it could and submitted only to the demands of the law.

In *Broadstreet* v. *Clark,* 65 Iowa, 670, the Supreme Court of the State decided that exemption laws pertained to the remedy and were not a defense in that State.   This ruling is repeated in *Willard* v. *Sturm,* 98 Iowa, 555, and applied to the proceedings in garnishment now under review.

It follows from these views that the Iowa court had jurisdiction, and that the Kansas courts did not give to the proceedings in Iowa the faith and credit they had there, and were hence entitled to in Kansas.

The judgment is reversed and the case remanded for further proceedings not inconsistent with this opinion.[20]

---

[20]*Louisville & Nashville Ry.* v. *Nash, 118 Ala. 477; Cooper v. Beers, 143 Ill. 25.*

CHAPTER X.

CAPACITY OF PERSONS.

NICHOLS & SHEPARD v. MARSHALL, 1899.

[108 Iowa 518.]

DEEMER, J.—Defendant is a married woman domiciled in this state. On or about the ninth day of July, 1894, she signed the note in suit, in the state of Indiana, at which place she was temporarily visiting, as surety for Milton W. Gregory. The note was made payable at the Indiana National Bank of Indianapolis. The laws of Indiana (section 6964, Burns' Rev. St.) provide that "a married woman shall not enter into any contract of suretyship, whether as indorser, guarantor, or in any other manner; and such contract, as to her, shall be void." It is insisted on behalf of appellant that as defendant was domiciled in this state at the time she made the note, her capacity to contract followed her into the state of Indiana, and validated her contract made in that commonwealth, and that the right of a married woman to make a contract relates to her contractual capacity, and, when given by the law of the domicile, follows the person. Our statutes permit the making of contracts of suretyship by married women, and, if appellant's postulate be correct, it follows that plaintiff is entitled to recover. The general rule seems to be, however, that the validity, nature, obligation, and interpretation of contracts are to be governed by the *lex loci contractus aut actus*. *Savary v. Savary*, 3 Iowa, 272; *Boyd v. Ellis*, 11 Iowa, 97; *Arnold v. Potter*, 22 Iowa, 194; *McDaniel v. Railway Co.*, 24 Iowa, 417; *Burrows v. Stryker*, 47 Iowa, 477; *Bigelow v. Burnham*, 90 Iowa, 300. The rule is also well settled that personal status is to be determined by the *lex domicilii*. *Ross v. Ross*, 129 Mass. 243. Continental jurists have generally maintained that personal laws of the domicil, affecting the status and capacity of all inhabitants of a particular class, bind them, wherever they may go, and that the validity of all contracts, in so far as the capacity of the parties to contract is involved, depends upon the *lex domicilii*. Thus, the Code of Napoleon enacts, "The laws concerning the status and capacity of persons govern Frenchmen, even when residing in a foreign country." See, also, Story Conflict of Laws (8th ed.), sections 63-66; Wharton Conflict of Laws (2d ed.), section 114. Some of the English cases have also followed this rule. *Guepratte v. Young*, 4 De Gex & S. 217, 5 Eng. Ruling Cas. 848; *Sottomayor v. De Barros*, 47 Law J. Prob. 23, 5 Eng. Ruling Cas. 814. But see, apparently to the contrary, *Burrows v. Jemino*, 2 Strange, 733; *Heriz v. De Casa Riera*, 10 Law J. Ch. 47. We do not think the continental rule is applicable to our situation and condition. A state has the undoubted right to define the capacity or incapacity of its inhabitants, be they residents or temporary visitors; and in this country, where travel is so common, and business has so little regard for state lines, it is more just, as well as more convenient, to have regard to the laws of the place of contract, as a uniform rule operating on all contracts, and which the contracting parties may be presumed to have had in contemplation when making their contracts, than to require them, at their peril, to know the domicile of those with whom they deal, and to ascertain the law of that domicile, however remote, which in many cases could not be done without such delay as would greatly cripple the power of contracting abroad at all. Indeed, it is a rule of almost·universal application that the law of the state where the contract is made and where it is to be performed enters into, and becomes a part of that contract, to the same extent and with the same effect as if written into the contract at length. Each state must prescribe for itself who of its residents have capacity to contract, and what changes shall be made, if any, in the disabilities imposed by the common law. Thus, in *Thompson v. Ketchum*, 8 Johns. 192, the note was made in Jamaica. The defense was infancy, according to the laws of New York. It was determined that the transaction was subject to the laws of the place of contract, and that infancy was a defense, or not, according to the laws of Jamaica. Mr. Justice Story, in his commentaries on Conflict of Laws, says: "In regard to questions of minority or majority, competency or incompetency to marry, incapacities incident to coverture, guardianship, emancipation, and other personal qualities and disabilities, the law of the domicile of birth, or the law of any other acquired and fixed domicile, is not generally to govern, but the *lex loci contractus aut actus,* where the contract is made or the act done." Story, Conflict of Laws, sections 103, 241. See, also, 2 Kent Commentaries, 233, note; 2 Kent Commentaries, 458; 2 Kent Commentaries, 459, note. It will be observed that Chancellor Kent, in some passages of his text, seems to incline to the civilian doctrine, yet the notes clearly indicates that he concurs with Justice Story. See further, on this subject, Story Conflict of Laws (4th ed.), sections 101, 102. The case of *Pearl v. Hansborough*, 9 Humph. 426, is almost exactly in point. In that case a married woman, domiciled with her husband in the state of Mississippi, by the law of which a purchase by a married woman was valid, and the property purchased went to her separate use, bought personal property in Tennessee, by the law of which married women were incapable of contracting. The contract was held void and unenforceable in Tennessee. See, also, *Male v. Roberts*, 3 Esp, 163; *Milliken v. Pratt*, 125 Mass. 374; *Carey v. Mackey*, 82 Me. 516, 17 Am. St. 500 (20 Atl. Rep. 84); *Baum v. Birchall*, 150 Pa. St. 164 (24 Atl. Rep. 620); 2 Parsons Contracts (8th ed.), *574, note; 2 Parsons Contracts, *575-*578. *Saul v. Creditors*, 5 Mart. (N. S.) 569, seems to be opposed to this rule. But as the case is from Louisiana, which state follows the civil law, it is not an authority. We may safely affirm, with Chancellor Kent, that while the continental jurists generally adopt the law of domicile, supposing it to come in conflict with the law of the place of contract, the English common law adopts the *lex loci contractus*. Lord Eldon, in *Male v. Roberts, supra*, said: "It appears from the evidence in this case that the cause of action arose in Scotland, and the contract must be therefore governed by the laws of that country, where the contract arises. Would infancy be a good defense by the laws of Scotland, had the action been commenced there? What the law of Scotland is with respect to the right of recovering against an infant for necessaries, I cannot say; but, if the law of Scotland is that such a contract as the present could not be enforced against an infant, that should have been given in evidence, and I hold myself not warranted in saying that such a contract is void by the laws of Scotland because it is void by the law of England. The law of the country where the contract arose must govern the contract, and what that law is should be given in evidence to me as a fact. No such evidence has been given, and I cannot take the fact of what that law is without evidence." It would seem, in this case, though not distinctly stated, that both parties were domiciled in England. The result of the application of these rules is that the contract was void where executed, and will not be enforced by the courts of this state.—AFFIRMED.[21]

---

[21]**Contracts.**—It has been doubted whether the personal competency or incompetency of an individual to contract depends on the law of the place where the contract is made or on the law of the place where the contracting party is domiciled. Perhaps in this country the question is not finally settled, though the preponderance of opinion here as well as abroad seems to be in favor of the law of the domicil. *Cooper v. Cooper, H. L. 13 App. Cas. 88 (1888); Freeman's Appeal, 68 Conn. 533; Woodward v. Woodward, 87 Tenn. 644.*

Capacity to Deed or Mortgage Land.—Capacity to convey or encumber an interest in land is governed by the law of the *situs*, and not by the law of the domicil. This is the general ruling in the United States in whatsoever court the question may arise, domestic or foreign. This rule applies to questions of infancy, coverture, majority, and of legal capacity generally. *Cochran v. Benton, 126 Ind. 58; Post v. First Natl. Bnk., 138 Ill. 559.*

FOREIGN CORPORATIONS.

BANK OF AUGUSTA v. EARLE, 1839.

[13 Pet. (U. S.) 519.]

1. Foreign Corporation Defined.
2. Extra-territorial Powers of Corporations.
3. Power of a State to Exclude Foreign Corporations.
4. What Constitutes "Doing Business" in the State.
5. Actions By and Against Foreign Corporations.

TANEY, Ch. J., delivered the opinion of the court.—These three cases involve the same principles, and have been brought before us by writs of error directed to the circuit court for the southern district of Alabama. The first two have been fully argued by counsel; and the last submitted to the court upon the arguments offered in the other two. There are some shades of difference in the facts, as stated in the different records, but none that can affect the decision. We proceed, therefore, to express our opinion on the first case argued, which was the *Bank of Augusta* v. *Joseph B. Earle.* The judgment in this case must decide the others.

The questions presented to the court arise upon a case stated in the circuit court in the following words:—"The defendant defends this action upon the following facts, that are admitted by the plaintiffs; that plaintiffs are a corporation, incorporated by an act of the legislature of the state of Georgia, and have powers usually conferred upon banking institutions, such as to purchase bills of exchange, etc. That the bill sued on was made and indorsed, for the purpose of being discounted by Thomas McGran, the agent, of said bank, who had funds of the plaintiffs in his hands, for the purpose of purchasing bills, which funds were derived from bills and notes discounted in Georgia by said plaintiffs, and payable in Mobile; and the said McGran, agent as aforesaid, did so discount and purchase the said bill sued on, in the city of Mobile, state aforesaid, for the benefit of said bank, and with their funds, and to remit said funds to the said plaintiffs. If the court shall say, that the facts constitute a defence to this action, judgment will be given for the defendant, otherwise for plaintiffs, for the amount of the bill, damages, interest and costs; either party to have the right of appeal or writ of error to the supreme court, upon this statement of facts, and the judgment thereon."

Upon this statement of facts, the court gave judgment for the defendant; being of opinion, that a bank incorporated by the laws of Georgia, with a power, among other things, to purchase bills of exchange, could not lawfully exercise that power in the state of Alabama; and that the contract for this bill was, therefore, void, and did not bind the parties to the payment of the money.

It will at once be seen, that the questions brought here for decision are of a very grave character; and they have received from the court an attentive examination. A multitude of corporations, for various purposes, have been chartered by the several states; a large portion of certain branches of business has been transacted by incorporated companies, or through their agency; and contracts to a very great amount have, undoubtedly, been made by different corporations, out of the jurisdiction of the particular state by which they were created. In deciding the case before us, we, in effect, determine whether these numerous contracts are valid, or not. And if, as has been argued at the bar, a corporation, from its nature and character, is incapable of making such contracts; or if they are inconsistent with the rights and sovereignty of the states in which they are made, they cannot be enforced in courts of justice.

Much of the argument has turned on the nature and extent of the powers which belong to the artificial being called a corporation; and the rules of law by which they are to be measured. On the part of the plaintiff in error, it has been contended, that a corporation, composed of citizens of other states, is entitled to the benefit of that provision in the constitution of the United States which declares that "the citizens of each state shall be entitled to all privileges and immunities of citizens in the several states;" that the court should look behind the act of incorporation, and see who are the members of it; and if, in this case, it should appear, that the corporation of the Bank of Augusta consists altogether of citizens of the state of Georgia, that such citizens are entitled to the privileges and immunities of citizens in the state of Alabama; and as the citizens of Alabama may, unquestionably, purchase bills of exchange in that state, it is insisted, that the members of this corporation are entitled to the same privilege, and cannot be deprived of it, even by express provisions in the constitution or laws of the state. The case of the *Bank of the United States* v. *Deveaux,* 5 Cranch 61, is relied on to support this position.

It is true, that in the case referred to, this court decided, that in a question of jurisdiction, they might look to the character of the persons composing a corporation; and if it appeared that they were citizens of another state, and the fact was set forth, by proper averments, the corporation might sue in its corporate name, in the courts of the United States. But in that case, the court confined its decision, in express terms, to a question of jurisdiction—to a right to sue—and evidently went even so far, with some hesitation. We fully assent to the propriety of that decision; and it has ever since been recognized as authority in this court. But the principle has never been extended any further than it was carried in that case; and has never been supposed to extend to contracts made by a corporation; especially in another sovereignty. If it were held to embrace contracts, and that the members of a corporation were to be regarded as individuals carrying on business in their corporate name, and therefore, entitled to the privileges of citizens, in matters of contract, it is very clear, that they must, at the same time, take upon themselves the liabilities of citizens, and be bound by their contracts in like manner. The result of this would be, to make a corporation a mere partnership in business, in which each stockholder would be liable, to the whole extent of his property, for the debts of the corporation; and he might be sued for them, in any state in which he might happen to be found. The clause of the Constitution referred to, certainly never intended to give to the citizens of each state the privileges of citizens in the several states, and at the same time to exempt them from the liabilities which the exercise of such privileges would bring upon individuals who were citizens of the state. This would be to give the citizens of other states far higher and greater privileges than are enjoyed by the citizens of the state itself. Besides, it would deprive every state of all control

over the extent of corporate franchises proper to be granted in
the state; and corporations would be chartered in one, to carry
on their operations in another. It is impossible, upon any sound
principle, to give such a construction to the article in question.
Whenever a corporation makes a contract, it is the contract of
the legal entity—of the artificial being created by the charter—
and not the contract of the individual members. The only rights
it can claim are the rights which are given to it in that character,
and not the rights which belong to its members as citizens of a
state; and we now proceed to inquire, what rights the plaintiffs
in error, a corporation created by Georgia, could lawfully exercise
in another state; and whether the purchase of the bill of exchange
on which this suit is brought, was a valid contract, and obligatory
on the parties.

The nature and character of a corporation created by a
statute, and the extent of the powers which it may lawfully exercise, have upon several occasions been under consideration in this
court. In the case of *Head* v. *Providence Insurance Company*,
2 Cranch 127, Chief Justice MARSHALL, in delivering the opinion
of the court, said, "without ascribing to this body, which in its
corporate capacity is the mere creature of the act to which it owes
its existence, all the qualities and disabilities annexed by the common law to ancient institutions of this sort, it may correctly be
said, to be precisely what the incorporating act has made it; to
derive all its powers from that act, and to be capable of exerting
its faculties only in the manner which that act authorizes. To this
source of its being, then, we must recur to ascertain its powers,
and to determine whether it can complete a contract by such com-
munications as are in this record." In the case of *Dartmouth
College* v. *Woodward*, 4 Wheat. 636, the same principle was again
decided by the court. "A corporation," said the court, "is an artificial being, invisible, intangible, and existing only in contemplation of law. Being a mere creature of the law, it possesses only
those properties which the charter of its creation confers upon it,
either expressly, or as incidental to its very existence." And in
the case of the *Bank of the United States* v. *Dandridge*, 12
Wheat. 64, where the question in relation to the powers of corporations and their mode of action, were very carefully considered,
the court said, "But whatever may be the implied powers of aggregate corporations, by the common law, and the modes by which
those powers are to be carried into operation; corporations created
by statute, must depend, both for their powers and the mode of

exercising them, upon the true construction of the statute itself."

It cannot be necessary to add to these authorities. And it may be safely assumed, that a corporation can make no contracts, and do no acts, either within or without the state which creates it, except such as are authorized by its charter; and those acts must also be done, by such officers or agents, and in such manner as the charter authorizes. And if the law creating a corporation, does not, by the true construction of the words used in the charter, give it the right to exercise its powers beyond the limits of the state, all contracts made by it in other states would be void.

The charter of the Bank of Augusta authorizes it, in general terms, to deal in bills of exchange; and consequently, gives it the power to purchase foreign bills as well as inland; in other words, to purchase bills payable in another state. The power thus given, clothed the corporation with the right to make contracts out of the state, in so far as Georgia could confer it. For whenever it purchased a foreign bill, and forwarded it to an agent to present for acceptance, if it was honored by the drawee, the contract of acceptance was necessarily made in another state; and the general power to purchase bills, without any restriction as to place, by its fair and natural import authorized the bank to make such purchases, wherever it was found most convenient and profitable to the institution; and also to employ suitable agents for that purpose. The purchase of the bill in question was, therefore, the exercise of one of the powers which the bank possessed under its charter; and was sanctioned by the law of Georgia creating the corporation, so far as that state could authorize a corporation to exercise its powers beyond the limits of its own jurisdiction.

But it has been urged in the argument, that notwithstanding the powers thus conferred by the terms of the charter, a corporation, from the very nature of its being, can have no authority to contract out of the limits of the state; that the laws of a state can have no extra-territorial operation; and that as a corporation is the mere creature of the law of the state, it can have no existence beyond the limits in which that law operates; and that it must necessarily be incapable of making a contract in another place. It is very true, that a corporation can have no legal existence out of the boundaries of the sovereignty by which it is created. It exists only in contemplation of law, and by force of the law; and where that law ceases to operate, and is no longer obligatory, the corporation can have no existence. It must dwell in the place of its creation, and cannot migrate to another sovereignty. But although it must live and have its being in that state only, yet it does not by any means follow, that its existence there will not be recognized in other places; and its residence in one state creates no insuperable objection to its power of contracting in another. It is, indeed, a mere artificial being, invisible and intangible; yet it is a person, for certain purposes, in contemplation of law, and has been recognized as such by the decisions of this court. It was so held, in the case of the *United States* v. *Amedy*, 11 Wheat. 412, and in *Beaston* v. *Farmers' Bank of Delaware*, 12 Pet. 125. Now, natural persons, through the intervention of agents, are continually making contracts in countries in which they do not reside; and where they are not personally present when the contract is made; and nobody has ever doubted the validity of these agreements. And what greater objection can there be to the capacity of an artificial person, by its agents, to make a contract, within the scope of its limited powers, in a sovereignty in which it does not reside; provided such contracts are permitted to be made by them by the laws of the place?

The corporation must, no doubt, show, that the law of its creation gave it authority to make such contracts, through such agents. Yet, as in the case of a natural person, it is not necessary that it should actually exist in the sovereignty in which the contract is made. It is sufficient, that its existence as an artificial person, in the state of its creation, is acknowledged and recognized by the law of the nation where the dealing takes place; and that it is permitted, by the laws of that place, to exercise there the powers with which it is endowed.

Every. power, however, of the description of which we are speaking, which a corporation exercises in another state, depends for its validity upon the laws of the sovereignty in which it is exercised; and a corporation can make no valid contract, without their sanction, express or implied. And this brings us to the question which has been so elaborately discussed; whether, by the comity of nations, and between these states, the corporations of one state are permitted to make contracts in another. It is needless to enumerate here the instances in which, by the general practice of civilized countries, the laws of the one, will, by the comity of nations, be recognized and executed in another, where the right of individuals are concerned. The cases of contracts made in a foreign country are familiar examples; and courts of justice have always expounded and executed them, according to the laws of the place in which they were made; provided that law was not repugnant to the laws or policy of their own country. The comity thus extended to other nations, is no impeachment of severeignty. It is the voluntary act of the nation by which it is offered; and is inadmissible, when contrary to its policy, or prejudicial to its interests. But it contributes so largely to promote justice between individuals, and to produce a friendly intercourse between the sovereignties to which they belong, that courts of justice have continually acted upon it, as a part of the voluntary law of nations. It is truly said, in Story's Conflict of Laws 37, that "In the silence of any positive rule, affirming or denying, or restraining the operation of foreign laws, courts of justice presume the tacit adoption of them by their own government, unless they are repugnant to its policy, or prejudicial to its interests. It is not the comity of the courts, but the comity of the nation, which is administered, and ascertained in the same way, and guided by the same reasoning by which all other principles of municipal law are ascertained and guided."

Adopting, as we do, the principle here stated, we proceed to inquire, whether, by the comity of nations, foreign corporations are permitted to make contracts within their jurisdiction; and we can perceive no sufficient reason for excluding them, when they are not contrary to the known policy of the state, or injurious to its interests. It is nothing more than the admission of the existence of an artificial person, created by the law of another state, and clothed with the power of making certain contracts; it is but the usual comity of recognizing the law of another state. In England, from which we have received our general principles of jurisprudence, no doubt appears to have been entertained, of the right of a foreign corporation to sue in its courts, since the case *Henriquez* v. *Dutch West India Company*, decided in 1729, 2 Ld. Raym. 1532. And it is a matter of history, which this court are bound to notice, that corporations created in this country, have been in the open practice, for many years past, of making contracts in England, of various kinds, and to very large amounts; and we have never seen a doubt suggested there, of the validity of these contracts, by any court or any jurist. It is impossible to imagine, that any court in the United States would refuse to execute a contract, by which an American corporation had borrowed money in England; yet if the contracts of corporations made out of the state by which they were created, are void, even contracts of that description could not be enforced.

It has, however, been supposed, that the rules of comity be-

tween foreign nations do not apply to the states of this Union;
that they extend to one another no other rights than those which
are given by the Constitution of the United States; and that the
courts of the general government are not at liberty to presume,
in the absence of all legislation on the subject, that a state has
adopted the comity of nations toward the other states, as a part
of its jurisprudence; or that it acknowledges any rights but those
which are secured by the Constitution of the United States. The
court think otherwise. The intimate union of these states, as
members of the same great political family; the deep and vital
interests which bind them so closely together; should lead us, in
the absence of proof to the contrary, to presume a greater degree
of comity, and friendship, and kindness toward one another, than
we should be authorized to presume between foreign nations.
And when (as without doubt must occasionally happen) the interest or policy of any state requires it to restrict the rule, it has but
to declare its will, and the legal presumption is at once at an end.
But until this is done, upon what grounds could this court refuse
to administer the law of international comity between these states?
They are sovereign states; and the history of the past, and the
events which are daily occurring, furnish the strongest evidence
that they have adopted towards each other the laws of comity, in
their fullest extent. Money is frequently borrowed in one state,
by a corporation created in another. The numerous banks established by different states are in the constant habit of contracting
and dealing with one another. Agencies for corporations engaged
in the business of insurance and of banking have been established
in other states, and suffered to make contracts, without any objection on the part of the state authorities. These usages of commerce and trade have been so general and public, and have been
practiced for so long a period of time, and so generally acquiesced
in by the states, that the court cannot overlook them, when a
question like the one before us is under consideration. The
silence of the state authorities, while these events are passing
before them, show their assent to the ordinary laws of comity
which permit a corporation to make contracts in another state.
But we are not left to infer it merely from the general usages
of trade, and the silent acquiescence of the states. It appears
from the cases cited in the argument, which it is unnecessary to
recapitulate in this opinion, that it has been decided in many of
the state courts, we believe in all of them where the question has
arisen, that a corporation of one state may sue in the courts of

another. If it may sue, why may it not make a contract? The right to sue is one of the powers which it derives from its charter. If the courts of another country take notice of its existence as a corporation, so far as to allow it to maintain a suit, and permit it to exercise that power; why should not its existence be recognized for other purposes, and the corporation permitted to exercise another power, which is given to it by the same law and the same sovereignty—where the last-mentioned power does not come in conflict with the interest or policy of the state? There is certainly nothing in the nature and character of a corporation which could justly lead to such a distinction; and which should extend to it the comity of suit, and refuse to it the comity of contract. If it is allowed to sue, it would, of course, be permitted to compromise, if it thought proper, with its debtor; to give him time; to accept something else in satisfaction; to give him a release; and to employ an attorney for itself to conduct its suit. These are all matters of contract, and yet are so intimately connected with the right to sue, that the latter could not be effectually exercised, if the former were denied.

We turn, in the next place, to the legislation of the states. So far as any of them have acted on this subject, it is evident, that they have regarded the comity of contract, as well as the comity of suit, to be a part of the law of the state, unless restricted by statute. Thus, a law was passed by the state of Pennsylvania, March 10th, 1810, which prohibited foreigners and foreign corporations from making contracts of insurance against fire, and other losses mentioned in the law. In New York, also, a law was passed, March 18th, 1814, which prohibited foreigners and foreign corporations from making in that state insurances against fire; and by another law, passed April 21st, 1818, corporations chartered by other states are prohibited from keeping any office of deposit for the purpose of discounting promissory notes, or carrying on any kind of business which incorporated banks are authorized by law to carry on. The prohibition of certain specified contracts by corporations, in these laws, is, by necessary implication, an admission that other contracts may be made by foreign corporations in Pennsylvania and New York; and that no legislative permission is necessary to give them validity. And the language of these prohibitory acts most clearly indicates, that the contracts forbidden by them might lawfully have been made, before these laws were passed. Maryland has gone still further in recognizing this right. By a law passed in 1834, that state has prescribed the manner in which corporations, not chartered by the state, "which shall transact or shall have transacted business" in the state, may be sued in its courts, upon contracts made in the state. The law assumes, in the clearest manner, that such contracts were valid, and provides a remedy by which to enforce them.

In the legislation of congress also, where the states and the people of the several states are all represented, we shall find proof of the general understanding in the United States, that by the law of comity among the states, the corporations chartered by one were permitted to make contracts in the others. By the act of congress of June 23d, 1836 (5 U. S. Stat. 52), regulating the deposits of public money, the secretary of the treasury was authorized to make arrangements with some bank or banks, to establish an agency in the states and territories where there was no bank, or none that could be employed as a public depository, to receive and disburse the public money which might be directed to be there deposited. Now, if the proposition be true, that a corporation created by one state cannot make a valid contract in another, the contracts made through this agency, in behalf of the bank, out of the state where the bank itself was chartered, would all be void, both as respected the contracts with the government and the individuals who dealt with it. How could such an agency, upon the principles now contended for, have conformed any of the duties for which it was established?

But it cannot be necessary to pursue the argument further. We think it is well settled, that by the law of comity among nations, a corporation created by one sovereignty is permitted to make contracts in another, and to sue in its courts; and that the same law of comity prevails among the several sovereignties of this Union. The public, and well-known, and long-continued usages of trade; the general acquiesence of the states; the particular legislation of some of them, as well as the legislation of congress; all concur in proving the truth of this proposition.

But we have already said, that this comity is presumed from the silent acquiescence of the state. Whenever a state sufficiently indicates that contracts which derive their validity from its comity are repugnant to its policy, or are considered as injurious to its interests; the presumption in favor of its adoption can no longer be made. And it remains to inquire, whether there is anything in the constitution or laws of Alabama, from which this court would be justified in concluding that the purchase of the bill in question was contrary to its policy.

The constitution of Alabama contains the following provisions in relation to banks: "One state bank may be established, with such number of branches as the general assembly may, from time to time, deem expedient, provided that no branch bank shall be established, nor bank charter renewed, under the authority of this state, without the concurrence of two-thirds of both houses of the general assembly; and provided also, that not more than one bank or branch bank shall be established, nor bank charter renewed, but in conformity to the following rules: 1. At least two-fifths of the capital stock shall be reserved for the state. 2. A proportion of power, in the direction of the bank, shall be reserved to the state, equal at least to its proportion of stock therein. 3. The state and individual stockholders shall be liable respectively for the debts of the bank, in proportion to their stock holden therein. 4. The remedy for collecting debts shall be reciprocal, for and against the bank. 5. No bank shall commence operations, until half of the capital stock subscribed for be actually paid in gold and silver; which amount shall, in no case, be less than $100,000.

Now, from these provisions in the constitution, it is evidently the policy of Alabama, to restrict the power of the legislature in relation to bank charters, and to secure to the state a large portion of the profits of banking, in order to provide a public revenue; and also to make safe the debts which should be contracted by the banks. The meaning, too, in which that state used the word bank, in her constitution, is sufficiently plain, from its subsequent legislation. All of the banks chartered by it, are authorized to receive deposits of money, to discount notes, to purchase bills of exchange, and to issue their own notes, payable on demand, to bearer. These are the usual powers conferred on the banking corporations in the different states of the Union; and when we are dealing with the business of banking in Alabama, we must undoubtedly attach to it the meaning in which it is used in the constitution and laws of the state. Upon so much of the policy of Alabama, therefore, in relation, to banks as is disclosed by its constitution, and upon the meaning which that state attaches to the word bank, we can have no reasonable doubt. But before this court can undertake to say, that the discount of the bill in question was illegal, many other inquiries must be made, and many other difficulties must be solved. Was it the policy of Alabama, to exclude all competition with its own banks, by the corporations of other states? Did the state intend, by these provisions in its

constitution, and these charters to its banks, to inhibit the circulation of the notes of other banks, the discount of notes, the loan
of money, and the purchase of bills of exchange? Or did it
design to go still further, and forbid the banking corporations of
other states from making a contract of any kind within its territory? Did it mean to prohibit its own banks from keeping mutual
accounts with the banks of other states, and from entering into
any contract with them, express or implied? Or did she mean
to give to her banks the power of contracting, within the limits
of the state with foreign corporations, and deny it to individual
citizens? She may believe it to be the interest of her citizens, to
permit the competition of other banks in the circulation of notes,
in the purchase and sale of bills of exchange, and in the loan of
money. Or she may think it to be her interest, to prevent the
circulation of the notes of other banks; and to prohibit them from
sending money there to be employed in the purchase of exchange,
or making contracts of any other description.

The state has not made known its policy upon any of these
points. And how can this court, with no other light before it,
undertake to mark out, by a definite and distinct line, the policy
which Alabama has adopted in relation to this complex and intri-
cate question of political economy? It is true, that the state is the
principal stockholder in her own banks. She has created seven;
and in five of them, the state owns the whole stock; and in the
others, two-fifths. This proves that the state is deeply interested
in the successful operation of her banks, and it may be her policy
to shut out all interference with them. In another view of the
subject, however, she may believe it to be her policy to extend
the utmost liberality to the banks of other states; in the expectation that it would produce a corresponding comity in other
states towards the banks in which she is so much interested. In
this respect, it is a question chiefly of revenue, and of fiscal policy.
How can this court, with no other aid than the general principles
asserted in her constitution, and her investments in the stocks
of her own banks, undertake to carry out the policy of the state
upon such a subject, in all of its details, and decide how far it
extends, and what qualifications and limitations are imposed upon
it? These questions must be determined by the state itself, and
not by the courts of the United States. Every sovereignty would,
without doubt, choose to designate its own line of policy; and
would never consent to leave it as a problem to be worked out by
the courts of the United States, from a few general principles,

which might very naturally be misunderstood or misapplied by the court. It would hardly be respectful to a state, for this court to forestall its decision, and to say, in advance of her legis- lation, what her interest or policy demands. Such a course would savor more of legislation than of judicial interpretation.

If we proceed from the constitution and bank charters to other acts of legislation by the state, we find nothing that should lead us to a contrary conclusion. By an act of assembly of the state, passed January 12th, 1827, it was declared unlawful for any person, body corporate, company or association, to issue any note for circulation as a bank-note, without the authority of law; and a fine was imposed upon any one offending against this statute. Now, this act protected the privileges of her own banks, in relation to bank-notes only; and contains no prohibition against the purchase of bills of exchange, nor against any other business by foreign banks, which might interfere with her own bank- ing corporations. And if we were to form our opinion of the policy of Alabama from the provisions of this law, we should be bound to say, that the legislature deemed it to be the interest and policy of the state, not to protect its own banks from compe- tition in the purchase of exchange, nor in anything but the issuing of notes for circulation. But this law was repealed by a subse- quent law, passed in 1833, repealing all acts of assembly not com- prised in a digest then prepared and adopted by the legislature. The law of 1827 above mentioned was not contained in this digest, and was consequently repealed. It has been said at the bar, in the argument, that it was omitted from the digest by mistake, and was not intended to be repealed. But this court cannot act judici- ally upon such an assumption. We must take their laws and policy to be such as we find them in their statutes. And the only inference that we can draw from these two laws, is, that after having prohibited, under a penalty, any competition with their banks, by the issue of notes for circulation, they changed their policy, and determined to leave the whole business of bank- ing open to the rivalry of others. The other laws of the state, therefore, in addition to the constitution and charters, certainly would not authorize this court to say, that the purchase of bills by the corporations of another state was a violation of its policy.

The decisions of its judicial tribunals lead to the same result. It is true, that in the case of the *State* v. *Stebbins*, 1 Stew. 312, the court said, that since the adoption of their constitution, bank- ing in that state was to be regarded as a franchise. And this case has been much relied on by the defendant in error. Now, we are satisfied, from a careful examination of the case, that the word franchise was not used, and could not have been used, by the court, in the broad sense imputed to it in the argument. For if banking includes the purchase of bills of exchange, and all banking is to be regarded as the exercise of a franchise, the decision of the court would amount to this—that no individual citizen of Alabama could purchase such a bill. For franchises are special privileges conferred by government upon individuals, and which do not belong to the citizens of the country, generally, of common right. It is essential to the character of a franchise, that it should be a grant from the sovereign authority, and in this country, no franchise can be held, which is not derived from a law of the state. But it cannot be supposed, that the constitution of Alabama intended to prohibit its merchants and traders from purchasing or selling bills of exchange; and to make it a monopoly in the hands of their banks. And it is evident, that the court of Alabama, in the case of the *State* v. *Stebbins,* did not mean to assert such a principle. In the passage relied on, they are speaking of a paper circulating currency, and asserting the right of the state to regulate and to limit it.

The institutions of Alabama, like those of the other states, are founded upon the great principles of the common law; and it is very clear, that at common law, the right of banking, in all its ramifications, belonged to individual citizens; and might be exercised by them at their pleasure. And the correctness of this principle is not questioned in the case of the *State* v. *Stebbins.* Undoubtedly, the sovereign authority may regulate and restrain this right; but the constitution of Alabama purports to be nothing more than a restriction upon the power of the legislature, in relation to banking corporations; and does not appear to have been intended as a restriction upon the rights of individuals. That part of the subject appears to have been left, as is usually done, for the action of the legislature, to be modified according to circumstances; and the prosecution against Stebbins was not founded on the provisions contained in the constitution, but was under the law of 1827 above mentioned, prohibiting the issuing of bank-notes. We are fully satisfied, that the state never intended, by its constitution, to interfere with the right of purchasing or selling bills of exchange; and that the opinion of the court does not refer to transactions of that description, when it speaks of banking as a franchise.

The question then recurs—Does the policy of Alabama deny to the corporations of other states the ordinary comity between nations? or does it permit such a corporation to make those contracts which from their nature and subject-matter, are consistent with its policy, and are allowed to individuals? In making such contracts, a corporation, no doubt, exercises its corporate franchise. But it must do this, whenever it acts as a corporation, for its existence is a franchise. Now, it has been held in the court of Alabama itself, in 2 Stew. 147, that the corporation of another state may sue in its courts; and the decision is put directly on the ground of national comity. The state, therefore, has not merely acquiesced by silence, but her judicial tribunals have declared the adoption of the law of international comity, in the case of a suit. We have already shown, that the comity of suit brings with it the comity of contract; and where the one is expressly adopted by its courts, the other must also be presumed, according to the usages of nations, unless the contrary can be shown.

The cases cited from 7 Wen. 276, and from 2 Rand. 465, cannot influence the decision in the case before us. The decisions of these two state courts were founded upon the legislation of their respective states, which was sufficiently explicit to enable their judicial tribunals to pronounce judgment on their line of policy. But because two states have adopted a particular policy, in relation to the banking corporation of other states, we cannot infer, that the same rule prevails in all of the other states. Each state must decide for itself. And it will be remembered, that it is not the state of Alabama which appears here to complain of an infraction of its policy. Neither the state, nor any of its constituted authorities, have interferred in this controversy. The objection is taken by persons who were parties to those contracts; and who participated in the transactions which are now alleged to have been in violation of the laws of the state.

It is but justice to all the parties concerned, to suppose that these contracts were made in good faith, and that no suspicion was entertained by either of them, that these engagements could not be enforced. Money was paid on them by one party, and received by the other. And when we see men dealing with one another openly in this manner, and making contracts to a large amount, we can hardly doubt, as to what was the generally-received opinion in Alabama, at that time, in relation, to the right of the plaintiffs to make such contracts. Everything now urged as proof of her policy, was equally public and well known, when these bills were negotiated. And when a court is called on to declare contracts thus made to be void, upon the ground that they conflict with the policy of the state; the line of that policy should be very clear and distinct, to justify the court in sustaining the defence. Nothing can be more vague and indefinite than that now insisted on as the policy of Alabama. It rests altogether on speculative reasoning as to her supposed interests; and is not supported by any positive legislation. There is no law of the state which attempts to define the rights of foreign corporations.

We, however, do not mean to say, that there are not many subjects upon which the policy of the several states is abundantly evident, from the nature of their institutions, and the general scope of their legislation; and which do not need the aid of a positive and special law to guide the decisions of the courts. When the policy of a state is thus manifest, the courts of the United States would be bound to notice it, as a part of its code of laws; and to declare all contracts in the state, repugnant to it, to be illegal and void. Nor do we mean to say, whether there may not be some rights under the constitution of the United States, which a corporation might claim, under peculiar circumstances, in a state other than that in which it was chartered. The reasoning, as well as the judgment of the court, is applied to the matter before us; and we think the contracts in question were valid, and that the defence relied on by the defendants cannot be sustained. The judgment of the circuit court in these cases must, therefore, be reversed, with costs.[22]

---

[22]**Foreign Corporation Defined.**—A foreign corporation is one created by or under the laws of another state or country. Although a collection of individuals, it has a separate and distinct individuality, and in law it is considered a person, an artificial person.

A corporation is a "citizen" of the state where it was created. *Baltimore & O. R. Co. v. Harris, 12 Wall. 65; Shaw v. Mining Co., 145 U. S. 444, 12 Sup. Ct. 935.* A corporation is to be deemed a "citizen" within the meaning of the acts of Congress defining the jurisdiction of the federal courts. *People v. Utica Ins. Co., 15 Johns. (N. Y.) 358; Denny v. Schram, 6 Wash. 134, 32 Pac. 1002.* A corporation is not a "citizen" within the meaning of the provision of the federal constitution that "the citizens of each state shall be entitled to all the privileges and immunities of citizens in the several states." *Paul v. Virginia, 8 Wall. 168; Blake v. McClung, 172 U. S. 239; Ducat v. City of Chicago, 48 Ill. 172; Tatem v. Wright, 23 N. J. L. 429.*

A corporation is not a person within the meaning of the constitutional provision that no state shall deny to any "person" within its jurisdiction the equal protection of its laws. *Pembina Mining Co. v. Penn., 125 U. S. 181, 8 Sup. Ct. 737.*

Extra-terratorial Powers.—A corporation can, by its agents, go into another state and carry on business there providing it keeps within the powers conferred by its charter, and such business is not contrary to the laws or policy of the state where it attempts to carry on business. *Kennebec v. Augusta Ins. Co., 6 Gray (Mass.) 580; Santa Clara Academy v. Sullivan, 116 Ill. 375, 6 N. E. 183; Lancaster v. Improvement Co., 140 N. Y. 576, 35 N. E. 964; Cowell v. Springs, 100 U. S. 59; Thompson v. Waters, 25 Mich. 214.*

In order to exclude the foreign corporation, there must be some express prohibition against such corporation, or else the general policy of the laws must be against it. *Demarest v. Flack, 128 N. Y. 205, 28 N. E. 645; Lancaster v. Improvement Co., 140 N. Y. 576, 35 N. E. 964; Bard v. Poole, 12 N. Y. 495; Cowell v. Springs, 100 U. S. 59.*

A foreign corporation may not do an act for doing which a special franchise is required. *Dodge v. Council Bluffs, 57 Iowa 560; Middle Bridge Co. v. Marks, 26 Me. 326.*

It may not do an act contrary to the public policy of the state. *American Soc. v. Gartrell, 23 Ga. 448.*

Public policy is that principle of the law which holds that no person can lawfully do that which has a tendency to be injurious to the public or against the public good. It is a variable quantity, and changes with the habits, capacities, and opportunities of the public.

Public policy is manifested by public acts, legislative and judicial, and not by private opinion, however eminent. *Giant Powder Co. v. Oregon Ry., 42 Fed. Rep. 470.* The exercise of comity in admitting or restraining the application of the laws of another country must rest in sound judicial discretion, dictated by the circumstances of the case. *Edgerly v. Bush, 81 N. Y. 199.*

The powers of a foreign corporation are determined by its charter, the law of its domicil, the law of the place where it attempts to do business, and comity, and all persons who deal with it must take notice of the limitations upon its charter. *Canada Ry. Co. v. Gebhard, 109 U. S. 527, 3 Sup. Ct. 363; Rue v. Railway Co., 74 Tex. 474, 8 S. W. 533; Runyan v. Coster, 14 Pet. 122.*

Power to Exclude Corporations.—A state or country may exclude foreign corporations altogether, or it may impose such terms as it chooses as a condition of allowing them to carry on business. The whole matter rests in the discretion of the state or country. *Paul v. Virginia, 8 Wall. 168; Liverpool Ins. Co. v. Massachusetts, 10 Wall. 566.* If a foreign corporation carries on business in a state without complying with the conditions imposed by the state, such contracts of the corporation are absolutely void. *In re Comstock, 3 Sawyer 218; Reliance Ins. Co. v. Sawyer, 160 Mass. 413, 36 N. E. 59; Cincinnati v. Rosenthal, 55 Ill. 85.* Some courts hold that a non-compliance with state laws renders the corporation liable to expulsion, but permits the contracts to stand. *Washburn Mill Co. v. Bartlett, 3 N. D. 138, 54 N. W. 544; Wright v. Lee, 4 S. D. 237, 55 N. W. 931.*

What Constitutes "Doing Business" in the State.—If a foreign corporation does any substantial part of its business in the state, it is said to be doing business in the state. A single act of the foreign corporation, if the act is of its ordinary business, constitutes doing business in the state. *People v. Wemple, 131 N. Y. 64, 29 N. E. 1002; Ginn v. Security Co., 92 Ala. 135, 8 South. Rep. 388.* The Supreme Court of the United States has held that a single act is not "doing business" in the state. *Cooper v. Manufacturing Co., 113 U. S. 727.*

Actions by and Against Foreign Corporations.—As a matter of comity, a corporation may sue in another state or country. But to sue a foreign corporation certain conditions must exist: First, it must appear that the corporation was carrying on business in the state; second, that the business was managed by some agent of the corporation; third, the existence of some local law making such corporation amenable to suit there as a condition, express or implied, of doing business in the state. *United States v. Am. Bell Tel. Co., 29 Fed. Rep. 17.* In a recent case, it has been held that service may be made upon its regularly appointed agents, even in the absence of a state statute conferring such authority. *Barrow v. Kane, 170 U. S. 100; Mutual Life Ins. v. Spratley, 172 U S. 602.*

GUARDIAN AND WARD.

IN RE STOCKMAN, 1888.

[71 Mich. 180.]

1. Guardian of the Person of the Ward.
2. Testamentary and Statutory Guardians.
3. Who May be Appointed Guardian.
4. Discretion of the Court.
5. Rights of Foreign Guardians.

SHERWOOD, C. J. Lucile Stockman is now nine years of age, and resides with her maternal grandparents in Port Huron, who are her guardians in this state, having received their appointment as such on October 19, 1885. The *paternal* grandparents reside in Washington, D. C., and were duly appointed testamentary guardians for Lucile in that city on September 4, 1885. The child's father and mother are both dead. The testamentary guardians are the petitioners in this case, and they seek to recover by the writ of *habeas corpus* this infant girl from the Michigan guardians. Mrs. Stockman, the mother of Lucile, died in the city of Washington on November 24, 1879, and Hugh R. Stockman, the father, died in the same city on August 23, 1885.

These parents were married in April, 1877, at Port Huron, Mrs. Stockman being only about 16 years of age when married. They remained in Port Huron until some time in July, 1877. There were some unpleasant things occurred in the manner the husband brought about the marriage, and it only need be said they were of a character not calculated to greatly increase the estimate which would most likely be accorded to him by a well-ordered and virtuous community. The wife's parents were a well-to-do and respectable family, who had resided in Port Huron more than 20 years, reputable people in good standing. While in Port Huron the newly-married couple boarded at the Huron House, and Mrs. Stockman was allowed to visit her mother but once, and then for the purpose of getting her trunk before they left the city, and the mother never saw Mrs. Stockman again but once until a few hours before she died. They lived during their marriage in Georgia and in Washington.

After the birth of the child, Lucile, which occurred while they were in Georgia, the mother was allowed to come to Port Huron for a few weeks in July and August, 1879, and then returned to Washington, where she died. Her mother was telegraphed to go to Washington about 48 hours before Mrs. Stockman died, and she was permitted to have the company of Mrs. Shaw, her mother, about 24 hours before she passed away. Before she died, Mrs. Stockman asked her husband to allow her mother, Mrs. Shaw, to take Lucile and keep her, and Mr. Stockman promised her that he would do so. And after the funeral he told Mrs. Shaw of the request his wife had made, and the promise he gave her, and then and there urged Mrs. Shaw to take the child, and do as his wife requested; and upon her suggestion that she would be willing to take her, and bring her up, but was afraid he might afterwards change his mind, and take the child from her, he affirmed he would not, saying:

"Oh, no, mother. You may have no fear. You take the child and bring her up pure and virtuous, like her mother, and that is all I ask."

Mrs. Shaw then promised him she would take her as requested by her daughter and him, and bring up the child as one of her own.

Mr. Stockman seemed very poor at this time. The only home he had ever furnished for his wife and child was in the family of his father and mother, and at their house; and after paying sundry bills for medicine for Mrs. Stockman before she died, and lending him $50 to help pay his wife's funeral expenses, she took the child Lucile, and brought her to her home in Port Huron, where she and her husband have cared for, supported, maintained, and educated her ever since.

When Mrs. Shaw took the child she was about 17 months old, and, the evidence shows, poor and sickly. She is now healthy, and enjoying her home and the family of her grandparents, where there are several children associates. She is also receiving such Christian education and other advantages as a large and prosperous Michigan city affords; and the testimony is to the effect that she desires to remain with her grandparents in Michigan, where she is contented and happy, and does not want to go and live with her paternal grandparents in Washington, and the maternal grandparents are anxious to have her remain with them, and are willing to maintain, educate, and support her from their own means, and at their own expense.

In the month of August, 1882, and after the child had been at Port Huron about 3 years, Mr. Stockman visited his daughter at Mr. and Mrs. Shaw's, and, after being there a few days, said he wanted to take her to Washington with him to spend the winter, and Mrs. Shaw could have her again in the spring, and was allowed to take her under his promise that the grandmother could have her again in the spring. Mrs. Shaw went for her in the month of April, 1883, when Mr. Stockman made trouble in getting her, and finally would not allow Mrs. Shaw to bring her away unless she would sign a writing, agreeing to return the child to him whenever he should call for her. Lucile was at the time not well, and these conditions, demanded of Mrs. Shaw before she could gain possession of the child, greatly embarrassed her, and, feeling that she could not leave her in Washington, she signed an instrument purporting to be of the effect stated. She then took the little girl and returned to Port Huron with her. Mrs. Shaw avers that she was compelled to sign said written agreement before she could get away the child, who was then sick, and, fearing she might die if allowed to remain there, she was ready to do almost anything to get her away, and she was thus compelled, at the risk, she believes, of the life of the child, and against her will, to sign said written instrument.

After their return to Port Huron, Lucile soon recovered her health, and she was permitted to remain undisturbed with Mrs. Shaw until on or about September 18, 1883, when Mr. Stockman came to the house of Mrs. Shaw, in Port Huron, and unceremoniously took the child away with the avowed purpose of taking her to Washington. This he was not allowed to do by Mr. Shaw, who found him with the child in the city, making preparations to leave with her. Shaw took her from Mr. Stockman, and went home with her. Mr. Stockman thereupon applied to the circuit court for the county of St. Clair for a writ of *habeaus corpus* to recover the child. Mr. and Mrs. Shaw appeared, and filed their answer, contesting his right to Lucile upon the following grounds:

1. That by reason of the request of the dying mother, and consummated after her death by the agreement of Mr. Stockman with Mrs. Shaw, that she should have the care and custody of the child during her infancy, she was entitled to take her away.

2. That Mr. Stockman was an unfit person to have the care, companionship, custody, or education of the child; that he was

intemperate in his habits; habitually used intoxicating liquor; that he had an ungovernable temper, and could not control his passions, and was a man of improper and immoral habits.

3. That he was extremely cross and cruel in his conduct towards Lucile, and without any sufficient cause would frequently inflict upon her severe blows, and cruel and improper punishment.

4. That he improperly treated the child when sick; compelled and forced her to take medicine of his own preparation, and contrary to the advice of physicians.

5. That he held improper relations and intercourse with bad women, and allowed them in his own rooms, in the presence of Lucile; and that he is financially unable to support the child; that he had no home of his own, was out of health, and was out of business.

The circuit judge ordered the case tried before a jury, and upon the first trial the jury disagreed, and upon the second trial, which occurred about a month thereafter, the jury rendered a verdict that Mr. and Mrs. Shaw should retain the custody of the child. This verdict was afterwards sought to be set aside in the circuit court, but the motion was denied by the circuit judge on May 27, 1884.

On June 23, 1884, Mr. Stockman filed his petition in this Court, and obtained a writ of *habeas corpus* to obtain his daughter. The application was substantially upon the same grounds as had been urged in the circuit court, and was heard upon the same testimony, with some unimportant additions, in this Court on October 18, 1884. The Court, being equally divided in opinion as to what should be done in the premises, caused to be entered the following order on January 30, 1885:

"In this case, the Court being equally divided in opinion as to the judgment that should be entered, the clerk is directed to make an entry to that effect, and the writ is dismissed for that cause, and without any decision upon the rights of the parties, and without prejudice either to any existing right or adjudication, or to any future remedy."

Here the matter was allowed to rest until Mr. Stockman died, in August, 1885. Previous to his death, which occurred at his father's in the city of Washington, and on February 20, 1885, he made a last will, in which he appointed his father and mother guardians of Lucile. They qualified, and letters of testamentary guardianship were duly issued to them in the orphans' court of the District of Columbia on September 4, 1885. In and by the will the testator directs his guardians to obtain the legal control of Lucile, and, if necessary to that end, they are directed to use all his property; and if they do not succeed, then he gives his property to his father and mother, if living, and, if not, he gives it in equal shares to his brother and sisters, and recites in his will that Mr. and Mrs. Shaw had committed perjury in their endeavors to retain the child.

In pursuance of and in accordance with the requirements of this will, Mr. Andrew H. Stockman and Anna B. Stockman, his wife, the father and mother of the testator, applied for and obtained a writ of *habeas corpus* from this Court to obtain the custody of their testamentary ward, Lucile, on February 8, 1887.

The petition for the writ does not vary materially in its statement of the facts from those contained in the other application, except, in addition thereto, it states that Mr. and Mrs. Shaw refused to deliver up Lucile to the testamentary guardians when requested; and that at the time the testator died a large sum of money was due him for military service, and which now belongs to Lucile; and that he had some personal property besides, all of which the testamentary guardians had secured and then had; and that, under the decision of the pension office, all of the pension moneys to which Lucile is entitled on account of the service of her father are now being paid to the testamentary guardians; that such pension money and personal estate are sufficient to support the ward; and, further, that they are able, and have property enough, to support her, if necessary, aside from the pension money; and that the respondents, Mr. and Mrs. Shaw, have changed the name of Lucile from Stockman to Shaw, for the purpose of preventing identification, and have had her christened by that name.

The respondents file their answer to the petition, which is in substance the same as that made to the other writs issued, with the further statements that the said Anna B. Stockman allowed the deceased in his life-time to live and cohabit at her house with a harlot. They deny that they have changed, or attempted to change, the name of the child, and aver that they are Lucile's duly-appointed guardians in this State. The answer then proceeds as follows:

"These respondents further state, the said Francis H. Shaw upon information and belief, and the said Marietta H. Shaw from her knowledge acquired as aforesaid, that the peititioners are unfit persons to have the care and custody of the little girl Lucile

Stockman, and that by reason of the great change that would take place in her mode of living, and by reason of the great cruelty which would be practiced towards the said infant by the said Anna B. Stockman, they fear that her life would be in danger, and that she would live but a short time; and upon information and belief they state that the said petitioners are persons without any moral restraint whatever; and that in matters of religion they are without any attachment to any Christian or moral community whatever; and that their surroundings and education would taint and destroy the good moral character of said infant Lucile; and they ask the protection of this Court for such child; and that the facts and circumstances of the petition, and this answer, may be inquired into; and that by the judgment of this Court the prayer of the petitioners may be denied.

"These respondents further state, upon information and belief, that the only object and purpose which the petitioners have in obtaining the custody of said child is to enable them to have some pretext for expending whatever money the said infant may be entitled to under the provisions of the act of Congress of the United States and under the provisions of the will, as set forth in said petition; and they state, upon information and belief, that there is no adequate security filed in any court in Washington to protect the estate of said infant from loss or speculation in case her custody and control should be transferred to the petitioners; and they refer to the affidavit hereto attached as a part of this answer."

The respondents also submit all the testimony upon the former trial, when the matter was before the jury. Such is substantially the issue as made up before us now for consideration.

The superior rights of a father to his child to those of the grandparents, all things else being equal, are no longer before us. It has now come to the single question and consideration whether the paternal or maternal grandparents shall have the care and custody. So far as the desires of the parents are concerned, the father's last wish was that his parents might have such care, and, so far as the mother's feelings in the matter is concerned, it was her dying request that her parents might have the care and training of her infant daughter, and at that time such were his wishes in the matter. I have reviewed all the evidence in this case, and, after applying to it all the knowledge and experience I possess, I must say that at this time, when he was stirred up by all the feelings of his better nature, and they had so far got control of his passions and prejudices as to allow his reason, his judgment, and affections to dictate what, under all the circumstances, would be best for the future welfare of his little child, in his wishes then expressed and the promise he gave to his dying wife, and the request he made of her mother that she would—

"Take the child and bring her up pure and virtuous, like her mother," saying, "that is all I ask,"—

He gave expression to the true sentiments of his heart, approved by his reason and his judgment; and it was the wisest and best conclusion he could have possibly reached, and in my opinion it ought not now to be disturbed.

The child is a girl. That mother knew better than any one else of its care and many wants and requirements through the period of its infancy and childhood, during a motherless future, and she knew that no one else could have the patience and affection for the little one, and minister those wants, to the extent of her own mother. Others might be found to take the charge but none could do it so well. There is no question but that Mrs. Shaw and her husband are competent, able, and well qualified for the duties the guardianship of this granddaughter imposes upon them, and it is a pleasure to them to discharge that duty. The child likes them, and is contented and happy with them. Why should this Court send her to a home where she does not wish to go, to friends she does not know, who have never expressed a desire for her, save to gratify the spleen and prejudice of a father, who by his will left to his daughter as her principal legacy the hatred he bore towards her mother's parents, to a climate not congenial to her health, and which brought her mother to a premature grave?

It is claimed by counsel for the Stockmans that the law is inexorable, and requires this to be done. I cannot agree with counsel upon this subject. Courts have a general superintending power over all infants, and the primary guardianship of the parent over his child lasts no longer than he is found to be competent, and discharges his duty which nature has laid upon him, properly; and when he fails to do this, the proper court may interfere, and charge another with the discharge of this duty. The good of society and the welfare of the State require this, and can never require less. Primarily, the court is the guardian of all orphan children, and will give the proper directions as to their care and support until such time as a guardian shall be appointed; and it is then its duty to see to it that the duties of the trust are properly discharged.

Guardians for infants may be appointed by the last will of the parent instead of by the court, in which case the court will recognize their authority and their control of the ward so long as it is right and proper, and for the best interest of the ward. The powers of a testamentary guardian are just the same precisely as are those of a guardian appointed by the court, and are allowed to be exercised or withheld for the same reasons. Who shall or may be appointed guardian is within the discretion of the court. Relatives of the infant are usually selected, and those nearest of kin are usually preferred when otherwise competent, and as between those entitled the question to be determined in making the selection is, and always should be, what will be for the best interest of the ward under all the circumstances? It should control everything else.

In looking into the circumstances in this case it seems to me but one conclusion can be reached, and that is that this child should be permitted to remain where she now is, with her maternal grandparents. The testimony shows they are doing all that is necessary for her enjoyment, her education, her health, her comfort, and welfare, and without expense to the ward or her estate. Her acquaintances, her associates, her friends, are all there, and she has all the advantages for moral and intellectual culture, with the accomplishments to be acquired in the best society; and were the change made as desired by petitioners, we are not sure she could have the benefit of all these. And I feel quite certain she would not. She is just at this time of an age when she needs the guardianship of the most exemplary and circumspect. She has now arrived at an age when impressions will become most lasting, and it is of the greatest importance to her future welfare that they should be correct. I do not think this Court would be justified in trying the experiment of transferring her custody to the grandparents at Washington, even though they were equally competent with those at Port Huron; a fact, however, I regret to say, I have been unable to find from the testimony. I am not prepared to give my assent to an experiment fraught with the danger of destroying the happiness of this innocent young girl's future life. There is no law which requires this Court to make such a decision, and justice to the dead as well as to the living protests against it.

Mr. and Mrs. Shaw have been duly appointed guardians of the child in this State. Under the agreement which was made by the father, on request of the mother, with Mrs. Shaw when

19

she brought the child to Port Huron, that place became the child's residence, and it was not changed by the agreement which Mrs. Shaw subsequently signed under duress in Washington. By virtue of the letters of guardianship the respondents have also the lawful custody of their ward, and the testamentary guardians never had any right to such custody, except that which comity gave them, and which can never be properly enforced in this State, under the circumstances appearing in this case. Laws of 1883, p. 3; Laws of 1887, p. 147; How. Stat. § 6312; *In re Rice*, 42 Mich. 528 (4 N. W. Rep. 284); *Johnstone v. Beattie*, 10 Clark & F. 42; *Morrell v. Dickey*, 1 Johns. Ch. 153; *Kraft v. Wickey*, 4 Gill & J. 332; Story Confl. Law, §§ 494-504; *Overseers v. Overseers*, 5 Cow. 527; *Riley v. Riley*, 3 Day, 74; *Fenwick v. Sear's Adm'rs*, 1 Cranch, 259; Whart Confl. Laws, §§ 261-264; Reeve, Dom. Rel. 454; *Creuze v. Hunter*, 2 Cox, Ch. 242; *De Manneville v. De Manneville*, 10 Ves. 52; *Wood v. Wood*, 5 Paige, 596, 605; *Leonard v. Putnam*, 51 N. H. 247; *Hubbard's Case*, 22 Alb. Law J. 315; *Ex parte Watkins*, 2 Ves. Sr. 470; *Woodworth v. Spring*, 4 Allen, 321; *Townsend v. Kendall*, 4 Minn. 412; *Boyd v. Glass*, 34 Ga. 253; *In re Turner*, 41 Law, J. (Q. B.) 142; *Rowe v. Rowe*, 28 Mich. 353; *Corrie v. Corrie*, 42 Id. 509 (4 N. W. Rep. 213); *People v. Brown*, 35 Hun, 324; 2 Lead. Cas. Eq. (White & T. Notes), 1528; Hoch. Inf. § 56; *Gishwiler v. Dodez*, 4 Ohio St. 615; *McLoskey v. Reid*, 4 Bradf. Surr. 334; *Ex parte Dawson*, 3 Id. 130; *Bennet v. Bennet*, 13 N. J. Eq. 114; Tyler, Inf. 283, 285-292; *Dumain v. Gwynne*, 10 Allen, 270; *In re Spence*, 2 Phil. Ch. 247.

Comity cannot be considered in a case like this, when the future welfare of the child is the vital question in the case. The good of the child is superior to all other considerations. It is the polar star to guide to the conclusion in all cases of infants, whether the question is raised upon a writ of *habeas corpus* or in a court of chancery. The infant's desire in determining where she shall reside, if of sufficient age and uninfluenced, is always listened to with interest, and in this case we have it marked and most emphatic. She wants to remain where she is.

I think the duty of the Court in this case is plain and clear. I have no doubt of Mrs. Shaw's right to the custody of this child under the contract she made with her father at the death-bed of her mother, and I am entirely satisfied that she is now receiving the care she needs, and that her education is properly attended to, and that she is happy in her home and surroundings, and that she never could be at Washington, under the guardianship of her paternal grandparents.

In my judgment the writ should be denied, with costs, and the child should be allowed to remain where she now is, with Mr. and Mrs. Shaw, in Port Huron.

MORSE and LONG, JJ., concurred with SHERWOOD, C. J.

LAMAR v. MICOU, 1884.

[112 U. S. 452.]

1. Guardian of the Property of the Ward.
2. Degree of Care to be Exercised over Ward's Property.
3. What Law Determines the Guardian's Liability.
4. Power of Foreign Guardians to Sue and be Sued.

This was an appeal by the executor of a guardian from a decree against him upon a bill in equity filed by the administratrix of his ward.

The original bill, filed on July 1, 1875, by Ann C. Sims, a citizen of Alabama, as administratrix of Martha M. Sims, in the Supreme Court of the State of New York, alleged that on December 11, 1855, the defendant's testator, Gazaway B. Lamar, was duly appointed, by the surrogate of the county of Richmond in that State, guardian of the person and estate of Martha M. Sims, an infant of six years of age, then a resident of that county, and gave bond as such, and took into his possession and control all her property, being more than $5,000; that on October 5, 1874, he died in New York, and on November 10, 1874, his will was there admitted to probate, and the defendant, a citizen of New York, was appointed his executor; and that he and his executor had neglected to render any account of his guardianship to the surrogate of Richmond county or to any court having cognizance thereof, or to the ward or her administratrix; and prayed for an account, and for judgment for the amount found to be due.

The defendant removed the case into the Circuit Court of the United States for the Southern District of New York; and there filed an answer, averring that in 1855, when Lamar was appointed guardian of Martha M. Sims, he was a citizen of Georgia, and she was a citizen of Alabama, having a temporary residence in the city of New York; that in the spring of 1861 the States of Georgia and Alabama declared themselves to have seceded from the United States, and to constitute members of the so-called Confederate States of America, whereupon a state of war arose between the United States and the Confederate States, which continued to be flagrant for more than four years after; that Lamar and Martha M. Sims were in the spring of 1861 citizens and residents of the States of Georgia and Alabama respectively, and citizens of the Confederate States, and were engaged in aiding and abetting the State of Georgia and the so-called Confederate States in their rebellion against the United States, and she continued to aid and abet until the time of her death, and he continued to aid and abet till January, 1865; that the United States by various public acts declared all his and her property, of any kind, to be liable to seizure and confiscation by the United States, and they both were, by the various acts of Congress of the United States, outlawed and debarred of any access to any court of the United States, whereby it was impossible for Lamar to appear in the Surrogate's Court of Richmond county to settle and close his accounts there, and to be discharged from his liability as guardian, in consequence whereof the relation of guardian and ward, so far as it depended upon the orders of that court, ceased and determined; that, for the purpose of saving the ward's property from seizure and confiscation by the United States, Lamar, at the request of the ward and of her natural guardians, all citizens of the State of Alabama, withdrew the funds belonging to her from the city of New York, and invested them for her benefit and account in such securities as by the laws of the States of Alabama and Georgia and of the Confederate States he might lawfully do; that in 1864, upon the death of Martha M. Sims, all her property vested in her sister, Ann C. Sims, as her next of kin, and any accounting of Lamar for that property was to be made to her; that on March 15, 1867, at the written request of Ann C. Sims and of her natural guardians, Benjamin H. Micou was appointed her legal guardian by the Probate Court of Montgomery County, in the State of Alabama, which was at that time her residence, and Lamar thereupon accounted for and paid over all property, with which he was chargeable as guardian of Martha M. Sims, to Micou, as her guardian, and received from him a full release therefor; and that Ann C. Sims when she became of age ratified and confirmed the same. To that answer the plaintiff filed a general replication.

The case was set down for hearing in the Circuit Court upon the bill, answer and replication, and a statement of facts agreed by the parties, in substance as follows:

On November 23, 1850, William W. Sims, a citizen of Georgia, died at Savannah in that State, leaving a widow, who was appointed his administratrix, and two infant daughters, Martha M. Sims, born at Savannah on September 8, 1849, and Ann C. Sims, born in Florida on June 1, 1851. In 1853 the widow married the Rev. Richard M. Abercrombie, of Clifton, in the county of Richmond and State of New York.

On December 11, 1855, on the petition of Mrs. Abercrombie, Gazaway B. Lamar, an uncle of Mr. Sims, and then residing at Brooklyn in the State of New York, was appointed by the surrogate of Richmond County guardian of the person and estate of each child "until she shall arrive at the age of fourteen years, and until another guardian shall be appointed;" and gave bond to her, with sureties, "to faithfully in all things discharge the duty of a guardian to the said minor according to law, and render a true and just account of all moneys and other property received by him, and of the application thereof, and of his guardianship in all respects, to any court having cognizance thereof;" and he immediately received from Mrs. Abercrombie in money $5,166.89 belonging to each ward, and invested part of it in January and April, 1856, in stock of the Bank of the Republic at New York, and part of it in March and July, 1857, in stock of the Bank of Commerce at Savannah, each of which was then paying, and continued to pay until April, 1861, good dividends annually, the one of ten and the other of eight per cent.

In 1856, several months after Lamar's appointment as guardian, Mr. and Mrs. Abercrombie removed from Clifton, in the State of New York, to Hartford, in the State of Connecticut, and there resided till her death in the spring of 1859. The children lived with Mr. and Mrs. Abercrombie, Lamar as guardian paying Mr. Abercrombie for their board, at Clifton and at Hartford, from the marriage until her death; and were then removed to Augusta in the State of Georgia, and there lived with their paternal grandmother and her unmarried daughter and only living child, their aunt; Lamar as guardian continuing to pay their board. After 1856 neither of the children ever resided in the State of New York. On January 18, 1860, their aunt was married to Benjamin H. Micou, of Montgomery, in the State of Alabama, and the children and their grandmother thereafter lived with Mr. and Mrs. Micou at Montgomery, and the children were educated and supported at Mr. Micou's expense.

From 1855 to 1859 Lamar resided partly in Georgia and

partly in New York. In the spring of 1861 he had a temporary residence in the city of New York, and upon the breaking out of the war of the rebellion, and after removing all his own property, left New York, and passed through the lines to Savannah, and there resided, sympathizing with the rebellion, and doing what he could to accomplish its success, until January, 1865, and continued to have his residence in Savannah until 1872 or 1873, when he went to New York again, and afterwards lived there. Mr. and Mrs. Micou also sympathized with the rebellion and desired its success, and each of them, as well as Lamar, failed during the rebellion to bear true allegiance to the United States.

At the time of Lamar's appointment as guardian, ten shares in the stock of the Mechanics Bank of Augusta in the State of Georgia, which had belonged to William W. Sims in his life-time, stood on the books of the bank in the name of Mrs. Abercrombie, as his administratrix, of which one-third belonged to her as his widow, and one-third to each of the infants. In January, 1856, the bank refused a request of Lamar to transfer one-third of that stock to him as guardian of each infant, but afterwards paid to him as guardian from time to time two-thirds of the dividends during the life of Mrs. Abercrombie, and all the dividends after her death until 1865. During the period last named, he also received as guardian the dividends on some other bank stock in Savannah, which Mrs. Abercrombie owned, and to which, on her death, her husband became entitled. Certain facts, relied on as showing that he, immediately after his wife's death, made a surrender of her interest in the bank shares to Lamar, as guardian of her children, are not material to the understanding of the decision of this court, but are recapitulated in the opinion of the Circuit Court. 7 Fed. Rep. 180-185.

In the winter of 1861-62, Lamar, fearing that the stock in the Bank of the Republic at New York, held by him as guardian, would be confiscated by the United States, had it sold by a friend in New York; the proceeds of the sale, which were about twenty per cent. less than the par value of the stock, invested at New York in guaranteed bonds of the cities of New Orleans, Memphis, and Mobile, and of the East Tennessee and Georgia Railroad Company; and those bonds deposited in a bank in Canada.

Lamar from time to time invested the property of his wards, that was within the so-called Confederate States, in whatever seemed to him to be the most secure and safe—some in Confederate States bonds, some in the bonds of the Individual States which composed the confederacy, and some in bonds of cities and of railroad corporaticns and stock of banks within these States.

On the money of his wards, accruing from dividends on bank stock, and remaining in his hands, he charged himself with interest until the summer of 1862, when, with the advice and aid of Mr. Micou, he invested $7,000 of such money in bonds of the Confederate States and of the State of Alabama; and in 1863, with the like advice and aid, sold the Alabama bonds for more than he had paid for them, and invested the proceeds also in Confederate State bonds; charged his wards with the money paid, and credited them with the bonds; and placed the bonds in the hands of their grandmother, who gave him a receipt for them and held them till the end of the rebellion, when they, as well as the stock in the banks at Savannah, became worthless.

Martha M. Sims died on November 2, 1864, at the age of fifteen years, unmarried and intestate, leaving her sister Ann C. Sims her next of kin. On January 12, 1867, Lamar, in answer to letters of inquiry from Mr. and Mrs. Micou, wrote to Mrs. Micou that he had saved from the wreck of the property of his niece, Ann C. Sims, surviving her sister, three bonds of the city of Memphis, indorsed by the State of Tennessee, one bond of the city of Mobile, and one bond of the East Tennessee and Georgia Railroad Company, each for $1,000, and with some coupons past due and uncollected; and suggested that by reason of his age and failing health, and of the embarrassed state of his own affairs, Mr. Micou should be appointed in Alabama guardian in his stead. Upon receipt of this letter Mrs. Micou wrote to Lamar, thanking him for the explicit statement of the niece's affairs, and for the care and trouble he had with her property; and Ann C. Sims, then nearly sixteen years old, signed a request, attested by her grandmother and by Mrs. Micou, that her guardianship might be transferred to Mr. Micou, and that he might be appointed her guardian. And on March 15, 1867, he was appointed guardian of her property by the Probate Court of the county of Montgomery and State of Alabama, according to the laws of that State, and gave bond as such.

On May 14, 1867, Lamar sent to Micou complete and correct statements of his guardianship account with each of his wards, as well as all the securities remaining in his hands as guardian of either, and a check payable to Micou a guardian of Ann C. Sims for a balance in money due her; and Micou, as such guardian, signed and sent to Lamar a schedule of and receipt for the property, describing it specifically, by which it appeared that the bonds of the cities of New Orleans and Memphis and of the East Ten nessee and Georgia Railroad Company were issued, and the Mem phis bonds, as well as the railroad bonds, were indorsed by the State of Tennessee, some years before the breaking out of the re bellion. Micou thenceforth continued to act in all respects as the only guardian of Ann C. Sims until she became of age on June 1, 1872.

No objection or complaint was ever made by either of the wards, or their relatives, against Lamar's transactions or invest ments as guardian, until July 28, 1874, when Micou wrote to Lamar, informing him that Ann C. Sims desired a settlement of his accounts; and that he had been advised that no credits could be allowed for the investments in Confederate State bonds, and that Lamar was responsible for the security of the investments in other bonds and bank stock. Lamar was then sick in New York, and died there on October 5, 1874, without having answered the letter.

Before the case was heard in the Circuit Court, Ann C. Sims died on May 7, 1878; and on June 20, 1878, Mrs. Micou was ap pointed in New York, administratrix *de bonis non* of Martha M. Sims, and as such filed a bill of revivor in this suit. On October 3, 1878, the defendant filed a cross bill, repeating the allegations of his answer to the original bill, and further averring that Ann C. Sims left a will, which had been admitted to probate in Mont gomery County in the State of Alabama, and afterwards in the county and State of New York, by which she gave all her prop erty to Mrs. Micou, who was her next of kin; and that Mrs. Micou was entitled to receive for her own benefit whatever might be recovered in the principal suit, and was estopped to deny the lawfulness or propriety of Lamar's acts, because whatever was done by him as guardian of Martha M. Sims in her lifetime, or as guardian of the interests of Ann C. Sims as her next of kin, was authorized and approved by Mrs. Micou and her mother and hus band as the natural guardians of both children. Mrs. Micou, as plaintiff in the bill of revivor, answered the cross bill, alleging that Ann succeeded to Martha's property as administratrix, and not as her next of kin, admitting Ann's will and the probate there of, denying that Mrs. Micou was a natural guardian of the chil dren, and denying that she approved or ratified Lamar's acts as guardian. A general replication was filed to that answer.

Upon a hearing on the pleadings and the agreed statement

of facts, the Circuit Court dismissed the cross bill, held all Lamar's investments to have been breaches of trust, and entered a decree referring the case to a master to state an account. The case was afterwards heard on exceptions to the master's report, and a final decree entered for the plaintiff for $18,705.19, including the value before 1861 of those bank stocks in Georgia of which Lamar had never had possession. The opinion delivered upon the first hearing is reported in 17 Blatchford, 378, and in 1 Fed. Rep. 14, and the opinion upon the second hearing in 7 Fed. Rep. 180. The defendant appealed to this court.

Mr. Justice GRAY delivered the opinion of the court. He recited the facts as above stated, and continued:

The authority of the Surrogate's Court of the county of Richmond and State of New York to appoint Lamar guardian of the persons and property of infants at the time within that county, and the authority of the Supreme Court of the State of New York, in which this suit was originally brought, being a court of general equity jurisdiction, to take cognizance thereof, are not disputed; and upon the facts agreed it is quite clear that none of the defences set up in the answer afford any ground for dismissing the bill.

The war of the rebellion, and the residence of both wards and guardian within the territory controlled by the insurgents, did not discharge the guardian from his responsibility to account after the war, for property of the wards which had at any time come into his hands or which he might by the exercise of due care have obtained possession of. A state of war does not put an end to pre-existing obligations, or transfer the property of wards to their guardians, or release the latter from the duty to keep it safely, but suspends until the return of peace the right of any one residing within the enemy's country to sue in our courts. *Ward* v. *Smith*, 7 Wall. 447; *Montgomery* v. *United States*, 15 Wall. 395, 400; *Insurance Co.* v. *Davis*, 95 U. S. 425, 430; *Kershaw* v. *Kelsey*, 100 Mass. 561, 563, 564, 570; 3 Phillmore International Law (2d ed.) § 589.

The appointment of Micou in 1867 by a court of Alabama to be guardian of the surviving ward, then residing in that State, did not terminate Lamar's liability for property of his wards which he previously had or ought to have taken possession of. The receipt given by Micou was only for the securities and money actually handed over to him by Lamar; and if Micou had any authority to discharge Lamar from liability for past mismanagement of either ward's property, he never assumed to do so.

The suggestion in the answer, that the surviving ward, upon coming of age, ratified and approved the acts of Lamar as guardian, finds no support in the facts of the case.

The further grounds of defence, set up in the cross bill, that Micou participated in Lamar's investments, and that Mrs. Micou approved them, are equally unavailing. The acts of Micou, before his own appointment as guardian, could not bind the ward. And admissions in private letters from Mrs. Micou to Lamar could not affect the rights of the ward, or Mrs. Micou's authority, upon being afterwards appointed administratrix of the ward, to maintain this bill as such against Lamar's representative, even if the amount recovered will inure to her own benefit as the ward's next of kin. 1 Greenl. Ev. § 179.

The extent of Lamar's liability presents more difficult ques tions of law, now for the first time brought before this court.

The general rule is everywhere recognized, that a guardian or trustee, when investing property in his hands, is bound to act honestly and faithfully, and to exercise a sound discretion, such as men or ordinary prudence and intelligence use in their own affairs. In some jurisdictions, no attempt has been made to establish a more definite rule; in others, the discretion has been confined, by the legislature or the courts, within strict limits.

The Court of Chancery, before the Declaration of Independence, appears to have allowed some latitude to trustees in making investments. The best evidence of this is to be found in the judgments of Lord Hardwicke. He held, indeed, in accordance with the clear weight of authority before and since, that money lent on a mere personal obligation, like a promissory note, without security, was at the risk of the trustee. *Ryder* v. *Bickerton,* 3 Swanston, 80, note; *S. C.* 1 Eden, 149, note; *Barney* v. *Saunders,* 16 How. 535, 545; Perry on Trusts, § 453. But in so holding, he said: "For it should have been on some such security as binds land, of something, to be answerable for it." 3 Swanston, 81, note. Although in one case he held that a trustee, directed by the terms of his trust to invest the trust money in government funds or other good securities, was responsible for a loss caused by his investing in South Sea stock; and observed that neither South Sea stock nor bank stock was considered a good security, because it depended upon the management of the governor and directors, and the capital might be wholly lost. *Trafford* v. *Boehm,* 3 Atk. 440, 444; yet in another case he declines to charge a trustee for a loss on South Sea stock which had fallen in value since the trustee received it; and said that "to compel trustees to make up a deficiency, not owing to their wilful default, is the harshest demand that can be made in a court of equity." *Jackson* v. *Jackson*, 1 Atk. 513, 514; *S. C.* West Ch. 31, 34. In a later case he said: "Suppose a trustee, having in his hands a considerable sum of money, places it out in the funds, which afterwards sink in their value, or on a security at the time apparently good, which afterwards turns out not to be so, for the benefit of the *cestui que trust*, was there ever an instance of the trustee's being made to answer the actual sum so placed out? I answer, no. If there is no *mala fides*, nothing wilful in the conduct of the trustee, the court will always favor him. For as a trust is an office necessary in the concerns between man and man, and which, if faithfully discharged, is attended with no small degree of trouble and anxiety, it is an act of great kindness in any one to accept it; to add hazard or risk to that trouble, and subject a trustee to losses which he could not foresee, and consequently not prevent, would be a manifest hardship, and would be deterring every one from accepting so necessary an office." That this opinion was not based upon the fact that in England trustees usually receive no compensation is clearly shown by the Chancellor's adding that the same doctrine held good in the case of a receiver, an officer of the court, and paid for his trouble; and the point decided was that a receiver, who paid the amount of rents of estates in his charge to a British tradesman of good credit, taking his bills therefor on London, was not responsible for the loss of the money by his becoming bankrupt. *Knight* v. *Plymouth*, 1 Dickens, 120, 126, 127; *S. C.* 3 Atk. 480. And the decision was afterwards cited by Lord Hardwicke himself showing that when trustees act by other hands, according to the usage of business, they are not answerable for losses. *Ex parte Belchier*, Ambler, 219; *S C.* 1 Kenyon, 38, 47.

In later times, as the amount and variety of English government securities increased, the Court of Chancery limited trust investments to the public funds, disapproved investments either in bank stock, or in mortgages of real estate, and prescribed so strict a rule that Parliament interposed; and by the statutes of 22 & 23 Vict. ch. 35, and 23 & 24 Vict. ch. 38, and by general orders in chancery, pursuant to those statutes, trustees have been authorized to invest in stock of the Bank of England or of Ireland, or upon mortgage of freehold or copyhold estates, as well as in the public funds. Lewin on Trusts (7th ed.) 282, 283, 287.

In a very recent case, the Court of Appeal and the House of Lords, following the decisions of Lord Hardwicke, in *Knight* v. *Plymouth* and *Ex parte Belchier*, above cited, held that a trustee investing trust funds, who employed a broker to procure securities authorized by the trust, and paid the purchase money to the broker, if such was the usual and regular course of business of persons acting with reasonable care and prudence on their own account, was not liable for the loss of the money by fraud of the broker. Sir George Jessel, M. R., Lord Justice Bowen, and Lord Blackburn affirmed the general rule that a trustee is only bound to conduct the business of his trust in the same manner that an ordinary prudent man of business would conduct his own; Lord Blackburn adding the qualification that "a trustee must not choose investments other than those which the terms of his trust permit." *Speight* v. *Gaunt*, 22 ch. D. 727, 739, 762; 9 App. Cas. 1, 19.

In this country, there has been a diversity in the laws and usages of the several States upon the subject of trust investments.

In New York, under Chancellor Kent, the rule seems to have been quite undefined. See *Smith* v. *Smith*, 4 Johns. Ch. 281, 285; *Thompson* v. *Brown*, 4 Johns. Ch. 619, 628, 629, where the chancellor quoted the passage above cited from Lord Hardwicke's opinion in *Knight* v. *Plymouth*. And in *Brown* v. *Campbell*, Hopk. Ch. 233, where an executor in good faith made an investment, considered at the time to be advantageous, of the amount of two promissory notes, due to his testator from one manufacturing corporation, in the stock of another manufacturing corporation, which afterwards became insolvent, Chancellor Sanford held that there was no reason to charge him with the loss. But by the latter decisions in that State investments in bank or railroad stock have been held to be at the risk of the trustee, and it has been intimated that the only investments that a trustee can safely make without an express order of the court are in government or real estate securities. *King* v. *Talbot*, 40 N. Y. 76, affirming *S. C.* 50 Barb. 453; *Ackerman* v. *Emott*, 4 Barb. 626; *Mills* v. *Hoffman*, 26 Hun. 594; 2 Kent Com. 416, note *b*. So the decisions in New Jersey and Pennsylvania tend to disallow investments in the stock of banks or other business corporations, or otherwise than in the public funds or in mortgages of real estate. *Gray* v. *Fox*, Saxon, 259, 268; *Halstead* v. *Meeker*, 3 C. E. Green, 136; *Lathrop* v. *Smalley*, 8 C. E. Green, 192; *Worrell's Appeal*, 9 Penn. St. 508, and 23 Penn. St. 44; *Hemphill's Appeal*, 18 Penn. St. 303; *Ihmsen's Appeal*, 43 Penn. St. 431. And the New York and Pennsylvania courts have shown a strong disinclination to permit investments in real estate or securities out of their jurisdiction. *Ormiston* v. *Olcott,* 84 N. Y. 339; *Rush's Estate,* 12 Penn. St. 375, 378.

In New England, and in the Southern States, the rule has been less strict.

In Massachusetts, by a usage of more than half a century, approved by a uniform course of judicial decision, it has come to be regarded as too firmly settled to be changed, except by the legislature, that all that can be required of a trustee to invest is that he shall conduct himself faithfully and exercise a sound discretion, such as men of prudence and intelligence exercise in the permanent disposition of their own funds, having regard not only to the probable income, but also to the probable safety of the capital; and that a guardian or trustee is not precluded from investing in the stock of banking, insurance, manufacturing or railroad corporations, within or without the State. *Harvard College* v. *Amory,* 9 Pick. 446, 461; *Lovell* v. *Minot,* 20 Pick. 116, 119; *Kinmonth* v. *Brigham,* 5 Allen, 270, 277; *Clark* v. *Garfield,* 8 Allen, 427; *Brown* v. *French,* 125 Mass. 410; *Bowker* v. *Pierce,* 130 Mass. 262. In New Hampshire and in Vermont, investments, honestly and prudently made, in securities of any kind that produce income, appear to be allowed. *Knowlton* v. *Bradley,* 17 N. H. 458; *Kimball* v. *Reding,* 11 Foster, 352, 374; *French* v. *Currier,* 47 N. H. 88, 99; *Barney* v. *Parsons,* 54 Vermont, 623.

In Maryland, good bank stock, as well as government securities and mortgages on real estate, has always been considered a proper investment. *Hammond* v. *Hammond,* 2 Bland. 306, 413; *Gray v. Lynch,* 8 Gill, 403; *Murray* v. *Feinour,* 2 Maryland Ch. 418. So in Mississippi, investment in bank-stock is allowed. *Smyth* v. *Burns,* 25 Mississippi, 422.

In South Carolina, before the war, no more definite rule appears to have been laid down than that guardians and trustees must manage the funds in their hands as prudent men manage their own affairs. *Boggs* v. *Adger,* 4 Rich. Eq. 408, 411; *Spear* v. *Spear,* 9 Rich. Eq. 184, 201; *Snelling* v. *McCreary,* 14 Rich. Eq. 291, 300.

In Georgia, the English rule was never adopted; a statute of 1845, which authorized executors, administrators, guardians and trustees, holding any trust funds, to invest them in securities of the State, was not considered compulsory; and before January 1, 1863 (when the statute was amended by adding a provision

that any other investment of trust funds must be made under a
judicial order, or else be at the risk of the trustee), those who lent
the fund at interest, on what was at the time considered by prudent men to be good security, were not held liable for loss without their fault. Cobb's Digest, 333; Code of 1861, § 2308;
Brown v. *Wright*, 39 Georgia, 96; *Moses* v. *Moses*, 50 Georgia,
9, 33.

In Alabama, the Supreme Court, in *Bryant* v. *Craig*, 12
Alabama, 354, 359, having intimated that a guardian could not
safely invest upon either real or personal security without an
order of court, the legislature, from 1852, authorized guardians
and trustees to invest on bond and mortgage, or on good personal
security, with no other limit than fidelity and prudence might require. Code of 1852, § 2024; Code of 1867, § 2426; *Foscue* v.
Lyon, 55 Alabama, 440, 452.

The rules of investment varying so much in the different
States, it becomes necessary to consider by what law the management and investment of the ward's property should be governed.

As a general rule (with some exceptions not material to the
consideration of this case) the law of the domicil governs the
status of a person, and the disposition and management of his
movable property. The domicil of an infant is universally held
to be the fittest place for the appointment of a guardian of his
person and estate; although for the protection of either, a guardian may be appointed in any State where the person or any property of an infant may be found. On the continent of Europe,
the guardian appointed in the State of the domicil of the ward is
generally recognized as entitled to the control and dominion of
the ward and his movable property everywhere, and guardians
specially appointed in other States are responsible to the principal
guardian. By the law of England and of this country, a guardian
appointed by the courts of one State has no authority over the
ward's person or property in another State, except so far as
allowed by the comity of that State, as expressed through its
legislature or its courts; but the tendency of modern statutes and
decisions is to defer to the law of the domicil, and to support the
authority of the guardian appointed there. *Hoyt* v. *Sprague*, 103
U. S. 613, 631, and authorities cited; *Morrell* v. *Dickey*, 1 Johns.
Ch. 153; *Woodworth* v. *Spring*, 4 Allen, 321; *Milliken* v. *Pratt*,
125 Mass. 374, 377, 378; *Leonard* v. *Putnam*, 51 N. H. 247;
Commonwealth v. *Rhoads*, 37 Penn. St. 60; *Sims* v. *Renwick*, 25
Georgia, 58; Dicey on Domicil, 172-176; Westlake Private Inter-

national Law (2d ed.) 48-50; Wharton Conflict of Laws (2d ed.) §§ 259-268.

An infant cannot change his own domicil. As infants have the domicil of their father, he may change their domicil by changing his own; and after his death the mother, while she remains a widow, may likewise, by changing her domicil, change the domicil of the infants; the domicil of the children, in either case, following the independent domicil of their parent. *Kennedy v. Ryall*, 67 N. Y. 379; *Potinger v. Wightman*, 3 Meriv. 67; *Dedham v. Natick*, 16 Mass. 135; Dicey on Domicil, 97-99. But when the widow, by marrying again, acquires the domicil of a second husband, she does not, by taking her children by the first husband to live with her there, make the domicil which she derives from her second husband their domicil; and they retain the domicil which they had, before her second marriage, acquired from her or from their father. *Cumner v. Milton*, 3 Salk. 259; *S. C.* Holt, 578; *Freetown v. Taunton*, 16 Mass. 52; *School Directors v. James*, 2 Watts & Sergeant, 568; *Johnson v. Copeland*, 35 Alabama, 521; *Brown v. Lynch*, 2 Bradford, 214; *Mears v. Sinclair*, 1 West Virginia, 185; Pothier Introduction Generale aux Coutumes, No. 19; 1 Burge Colonial and Foreign Law, 39; 4 Phillimore International Law (2d ed.) § 97.

The preference due to the law of the ward's domicil, and the importance of a uniform administration of his whole estate, require that, as a general rule, the management and investment of his property should be governed by the law of the State of his domicil, especially when he actually resides there, rather than by the law of any State in which a guardian may have been appointed or may have received some property of the ward. If the duties of the guardian were to be exclusively regulated by the law of the State of his appointment, it would follow that in any case in which the temporary residence of the ward was changed from State to State, from considerations of health, education, pleasure or convenience, and guardians were appointed in each State, the guardians appointed in the different States, even if the same persons, might be held to diverse rules of accounting for different parts of the ward's property. The form of accounting, so far as concerns the remedy only, must indeed be according to the law of the court in which relief is sought; but the general rule by which the guardian is to be held responsible for the investment of the ward's property is the law of the place of the domicil of the ward. Bar International Law, § 106 (Gillespie's translation), 438; Wharton Conflict of Laws, § 259.

It may be suggested that this would enable the guardian, by changing the domicil of his ward, to choose for himself the law by which he should account. Not so. The father, and after his death the widowed mother, being the natural guardian, and the person from whom the ward derives his domicil, may change that domicil. But the ward does not derive a domicil from any other than a natural guardian. A testamentary guardian nominated by the father may have the same control of the ward's domicil that the father had. *Wood* v. *Wood,* 5 Paige, 596, 605. And any guardian, appointed in the State of the domicil of the ward, has been generally held to have the power of changing the ward's domicil from one county to another within the same State and under the same law. *Cutts* v. *Haskins,* 9 Mass. 543; *Holyoke* v. *Haskins,* 5 Pick. 20; *Kirkland* v. *Whately,* 4 Allen, 462; *Anderson* v. *Anderson,* 42 Vermont, 350; *Ex parte Bartlett,* 4 Bradford, 221; *The Queen* v. *Whitby,* L. R. 5 Q. B. 325, 331. But it is very doubtful, to say the least, whether even a guardian appointed in the State of the domicil of the ward (not being the natural guardian or a testamentary guardian) can remove the ward's domicil beyond the limits of the State in which the guardian is appointed and to which his legal authority is confined. *Douglas* v. *Douglas,* L. R. 12 Eq. 617, 625; *Daniel* v. *Hill,* 52 Alabama 430; Story Conflict of Laws, § 506, note; Dicey on Domicil, 100, 132. And it is quite clear that a guardian appointed in a State in which the ward is temporarily residing cannot change the ward's permanent domicil from one State to another.

The case of such a guardian differs from that of an executor of, or a trustee under, a will. In the one case, the title in the property is in the executor or the trustee; in the other, the title in the property is in the ward, and the guardian has only the custody and management of it, with power to change its investment. The executor or trustee is appointed at the domicil of the testator; the guardian is most fitly appointed at the domicil of the ward, and may be appointed in any State in which the person or any property of the ward is found. The general rule which governs the administration of the property in the one case may be the law of the domicil of the testator; in the other case, it is the law of the domicil of the ward.

As the law of the domicil of the ward has no extra-territorial effect, except by the comity of the State where the property is situated, or where the guardian is appointed, it cannot of course prevail against a statute of the State in which the question is presented for adjudication, expressly applicable to the estate of a ward domiciled elsewhere. *Hoyt* v. *Sprague,* 103 U. S. 613. Cases may also arise with facts so peculiar or so complicated as to modify the degree of influence that the court in which the guardian is called to account may allow to the law of the domicil of the ward, consistently with doing justice to the parties before it. And a guardian, who had in good faith conformed to the law of the State in which he was appointed, might perhaps be ex- cused for not having complied with stricter rules prevailing at the domicil of the ward. But in a case in which the domicil of the ward has always been in a State whose law leaves much to the discretion of the guardian in the matter of investments, and he has faithfully and prudently exercised that discretion with a view to the pecuniary interests of the ward, it would be inconsis- tent with the principles of equity to charge him with the amount of the moneys invested, merely because he has not complied with the more rigid rules adopted by the courts of the State in which he was appointed.

The domicil of William W. Sims during his life and at the time of his death in 1850 was in Georgia. This domicil continued to be the domicil of his widow and of their infant children until they acquired new ones. In 1853, the widow, by marrying the Rev. Mr. Abercrombie, acquired his domicil. But she did not, by taking the infants to the home, at first in New York and after- wards in Connecticut, of her new husband, who was of no kin to the children, was under no legal obligation to support them, and was in fact paid for their board out of their property, make his domicil, or the domicil derived by her from him, the domicil of the children of the first husband. Immediately upon her death in Connecticut, in 1859, these children, both under ten years of age, were taken back to Georgia to the house of their father's mother and unmarried sister, their own nearest surviving relatives; and they continued to live with their grandmother and aunt in Georgia until he marriage of the aunt in January, 1860, to Mr. Micou, a citizen of Alabama, after which the grandmother and the children resided with Mr. and Mrs. Micou at their domicil in that State.

Upon these facts, the domicil of the children was always in Georgia from their birth until January, 1860, and thenceforth was either in Georgia or in Alabama. As the rules of investment prevailing before 1863 in Georgia and in Alabama did not sub- stantially differ, the question in which of those two States their domicil was is immaterial to the decision of this case; and it is therefore unnecessary to consider whether their grandmother was their natural guardian, and as such had the power to change their domicil from one State to another. See Hargrave's note 66 to Co. Lit. 88 *b;* Reeve Domestic Relations, 315; 2 Kent. Com. 219; Code of Georgia of 1861, §§ 1754, 2452; *Darden* v. *Wyatt,* 15 Georgia, 414.

Whether the domicil of Lamar in December, 1855, when he was appointed in New York guardian of the infants, was in New York or in Georgia, does not distinctly appear, and is not material; because, for the reasons already stated, wherever his domicil was, his duties as guardian in the management and investment of the property of his wards were to be regulated by the law of their domicil.

It remains to apply the test of that law to Lamar's acts or omissions with regard to the various kinds of securities in which the property of the wards was invested.

1. The sum which Lamar received in New York in money from Mrs. Abercrombie he invested in 1856 and 1857 in stock of the Bank of the Republic at New York, and of the Bank of Commerce at Savannah, both of which were then, and continued till the breaking out of the war, in sound condition, paying good dividends. There is nothing to raise a suspicion that Lamar, in making these investments, did not use the highest degree of prudence; and they were such as by the law of Georgia or of Alabama he might properly make. Nor is there any evidence that he was guilty of neglect in not withdrawing the investment in the stock of the Bank of Commerce at Savannah before it became worthless. He should not therefore be charged with the loss of that stock.

The investment in the stock of the Bank of the Republic of New York being a proper investment by the law of the domicil of the wards, and there being no evidence that the sale of that stock by Lamar's order in New York in 1862 was not judicious, or was for less than its fair market price, he was not responsible for the decrease in its value between the times of its purchase and of its sale. He had the authority, as guardian, without any order of court, to sell personal property of his ward in his own possession, and to reinvest the proceeds. *Field* v. *Schieffelin,* 7 Johns. Ch. 150; *Ellis* v. *Essex Merrimack Bridge,* 2 Pick. 243. That his motive in selling it was to avoid its being confiscated by the United States does not appear to us to have any bearing on the rights of these parties. And no statute under which it could have been confiscated has been brought to our notice. The act of July 17, 1862, ch. 195, § 6, cited by the appellant, is limited to property of persons engaged in or abetting armed rebellion, which could hardly be predicated of two girls under thirteen years of age. 12 Stat. 591. Whatever liability, criminal or civil, Lamar, may have incurred or avoided as towards the United States, there was nothing in his selling this stock, and turning it into money, of which his wards had any right to complain.

As to the sum received from the sale of the stock in the Bank of the Republic, we find nothing in the facts agreed by the parties, upon which the case was heard, to support the argument that Lamar, under color of protecting his wards' interests, allowed the funds to be lent to cities and other corporations which were aiding in the rebellion. On the contrary, it is agreed that that sum was applied to the purchase in New York of guaranteed bonds of the cities of New Orleans, Memphis and Mobile, and of the East Tennessee and Georgia Railroad Company; and the description of those bonds, in the receipt afterwards given by Micou to Lamar, shows that the bonds of that railroad company, and of the cities of New Orleans and Memphis, at least, were issued some years before the breaking out of the rebellion, and that the bonds of the city of Memphis and the railroad company were at the time of their issue indorsed by the State of Tennessee. The company had its charter from that State, and its road was partly in Tennessee and partly in Georgia. Tenn. St. 1848, ch. 169. Under the discretion allowed to a guardian or trustee by the law of Georgia and of Alabama, he was not precluded from investing the funds in his hands in bonds of a railroad corporation, indorsed by the State by which it was chartered, or in bonds of a city. As Lamar, in making these investments, appears to have used due care and prudence, having regard to the best pecuniary interests of his wards, the sum so invested should be credited to him in this case, unless, as suggested at the argument, the requisite allowance has already been made in the final decree of the Circuit Court in the suit brought by the representative of the other ward, an appeal from which was dismissed by this court for want of jurisdiction in 104 U. S. 465.

2. Other moneys of the wards in Lamar's hands, arising either from dividends which he had received on their behalf, or from interest with which he charged himself upon sums not invested, were used in the purchase of bonds of the Confederate States, and of the State of Alabama.

The investment in bonds of the Confederate States was clearly unlawful, and no legislative act or judicial decree or decision of any State could justify it. The so-called Confederate government was in no sense a lawful government, but was a mere government of force, having its origin and foundation in rebellion against the United States. The notes and bonds issued in its name and for its support had no legal value as money or property, except by agreement or acceptance of parties capable of contracting with each other, and can never be regarded by a court sitting under the authority of the United States as securities in which trust funds might be lawfully invested. *Thorington* v. *Smith,* 8 Wall. 1; *Head* v. *Starks,* Chase, 312; *Horn* v. *Lockhart,* 17 Wall. 570; *Confederate Note Case,* 19 Wall. 548; *Sprott* v. *United States,* 20 Wall. 459; *Fretz* v. *Stover,* 22 Wall. 198; *Alexander* v. *Bryan,* 110 U. S. 414. An infant has no capacity, by contract with his guardian, or by assent to his unlawful acts, to affect his own rights. The case is governed in this particular by the decision in *Horn* v. *Lockhart,* in which it was held that an executor was not discharged from his liability to legatees by having invested funds, pursuant to a statute of the State, and with the approval of the probate court by which he had been appointed, in bonds of the Confederate States, which became worthless in his hands.

Neither the date nor the purpose of the issue of the bonds of the State of Alabama is shown, and it is unnecessary to consider the lawfulness of the investment in those bonds, because Lamar appears to have sold them for as much as he had paid for them, and to have invested the proceeds in additional Confederate States bonds, and for the amount thereby lost to the estate he was accountable.

3. The stock in the Mechanics' Bank of Georgia, which had belonged to William W. Sims in his lifetime, and stood on the books of the bank in the name of his administratrix, and of which one-third belonged to her as his widow, and one-third to each of the infants, never came into Lamar's possession; and upon a request made by him, the very next month after his appointment, the bank refused to transfer to him any part of it. He did receive and account for the dividends; and he could not, under the law of Georgia concerning foreign guardians, have obtained possession of property of his wards within that State without the consent of the ordinary. Code of 1861, §§ 1834-1839. The attempt to charge him for the value of the principal of the stock must fail

for two reasons: First. This very stock had not only belonged to the father of the wards in his lifetime, but it was such stock as a guardian or trustee might properly invest in by the law of Georgia. Second. No reason is shown why this stock, being in Georgia, the domicil of the wards, should have been transferred to a guardian who had been appointed in New York during their temporary residence there.

The same reasons are conclusive against charging him with the value of the bank stock in Georgia, which was owned by Mrs. Abercrombie in her own right, and to which Mr. Abercrombie became entitled upon her death. It is therefore unnecessary to consider whether there is sufficient evidence of an immediate surrender by him of her interest to her children.

The result is, that

Both the decrees of the Circuit Court in this case must be reversed, and the case remanded for further proceedings in conformity with this opinion.[23]

---

[23]A guardian appointed by a foreign court over wards who are foreigners may be allowed to retain his control over the wards, or a new guardian may be appointed to protect such wards. *Nugent v. Vetzera, Law Reports, 2 Equity 704.* A foreign guardian has no authority over the person or property of his ward. *Woodworth v. Spring, 4 Allen (Mass.) 321.* A foreign guardian cannot sue or be sued, nor can he be called to account in any court but the one that appointed him. *Morgan v. Potter, 157 U. S. 195; McCleary v. Menke, 109 Ill. 294; Donley v. Shields, 14 Ohio 359; Burnet v. Burnet, 12 B. Monroe 323.*

A state may allow a foreign guardian of a non-resident to get control of the ward's personal property. This is usually accomplished by applying to the probate court. *Grimmett v. Witherington, 16 Ark. 377; In re Benton, 92 Iowa 202, 60 N. W. 614.* As a rule a guardian is appointed in each state in which the ward has personal property. However, the guardian appointed at the domicil may be appointed ancillary guardian also. *Hoyt v. Sprague, 103 U. S. 613; Jefferson v Glover, 46 Miss. 510.*

A guardian has no power over real property in another state or country. *Watts v. Wilson, 93 Ky. 495, 20 S. W. 505; Smith v. Wiley, 22 Ala. 396; Grist v. Forehand, 36 Miss. 69.*

CHAPTER XI.

LEGITIMATION AND ADOPTION.

BLYTHE v. AYRES, 1892.

[96 Cal. 532.]

1. Legitimation by Subsequent Acts of the Parents.   2. The Law Applied to Acts of Legitimation.

APPEAL by the "Williams heirs" from a judgment of the Superior Court of the city and county of San Francisco declaring Florence Blythe to be the sole heir of Thomas H. Blythe, deceased.

The court below found that the real name of the deceased was Thomas H. Williams, that he had no heirs in the direct line except the plaintiff, Florence Blythe, and that the persons known as the "Williams heirs" were next of kin to him in the collateral line. There are numerous other claimants, who contest the finding in favor of the Williams heirs, on behalf of whom briefs were permitted to be filed upon this appeal by their counsel as *amici curiae*. Further facts are stated in the opinion.

GAROUTTE, J.—This is an action instituted under section 1664 of the Code of Civil Procedure by the plaintiff, a minor, through her guardian, to determine the heirship and title to the estate of Thomas H. Blythe, deceased. The section provides that in all estates being administered, or that may hereafter be administered, any person claiming to be heir to the deceased, or entitled to distribution in whole or in part of such estate, may, at any time after the expiration of one year from the issuance of letters testamentary or of administration, file a petition in the matter of such estate, praying the court to ascertain and declare the rights of all persons to said estate and all interests therin, and to whom distribution thereof should be made. The case is most important, from any view. The defendants, claiming to be collateral kindred, are numbered by the hundred, many of them represented by separate counsel of great ability and experience in the law; the property interests involved are very large; the trial in the *nisi prius* court extended continuously through the greater portion of a year; the facts are novel, and the principles of law applicable many and complicated.

Plaintiff's claim is based upon sections 230 and 1387, respectively of the Civil Code of California. Section 230 reads as follows:—

"Sec. 230. The father of an illegitimate child, by publicly acknowledging it as his own, receiving it as such, with the consent of his wife, if he is married, into his family, and otherwise treating it as if it were a legitimate child, thereby adopts it as such; and such child is thereupon deemed for all purposes legitimate from the time of its birth. The foregoing provisions of this chapter do not apply to such an adoption."

Section 1387, as far as it pertains to the matters involved in this litigation, provides:—

"Sec. 1387. Every illegitimate child is an heir of the person who, in writing, signed in the presence of a competent witness, acknowledges himself to be the father of such child."

As a result of the trial, the court filed findings of fact, and its conclusions of law based thereon are to the effect that the plaintiff, Florence Blythe, was and is the child of Thmas H. Blythe, deceased; that said Thomas H. Blythe legally adopted her under the provision of section 230 of the Civil Code; that she is his lawful heir, and the only person entitled to have and receive distribution of the estate of said Thomas H. Blythe, deceased.

The principles of law and the facts of the case bearing upon her contention under these respective provisions of the code are entirely dissimilar, involving a separate discussion; and in the construction of section 230, our investigation also necessarily divides itself into two distinct branches.

1. Was plaintiff so domiciled with relation to her putative father's domicile as to have rendered any action of his looking to adoption available for that purpose? or, placing the interrogatory in the clear and emphatic language of appellants' counsel (to which interrogatory they all with great confidence give answer, Yes), Was she so domiciled or so situated that she could not be subject to the laws of California, and be by those laws transmuted from bastardy to legitimacy?

2. If her situation endowed her with the capacity for legitimation, did the acts of Blythe bring her within the requirements of the statute?

The facts found by the court which face us while we are engaged in a consideration of the first branch of this subject may be succinctly and substantially stated as follows:—

1. That plaintiff was born in England, upon December 18, 1873, and was the issue of Thomas H. Blythe and Julia Perry;

2. That Julia Perry was a native of England, domiciled therein, and continued to there reside until one month after the death of said Blythe;

3. That plaintiff remained in England until after the death of Blythe, when she came to California, and said Blythe was never at any time within any of the countries of Europe after the twenty-ninth day of August, 1873;

4. That said Blythe was a citizen of the United States, and of the state of California, domiciled in said state, and died intestate therein, April 4, 1883, leaving surviving him no wife, no father, no mother, and no child, save and except said Florence Blythe, the plaintiff herein;

5. That said Thomas H. Blythe and said Julia Perry never were married, and said plaintiff was begotten while said Blythe was temporarily sojourning in England, and was born after said Blythe's return to California, and that said Blythe never was married.

Before passing to the merits of the discussion, we pause a moment to say that the verb "adopts," as used in section 230, is used in the sense of "legitimates," and that the acts of the father of an illegitimate child, if filling the measure required by that statute, would result, strictly speaking, in the legitimation of such child, rather than its adoption. Adoption, properly considered, refers to persons who are strangers in blood; legitimation, to persons where the blood relation exists. (See law dictionaries,— Bouvier's, Black's, Anderson's and Rapalje's.) This is the distinguishing feature between adoption and legitimation, as recognized by all the standard law-writers of the day who have written upon the subject; and for the reason that the text-writers and the decisions of courts, to which we shall look for light and counsel, treat the subject as a question of legitimation, we shall view the matter from that stand-point.

The section is broad in its terms. It contains no limitations or conditions, and to the extent of the power vested in the legislature of the state, applies to all illegitimates, wherever located and wherever born. The legislature has not seen fit to make any exception to its operation, and as was said by Taney, C. J., in *Brewer* v. *Blougher*, 14 Pet. 178, when considering a quite similar provision of a statute: "In the case before us, the words are general, and include all persons who come within the description of illegitimate children, ... and when the legislature speaks in general terms of children of that description without making any exceptions, we are bound to suppose they design to include the whole class."

Bar, in his work on International Law (p. 434), says: "Legitimation of bastards, either by subsequent marriage or by an act of the government (*Rescriptum principis*), is nothing but a legal equalization of certain children illegitimately begotten with legitimate children." In other words, the object and effect of section 230 is to change the *status* and capacity of an illegitimate child to the *status* and capacity of a child born in lawful wedlock.

This case, upon its facts, presumably stands alone in legal jurisprudence, for counsel, in the exercise of great learning and unexampled industry, have failed to parallel it. We have here a father at all times domiciled in the state of California, a mother at all times domiciled in England, and an illegitimate child born in England, and continuously there residing until the death of her father in California. As to the effect of our statutes upon such a state of facts, the consideration of the matter of domicile of these parties, and the principles of law applicable thereto, is a most important element to its proper determination, and it is a source of some satisfaction to be able to say that there are elementary principles pertaining to this subject of domicile, even though few in number, upon which practically all the text-writers stand on common ground, to wit:—

1. The domicile of the mother is the domicile of the illegitimate child, and the place of birth of the child is an immaterial element.

2. In a case of *legitimatio per subsequens matrimonium*, the place of marriage does not affect the question.

3. Legitimation by a subsequent marriage depends upon the law of the domicile of the father; Dicey on Domicile, 181, and other text-writers, supported by many authorities, holding that the domicile of the father at the date of the birth is the vital inquiry. and other authority (Fraser on Parent and Child, 62; Bar on International Law, 434; Savigny on Private International Law, 302) holding that the domicile of the father at the date of marriage is the determinative fact.

Inasmuch as the deceased, Blythe, was domiciled in California both at the time of the birth of the child and at the time he performed the acts which it is claimed resulted in legitimation, this question does not become an issue in the case, and we are not called upon to dispel the clouds of doubt that envelop it.

The contention of appellants that the *status* of a person resid-

ing in a foreign country and a subject thereof cannot be changed
by acts performed in California, under a provision of the law of
our state legislature, cannot be supported as a rule without many
exceptions, and to the extent of those exceptions, a state law
must be held, by its own courts at least, to have extraterritorial
operation.   And this principle of the foreign operation of state
laws even goes to the extent that in many instances such laws are
recognized and given effect by the courts of that particular foreign jurisdiction.   The doctrine of extraterritorial operation of
state laws is fully exemplified in the case of *Hoyt* v. *Thompson,*
5 N. Y. 340, where the court says: "It is a conceded principle,
that the laws of a state have no force, *proprio vigore,* beyond its
territorial limits, but the laws of one state are ferquently permitted by the courtesy of another to operate in the latter for the pro-
motion of justice, where neither that state nor its citizens will
suffer any inconvenience from the application of the foreign law.
This courtesy, or comity, is established, not only from motives
of respect for the laws and institutions of the foreign countries,
but from consideration of mutual utility and advantage."

The case of *Burton* v. *Burton,* 1 Keyes, 359, is a striking
illustration of the operation of a law of the United States in affixing a different *status* to a foreign subject resident in a foreign
country.   In that case, after plaintiff's marriage to Burton in a
foreign land, he himself being a foreign resident and subject at
the time, he emigrated to the state of New York, was naturalized,
and there died.   Although an actual resident of England at all
times, upon the death of her husband she came to New York, and
claimed her right of dower, upon the ground that she was a citizen of the United States, made so by virtue of the naturalization
of her husband under a general act of Congress to that effect, and
her claim was upheld.   In conclusion, the court uses this language: "It is said, furthermore, that she did not, by residence,
or in any other way, assume the allegiance of the United States,
or give her assent to the citizenship conferred by the act.   This,
however, was not necessary, to entitle her to claim its benefits."
In *Headman* v. *Rose,* 63 Ga. 458, the same question was again
presented, and that court said: "When the claim was first presented here as to whether Mrs. Rose could claim to be a citizen
of the United States under the provisions of that act of Congress
(having never been in the United States until after the death of
her husband), we were all inclined to the opinion that she could
not, but upon a more careful examination of that statute, in the

light of the interpretation which has been given to it by the supreme court of North Carolina in *Kane* v. *McCarthy*, 63 N. C. 299, and by the court of appeals of New York in *Burton* v. *Burton*, 1 Keyes, 371, and in *Kelley* v. *Owen*, 7 Wall. 496, in which the supreme court of the United States cites the case of *Burton* v. *Burton*, 1 Keyes, 359, approvingly, we hold and decide that if Mary Rose was married to William Rose, the intestate, and he was a naturalized citizen of the United States, then she, by the terms and provisions of the act of Congress of 1855, was also a citizen of the United States." It will be noticed that these decisions are not based upon the principle that the domicile of the husband was the domicile of the wife, and that consequently she was deemed to be in this country at the date of his naturalization, and therefore came under the operation of the act, but they rest upon the broad principle that Congress has not only the power to say what aliens shall become citizens of the United States, but what acts shall create such citizenship. The fact that these cases bear upon the political *status* of the party, rather than upon his civil *status*, does not weaken their force as authority here. In principle, no distinction can be discerned in this regard. In both cases there is involved an exercise of the same sovereign power. This doctrine has been carried to still greater lengths in criminal cases, where a crime has been committed in a foreign jurisdiction. In the Warrender case, 2 Clark & F. 539, Lord Brougham remarked: "But it may be said that the offense being committed abroad, and not within the Scotch territory, prevents the application to it of the Scotch criminal law. To this it may, however, be answered, that where a person has his domicile in a given country, the laws of that country to which he owes allegiance may visit even criminal offenses committed by him out of its territory. Of that we have many instances in our own jurisprudence; murder and treason committed by Englishmen abroad are triable in England, and punishable here. Nay, by the bill which I introduced in 1811, and which is constantly acted upon, British subjects are liable to be convicted of felony for slave-trading, in whatever part of the world committed by them."

Section 215 of the Civil Code is as follows:—

"Sec. 215. A child born before wedlock becomes legitimate by the subsequent marriage of its parents."

This section takes a wide range; its operation is not confined within state lines; it is as general as language can make it; oceans furnish no obstruction to the effect of its wise and beneficent provisions; it is manna to the bastards of the world. If Blythe, subsequent to the birth of plaintiff, had returned to England and married Julia Perry, such marriage, under the provision of law just quoted, *ipso facto*, would have resulted in the legitimation of Florence Blythe. Then, in answer to the interrogatory of appellants already noticed, we say that she was so domiciled that by the laws of California she could have been changed from bastardy to legitimacy. Our statute, conjoined with principles of international law, would have changed her bastardy to legitimacy in the world at large; and regardless of international law, and regardless of all law of foreign countries, our statute law alone would have made her legitimate in the world at large, whenever and however that question should present itself in the courts of California. And we also have here a most striking illustration of the extraterritorial operation of California law. We have the effect of a statute of this state attaching to a state of facts where the mother and child were never in California, but residing and domiciled in England, and the marriage taking place in England; and California law, as stated, has the effect upon that child to give it a different domicile, and completely change its *status*. Such would not only be the effect of this law upon the child viewed by California courts, but such would be its effect viewed by the courts of England, where the child was domiciled, and that, too, notwithstanding no provisions of law are there found for the legitimation of bastards. This assumption of Blythe's marriage to Julia Perry, in its facts, forms an exact photograph of the celebrated case of *Munro* v. *Munro*, found in 1 Rob. App. 492,—a case crystallizing the judicial thought of the age upon the subject, and commanding the respect of all writers and judges upon the law of domicile. We shall make copious references and indulge in liberal quotations from that decision, for its legal soundness never has been questioned, and as we view the subject, it casts a flood of light upon many matters involved in the investigation at hand.

Munro, a Scotch gentleman of fortune domiciled in Scotland, which upon a visit to London, cohabited with an Englishwoman domiciled in England, and a child was the result of such cohabitation. He subsequently married the woman in England, and it was held, under the law of Scotland, by the House of Lords sitting as a court of appeal (although if it had been a case appealed from the English courts, the decision would, undoubtedly, have been the same), that such child was thereby legitimated, Scottish law providing for legitimation *per subséquens matrimonium*. It was there said: "It is maintained that the pursuer having been born in England of an Englishwoman not married at the time of the birth, she was born an illegitimate child; that that *status* of illegitimacy was indelible by the law of England; and that a subsequent marriage, even taking it to be a Scotch marriage, could not legitimate the child, or wipe off the indelible stain of illegitimacy. We cannot assent to this proposition, and with all possible deference to any different opinions, we know of no authority for it in the law of Scotland, or among the jurists and writers on general law, in the application here attempted to be made of it.

To say, again, that because the child was born in England of and English mother, her illegitimacy is indelible, if this means that it is indelible by the law of England, and under the law of England, is to say no more than that the law of England has not adopted the rule of legitimation *per subsequens matrimonium;* but if it be meant that because a child was born in England it cannot become legitimate in Scotland by a Scotch marriage, is a question to be determined by the law of Scotland, it is a *petitio principi* for which there is no authority whatever in that law.

We are here in a Scotch question and in a Scotch court, applying a plain rule of our law, and unless that law says that if a child be born in England it shall not have the benefit of the rule, we do not see how it is at all material that it could not enjoy it if the law of England were to be applied to the case; but we know of no exception in the law of Scotland, nor, as far as we are informed, is there any such exception recognized in the law of any country which holds the principle of legitimation *per subsequens matrimonium.* We are not here giving any opinion on a point about which it does not belong to us to form any judgment. We are not inquiring what the law of England might decide if the pursuer, or any person similarly situated, were making a claim in an English court of law in respect of property within their jurisdiction. . . . . We are aware that conflicts of law may take place, and there is no help for it when they do occur; but the question before us is a purely Scotch question, to be ruled by general principles, no doubt, but still with reference to the law of Scotland in that particular point, and we cannot, in consistency with the established principles of that law, hold that this pursuer could not become legitimated by the marriage of her parents, when or wheresoever she may have been born. It appears to us to be very clear that the circumstance of the mother being *English* adds nothing at all to the supposed difficulty in the place of the pursuer's

birth. She was certainly illegitimate by the law of England, and
by the law of Scotland also, at the time of her birth, and she would
have been so equally though her mother had been a Scotchwoman.
Lord Mackenzie said: 'I cannot help entertaining doubt whether
the indelibility of English bastardy has any meaning beyond this,
that an English bastard is not legitimated by an English marriage. .   But suppose it were true that English bastardy is
indelible, not only against a marriage in England, but against a
marriage all the world over,—I say, suppose there was produced
a statute providing and declaring that an English bastard born
in England should remain a bastard all the world over, notwithstanding anything, that could be done in any country,—I ask,
could we give it effect? Could we acknowledge the authority of
such a statute? I think we will be bound to say that the English
Parliament might rule the fate of the bastards in England, but
that its laws were not entitled to extend to other countries, and
that there was no principle of the law of nations which would
give effect to such a statute.' " In summing up his conclusions,
the Lord Chancellor, after holding Munro to be domiciled in Scotland, said: "If that be a correct conclusion from the evidence, it
follows that the appellant in *Munro* v. *Munro,* being the child of
a domiciled Scotchman, had at the moment of her birth a capacity
of being legitimatized by the subsequent marriage of her parents
for all civil purposes in Scotland, and that she, accordingly, by
their subsequent marriage in 1801, became legitimated, and, as
such, capable of succeeding to the property in question."

The foregoing views of learned judges are in direct conflict
with the arguments of appellants' counsel in this case; and such
views were declared to be the law, after able arguments there
made upon the same lines as here presented. Appellants insist
that the domicile of the child irrevocably fixes that child's *status.*
In this case, subsequent to the child's birth, Julia Perry married
a domiciled Englishman; hence her domicile was permanently
established in England, and for that reason the child's domicile,
being the mother's domicile, was permanently established there.
Under appellants' reasoning, this state of facts would forever
debar the child from legitimation, for even its presence in California would avail nothing as against its English domicile. If
such be good law, section 226 of the Civil Code, expressly
authorizing the adoption of minors of other states, is bad law, for
it is squarely in conflict with those views.

We find in Story's work upon Conflict of Laws (sec. 105 a)

the following: "6· As to issue born before the marriage, if by
the law of the country where they are born they would be legitimated by the subsequent marriage of their parents, they will by
such subsequent marriage (perhaps in any country, but at all
events in the same country) become legitimate, so that this character of legitimacy will be recognized in every other country. If
illegitimate there, the same character will belong to them in every
other country." But Judge Story's citations in its support do not
clearly bear him out, and legal authority to the effect that the place
of birth forms no element in the case vastly preponderates.

We have in *Loring* v. *Thorndike*, 5 Allen, 257, a case involving additional elements, and therefore additional complications,
even to those found in the Munro case. The man was domiciled
in Massachusetts. The woman was domiciled in Mayence. The
illegitimate children were born in Frankfort-on-the-Main, and the
marriage occurred in that city. To accomplish legitimation, the
Massachusetts law required not only a subsequent marriage, but
a subsequent acknowledgement of the child. Upon this state of
facts, and this provision of law, the child was held legitimate by
the Massachusetts court, even though the acts of acknowledgment occurred in a foreign country. In the case of *In re Grove*,
L. R. 40 Ch. Div., 216, Lord Chief Justice Cotton said: "What is
really necessary, I think, is, that the father should at the time of
the birth of the child be domiciled in the country allowing legitimation, so as to give to the child the capacity of being made
legitimate by a subsequent marriage; but it is the subsequent marriage which gives the legitimacy to the child, who has at its birth,
in consequence of its father's domicile, the capacity of being made
legitimate by a subsequent marriage." In the same case, Lord
Justice Fry stated: "The appellant claims through Sarah Thomegay, who was born in 1744, in this country [England], and was
an illegitimate child of Marc Thomegay and Martha Powis. At
birth that child took the domicile of its mother, and it took the
status of illegitimacy according to the law of the domicile of its
mother, and it took also the capacity to change that *status* of illegitimacy for one of legitimacy, provided that, according to the
law of the domicile of the father, the subsequent marriage would
work legitimation. The position of such a child, therefore, is
curious, taking domicile and *status* from the mother, but taking
the potentiality of changing its *status* from its putative father."
In the case of *Shedden* v. *Patrick*, 1 Macq. 535, the father being
domiciled in the state of New York at the date of the child's birth,

and there being no law of legitimation in New York, the child was declared illegitimate by the English courts.

Appellants' counsel confidently insist that *Ross* v. *Ross*, 129 Mass. 243, 37 Am. Rep. 321, is valuable as an authority to support their views. After a careful examination of the opinion in that case, we are unable to preceive its force as authority here. A child was legally adopted in Pennsylvania. The adoptive parent removed with the child to Massachusetts, where the father became domiciled, and there died, leaving real estate in that commonwealth. The litigation arose upon a question as to who was entitled to inherit, and the court said: "We are therefore of the opinion that the legal *status* of the child of intestate, once acquired by the demandant under a statute and by a judicial decree of the state of Pennsylvania, while the parties were domiciled there, continued after their removal into this commonwealth, and that by virtue thereof the demandant is entitled to maintain this action." Respondent's position in this case controverts no principle of law there declared, and it is difficult to see how the court could have arrived at a different conclusion. The judgment would have been the same if the father had never changed his domicile to Massachusetts, and probably the same if there had been no law of adoption whatever in that state. *Miller* v. *Miller*, 91 N. Y. 315, 43 Am. Rep. 669, in principle, seems to have been that character of case, and the same conclusions were there arrived at by the court. In the celebrated case of *Birtwhistle* v. *Vardill*, 2 Clark & F. 840, to which the learned chief justice refers in his opinion in the Ross case, the decision would have undoubtedly been in line with *Ross* v. *Ross*, 129 Mass. 243, 37 Am. Rep. 321, if, in lieu of the Statute of Merton, England's law of descent had been similar to the Massachusetts provision. The case of *Foster* v. *Waterman*, 124 Mass. 592, involves nothing but a single question of statutory construction, and in no manner supports the proposition that a resident of one state cannot adopt a child under the adoption laws of another state, where such child is domiciled, but *Appeal of Wolf*, 13 Alt. Rep. 760, does hold directly to the contrary of such contention.

The doctrine of indelibility of bastardy in England is not correct in its broadest sense, for it is in the power of Parliament to legitimate bastards at any time. Neither is the rule universal that a child legitimate in one country is legitimate in all the world. This principle of different *status* in different countries finds a striking illustration in Lolly's case, reviewed and dissented from by Lord Brougham in *Warrender* v. *Warrender*, 2 Clark & F. 539. In that case the facts disclose that Lolly was married in England, divorced in Scotland, and upon his return to England and making a second marriage, he was then tried and convicted of bigamy. Here we have a state of facts where, under the respective laws of England and Scotland, Lolly, after his divorce and prior to his second marriage, was a married man in England and an unmarried man in Scotland, and after his second marriage he had a lawful wife in Scotland and a different lawful wife in England, thus having two lawful wives at the same time. It can hardly be said that Lolly's *status* was the same in both countries. A similar principle is applied to the legitimacy of children by subsequent marriage. The provisions of section 215 would operate upon and legitimate a child born of a father who, at the time of its conception and birth, was the husband of another woman, or would apply to an incestuous bastard. Such was expressly declared to be the law under a similar provsion of a state statute in the case of *Hawbecker* v. *Hawbecker*, 43 Md. 516, the court saying: "No doubt, the legislature, in thus mitigating the severe rule of the common law, intended to hold out to the sinning parents an inducement to marry, and thus put a stop to the mischiefs of further illicit intercourse between them, *but, in our opinion, the main purpose and intent of the enactment we are now considering was to remove the taint and disabilities of bastardy from the unoffending children whenever their parents did marry, without regard to the deepness of guilt on the part of their parents in which they were conceived and born.*" Such a child, under the canon law, would be deemed an adulterine or incestuous bastard, incapable of legitimation, and in the courts of certain countries where the law controls would not be recognized as legitimate. Thus is presented a case, and by no means an anomalous one, where the child would be legitimate in California, and illegitimate by the laws of various other countries. (See Fraser on Parent and Child, 56 subd. 10.)

We have quoted thus extensively from the authorities upon the subject of domicile as specially bearing upon the question of *legitimatii per subsequens matrimonium,* for the reason that we are unable to perceive any difference in the general principles of law bearing upon that character of legitimation and in those principles bearing upon other forms of legitimation authorized by the same statute. The only distinction claimed by appellants is, that legitimation founded upon subsequent marriage is based upon the fiction of law that a previous consent existed, and the marriage related back to that time. Upon this point it would seem all-sufficient to say that our statute does not recognize such a fiction, and its effective operation in no wise depends upon the assumption of its presence. Times are not what they once were, and we live in an age too practical to build our law upon the unstable foundation of fictions. In *Birtwhistle* v. *Vardill*, 2 Clark & F. 840, Tyndall, L. C. J., in speaking upon this question, says: "Pothier, on the other hand, when he speaks of the effect of a subsequent marriage in legitimating children born before it, disclaims the authority of the canon law, nor does he mention any fiction of an antecedent marriage, but rests the effect upon the positive law of the country. He first instances the custom of Troyes, and then adds :   . . that it is a common right, received throughout the whole kingdom." Schouler on Domestic Relations (sec. 226) says: "The principle to which the law of legislation *per subsequens matrimonium* is to be referred has been a subject of controversy. The canonists base the law, not on general views of expediency and justice, but upon a fiction which they adopted in order to reconcile the new law with established rules; for, assuming that, as a general rule, children are not legitimate unless born in lawful wedlock, they declare that by a fiction of law parents were married when the child was born. Such reasoning, by no means uncommon when the wise saw more clearly what was right than why it was so, has not stood the test of modern logic, and the Scotch courts have placed the rule once more where its imperial founders left it, namely, on the ground of general policy and justice."

Upon principle, no distinction can be made between the rules of law applicable to these various forms of legitimation. Many of the states of this Union, in order to effect those ends, require, in addition to a subsequent marriage, that the father (in some state, both father and mother) shall also acknowledge the child. This is the case of *Loring* v. *Thorndike*, 5 Allen, 257, where the marriage not only took place in foreign territory, but as is said in *Ross* v. *Ross*, 129 Mass. 259, the facts of the acknowledgment occurred in a foreign jurisdiction. Thus Massachusetts law required marriage *and* acknowledgment, and invoked the rule of domicile of the father to establish the capacity of the child for legitimation. Section 2405 of the Revised Code of Alabama allows legitimation of a bastard child simply by acknowledgment of the father in writing, certified and recorded. No consent of the mother is required; no notice to or consent of the child is demanded. If such a statute were found within the lids of the Civil Code in this state, under the facts of this case as they appear upon the question of domicile, Blythe, by following the requirements of the provision of law there laid down, could legitimate his illegitimate child. California law (Civ. Code, sec. 215) declares that marriage *ipso facto* results in legitimation, and section 230 declares that acknowledgment accompanied by certain other acts shall result in legitimation. If the principle of the domicile of the father is good law where marriage and acknowledgment are both required to accomplish the result, that principle is no less good law when applied to marriage alone under section 215, or when applied to acknowledgment alone under the Alabama Code, or when applied to acknowledgment accompanied by other acts under section 230 of the Civil Code of this state.

Dicey says (p. 192): "Question. What is the effect, according to English law, of a person being made legitimate by the authority of a foreign sovereign? Suppose that a person born illegitimate is legitimated by a decree of the Czar of Russia; will such a person be held legitimate here? There is no English authority on the subject. The most probable answer is (it is conceived), that the effect of such a decree would, like the effect of a subsequent marriage of the parents, depend on the domicile of such person's father at the time of the birth. *Suppose, that is to say, that D, the child's father, were domiciled in Russia at the time of the child's birth, the decree would have the effect of making the child legitimate in England.* A person, on the other hand, born of a father domiciled in England could not be made legitimate here by the force of any foreign law."

Bar, in his International Law, has discussed this identical question at length, although it can scarcely be said to be even incidentally mentioned in the works of either Savigny, Foote, Phillimore, or Schaffner. He says (sec. 198): "In what we have said we have proceeded on the footing that legitimation, if the consent of the child be validly given, is dependent solely on the personal law of the father, and that, therefore, if this law allows legitimation by an act of the head of the state, it matters not to inquire whether some other legal system, in particular the personal law which the child has hitherto enjoyed, recognizes this legitimation; but that, on the contrary, legitimation *per rescriptum* is to be regarded in international law on exactly the same footing as legitimation *per subsequens matrimonium*. This opinion, which, as we think, is the prevailing opinion in German juris-prudence, and in which, too, Fiore (sec. 149), Phillimore (sec. 542), and Wharton (sec. 249) concur, has, however, often been disputed. In the first place, it has been said that an act of that kind by a sovereign must 'necessarily have its operation confined to the dominion of that sovereign, for he has no authority be-yond these limits; but if it be true, generally, that the personal law of the father is the rule, that law must be allowed to say that legitimation can take place by means of an act of that kind. The legitimation is to be recognized, not because the sovereign is to exercise sovereign rights in another country, but because the per-sonal law is to have effect there. The opposite opinion, which is held by older writers, is no doubt explained, and to some extent justified, by the imperfect legal capacity which in the middle ages, and in many territories down to later times, clung to the bastard, especially, too, as the sole result of legitimation, even in the ter-ritory of the sovereign who bestowed it, was in many cases merely to withdraw the estate of the person so legitimated, upon his death, from the grasp of his sovereign, etc. . . . . But, in the second place, the more modern French school, while they reject the view of the older writers as to the effect of the legitimation being necessarily confined to the territory of the sovereign who bestows it, refuse to recognize this kind of legitimation, unless it is also recognized in the personal law which the child has hitherto enjoyed. In this way, one who has hitherto been a French child, in respect that the Civil Code has never sanctioned legitimation *per rescriptum,* can never be legitimated by the act of a foreign sovereign. But Laurent, in arguing in support of this doctrine that legitimation touches the *status* of persons, and that this *status* must be determined everywhere of Frenchmen by the law of France, proves too much. This rule would have to hold, also, in the case of legitimation by subsequent marriage, so that in this case, also, the personal law of the child would be the only rule.

In this connection, and as bearing directly and emphatically upon the general principles involved in the solution of the impor-tant question presented by this branch of the case, we again quote from Bar (sec. 194): "If the personal law of the child requires more conditions to be observed before it will pronounce that a child has been legitimated, the reason of that is, not any anxiety for the interest of the child, so much as for that of the father and his family, e. g., the other children, his collateral relations; but the state, to which the child has up to that moment belonged, has no interest in that matter, and if that legal system which is charged with the protection of the family is willing to hold the child legitimated, there is in truth no conflict between the two systems. That system to which the child has hitherto belonged says: 'If the father belonged to me, I would not hold the child to be legitimated.' That involved no contradiction of the other system, which says: 'Since the father belongs to me, I do hold the child to be legitimated.' No doubt we must assume that assent of the child is given in due legal form, for legitimation can only take place against the child's wish if the personal law of the child forces that upon him or her; but in by far the greater number of cases it will be beyond all doubt that the legitimation is advantageous to the child, and the child or its guardian can subsequently signify its approval of and found upon it."

Legitimation is the creature of legislation. Its existence is solely dependent upon the law and policy of each particular sovereignty. The law and policy of this state authorize and encourage it, and there is no principle upon which California law and policy, when invoked in California courts, shall be made to surrender to the antagonistic law and policy of Great Britain. It was said in *Munro* v. *Munro*, 1 Rob. App. 492: "We are here in a Scotch question and in a Scotch court, applying a plain rule of our law, and unless that law says that if a child be born in England it shall not have the benefit of the rule, we do not see how that it is at all material that it could not enjoy it if the law of England were to be applied to the case"; and again: "We are not inquiring what the law of England might decide if the person were making a claim in an English court of law in respect of property within their jurisdiction." And we say here, plaintiff was the child of Blythe, who was a domiciled citizen of the state of California. She founds her claim upon the statutes of this state, and is now here invoking the jurisdiction of the courts of this state. It is a question of California law to be construed in California courts, and we see nothing in our constitution or statutory law, or in international law, to have prevented Blythe from making the plaintiff his daughter in every sense that the word implies. In conclusion, we hold that Blythe being domiciled in the state of California both at the time of the birth of plaintiff and at the time he performed the acts which it is claimed resulted in the legitimation of plaintiff, and California law authorizing the legitimation of bastards by the doing of certain acts, it follows that Florence

Blythe, the plaintiff, at all times was possessed of a capacity for legitimation, under section 230 of the Civil Code of this state.

We pass to an examination of the second branch of the discussion involved in the consideration of section 230; namely, if plaintiff's situation endowed her with the capacity for legitima tion, did the acts of Blythe bring her within the requirements of the statute? Those requirements are: 1. He shall publicly ac knowledge the child as his own; 2. He shall receive it as his child, with the consent of his wife, if he is married, into his family; 3. He shall otherwise treat it as if it were a legitimate child.

As to these matters, the trial court found in detail the facts to be, that Blythe had fulfilled every requirement of the statute. These findings are strenuously attacked as being unsupported by the evidence, and we are called upon to pass upon its sufficiency in this regard.

This section of the code is entitled to a liberal construction, because section 4 provides: "The rule of the common law, that statutes in derogation thereof are to be strictly construed, has no application to this code. The code establishes the law of this state respecting the subjects to which it relates, and its provisions . . . . are to be liberally construed, with a view to effect its objects and to promote justice." By virtue of this provision, the court, in the case of *In re Jessup*, 81 Cal. 419, has expressly declared that this section shall have a liberal construction, but, as there said, "liberal construction does not mean enlargement or restriction of a plain provision of a written law. If a provision of the code is plain and unambiguous, it is the duty of the court to enforce it as it is written. If it is ambiguous or doubtful, or susceptible of different constructions or interpretations, then such liberality of construction is to be indulged in as, within the fair interpretation of its language, will effect its apparent object and promote justice.'

Did Blythe acknowledge the plaintiff to be his own child? The word "acknowledge" has no technical meaning, and in its ordinary acceptation is defined, by Webster, "to own or admit the knowledge of." It is not necessary to dwell at great length upon this special element nesessary to satisfy the statute. Under the evidence, it can hardly be considered debatable. Blythe declared the plaintiff to be his child, to all persons, upon all occasions. He was garrulous upon the subject. Aside from his business occupations, his mind ever rested upon his relations to the child, and it was his common topic of conversation. If necessary to this decision, it could almost be held that he shouted it from the house-tops. He acknowledged the child to its mother and to its grand-mother before it was born, and subsequently, in no single in-stance, was he ever heard to deny its paternity. It was named and baptized Florence Blythe at his request, and ever after has been known to the world as Florence Blythe. Authority is not necessary to be cited to support this branch of the case, but *In re Jessup*, 81 Cal. 419, is not only in accord with this position, but conclusive in its favor. This acknowledgment was also public, for, as we have seen, the thought of concealment of the paternity of the child never entered his mind. Why should it, when it is entirely apparent from the evidence that he was proud of such paternity?

2. Did Blythe receive it as his child, with the consent of his wife, into his family? Blythe had no wife, and that element of the statute is eliminated from the case. No construction of the statute, however rigid, would hold the existence of a wife neces-sary, before the benefits to be derived under this section could pos-sibly attach to an illegitimate child. This question of the wife's consent can only be a material element when there is a wife to consent. *In re Jessup*, 81 Cal. 419, fully recognizes and necessar-ily adopts this principle, for in that case, as here, the father of the child had no wife to consent, and such fact would thus have de-feated plaintiff's claims at the very threshold of the litigation. It may be conceded, for the purposes of this case, that if Blythe had a family, such child must have been received therein, or the statute would not have been satisfied; but, as we have seen, if Blythe had no wife to consent, that requirement has no standing here; so if he had no family into which the child could have been re-ceived, that element is foreign to the case. Under the rule of liberal construction laid down in the case of *In re Jessup*, 81 Cal. 419, such must necessarily be the law. To give that meaning to the statute by which all men who have no families are debarred from legitimating their illegitimate offspring would be to give the section a harsh and illiberal construction. Unless the provision is so plain and explicit as to amount to an express inhibition to that effect, upon every principle of right and justice we could not so hold. The rule of construction as declared in the Jessup case is, that if the statute is ambiguous or doubtful, or susceptible of different constructions or interpretations, then such construction is to be indulged as, within, the fair interpretation of its lan-guage, will effect its apparent object and purpose. Section 1866

of the Code of Civil Procedure further provides: "When a statute or instrument is equally susceptible of two interpretations,
one in favor of natural right, and the other against it, the former
is to be adopted." Applying these tests of statutory construction
to this provision, but one result can flow therefrom, and that is,
the existence of a family, no more than the existence of a wife,
is an indispensable element to a complete and perfect adoption
(or legitimation, more properly speaking) under this provision
of law. This view is fully borne out by the decision in *In re
Jessup*, 81 Cal. 419. It is said in the decision of the court in that
case, referring to Jessup: "As he had no home and no family in
the strict sense of a 'collective body of persons who live in one
house and under one head or manager, a household including
parents, children, and servants,' it would not be a fair or liberal
construction to say that the child had not been adopted or acknowledged because he had not been received in such a home or
made a member of such fammily." It is needless to say that the
Jessup case was considered with the care that its importance demanded, for the record discloses that fact; and it may be suggested that upon this question alone the court stood together. Indeed, the learned counsel representing appellants in that case
throughout their arguments conceded such to be the law. Blythe
had no family. The court found that he was living with a mistress in San Francisco from the year 1880 to the time of his
death. He appears to have lived in lodging-houses during all
these years. He had no relations, save of the collateral line, and
they were at all times residing in a foreign country. He had
not seen them or communicated with them for more than ten
years prior to his death, and at no time had he seen any of them,
or communicated with any of them, since Florence Blythe, the
plaintiff, was born. If he had a family, either his mistress or
these collateral kindred constituted that family. Such cannot be
the fact, and it would be a travesty upon the word to so hold. It
was held in the Jessup case that the father had a family, in the
sense of brothers and sisters, with whom he was brought into frequent contact, and from whom he concealed and denied the paternity of the child, and for these reasons, and others, the court held
there was no adoption. There are no facts in this case in the
slightest degree comparable to those there presented. In that
case, the language of the court as to this point bears directly upon
the question of acknowledgment, and not as to the reception into
the family; and we have already seen that a public acknowledg-

ment was made by Blythe against which nothing can be said. If the term "receiving it into his family" does not necessarily mean an actual reception into an actual family, but may mean a constructive reception into a constructive family, then such measure of requirement is filled to the brim. Plaintiff was baptized in Blythe's name at his request. Their correspondence indicates hearts filled with mutual affection. Her picture looked down upon him from its place upon the wall. At his rooms her name was a household word.

We pass to the examination of the remaining element of the statute, to wit: "He shall otherwise treat it as a legitimate child." If the father has publicly acknowledged the child to be his child, and has taken it into his family, it would seem but little remained to be done to wash away forever the stain of bastardy. The public acknowledgment of the child is the main fact. It is the important factor, in the eyes of the statute. If the child was publicly acknowledged and received into the family, it would be a novel case where a court of equity would close its doors and refuse to declare a legitimation because the child was poorly clothed and illy fed. That case has not yet arisen, and it is hoped and believed it never will. The statute clearly means that the father must treat his illegitimate child as he would naturally treat his legitimate child, not as the majority of men in his financial circumstances would or should treat their children. Every man furnishes the rule by which he must be measured. No imaginary standard of excellence can be created, and then it be demanded that Blythe shall rise to that standard. If appellants' contention be true, a child whose father was an ignorant man believing education an evil to be shunned, and who therefore denied an education to the child, could not be granted legitimation. Upon appellants' theory, an illegitimate child whose father was a miser would be compelled to bear forever the stain of bastardy. While Blythe was a man of large property interests, his estates were heavily involved. Money was required in many channels, and it is not probable that he had any surplus of cash on hand. Plaintiff was well clothed and well fed. It appears that at no time was she deprived of the necessaries of life. She resided at all times either with her mother or her grandmother. Blythe furnished something near $150 a year for her support; certainly during her infancy this was entirely sufficient, and no complaints were made to him that more money was needed to meet her wants. At all these times he himself was either stopping in a log house in the mountains of

Trinity, or living with his mistress in lodgings in San Farncisco, surrounded by his dogs, birds, and cats, while his hens were located upon the roof. It may well be inferred from the simplicity of his own life as indicated by the foregoing circumstances, that if legitimate children had been born to him, they would have been treated, as far as pecuniary expenditures were concerned, upon the same lines as this illegitimate child was treated. He made a will, which was subsequently lost or destroyed, wherein he provided for her. He corresponded with her as a father would correspond with his little daughter. He had her christened in the name of Florence Blvthe. Her health, her education, and her religion were matters in which he exercised the utmost concern. She occupied his thoughts, and her name was upon his lips in his dying hour. For these reasons, it may well be said that "he otherwise treated her as a legitimate child."

We pass to an examination of section 1387 of the Civil Code, upon which plaintiff relies to constitute herself an heir of Thomas H. Blythe, deceased. That section declares, *inter alia,* that "every illegitimate child is an heir of the person who, in writing, signed in the presence of a competent witness, acknowledges himself to be the father of such child." It is unnecessary to decide whether this provision affects the *status* of a child, or whether it is alone a statute of descent. If it either directly or indirectly touches upon *status,* our views upon the question, as herein previously expressed, are applicable. If it is a statute of descent, pure and simple,—and *Estate of Magee,* 63 Cal. 414, seems to so declare in explicit terms,—then the plaintiff is entitled to all the benefits of it, regardless of domicile, *status,* or extraterritorial operation of state laws.

The rules of liberal construction applicable to section 230 are likewise to be invoked in the consideration of section 1387; and the obvious purpose and intent of the legislature in making this enactment was to entitle illegitimate children to inherit their father's estate, the same as legitimate children. Did the intestate, Blythe, in writing, signed in the presence of a competent witness, acknowledge that he was the father of the claimant, Florence Blythe? Upon an inspection of the provision, we see that the word "acknowledge" must be viewed in the light of its ordinary acceptation, and it is therefore used in exactly the same sense as when found in section 230. The acts required to constitute the acknowledgment are not laid down in the statute. No stated form of acknowledgment is there found by which we may be guided. Again, we mus. take this statute as we find it. We are not here to construct a statute, but to construe a statute. We can neither interpolate nor eliminate, and we are bound to assume that the legislature enacted the law as it now stands with a due comprehension of the meaning of words and of the rules of statutory construction, and that they incorporated into the act all that was intended, and that they intended that effect should be given to all that was found therein.

The writings relied upon in this case to bring plaintiff within the provisions of the statute are various letters, written at different times, by Blythe to his daughter and her grandfather, which letters were signed by him in the presence of W. H. H. Hart, who was a competent witness. These letters, as to the question of acknowledgment of relationship, are of the same general character and import, and our investigation will be limited to the consideration of two of them, one a letter to the grandfather, and the other a letter to the daughter, either of which, to our minds, fully satisfies the statute. He writes a letter to the plaintiff, from which we quote:—

"*My Darling Child,*—You have made your father very happy by writing to him your little letter. . . . But I feel sad to learn that my own dear child has been sick, and her papa not being near to help her. You say you wonder when you shall see your dear papa. Well, my dear child, it is about like this: Your papa . After that your papa will leave San Francisco, ... and have his dear Florence with him always. . . I should like my dear daughter to write to her papa a letter once every month. . . . . Grant is now lying at my feet, while his master is writing his first letter to his own darling child, far away. . . . . May God bless you, my dear child. From your loving father,

"THOMAS H. BLYTHE."

The letter to the grandfather was read to said Hart, and signed in his presence. We quote: "I look at the proposed baptism of dear Flora as a matter of very deep importance. After full deliberation, I think it best to have Flora brought up in the Episcopal Church,—Church of England. You will, therefore, please have my daughter christened at once, and have her named after her father, Florence Blythe."

There can be but one construction placed upon these letters, and that is, they mean that Florence was the daughter of Thomas H. Blythe,—"his own dear child." These letters acknowledge the relationship of father and daughter, not hesitatingly and

grudgingly, but willingly, gladly, and entirely. When a father
says, "You are my own darling child," "I am your father; you
shall be baptized in my name, and loved, cherished, and protected
always," the subject is exhausted, the cup of acknowledgment is
filled to overflowing. If letters are entitled to be used as writings
to prove the fact of acknowledgment, these letters prove that fact.
It was decided in *Bailey* v. *Boyd,* 59 Ind. 297, under a statute requiring the father to acknowledge his illegitimate child subsequent
to marriage, before such child should be held legitimate, that "it
was not necessary that this acknowledgment should have been
expressed in words, but it may fairly be inferred from the acts
and conduct of the elder Bazil." But it is now insisted that the
writing must be a writing specially prepared for the sole object
of making the illegitimate child an heir of the father. The
adjudications of courts are not favorable to this view. In the
case of *Rice* v. *Efford,* 3 Hen. & M. 227, it was held that the
recognition of the illegitimate child in a will as the testator's child,
the will being void as a will, was sufficient to entitle him to inherit.
Chief Justice Tucker, in this connection, saying in *Stones* v.
Keeling, reported in the same volume, upon the following page:
"The act of 1785, it should be remembered, relates to the disposition of property only, and proceeds to show who shall be
admitted to share the property of a person dying intestate, notwithstanding any former legal bar to a succession thereto, and in
that light the law ought to receive the most liberal construction,
it being evidently the design of the legislature to establish the
most liberal and extensive rules of succession to estates in favor
of all in whose favor the intestate himself, had he made a will,
might have been supposed to be influenced, and here there can be
no doubt, had he died testate, that these daughters would have
been the first object of his care." Reading the present case in the
light of the evidence furnished by the record, there can be no
doubt but if Blythe had died testate, Florence would have been
the first object of his care. In *Succession of Fletcher,* 11 La.
Ann. 60, Henry Fletcher, in an act of manumission made before
a notary and witnesses, described the party enfranchised by his
act as his "natural daughter, slave," and such was held to be a
sufficient acknowledgment of paternity, under a statute which
declared that "the acknowlegment of an illegitimate child shall
be made by a declaration executed before a notary public, in the
presence of two witnesses." In that case the court, citing French
authorities, held: "It is said that the words 'natural daughter,

slave,' were terms of description foreign to the purpose of the act, used to manumit a slave, and not to acknowledge her paternity, but no form is prescribed for such an acknowledgment, save only that the declaration be made before a notary public, in presence of two witnesses. If the declaration be thus made, it seems to be immaterial whether it be the main object of the act, or not." In *Remy* v. *Municipality*, 11 La. Ann. 159, the court, in referring to the acknowledgment of paternity made in a will, said: "This document, it is true, was intended to be a will, and has never been admitted to probate as such, but though not binding as a will, it is certainly good as an acknowledgment of paternity, made in due form." Section 1387 is essentially a statute of inheritance, and there is no more fitting place for the father to recognize the moral duty enjoined upon him toward his illegitimate offspring than by acknowledging that child in his last will and testament in accordance with the provisions of that section; and the fact that the acknowledgment was subsidiary to the main object and purpose of the testator in making the document would not thereby weaken the effect of the writing as an acknowledgment.

Under the statute of Indiana, marriage and subsequent acknowledgment of the paternity of the child by the father constituted a legitimation of the child, and in the case of *Brock* v. *State*, 85 Ind. 397, where the father married the woman and acknowledged the child for the sole purpose of escaping a prosecution for bastardy, and with the intention at the time of the marriage to immediately abandon the mother and child, it was held that such intentions were entirely immaterial, and that his acts created a legitimation.

In *Crane* v. *Crane*, 31 Iowa, 296, the question here involved squarely presented itself. The statute of Iowa provided for legitimation by a recognition in writing of the illegitimate child by the father. Two propositions upon which appellants insist are directly decided against them in that case. It was held that a formal writing of recognition was not necessary, but that letters to a friend would suffice, and it was further held that the references to the child in the letters were sufficient to constitute recognition. The references by the father in those letters to the child as his child, while quite clear, are weak, vague, and unconvincing when compared to the references upon the same subject found in the letters of Blythe. A majority of the states of this Union, and also various countries of Europe, require the illegitimate child to be recognized or acknowledged by the father before legitimation takes piace, yet no authority has been cited from any state or country (and we therefore confidently assume there is none), except the case of *Pina* v. *Peck*, 31 Cal. 359, to which our atten tion shall be presently directed, which holds that a formal recog nition or formal acknowledgment is necessary, in order to consti tute a legitimation.

It is insisted that the witness Hart should have subscribed his name to the writing as a witness thereto, but "competent wit ness" and "subscribing" or "attesting" witness are in no sense synonymous terms. In *In the matter of Noble*, 124 Ill. 270, the court says: " 'Credible witnesses,' as used in the statute relating to wills, has been construed, both in England and this country, to mean *competent witnesses;* that is, such persons as are not legally disqualified from testifying in courts of justice by reason of men tal incapacity, interest, or the commission of crime, or other cause excluding them from testifying generally, or rendering them incompetent in respect of the particular subject-matter or in the particular suit." As before remarked, it is not the duty of the court to add to or subtract from the words of the statute. We must construe it as it stands enacted. If the legislature had intended such witness to be a "subscribing" or "attesting" witness, it was easy for it to have said so. Not having so declared, it would be judicial legislation for this court to so hold the statute to be. Section 1940 of the Code of Civil Procedure provides that a writing may be proved by any one who saw it executed, and we cannot say but that such proof was contemplated by the legisla ture when it framed this provision of the statute. Our codes contain many instances where the term "attesting witness" or "subscribing witness" is used, when the signature of the witness is required to give life to a written instrument, and we must pre sume that the legislature did not intend that the writing should be signed, when it did not so declare. In all the statutes of the varicus states, wherever the signature of a witness to any docu ment is required, we find the statute either using the words "attesting witness" or "subscribing witness." Under the liberal rules of construction by which this court must be guided, and under the principle laid down by Chief Justice Tucker in *Stones* v. *Keeling*, 3 Hen. & M. 228, we are not called upon to defeat this plaintiff's claims by holding that the words "competent wit ness," as used in the statute, should be construed to mean "attest ing" or "subscribing" witness. The law of Pennsylvania requires that the will of a married woman shall be executed in the presence of two witnesses, and the court said, in *Combs's Appeal*, 105 Pa. St. 159; "Such witnesses were not required to subscribe their names thereto." If more need be said on this behalf, we would suggest that this statute was originally copied from a statute of the state of Maine, which also used the words "competent witness"; but subsequently the legislature of that state amended the statute by causing it to read, *"and attested by a* competent witness," that legislature thus recognizing not only the fact that legislation was necessary in order that the witness should be required to sign the writing, but also that it was a matter with which the legislature should deal and with which the courts had no concern. It is a familiar principle of statutory construction that a statute taken and enacted from the laws of another state carries with it the construction given to it by the laws of that state. The amendment made to the statute of Maine clearly indicates what construction was there given this provision of section 1387.

In speaking as to the construction of statutes relating to the form and manner of making wills, the court said in *In the Matter of Simpson*, 56 How. Pr. 126: "The restrictions which from motives of prudence are thrown around the right should be construed liberally in favor of the testament, and forms should not be required which the legislature has not plainly prescribed." The question as to the wisdom and policy of this provision is not a matter for our consideration. This court is not the forum to administer relief for evil in this law, if evil there be. If the law is not what it should be, let the legislature follow the course adopted by the state from which it took the law, and amend the statute in this regard, as that state has done. As the law is now written, compliance has been had with it, and having determined that matter, the investigation is concluded, as far as this court is concerned.

It is further insisted that the letters, when placed in the crucible by which they are to be tested, are found wanting, because it is said that the writing must be complete in itself; that is, it must show upon its face that the child is an illegitimate child, and that it was signed in the presence of a competent witness. We find nothing in the law subjecting the writing to any such test. The statute does not require it. Such recitals would not add one jot to the weight and credit to be given to the writing by the court, if they were there found stated. They would have no more weight and be of no more avail in arriving at a final deter-

mination of the merits of the cause, than if Blythe had said in the
writing, "I made this writing, and the facts therein stated are
true." A statement in the writing that it was signed in the presence of a competent witness could not be evidence of that fact;
no more would a reference in the writing to the child as an illegitimate child establish such illegitimacy. In *Grant* v. *Mitchell*,
83 Me. 26, the court, in speaking to this question, said: "In either
case, it must first appear that the child is illegitimate. The statute does not, nor does it purport to, act upon any other; nor does
the subsequent marriage, adoption, or acknowledgment have any
tendency to prove this fact. Whatever may be the effect of the
acknowledgment in showing the paternity of one proved to be
illegitimate, it annot be taken as proof of the illegitimacy."
Blythe, in writing, acknowledged himself to be the father of
Florence Blythe; Florence Blythe is an illegitimate child; therefore, Blythe acknowledged himself to be the father of an illigiti-
mate child. This logic is unassailable, and no sound reason can be
adduced why the acknowledgment should contain a declaration of
bastardy.

Bearing upon both branches of this case, as to the policy of
the law, and the true principle of construction to be invoked, we
quote the apt language of Beatty, C. J., in the Jessup case (81 Cal.
435), and the views there expressed in no wise conflict with the
principles declared in the main opinion of the court. He says:
"The only argument that can be made against his claim to inherit
his father's estate rests upon a strict construction of the statutes,
remedial in their nature, designed to secure to innocent unfor-
tunates in his situation a just share of the rights to which they
are by nature as fully entitled as are legitimate offspring. No
doubt a strong argument can be built on this basis of strict construction against the decision of the superior court. But I adhere
to the view so strongly put and so satisfactorily maintained by
Justice Works in his opinion, that in cases of this kind the only
strictness required is in proof of paternity. That being satisfactorily established by plenary proof, I think courts should lean
strongly in favor of a finding that the father of an illegitimate
child has done what every honest and humane man should be not
only willing and eager to do, and what a just law would compel
the unwilling to do. I also think it a wholly unauthorized construction of the statute to hold that the acts of recognition, acknowledgment, etc., necessary to legitimize a natural child should
be performed with the express intention on the part of the father

of accomplishing that object. If the acts are in themselves such as the statute prescribes, I think they confer legitimacy without any reference to the intent with which they are performed. There is no danger to morality in recognizing the natural rights of illegitimate children as against their fathers, or other claimants of their estates, and there is no danger of encouraging the fabrication of spurious claims so long as strict proof of paternity is insisted upon."

The foregoing views are not in harmony with the principles declared in the elaborate opinion of Mr. Justice Rhodes in the case of *Pina* v. *Peck*, 31 Cal. 359, and upon which decision appellants in the main rest this branch of their case. It is not our intention to analyze the soundness of the legal principles there laid down, otherwise than may have been incidentally done in what we have already said. Still, we might be allowed to say, no authority of courts or men learned in the law is presented in that opinion to support the views there declared, although, as we have seen, authority is not wanting to the contrary. *Pina* v. *Peck*, 31 Cal. 359, is not authority in this case, for two sufficient reasons: 1. But four justices participated in the decision (Justice Sanderson not taking part), and two of these justices concurred alone in the judgment. This fact entirely destroys the effect of the decision as an authority upon any and all matters therein discussed. 2. Justice Rhodes says at the very inception of his opinion: "It is contended by the defendants that this provision of the statute is in derogation of the common law, and must, therefore, be strictly construed. That doctrine was announced and applied by the court in the estate of Samuel Sanford, and we are of opinion that the ruling is correct, beyond a doubt. *As a consequence resulting from the operation of this rule*, the acknowledgment must conform to the statute, and be complete in itself; that is to say, it must not require the aid of extrinsic evidence. When the parties are identified, and the instrument in writing is produced and proven, the court must be able to say from the instrument that the person who signed it thereby acknowledged himself to be the father of the illegitimate child therein named." Thus this decision was expressly based upon strict and rigid rules of statutory construction, and as we have seen, those rules of construction have now been entirely displaced, as to the codes, by rules liberal and humane in their character. That decision being expressly based upon strict rules of construction, and strict rules of construction now being abolished, it cannot

be said to be binding authority in a case which we are called upon
to decide by an application of statutory rules of liberal construction. It is insisted that the following rule of construction, as
declared by Judge Cooley in his Constitutional Limitations (p.
66), must be invoked in this case, to wit: "It has ever properly
been held that the legislature, by enacting without material alter-
ation a statute which has been judicially expounded by the
highest court of the state, must be presumed to have intended that
the same words should be received in the new statute in the sense
which had been attributed to them in the old." There can be no
question that if the rules of statutory construction were the same
now as when *Pina v. Peck*, 31 Cal. 359, was decided, and the
views there expressed had been adopted by a majority of the
court, this principle of the construction of statutes would have
controlling effect in this case, but it is equally true that if the rules
of construction have been changed, such principle, in the very
nature of things, could not maintain.

For the foregoing reasons, let the judgment be affirmed.

PATERSON, J., and SHARPSTEIN, J., concurred.[24]

---

[24] As a general rule, in this country, the law of the father's domicil at
the time of the marriage, determines whether such child is made legitimate
by the subsequent marriage of the parents. If such law recognizes legitimation by subsequent marriage of the parents, the child is legitimate everywhere. *Fowler v. Fowler, 131 N. C. 169, 42 S. E. 563, 59 L. R. A. 317;
Straeder v. Graham, 51 U. S. 10; Stewart v. Stewart, 31 N. J. Eq. 407;
Sunderland Estate, 60 Iowa 732.* The English rule seems to be that it is
the law of the father's domicil at the time of the birth of the child which
should determine the effect of a subsequent marriage of the parents, and
not the law of the father's domicil at the time of marriage. *Dicey Conflict
of Laws, 497, 761,* and cases cited.

MARRIAGE.

COMMONWEALTH v. LANE, 1873.

[113 Mass. 458.]

1. General Rule as to Validity of   3. To What Extent are Foreign Mar-
    Marriage.   riages Recognized.
2. Exceptions to the General Rule.   4. Extra-territorial Effect of Re-
                                             strictions on Marriages.

GRAY, C. J. The report finds that the defendant was lawfully married to his first wife in this Commonwealth; that she
obtained a divorce here from the bond of matrimony, for his

adultery; that he was afterwards, while still a resident of this Commonwealth, married to a second wife in the State of New Hampshire, and cohabited with her in this Commonwealth, the first wife being still alive; and the question is whether he is indictable for polygamy, under the Gen. Sts. c. 165, § 4.

It is provided by our statutes of divorce that, in cases of divorce from the bond of matrimony, the innocent party may marry again as if the other party were dead; but that any marriage contracted by the guilty party during the life of the other, without having obtained leave from this court to marry again, shall be void, and such party shall be adjudged guilty of polygamy. Gen. Sts. c. 107, §§ 25, 26. St. 1864, c. 216.

The marriage act, Gen. Sts. c. 106, specifies, in §§ 1-3, what marriages shall be void by reason of consanguinity or affinity; in § 4, that all marriages contracted while either of the parties has a former wife or husand living, except as provided in c. 107, shall be void; in § 5, that no insane person or idiot shall be capable of contracting marriage; and in § 6 as follows: "When persons resident in this state, in order to evade the preceding provisions, and with an intention of returning to reside in this state, go into another state or country, and there have their marriage solemnized, and afterwards return and reside here, the marriage shall be deemed void in this state."

All these sections, except the last, are manifestly directed and limited to marriages within the jurisdiction of this Commonwealth; and the last has no application to this case, because it does not appear to have been proved or suggested at the trial that the parties to the second marriage went out of this state to evade our laws, or even that the second wife had resided in this state or knew of the previous marriage and divorce.

By the Gen. Sts. c. 165, § 4, "whoever, having a former husband or wife living, marries another person, or continues to cohabit with such second husband or wife in this state," shall (except when the first husband or wife has for seven years been absent and not known to the other party to be living, or in case of a person legally divorced from the bonds of matrimony and not the guilty cause of such divorce) be deemed guilty of polygamy and punished accordingly.

This statute is not intended to make any marriages unlawful which are not declared to be unlawful by other statutes, nor to punish cohabitation under a lawful marriage. Its object is to prohibit unlawful second marriages, whether the parties are actually married in this Commonwealth, or continue after being married elsewhere to cohabit here. But in either alternative, in order to sustain the indictment, the second marriage must be unlawful. It is not enough that the marriage is such as would be unlawful if contracted in this Commonwealth; it must be a marriage which, being contracted where it was, is unlawful here.

The marriage in New Hampshire is stated in the report to have been "according to the forms of law;" and it appears by the statutes of New Hampshire, therein referred to, that the only provision relating to the invalidity of marriages on account of the incompetency of parties to contract them is as follows: "All marriages prohibited by law, on account of the consanguinity or affinity of the parties, or where either has a former wife or husband living, knowing such wife or husband to be alive, if solemnized in this state, shall be absolutely void without any decree of divorce or other legal process." Gen. Sts. of N. H. (1867), c. 163, § 1. That provision clearly does not extend to a case in which the former wife, having obtained a divorce from the bond of matrimony, was absolutely freed from all obligation to the husband, and in which, as observed by Mr. Justice Wilde, in a like case, "notwithstanding the restraints imposed on the husband, he being the guilty cause of the divorce, the dissolution of the marriage contract was total, and not partial." *Commonwealth* v. *Putnam,* 1 Pick. 136, 139. The marriage in New Hampshire must therefore be taken to have been valid by the law of that state.

The question presented by the report is therefore reduced to this: If a man who has been lawfully married in this Commonwealth, and whose wife has obtained a divorce *a vinculo* here because of his adultery, so that he is prohibited by our statutes from marrying again without leave of this court, is married, without having obtained leave of the court, and being still a resident of this Commonwealth, to another woman in another state, according to its laws, and afterwards cohabits with her in this Commonwealth, is his second marriage valid here?

The determination of this question depends primarily upon the construction of our statutes, but ultimately upon fundamental principles of jurisprudence, which have been clearly declared by the judgments of our predecessors in this court, and in the light of which those statutes must be read in order to ascertain their just extent and effect.

What marriages between our own citizens shall be recognized as valid in this Commonwealth is a subject within the power of the Legislature to regulate. But when the statutes are silent, questions of the validity of marriages are to be determined by the *jus gentium*, the common law of nations, the law of nature as generally recognized by all civilized peoples.

By that law, the validity of a marriage depends upon the question whether it was valid where it was contracted; if valid there, it is valid everywhere.

The only exceptions admitted by our law to that general rule are of two classes: 1st. Marriages which are deemed contrary to the law of nature as generally recognized in Christian countries; 2d. Marriages which the Legislature of the Commonwealth has declared shall not be allowed any validity, because contrary to the policy of our own laws.

The first class includes only those void for polygamy or for incest. To bring it within the exception on account of polygamy, one of the parties must have another husband or wife living. To bring it within the exception on the ground of incest, there must be such a relation between the parties contracting as to make the marriage incestuous according to the general opinion of Christendom; and, by that test, the prohibited degrees include, beside pesons in the direct line of consanguinity, brothers and sisters only, and no collateral kindred. *Wightman* v. *Wightman*, 4 Johns. Ch. 343, 349-351. 2 Kent Com. 83. Story Confl. § 114. *Sutton* v. *Warren*, 10 Met. 451. *Stevenson* v. *Gray*, 17 B. Mon. 193. *Bowers* v. *Bowers*, 10 Rich. Eq. 551.

A marriage abroad between persons more remotely related, not absolutely void by the law of the country where it was celebrated, is valid here, at least until avoided by a suit instituted for the purpose, even if it might have been so avoided in that country; and this is so, whether the relationship between the parties is one which would not make the marriage void if contracted in this Commonwealth, as in the case of a marriage between a widower and his deceased's wife's sister, or one which would invalidate a marriage contracted here as in the case of a marriage between aunt and nephew.

In *Greenwood* v. *Curtis*, 6 Mass. 358, 378, 379, Chief Justice Parsons said: "If a foreign state allows of marriages incestuous by the law of nature, as between parent and child, such marriage could not be allowed to have any validity here. But marriages not naturally unlawful, but prohibited by the law of one state, and not of another, if celebrated where they are not prohibited, would be holden valid in a state where they are not allowed. As in this state a marriage between a man and his deceased wife's sister is lawful, but it is not so in some states; such a marriage celebrated here would be valid in any other state, and the parties entitled to the benefits of the matrimonial contract." This distinction was approved by Chancellor Kent and by Judge Story. 2 Kent Com. 85, note *a*. Story Confl. § 116.

In *The Queen* v. *Wye,* 7 A. & E. 761, 771 ; *S. C.* 3 N. & P. 6, 13, 14; it was decided that the marriage of a man with his mother's sister in England before the St. of 5 & 6 Will. IV. *c.* 54, though voidable by process in the ecclesiastical courts, was, until so avoided, valid for all civil purposes, including legitimacy and settlement. In accordance with that decision, it was held in *Sutton* v. *Warren,* 10 Met. 451, that such a marriage contracted in England, and never avoided there, must, upon the subsequent removal of the parties to Massachusetts, and the question arising collaterally in an action at common law, be deemed valid here, although, if contracted in this Commonwealth, it would have been absolutely void.

A marriage which is prohibited here by statute, because contrary to the policy of our laws, is yet valid if celebrated elsewhere according to the law of the place, even if the parties are citizens and residents of this Commonwealth, and have gone abroad for the purpose of evading our laws, unless the Legislature has clearly enacted that such marriages out of the state shall have no validity here. This has been repeatedly affirmed by well considered decisions.

For example, while the statues of Massachusetts prohibited marriages between white persons and negroes or mulattoes, a mulatto and a white woman, inhabitants of Massachusetts, went into Rhode Island, and were there married according to its laws, and immediately returned into Massachusetts; and it was ruled by Mr. Justice Wilde at the trial, and affirmed by the whole court, that the marriage, even if the parties went into Rhode Island to evade our laws, yet, being good and valid there, must upon general principles be so considered here, and that the wife therefore took the settlement of her husband in this Commonwealth. *Med. way* v. *Needham,* 16 Mass. 157.

So it has been held that a man, from whom his wife had obtained in this state a divorce *a vinculo* for his adultery, which by our statutes disabled him from contracting another marriage, might lawfully marry again in another state according to its laws;

that the children of such marriage took the settlement of their father in this Commonwealth; and that the new wife was entitled to dower in his lands here, even if the wife as well as the husband was domiciled here, and knew of the previous divorce and its cause, and went into the other state to evade our laws—so long as our statutes did not declare a marriage contracted there with such intent to be void here. *West Cambridge* v. *Lexington*, 1 Pick. 506. *Putnam* v. *Putnam*, 8 Pick. 433. See also *Dickson* v. *Dickson*, 1 Yerger, 110; *Ponsford* v. *Johnson*, 2 Blatchf. C. C. 51; 2 Kent Com. 91-93.

The principles upon which these decisions proceeded were recognized in all the English cases decided before the American Revolution, although it is true, as has since been pointed out, that the particular question in each of them related rather to the forms required than to the capacity of the parties.

Lord Hardwicke's Marriage Act in 1752 provided that all marriages of minors, solemnized by license without the consent of parents or guardians, should be void. St. 26 Geo. II. *c.* 33, § 11. Yet in the first case which arose under that act, in which an English boy eighteen years old went abroad with an English woman, and was there married to her without such consent, Lord Hardwicke, sitting as chancellor, assumed that if the marriage had been valid by the law of the country in which it was celebrated, it would have been valid in England, saying: "It will not be valid here unless it is so by the laws of the country where it was had; and so it was said by Murray, attorney general, to have been determined lately at the Delegates." And it would seem by the report that the woman defeated an application to the Ecclesiastical Court to annul the marriage, by refusing to appear there. *Butler* v. *Freeman*, Ambl. 301.

The case, thus referred to as determined at the Delegates, was evidently *Scrimshire* v. *Scrimshire*, decided by Sir Edward Simpson in the Consistory Court in 1752. Of that opinion, Sir George Hay, in *Harford* v. *Morris*, 2 Hagg. Con. 423, 431, said, "Every man has allowed the great and extensive knowledge of the judge;" and Sir William Wynne, in *Middleton* v. *Janverin*, 2 Hagg. Con. 437, 446, remarked that he remembered to have heard that the judgment was founded on great deliberation, and that Lord Hardwicke was consulted on it.

In *Scrimshire* v. *Scrimshire*, Sir Edward Simpson, in delivering judgment, said: "The question being in substance this,

Whether, by the law of this country, marriage contracts are not
to be deemed good or bad according to the law of the country in
which they are formed; and whether they are not to be construed
by that law? If such be the law of this country, the rights of
English subjects cannot be said to be determined by the laws of
France, but by those of their own country, which sanction and
adopt this rule of decision." "All nations allow marriage contracts; they are *juris gentium*, and the subjects of all nations are
equally concerned in them; and from the infinite mischief and
confusion that must necessarily arise to the subjects of all nations,
with respect to legitimacy, succession and other rights, if the
respective laws of different countries were only to be observed, as
to marriages contracted by the subjects of those countries abroad,
all nations have consented, or must be presumed to consent, for
the common benefit and advantage, that such marriages should
be good or not, according to the laws of the country where they
are made. It is of equal consequence to all, that one rule in these
cases should be observed by all countries—that is, the law where
the contract is made." And he declared the marriage in that
case to be invalid, only because it appeared to be wholly null and
void by the laws of France, where it was celebrated. 2 Hagg.
Con. 395, 407, 408, 417, 421.

In *Compton* v. *Bearcroft*, (1767-69,) where the parties, both
being English subjects and the libellant a minor, ran away and
were married in Scotland, a libel for the nullity of the marriage
was dismissed by Sir George Hay in the Court of Arches, upon
the ground that Lord Hardwicke's Act did not extend to Scotland; but by the Court of Delegates on appeal, consisting of
Justices Gould and Aston, Baron Perrott, and two doctors of
civil law, upon the broader ground that the marriage was good by
the *lex loci.* 2 Hagg. Con. 430, 443, 444 & note; *S. C.* Bul.
N. P. 113, 114. See also *Ilderton* v. *Ilderton*, 2 H. Bl. 145;
Dalrymple v. *Dalrymple*, 2 Hagg. Con. 54, 59; *Ruding* v. *Smith*,
Ib. 371, 390, 391; *Steele* v. *Braddell*, Milward, 1, 21.

In a recent case in the House of Lords, the cases of *Medway*
v. *Needham*, 16 Mass. 157, and *Sutton* v. *Warren*, 10 Met. 451,
above cited, have been severely criticised, and pointedly denied
to be law. *Brook* v. *Brook*, 9 H. L. Cas. 193; *S. C.* 3 Sm. &
Giff. 481. As that court is the one of all foreign tribunals, the
opinions of which, owing to the learning, experience and ability
of the judges, we are accustomed to regard with the most respect,
it becomes necessary to examine with care the scope of that deci-

sion, and the soundness of the reasons assigned for it; and in order to make this examination intelligible, it will be convenient first to refer to the English statutes and to some earlier decisions.

Several statutes of Henry VIII., which it is unnecessary to state in detail, declared marriages within certain degrees of consanguinity and affinity, and among others the marriage of a widower with his deceased wife's sister, to be "contrary to God's law as limited and declared by act of Parliament." Sts. 25 Hen. VIII. *c. 22*; 28 Hen. VIII. *cc. 7, 16*; 32 Hen. VIII. *c. 38*. While those statutes remained unaltered, a period of nearly three hundred years, such marriages were held by the judges not to be absolutely void, but voidable only by suit in the ecclesiastical courts during the lifetime of both parties, and, if not so avoided, were treated as valid, the wife entitled to dower, and the children of the marriage legitimate. Co. Lit. 33. *Hinks* v. *Harris*, 4 Mod. 182; *S. C.* 12 Mod. 35; Carth. 271; 2 Salk. 548. Lord Hardwicke, in *Brownsword* v. *Edwards*, 2 Ves. Sen. 243, 245. 1 Bl. Com. 434, 435. *Elliott* v. *Gurr*, 2 Phillim. 16. *The Queen* v. *Wye*, 7 A. & E. 761, 771; *S. C.* 3 N. & P. 6, 13, 14. *Westby* v. *Westby*, 2 Dru. & War. 502, 515, 516; *S. C.* 1 Con. & Laws. 537, 544, 545; 4 Irish Eq. 585, 593.

The St. of 5 & 6 Will. IV. *c.* 54, commonly known as Lord Lyndhurst's Act, provided, as to marriages between persons within the prohibition degrees of affinity, as follows: 1st, that such marriages, celebrated before the passage of the act, should not be annulled, except in a suit already pending in the ecclesiastical courts; 2d, that such marriages, thereafter celebrated, should be absolutely null and void to all intents and purposes whatever; 3d, that nothing in this act should be construed to extend to Scotland.

The marriage of a widower with the sister of his deceased wife, in England, after this statute, was held to be within the prohibited degrees and utterly void. *The Queen* v. *Chadwick*, 11 Q. B. 173, 234.

A case afterwards came before the Scotch courts, in which an English citizen married his deceased wife's sister in England; the validity of the marriage was not disputed during her life, and she died before the St. of Will. IV.; and the question was, whether the children of the marriage could inherit his lands in Scotland. The Scotch courts, in a series of very able opinions, held that they could, upon the ground that by the law of England, the marriage, not having been challenged in the lifetime of both parties, could not in any form be declared invalid in England, and the children were legitimate there, and must therefore be deemed legitimate in Scotland. *Fenton* v. *Ligingstone,* 16 Ct. of Sess. Cas. (2d Series) 104, and 18 Ib. 865. The House of Lords, on appeal, reversed that decision, and held that, although the marriage had, by reason of the peculiar rules governing the English courts of temporal and ecclesiastical jurisdiction, become irrevocable there, yet it was always illegal; and that, those rules not being applicable in the Scotch courts, the legitimacy of the children in Scotland depended upon the question whether the marriage was illegal by the law of Scotland. *S. C.* 3 Macq. 497. The Scotch court thereupon decided that the marriage was illegal, and that the children were incapable of inheriting lands in Scotland. *S. C.* 23 Ct. of Sess. Cas. (2d Series) 366.

In *Brook* v. *Brook, ubi supra,* a widower and the sister of his deceased wife, being lawfully domiciled in England, while on a temporary visit to Denmark, had a marriage solemnized between them, which was by the laws of Denmark lawful and valid to all intents and purposes whatsoever. In a suit in equity, brought after the death of both parties, to ascertain the rights of the children in their father's property, the House of Lords, in accordance with the opinions of Lords Campbell, Cranworth, St. Leonards and Wensleydale, and affirming a decree rendered by Vice Chancellor Stuart, assisted by Mr. Justice Cresswell, held that the marriage in Denmark was wholly void by the St. of Will. IV., and that the children of that marriage were bastards.

The decision was put, by the learned judges who concurred in it, upon three different grounds.

The first ground was that the St. of Will. IV. disqualified English subjects everywhere from contracting such a marriage. This ground was taken in the court below, and by Lord St. Leonards in the House of Lords. 3 Sm. & Giff. 522, 525. 9 H. L. Cas. 234–238. But it was expressly disclaimed by Lord Campbell, Lord Cransworth and Lord Wensleydale, the two former of whom expressed opinions that the statute did not extend to all the colonies, and all three declared that they did not think its purpose was to put an end to such marriages by British subjects throughout the world. 9 H. L. Cas. 214, 222, 240.

The second ground, which was suggested by Mr. Justice Cresswell and Lord Wensleydale only, and is opposed to all the American authorities, was that the case justly fell within the first exception, stated in Story Confl. § 114, of marriages involving polygamy and incest. 3 Sm. & Giff. 513. 9 H. L. Cas. 241, 245. In view of that position, it may be observed that in an earlier case, in which Lord Wensleydale himself (then Baron Parke) delivered the opinion, a marriage of a widower with his deceased wife's sister, before the St. of Will. IV., was prevented from being made irrevocable by that statute, only by the institution, a week before its passage, of a suit for nullity in the Ecclesiastical Court by the father of the supposed wife; and by the decision of the Privy Council, that because, if the marriage was not set aside, the birth of a child of the marriage would impose a legal obligation upon the grandfather to maintain the child in the event of its being poor, lame or impotent, and unable to work, he had, according to the rules of the ecclesiastical courts, a sufficient interest, "although of an extremely minute and contingent character," to support such a suit. *Sherwood* v. *Ray,* 1 Moore P. C. 353, 401, 402.

The third ground, upon which alone all the law lords agreed, was that the St. of Will. IV. made all future marriages of this kind between English subjects, having their domicil in England, absolutely void, because declared by act of Parliament to be contrary to the law of God, and must therefore be deemed to include such marriages, although solemnized out of the British dominions.

The law of England, as thus declared by its highest legislative and judicial authorities, is certainly presented in a remarkable aspect. 1st. Before the St. of Will. IV., marriages within the prohibited degrees of affinity, if not avoided by a direct suit for the purpose during the lifetime of both parties, had the same effect in England, in every respect, as if wholly valid. 2d. This statute itself made such marriages, already solemnized in England, irrevocably valid there, if no suit to annul them was already pending. 3d. It left such marriages in England, even before the statute, to be declared illegal in the Scotch courts, at least so far as rights in real estate in Scotland were concerned. 4th. According to the opinion of the majority of the law lords, it did not invalidate marriages of English subjects in English colonies, in which a different law of marriage prevailed. 5th. But it did make future marriages of this kind, contracted either in England or in a foreign country, by English subjects domiciled in England, absolutely void, because declared by the British Parliament to be contrary to the law of God.

The judgment proceeds upon the ground that an act of Parliament is not merely an ordinance of man, but a conclusive declaration of the law of God; and the result is that the law of God, as declared by act of Parliament and expounded by the House of Lords, varies according to time, place, length of life of parties, pecuniary interests of third persons, petitions to human tribunals, and technical rules of statutory construction and judicial procedure.

The case recalls the saying of Lord Holt, in *London* v. *Wood*, 12 Mod. 669, 687, 688, that "an act of Parliament can do no wrong, though it may do several things that look pretty odd;" and illustrates the effect of narrow views of policy, of the doctrine of "the omnipotence of Parliament," and of the consequent unfamiliarity with questions of general jurisprudence, upon judges of the greatest vigor of mind, and of the profoundest learning in the municipal law and in the forms and usages of the judicial system of their own country.

Such a decision, upon such reasons, from any tribunal, however eminent, can have no weight in inducing a court, not bound by it as authority, to overrule or disregard its own decisions.

The provision of the Gen. Sts. *c*. 107, § 25, forbidding the guilty party to a divorce to contract another marriage, during the life of the other party, without leave of this court, on pain of being adjudged guilty of polygamy, does not create a permanent incapacity, like one arising from consanguinity or affinity. It is rather in the nature of the imposition of a penalty, to which it would be difficult to give any extra-territorial operation. *West Cambridge* v. *Lexington*, 1 Pick. 506, 510, 512. *Clark* v. *Clark*, 8 Cush. 385, 386. Upon the principles and authorities stated in the earlier part of this opinion, it certainly cannot invalidate a subsequent marriage in another state according to its laws, at least without proof that the parties went into that state and were married there with the intent to evade the provisions of the statutes of this Commonwealth. No such intent being shown in this case, we need not consider its effect, if proved, nor whether the indictment is in due form. See *Commonwealth* v. *Putnam*, 1 Pick. 136, 139; *Commonwealth* v. *Hunt*, 4 Cush. 49.

New trial ordered.

UNITED STATES v. RODGERS, 1901.

[109 Fed. Rep. 886.]

J. B. McPHERSON, District Judge. The relator is a naturalized citizen of the United States, and is the husband of Rosa

Devine, and the father of her idiot son, William. Rosa and William are Russian Jews, whom the commissioner of immigration at the port of Philadelphia has ordered to be deported, on the ground that both are aliens, and that William is an idiot, and Rosa is a pauper that is likely to become a public charge. The alienage of both is denied upon the ground that when the husband and father became a citizen the wife and child ceased to be aliens; and this is the only point to be decided. The decision is admitted to depend upon the answer to be given to the question whether Rosa is the relator's lawful wife, or, rather, whether she is to be so regarded in this state; for she is her husband's niece, and such a marriage, if originally celebrated in Pennsylvania, would be void: Act 1860, § 39 (P. L. 393) ; 1 Purd. Dig. (Ed. 1872) p. 54. Among the Jews in Russia, however, where the ceremony took place, it has been satisfactorily proved that a marriage between uncle and niece is lawful, and, being valid there, the general rule undoubtedly is that such a marriage would be regarded everywhere as valid. But there is this exception, at least, to the rule: If the relation thus entered into elsewhere, although lawful in the foreign country, is stigmatized as incestuous by the law of Pennsylvania, no rule of comity requires a court sitting in this state to recognize the foreign marriage as valid. I think the following quotation from Dr. Reinhold Schmid, a Swiss jurist of eminence, to be found in Whart. Confl. Laws (2d Ed.) § 175, correctly states the proper rule upon this subject ·

"When persons married abroad take up their residence with us, it is agreed on all sides that the marriage, so far as its formal requisites are concerned, cannot be impeached, if it corresponds either with the laws of the place where the married pair had their domicile, or with those where the marriage was celebrated. But we must not construe this as implying that the juridical validity of the marriage depends absolutely on the laws of the place under whose dominion it was constituted; for the fact that a marriage was void by the laws of a prior domicile is no reason why we should declare it void if it united all the requisites of a lawful marriage as they are imposed by our laws. So far as concerns the material conditions of the contract of marriage, we must distinguish between such hindrances as would have impeded marriage, but cannot dissolve it when already concluded, and such as would actually dissolve a marriage if celebrated in the face of

them. A matrimonial relation that in the last sense is prohibited
by our laws cannot be tolerated in our territory, though it was
entered into by foreigners before they visited us. We will, therefore, tolerate no polygamous or incestuous unions of foreigners
settling within our limits."

Other authority may be found in State v. Brown, 47 Ohio
St. 102, 23 N. E. 747, where it is said, in determining the effect
of a statute that forbade sexual intercourse between persons
nearer of kin than cousins

"We hold, therefore, that by section 7091, Rev. St., sexual
commerce as between persons nearer of kin than cousins is prohibited, whether they have gone through the form of intermarriage or not; nor is it material that the marriage was celebrated
in a country where it was valid, for we are not bound upon principles of comity, to permit persons to violate our criminal laws,
adopted in the interest of decency and good morals, and based
upon principles of sound public policy, because they have assumed,
in another state or country, where it was lawful, the relations
which led to the acts prohibited by our laws."

See, also, Inhabitants of Medway v. Inhabitants of Needham,
16 Mass. 157, 8 Am. Dec. 131, and In re Stull's Estate, 183 Pa.
625, 39 Atl. 16, 39 L. R. A. 539.

In view of this exception to the general rule, it seems to me
to be impossible to recognize this marriage as valid in Pennsylvania, since a continuance of the relation here would at once
expose the parties to indictmment in the criminal courts, and to
punishment by fine and imprisonment in the penitentiary. In
other words, this court would be declaring the relation lawful,
while the court of quarter sessions in Philadelphia county would
be obliged to declare it unlawful. Whatever may be the standard
of conduct in another country, the moral sense of this community
would undoubtedly be shocked at the spectacle of an uncle and
niece living together as husband and wife; and I am, of course,
bound to regard the standard that prevails here, and to see that
such an objectionable example is not presented to the public. A
review of the Pennsylvania legislation affecting the marriage of
uncle and niece will be found in Parker's Appeal, 44 Pa. 309. It is
accordingly ordered that Rosa and William Devine be remanded.[25]

---

[25]As a general rule, mutual present consent lawfully expressed makes a
good common law marriage. Cohabitation adds nothing to its legal effect.

Bishop, Mar. & Div. Sec. 3³7; Dumaresly v. Fishly, 10 Ky. 368; Rose v. Clark, 8 Paige 574; Richard v. Brehm, 73 Pa. 140. In Michigan, the present consent is not sufficient to constitute a valid common law marriage, the consent must be followed by cohabitation. *Lorimer v. Lorimer, 124 Mich. 631.*

The "sealing ceremony" of the Mormon church, whereby the parties agreed and were declared by a church official to be married, created a valid marriage, though the parties had never lived together. *Hilton v. Roylance, Utah, 69 Pac. Rep. 660.* The case of *Hyde v. Hyde, L. R. 1 Prob. & Div. 130,* refused to recognize as valid in England, a marriage contracted in Utah. The court held that a union formed between a man and woman in a foreign country, although it may bear the name of a marriage, is not a valid marriage according to the law of England, unless it is formed on the same basis as marriages throughout Christendom, and be in its essence the voluntary union for life of one man and one woman, to the exclusion of all others.

A marriage by a woman to her deceased husband's brother, held valid in England. *Husey-Hunt v. Bozzelli, 1 Chan. 751 (1902).* A marriage on the high seas in order to evade the laws of the state is void. *Norman v. Thomson, 121 Cal. 620 (1898).* Indian marriages in accordance with the custom of the tribe are valid in this country although such marriages are polygamous. *Earl v. Godley, 142 Minn. 361.* A negro man and a white woman both domiciled in Virginia went to Washington, D. C., and were married. Ten days later they returned to Virginia. Such marriages are void in Virginia. The parties were held liable to criminal prosecution. *Kinney v. Commonwealth, 30 Grat. (Va.) 858.*

In many states, laws have been passed providing, in case of divorce, that the guilty party shall not marry during the lifetime of the innocent consort.

What is the effect of such a law or decree where the prohibited party goes into another state and is there married? Some courts hold the second marriage valid. The disability to marry again is treated as a penalty and is not recognized or enforced in other states. *Dickson v. Dickson, 1 Yerg. (Tenn.) 110, 24 Am. Dec. 444; Putnam v. Putnam, 8 Pick. (Mass.) 433; Van Voorhis v. Brintnall, 86 N. Y. 18, 40 Am. Rep. 505; Wilson v. Holt, 83 Ala. 528, 3 So. Rep. 321; Succession of Hernandez, 46 La. Am. 962, 24 L. R. A. 831; Crawford v. State, 73 Miss. 172, 18 So. Rep. 848, 35 L. R. A. 224; Thorp v. Thorp, 90 N. Y. 602: Moore v. Hegeman, 92 N. Y. 521, 44 Am. Rep. 408.* Some courts hold the second marriage invalid. *Pennegar v. State, 87 Tenn. 244, 10 S. W. 305, 2 L. R. A. 703; West Cambridge ₁. Lexington, 1 Pick. (Mass.) 506; 11 Am. Dec. 231.* May the guilty party on his return to his domicil, and for cohabitation there with his second wife, be punished for lewdness, fornication, adultery, or bigamy? The courts have answered this in the negative. *State v. Weatherby, 43 Me. 248, 69 Am. Dec. 59; Crawford v. State, 73 Miss. 172, 35 L. R. A. 224; Can. v. Putnam, 1 Pick. (Mass.) 136; People v. Hovey, 5 Barb. (N. Y.) 117.*

If the statute is made specific enough, the guilty party may be punished on his return to his domicil. *Com. v. Lane, 113 Mass. 458, 18 Am. Rep. 509; State v. Kennedy, 76 N. C. 251, 22 Am. Rep. 683.* In the case of *Thorp v. Thorp, 90 N. Y. 602,* the court held that such second marriage did not constitute a contempt of court.

PROPERTY RIGHTS OF HUSBAND AND WIFE AS
AFFECTED BY THE MARRIAGE.

LONG v. HESS, 1895.

[154 Ill. 482.]

This was a bill in chancery, brought by William Long and
Catherine Gleim, against George Hess, Henry Hess, Louis Hess
and Mary Kopf, the children, Christina Hess, the widow, and
Louis Hess, the executor, of Jacob Hess, deceased, to set aside
the will of Jacob Hess, and to declare a trust in favor of com
plainants in two-sixths of the estate of the testator. Jacob Hess
died March 29, 1891, in LaSalle county, where he had lived for
many years, leaving an estate consisting almost exclusively of
lands situate in that county, and leaving a last will, by which he
gave his entire estate to his widow for life, and after providing
for the payment of $100 each to the complainants, divided the
remainder among his four children above named.

Jacob Hess and Christina, his wife, were both natives of the
Grand Duchy of Hesse, now a part of the German Empire. Prior
to their marriage, in 1846, Christina Hess was the widow of
Bernhardt Lang, then lately deceased, and the complainants are
her children by her former marriage. She was then the owner of
a small amount of property, consisting of a dwelling house and
certain small tracts of land, but the amount and value of her
property are not clearly shown by the evidence. Jacob Hess was
at the same time the owner of a tract of land of the value of 350
florins, and of 150 florins in cash. Jacob Hess and Christina
Lang being about to be married, the following ante-nuptial contract, as is claimed, was executed between them:

"*Know all men by these presents*, that, on the day hereinafter written, a true and irrevocable marriage contract has been
agreed upon and concluded between Jacob Hess, single, lawful
son of Adam Hess, citizen and baker of Beerfelden, as bride-
groom, party of the first part, and Christina Lang, widow, of
Beerfelden, as bride, party of the second part, as follows, to-wit:
The said parties have resolved to take one another as husband
and wife, to remain in joy and sorrow until death shall separate
them, and to have their marriage solemnized in the near future
by a priest. As regards their worldly success and subsistence,

the bride agrees to receive the groom to live at her house. The groom to bring into the marriage that piece of land situated at Unter Beerfelden (district of Hetzbach), described at 86.144, N. 376.4, 1815 Klftr., and valued at 350 florins, also in cash 150 florins, (in words one hundred and fifty florins.) It is further agreed that the two children of the bride, of her first marriage, shall have an advancement of 100 florins, (in words one hundred florins,) with the understanding that in case of the death of one of the said children the surviving child is to inherit the whole of the said advancement. As to everything else the said two children of the first marriage and those to be begotten in this marriage shall inherit equally, share and share alike. In all other cases not especially enumerated herein the contracting parties subject themselves to the general laws of Germany, especially the rules and customs of the country.

"Beerfelden, May 11, 1846.

> JAKOB HESS, *Groom,*
> ANNA CHRISTINA LANG, *Bride,*
> EVA CHRISTINA HESS, *Widow.*
> ANDREAS SCHMAHL.

"Authenticated: NEWER, *Mayor."*

Shortly after these proceedings Jacob Hess and Christina Lang were married, and as the fruit of such marriage their four children, now defendants in this suit, were afterwards born. After their marriage Hess and wife lived in the house belonging to the wife, the complainants, then young children, being members of the family. There seems to have been a small bakery on the premises, and Hess, during the time he continued to live in Germany, carried on the business of a baker.

In May, 1851, Hess and wife sold the property they owned in Germany, the amount realized therefrom being a little over 1000 florins, or about $400, and they then came to this country, bringing the complainants with them. They first settled at Buffalo, New York, where Hess seems to have carried on the business of a baker in a small way. About the year 1858 he removed with his family to LaSalle county, in this State, where he resided up to the time of his death, and where he accumulated the estate which he attempted to dispose of by will. There is no evidence, nor does it seem to be claimed, that any portion of the avails of the property sold in Germany went into or formed a part of the estate which he owned at his death.

23

The complainants insist that the ante-nuptial contract above set forth is to be construed and enforced according to the rules of law in force in the Grand Duchy of Hesse at the time it was entered into; that by that law the complainants were adopted by Jacob Hess, and became heirs of his estate jointly with the·children born of the marriage then about to be solemnized; that their right to succeed to the estate of Hess at his death was a vested right, and one which, under the law where the contract was made, was incapable of being divested by will, and therefore that the will is void as to them, or, at least, that the devisees should be held to have taken the lands devised to them subject to the complainants' rights, and that the devisees should be charged as trustees for their benefit.

The deposition of an attorney residing in Hesse, and learned in the laws in force in that Grand Duchy at that time, was taken on behalf of the complainants, and it is claimed that the local law in force there at that time was substantially as above stated. A motion to suppress his deposition upon the ground, among other things, that it was not taken in conformity with the statute, was made by the defendants and overruled by the court. The cause afterward coming on to be heard on pleadings and proofs, the court found the equities of the case to be with the defendants, and entered a decree dismissing the bill at the costs of the complainants. From that decree the complainants have now appealed to this court.

BAILEY, J.: The defendants, in whose favor the decree was rendered, now urge, with a considerable degree of earnestness, that the court below erred in refusing to suppress the deposition taken in Germany, on the ground that the manner in which it was taken was a clear departure from that prescribed by the statute for taking the depositions of foreign witnesses. All we need say upon that point is, that the question thus raised is not before us for decision. The court below refused to suppress the deposition and considered it as evidence on the final hearing, but upon all the evidence as thus presented the decision of the court was in the defendants' favor and the complainants have appealed. The defendants have assigned no cross-errors, and they must therefore be deemed to be content with the decision of their motion to suppress, and so, for all the purposes of this appeal, the deposition, however irregularly it may have been taken, must be regarded as having been rightfully retained and considered as evidence at the hearing.

The only question presented by the record is as to the legal effect upon the property acquired by Jacob Hess in this State, of the ante-nuptial contract entered into in Germany between him and his then intended wife. It is claimed that the contract, when considered in connection with the judicial proceedings had thereon, constituted, in legal effect, an adoption of the complainants by Hess, so as to place them upon the same footing, as far as succession to his property and estate was concerned, with the children afterwards born of the marriage then in contemplation; and it is further contended, that by the rules of law in force where the contract was made, and which entered into and formed a part of it, the property then owned by Hess and by his intended wife, as well as that afterwards acquired by them, became communal property, in which the children of the family, both natural and adopted, acquired a vested right, and that Hess could not, by will, divest their right to succeed to such estate as he might leave at his death.

After considering all the evidence, we are left in very grave doubt whether the laws of the Grand Duchy of Hesse, upon which reliance is placed, are sufficiently proved. But waiving that point, and assuming that the proof is sufficient, and that the rules of law prevailing in Hesse at the date of the contract were as the complainants contend, the question remains whether the ante-nuptial contract should be enforced in this State as to property, and especially real property, subsequently acquired by Hess in this State.

It should be remembered that at the date of the contract the parties were living at Beerfelden, in the Grand Duchy of Hesse, and, so far as appears, were intending to remain there permanently. There is nothing, either in the contract itself or in the evidence, having the least tendency to show that their removal to any other place was then contemplated. The evidence furnished by the contract is all in the direction of showing that their intention was to make Beerfelden their permanent home. The agreement on the part of the bride was, "to receive the groom to live at her house," and the contract, after certain stipulations as to the property brought into the marriage by the groom, and as to the rights of the children of the bride by her former-marriage, concludes with the provision, that "in all other cases not especially enumerated herein the contracting parties subject themselves to the general laws of Germany, especially the rules and customs of the country." In point of fact, Jacob Hess, after his marriage, took up his residence at his wife's house and made that his domicil, and thereupon engaged at that place in the business of a baker, which he carried on for five years. He then sold out his property there and emigrated to the United States.

It should also be observed that there is a total absence of any express provision in the contract making it applicable to the future acquisitions of the contracting parties. It deals with the property they then possessed, but makes no reference to such as they might afterwards gain. The only language in the contract on which any reliance is placed as having reference to future acquisitions is the following: "As regards their worldly success and subsistence, the bride agrees to receive the groom to live at her house. If these words are correctly translated from the original German, in which the contract was written—and we have heard no suggestion that they are not,—they are, to say the least, extremely ambiguous, and we are able to put upon them no rational construction which would make out of them an agree ment to subject the future acquisitions of the parties to the pro visions of the contract. The most probable and natural inter- pretation of the words would seem to be, that, with a view to pro viding for the worldly success and the subsistence of the family, the bride agreed to receive the groom to live at her house. They can not, without importing into them a meaning which does not appear upon their face, be held to have any direct reference to the future acquisitions of the contracting parties, and especi- ally their acquisitions after emigrating from their then residence and making their permanent domicil in a foreign country.

The property rights of husband and wife, as affected by the marriage contract itself, or by an ante-nuptial agreement, where the marriage or the ante-nuptial agreement has been entered into in a foreign country, have always presented questions of no little perplexity and difficulty. Story, in his treatise on the Con- flict of Laws, (sec. 143,) says: "The principal difficulty is not so much to ascertain what rule ought to govern in cases of express nuptial contract, at least where there is no change of domicil, as what rule ought to govern in cases where there is no such contract, or no contract which provides for the emergency. Where there is an express nuptial contract, that, if it speaks fully to the very point, will generally be admitted to govern all the property of the parties, not only in the matrimonial domicil, but in every other place, under the same limitations and restrictions as apply to other cases of contract. But where there is no express nuptial contract at all, or none speaking to the very point, the question, what rule ought to govern, is surrounded with more difficulty." The learned author then, after an extended examination of the opinions of the leading law writers in this country and in Europe, and also of the decisions of the Supreme Court of Louisiana, (the only court which, at that time, seems to have given these questions elaborate and careful consideration,) lays down the following propositions, which, as he says, although not universally established or recognized in America, have much domestic authority for their support and have none in opposition to them:

"(1) Where there is a marriage between parties in a foreign country, and an express contract respecting their rights and property, present and future, that, as a matter of contract, will be held equally valid everywhere, unless, under the circumstances, it stands prohibited by the laws of the country where it is sought to be enforced. It will act directly on movable property everywhere. But as to immovable property in a foreign territory it will, at most, confer only a right of action, to be enforced according to the jurisprudence *rei sitæ*. (2) Where such an express contract applies, in terms or intent, only to present property, and there is a change of domicil, the law of the actual domicil will govern the rights of the parties as to all future acquisitions. (3) Where there is no express contract, the law of the matrimonial domicil will govern as to all rights of the parties to their present property in that place and as to all personal property everywhere, upon the principle that movables have no situs, or, rather, that they accompany the person everywhere. As to immovable property the law *rei sitæ* will prevail. (4) Where there is no change of domicil, the same rule will apply to future acquisitions as to present property. (5) But where there is a change of domicil, the law of the actual domicil, and not the matrimonial domicil, will govern as to all future acquisitions of movable property, and as to all immovable property the law *rei sitæ*." Story on Conflict of Laws, sec. 184 *et seq.*

The propositions thus laid down by Judge Story seem to have received the general approval of the courts of this counrty, so far as there has been occasion to consider them since he wrote. Thus, in *Fuss* v. *Fuss,* 24 Wis. 256, parties domiciled in Prussia were married there, and afterward entered into a post-nuptial contract, whereby each granted and transferred to the other all real and personal property which should belong to the donator on the day of his death. The wife, at the time, owned real estate in Prussia, over which, by the laws of that country, she had full control and right of disposal. Several years afterward the property was sold, the husband taking the money and investing it in land in Wisconsin, to which the parties removed, and on which they resided until the husband's death. He also, during his lifetime, acquired other property, both real and personal, situate in Wisconsin, which he owned on the day of his death. By his last will the husband devised and bequeathed all his property, both real and personal, to his widow for life, with remainder to the brothers and sisters of the testator. On bill filed by the widow, claiming that, by force of the post-nuptial contract, she was entitled to an estate in fee in the lands and to the absolute ownership of the personal property left by her husband, it was held that there was nothing in the contract which spoke to the very point,—that it contained nothing which manifested any intention in the parties to regulate or control by it, according to the law of their matrimonial domicil, the future acquisitions and gains of property in any foreign State or territory or any property which should be held by the husband in such State or territory, and, consequently, that the property acquired and owned by the husband in Wisconsin in his own name was subject to be disposed of by him, by will or otherwise, according to the laws of that State, and that the widow's rights therein were not determined by the contract.

In *Castro* v. *Illies*, 22 Texas, 479, substantially the same doctrine was laid down, although, as that case arose out of a controversy between a wife claiming under an ante-nuptial contract and execution creditors of the husband, the decision is not in all respects so directly in point as the one last cited. There parties domiciled in Paris, France, executed an ante-nuptial contract and married in Paris. Some years afterward they emigrated to this country and became domiciled in Texas, where the husband subsequently acquired certain real property. It was claimed that by the rules of the French law the contract vested in the wife a certain interest in the property acquired by her husband which was not subject to seizure for her husband's debts, but it was held that as there were in the contract no words "speaking to the very point,"—that is, no words making the contract specifically applicable to property subsequently acquired by the husband in a State or country foreign to that in which the contract was made,—it had no operation upon lands subsequently acquired by the husband in Texas.

In *Besse* v. *Pellochoux*, 73 Ill. 285, an ante-nuptial contract was made between parties domiciled in Switzerland in regard to property to be occupied during the marriage, it appearing that the contract contemplated no change of domicil, but was to be performed in the place where it was made, and it was held that the contract did not affect real estate acquired in this State by the husband after their emigration to this country. In the opinion the doctrine laid down by Judge Story was cited with approval, and it was said that in that case there was nothing in the contract "speaking to the very point,"—that manifested any intention that all future acquisitions of property in foreign countries should be controlled by it.   See, also, *Lyon* v. *Knott*, 26 Miss. 548; *Kneeland* v. *Ensley*, Meigs, 620: *Saul* v. *Creditors*, 5 Martin (N. S.) 569; *LeBreton* v. *Myers*, 8 Paige, 261; *Gale* v. *Davis' Heirs*, 4 Martin (O. S.), 645.

The case of *Decouche* v. *Savetier*, 3 Johns. Ch. 190, is one where an ante-nuptial contract, entered into by the parties in Paris, was enforced in this country in favor of the wife, to the exclusion of the husband's relatives. But there the contract expressly provided that there shall be a community of property between them, according to the custom of Paris, which is to govern the disposition of the property, though the parties should hereafter settle in countries where the laws and usages are different or contrary." There the intention to make the contract applicable to property afterward acquired in foreign countries was expressly made to appear by "words speaking to the very point."

Considerable reliance is placed by the complainants upon the case of *Scheferling* v. *Huffman*, 4 Ohio St. 241, where the ante-nuptial contract entered into by the parties in Germany, in which it was agreed that all the property of the intended wife which she then owned or which should be mutually acquired by the parties during coverture should be the property of the wife, was sustained and enforced, and held to apply to the property acquired by them in the State of Ohio after their emigration to this country. It will be noticed, however, that in that case the contract, by its express terms, was made applicable not only to the property then owned by the intended wife, but also to all property acquired during the continuance of the marriage. It is therefore clearly distinguishable from the present case, where no express provision is made applicable to property acquired in this State after the parties became domiciled here.

We are therefore of the opinion that the ante-nuptial contract in this case is not applicable to real property acquired by Hess in this State after his emigration to this country, but that such property was subject to disposition by him, by deed or will, according to the laws of this State. His will, therefore, must be valid, so as to vest in his devisees a title which must prevail over any rights derived by the complainants from the ante-nuptial contract.

We are unable to see that any peculiar force is to be given to the fact that complainants, at the time Jacob Hess and wife emigrated to this country, were infants, and therefore incapable of consenting to a change of their domicile, or of waiving any rights which were secured to them by the contract. As the contract can not be held to have any application to the property sought to be reached in this case, no rights of theirs were affected by their being brought to this country, and they had nothing to waive. Even if it be admitted that, by reason of their legal adoption by Jacob Hess, they would have been entitled to succeed to his estate, at his death, as his heirs-at-law, the ante-nuptial contract furnished no obstacle to the exercise by Hess of his right to dispose of his estate by will, and he having done so, nothing was left to descend to the complainants as his heirs-at-law. Although the complainants may have acquired the status of adopted children and heirs-at-law by the contract and judicial proceedings had in Germany, their inheritance of after-acquired real estate situated in this State must be in accordance with our laws, and by our laws a testator has an absolute right to dispose of his property by will, even to the exclusion alike of his natural or his adopted children.

We are of the opinion that the decree of the circuit court is justified by the evidence, and it will accordingly be affirmed.[26]

---

[26]"The authorities are quite generally in accord in selecting the matrimonial domicil as the place which shall furnish the law regulating the interests of husband and wife in the movable property of either, which was *in esse* when the marriage took place. Perplexing questions sometimes arise as to what place shall be deemed the true matrimonial domicil in the sense of this rule. Mr. Justice Story supposes a case where neither of the parties has a domicil in the place where the marriage was celebrated, and the parties were there *in transitu,* or during a temporary residence, or on a journey made for that sole purpose *animo revertendi,* and says that the principle maintained by foreign jurists in such cases would be that the actual or intended domicil of the parties would be deemed to be the

true matrimonial domicil; or, to express the doctrine in a more general form, that the law of the place where, at the time of the marriage, the parties intended to fix their domicil would govern all the rights resulting from the marriage.

"He also supposes the case of a man domiciled in one state marrying a lady domiciled in another state, and says that foreign jurists would hold that the matrimonial domicil would be the domicil of the husband if it was the intention of the parties to fix their residence there, or the domicil of the wife if it was their intention to fix their residence there, or in a different place from the domicil of either the husband or wife if they intended to establish their matrimonial domicil in some other place. He then refers to the decisions of the courts of Louisiana, adopting the same principle, and concludes that, under these circumstances, where there is such a general consent of foreign jurists to the doctrine thus recognized in America, it is not, perhaps, too much to affirm that a contrary doctrine will scarcely hereafter be established; for, in England as well as in America, in the interpretation of other contracts, the laws of the place where they are to be performed has been held to govern." *Harral v. Harral, 39 N. J. Eq. 279; Townes v. Durbin, 3 Met. (Ky.) 352; Castleman v. Jeffries, 60 Ala. 380.*

When personal property becomes the husband's by the law of the domicil, a subsequent change of domicil will not change his rights. *Cahalan v. Munroe, 70 Ala. 271.* When personal property remains in wife, subsequent change of domicil will not change her rights. *Reid v. Gray, 37 Pa. 508.* As to wife's rights in husband's property see *Kraemer v. Kraemer, 52 Cal. 302.*

CHAPTER XII.

PERSONAL PROPERTY AND REAL PROPERTY.

GREEN v. VAN BUSKIRK, 1866, 1886.

[5 Wall. 307, 7 Wall. 139.]

1. Extra-territorial Effect of Transfers of Personal Property.
2. Conditional Sales of Personal Property.
3. Mortgages of Personal Property.
4. Gifts of Personal Property.
5. Conveyances of Real Property.

MOTION to dismiss a writ of error to the Supreme Court of the State of New York.

The Constitution of the United States declares (Section 1, Article IV) that *full faith and credit* shall be given in each State to the public acts, records, *and judicial proceedings* of every other State; and that Congress may by general laws prescribe the manner in which such acts, records, and proceedings shall be proved, and the *effect* thereof.

Under the power here conferred, Congress, by act of 1790, May 26, 1 Stat. at Large, 122, provides that records, authenticated in a way which it prescribes, shall "have such faith and credit given to them in ever other court of the United States, as they have by law or usage in the court from which they are taken."

With this provision of the Constitution and this law in force, Bates being the owner of certain iron safes at Chicago, in the State of Illinois, on the 3d day of November, 1857, executed and delivered, in the State of New York, to Van Buskirk and others, a chattel mortgage of them. On the 5th day of the same month Green caused to be levied on the same safes a writ of attachment, sued by him out of the proper court in Illinois, against the property of Bates. The attachment suit proceeded to judgment, and the safes were sold in satisfaction of Green's debt. Van Buskirk, Green, and Bates, were all citizens of New York. Green's attachment was levied on the safes as the property of Bates, before the possession was delivered to Van Buskirk, and before the mortgage from Bates to him was recorded, and before notice of its existence.

Van Buskirk afterwards sued Green, in the New York

courts, for the value of the safes thus sold under his attachment, and Green pleaded the proceeding in the court of Illinois in bar of the action. In this suit thus brought by him in the New York courts, Van Buskirk obtained judgment, and the judgment was affirmed in the highest court of the State of New York. From this affirmance Green took a writ of error to this court, assuming the case to fall within the twenty-fifth section of the Judiciary Act, which gives such writ in any case wherein is drawn in question a clause of the Constitution of the United States, and the decision is against the title, right, or privilege especially set up. His assumption was that the faith and credit which the judicial proceedings in the courts of the State of Illinois had by law and usage in that State, were denied to them by the decision of the courts of New York, and that in such denial, those courts decided against a right claimed by him under the above-mentioned Section 1, Article IV, of the Constitution, and the act of Congress of May 26th, 1790, on the subject of it.

Mr. Justice MILLER delivered the opinion of the court.

The section of the Constitution discussed in this case, declares that "full faith and credit shall be given in each State to the public acts, records, and judicial proceedings of every other State. And that Congress may, by general laws, prescribe the manner in which such acts, records, and proceedings shall be proved, and the *effect* thereof."

The act of 1790 was intended to be an exercise of the power conferred upon Congress by this section. In the leading case of *Mills* v. *Duryee*, 7 Cranch, 481, this court held that the act in question did declare the effect of such judicial records, and that it should be the same in other States as that in which the proceedings were had. In the case of *Christmas* v. *Russell, supra*, last preceding case, p. 290' decided at the present term of the court, we have reaffirmed this doctrine, and have further declared that no State can impair the effect thus to be given to judicial proceedings in her sister State, by a statute of limitation intended to operate on demands which may have passed into judgment by such proceedings, as though no such judgment had been rendered.

The record before us contains the pleadings in the case, the facts found by the court, and the conclusions of law arising thereon. And notwithstanding the inverted manner in which the court has stated its legal conclusions, it seems clear that it did pass upon the effect of the judicial proceedings in Illinois

upon the title of the property in contest. The case is not varied
by declaring that the mortgage made and delivered in New York
overreached the subsequent attachment in Illinois. According to
the view taken by that court, Van Buskirk, the plaintiff, had
title to the property under the laws of New York by virtue of
his mortgage, and the question to be decided was whether the
proceedings in Illinois were paramount in their effect upon the
title to the New York mortgage.

It is said that Van Buskirk being no party to the proceedings in Illinois was not bound by them, but was at liberty to
assert his claim to the property in any forum that might be open
to him; and, strictly speaking, this is true. He was not bound
by way of estoppel, as he would have been if he appeared and submitted his claim, and contested the proceedings in attachment.
He has a right to set up any title to the property which is superior
to that conferred by the attachment proceedings, and he has the
further right to show *that the property was not liable to the attachment*—a right from which he would have been barred if
he had been a party to that suit. And the question of the liability
of the property in controversy to that attachment is the question
which was raised by the suit in New York, and which was there
decided. That court said that this question must be decided by the
laws of the State of New York, because that was the domicile of
the owner at the time the conflicting claims to the property
originated.

We are of opinion that the question is to be decided by the
effect given by the laws of Illinois, where the property was situated, to the proceedings in the courts of that State, under which it
was sold.

There is no little conflict of authority on the general question as to how far the transfer of personal property by assignment or sale, made in the country of the domicil of the owner, will
be held to be valid in the courts of the country where the property is situated, when these are in different sovereignties. The
learned author of the Commentaries on the Conflict of Laws, has
discussed the subject with his usual exhaustive research. And
it may be conceded that as a question of comity, the weight of his
authority is in favor of the proposition that such transfers will
generally be respected by the courts of the country where the
property is located, although the mode of transfer may be different from that prescribed by the local law. The courts of
Vermont and Louisiana, which have given this question the

fullest consideration, have, however, either decided adversely to this doctrine or essentially modified it. *Taylor* v. *Boardman*, 25 Vermont, 589; *Ward* v. *Morrison,* Id. 593; *Emerson* v. *Partridge,* 27 Vermont, 8; *Oliver* v. *Towne,* 14 Martin's Louisiana, 93; *Norris* v. *Mumford,* 4 Id. 20. Such also seems to have been the view of the Supreme Court of Massachusetts. *Lanfear* v. *Sumner,* 17 Massachusetts, 110.

But after all, this is a mere principle of comity between the courts, which must give way when the statutes of the country where property is situated, or the established policy of its laws prescribe to its courts a different rule. The learned commentator, already referred to, in speaking of the law in Louisiana which gives paramount title to an attaching creditor over a transfer made in another State, which is the domicil of the owner of the property, says: "No one can seriously doubt that it is competent for any State to adopt such a rule in its own legislation, since it has perfect jurisdiction over all property, personal as well as real, within its territorial limits. Nor can such a rule, made for the benefit of innocent purchasers and creditors, be deemed justly open to the reproach of being founded in a narrow or a selfish policy." Story on the Conflict of Laws, § 390. Again, he says: "Every nation, having a right to dispose of all the property actually situated within it, has (as has been often said) a right to protect itself and its citizens against the inequalities of foreign laws, which are injurious to their interests."

Chancellor Kent, in commenting upon kindred subject, namely, the law of contracts, remarked, 2 Commentaries, 599: "But, on this subject of conflicting laws, it may be generally observed that there is a stubborn principle of jurisprudence that will often intervene and act with controlling efficacy. This principle is, that where the *lex loci contractus* and the *lex fori,* as to conflicting rights acquired in each, come in direct collision, the comity of nations must yield to the positive law of the land."

In the case of *Milne* v. *Moreton,* 6 Binney, 361, the Supreme Court of Pennsylvania says, that "every country has a right of regulating the transfer of all personal property within its territory; but when no positive regulation exists, the owner transfers it at his pleasure."

The Louisiana court, in a leading case on this subject, gives in the following language, a clear statement of the foundation of this principle: "The municipal laws of a country have no force beyond its territorial limits, and when another government permits these to be carried into effect within her jurisdiction, she does so upon a principle of comity. In doing so, care must be taken that no injury is inflicted on her own citizens, otherwise justice would be sacrificed to comity. . . . If a person sends his property within a jurisdiction different from that where he resides, he impliedly submits it to the rules and regulations in force in the country where he places it."

Apart from the question of authority, let us look at some of the consequences of the doctrine held by the court of New York.

If the judgment rendered against the plaintiff in error is well founded, then the sheriff who served the writ of attachment, the one who sold the property on execution, any person holding it in custody pending the attachment proceedings, the purchaser at the sale, and all who have since exercised control over it, are equally liable.

If the judgment in the State of Illinois, while it protects all such persons against a suit in that State, is no protection anywhere else, it follows that in every case where personal property has been seized under attachment, or execution against a non-resident debtor, the officer whose duty it was to seize it, and any other person having any of the relations above described to the proceeding, may be sued in any other State, and subjected to heavy damages by reason of secret transfers of which they could know nothing, and which were of no force in the jurisdiction where the proceedings were had, and where the property was located.

Another consequence is that the debtor of a non-resident may be sued by garnishee process, or by foreign attachment as it is sometimes called, and be compelled to pay the debt to some one having a demand against his creditors; but if he can be caught in some other State, he may be made to pay the debt again to some person who had an assignment of it, of which he was ignorant when he was attached.

The article of the Constitution, and the act of Congress relied on by the plaintiff in error, if not expressly designed for such cases as these, find in them occasions for their most beneficent operation.

We do not here decide that the proceedings in the State of Illinois have there the effect which plaintiff claims for them; because that must remain to be decided after argument on the merits of the case. But we hold that the effect which these proceedings have there, by the law and usage of that State, was a question necessarily decided by the New York courts, and that it was decided against the claim set up by plaintiff in error under the constitutional provision and statute referred to, and that the case is therefore properly here for review.

MOTION TO DISMISS OVERRULED.

Mr. Justice DAVIS delivered the opinion of the court.

That the controversy in this case was substantially ended when this court refused (5 Wallace, 312) to dismiss the writ of error for want of jurisdiction, is quite manifest by the effort which the learned counsel for the defendants in error now make, to escape the force of that decision.

The question raised on the motion to dismiss was, whether the Supreme Court of New York, in this case, had decided against a right which Green claimed under the Constitution, and an act of Congress. If it had, then this court had jurisdiction to entertain the writ of error, otherwise not.

It was insisted on the one side, and denied on the other, that the faith and credit which the judicial proceedings in the courts of the State of Illinois had by law and usage in that State, were denied to them by the Supreme Court of New York, in the decision which was rendered.

Whether this was so or not, could only be properly considered when the case came to be heard on its merits; but this court, in denial of the motion to dismiss, *held* that the Supreme Court of New York necessarily decided *what* effect the attachment proceedings in Illinois had by the law and usage in that State; and as it decided against *the* effect which Green claimed for them, this court had jurisdiction, under the clause of the Constitution which declares "that full faith and credit shall be given in each State to the public acts, records, and judicial proceedings in every other State, and the act of Congress of 1790, which gives to those proceedings the same faith and credit in other States, that they have in the State in which they were rendered.

This decision, supported as it was by reason and authority, left for consideration, on the hearing of the case, the inquiry, whether the Supreme Court of New York did give to the attachment proceedings in Illinois the same effect they would have received in the courts of that State.

By the statutes of Illinois, any creditor can sue out a writ of attachment against a non-resident debtor, under which the officer is required to seize and take possession of the debtor's property, and if the debtor cannot be served with process, he is notified by publication, and if he does not appear, the creditor, on making proper proof, is entitled to a judgment by default for his claim, and a special execution is issued to sell the property attached. The judgment is not a lien upon any other property than that attached; nor can any other be taken in execution to satisfy it. These statutes further provide, that mortgages on personal property have no validity against the rights and interests of third persons, without being acknowledged and recorded, unless the property be delivered to and remain with the mortgagee.

And so strict have the courts of Illinois been in construing the statute concerning chattel mortgages, that they have held, if the mortgage cannot be acknowledged in the manner required by the act, there is no way of making it effective, except to deliver the property, and that even actual notice of the mortgage to the creditor, if it is not properly recorded, will not prevent him from attaching and holding the property (*Henderson* v. *Morgan*, 26 *Illinois*, 431; *Porter* v. *Dement*, 35 Id. 479).

The policy of the law in Illinois will not permit the owner of personal property to sell it and still continue in possession of it. If between the parties, without delivery, the sale is valid, it has no effect on third persons who, in good faith, get a lien on it; for an attaching creditor stands in the light of a purchaser, and as such will be protected (*Thornton* v. *Davenport*, 1 Scammon, 296; *Strawn* v. *Jones*, 16 Illinois, 117.) But it is unnecessary to cite any other judicial decisions of that State but the cases of *Martin* v. *Dryden* (1 Gilman, 187), and *Burnell* v. *Robertson* (5 Id. 282), which are admitted in the record to be a true exposition of the laws of Illinois on the subject, to establish that *there* the safes were subject to the process of attachment, and that the proceedings in attachment took precedence of the prior unrecorded mortgage from Bates.

If Green, at the date of the levy of his attachment, did not know of this mortgage, and subsequently perfected his attachment by judgment, execution, and sale, the attachment held the property, although at the date of the levy of the execution he did know of it. The lien he acquired, as a *bona fide* creditor, when he levied his attachment without notice of the mortgage, he had the right to perfect and secure to himself, notwithstanding the fact that the mortgage existed, was known to him, before the judicial proceedings were completed. This doctrine has received the sanction of the highest court in Illinois through a long series of decisions, and may well be considered the settled policy of the State on the subject of the transfer of personal property. If so, the effect which the courts there would give to these proceedings in attachment, is too plain for controversy. It is clear, if Van Buskirk had selected Illinois, instead of New York, to test the liability of these safes to seizure and condemnation, on the same evidence and pleadings, their seizure and condemnation would have been justified.

It is true, the court in Illinois did not undertake to settle in the attachment suit the title to the property, for that question was not involved in it, but when the true state of the property was shown by other evidence, as was done in this suit, then it was obvious that by the laws of Illinois it could be seized in attachment as Bate's property.

In order to give due force and effect to a judicial proceeding, it is often necessary to show by evidence, outside of the record, the predicament of the property on which it operated. This was done in this case, and determined the effect the attachment proceedings in Illinois produced on the safes, which effect was denied to them by the Supreme Court of New York.

At an early day in the history of this court, the act of Congress of 1790, which was passed in execution of an express power conferred by the Constitution, received an interpretation which has never been departed from (*Mills* v. *Duryee,* 1 Cranch, 481) and obtained its latest exposition in the case of *Christmas* v. *Russell* (5 Wallace, 290).

The act declares that the record of a judgment (authenticated in a particular manner), shall have the same faith and credit as it has in the State court from whence it is taken. And this court say: "Congress have therefore declared the effect of the record, by declaring what faith and credit shall be given to it;" and that "it is only necessary to inquire in every case what is the effect of a judgment in the State where it is rendered."

It should be borne in mind in the discussion of this case, that the record in the attachment suit was not used as the foundation of an action, but for purposes of defence. Of course Green could not sue Bates on it, because the court had no jurisdiction of his person; nor could it operate on any other property belonging to Bates than that which was attached. But, as by the law of Illinois, Bates was the owner of the iron safes when the writ of attachment was levied, and as Green could and did lawfully attach

24

them to satisfy his debt in a court which had jurisdiction to render the judgment, and as the safes were lawfully sold to satisfy that judgment, it follows that when thus sold the right of property in them was changed, and the title to them became vested in the purchasers at the sale. And as to the effect of the levy, judgment and sale is to protect Green if sued in the courts of Illinois, and these proceedings are produced for his own justification, it ought to require no argument to show that when sued in the court of another State for the same transaction, and he justifies in the same manner, that he is also protected. Any other rule would destroy all safety in derivative titles, and deny to a State the power to regulate the transfer of personal property within its limits and to subject such property to legal proceedings.

Attachment laws, to use the words of Chancellor Kent, "are legal modes of acquiring title to property by operation of law." They exist in every State for the furtherance of justice, with more or less liberality to creditors. And if the title acquired under the attachment laws of a State, and which is valid there, is not to be held valid in every other State, it were better that those laws were abolished, for they would prove to be a snare and a delusion to the creditor.

The Vice-Chancellor of New York, in *Cochran v. Fitch* (1 Sandford Ch. 146) when discussing the effect of certain attachment proceedings in the State of Connecticut, says: "As there was no fraud shown, and the court in Connecticut had undoubted jurisdiction *in rem* against the complainant, it follows that I am bound in this State to give to the proceedings of that court the same faith and credit they would have in Connecticut." As some of the judges of New York had spoken of these proceedings in another State, without service of process or appearance, as being nullities in that state and void, the same vice-chancellor says: "But these expressions are all to be referred to the cases then under consideration, and it will be found that all those were suits brought upon the foreign judgment as a debt, to enforce it against the person of the debtor, in which it was attempted to set up the judgment as one binding on the person."

The distinction between the effect of proceedings by foreign attachments, when offered in evidence as the ground of recovery against the person of the debtor, and their effect when used in defence to justify the conduct of the attaching creditor, is manifest and supported by authority (*Cochran v. Fitch*, 1 Sandford, Ch. 146; *Kane v. Cook*, 8 California, 449). Chief Justice Parker, in *Hall v. Williams* (6 Pickering 232) speaking of the force and effect of judgments recovered in other States, says: "Such a judgment is to conclude as to everything over which the court which rendered it had jurisdiction. If the property of the citizen of another State, within its lawful jurisdiction, is condemned by lawful process there, the decree is final and conclusive."

It would seem to be unnecessary to continue this investigation further, but our great respect for the learned court that pronounced the judgment in this case, induces us to notice the ground on which they rested their decision. It is, that the law of the State of New York is to govern this transaction, and not the law of the State of Illinois where the property was situated; and as, by the law of New York, Bates had no property in the safes at the date of the levy of the writ of attachment, therefore none could be acquired by the attachment. The theory of the case is, that the voluntary transfer of personal property is to be governed everywhere by the law of the owner's domicile, and this theory proceeds on the fiction of law that the domicile of the owner draws to it the personal estate which he owns wherever it may happen to be located. But this fiction is by no means of universal application, and as Judge Story says, "yields whenever it is necessary for the purposes of justice that the actual *situs* of the thing should be examined." It has yielded in New York on the power of the State to tax the personal property of one of her citizens, situated in a sister State (*The People ex. rel. Hoyt* v. *The Commissioner of Taxes*, 23 New York, 225), and always yields to "laws for attaching the estate of non-residents, because such laws necessarily assume that property has a *situs* entirely distinct from the owner's domicile." If New York cannot compel the personal property of Bates (one of her citizens) in Chicago to contribute to the expenses of her government, and if Bates had the legal right to own such property there, and was protected in its ownership by the laws of the State; and as the power to protect implies the right to regulate, it would seem to follow that the dominion of Illinois over the property was complete, and her right perfect to regulate its transfer and subject it to process and execution in her own way and by her own laws.

We do not propose to discuss the question how far the transfer of personal property lawful in the owner's domicile will be respected in the courts of the country where the property is located and a different rule of transfer prevails. It is a vexed question, on which learned courts have differed; but after all there is no absolute right to have such transfer respected, and it is only on a principle of comity that it is ever allowed. And this principle of comity always yields when the laws and policy of the State where the property is located has prescribed a different rule of transfer with that of the State where the owner lives.

We have been referred to the case of *Guillander* v. *Howell* (35 New York Reports, 657), recently decided by the Court of Appeals of New York, and as we understand the decision in that case, it harmonizes with the views presented in this opinion. A citizen of New York owning personal property in New Jersey made an assignment, with preferences to creditors, which was valid in New York but void in New Jersey. Certain creditors in New Jersey seized the property there under her foreign attachment laws and sold it, and the Court of Appeals recognized the validity of the attachment proceeding, and disregarded the sale in New York. That case and the one at bar are alike in all respects except that the attaching creditor there was a citizen of the State in which he applied for the benefit of the attachment laws, while Green, the plaintiff in error, was a citizen of New York; and it is insisted that this point of difference is a material element to be considered by the court in determining this controversy, for the reason that the parties to this suit, as citizens of New York, were bound by its laws. But the right under the Constitution of the United States and the law of Congress which Green invoked to his aid is not at all affected by the question of citizenship. We cannot see why, if Illinois, in the spirit of enlightened legislation, concedes to the citizens of other States equal privileges with her own in her foreign attachment laws, that the judgment against the personal estate located in her limits of a non-resident debtor, which a citizen of New York lawfully obtained there, should have a different effect given to it under the provisions of the Constitution and the law of Congress, because the debtor, against whose property it was recovered, happened also to be a citizen of New York.

The judgment of the Supreme Court of the State of New York is REVERSED, and the cause remitted to that court with instructions to enter

JUDGMENT FOR THE PLAINTIFF IN ERROR.

BARNETT v. KINNEY, 1893.

[147 U. S. 476.]

This was an action of replevin commenced in the District Court of Alturas County, Territory of Idaho, on December 12,

1887, by Josiah Barnett against P. H. Kinney to recover the possession of certain goods and chattels mentioned in the complaint and for damages and costs. The case was submitted to the court for trial, a jury having been expressly waived, upon an agreed statement of facts, and the court made its findings of fact as follows: That on November 23, 1887, M. H. Lipman was a citizen of the United States and of the Territory of Utah, residing and doing business at Salt Lake City, and was possessed and the owner of real and personal property in Utah, and of certain personal property at Hailey, in Alturas County, Idaho; and that he was indebted to divers persons, (none of whom were then, or at the time of trial, citizens, residents and inhabitants of Idaho), and was insolvent, and on that day duly made, executed and delivered to Barnett, as his assignee, a deed of assignment in writing, which was accepted by Barnett, who assumed the execution thereof; that by the assignment, Lipman sold, transferred, assigned and delivered to Barnett all his property, real and personal, wherever found, in trust, to take possession and convert the same into cash, and pay the necessary expenses, and then his creditors, according to certain classes named in the assignment, preferences being made thereby in favor of certain creditors, as against others, all being designated by classes; that on November 25, 1887, Barnett, as assignee, took actual possession of the personal property situated in Idaho, and on November 26, and before the property was taken by Kinney, filed the assignment for record in the proper office in Alturas County; and that Kinney had actual knowledge and notice in these premises. It was further found that the assignment "was and is valid by the laws of the Territory of Utah;" that Lipman was indebted to the St. Paul Knitting Works, a corporation organized and existing under the laws of the State of Minnesota, the liability having been incurred by him as a citizen, resident and inhabitant of Utal, and in the transaction of his business there; that on November 26, 1887, and while Barnett was in actual possession, Kinney, who was sheriff of Alturas County, under a writ of attachment in favor of that corporation and against Lipman, took possession of the property; and that thereupon this action of replevin was commenced and the possession of the property delivered to Barnett, who had sold the same and retained the proceeds subject to the final disposition of the action. It was further found that prior to the taking of the property from Barnett by Kinney under the writ of attachment and after the assignment had been recorded, Kinney, as sheriff, had taken it from Barnett's possession under a writ of attachment issued at the suit of a firm located in Nebraska against Lipman, and it had been retaken from Kinney in an action of claim and delivery brought by Barnett against him, which action was still pending. It was also found that the goods had been shipped from Lipman's store in Utah in September, 1887, to Alturas County, and that Lipman from September, 1887, up to the time of making the assignment, had been doing business in Idaho in the running of a branch store at Hailey, in Alturas County; and that at the time of bringing this action defendant was wrongfully detaining the property from the possession of plaintiff.

The court found as conclusions of law that the assignment, a copy of which was annexed to the finding of facts, was a good and valid instrument, and conveyed title to the property in question and that the plaintiff at the time of bringing the action and the trial was entitled to the possession of the property, and to judgment therefor, and for nominal damages and costs. Judgment having been entered, an appeal was prosecuted to the Supreme Court of the Territory, by which it was reversed, and the cause remanded to the District Court with instructions to enter judgment for the defendant. The record shows that the case had been tried in the District Court before the then Chief Justice of the Territory, and that a change had taken place in that office when the hearing was had on appeal. Of the three members composing the Supreme Court, one was for reversal and another for affirmance, while the Chief Justice had been of counsel between the same parties in a case in the same District Court, but "with a different attaching creditor," and he stated that he had not participated in the discussion of the case, but, his associates having reached opposite conclusions, the disagreeable duty rested upon him of "breaking the dead-lock," which he did by concuring in the opinion for reversal. The majority opinion is to be found in 23 Pac. Rep. 922, and the dissent in 24 Pac. Rep. 624. The case was brought by appeal to this court.

Mr. Chief Justice FULLER, after stating the case, delivered the opinion of the court.

The Supreme Court of the Territory held that a non-resident could not make an assignment, with preferences, of personal property situated in Idaho, that would be valid as against a non-resident attaching creditor, the latter being entitled to the same rights as a citizen of Idaho; that the recognition by one State of the laws of another State governing the transfer of property rested on the principle of comity, which always yielded when the policy of the State where the property was located had prescribed a different rule of transfer from that of the domicil of the owner; that this assignment was contrary to the statutes and the settled policy of Idaho, in that it provided for preferences; that the fact that the assignee had taken and was in possession of the property could not affect the result; and that the distinction between a voluntary and an involuntary assignment was entitled to no con sideration.

Undoubtedly there is some conflict of authority on the ques tion as to how far the transfer of personal property by assign ment or sale, lawfully made in the country of the domicil of the owner, will be held to be valid in the court of another country, where the property is situated and a different local rule prevails.

We had occasion to consider this subject somewhat in *Cole v. Cunningham,* 133 U. S. 107, 129, and it was there said: "*Great contrariety* of state decision exists upon this general topic, and it may be fairly stated that, as between citizens of the state of the forum, and the assignee appointed under the laws of another state, the claim of the former will be held superior to that of the latter by the courts of the former; while, as between the assignee and citizens of his own state and the state of the debtor, the laws of such state will ordinarily be applied in the state of the litigation, unless forbidden by, or inconsistent with, the laws of policy of the latter. Again, although, in some of the states, the fact that the assignee claims under a decree of a court or by virtue of the law of the state of the domicil of the debtor and the attach- ing creditor, and not under a conveyance by the insolvent, is re- garded as immaterial, yet, in most, the distinction between invol- untary transfers of property, such as work by operation of law, as foreign bankrupt and insolvent laws, and a voluntary con- veyance, is recognized. The reason for the distinction is that a *voluntary transfer,* if valid where made, ought generally to be valid everywhere, being the exercise of the personal right of the owner to dispose of his own, while an *assignment by operation of law* has no legal operation out of the state in which the law was passed. This is a reason which applies to citizens of the actual *situs* of the property when that is elsewhere than 'at the domicil of the insolvent, and the controversy has chiefly been as

to whether property so situated can pass even by a voluntary conveyance."

We have here a voluntary transfer of his property by a citizen of Utah for the payment of his debts, with preferences, which
transfer was valid in Utah, where made, and was consummated
by the delivery of the property in Idaho, where it was situated,
and then taken on an attachment in favor of a creditor not a
resident or citizen of Idaho. Was there anything in the statutes
or established policy of Idaho invalidating such transfer?

Title XII of Part Second of the Revised Statutes of the Territory of Idaho, entitled "Of proceedings in insolvency," (Rev.
Stats. Idaho, §§ 5875 to 5932,) provided that "no assignment of
any insolvent debtor, otherwise than as provided in this title, is
legal or binding on creditors;" that creditors should share *pro
rata*, "without priority or preference whatever;" for the discharge
of the insolvent debtor upon compliance with the provisions of
the title, by application for such discharge by petition to the District Court of the county in which he had resided for six months
next preceding, with schedule and inventory annexed, giving a
true statement of debts and liabilities and a description of all the
insolvent's estate, including his homestead, if any, and all property exempt by law from execution. The act applied to corporations and partnerships, and declared that if the partners resided
in different counties, that court in which the petition was first filed
should retain jurisdiction over the case. Nothing is clearer from
its various provisions than that the statute had reference only to
domestic insolvents. As pointed out by Judge Berry in his dissenting opinion, the first section of the fifty-eight upon this subject, in providing that "every insolvent debtor may, upon compliance with the provisions of this title, be discharged from his
debts and liabilities," demonstrates this. The legislature of Idaho
certainly did not attempt to discharge citizens of other jurisdictions from their liabilities, nor intend that personal property in
Idaho, belonging to citizens of other States or Territories, could
not be applied to the payment of their debts unless they acquired
a six months' residence in some county of Idaho, and went through
its insolvency court.

The instrument in controversy did not purport to be executed under any statute, but was an ordinary common law assignment with preferences, and as such was not, in itself, illegal.
Jewell v. Knight, 123 U. S. 426, 434. And it was found as a fact
that it was valid under the laws of Utah. While the statute of

Idaho prescribed *pro rata,* distribution without preference, in assignments under the statute, it did not otherwise deal with the disposition of his property by a debtor nor prohibit preferences between non-resident debtors and creditors through an assignment valid by the laws of the debtor's domicil. No just rule required the courts of Idaho, at the instance of a citizen of another state, to adjudge a transfer, valid at common law and by the law of the place where it was made, to be invalid, because preferring creditors elsewhere, and, therefore, in contravention of the Idaho statute and the public policy therein indicated in respect of its own citizens, proceeding thereunder. The law of the *situs* was not incompatible with the law of the domicil.

In *Halsted* v. *Strauss,* 32 Fed. Rep. 279, 280, which was an action in New Jersey involving an attachment there by a New York creditor as against the voluntary assignee of a New York firm, the property in dispute being an indebtedness of one Strauss, a resident of New Jersey, to the firm, Mr. Justice Bradley remarked: "It is true that the statute of New Jersey declares that assignments in trust for the benefit of creditors shall be for their equal benefit, in proportion to their several demands, and that all preferences shall be deemed fraudulent and void. (But this law applies only to New Jersey assignments, and not to those made in other States, which affect property or creditors in New Jersey.) It has been distinctly held by the courts of New Jersey that a voluntary assignment made by a non-resident debtor, which is valid by the law of the place where made, cannot be impeached in New Jersey, with regard to property situated there, by non-resident debtors. *Bentley* v. *Whittemore,* 4 C. E. Green, (19 N. J. Eq.) 462; *Moore* v. *Bonnell,* 2 Vroom (31 N. J. Law,) 90. The execution of foreign assignments in New Jersey will be enforced by its courts as a matter of comity, except when it would injure its own citizens; then it will not. If Deering, Milliken & Co. were a New Jersey firm they could successfully resist the execution of the assignment in this case. But they are not; they are a New York firm. New York is their business residence and domicil. The mere fact that one of the partners resides in New Jersey cannot alter the case. The New Jersey courts in carrying out the policy of its statutes for the protection of its citizens, by refusing to carry into effect a valid foreign assignment, will be governed by reasonable rules of general jurisprudence; and it seems to me that to refuse validity to the assignment in the present case would be unreasonable and uncalled for."

In *May* v. *First National Bank*, 122 Illinois, 551, 556, the Supreme Court of Illinois held that the provision in the statute of that State prohibiting all preferences in assignments by debtors applied only to those made in the State, and not to those made in other States; that the statute concerned only domestic assignments and domestic creditors; and the court, in reference to the contention that, if not against the terms, the assignment was against the policy of the statute, said: "An assignment giving preference, though made without the State, might, as against creditors residing in this State, with some reason, be claimed to be invalid, as being against the policy of the statute in respect of domestic creditors—that it was the policy of the law that there should be an equal distribution in respect to them. But as the statute has no application to assignments, made without the State, we cannot see that there is any policy of the law which can be said to exist with respect to such assignments, or with respect to foreign creditors, and why non-residents are not left free to execute voluntary assignments, with or without preferences, among foreign creditors, as they may see fit, so long as domestic creditors are not affected thereby, without objection lying to such assignments that they are against the policy of our law. The statute was not made for the regulation of foreign assignments, or for the distribution, under such assignments, of a debtor's property among foreign creditors."

In *Frank* v. *Bobbitt*, 155 Mass. 112, a voluntary assignment made in North Carolina and valid there, was held valid and enforced in Massachusetts as against a subsequent attaching creditor of the assignors, resident in still another State, and not a part to the assignment. The Supreme Judicial Court observed that the assignment was a voluntary and not a statutory one; that the attaching creditors were not resident in Massachusetts; that at common law in that State an assignment for the benefit of reditors which created preferences was not void for that reason; and that there was no statute which rendered invalid such an assignment when made by parties living in another State, and affecting property in Massachusetts, citing *Train* v. *Kendall*, 137 Mass. 366. Referring to the general rule that a contract, valid by the law of the place where made, would be regarded as valid elsewhere, and stating that "it is not necessary to inquire whether this rule rests on the comity which prevails between different states and countries, or is a recognition of the general right which everyone has to dispose of his property or to contract concerning it as he chooses," the court said that the only qualification annexed to voluntary assignments made by debtors living in another State had been "that this court would not sustain them if to do so would be prejudicial to the interests of our own citizens or opposed to public policy." And added: "As to the claim of the plaintiffs that they should stand as well as if they were citizens of this State, it may be said, in the first place, that the qualification attached to foreign assignments is in favor of our own citizens as such, and in the next place, that the assignment being valid by the law of the place where it was made, and not adverse to the interests of our citizens nor opposed to public policy, no cause appears for pronouncing it invalid." And see, among numerous cases to the same effect, *Butler* v. *Wendell*, 57 Michigan, 62; *Receiver* v. *First National Bank*, 7 Stewart, (34 N. J. Eq. 450); *Egbert* v. *Baker*, 58 Connecticut, 319; *Chafee* v. *Fourth National Bank of New York*, 71 Maine, 514; *Ockerman* v. *Cross*, 54 N. Y. 29; *Weider* v. *Maddox*, 66 Texas, 372; *Thurston* v. *Rosenfield*, 42 Missouri, 474.

We do not regard our decision in *Green* v. *Van Buskirk*, 5 Wall. 307; 7 Wall. 139, as to the contrary. That case was fully considered in *Cole* v. *Cunningham, supra,* and need not be reëxamined. The controversy was between two creditors of the owner of personalty in Illinois, one of them having obtained judgment in a suit in which the property was attached and the other claiming under a chattel mortgage. By the Illinois statute such a mortgage was void as against third persons, unless acknowledged and recorded as provided, or unless the property was delivered to and remained with the mortgagee, and the mortgage in that case was not acknowledged and recorded, nor had possession been taken. All parties were citizens of New York, but that fact was not considered sufficient to overcome the distinctively politic and coercive law of Illinois.

In our judgment the Idaho statute was inapplicable and the assignment was in contravention of no settled policy of that Territory. It was valid at common law, and valid in Utah, and the assignee having taken possession before the attachment issued, the District Court was right in the conclusions of law at which it arrived.

The judgment is reversed and the cause remanded to the Supreme Court of the State of Idaho for further proceedings not inconsistent with this opinion.

Judgment reversed.

HERVEY v. LOCOMOTIVE WORKS, 1876.

[93 U. S. 664.]

ERROR to the Circuit Court of the United States for the Southern District of Illinois.

On the twenty-first day of August, 1871, the Rhode Island Locomotive Works entered into a contract with J. Edwin Conant & Co., as follows:—

"This agreement made this twenty-first day of August, 1871, by and between the Rhode Island Locomotive Works of Providence, R. I., party of the first part, and J. Edwin Conant & Co., contractors for the Chicago & Illinois Southern Railroad Co., party of the second part, witnesseth:

"That whereas the said party of the first part is the owner of one locomotive-engine and tender complete, named Alfred N. Smyser, No. 3; and whereas the said party of the second part is desirous of using and eventually purchasing the same: now, therefore, in consideration of the sum of one dollar to the said party of the first part by the said party of the second part in hand paid, the receipt whereof is hereby acknowledged, and in consideration of the covenants and agreements hereinafter contained, the said party of the first part agrees to let and lease, and hereby does let and lease, to the said party of the second part, and the said party of the second part agrees to have and take from the said party of the first part, the said one locomotive-engine and tender, with the right to place the same upon its railroad, and to use the same in the usual manner in transacting the business of the said railroad; and in consideration thereof the said party of the second part hereby covenants and agrees to pay to the said party of the first part for the use and rent of the same the sum of $12,093.96 in notes, as follows:—

10% cash	$1,150.00
One note due Feb. 24, 1872 . .	3,580.16
One " " May 24, 1872	3,647.90
One " " Aug. 24, 1872	3,715.90
	$12,093.96

"And the said party of the second part hereby further covenants and agrees, during the time hereby demised, to keep and maintain the said one locomotive-engine and tender in as good condition as it now is, reasonable and ordinary wear and tear excepted; but it is understood and agreed, that any injury by collision, by running off the track, or by fire, or by destruction from any cause, is not to be considered reasonable and ordinary wear and tear.

"And the said party of the first part, in consideration of the foregoing, further covenants and agrees, that in case said party of the second part shall pay the said notes promptly, as hereinbefore set forth, upon payment of the last-mentioned note, viz., $3,715.90, and all renewals of same, it will grant, sell, assign, transfer, and convey to the said party of the second part the said one locomotive-engine and tender in the condition it then is, to have and to hold the same to the said party of the second part, its legal representatives, successors, and assigns forever. And the said party of the second part further covenants and agrees, that if it shall fail to make any of the said payments when due, then the said party of the first part shall be at liberty, and it shall be lawful for it, to enter upon and take possession of the said one locomotive-engine and tender, and to that end to enter upon the road and other property of said party of the second part.

"And the second party of the second part further covenants and agrees, that, in case of any default on its part in any of the payments, as hereinbefore provided, it will, within thirty days thereafter, deliver the said one locomotive-engine and tender to the said party of the first part.

"And the said party of the first part shall thereafter, upon thirty days' written notice to the said party of the second part of the times and place of sale, proceed to sell the one locomotive-engine and tender, and shall apply the proceeds of such sales, first, to the payment of the expenses of the sale; second, to the payment of any balance then due, or thereafter to become due, for or on account of the rent, as hereinbefore provided; and, if after these payments there shall remain any balance of the proceeds of the sale, the same shall be paid to the said party of the second part.

"And the said party of the second part further covenants agrees, that they will not in any way exercise or claim the right to release, incumber, or in any way dispose of said one locomotive-engine and tender, or employ them during the term of this lease in any other way than in the service of J. Edwin Conant & Co., contractors for the Chicago & Illinois Southern Railroad Company, or in any way or manner interfere with the said party of the first part in repossessing and retaking said one locomotive-engine and

tender, should default be made in any of the hereinbefore provided
for payments, but the full legal right and title of said one locomotive-engine and tender shall and does remain in the Rhode Island
Locomotive Works, as fully, to all intents and purposes, as though
the lease had not been made.

"And the said party of the first part hereby covenants and
agrees, that if the said party of the second part shall and do well
and truly make each of the payments aforesaid at the times hereinbefore specified, without any let or hindrance or delay whatever as
to any or either of said payments, that upon the last-mentioned
payment, viz., $3,715.90, and all renewals being made, as well as
each and all of the other said payments, the said party of the first ·
part will and shall convey the said one locomotive-engine and tender to the said party of the second part, and give them a full
acquittance for the same, and that the title thereto shall *ipso facto,*
by the completion of such payment, vest in the said J. Edwin Conant & Co., contractors for the Chicago & Illinois Southern Railroad Company.

"In witness whereof, the parties hereto have hereunto set the
corporate seal, by the respective officers duly authorized.

"RHODE ISLAND LOCOMOTIVE WORKS.

"EDW. P. MASON, *Treasurer.*	SEAL RHODE ISLAND
"J. EDWIN CONANT & CO.,	LOCOMOTIVE WORKS,
Contractors C. & Ill. So. R. R."	PROVIDENCE, R. I.

Which agreement was indorsed as follows:—

"STATE OF ILLINOIS, CUMBERLAND COUNTY:

"I hereby certify that the within instrument was filed in this
office for record on the twenty-eighth day of January, 1873, at
two o'clock P. M., and duly recorded in book D of mortgages, page
485, and examined.

"ANDREW CARSON,

"*Clerk and Ex-Officio Recorder.*"

It was admitted that the agreement was executed at its place
of business, in Rhode Island, by the Rhode Island Locomotive
Works, and in New York by Conant & Co., where they resided;
that Conant & Co. paid no part of the principal of the purchase-
money except the amount admitted on the face of the agreement;
and that they obtained possession of said engine and its tender
under said agreement, and took it to Illinois.

On the 28th of October, 1871, by virtue of a writ of attachment issued out of the Court of Common Pleas of Coles County, Illinois, in an action of assumpsit wherein Conant & Co. were defendants, the sheriff seized the Smyser as their property, and sold it to the plaintiff in error, Hervey.

On the 29th of January, 1873, the marshal of the United States for the southern district of Illinois took possession of the Smyser under a writ of replevin sued out of the Circuit Court of the United States for that district by the Rhode Island Locomotive Works against Hervey, and the Paris and Decatur Railroad Company.

At the trial, the court below found a special verdict as follows:—

That the lease offered in evidence by plaintiff was a subsisting executory contract between the parties thereto.

That the plaintiff had not parted with the legal possession of the locomotive in controversy.

That the plaintiff had never received payment for the locomotive in controversy other or further than as stated in the face of their lease.

That the plaintiff delivered to Conant & Co. the said locomotive to be used by them in Illinois, and that said locomotive was so used in that State.

That the possession of Conant & Co. was the possession of the plaintiff.

That the defendant obtained possession of the locomotive in controversy in due form of law, under execution, levy, and sale, in pursuance of a valid judgment obtained in a court of competent jurisdiction, after due service upon the parties thereto in a suit against Conant & Co.

That a sale under said execution was, by an officer duly authorized thereto, made to the defendant, Robert G. Hervey, and that payment was made, in the full amount bid at said sale, by said Hervey to said officer, and that the said officer delivered the said locomotive to said Hervey.

That, subsequent to such sale and delivery by said officer to said Hervey, plaintiffs placed upon record, in the proper recorder's office in the county of Coles, in the State of Illinois, where the said property was held, the said lease, in the chattel-mortgage records in said county.

That said recording of said lease was more than one year subsequent to the sale of said locomotive under said execution and levy.

That said sale by said officer to said Hervey was under a special execution, as shown by the public records of said Coles County.

Whereupon the court found for the plaintiff, and gave judgment accordingly.

MR. JUSTICE DAVIS delivered the opinion of the court.

It was decided by this court in *Green* v. *Van Buskirk*, 5 Wall. 307, 7 id. 139, that the liability of property to be sold under legal process, issuing from the courts of the State where it is situated, must be determined by the law there, rather than that of the jurisdiction where the owner lives. These decisions rest on the ground that every State has the right to regulate the transfer of property within its limits, and that whoever sends property to it impliedly submits to the regulations concerning its transfer in force there, although a different rule of transfer prevails in the jurisdiction where he resides. He has no absolute right to have the transfer of property, lawful in that jurisdiction, respected in the courts of the State where it is found, and it is only on a prin ciple of comity that it is ever allowed. But this principle yields when the laws and policy of the latter State conflict with those of the former.

The policy of the law in Illinois will not permit the owner of personal property to sell it, either absolutely or conditionally, and still continue in possession of it. Possession is one of the strongest evidences of title to this class of property, and cannot be rightfully separated from the title, except in the manner pointed out by statute. The courts of Illinois say that to suffer without notice to the world the real ownership to be in one person, and the ostensible ownership in another, gives a false credit to the latter, and in this way works an injury to third persons. Accordingly, the actual owner of personal property creating an interest in another, to whom it is delivered, if desirous of preserving a lien on it, must comply with the provisions of the Chattel-Mortgage Act. R. S. Ill. 1874, 711, 712. It requires that the instrument of conveyance, if it have the effect to preserve a mortgage or lien on the property, must be recorded, whether the party to it be a resident or non-resident of the State. If this be not done, the instrument, so far as third persons are concerned, has no validity.

Secret liens which treat the vendor of personal property, who has delivered possession of it to the purchaser, as the owner until the payment of the purchase-money, cannot be maintained in Illinois. They are held to be constructively fraudulent as to creditors, and the property, so far as their rights are concerned, is considered as belonging to the purchaser holding the possession. *McCormick* v. *Hadden,* 37 Ill. 370; *Ketchum* v. *Watson,* 24 id. 591. Nor is the transaction changed by the agreement assuming the form of a lease. In determining the real character of a contract, courts will always look to its purpose, rather than to the name given to it by the parties. If that purpose be to give the vendor a lien on the property until payment in full of the purchase-money, it is liable to be defeated by creditors of the purchaser who is in possession of it. This was held in *Murch* v. *Wright,* 46 id. 488. In that case the purchaser took from the seller a piano at the price of $700. He paid $50 down, which was called rent for the first month, and agreed to pay, as rent, $50 each month, until the whole amount should be paid, when he was to own the piano. The court held, "that it was a mere subterfuge to call this transaction a lease," and that it was a conditional sale, with the right of rescission on the part of the vendor, in case the purchaser should fail in payment of his installments,—a contract legal and valid as between the parties, but subjecting the vendor to lose his lien in case the property, while in possession of the purchaser, should be levied upon by his creditors. That case and the one at bar are alike in all essential particulars.

The engine Smyser, the only subject of controversy in this suit, was sold on condition that each and all of the installments should be regularly paid, with a right of rescission on the part of the vendor in case of default in any of the specified payments.

It is true the instrument of conveyance purports to be a lease, and the sums stipulated to be paid are for rent; but this form was used to cover the real transaction, as much so as was the rent of the piano in *Murch* v. *Wright, supra.* There the price of the piano was to be paid in thirteen months, and here, that of the engine, $12,093.96, in one year. It was evidently not the intention that this large sum should be paid as rent for the mere use of the engine for one year. If so, why agree to sell and convey the full title on the payment of the last installment? In both cases, the stipulated price of the property was to be paid in short installments, and no words employed by the parties can have the effect of changing the true nature of the contracts. In the case at bar the agreement contemplated that the engine should be removed to the State of Illinois, and used by Conant & Co., in the prosecution of their business as constructors of a railroad. It was accordingly taken there and put to the use for which it was purchased; but while in the possession o.' Conant & Co., who exercised complete ownership over it, it was seized and sold, in the local courts of Illinois, as their property. These proceedings were valid in the jurisdiction where they took place, and must be respected by the Federal tribunals.

The Rock Island Locomotive Works took the risk of losing its lien in case the property, while in the possession of Conant & Co., should be levied on by their creditors, and it cannot complain, as the laws of Illinois pointed out a way to preserve and perfect its lien.

By stipulation the judgment of the court below is affirmed as to the locomotive Olney, No. 1.

As to the locomotive and tender called Alfred N. Smyser, No. 3,   *Judgment reversed.*

MARVIN SAFE CO. v. NORTON, 1886.

[48 N. J. L. 410.]

On May 1st, 1884, one Samuel N. Schwartz, of Hightstown, Mercer county, New Jersey, went to Philadelphia, Pennsylvania, and there, in the office of the prosecutors, executed the following instrument:

"May 1st, 1884.

'*Marvin Safe Company:*

"Please send, as per mark given below, one second-hand safe, for which the undersigned agrees to pay the sum of eighty-four dollars ($84), seven dollars cash, and balance seven dollars per month. Terms cash, delivered on board at Philadelphia or New York, unless otherwise stated in writing. It is agreed that Marvin Safe Company shall not relinquish its title to said safe, but shall remain the sole owners thereof until above sum is fully paid in money. In event of failure to pay any of said installments or notes, when same shall become due, then all of said installments or notes remaining unpaid shall immediately becomes due. The Marvin Safe Company may, at their option, remove said safe without legal process. It is expressly understood that there are no conditions whatever not stated in this memorandum, and the undersigned agrees to accept and pay for safe in accordance therewith.

SAMUEL N. SCHWARTZ.

"Mark—Samuel L. Schwartz, Hightstown, New Jersey.
"Route—New Jersey.
"Not accountable for damages after shipment."

Schwartz paid the first installment of $7 May 1st, 1884, and the safe was shipped to him the same day. He afterwards paid two installments, of $7 each, by remittance to Philadelphia by check. Nothing more was paid.

On July 30th, 1884, Schwartz sold and delivered the safe to Norton for $55. Norton paid him the purchase money. He bought and paid for the safe without notice of Schwartz's agreement with the prosecutors. Norton took possession of the safe and removed it to his office. Schwartz is insolvent and has absconded.

The prosecutor brought trover against Norton, and in the court below the defendant recovered judgment, on the ground that the defendant, having bought and paid for the safe *bona fide*, the title to the safe, by the law of Pennsylvania, was transferred to him.

The opinion of the court was delivered by

DEPUE, J. The contract expressed in the written order of May, 1884, signed by Schwartz, is for the sale of the property to him conditionally, the vendor reserving the title, notwithstanding delivery, until the contract price should be paid. The courts of Pennsylvania make a distinction between the bailment of a chattel, with power in the bailee to become the owner on payment of the price agreed upon, and the sale of a chattel with a stipulation that the title shall not pass to the purchaser until the contract price shall be paid. On this distinction the courts of that state hold that a bailment of chattels, with an option in the bailee to become the owner on payment of the price agreed upon, is valid, and that the right of the bailor to resume possession on nonpayment of the contract price is secure against creditors of the bailee and *bona fide* purchasers from him; but that upon the delivery of personal property to a purchaser under a contract of sale, the reservation of title in the vendor until the contract price is paid is void as against creditors of the purchaser or a *bona fide* purchaser from him. *Clow v. Woods*, 5 *S. & R.* 275; *Enlow v. Klein*, 79 *Penna. St.* 488; *Haak v. Linderman*, 64 *Id.* 499; *Stadfeld v. Huntsman*, 92 *Id.* 53; *Brunswick v. Hoover*, 95 *Id.* 508; 1 *Benj. on Sales* (*Corbin's ed.*) § 446; 30 *Am. Law Reg.* 224, *Note to Lewis v. McCabe.*

In the most recent case in the Supreme Court of Pennsylvania Mr. Justice Sterrett said: "A present sale and delivery of personal property to the vendee, coupled with an agreement that the title shall not vest in the latter unless he pays the price agreed upon

at the time appointed therefor, and that in default of such payment the vendor may recover possession of the property, is quite
different in its effect from a bailment for use, or, as it is sometimes called, a lease of the property, coupled with an agreement
whereby the lessee may subsequently become owner of the property
upon payment of a price agreed upon. As between the parties
to such contracts, both are valid and binding; but as to creditors,
the latter is good while the former is invalid." *Forest* v. *Nelson,*
19 *Rep.* 38; 108 *Penna St.* 481.

The cases cited show that the Pennsylvania courts hold the
same doctrine with respect to *bona fide* purchasers as to creditors.

In this state, and in nearly all of our sister states, conditional
sales—that is, sales of personal property on credit, with delivery of
possession to the purchaser and a stipulation that the title shall remain in the vendor until the contract price is paid—have been held
valid, not only against the immediate purchaser, but also against
his creditors and *bona fide* purchasers from him, unless the vendor
has conferred upon his vendee *indicia* of title beyond mere possession, or has forfeited his right in the property by conduct which
the law regards as fraudulent. The cases are cited in *Cole* v.
Berry, 13 *Vroom* 308; *Midland R. R. Co.* v. *Hitchcock,* 10 *Stew.
Eq.* 549, 559; 1 *Benj. on Sales (Corbin's ed.)* §§ 437-460; 1
Smith's Lead. Cas. (8th ed.) 33-90; 30 *Am. Law Reg.* 224, *note
to Lewis* v. *McCabe;* 15 *Am. Law Rev.* 380, *tit.* "*Conversion
by purchase*" The doctrine of the courts of Pennsylvania is founded upon the doctrine of *Twyne's Case,* 3 *Rep.* 80,
and *Edwards* v. *Harbin,* 2 *T. R.* 587, that the possession of chattels
under a contract of sale without title is an indelible badge of fraud
—a doctrine repudiated quite generally by the courts of this country, and especially in this state. *Runyon* v. *Groshon,* 1 *Beas.* 86;
Broadway Bank v. *McElrath,* 2 *Id.* 24; *Miller* ads. *Pancoast,* 5
Dutcher 250. The doctrine of the Pennsylvania courts is disapproved by the American editors of Smith's Leading Cases in the
note to *Twyne's Case,* 1 *Sm. Lead. Cas. (8th ed.)* 33, 34, and by
Mr. Landreth in his note to *Lewis* v. *McCabe,* 30 *Am. Law Reg.*
224; but nevertheless the Supreme Court of that state, in the latest
case on the subject—*Forest* v. *Nelson,* decided February 16th,
1885—has adhered to the doctrine. It must therefore be regarded
as the law of Pennsylvania that upon a sale of personal property
with delivery of possession to the purchaser, an agreement that
title should not pass until the contract price should be paid is
valid as between the original parties, but that creditors of the pur-

chaser, or a purchaser from him *bona fide,* by a levy under execution or a *bona fide* purchase, will acquire a better title than the original purchaser had—a title superior to that reserved by his vendor. So far as the law of Pennsylvania is applicable to the transaction it must determine the rights of these parties.

The contract of sale between the Marvin Safe Company and Schwartz was made at the company's office in Philadelphia. The contract contemplated performance by delivery of the safe in Philadelphia to the carrier for transportation to Hightstown. When the terms of sale are agreed upon, and the vendor has done everything that he has to do with the goods, the contract of sale becomes absolute. *Leonard* v. *Davis,* 1 *Black* 476; 1 *Benj. on Sales,* § 308. Delivery of the safe to the carrier in pursuance of the contract was delivery to Schwartz, and was the execution of the contract of sale. His title, such as it was, under the terms of the contract was thereupon complete.

The validity, construction and legal effect of a contract may depend either upon the law of the place where it is made or of the place where it is to be performed, or, if it relate to movable property, upon the law of the *situs* of the property, according to circumstances; but when the place where the contract is made is also the place of performance and of the *situs* of the property, the law of that place enters into and becomes part of the contract, and determines the rights of the parties to it. *Fredericks* v. *Frazer,* 4 *Zab.* 162; *Dacosta* v. *Davis, Id.* 319; *Bulkley* v. *Honold,* 19 *How.* 390; *Scudder* v. *Union National Bank,* 91 *U. S.* 406; *Pritchard* v. *Norlon,* 106 *Id.* 124; *Morgan* v. *N. O., M. & T. R. R. Co.,* 2 *Woods* 244; *Simpson* v. *Fogo,* 9 *Jur.* (*N. S.*) 403; *Whart. Confl. of Law,* §§ 341, 345, 401, 403, 418; *Parr* v. *Brady,* 8 *Vroom* 201. The contract between Schwartz and the company having been made, and also executed in Pennsylvania by the delivery of the safe to him, as between him and the company Schwartz's title will be determined by the law of Pennsylvania. By the law of that state the condition expressed in the contract of sale that the safe company should not relinquish title until the contract price was paid, and that on the failure to pay any of the installments of the price the company might resume possession of the property, was valid as between Schwartz and the company. By his contract Schwartz obtained possession of the safe and a right to acquire title on payment of the contract price; but until that condition was performed the title was in the company. In this situtaion of affairs the safe was brought into this state, and the property became sub ject to our laws.

The contract of Norton, the defendant, with Schwartz for the purchase of the safe was made at Hightstown in this state. The property was then in this state, and the contract of purchase was executed by delivery of possession in this state. The contract of purchase, the domicile of the parties to it, and the *situs* of the subject matter of purchase were all within this state. In every respect the transaction between Norton and Schwartz was a New Jersey transaction. Under these circumstances, by principles of law which are indisputable, the construction and legal effect of the contract of purchase, and the rights of the purchaser under it are determined by the law of this state. By the law of this state Norton, by his purchase, acquired only the title of his vendor— only such title as the vendor had when the property was brought into this state and became subject to our laws.

It is insisted that inasmuch as Norton's purchase, if made in Pennsylvania, would have given him a title superior to that of the safe company, that therefore his purchase here should have that effect, on the theory that the law of Pennsylvania, which subjected the title of the safe company to the rights of a *bona fide* purchaser from Schwartz, was part of the contract between the company and Schwartz. There is no provision in the contract between the safe company and Schwartz that he should have power, under any circumstances, to sell and make title to a purchaser. Schwartz's disposition of the property was not in conformity with his contract, but in violation of it. His contract, as construed by the laws of Pennsylvania, gave him no title which he could lawfully convey. To maintain title against the safe company Norton must build up in himself a better title than Schwartz had. He can accomplish that result only by virtue of the law of the jurisdiction in which he acquired his rights.

The doctrine of the Pennsylvania courts that a reservation of title in the vendor upon a conditional sale is void as against creditors and *bona fide* purchasers, is not a rule affixing a certain construction and legal effect to a contract made in that state. The legal effect of such a contract is conceded to be to leave property in the vendor. The law acts upon the fact of possession by the purchaser under such an arrangement, and makes it an indelible badge of fraud and a forfeiture of the vendor's reserved title as in favor of creditors and *bona fide* purchasers. The doctrine is founded upon considerations of public policy adopted in that state, and applies to the fact of possession and acts of ownership under such a contract, without regard to the place where the contract was made, or its legal effect considered as a contract. In *McCabe v. Blymyry,* 9 *Phila. Rep.* 615, the controversy was with respect to the rights of a mortgagee under a chattel mortgage. The mortgage had been made and recorded in Maryland, where the chattel was when the mortgage was given, and by the law of Maryland was valid though the mortgagor retained possession. The chattel was afterwards brought into Pennsylvania, and the Pennsylvania court held that the mortgage, though valid in the state where it was made, would not be enforced by the courts of Pennsylvania as against a creditor or purchaser who had acquired rights in the property after it had been brought to that state; that the mortgagee, by allowing the mortgagor to retain possession of the property and bring it into Pennsylvania, and exercise notorious acts of ownership, lost his right under the mortgage as against an intervening Pennsylvania creditor or purchaser, on the ground that the contract was in contravention of the law and policy of that state. Under substantially the same state of facts this court sustained the title of a mortgagee under a mortgage made in another state, as against a *bona fide* purchaser who had bought the property of the mortgagor in this state, for the reason that the possession of the chattel by the mortgagor was not in contravention of the public policy of this state. *Parr* v. *Brady,* 8 *Vroom* 201.

The public policy which has given rise to the doctrine of the Pennsylvania courts is local, and the law which gives effect to it is also local, and has no extra-territorial effect. In the case in hand the safe was removed to this state by Schwartz as soon as be became the purchaser. His possession under the contract has been exclusively in this state. That possession violated no public policy—not the public policy of Pennsylvania, for the possession was not in that state; nor the public policy of this state, for in this state possession under a conditional sale is regarded as lawful, and does not invalidate the vendor's title unless impeached for actual fraud. If the right of a purchaser, under a purchase in this state, to avoid the reserved title in the original vendor on such grounds be conceded, the same right must be extended to creditors buying under a judgment and execution in this state; for, by the law of Pennsylvania, creditors and *bona fide* purchasers are put upon the same footing. Neither on principle nor on considerations of convenience or public policy can such a right be conceded. Under such a condition of the law confusion and uncertainty in the title to property would be introduced, and the transmission of the title to movable property, the *situs* of which is in this state, would depend, not upon our laws, but upon the laws and public policy of sister states or foreign countries. A purchaser of chattels in this state, which his vendor has obtained in New York or in most of our sister states under a contract of conditional sale, would take no title; if obtained under a conditional sale in Pennsylvania, his title would be good; and the same uncertainty would exist in the title of purchasers of property so circumstanced at a sale under judgment and execution.

The title was in the safe company when the property in dispute was removed from the State of Pennsylvania. Whatever might impair that title—the continued possession and exercise of acts of ownership over it by Schwartz and the purchase by Norton —occurred in this state. The legal effect and consequences of those acts must be adjudged bv the law of this state. By the law of this state it was not illegal nor contrary to public policy for the company to leave Schwartz in possession as ostensibe owner, and no forfeiture of the company's title could result therefrom. By the law of this state Norton, by his purchase, acquired only such title as Schwartz had under his contract with the company. Nothing has occurred which by our law will give him a better title.

The judgment should be reversed.

CLEVELAND MACHINE WORKS v. LANG, 1892.

[67 N. H. 348.]

REPLEVIN, for two machines, hereinafter described, situate in the Granite Mills in Northfield, and attached as both real and personal estate by the defendant, a deputy sheriff, on a writ in favor of Denny, Rice & Co. against Edward P. Parsons. Plea, the general issue, and a brief statement that the machines were the property of said Parsons, and that they had become annexed to the Granite Mills and liable to attachment as part of the realty. Facts found by the court.

The negotiations for the machines were had and completed with the plaintiffs at their place of business in Worcester, Mass., by one Green, as agent for Parsons who resided in Boston. Aside from the agreement of the plaintiffs to send one of their employés to Northfield to set up the machines, which they did, the terms of the contract were as follows·

"TILTON, N. H., Oct. 14, 1890.

"Borrowed and received of Cleveland Machine Works, Worcester, Mass., the following macninery. If the price set against them is paid as per memorandum below, the property is then to belong to Edward P. Parsons, otherwise it remains the property of the said Cleveland Machine Works. Notes and drafts, if given, are not to be considered as payments until they are paid; and all part payments are to be forfeited by the non-payment of balance at time stated. In the meantime the said Edward P. Parsons is to keep the property in good order, and may use it free from any other charge; and the said Edward P. Parsons further agrees to pay such price as per memorandum below, and to keep the property sufficiently insured for the benefit of the said Cleveland Machine Works. List of machinery included in the above agreement as follows, with prices annexed:

One 10-4 Cloth Dryer with No. 8 Exhauster, 1,000 feet Heater, and clothing of brass wire set in leather and paper, $1,100.00
Terms of payment: $300.00 cash thirty days after shipment, balance four months note, $800.00, dated at time of shipment and interest added.
One 90-inch Blanket Gig and one set of slats, 215.00
Terms of payment: $50.00 cash thirty days after shipment, balance ($165.00) five months note, dated at time of shipment, with interest added.

EDWARD P. PARSONS."

This paper was signed by Parsons in Boston, and delivered to the plaintiffs before the machines were shipped, but it has never been recorded in Northfield, or elsewhere in this state. Soon afterwards the plaintiffs shipped the machines from Worcester, Parsons paying the freight to Northfield. The machines were placed in his mill, and used therein until his failure, which occurred shortly afterwards. The dryer weighed 7,000 pounds and the gig 3,800 pounds. The gig was not fastened to the floor at all, and the dryer by only two or three screws. Parsons never paid but $100 on the contract, and never claimed the machines to be his property. At the time of the Denny, Rice & Co. attachment, neither they nor the defendant had notice of the plaintiffs' lien.

CLARK, J. By the terms of the contract the machines were to remain the property of the Cleveland Machine Works until paid for. The contract was negotiated in Massachusetts, by citizens of Massachusetts, respecting property situated in Massachusetts.

The shipment of the machines at Worcester—Parsons paying the freight from that point—made Worcester the place of delivery, and vested in Parsons all the right and interest he ever acquired in the property. The agreement to send a man to set up the machines at Northfield was not a condition precedent to the vesting of the conditional title in Parsons, any more than an agreement to furnish instruction as to the mode of operating the machines would have been. The written agreement shows that the parties understood that the conditional title passed upon the shipment of the machines, by fixing the time of payment from that date. The contract was a conditional sale of chattels in Massachusetts, negotiated and completed there by Massachusetts parties, and valid by the law of Massachusetts; and being valid where it was made, its validity was not affected by the subsequent removal of the property to New Hampshire. *Sessions* v. *Little,* 9 N. H. 271; *Smith* v. *Godfrey,* 28 N. H. 379; *Stevens* v. *Norris,* 30 N. H. 466.

As a general rule, contracts respecting the sale or transfer of personal property, valid where made and where the property is situated, will be upheld and enforced in another state or country, although not executed according to the law of the latter state, unless such enforcement would be in contravention of positive law and public interests. A personal mortgage of property in another state, executed and recorded according to the laws of that state, is valid against the creditors of the mortgagor attaching the property in this state, although the mortgage is not recorded here. *Offutt* v. *Flagg,* 10 N. H. 46; *Ferguson* v. *Clifford,* 37 N. H. 86. A mortgagor of horses in Massachusetts, bringing them into this state, cannot subject them to a lien for their keeping against the Massachusetts mortgagee. *Sargent* v. *Usher,* 55 N. H. 287. A boarding-house keeper's lien under the laws of Massachusetts is not lost by bringing the property into this state. *Jaquith* v. *American Express Co.,* 60 N. H. 61.

Formerly by the laws of Vermont a chattel mortgage was invalid against creditors of the mortgagor if the property remained in his possession. But it was held in Vermont and in New Hampshire that a mortgage of personal property in New Hampshire, duly executed and recorded according to the law of New Hampshire, was valid against creditors of the mortgagor attaching the property in his possession in Vermont. *Cobb* v. *Buswell,* 37 Vt. 337; *Lathe* v. *Schoff,* 60 N. H. 34. In

Cobb v. *Buswell* the property was taken to Vermont with the consent of the mortgagee, and in *Lathe* v. *Schoff* it was understood, when the mortgage was executed, that the horses mortgaged were to be removed to Vermont by the mortgagor and kept there after the season of summer travel closed. So a chattel mortgage made by a citizen of Massachusetts temporarily in New York with the mortgaged property, if valid by the law of New York, is valid against the creditors of the mortgagor attaching the property in his possession in Massachusetts. *Langworthy* v. *Little,* 12 Cush. 109.

The law of New Hampshire respecting conditional sales has no extra-territorial force, and does not apply to sales made out of the state. Neither the parties nor the subject-matter of the contract respecting the machines were within its operation. If the conditional sale had been made in this state before the statute was enacted requiring an affidavit of the good faith of the transaction and a record in the town clerk's office, it would not have been affected by the statute. When the machines were brought to this state, there was no provision of the statute for recording the plaintiffs' lien. There was no change or transfer of title in this state, and the title of the plaintiffs, valid against creditors under a contract completed in Massachusetts, was not destroyed by the removal of the property to New Hampshire.

Smith v. *Moore,* 11 N. H. 55, cited by the defendant as sustaining the position that the plaintiffs' lien was destroyed because there was no law in this state providing for a record in such a case, is an authority against the defendant. In that case the property was in this state when the mortgage was made, the mortgagor residing out of the state. The court say,—"If the property had been situated out of the state when the mortgage was made, and the mortgage had been valid according to the law of the place, a subsequent removal of the property to this state would not have affected its validity," citing *Offutt* v. *Flagg,* 10 N. H. 46.

Conditional sales were valid in this state without record until January 1, 1886. *McFarland* v. *Farmer,* 42 N. H. 386; *Holt* v. *Holt,* 58 N. H. 276; *Weeks* v. *Pike,* 60 N. H. 447. The statute of 1885, *c.* 30, had no application to contracts between parties residing out of the state, and made no provision for recording such contracts. The fact that the contract is not within the statute is an answer to the position that the plaintiffs' title is to be tested by the law of New Hampshire.

The attachment of the real estate gave the defendant no possession of or right of property in the machines. *Scott* v. *Manchester Print Works*, 44 N. H. 507. By attaching them as personal property, the defendant claims to hold the possession and property in them, as the property of Parsons, for the benefit of the attaching creditors. If Parsons had an attachable interest subject to the plaintiffs' lien, the defendant's claim to hold the entire property under the attachment entitles the plaintiffs to maintain replevin, if they have any title to the machines and there is no estoppel. As between the plaintiffs and Parsons, the machines were the property of the plaintiffs. They were never the property of Parsons. He was simply a bailee, and never claimed to own them.

"Judgment and execution liens attach to the defendant's real, instead of his apparent, interest in the property. It follows from this that the sale made under such a lien can ordinarily transfer no interest beyond that in fact held by the defendant when the lien attached, or acquired by him subsequently thereto and before the sale." Freem. Ex., *s.* 335. A purchaser at a sheriff's sale, there being no estoppel, acquires no title to property not belonging to the debtor. *Bryant* v. *Whitcher*, 52 N. H. 158.

An attaching creditor is not in the position of a purchaser for a valuable consideration without notice of any defect of title. The defendant, and the creditors of Parsons whom he represents, do not occupy the relation of *bona fide* vendees or mortgagees for value without notice. They stand no better than Parsons, who never owned or claimed to own the machines. Their claim to hold the property against the plaintiffs' title is based upon Parson's ownership, and not upon any attempted transfer of title by him to them; and as he had no title they took nothing by the attachment.

The case has no analogy to an attachment of property to which the debtor has a voidable title valid until rescinded (*Bradley* v. *Obear*, 10 N. H. 477), or to the numerous class of cases where the debtor once had a valid title which he has conveyed or transferred in fraud of creditors.

As Parsons had no title to the machines, and as no legal or equitable ground of estoppel to the assertion of the plaintiffs' title is shown, the plaintiffs are entitled to judgment.

Judgment for the plaintiffs.

EMERY v. CLOUGH, 1885.

[63 N. H. 552.]

BILL IN EQUITY, under Gen. Laws, *c.* 209, *s.* 2, for discovery, and the restoration of a municipal bond for $1,000, alleged to belong to the estate of William Emery, the plaintiff's intestate, unlawfully withheld by the defendant; also a suit at law to recover $280 of money claimed to be in the hands of the defendant belonging to the estate. Facts found by the court.

The legal domicile of said William Emery during his whole life was at Loudon, in this state. May 21, 1882, being very sick while temporarily at Montpelier, Vt., he delivered to the defendant as a *donatio causa mortis,* the bond in question, and six days afterwards also delivered to her, as like gifts to several persons residing in Loudon, the sum of $280, to be by her distributed to the parties by him designated, after his death. No one was present when the bond and money were delivered by William to the defendant, and the defendant offers no evidence to prove the same, except her own testimony, and a memorandum signed by William but not witnessed. The plaintiff objected to the evidence offered as incompetent and insufficient. The memorandum may be referred to in argument. No attempt has been made by defendant or any one else to prove the above gifts, according to the requirements of Gen. Laws, *c.* 193, *s.* 17.

SMITH, J. It is contended on the part of the defendant that the transaction in Vermont, whereby the defendant became possessed of the bond, was a *donatio causa mortis,* valid as an executed contract under the laws of Vermont, and therefore valid here. The plaintiff contends that the transaction was in the nature of a testamentary disposition of property, and if valid in Vermont as a *donatio causa mortis,* it is not valid in this state because it was not proved by the testimony of two indifferent witnesses upon petition by the donee to the probate court to establish the gift, filed within sixty days after the decease of the donor. G. L., *c.* 193, *s.* 17. The domicile of the parties at the time of the delivery of the bond to the defendant, and ever afterwards, to the death of the donor, being in this estate, it is claimed that the neglect of the defendant to establish the gift in the probate court is fatal to her right to retain the bond. Every requisite to constitute a valid gift *causa mortis* under the laws of Vermont, where the parties were temporarily residing at the time of the delivery of the bond, was complied with. *Holley v. Adams*, 16 Vt. 206; *Caldwell v. Ren frew*, 33 Vt. 213; *French v. Raymond*, 39 Vt. 623. Every requisite, also, to constitute such a gift under the laws of New Hamp shire was complied with except the *post mortem* proceedings required by our statute. The question therefore is, whether the *lex loci* or the *lex domicilii* governs; and the answer to this question depends upon the legal character and effect of such gifts.

A gift *causa mortis* is often spoken of in the books as a testamentary disposition of property, or as being in the nature of a legacy. *Jones v. Brown*, 34 N. H. 439; 1 Wms. Ex'rs, 686, *n.* 1. And such was the doctrine of the civil law. 2 Kent Com. 444, and authorities cited in note *b*. Such gifts are always made upon condition that they shall be revocable during the life-time of the donor, and that they shall revest in case he shall survive the donee, or shall be delivered from the peril of death in which they were made. The condition need not be expressed, as it is always implied when the gift is made in the extremity of sickness, or in contemplation of death. It is sometimes, perhaps generally, said in the English cases that a gift *causa mortis* does not vest before the donor's death; but in *Nicholas v. Adams*, 2 Whart. (Pa.) 17, *Gibson*, C. J., considered this to be inaccurate, holding that this gift, like every other, is not executory, but executed in the first instance by delivery of the thing, though defeasible by reclamation, the contingency of survivorship, deliverance from peril, or from some other act inconsistent with the gift, and indicating the donor's purpose to resume the possession of the gift. 1 Wms. Ex'rs 686, *n.* 1; *Marshall v. Berry*, 13 Allen 43, 46.

A gift *causa mortis* resembles a testamentary disposition of property in this,—that it is made in contemplation of death, and is revocable during the life of the donor. It is not, however, a testament, but in its essential characteristics is, what its name indicates, a gift. Actual delivery by the donor in his life-time is necessary to its validity, or if the nature of the property is such that it is not susceptible of corporeal delivery, the means of obtaining possession of it must be delivered. The donee's possession must continue during the life of the donor, for recovery of possession by the latter is a revocation of the gift. But in case of a legacy, the possession remains with the testator until his decease. The title to a gift *causa mortis* passes by the delivery, defeasible only in the life-time of the donor, and his death perfects the title in the donee by terminating the donor's right or power of defeasance. The property passes from the donor to the donee directly, and not through the executor or administrator, and after his death it is liable to be divested only in favor of the donor's creditors. In this respect it stands the same as a gift *inter vivos*. It is defeasible in favor of creditors, not because it is testamentary, but because, as against creditors, one cannot give away his property. A gift *causa mortis* is not subject to probate, nor to contribution with lagacies in case the assets are insufficient, nor to any of the incidents of administration. It is not revocable by will, for, as a will does not operate until the decease of the testator, and the donor, at his decease, is divested of his property in the subject of the gift, no right or title in it passes to his representatives. The donee takes the gift, not from the administrator, but against him, and no act or assent on the part of the administrator is necessary to perfect the title of the donee. *Cutting* v. *Gilman*, 41 N. H. 147, 151; *Marshall* v. *Berry, supra; Doty* v. *Willson*, 47 N. Y. 580, 585; *Dole* v. *Lincoln*, 31 Me. 422; *Chase* v. *Redding*, 13 Gray 418; *Basket* v. *Hassell*, 107 U. S. 602; 1 Wms. Ex'rs 686, *n.* 1. A valid gift *inter vivos* may be made on similar terms. *Worth* v. *Case*, 42 N. Y. 362; *Dean* v. *Carruth*, 108 Mass. 242; *Warren* v. *Durfee*, 126 Mass. 338.

A gift *causa mortis* in some respects may be said to resemble a contract, the mutual consent and concurrent will of both parties being necessary to the validity of the transfer. 2 Kent Com. 437, 438; 1 Pars. Cont. 234. Contracts are commonly understood to mean engagements resulting from negotiation. 2 Kent Com. 437. And in *Peirce* v. *Burroughs*, 58 N. H. 302, it was held that the assent of both parties is as necessary to a gift as to a contract.

Prior to the passage of *c.* 106, Laws of 1883, the law required a will to be executed according to the law of the testator's domicile at the time of his death. *Saunders* v. *Williams*, 5 N. H. 213; *Heydock's Appeal*, 7 N. H. 496. The distribution of the estate of a deceased person among the heirs or legatees is to be made according to the law of the domicile of the testator or intestate at the time of his death. *Leach v. Pillsbury*, 15 N.H. 137. But the plaintiff's intestate did not die possessed of the bond in suit. It did not vest in his administrator, and is not assets of his estate. The defeasible title which vested in the defendant at the time of the delivery was not defeated by the donor in his life-time, and his right and power to defeat it ceased with his death. A gift *causa mortis* is not a testament. If it is a contract, in this case it was executed in Vermont in the life of the plaintiff's intestate. If it is not a contract, as that term is commonly understood, it is a gift which received the assent of both parties, and nothing remained to perfect the conditional title of the defendant before the decease of the donor. The transfer of the bond being, therefore, either an executed contract or a perfected gift in Vermont, and valid under the laws of Vermont, is valid here; and no question arises whether our statute (G. L., c. 193, s. 17) affects the contract or the remedy. That section applies to gifts made in this state.

As to the sum of $280, the money was deliverd to the defendant as gifts *causa mortis* to sundry persons then and now residing in this state designated by the donor, to be by the defendant delivered to them after his decease. Delivery to a third person for the donee's use is as effectual as delivery to the donee. *Cutting v. Gilman*, 41 N. H. 147, 151, 152, and authorities cited; *Drury v. Smith*, 1 P. Wms. 404; *Marshall v. Berry*, 13 Allen 43. And there is no suggestion that the gift of the money stands differently from that of the bond.

The question as to mode of proof remains to be considered. In the first case, it has not been shown and it does not appear that injustice will be done by excluding the defendant from testifying. G. L., c. 228, ss. 13, 16, 17. As that question has not been passed upon at the trial term it is still open, and the ruling of the judge will be subject to exception and revision. The written memorandum on the envelope containing the bond, signed by the plaintiff's intestate and produced by the defendant, reads as follows: "Given to Hannah K. Clough on condition if I regain my health it is to be returned to me in good faith, otherwise the gift is absolute. William Emery." This memorandum is evidence sufficient to establish a gift *causa mortis*. *Curtis v. Portland Savings Bank*, 77 Me., 151 —S. C., 52 Am. R. 750. It contains a statement of no more than is always implied when such a gift is made. The donor could not tell whether he should die, or recover from his sickness. If he should recover, the law would hold the gift void. *Grymes v. Hone*, 49 N. Y. 17, 21.

In the second case, the defendant is a nominal party. The real defendants are the donees. The facts stated show no reason why she should not be allowed to testify, and injustice might be done if she were excluded. *Drew v. McDaniel, Adm'r*, 60 N. H. 480; *Welch v. Adams*, 63 N. H. 344, 351.

Case discharged.[27]

---

[27]A mortgage of personal property valid where executed and where the property was located at the time is valid in other states, and the rights

of the mortgagee are vested rights and can not be taken away. However, a state may provide for the recording of chattel mortgages executed in another state within a reasonable time after the mortgaged property is brought into the state, this is to protect creditors and purchasers in good faith for value.
.*Greenville Nat. Bank v. Evans Co. 9 Okla. 353; Langworthy v. Little, 12 Cush. 109.*

A chattel mortgage in one state may not be vaild in another state. Chattel mortgage laws have no force beyond the jurisdiction of the sovereignty enacting them. *Vinnig v. Millar, 109 Mich. 205*, and cases cited.

A chattel mortgage made in Missouri by a person domiciled there, to a citizen of Kansas, upon property situated in Kansas, is governed by the law of Kansas. *Mackey v. Pettijohn, 6 Kans. App. 57.*

Real Property.—No lands can be acquired or passed unless according to the laws of the state in which they are situate. *Clark v. Graham, 6 Wheat. 577; Swank v. Hufnagle, 111 Ind. 453, 12 N. E. 303; Shattuck v. Bates, 92 Wis. 633, 66 N. W. 706.* The *nature, extent of interest,* and *validity* of conveyance are determined by the law of the place where the land is situated. *Glover v. U. S., 29 Ct. Cl. 236; Danner v. Brewer, 69 Ala. 191; Moore v. Church, 70 Iowa 208; Fessenden v. Taft, 65 N. H. 39, 17 Atl. Rep. 713.* A deed valid according to the law of the place where the land is situated is a good conveyance, although it is not a good deed according to the law of the place of making. *Post v. Nat. Bank, 138 Ill. 559, 28 N. E. 978; Manton v. Seiberling, 107 Iowa 534, 78 N. W. 194.*

A deed of lands situated in North Carolina executed in South Carolina by a married woman living there, was in due form executed and acknowledged, according to the laws of South Carolina, with covenants of warranty. *Held,* that while both deed and covenant were valid by the laws of South Carolina, both were void in North Carolina, as the deed was defectively acknowledged; that the deed being void, the covenant worked no estoppel against the maker, although valid where made. *Smith v. Ingram, 130 N. C. 100, 40 S. E. 984.* There is great confusion upon the question involved in this case. Some courts have expressly held the opposite. *Phelps v. Decker, 10 Mass. 267; Polson v. Stewart, 167 Mass. 211, 45 N. E. 737, 36 L. R. A. 177, 57 Am. St. Rep. 452.* Certain authorities have taken the broad ground that all controversies affecting real estate must be settled by the *lex situs. Johnston v. Gawtry, 11 Mo. App. 322.* On the other hand, it has been held that covenants are personal contracts and if valid where made are valid and enforcible everywhere. *Oliver v. Loye, 59 Miss. 320.* Others have noted a distinction between covenants running with the land and those not running with the land. The latter would be valid in other jurisdictions even if inoperative according to the law of the place where the land is. *Bethell v. Bethell, 54 Ind. 428.* A covenant of warranty is an accessory contract. *Holland, Jurisprudence (5th ed.) 261.* On principle it then seems that when there is in effect no principal contract, no collateral agreement which rests merely on the existence of the main obligation can be supported. *Michigan Law Review (Nov., 1902) page 141.*

CHAPTER XIII.

CONTRACTS.

SIR JOSEPH HOLLAND (Jurisprudence Chap. XII, p. 181) says:

"In the fuller language of Savigny an obligation is the "*control* over another person, yet not over this person in all "respects (in which case his personality would be destroyed) but "over single acts of his which must be conceived of as substracted "from his free will and subjected to our will; or according to "Kant, 'the possession of the will of another as a means of deter- "mining it through your own in accordance with the law of free- "dom to a definite act.' An obligation, as its etymology denotes, "is a tie, whereby one person is bound to perform some act for the "benefit of another. In some cases the two parties agree thus to "be bound together. In other cases they are bound without their "consent. *In every case it is the law which ties the knot; and its* "*untying, solutio, is competent only to the same authority.* There "are cases in which a merely moral duty giving rise to what is "called a natural as opposed to a civil obligation will incidentally "receive legal recognition. As if a person pays a debt barred by "statute of limitations he will not be allowed to receive the "money, though paid in ignorance."

MR. JUSTICE MARKBY (Elements of Law considered with reference to principles of general jurisprudence) says:

"It seems in some cases to have been thought that it was an "easier process to arrive at liability when there was intention "than when there was none; it being apparently forgotten that the "affixing of liability is an independeht process to which the pre- "liminary requisite and the only one is the sovereign will."

LORD JUSTICE TURNER said (*Pen. etc., Nav. Co.* v. *Shand*, 3 Moore, P. C., N. S., 290-1):

"The general rule is that the law of the country where a "contract is made governs as to the nature, the obligation, and

"the interpretation of it. The parties to a contract are either the
"subjects of the power there ruling, or, as temporary residents, owe
"it a temporary allegiance. In either case, equally, they must be
"understood to submit to the law there prevailing, and to agree
"to its action upon their contracts. It is, of course, immaterial
"that such agreement is not expressed in terms. It is equally an
"agreement in fact, presumed *de jure;* and a foreign court, inter-
"preting or enforcing it on any contrary rule, defeats the intention
"of the parties, as well as neglects to observe the recognized
"comity of nations."

EQUITABLE LIFE ASSURANCE CO. v. CLEMENTS, 1891.

[140 U. S. 226.]

THIS was an action brought by Alice L. Wall, a citizen of
Missouri and widow of Samuel E. Wall, and prosecuted by Benjamin F. Pettus, her administrator, against the Equitable Life
Assurance Society of the United States, a corporation of New
York and doing business in Missouri, on a policy of insurance
executed by the defendant at his office in the city of New York
on December 23, 1880, upon the life of Samuel E. Wall, by which,
in consideration of the payment of $136.25 by him, and of the
payment of a like sum on or before December 15 in each year
during the continuance of the contract, it promised to pay to Alice
L. Wall, his wife, $5,000 at his office in the city of New York,
within sixty days after satisfactory proofs of his death.

"And further, that if the premiums upon this policy for not
less than three complete years of assurance shall have been duly
received by said society, and this policy should thereafter become
void in consequence of default of payment of a subsequent premium, said society will issue, in lieu of such policy, a new paid-up
policy, without participation in profits, in favor of said Alice L.
Wall, if living," "for the entire amount which the full reserve on
this policy, according to the present legal standard of the State
of New York, will then purchase as a single premium, calculated
by the regular table for single-premium policies now published
and in use by the society: Provided, however, that this policy shall
be surrendered, duly receipted, within six months of the date of
default in the payment of premium, as mentioned above.

"This policy is issued and accepted upon the condition that
the provisions and requirements printed or written by the society
upon the back of this policy are accepted by the assured as part of

this contract as fully as if they were recited at length over the signatures hereto affixed."

Among the provisions and requirements printed on the back of the policy were the following:

"4. All premiums are due in the city of New York, at the date named in the policy; but at the pleasure of the society suitable persons may be authorized to receive such payments at other places, but only on the production of the society's receipt therefor, signed by the president, vice-president, actuary, secretary or assistant secretary, and countersigned by the person to whom the payment is made. No payment made to any person, except in exchange for such receipt, will be recognized by the society. All premiums are considered payable annually in advance; when the premium is made payable in semi-annual or quarterly installments, that part of the year's premiums, if any, which remains unpaid at the maturity of this contract, shall be regarded as an indebtedness to the society on account of this contract, and shall be deducted from the amount of the claim; and if any premium or installment of a premium on this policy shall not be paid when due, this policy shall be void; nevertheless nothing herein shall be construed to deprive the holder of this policy of the privilege to demand and receive paid-up insurance in accordance with the agreement contained in this policy.

"5. The contract between the parties hereto is completely set forth in this policy and the application therefor, taken together, and none of its terms can be modified, nor any forfeiture under it waived, except by an agreement in writing, signed by the president, vice-president, actuary, secretary or assistant secretary of the society, whose authority for this purpose will not be delegated.

"6. If any statement made in the application for this policy be in any respect untrue, this policy shall be void."

The application for the policy was dated at Windsor in the State of Missouri, December 15, 1880, addressed to the defendant, and signed by Samuel E. Wall and Alice L. Wall; and the parts of it relied on by the defendants were as follows:

"27. Does the person for whose benefit the assurance is effected, in consideration of the agreements contained in the policy hereby applied for (providing for paid-up insurance in the event of surrender of the policy at certain periods and under certain conditions specified), waive and relinquish all right or claim to any other surrender value than that so provided, whether required by a statute of any State or not?" "Yes."

"It is hereby declared and agreed that all the statements and answers written on this application are warranted to be true, and are offered to the society as a consideration of the contract, which shall not take effect until the first premium shall have been actually paid during the life of the person herein proposed for assurance."

The petition alleged that, in consideration of the sum of $136.25 paid to the defendant by Samuel E. Wall, and of the further agreement on his part to pay to the defendant an annual premium of $136.25 on or before December 15 in each year during the continuance of the contract, the defendant "made, executed and delivered to said Samuel E. Wall, who was then and all the times hereinafter mentioned a resident of the State of Missouri, and in which state the said policy was delivered and the said premiums paid," the policy of insurance, above stated.

The answer admitted that said Wall was a resident of the State of Missouri, and that the policy of insurance, "after being applied for to and executed by the defendant, was, at the request of the said Wall, transmitted to the State of Missouri and was delivered to said Wall in said State," and "that the annual premiums due on said policy on December 15, 1881, and December 15, 1882, were paid, as also the cash premium due when said policy was issued."

The plaintiff alleged in the petition, and proved at the trial, that Samuel E. Wall failed to pay the premium due December 15, 1883; that he died January 21, 1884; that the defendant, on notice of his death, denied its liability, and thereby waived further proof thereof; that on December 15, 1883, the policy had acquired a net value of $161.05, as computed upon the American experience table of mortality, with four and a half per cent annual interest; that neither Wall nor his wife was then indebted to the defendant, on account of past premiums on the policy, or otherwise; that his age at that time was thirty-nine years; and that three-fourths of such net value, applied and taken as a net single premium for temporary insurance for the full amount written in the policy, would continue the policy in force until August 30, 1886.

The plaintiff claimed the full amount of the policy, with interest, by virtue of the provisions of the Revised Statutes of Missouri of 1879, which are copied in the margin.

The grounds of defence relied on were: 1st. That the policy was a contract governed by the laws of the State of New

York and not by the laws of the State of Missouri. 2d. That if it was governed by the laws of Missouri, then the stipulations in the policy and in the application therefor were valid and binding on the plaintiff as a waiver of the provisions of § 5983 of the Revised Statutes of Missouri.

The court, on motion of the plaintiff, ordered the parts of the answer which set up these defences to be struck out, delivering the opinion reported in 32 Fed. Rep. 273; and afterwards, upon a submission of the case to its decision without a jury, declined to sustain these defences, and rendered judgment for the plaintiff in the sum of $6,125. The defendant duly excepted to these rulings, and sued out this writ of error.

MR. JUSTICE GRAY, after stating the case as above, delivered the opinion of the court.

Upon the question whether the contract sued on was made in New York or in Missouri, there is nothing in the record, except the policy and application, the petition and answer, by which the facts appear to have been as follows: The assured was a resident of Missouri, and the application for the policy was signed in Missouri. The policy, executed at the defendant's office in New York, provides that "the contract between the parties hereto is completely set forth in this policy and the application therefor, taken together." The application declares that the contract "shall not take effect until the first premium shall have been actually paid during the life of the person herein proposed for assurance." The petition alleges that that premium and two annual premiums were paid in Missouri. The answer expressly admits the payment of the three premiums, and, by not controverting that they were paid in Missouri, admits that fact also, if material. Missouri Rev. Stat. 1879, § 3545. The petition further alleges that the policy was delivered in Missouri; and the answer admits that the policy was, "at the request of the said Wall, transmitted to the State of Missouri and was delivered to said Wall in said State." If this form of admission does not imply that the policy was at the request of Wall transmitted to another person, perhaps the company's agent, in Missouri, and by him there delivered to Wall, it is quite consistent with such a state of facts; and there is no evidence whatever, or even averment, that the policy was transmitted by mail directly to Wall, or that the company signified to Wall its acceptance of his application in any other way that by the delivery of the policy to him in Missouri. Upon this record, the conclusion is inevitable that the policy never became a completed contract, binding either party to it, until the delivery of the policy and the payment of the first premium in Missouri; and consequently that the policy is a Missouri contract and governed by the laws of Missouri.

By the revised statutes of Missouri of 1879, in force when this policy was made, it was enacted as follows: By § 5983, "no policy of insurance on life, hereafter issued by any life insurance company authorized to do business in this State, shall, after payment upon it of two full annual premiums, be forfeited or become void, by reason of the nonpayment of premium thereon; but it shall be subject to the following rules of commutation, to wit:" The net value of the policy is to be computed, and the insurance is to continue in force for the full amount of the policy for such time as three-fourths of such net value will be a premium for, according to the rules of commutation prescribed in that section. By § 5984, the holder of the policy, within sixty days from the beginning of such temporary insurance, may elect to take a paid-up policy for such amount as the net value aforesaid would be a premium for. By § 5985, if the assured dies within the term of temporary insurance, as determined by § 5983 and there has been no breach of any other condition of the policy, "the company shall be bound to pay the amount of the policy, the same as if there had been no default in the payment of premium, anything in the policy to the contrary notwithstanding."

The manifest object of this statute, as of many statutes regulating the form of policies of insurance on lives or against fires, is to prevent insurance companies from inserting in their policies conditions of forfeiture or restriction, except so far as the statute permits. The statute is not directory only, or subject to be set aside by the company with the consent of the assured; but it is mandatory, and controls the nature and terms of the contract into which the company may induce the assured to enter. This clearly appears from the unequivocal words of command and of prohibition above quoted, by which, in § 5983, "no policy of insurance" issued by any life insurance company authorized to do business in this State "shall, after the payment of two full annual premiums, be forfeited or become void, by reason of the non-payment of premium thereon; but it shall be subject to the following rules of commutation:" and, in § 5985, that if the assured dies within the term of temporary insurance, as determined in the former section, "the company shall be bound to pay the amount of the policy," "anything in the policy to the contrary notwithstanding."

This construction is put beyond doubt by § 5986, which, by

specifying four cases (two of which relate to the form of the policy) in which the three preceding sections "shall not be applicable," necessarily implies that those sections shall control all cases not so specified, whatever be the form of the policy.

Of the cases so specified, the only ones in which the terms of the policy are permitted to differ from the plan of the statute are the first and second, which allow the policy to stipulate for the holder's receiving the full benefit, either in cash, or by a new paid-up policy, of the three-fourths of the net value, as determined by §§ 5983 and 5984. The other two cases specified do not contemplate or authorize any provision in the contract itself inconsistent with the statute; but only permit the holder to surrender the policy, either in lieu of a new policy, or for a consideration adequate in his judgment. In defining each of these two cases, the statute, while allowing the holder to make a new bargain with the company, at the time of surrendering the policy, and upon such terms as, on the facts then appearing, are satisfactory to him, yet significantly, and, it must be presumed, designedly, contains nothing having the least tendency to show an intention on the part of the legislature that the company might require the assured to agree in advance that he would at any future time surrender the policy or lose the benefit thereof, upon any terms but those prescribed in the statute.

It follows that the insertion, in the policy, of a provision for a different rule of commutation from that prescribed by the statute, in case of default of payment of premium after three premiums have been paid; as well as the insertion, in the application, of a clause by which the beneficiary purports to "waive and relinquish all right or claim to any other surrender value than that so provided, whether required by a statute of any State, or not;" is an ineffectual attempt to evade and nullify the clear words of the statute.   *Judgment affirmed.*

NORTHAMPTON MUTUAL INS. CO. v. TUTTLE, 1878.

[40 N. J. L. 476.]

Van Syckel, J. The plaintiff brought suit before a justice of the peace of the county of Warren, to recover the amount of an assessment made against the defendant upon a policy of insurance issued to him by the plaintiff company. The plaintiff recovered a judgment before the justice, which was reversed in the Warren Common Pleas, on the ground that the insurance company, plaintiff, was a foreign insurance company, and that the contract was a New Jersey contract, negotiated by an agent in New Jersey, contrary to our statute. *Nix. Dig.* 435, § 66; *Ib.* 436, § 73.

The policy was dated May 27th, 1872, and insured defendant for the term of one year. An assessment was made July 2d, 1872, which paid the company's losses to that date. The losses from July 2d, 1872, to January 14th, 1873, amounted to about $12,000, and this sum was the basis of the assessment for which the defendant was sued.

The property issued was in this state, where the defendant and Thatcher, one of the directors of the insurance company, resided when the policy was issued.

The application was signed by the defendant in this state, where Thatcher gave him a receipt, of which the following is a copy:

"Northampton Mutual Live Stock Insurance Company, of Northampton county, Pa.

"Received of Wm. Tuttle, for an insurance by the North ampton Mutual Live Stock Insurance Company against loss by death upon the animals described in application, the sum of one dollar and thirty cents, being the amount paid for membership for the term of one year from the 27th day of May, 1872, for which said company agrees to issue a policy to said applicant when the application is approved, and if not approved, the above amount to be refunded to the said applicant.

"J. B. THATCHER,
"Dated May 27th, 1872.   *Agent.*"

Article VI. of the by-laws of the company provided that the agent of the company should give a receipt for the premium paid, and that the insurance should take effect from that time, provided the application was approved by the board of directors, or its executive committee, after which the policy would be issued; and if not approved, the money would be refunded.

In this case the application for insurance was taken by Thatcher to Easton, in the State of Pennsylvania, where it was approved by the directors of the company, and the policy was there issued and sent by mail to the defendant, in New Jersey.

If the contract of insurance was made in the State of Pennsylvania, and was valid there, comity requires us to enforce it here. *Columbia Ins. Co. v. Kinyon,* 8 Vroom 33.

This case, therefore turns upon the question whether it was made in this state.

Thatcher acted as the agent of the company, with authority to receive applications. He received the defendant's application, with the premium, which he transmitted to the company at its place of business in Pennsylvania. By the express terms of the receipt given bv the agent to the defendant, the company had the option to approve the application and issue a policy, or to reject it and refund the premium. It was a mere proposition, from which the parties might have receded, and not a contract. Approval by the company was necessary to ripen into a contract. Not until then did the minds of the parties come together, and invest the transaction with the attributes of a valid agreement. The contract of insurance must be regarded as having been made when the company approved the defendant's application, and issued and transmitted to him their policy. *Hyde* v. *Goodnow*, 3 *N. Y.* 266; *Huntley* v. *Merrill*, 32 Barb. 626.

The contract must be held to have been made where the last act necessary to complete it was done.

Although there is some conflict in the cases, I think the weight of authority is, that when the offer of the insured was accepted, and the policy deposited in the postoffice by the company, properly addressed to the insured, the contract was made. It did not remain incomplete until the insured, by receiving the policy, was notified of the acceptance of his proposal.

In *McCulloch* v. *Eagle Insurance Company*, 1 Pick. 278, the Supreme Court of Massachusetts, on the Authority of Cooke *v.* Oxley, held that mailing a letter acceeding to terms offered did not complete the bargain, but the views expressed by the court were modified in a later case, reported in 10 *Pick.* 330.

In *Adams* v. *Lindsell*, 1 *B. & Ald.* 681, the bargain was declared to be perfected when the letter was put in the mail, giving notice to the other party of the acceptance of his offer.

This question is ably reviewed by Justice Marcy, in *Mactier* v. *Frith*, 6 Wend. 103, in which the Court of Errors overruled the decision of Chancellor Walworth, that to make a valid contract it is not only necessary that the minds of the contracting parties should meet on the subject of the contract, but that fact must be communicated to each other.

The same rule prevails in the Supreme Court of the United States. *Tayloe* v. *Merchants' Fire Insurance Company*, 9 How. 390.

It has also the unqualified approval of Chancellor Kent. *2 Kent's Com.* (6th ed.) 477.

The cases in this state are to the same effect. *Houghwout v. Boisaubin, 3 C. E. Green* 315; *Potts v. Whitehead, 5 C. E. Green* 55; *Commercial Insurance Company v. Hallock, 3 Dutcher* 645.

In the case last cited, Justice Elmer says: "It being well and satisfactorily established at law that the acceptance of a proposition, and the sending notice thereof by mail, complete the bargain, although the letter never reaches its destination, it follows that the company were bound by what they did on that day, and had no power afterwards to revoke it."

A bargain must be considered as closed when no mutual act remains to be done to entitle either party to enforce it.

Under the adjudged cases it seems to be clear that if the assured had suffered loss the instant after the policy was mailed, he could have resorted to it for indemnity.

The case in hand is stronger than any of the cases cited, for here, by the express terms of the receipt, there was a stipulation on the part of the company to issue a policy when the application was approved.

After the approval the company could not have receded from it, but would have been bound to issue the policy. Their obligation to do so did not depend upon notice of acceptance to the insured, but upon the fact of acceptance.

It being conceded that the approval of the application was given in Pennsylvania, and the policy mailed there, the contract must be adjudged to have been made in that state, and not in New Jersey.

The contract, therefore, is valid, and comity requires its enforcement here. *Columbia Fire Insurance Company v. Kinyon,* 8 Vroom 33.

By the constitution and by-laws of the company, it is provided, that if it should happen that the funds on hand be insufficient to pay all losses and expenses, the directors shall, by resolution, levy a tax on the members of the company, as their policies stand unexpired on the books of the company, said tax to be levied on the amount insured.

The assessment in this case was made in accordance with this by-law, which the defendant, as a member of the plaintiff company, is presumed to know, and is required to conform to. *Northampton Mutual Company v. Stewart,* 10 Vroom 486.

The judgment of the Warren Pleas, that the contract was void under the statute law of this state, was erroneous, and should be set aside.

JONES v. SURPRISE, 1886.

[64 N. H. 243.]

ASSUMPSIT, to recover a balance due for the sale of wines and spirituous liquors. Plea. the general issue, with a brief statement that the contract was void under Gen. Laws, c. 109, s. 18. Facts found by the court.

The plaintiffs were liquor dealers in Boston, and the defendant a saloonkeeper in Suncook at the time of the sale of the liquors in suit. The plaintiffs' agent solicited orders for the liquors in the defendant's saloon, and forwarded the orders to the plaintiffs in Boston, having no authority to make a contract for their sale. He informed the defendant that the liquors would be delivered to him at the plaintiffs' store-rooms in Boston. When he solicited the orders he had no knowledge of the provisions of s. 18, c. 109, Gen. Laws, and did not intend the violation of any law of this state. He knew at the time of the sale that the defendant bought for the purpose of selling in violation of law. The liquors were delivered to carriers in Boston for the defendant, and he paid the cost of transportation from Boston to Suncook where he received them. Their sale was authorized by the law of Massachusetts.

The plaintiffs claimed that the sale being valid by the law of Massachusetts, the law of this state prohibiting the taking or soliciting of orders did not invalidate it. They further claimed, that as the statute prohibits the taking of orders for spirituous or distilled liquors only, they can recover for the wines. There was evidence tending to show that the wines were intoxicating.

SMITH, J. It is made a criminal offence for any person not an agent to sell or keep for sale spirituous liquor, or for any person within this state to solicit or take an order for spirituous liquor to be delivered at any place without this state, knowing, or having reasonable cause to believe, that if so delivered the same will be transported to this state and sold in violation of our laws. G. L. c. 109, ss. 13, 18. One question in this case is, whether intoxicating wines are included within the terms of this statute. The legislature has defined intoxicating liquor as follows: "By the words 'spirit,' 'spirituous,' or 'intoxicating liquor,' shall be intended all spirituous or intoxicating liquor, and all mixed liquor, any part of which is spirituous or intoxicating, unless otherwise expressly declared." G. L., *c.* 1, *ss.* 1, 31. As intoxicating wines and other intoxicating fermented liquors are not expressly excluded from the operation of *ss.* 13, 18, 19, *c.* 109, of the Gen. Laws, the only conclusion is that they come within the prohibition of its terms. No reason appears why the legislature should prohibit the solicitation of orders for one class of intoxicating liquors and permit it as to others. The construction of statutes is governed by legislative definitions; that of indictments by the ordinary use of language. *State* v. *Adams,* 51 N. H. 568; *State* v. *Canterbury,* 28 N. H. 195; *State v. Butman,* 61 N. H. 511, 515.

The remaining question is, whether the plaintiffs can maintain an action in our courts for the price of liquors sold and delivered in a state where the sale is lawful, they having solicited and taken orders for the liquors in this state in violation of our laws. That their authorized agent, who solicited and took the orders, did not know the solicitation or taking of orders was prohibited, and did not intend the violation of any law, is immaterial. A person is presumed to know and understand not only the laws of the country where he dwells, but also those in which he transacts business. In *Hill* v. *Spear,* 50 N. H. 253 it was held by a majority of the court that mere solicitation by a dealer in liquors of orders in the future for spirituous liquors, even though he may have had reason to believe and did believe that the liquors would be resold by the purchaser in violation of the law of this state, is not such a circumstance as will affect the validity of a subsequent sale of such liquors in a state where the sale is not prohibited. Numerous decisions in England and in this country upon the subject were cited and discussed in that case, and an extended review of most of the same authorities may be found in *Tracy* v. *Talmage,* 14 N. Y. 162. Further discussion of the authorities is not called for at the present time. When *Hill* v. *Spear* was decided, the soliciting of orders for spirituous liquors to be delivered without the state was not prohibited. The present statute (G. L., *c.* 109, *ss.* 18, 19), first enacted in 1876 (Laws of 1876, *c.* 33), makes the mere soliciting or taking of such orders, or the going from place to place soliciting or taking such orders, with knowledge or reasonable cause to believe that the liquors will be transported to this state and sold in violation of law, without any other act in furtherance of the vendee's design, a criminal offence, punishable by fine or imprisonment. The plaintiffs' authorized agent, who solicited and took these orders from the defendant, knew the liquors were to be kept and sold by the

defendant in this state in violation of law.   His knowledge is in
law the knowledge of the plaintiffs.

The plaintiffs contend that inasmuch as the soliciting of
orders constituted no part of the contract when the soliciting was
not prohibited, the act of soliciting, now that it is made illegal,
cannot vitiate a contract of which it forms no part.   The case
is not affected by the plaintiffs' ability to prove a sale without
proof of the solicitation.   No people are bound to enforce or
hold valid in their courts of justice any contract which is injurious to their public rights, or offends their morals, or contravenes their policy, or violates public law.   And every independent community will judge for itself how far the rule of comity
between states is to be permitted to interfere with its domestic
interests and policy.   2 Kent Com. 457, 458; *Hill* v. *Spear*, 50 N.
H. 253, 262; *Bliss* v. *Brainard*, 41 N. H. 256, 258.   The object
of the statute of 1876 (G. L., c. 109, ss. 18, 19) was to discourage
the sale of liquor in other states to be transported to this state and
sold in violation of its statutes.   New Hampshire cannot prohibit
the sale of liquor in other states, but it can punish, as it does by
this statute, acts done in this state with the purpose of facilitating
sales of intoxicating liquors in other states to be transported to
this state and to be illegally sold here, in contravention of our
policy and to the injury of our citizens.   The statute was intended
to make such sales and transportation difficult, if not impossible,
by subjecting those who violate its provisions to the penalty of
fine or imprisonment.   Where a statute provides a penalty for an
act, this is a prohibition of the act.   In *Bartlett* v. *Vinor*, Carth.
252—*S. C.* Skin. 322, *Holt*, C. J., said,—"Every contract made
for or about any matter or thing which is prohibited or made
unlawful by any statute is a void contract, though the statute does
not mention that it shall not be so, but only inflicts a penalty on
the offenders, because a penalty implies a prohibition, though
there are no prohibitory words in the statute."   Accordingly it is
everywhere held that wherever an indictment can be sustained
for the illegal sale of liquors or other goods, there the price
cannot be recovered (*Bliss* v. *Brainard*, 41 N. H. 256, 268, *Smith*
v. *Godfrey*, 28 N. H. 384, *Caldwell* v. *Wentworth*, 14 N. H. 431,
Lewis v. *Welch*, 14 N. H. 294, *Pray* v. *Burbank*, 10 N. H. 377);
and if this was a New Hampshire contract the plaintiffs could
not recover.   The law does not help the seller to recover the
price of goods, the sale of which it interdicts.   The reason of this
rule applies in this case.   Although this contract was executed in
Massachusetts, it had its inception in this state, in direct violation

or our laws. Orders for these liquors were solicited and taken here by the plaintiffs' agent, sent here for that purpose; were transmitted by him to the plaintiffs; were accepted by them, and became the basis of the contract which they seek to enforce in this state. The orders are evidence for the plaintiffs as to price, quantity, and kinds of liquors purchased, as well as of an offer by the defendant to purchase, if, indeed, it is not true that the plaintiffs cannot prove their case without founding it upon the orders. Both the soliciting and the taking of the orders was an indictable offence, in which the agent was principal. The inciting, encouraging, and aiding another to commit a misdemeanor is itself a misdemeanor. Russ. on Crimes, 46, 47. The plaintiffs stand precisely as they would if they, instead of their agent, had solicited and taken the orders. G. L., c. 284, s. 7. Having aided, abetted, procured, and hired their agent to violate our laws by soliciting and taking orders for the very liquors embraced in this contract, they cannot with any grace invoke the remedy afforded by our laws to recover the price. No rule of comity requires us to enforce in favor of a non-resident a contract which had its origin in the open violation of law, and which would not be enforced in favor of our own citizens, especially when it is offensive to our morals, opposed to our policy, and injurious to our citizens. Its enforcement would tend to nullify the statute which the plaintiffs have caused to be violated. The law which prohibits an end, will not lend its aid in promoting the means designed to carry it into effect. It does not promote in one form that which it prohibits in another. *White* v. *Buss.* 3 Cush. 448, 450. The opinion in *Hill* v. *Spear* (p. 264) concedes that there could be no recovery if the plaintiffs had actively participated in an illegal act in effecting the sale, and is put upon the ground that Stewart, their agent, did not advise, request, or encourage any violation of the laws of this state.

In *Bliss* v. *Brainard*, 41 N. H. 256, 268, we said,—"Where a contract grows immediately out of, and is connected with, an illegal or immoral act, a court of justice will not lend its aid to enforce it. So, if the contract be in part connected with the illegal consideration, but growing immediately out of it, though it be in fact a new and separate contract, it is equally tainted by it." In that case the plaintiff sought to recover for the value of the casks in which the liquors were contained, and for the freight and cartage of the liquors, the sale of the liquors being unlawful. *Fowler*, J., said,—"Aside, therefore, from the positive provisions of the Massachusetts statute, withdrawing all protection from

vessels and casks when employed as the instruments for perpetu-
ating a violation of positive law, we think the sale of the casks
was so tainted with the illegality of the sale of the liquors, so
much a part of the *res gestae* of the main illegal and criminal
transaction, and so much the mere instrument whereby it was
accomplished, that no action can be maintained to recover their
price." For analogous reasons the plaintiffs in this case cannot
recover. Although this is a Massachusetts contract, valid in that
state, it is so tainted by the plaintiffs' illegal conduct in soliciting,
taking, and transmitting orders in violation of the statute, that
comity will not extend to them the remedy afforded by our laws.
The taking of such orders tends directly to encourage the illegal
sale of liquors in this state, and, being prohibited, it follows that
an action to recover the price of liquors sold and delivered pursuant to orders so solicited cannot be maintained in this state,
although the sale of intoxicating liquors in the state or country
where they are sold and delivered is not illegal. *Dunbar v.
Locke*, 62 N. H.—

Judgment for the defendant.

STAPLES v. KNOTT, 1891.

[128 N. Y. 403.]

GRAY, J. The promissory note in suit bears date at Washington, D. C., April 5, 1889; was made payable at a bank in
Watertown, N. Y., and carried interest at the rate of seven per
cent per annum. The appellant was indorser upon it, and defends
on the ground of usury. If the contract of the parties, which is
evidenced by this note, was governed by the laws of this state,
the defense should have prevailed; but if made under the laws of
the District of Columbia the judgment was right and should be
sustained.

The note was given in renewal of a balance due upon a prior
note, made by and between the same parties, which bore date at
Washington, D. C., April 5, 1888; was payable one year after
date at a bank in Washington; bore the same rate of interest and
was similarly indorsed. Some payments were made on account
of the principal, but, before its maturity, the maker requested of
plaintiff, a resident of Washington, by letter, to renew for the balance remaining due. Failing to receive any reply, he went on to
Washington, and there prevailed upon the plaintiff to agree to
take a new note for his debt. This note was then drawn by the
plaintiff and handed to the maker for execution, who took it back

to his home in Syracuse, N. Y., where his and the appellant's signatures were affixed, as maker and indorser respectively. It had been agreed with the plaintiff that, upon this new note being returned to him, he would send back the original note, and the appellant himself mailed the renewal note to the plaintiff in Washington.

These facts, which were not disputed, should make it perfectly obvious that there was here every essential to a valid contract under the laws of the plaintiff's domicile, and the only accompaniment lacking to a full local coloring was the foreign place named for payment. For the affixing of the signatures to the note by the maker and the indorser, however important as acts, was, yet, but a detail in the performance and execution of the contract which had been agreed upon with the plaintiff. But naming a New York bank as the place where the maker would provide for the payment of the note, did not characterize the contract in one way or the other. That arrangement was one simply for the convenience of the maker. It could have no peculiar effect. The transactions, which resulted in an agreement to extend the time for the payment of the debt and to accept a new note, took place wholly in the District of Columbia, and what else was enacted in the matter elsewhere neither added to nor altered the agreement of the parties. Though the engagement of the indorser, in a sense, was independent of that of the maker, that proposition is one which does not affect the local character of the contract, but which simply concerns the question of the enforcement of the indorser's liability. Whatever the previous knowledge of the appellant, as to the negotiations and the agreement for a renewal of the promise to pay between the maker of the old note and the plaintiff, the question is without importance. When he indorsed the note, which had been prepared and was brought to him, and sent it through the mail to the plaintiff, his engagement was with respect to a contract validly made according to the laws of the District of Columbia, and when the note was received by the plaintiff the transaction was then consummated in that place. In *Lee* v. *Selleck* (33 N. Y. 615) it was said, with respect to an indorsement in Illinois of a note made in New York, that the fact of the indorser writing his name elsewhere was of no moment. Upon delivery by his agent to the plaintiffs in New York, it became operative as a mutual contract.

The agreement, which was made in Washington for the giving of the promissory note in question, was the forbearance of a debt already due, upon which the appellant was liable; and the renewal of his engagement as indorser upon the note, without any qualification of his contract of indorsement, was in fact an act in ratification and execution of the previous agreement. That agreement between the plaintiff and the maker in Washington took its concrete legal form in a note, prepared there by the plaintiff, with a rate of interest sanctioned by the laws of his domicile, adopted by the appellant by indorsement in blank, and made operative as a mutual contract by delivery to plaintiff in Washington through the mails.

For the court to hold, because the note was not actually signed and indorsed in the District of Columbia, where the agreement, it evidenced, was made. or because it was made payable in another state, that the contract was void as contravening the usury laws of the place of signature and of payment, would be intolerable and against decisions of this court. (*Wayne Co. Sav. Bank* v. *Low*, 81 N. Y. 566; *Western T. & C. Co.* v. *Kilderhouse*, 87 id. 430; *Sheldon* v. *Haxtun*, 91 id. 124.)

I think the plaintiff was entitled to recover, as upon a contract made under the government of the laws of the District of Columbia and, therefore, valid and enforceable in any state.

The judgment should be affirmed, with costs.

All concur.   *Judgment affirmed.*

MILLIKEN v. PRATT. 1878.

[125 Mass. 374.]

CONTRACT to recover $500 and interest from January 6, 1872. Writ dated June 30, 1875. The case was submitted to the Superior Court on agreed facts, in substance as follows:

The plaintiffs are partners doing business in Portland, Maine, under the firm name of Deering, Milliken & Co. The defendant is and has been since 1850, the wife of Daniel Pratt, and both have always resided in Massachusetts. In 1870, Daniel, who was then doing business in Massachusetts, applied to the plaintiffs at Portland for credit, and they required of him, as a condition of granting the same, a guaranty from the defendant to the amount of five hundred dollars, and accordingly he procured from his wife the following instrument:

"Portland, January 29, 1870. In consideration of one dollar paid by Deering, Milliken & Co., receipt of which is hereby acknowledged, I guarantee the payment to them by Daniel Pratt of the sum of five hundred dollars, from time to time as he may want—this to be a continuing guaranty. Sarah A. Pratt."

This instrument was executed by the defendant two or three days after its date, at her home in Massachusetts, and there delivered by her to her husband, who sent it by mail from Massachusetts to the plaintiffs in Portland; and the plaintiffs received it from the postoffice in Portland early in February, 1870.

The plaintiffs subsequently sold and delivered goods to Daniel from time to time until October 7, 1871, and charged the same to him, and, if competent, it may be taken to be true, that in so doing they relied upon the guaranty. Between February, 1870, and September 1, 1871, they sold and delivered goods to him on credit to an amount largely exceeding $500, which were fully settled and paid for by him. This action is brought for goods sold from September 1, 1871, to October 7, 1871, inclusive, amounting to $860.12, upon which he paid $300, leaving a balance due of $560.12. The one dollar mentioned in the guaranty was not paid, and the only consideration moving to the defendant therefor was the giving of credit by the plaintiffs to her husband. Some of the goods were selected personally by Daniel at the plaintiffs' store in Portland, others were ordered by letters mailed by Daniel from Massachusetts to the plaintiffs at Portland, and all were sent by the plaintiffs by express from Portland to Daniel in Massachusetts, who paid all express charges. The parties were cognizant of the facts.

By a statute of Maine, duly enacted and approved in 1866, it is enacted that "the contracts of any married woman, made for any lawful purpose, shall be valid and binding, and may be enforced in the same manner as if she were sole." The statutes and the decisions of the court of Maine may be referred to.

Payment was duly demanded of the defendant before the date of the writ, and was refused by her.

The Superior Court ordered judgment for the defendant; and the plaintiffs appealed to this court.

GRAY, C. J. The general rule is that the validity of a contract is to be determined by the law of the state in which it is made; if it is valid there, it is deemed valid everywhere, and will sustain an action in the courts of a state whose laws do not permit such a contract. *Scudder* v. *Union National Bank*, 91 U. S. 406. Even a contract expressly prohibited by the statutes of the state in which the suit is brought, if not in itself immoral, is not necessarily nor usually deemed so invalid that the comity of the state, as administered by its courts, will refuse to entertain an action on such a contract made by one of its own citizens abroad in a state the laws of which permit it. *Greenwood* v. *Curtis,* 6 Mass. 358. *M'Intyre* v. *Parks,* 3 Met. 207.

If the contract is completed in another state, it makes no difference in principle whether the citizen of this state goes in person, or sends an agent, or writes a letter, across the boundary line between the two states. As was said by Lord Lyndhurst, "If I, residing in England, send down my agent to Scotland, and he makes contracts for me there, it is the same as if I myself went there and made them." *Pattison* v. *Mills,* 1 Dow & Cl. 342, 363. So if a person residing in this state signs and transmits, either by a messenger or through the postoffice, to a person in another state, a written contract, which requires no special forms or solemnities in its execution, and no signature of the person to whom it is addressed, and is assented to and acted on by him there, the contract is made there, just as if the writer personally took the executed contract into the other state, or wrote and signed it there; and it is no objection to the maintenance of an action thereon here, that such a contract is prohibited by the law of this Commonwealth. *M'Intyre* v. *Parks,* above cited.

The guaranty, bearing date of Portland, in the State of Maine, was executed by the defendant, a married woman, having her home in this Commonwealth, as collateral security for the liability of her husband for goods sold by the plaintiffs to him, and was sent by her through him by mail to the plaintiffs at Portland. The sales of the goods ordered by him from the plaintiffs at Portland, and there delivered by them to him in person, or to a carrier for him, were made in the State of Maine. *Orcutt* v. *Nelson,* 1 Gray, 536. *Kline* v. *Baker,* 99 Mass. 253. The contract between the defendant and the plaintiffs was complete when the guaranty had been received and acted on by them at Portland, and not before. *Jordan* v. *Dobbins,* 122 Mass. 168. It must therefore be treated as made and to be performed in the State of Maine.

The law of Maine authorized a married woman to bind herself by any contract as if she were unmarried. St. of Maine of 1866, c. 52. *Mayo* v. *Hutchinson,* 57 Maine, 546. The law of Massachusetts, as then existing, did not allow her to enter into a contract as surety or for the accommodation of her husband or of any third person. Gen. Sts. c. 108, § 3. *Nourse* v. *Henshaw,* 123 Mass. 96. Since the making of the contract sued on, and before the bringing of this action, the law of this Commonwealth has been changed, so as to enable married women to make such

contracts. St. 1874, *c.* 184. *Major* v. *Holmes,* 124 Mass. 108.
Kenworthy v. *Sawyer, ante,* 28.

The question therefore is, whether a contract made in another
state by a married woman domiciled here, which a married
woman was not at the time capable of making under the law of
this Commonwealth, but was then allowed by the law of that state
to make, and which she could now lawfully make in this Commonwealth, will sustain an action against her in our courts.

It has been often stated by commentators that the law of the
domicil, regulating the capacity of a person, accompanies and
governs the person everywhere. But this statement, in modern
times at least, is subject to many qualifications; and the opinions
of foreign jurists upon the subject, the principal of which are
collected in the treatises of Mr. Justice Story and Dr. Francis
Wharton on the Conflict of Laws, are too varying and contra-
dictory to control the general current of the English and American authorities in favor of holding that a contract, which by the
law of the place is recognized as lawfully made by a capable
person, is valid everywhere, although the person would not,
under the law of his domicil, be deemed capable of making it.

Two cases in the time of Lord Hardwicke have been sometimes supposed to sustain the opposite view. The first is *Ex
parte Lewis,* 1 Ves. Sen. 298, decided in the Court of Chancery
in 1749, in which a petition, under the St. of 4 Geo. II. *c.* 10, that
a lunatic heir of a mortgagee might be directed to convey to the
mortgagor, was granted by Lord Hardwicke, on the ground of
"there having been a proceeding before a proper jurisdiction, the
Senate of Hamburgh, where he resided, upon which he was
found *non compos,* and a curator or guardian appointed for him
and his affairs, which proceeding the court was obliged to take
notice of." But the foreign adjudication was thus taken notice
of as competent evidence of the lunacy only; and that the
authority of the foreign guardian was not recognized as extending to England is evident from the fact that the conveyance
prayed for and ordered was from the lunatic himself. The other
is *Morrison's case,* in the House of Lords in 1750, for a long
time principally known in England and America by the imperfect
and conflicting statements of counsel *arguendo* in *Sill* v. *Worswick,* 1 H. Bl. 677, 682; but in which, as the Scotch books of
reports show, the decision really was that a committee, appointed
in England, of a lunatic residing there, could not sue in Scotland
upon a debt due him, but that, upon obtaining a power of attor-

ney from the lunatic, they might maintain a suit in Scotland in his name; and Lord Hardwicke said that the law would be the same in England—evidently meaning, as appears by his own statement afterwards, that the same rule would prevail in England in the case of a foreigner who had been declared a lunatic, and as such put under guardianship in the country of his domicil. Morrison's Dict. Dec. 4595. 1 Cr. & Stew. 454, 459. *Thorne v. Watkins,* 2 Ves. Sen. 35, 37. Both those cases, therefore, rightly understood, are in exact accordance with the later decisions, by which it is now settled in Great Britain and in the United States, that the appointment of a guardian of an infant or lunatic in one state or country gives him no authority and has no effect in another, except so far as it may influence the discretion of the courts of the latter, in the exercise of their own independent jurisdiction, to appoint the same person guardian, or to decree the custody of the ward to him. *Ex parte Watkins,* 2 Ves. Sen. 470. *In re Houstoun,* 1 Russ. 312. *Johnson v. Beattie,* 10 Cl. & Fin. 42. *Stuart v. Bute,* 9 H. L. Cas. 440; S. C. 4 Macq. 1. *Nugent v. Vetzera,* L. R. 2 Eq. 704. *Woodworth v. Spring,* 4 Allen, 321. Story Confl. § 499.

Lord Eldon, when Chief Justice of the Common Pleas, and Chief Justice Kent and his associates in the Supreme Court of New York, held that the question whether an infant was liable to an action in the courts of his domicil, upon a contract made by him in a foreign country, depended upon the question whether by the law of that country such a contract bound an infant. *Male v. Roberts,* 3 Esp. 163. *Thompson v. Ketcham,* 8 Johns. 189.

Mr. Westlake, who wrote in 1858, after citing the decision of Lord Eldon, well observed, "That there is not more authority on the subject may be referred to its not having been questioned;" and summed up the law of England thus: "While the English law remains as it is, it must, on principle, be taken as excluding, in the case of transactions having their seat here, not only a foreign age of majority, but also all foreign determination of status or capacity, whether made by law or by judicial act, since no difference can be established between the cases, nor does any exist on the continent." "The validity of a contract made out of England, with regard to the personal capacity of the contractor, will be referred in our courts to the *lex loci contractûs;* that is, not to its particular provisions on the capacity of its domiciled subjects, but in this sense, that, if good where made, the contract will be held good here, and conversely." Westlake's Private International Law, §§ 401, 402, 404.

In a recent case, Lord Romilly, M. R., held that a legacy bequeathed by one domiciled in England to a boy domiciled with his father in Hamburgh, by the law of which boys do not become of age until twenty-two and the father is entitled as guardian to receive a legacy bequeathed to an infant, might be paid to the boy at his coming of age by the law of England, although still a minor by the law of his domicil, and in the meanwhile must be dealt with as an infant's legacy. *In re Hellmann's Will,* L. R. 2 Eq. 363.

The Supreme Court of Louisiana, in two cases which have long been considered leading authorities, strongly asserted the doctrine that a person was bound by a contract which he was capable by the law of the place, though not by the law of his own domicil, of making; as, for instance, in the case of a contract made by a person over twenty-one and under twenty-five years of age, in a state whose laws authorized contracts to be made at twenty-one, whereas by the laws of his domicil he was incapable of contracting under twenty-five. *Baldwin* v. *Gray,* 16 Martin, 192, 193. *Saul* v. *His Creditors,* 17 Martin, 569, 597 The same doctrine was recognized as well settled in *Andrews* v *His Creditors,* 11 Louisiana, 464, 476.

In other cases of less note in that state, the question of personal capacity was indeed spoken of as governed by the law of the domicil. *Le Breton* v. *Nouchet,* 3 Martin, 60, 70. *Barrera* v. *Alpuente,* 18 Martin, 69, 70. *Garnier* v. *Poydras,* 13 Louisiana, 177, 182. But in none of them was the statement necessary to the decision. In *Le Breton* v. *Nouchet,* the point adjudged was, that where a man and woman domiciled in Louisiana (by the law of which the wife retains her separate property) were married, with the intention of returning to Louisiana, in the Mississippi Territory (where the rule of the common law prevailed, by which the wife's personal property became her husband's), the law of Louisiana, in which the parties intended to continue to reside, governed their rights in the wife's property; and the further expression of an opinion that the rule would be the same if the parties intended to remain in the Mississippi Territory was purely *obiter dictum,* and can hardly be reconciled with later decisions of the same court. *Gale* v. *Davis,* 4 Martin, 645. *Saul* v. *His Creditors,* 17 Martin, 569. See also *Read* v. *Earle,* 12 Gray, 423. In *Barrera* v. *Alpuente,* the case was discussed in the opinion upon the hypothesis that the capacity to receive a legacy was governed by the law of the domicil; but the same result would have followed from holding that it was governed by the law of the place where the right accrued and was sought to be enforced. In *Garnier v. Poydras,* the decision turned on the validity of a power of attorney executed and a judicial authorization given in France, where the husband and wife had always resided.

In *Greenwood v. Curtis,* Chief Justice Parsons said, "By the common law, upon principles of national comity, a contract made in a foreign place, and to be there executed, if valid by the laws of that place, may be a legitimate ground of action in the courts of this state; although such contract may not be valid by our laws, or even may be prohibited to our citizens;" and that the Chief Justice considered this rule as extending to questions of capacity is evident from his subsequent illustration of a marriage contracted abroad between persons prohibited to intermarry by the law of their domicil. 6 Mass. 377–379. The validity of such marriages (except in case of polygamy, or of marriages incestuous according to the general opinion of Christendom) has been repeatedly affirmed in this Commonwealth. *Medway v. Need ham,* 16 Mass. 157. *Sutton v. Warren,* 10 Met. 451. *Commonwealth v. Lane,* 113 Mass. 458.

The recent decision in *Sottomayor v. De Barros,* 3 P. D. 1, by which Lords Justices James, Baggallay and Cotton, without referring to any of the cases that we have cited, and reversing the judgment of Sir Robert Phillimore in 2 P. D. 81, held that a marriage in England between first cousins, Portuguese subjects, resident in England, who by the law of Portugal were incapable of intermarrying except by a Papal dispensation, was therefore null and void in England, is utterly opposed to our law; and consequently the *dictum* of Lord Justice Cotton, "It is a well-recognized principle of law that the question of personal capacity to enter into any contract is to be decided by the law of domicil," is entitled to little weight here.

It is true that there are reasons of public policy for upholding the validity of marriages, that are not applicable to ordinary contracts; but a greater disregard of the *lex domicilii* can hardly be suggested, than in the recognition of the validity of a marriage contracted in another state, which is not authorized by the law of the domicil, and which permanently affects the relations and the rights of two citizens and of others to be born.

Mr. Justice Story, in his Commentaries on the Conflict of Laws, after elaborate consideration of the authorities, arrives at the conclusion that "in regard to questions of minority or majority, competency or incompetency to marry, incapacities incident to coverture, guardianship, emancipation, and other personal qualities and disabilities, the law of the domicil of birth, or the law of any other acquired and fixed domicil, is not generally to govern, but the *lex loci contractûs aut actûs*, the law of the place where the contract is made, or the act done;" or as he elsewhere sums it up, "although foreign jurists generally hold that the law of the domicil ought to govern in regard to the capacity of persons to contract; yet the common law holds a different doctrine, namely, that the *lex loci contractûs* is to govern." Story Confl. §§ 103, 241. So Chancellor Kent, although in some passages of the text of his Commentaries he seems to incline to the doctrine of the civilians, yet in the notes afterwards added unequivocally concurs in the conclusions of Mr. Justice Story. 2 Kent Com. 233 note, 458, 459 & note.

In *Pearl* v. *Hansborough.* 9 Humph. 426, the rule was carried so far as to hold that where a married woman domiciled with her husband in the State of Mississippi, by the law of which a purchase by a married woman was valid and the property purchased went to her separate use, bought personal property in Tennessee, by the law of which married women were incapable of contracting, the contract of purchase was void and could not be enforced in Tennessee. Some authorities, on the other hand, would uphold a contract made by a party capable by the law of his domicil, though incapable by the law of the place of the contract. *In re Hellmann's Will,* and *Saul* v. *His Creditors,* above cited. But that alternative is not here presented. In *Hill* v. *Pine River Bank,* 45 N. H. 300, the contract was made in the state of the woman's domicil, so that the question before us did not arise and was not considered.

The principal reasons on which continental jurists have maintained that personal laws of the domicil, affecting the status and capacity of all inhabitants of a particular class, bind them wherever they may go, appear to have been that each state has the rightful power of regulating the status and condition of its subjects, and, being best acquainted with the circumstances of climate, race, character, manners and customs, can best judge at what age young persons may begin to act for themselves, and whether and how far married women may act independently of

their husbands; that laws limiting the capacity of infants or
of married women are intended for their protection, and cannot
therefore be dispensed with by their agreement; that all civilized states recognize the incapacity of infants and married
women; and that a person, dealing with either, ordinarily has
notice, by the apparent age or sex, that the person is likely to
be of a class whom the laws protect, and is thus put upon inquiry
how far, by the law of the domicil of the person, the protection
extends.

On the other hand, it is only by the comity of other states
that laws can operate beyond the limit of the state that makes
them. In the great majority of cases, especially in this country,
where it is so common to travel, or to transact business through
agents, or to correspond by letter, from one state to another, it
is more just, as well as more convenient, to have regard to the
law of the place of the contract, as a uniform rule operating on
all contracts of the same kind, and which the contracting parties
may be presumed to have in contemplation when making their
contracts, than to require them at their peril to know the domicil
of those with whom they deal, and to ascertain the law of that
domicil, however remote, which in many cases could not be done
without such delay as would greatly cripple the power of contracting abroad at all.

As the law of another state can neither operate nor be executed in this state by its own force, but only by the comity of
this state, its operation and enforcement here may be restricted
by positive prohibition of statute. A state may always by express enactment protect itself from being obliged to enforce in
its courts contracts made abroad by its citizens, which are not
authorized by its own laws. Under the French code, for instance,
which enacts that the laws regulating the status and capacity of
persons shall bind French subjects, even when living in a foreign
country, a French court cannot enforce a contract made by a
Frenchman abroad, which he is incapable of making by the law
of France. See Westlake, §§ 399, 400.

It is possible also that in a state where the common law pre
vailed in full force, by which a married woman was deemed incapable of binding herself by any contract whatever, it might
be inferred that such an utter incapacity, lasting throughout the
joint lives of husband and wife, must be considered as so fixed
by the settled policy of the state, for the protection of its own
citizens, that it could not be held by the courts of that state to

yield to the law of another state in which she might undertake to contract.

But it is not true at the present day that all civilized states recognize the absolute incapacity of married women to make contracts. The tendency of modern legislation is to enlarge their capacity in this respect, and in many states they have nearly or quite the same powers as if unmarried. In Massachusetts, even at the time of the making of the contract in question, a married woman was vested by statute with a very extensive power to carry on business by herself, and to bind herself by contracts with regard to her own property, business and earnings; and, before the bringing of the present action, the power had been extended so as to include the making of all kinds of contracts, with any person but her husband, as if she were unmarried. There is therefore no reason of public policy which should prevent the maintenance of this action.

Judgment for the plaintiffs.

FLAGG v. BALDWIN, 1884.

[38 N. J. Eq. 219.]

MAGIE, J.

The bill in this case was filed for the foreclosure of a mortgage made by Jennie M. Flagg and William L. Flagg, her husband (who are the appellants), to Abram F. Baldwin (who is the respondent), upon lands in this state, to secure the payment of appellants' bond. The bond and mortgage were dated August 26th, 1880. The bond was in the ordinary form of a money obligation and was conditioned for the payment to respondent of $11,563.44, with interest, on demand. The mortgage recited that it was intended to secure the money which appellants had so bound themselves to pay, and that the amount of $11,563.44 was made up of $7,563.44, which was therein declared to be then due .rom appellants to respondents, and of $4,000 to be security for future advances.

From the proofs it appears that the sum of $7,563.44, so admitted to be due from appellants to respondent, was made up of different sums. One sum represented the loss which had been incurred by Mr. Flagg in a stock speculation which had been carried on by him and one Ripley with respondent, a stockbroker in New York. Another sum represented losses incurred by Mr. Flagg in a like speculation carried on by him and respondent in joint account. Another sum represented losses in-

curred in a like speculation originally carried on by Mr. Flagg
with respondent and afterwards transferred to and carried on by
Mrs. Flagg (under the control and management of her husband)
with respondent. The losses thus incurred were the result of
stock dealings for these respective parties upon a margin sometimes put up in cash, and in Mrs. Flagg's case in her own note,
which represented her margin.

The $4,000 of future advances were designed and intended
as a margin for a continuance of the stock speculation of Mrs.
Flagg to be carried on in her name under the management of
her husband with respondent, and the advances contemplated by
both parties were such as would cover and make good her losses
therein, if any.

Respondent's books show that the bond and mortgage were
credited to Mrs. Flagg's account for the sum of $11,563.44, and
that account had been charged with the previous losses. It appears further that the speculative stocks carried in that account
have all been closed out with the result of leaving a balance in
Mrs. Flagg's favor of $653.93. Since the mortgage entered into
the account, the effect is that there is due thereon the sum of
$10,909.51, with interest, and its foreclosure and the sale of the
mortgaged premises must be conceded unless some of the de
fences are sustained.

The main defence goes to the validity of the bond and mortgage, and contests them on the ground that the contracts out of
which they arose were wagering contracts and illegal and void,
and that the bond and mortgage securing an indebtedness arising
solely from such cause are tainted with the same illegality and
cannot be enforced.   ,

In coming to the consideration of the question thus raised, it
is obvious that it is important to determine at what place the
contracts contested were made. For if they are New Jersey
contracts and subject to our law, the sole question is whether
they are such contracts as are declared unlawful by the "act to
prevent gaming." *Rev. p. 458.* While if they are contracts
of another place, it must be preliminarily determined whether
they are objectionable by the law of the place of contract; or if
not. whether they will still be enforced by our courts.

The evidence seems to leave no room for doubt that the con
tracts in question are contracts made and to be performed in the
state of New York. The transactions anterior to the execution of
the bond and mortgage took place wholly within that state. By

the bond and mortgage the parties averred they resided in that state. The mortgagee did, in fact, reside there. The mortgage was acknowledged there. Delivery of the papers was made, and the remaining transactions took place there. Although the mortgage affected lands in this state, the above-stated facts establish, according to a long line of decisions, that the contracts were New York contracts. *Cotheal v. Blydenburgh, 1 Hal. Ch. 17; S. C., 1 Hal. Ch. 631; De Wolf v. Johnson, 10 Wheat. 367; Dolman v. Cook, 1 McCart. 56; Campion v. Kille, 1 McCart. 229; S. C., 2 McCart. 476; Atwater v. Walker, 1 C. E. Gr. 42.*

Where contracts of a particular kind are forbidden by the law of the state in which they are sought to be enforced, and the party seeking to enforce them relies on the fact that they were made in a foreign state and are valid contracts by the *lex loci contractus*, it has been held elsewhere that he is bound to aver and prove those facts. *Thatcher v. Morris, 11 N. Y. 437.*

But the rule which seems to have been established in this state requires one who defends against a foreign contract, if he relies on its being invalid by force of the *lex loci contractus*, to both set up and prove the foreign law. *Campion v. Kille, ubi supra; Dolman v. Cook, ubi supra; Uhler v. Semple, 5 C. E. Gr. 288.*

We have, then, to deal with transactions which took place within the state of New York and must be presumed to be governed by the laws of that state. Whatever may be the rule respecting the burden of setting up and proving the law of the foreign state under such circumstances, neither appellants nor respondent have furnished in their pleadings or proofs any information on the subject. In the absence of proof of the law of another state, the better opinion is that, at least with respect to states comprised in the territory severed from England by the revolution, the presumption is that the common law prevails. *White v. Knapp, 47 Barb. 549; Stokes. v. Macken, 62 Barb. 145; Holmes v. Broughton, 10 Wend. 75; Thurston v. Percival, 1 Pick. 415; Shepherd v. Nabors, 6 Ala. 631; Walker v. Walker, 41 Ala. 353; Thompson v. Monrow, 2 Cal. 99; Inge v. Murphy, 10 Ala. 885; Norris v. Harris, 15 Cal. 226; Titus v. Scantling, 4 Blackf. 89; Crouch v. Hall, 15 Ill. 263; Brown v. Pratt, 3 Jones (N. C.) Eq. 202.*

By the common law, contracts of wager and similar contracts were not objectionable *per se*. They were, in fact, enforced by the courts without any objection on the score of being dependent on a chance or casualty. Courts did, in some instances, refuse to enforce such contracts, but only when the subject of the wager was objectionable, as tending to encourage acts contrary to sound morals (*Gilbert* v. *Sykes, 16 East 150*) ; or being injurious to the feelings or interests of third persons (*De Costa* v. *Jones Cowp. 729*) ; or against public policy or public duty (*Atherfold* v. *Beard, 2 T. R. 610; Tappenden* v. *Randall, 2 B. & P. 467; Shirley* v. *Sankey, 2 P. & B. 130; Hartley* v. *Rice, 10 East 22*).

It has not been urged, nor does there seem to be ground for contending, that the transactions in question were such as by the common law would not be enforced.

We are therefore required to determine whether these contracts, made in the state of New York, and presumed to be governed, as to their validity, by the doctrines of the common law and not objectionable thereunder, are to be enforced in this state.

The common law under which such contracts were enforcable has been here altered by the passage of the act against gaming above referred to. By the first section, all wagers, bets or stakes made to depend on any lot, chance, casualty or unknown or contingent event are declared to be unlawful. By the third section, all bonds, mortgages or other securities made or given, where the whole or any part of the consideration shall be for money laid or betted in violation of the first section, or for repaying money knowingly advanced to help or facilitate such violation, are declared to be utterly void.

If the contracts now sought to be enforced would be obnoxious to these provisions of our statute, if made in this state, are we to enforce them because made in New York, where we are bound to presume the common law exists unaltered?

The enforcement of a foreign law and contracts dependent thereon for validity, within another jurisdiction and by the courts of another nation, is not to be demanded as a matter of strict right. It is permitted, if at all, only from the comity which exists between states and nations. Every independent community must judge for itself how far this comity ought to extend. Certain principles are well-nigh universally recognized as governing this subject. It is everywhere admitted that a contract respecting matter *malum in se,* or a contract *contra bonos mores,* will not be enforced elsewhere, however enforceable by the *lex loci contractus.* An almost complete agreement exists upon the proposition that a contract valid where made will not be enforced by the courts of another country, if, in doing so, they must violate the plain public policy of the country whose jurisdiction is invoked to enforce it, or if its enforcement would be injurious to the interest or conflict with the operation of the public laws of that country. *Story's Confl. Laws* § *244; 1 Addison Cont.* § *241; Forbes* v. *Cochrane, 2 B. & C. 448; Grell* v. *Levy, 16 C. B. (N. S.) 73; Hope* v. *Hope, 8 De G., M. & G. 731; 2 Kent's Com. 475; Bank of Augusta* v. *Earle, 13 Pet. 519; Ogden* v. *Saunders, 12 Wheat. 213; Blanchard* v. *Russell, 13 Mass. 1.* This proposition has been announced and applied in our own state. *Varnum* v. *Camp, 1 Gr. 326; Frazier* v. *Fredericks, 4 Zab. 162; Moore* v. *Bonnell, 2 Vr. 90; Bentley* v. *Whittemore, 4 C. E. Gr. 462; Watson* v. *Murray, 8 C. E. Gr. 257; Union L. & E. Co.* v. *Erie R. Co., 8 Vr. 23.*

Since the courts of each state must, at least in the absence of positive law, determine how for comity requires the enforcement of foreign contracts, it results that there is contrariety of view, and the proposition above stated is not universally admitted. Thus, in New York, a contract made in Kentucky, under a law of that state, establishing a lottery for the benefit of a college, was upheld, notwithstanding the law of New York prohibiting lotteries. *Com. of Ky.* v. *Bassford, 6 Hill 526.* Chief-Justice Nelson limited the cases of contracts not enforceable, though valid where made, to such as are plainly contrary to morality. He gave no consideration to the doctrine elsewhere settled, that excludes from enforcement, contracts opposed to the public policy or violative of a public law of the place of enforcement. In this view, he seems to be sustained by the court of appeals. *Thatcher* v. *Morris, 11 N. Y. 437.*

So in Massachusetts, a contract arising out of a completed sale of lottery tickets, in a state where such sale was lawful, was enforced by the courts, although such sale was there prohibited by statute. *McIntyre* v. *Parks, 3 Metc. 207.* But there was no discussion of principles by the court.

The courts of this state have expressed and enforced different views. Thus, in *Varnum* v. *Camp, 1 Gr. 326,* the question of the validity of a foreign assignment for the benefit of creditors, came before the supreme court. The assignment was made in New York, and was assumed to be valid by the law of that state. It created preferences, and by the law of this state, was fraudulent and void. The assignment was held unenforceable here. Chief-Justice Ewing, whose opinion was adopted by the court, puts the decision distinctly upon the ground that the assignment was one in violation of the policy of our laws, in hostility with their provisions, and which they declared to be fraudulent and void. In *Bentley* v. *Whittemore, 4 C. E. Gr. 462,* a similar question arose in this court, and the doctrine of *Varnum* v. *Camp* was restated and affirmed. The application of the doctrine was, however, limited to the protection of the residents and citizens of this state, for whose benefit its public policy was held to be adopted. With respect to non-residents, or citizens of other states, it was held that comity would require the recognition of foreign assignments, if valid where made. *Watson* v. *Murray, ubi sup.,* was the case of a bill filed for an account of a partnership transaction in a lottery in another state, where such a transaction was claimed to be lawful. The bill was dismissed on the advice of Vice-Chancellor Dodd. His conclusion was that such a transaction, though valid where made, should not be enforced here, because it was in violation of a public law of this state, and within the exceptions to the rule of comity requiring the enforcement of foreign contracts. He further argued that lotteries are not only illegal, but are to be judicially considered to be immoral. It is unnecessary to determine how far that view can be sustained. But with the conclusion arrived at I unhesitatingly agree. It is in accord with the decisions in *Varnum* v. *Camp* and *Bentley* v. *Whittemore.* It seems to me that no court can, on full consideration, deliberately adopt a rule that will require the enforcement of foreign contracts, violative of the public laws and subversive of the distinct public policy of the country whose laws and policy they are bound to enforce. No *comitas inter communitates* can compel such a sacrifice.

The limitations on the rule laid down in *Bentley* v. *Whittemore* do not come in question in this case. It appears that Mrs. Flagg was, in fact, a resident of this state at the time these contracts were made, and there is nothing to show a change of residence.

We are brought, then, to the question whether our law against gaming is such a public law and establishes such a public policy as to require us to refuse to enforce foreign contracts in conflict with it, in a case like that under consideration. I think this question must be answered in the affirmative.

It is true that, in *Dolman* v. *Cook* and *Campion* v. *Kille, ubi sup.,* foreign contracts, valid by the law of the state where made, were enforced here, although, by our law, they were usurious and declared to be void. No consideration seems to have been given to the question whether our usury law was such a law and evinced such a public policy as required us to refrain from enforcing foreign contracts in conflict with it. As we have seen, that consideration led our courts to reject foreign assignments violative of our laws, where the interests of our own citizens were concerned. But a plain distinction at once presents itself between a usury law and a law regulating assignments for the benefit of creditors, or a law against gaming. One affects only the parties to the contract, and is framed for the protection of the borrower. The others relate to the public or classes of the public who are interested therein and affected thereby.

But our law against gaming goes further than to merely prohibit the vice of avoid contracts tainted with it. It declares it unlawful, and so puts the contracts beyond the protection of the laws or the right of appeal to the courts. The reason and object of the law are obvious. The vice aimed at is not only injurious to the person who games, but wastes his property, to the injury of those dependent on him, or who are to succeed to him. It has its more public aspect, for if it be announced that a trustee has been false to his trust, or a public officer has embezzled public funds, by common consent the first inquiry is whether the defaulter has been wasting his property in gambling.

In my judgment, our law against gaming is of such a character, and is designed for the prevention of a vice, producing injury so widespread in its effect, the policy evinced thereby is of such public interest that comity does not require us to here enforce a contract which, by that law, is stigmatized as unlawful, and so prohibited.

It remains to determine whether the enforcement of these contracts will conflict with the provisions of this statute and the public policy thereby established. If so, it must be for the reason that the mortgage secures an indebtedness arising out of transactions that are wagers.

In considering this question, care should be taken not to trench upon legitimate and proper enterprises. The act is not intended to interfere with the right of buying and selling for speculation.

The line is to be drawn between what is legitimate speculation and what is unlawful wager. When property is actually bought, whether with money or with credit, the purchaser and owner may lawfully hold it for a future rise and risk a future

28

fall. With such transactions, the law does not pretend to inter
fere. They are within the line of lawful speculation.

But when, either without any disguise or under a guise which
simulates such legitimate enterprises, the real transaction is a
mere dealing in the differences between prices, *i. e.*, in the payments of future profits or future losses, as the event may be, then,
in my judgment, the line which separates lawful speculation from
illegal wagering is crossed, and the contract, under our law, becomes unlawful, and the securities for it void.

This proposition is sustained by all the cases, without an exception, that I can discover   The only disagreement relates to
the application of the doctrine.

Thus, in New York, the court of appeals, in *Kingsbury* v.
Kirwan, 77 N. Y. 612, declared that a contract for the purchase
and sale of property would be a wagering contract, if it was the
understanding that the property should not be delivered, but that
only the difference in the market price should be paid and received.   In *Bigelow* v. *Benedict, 70 N. Y. 202*, the same view
had been expressed, and it was also held that, although the form
of the contract was unobjectionable, yet if, in fact, it was a mere
cover for betting on the future price of a commodity, and no
actual sale or purchase was intended, the contract was one of
wager.

It is true that the same court has determined, though against
the protest of able and distinguished judges, that between the
broker purchasing on a margin and his customer, the relation of
principal and agent, and of pledgor and pledgee, exists. *Markham* v. *Jaudon, 41 N. Y. 235; Baker* v. *Drake, 66 N. Y. 518;
Gruman* v. *Smith, 81 N. Y. 25.*   It has been there held that a
broker can recover from his customer deficiencies arising from
sales of stocks bought on a margin, and that where, upon a margin, a broker made "short sales" of stock, which he borrowed
for that purpose, he might recover of his customer what was
expended in replacing the borrowed stock. *Wicks* v. *Hatch, 62
N. Y. 535; Knowlton* v. *Fitch, 52 N. Y. 288.*   But in these
cases, it does not seem to have been contended that the contract
was a mere cover for wager.   Such contention was made in
Kingsbury v. *Kirwan* and *Bigelow* v. *Benedict*, but it was held
that there was no sufficient evidence that the transactions were
not real.   Upon a review of all the cases in New York, they
establish, in my judgment, the correct doctrine that a contract
relating to differences only would be a wager contract.   But

they also hold that dealings on margin are not to be considered as dealings in mere differences. If, in any case, evidence sufficient to show that the margin dealings were mere covers for dealings in differences was produced, then, upon the principles there laid down, the contracts would be wagers.

In the courts of Pennsylvania, the same principles have been often enunciated. Thus, in *Smith* v. *Bouvier, 70 Pa. St. 325,* the court approved a charge to a jury which left to them to say whether the transactions embraced in the case were *bona fide* or were mere covers for gambling operations. See, also, *Fareira* v. *Gabell, 89 Pa. St. 89.* And in general, whenever the verdict of a jury established, or the evidence required the court to hold, that the transactions, however correct in point of form, were mere dealings in differences, they were declared to be wagers. *Brua's Appeal, 55 Pa. St. 294; Kirkpatrick* v. *Bonsall, 72 Pa. St. 155; Maxton* v. *Gheen, 75 Pa. St. 166; North* v. *Phillips, 89 Pa. St. 250; Dickson* v. *Thomas, 97 Pa. St. 278; Ruchizky* v. *De Haven, 97 Pa. St. 202; Patterson's Appeal, 16 Rep. 59.* The point of divergence between the New York and Pennsylvania cases is upon the relation existing between the customer and the broker who is managing a speculative account upon a margin. The New York cases treat the broker as a mere agent, and so as a pledgee of the stocks purchased on such an account. This result was reached by a divided court, Justices Grover and Woodruff delivering vigorous dissenting opinions. The latter especially points out, in a perspicuous and, in my judgment, convincing way, the plain difference between a stock broker dealing on margins and a broker or agent in ordinary transactions. *Markham* v. *Jaudon, 41 N. Y. 256.* In Pennsylvania, it is held that one who enters into a stock speculation on margins, with a stock broker, is to be considered as dealing with the broker as a principal, and not as an agent. *Ruchizky* v. *De Haven, sup. 2.* This view is, in my judgment, entirely correct. The customer who deals on margins knows no other person in the transaction but the broker. He has no claim upon, and is subject to no liability to any other person whatever.

The same doctrine has been announced by the supreme court of the District of Columbia (*Justh* v. *Holliday, 11 Wash. L. Rep. 418*), and by the United States circuit court in the district of Kansas. *Cobb* v. *Prell, 22 Am. Law Reg. (N. S.) 609.* To the latter case a note is appended, discussing the subject and collecting many cases.

In *Grizewood* v. *Blane, 11 C. B. 526*, it was held that a color-able contract for the sale and purchase of railway shares, when neither party intends to deliver or accept the shares, but merely to pay differences according to the rise and fall of the market, was a gaming contract, within the *8 and 9 Vic. c. 109 § 18*, which declares contracts by way of gaming and wagering void, and forbids recovery of any money won on a wager. The subsequent case of *Thacker* v. *Hardy, L. R. (4 Q. B. Div.) 685*, does not shake the authority of *Grizewood* v. *Blane,* but expressly approves it. Since, however, in the case of *Thacker* v. *Hardy,* a broker was permitted to recover of his customer indemnity for con-tracts entered into on a speculative account, although the broker knew the customer did not intend to accept the stock bought or deliver the stock sold for him, but expected the broker to so arrange matters that nothing but differences were to be payable by him, it has been much relied on by respondent's counsel. But, in that case, the broker was treated as a mere agent enter-ing into contracts for his principal, and so entitled to indemnity against any personal liability thereon. The ground of decision was that the contract, as between the customer and the other principal (the stock broker being treated as mere agent), was, at the most, void, but not illegal, and that the broker's right of indemnity was not affected thereby. Thus, Lindsley, J., by whom the case was tried without a jury, says that: "If gaming and wagering were illegal, I should be of opinion that the illegality of the transactions in which the plaintiff and defendant were en-gaged, would have tainted, as between them, whatever plaintiff had done in furtherance of their illegal designs, and would have precluded him from claiming, in a court of law, any indemnity from the defendant in respect of liabilities incurred." He points out that it had been held, under the English act of *8 and 9 Vict.,* above cited, that, although gaming and wagering contracts could not be enforced, they were not illegal. He draws the conclusion that the acts of the broker, not being in furtherance of an illegal transaction, and being directed by the customer, entitled him to indemnity against loss thereby. On appeal, the views of the trial judge were approved.

It will be observed that our statute declares such contracts not only void, but unlawful, and, further, that the relation of agency between the customer and broker, in such transactions on which the decision was grounded, is not, by the weight of author-ity in this country, recognized as the real relation of the parties.

For reasons above given, I think it clear that the customer and broker, in these margin transactions, deal as two principals, and not as principal and agent.

My conclusion is that these transactions, so far as affected by our law against gaming, are to be examined, to discover their real nature, and if, however unobjectionable their form may be, the real contract is merely in respect to differences, the contract is a wager, both void and unlawful.

On examining the transactions in question in this cause, with a view to discover their real character, I am compelled to the conclusion that, however they may have been made to imitate real transactions, they were in fact mere wagers. It never was contemplated, intended or agreed, by either party, that the stocks purchased or sold were to become or to be treated as the stocks of appellants. The real contract disclosed by the evidence was to receive and pay differences.

All the transactions were upon margins. They commenced by Flagg's depositing $1,000 with respondent, when he agreed to open the account, which was wholly a speculative account. Afterwards Flagg deposited $300 more. Then the wife's note for $4,500 was put in, and the account transferred to her name. Finally the bond and mortgage were given.

Upon these advances the purchases were very large. Respondent testifies that upon the margin of $1,300, stocks of a cash value of about $450,000 were purchased for the account between January 28th and June 16th, 1880. After the account was transferred to Mrs. Flagg's name, stocks to an amount between $600,000 and $700,000, were purchased between June 16th, 1880, and March 17th, 1881. Thus, in less than fourteen months, purchases aggregating over $1,000,000 were made. According to Flagg's statement, the account once held one thousand three hundred shares, of a par value of $1,300,000.

The certificates of the stocks were never transferred or delivered to appellants.

These enormous transactions were far beyond the ability of appellants at any time, and were known to be so. It appears that respondent was notified that the first advance was all that Flagg had to speculate with. The wife's note, and subsequently her bond and mortgage, were resorted to with the avowed purpose of binding her separate property. Respondent admits that he was informed and knew that Flagg was speculating for all that Mrs. Flagg and he had in the world.

Under such circumstances, it is idle to pretend that there was or could be any hope or expectation that appellants were to take or could be required to take these vast amounts of stock. For respondent to have tendered them, and demanded payment for them, would have been absurd in the extreme. The whole circumstances show that no such right to tender entered into the transaction. On the contrary, the contract plainly was that if the stocks bought advanced, the profit was to be realized by a sale. If they declined, the remedy of respondent to save himself was by a sale. The settlement was to be of the profits and losses thus ascertained.

If, in the absence of express stipulation, the reciprocal rights of tendering and demanding this stock would be presumed to enter into such a contract, the whole circumstances corroborate the testimony of Flagg, who swears that it was expressly understood that there was not to be any actual delivery of stocks, and that he should not be required to pay for them.

In the able opinion below much stress is laid on the fact that the purchases and sales for this account were actually made by respondent. He so testifies, and produces vouchers in corroboration of his statement. That the transactions were very large, and upon a petty advance, is not sufficient, probably, to permit us to reject this positive statement. But assuming it to be true that respondent actually purchased or sold every share of stock in this account, I am unable to perceive how the circumstance affects the conclusion in this case. If respondent was the mere agent of the appellants in transactions with third parties, there might be some significance attached to it. But such is not, as we have seen, the real nature of the relation between the parties. They were dealing, as to this transaction, as principals, and it was a matter of indifference whether respondent owned or bought the stock he agreed to carry. The transaction was precisely like that which Judge Woodruff, in the dissenting opinion in *Markham* v. *Jaudon,* characterized as "an executory agreement for a pure speculation in the rise and fall of stock, which the broker, on condition of indemnity against loss, agrees to carry through in his own name and on his own means or credit, accounting to him [the customer] for the profits, if any, and holding him responsible for the losses." Such an agreement is, within the principles above referred to, a wager.

Nor is the result altered by the fact that the broker has or attempts to retain perfect indemnity against loss on his part. As

I interpret the transactions, respondent, in consideration of commissions and interest on advances, agreed to buy and hold stock in anticipation of a rise; or to sell stock of his own, or borrowed for that purpose, in anticipation of a fall. The agreement required him to pay the profits of the transaction, which would otherwise be his, to appellants. On the other hand, appellants, in consideration of his thus carrying the stock bought, or providing the stock sold, agreed that in case of a rise or fall to a certain amount, the stock should be closed out, and the loss, which otherwise would fall on respondent, should be paid by them to him. This bargain contained all the elements of a wager. It is not less a wager because one of the parties obtained a guaranty for the performance of the bargain by the other party.

For these reasons my conclusion is that the transactions in question were wagers within the meaning of our law; that the securities given for them would be absolutely void if the contracts were made in this state; that although made in a foreign state, and not objectionable by the law which must be presumed (in the absence of proof) to govern them, they will not be, and ought not to be, enforced in this state, between these parties, because to enforce them would be opposed to a public policy on this subject of the vice of gaming, perspicuously shown by our law on that subject.

The decree below must be reversed, and a decree entered dismissing the bill. Appellants are entitled to their costs.

POLSON v. STEWART, 1897.

[167 Mass. 211.]

HOLMES, J. This is a bill to enforce a covenant made by the defendant to his wife, the plaintiff's intestate, in North Carolina, to surrender all his marital rights in certain land of hers. The land is in Massachusetts. The parties to the covenant were domiciled in North Carolina. According to the bill, the wife took steps which under the North Carolina statutes gave her the right to contract as a feme sole with her husband as well as with others, and afterwards released her dower in the defendant's lands. In consideration of this release, and to induce his wife to forbear suing for divorce, for which she had just cause, and for other adequate considerations, the defendant executed the covenant. The defendant demurs.

The argument in support of the demurrer goes a little

further than is open on ⁺he allegations of the bill.   It suggests
that the instrument which made the wife a "free trader," in the
language of the statute, did not go into effect until after the execution of the release of dower and of the defendant's covenant.
But the allegation is that the last mentioned two deeds were
executed after the wife became a free trader, as they probably
were in fact, notwithstanding their bearing date earlier than the
registration of the free trader instrument. We must assume
that at the date of their dealings together the defendant and his
wife had as large a freedom to contract together as the laws of
their domicil could give them.

But it said that the laws of the parties' domicil could not
authorize a contract between them as to lands in Massachusetts.
Obviously this is not true.   It is true that the laws of other
States cannot render valid conveyances of property within our
borders which our laws say are void, for the plain reason that
we have exclusive power over the *res. Ross* v. *Ross,* 129 Mass.
243, 246. *Hallgarten* v. *Oldham,* 135 Mass. 1, 7, 8. But the
same reason inverted establishes that the *lex rei sitæ* cannot
control personal covenants, nor purporting to be conveyances,
between persons outside the jurisdiction, although concerning a
thing within it. Whatever the covenant, the laws of North
Carolina could subject the defendant's property to seizure on
execution, and his person to imprisonment, for a failure to
perform it. Therefore, on principle, the law of North Carolina
determines the validity of the contract. Such precedents as there
are, are on the same side.   The most important intimations to the
contrary which we have seen are a brief note in Story, Confl. of
Laws, § 436, note, and the doubts expressed in Mr. Dicey's very
able and valuable book. Lord Cottenham stated and enforced
the rule in the clearest way in *Ex parte Pollard,* 4 Deac. 27, 40
et seq.; S. C. Mont. & Ch. 239, 250. So Lord Romilly in *Cood*
v. *Cood,* 33 *Beav.* 314, 322. So in Scotland, in a case like the
present, where the contract enforced was the wife's. *Findlater*
v. *Seafield, Faculty Decisions,* 553, Feb. 8, 1814. See also *Cun-
inghame* v. *Semple,* 11 Morison, 4462; Erskine, Inst. Bk. 3, tit.
2, § 40; Westlake, Priv. Int. Law (3d ed.) § 172 Rorer, Interstate
Law (2d ed.) 289, 290.

If valid by the law of North Carolina there is no reason
why the contract should not be enforced here. The general principle is familiar. Without considering the argument addressed
to us that such a contract would have been good in equity if

made here (*Holmes* v. *Winchester,* 133 Mass. 140, *Jones* v. *Clifton,* 101 U. S. 225, and *Bean* v. *Patterson,* 122 U. S. 496, 499), we see no ground of policy for an exception. The statutory limits which have been found to the power of a wife to release dower (*Mason* v. *Mason,* 140 Mass. 63, and *Peaslee* v. *Peaslee,* 147 Mass. 171, 181) do not prevent a husband from making a valid covenant that he will not claim marital rights with any person competent to receive a covenant from him. *Charles* v. *Charles,* 8 Grat. 486. *Logan* v. *Birkett,* 1 Myl. & K. 220. *Marshall* v. *Beall,* 6 How. 70. The competency of the wife to receive the covenant is established by the law of her domicil and of the place of the contract. The laws of Massachusetts do not make it impossible for him specifically to perform his undertaking. He can give a release which will be good by Massachusetts law. If it be said that the rights of the administrator are only derivative from the wife, we agree, and we do not for a moment regard any one as privy to the contract except as representing the wife. But if then it be asked whether she could have enforced the contract during her life, an answer in the affirmative is made easy by considering exactly what the defendant undertook to do. So far as occurs to us, he undertook three things: first, not to disturb his wife's enjoyment while she kept her property; secondly, to execute whatever instrument was necessary in order to release his rights if she conveyed; and thirdly, to claim no rights on her death, but to do whatever was necessary to clear the title from such rights then. All these things were as capable of performance in Massachusetts as they would have been in North Carolina. Indeed, all the purposes of the covenant could have been secured at once in the lifetime of the wife by a joint conveyance of the property to a trustee upon trusts properly limited. It will be seen that the case does not raise the question as to what the common law and the presumed law of North Carolina would be as to a North Carolina contract calling for acts in Massachusetts, or concerning property in Massachusetts, which could not be done consistently with Massachusetts law.

With regard to the construction of the defendant's covenant we have no doubt. It is "to surrender, convey, and transfer to said Kitty T. Polson Stewart, Jr., and her heirs, all the rights of him, the said Henry Stewart, Jr., in and to the lands and property above described, which he may have acquired by reason of the aforesaid marriage, and the said Kitty T. Polson Stewart,

Jr., is to have the full and absolute control and possession of all of said property free and discharged of all the rights, claims, or demands of every nature whatsoever of the said Henry Stewart, Jr." Notwithstanding the decision of the majority in *Rochon v. Lecatt*, 2 Stew. (Ala.) 429, we think that it would be quibbling with the manifest intent to put an end to all claims of the defendant if we were to distinguish between vested rights which had and those which had not yet become estates in the land, or between claims during the life of the wife and claims after her death. It is plain, too, that the words import a covenant for such further assurance as may be necessary to carry out the manifest object of the deed. See *Marshall v. Beall*, 6 How. 70; *Ward v. Thompson*, 6 Gill & Johns. 349; *Hutchins v. Dixon*, 11 Md. 29; *Hamrico v. Laird*, 10 Yerger, 222; *Mason v. Deese*, 30 Ga. 308; *McLeod v. Board*, 30 Tex. 238.

Objections are urged against the consideration. The instrument is alleged to have been a covenant. It is set forth, and mentions one dollar as the consideration. But the bill alleges others; to which we have referred. It is argued that one of them, forbearance to bring a well founded suit for divorce, was illegal. The judgment of the majority in *Merrill v. Peaslee*, 146 Mass. 460, 463, expressly guarded itself against sanctioning such a notion, and decisions of the greatest weight referred to in that case show that such a consideration is both sufficient and legal. *Newsome v. Newsome*, L. R. 2 P. & D. 306, 312. *Wilson v. Wilson*, 1 H. L. Cas. 538, 574. *Beasant v. Wood*, 12 Ch. D. 605, 622. *Hart v. Hart*, 18 Ch. D. 670, 685. *Adams v. Adams*, 91 N. Y. 381. *Sterling v. Sterling*, 12 Ga. 201. Then it is said that the wife's agreement in bar of her dower was invalid, because it had not the certificate that she had been examined, etc., as required by the North Carolina statutes annexed to the bill. Whether it was invalid or not, the defendant was content with it, and accepted the execution of it as a consideration. This being so, it would be hard to say that it was not one, even if without legal effect. Whether void or not, it is alleged to have been performed; and finally, if it was void, it was void on its face, as matter of law, and the husband must be taken to have known it, so that the most that could be done would be to disregard it; if that were done, the other considerations would be sufficient. See *Jones v. Waite*, 5 Bing, N. C. 341, 351. *Demurrer overruled.*

FIELD, C. J. I cannot assent to the opinion of a majority of the court. By our law husband and wife are under a general disability or incapacity to make contracts with each other. The decision in *Whitney* v. *Closson,* 138 Mass. 49, shows, I think, that the contract sued on would not be enforced if the husband and wife had been domiciled in Massachusetts when it was made. As a conveyance made directly between husband and wife of an interest in Massachusetts land would be void although the parties were domiciled in North Carolina when it was made, and by the laws of North Carolina were authorized to make such a conveyance, so I think that a contract for such a conveyance between the same persons also would be void. It seems to me illogical to say that we will not permit a conveyance of Massachusetts land directly between husband and wife, wherever they may have their domicil, and yet say that they may make a contract to convey such land from one to the other which our courts will specifically enforce. It is possible to abandon the rule *lex rei sitæ,* but to keep it for conveyances of land and to abandon it for contracts to convey land seems to me unwarrantable.

The question of the validity of a mortgage of land in this Commonwealth is to be decided by the law here, although the mortgage was executed elsewhere where the parties resided, and would have been void if upon land there situated. *Goddard* v. *Sawyer,* 9 Allen, 78. "It is a settled principle, that 'the title to, and the disposition of, real estate must be exclusively regulated by the law of the place in which it is situated.'" *Cutter* v. *Davenport,* 1 Pick. 81. *Osborn* v. *Adams,* 18 Pick 245. The testamentary execution of a power of appointment given by will in relation to land is governed by the *lex situs,* or the law of the domicil of the donor of the power. *Sewall* v. *Wilmer,* 132 Mass. 131.

The plaintiff, merely as administrator, cannot maintain the bill. *Caverly* v. *Simpson,* 132 Mass. 462, 464. The plaintiff must proceed on the ground that Mrs. Henry Stewart, Jr. acquired by the instruments executed in North Carolina the right to have conveyed or released to her and her heirs by her husband all the interest he had as her husband in her lands in Massachusetts; that this right descended on her death to her heirs, according to the law of Massachusetts; and that the plaintiff, being an heir, has acquired the interest of the other heirs, and therefore brings the bill as owner of this right. The plaintiff, as heir, claims by descent from Mrs. Stewart, and if the contract sued on is void as to her, it is void as to him.

It is only on the ground that the contract conveyed an equitable title that the plaintiff as heir has any standing* in court. His counsel founds his arguments on the distinction between a conveyance of the legal title to land and a contract to convey it. If the instrument relied on purported to convey the legal title, his counsel in effect admits that it would be void by our law. He accepts the doctrine stated in *Ross* v. *Ross,* 129 Mass. 243, 246, as follows: "And the validity of any transfer of real estate by act of the owner, whether *inter vivos* or by will, is to be determined, even as regards the capacity of the grantor or testator, by the law of the State in which the land is situated." As a contract purporting to convey a right in equity to obtain the legal title to land, he contends that it is valid. I do not dispute the cases cited with reference to contracts concerning personal property, but the rule at common law in regard to the capacity of parties to make contracts concerning real property, as I read the cases and text-books, is that the *lex situs* governs. *Cochran* v. *Benton,* 126 Ind. 58. *Doyle* v. *McGuire,* 38 Iowa, 410. *Sell* v. *Miller,* 11 Ohio St. 331. *Johnston* v. *Gawtry,* 11 Mo. App. 322. *Frierson* v. *Williams,* 57 Miss. 451.

Dicey on the Conflict of Laws is the latest text-book on the subject. He states the rule as follows ·

Page lxxxix. "(B). Validity of Contract. (i) Capacity.

"Rule 146. Subject to the exceptions hereinafter mentioned, a person's capacity to enter into a contract is governed by the law of his domicil (*lex domicilii*) at the time of the making of the contract.

"(1) If he has such capacity by that law, the contract is, in so far as its validity depends upon his capacity, valid.

"(2) If he has not such capacity by that law, the contract is invalid.

"Exception 1. A person's capacity to bind himself by an ordinary mercantile contract is (probably) governed by the law of the country where the contract is made (*lex loci contractus*) [?].

"Exception 2. A person's capacity to contract in respect of an immovable (land) is governed by the *lex situs.*"

Page xcii. "(A). Contracts with regard to Immovables.

"Rule 151. The effect of a contract with regard to an immovable is governed by the proper law of the contract [?].

"The proper law of such contract is, in general, the law of the country where the immovable is situate (*lex situs*)."

On page 517 *et seq.* he states the law in the same way, with·

numerous illustrations, but with some hesitation as to the law governing the form of contracts to convey immovables. See page xc., Rule 147, Exception 1. For American notes with cases, see page 527 *et seq.* In the Apppendix, page 769, note (B), he discusses the subject at length, and with the same result. Some of the cases cited are the following: *Succession of Larendon,* 39 La. An. 952; *Besse v. Pellochoux,* 73 Ill. 285; *Fuss v. Fuss,* 24 Wis. 256; *Moore v. Church,* 70 Iowa, 208; *Heine v. Mechanics & Traders Ins. Co.* 45 La. An. 770; *First National Bank of Attleboro v. Hughes,* 10 Mo. App. 7; *Ordronaux v. Rey,* 2 Sandf. Ch. 33; *Adams v. Clutterbuck,* 10 Q. B. D. 403; *Chapman v. Robertson,* 6 Paige, 627, 630.

Phillimore in 4 Int. Law (3d ed.), 596, states the law as follows:

"DCCXXXV. 1. The case of a contract respecting the *transfer* of immovable property illustrates the variety of the rules which the foreign writers upon private international law consider applicable to a contract to which a foreigner is a party: they say that,

"i. The capacity of the obligor to enter into the contract is determined by reference to the law of his domicil.

"ii. The like capacity of the obligee by the law of *his* domicil.

"iii. The mode of alienation or acquisition of the immovable property is to be governed by the law of the situation of that property.

"iv. The external form of the contract is to be governed by the law of the place in which the contract is made.

"It is even suggested by Fœlix, that sometimes the *interpretation* of the contract may require the application of a fifth law.

"DCCXXXVI. The Law of England, and the Law of the North American United States, require the application of the *lex rei sitæ* to all the four predicaments mentioned in the last section.

"DCCXXXVII. But a distinction is to be taken between contracts to transfer property and the contracts by which it is transferred. The former are valid if executed according to the *lex loci contractus;* the latter require for their validity a compliance with the forms prescribed by the *lex rei sitæ.* Without this compliance the *dominium* in the property will not pass."

To the same effect as to the capacity of the parties are Rattigan, Priv. Int. Law, 128; Whart. Confl. of Laws (2d ed.) § 296;

Story, Confl. of Laws (8th ed.) §§ 424-431, 435; Rorer, Inter-
state Law, 263; Nelson, Priv. Int. Law, 147, 260. See Westlake, Priv. Int. Law (3d ed.) §§ 156, 167 *et seq.*

On reason and authority I think it cannot be held that,
although a deed between a husband and his wife, domiciled in
North Carolina, of the rights of each in the lands of the other in
Massachusetts, is void as a conveyance by reason of the incapacity
of the parties under the law of Massachusetts to make and receive
such a conveyance to and from each other, yet, if there are covenants in the deed to make a good title, the covenants can be
specifically enforced by our courts, and a conveyance compelled,
which, if voluntarily made between the parties, would be void.

I doubt if all of the instruments relied on have been executed
in accordance with the statutes of North Carolina. By § 1828
of the statutes of that State set out in the papers, the wife
became a free trader from the time of registration. This I
understand is January 7, 1893. Exhibit B purports to have been
executed before that time, to wit, January 4, 1893. There does
not appear to have been any examination of the wife separate and
apart from her husband, as required by § 1835. If Exhibit B
fails, there is at least a partial failure of consideration for Exhibit
C. It is said that an additional consideration is alleged, viz. the
wife's forbearing to bring a suit for divorce. Whether this last
is a sufficient consideration for a contract I do not consider. It
is plain enough that there was an attempt on the part of the husband and wife to continue to live separate and apart from each
other without divorce, and to release to each other all the property
rights each had in the property of the other. If the release of
one fails, I think that this court should not specifically enforce
the release of the other; mutuality in this respect is of the essence
of the transaction. If the husband owned lands in Massachusetts, and had died before his wife, I do not think that Exhibit
B, even if it were executed according to the statutes of North
Carolina, and the wife duly examined and a certificate thereof
duly made, would bar her of her dower. Our statutes provide
how dower may be barred. Pub. Sts. c. 124, §§ 6-9. Exhibit
B is not within the statute. See *Mason* v. *Mason*, 140 Mass. 63.
Ante-nuptial contracts have been enforced here in equity so as to
operate as a bar of dower, even if they did not constitute a legal
bar. *Jenkins* v. *Holt*, 109 Mass. 261. But post-nuptial contracts, so far as I am aware, never have been enforced here so as
to bar dower, unless they conform to the statutes. *Whitney* v.

Closson, 138 Mass. 49. Whatever may be true of contracts between husband and wife made in or when they are domiciled in other jurisdictions, so far as personal property or personal liability is concerned, I think that contracts affecting the title to real property situate within the Commonwealth should be such as are authorized by our laws. I am of opinion that the bill should be dismissed.

SCUDDER v. UNION NATIONAL BANK, 1875.

[91 U. S. 406.]

ERROR to the Circuit Court of the United States for the Northern District of Illinois.

This was an action of assumpsit against William H. Scudder and others, constituting the firm of Henry Ames & Co., to recover the amount of a bill of exchange. Process was served only upon Scudder, who pleaded *non-assumpsit* and several special pleas.

The statute of Illinois on which one of the pleas is based provides that no action shall be brought whereby to charge the defendant upon any special promise to answer for the debt, default, or miscarriage of another person, "unless the promise or agreement upon which such action shall be brought, or some memorandum or note thereof, shall be in writing, and signed bv the party to be charged therewith, or some other person thereunto by him specially authorized."

The Missouri statute provides:—

"SECTION 1. No person within this State shall be charged as an acceptor of a bill of exchange, unless his acceptance shall be in writing, signed bv himself or his lawful agent.

"SECT. 2. If such acceptance be written on a paper other than the bill, it shall not bind the acceptor, except in favor of a person to whom such acceptance shall have been shown, and who, upon the faith thereof, shall have received the bill for a valuable consideration.

"SECT. 3. An unconditional promise in writing, to accept a bill before drawn, shall be deemed an actual acceptance in favor of every person to whom such written promise shall have been shown, and who, upon the faith thereof, shall have received the bill for a valuable consideration.

"SECT. 4. Every holder of a bill presenting the same for

accpetance may require that the acceptance be written on the bill; and a refusal to comply with such request shall be deemed a refusal to accept, and the bill may be protested for non-acceptance.

"Sect. 5. The preceding sections shall not be construed to impair the right of any person to whom a promise to accept a bill may have been made, and who, on the faith of such promise, shall have drawn or negotiated the bill, to recover damages of the party making such promise, on his refusal to accept such bill."

The parties went to trial; and the bank offered evidence tending to establish, that for over a year prior to the seventh day of July, 1871, the firm of Henry Ames & Co. were engaged in business at St. Louis, Mo., and that Leland & Harbach, commission merchants in Chicago, had from time to time bought lots of pork for said firm, on commission; that on the seventh day of July, 1871, the defendant Scudder, a member of said firm, came to Chicago at the request of Leland & Harbach, who were then in an embarrassed condition, owing to speculations in grain; that, on the same day, John L. Hancock delivered to Leland & Harbach 500 barrels of pork, which they had bought of him for Ames & Co., by their request and direction, at $16.25 per barrel, in May, to be delivered in July, of which purchase said Ames & Co. had been duly advised; that, in payment of said pork, Leland & Harbach gave Hancock their check on the Union National Bank of Chicago for $8,031; and that the charges for inspection and commissions made the total cost of the pork $8,125.

That Leland & Harbach, on the same day, shipped the pork to Ames & Co. at St. Louis, Mo., who received and sold it; and that, at the time the bill was drawn, Scudder, who was then present in the office of Leland & Harbach, consented to the receipt of said pork, and verbally authorized them to draw on Ames & Co. for the amount due therefor.

That a bill of exchange in words and figures following—

"8,125.00.   Chicago, July 7, 1871.

"Pay to the order of Union National Bank eight thousand one hundred and twenty-five dollars, value received, and charge to account of   Leland & Harbach.

"To Messrs. Henry Ames & Co., St. Louis, Mo."

—was on said seventh day of July, 1871, presented for discount at the Union National Bank by Leland & Harbach's clerk; and the vice-president of the bank declined to give Leland & Harbach credit for the bill without a bill of lading or other security. That the clerk then returned to Leland & Harbach's office, and stated the bank's objections, Scudder being present; and, in the presence and hearing of said defendant, Scudder, the clerk was told by Leland or Harbach to return to the bank, and tell the vice-president that Scudder, one of the firm of Ames & Co., was then in Chicago, and had authorized the drawing of said draft, and that it was drawn against 500 barrels of pork that day bought by Leland & Harbach for Henry Ames & Co., and duly shipped to them. That the clerk returned, and made the statement as directed; and the vice-president, upon the faith of such statement that the bill was authorized by defendants, discounted said bill, the proceeds were passed to Leland & Harbach's credit, and the check given by them to Hancock in payment of said pork was paid out of the proceeds of said draft.

The bank then offered in evidence the said bill of exchange with a notarial certificate of protest, showing that the bill was presented to Henry Ames & Co. for payment July 8, 1871, and duly protested for non-payment.

It was admitted that said Ames & Co. had never paid said bill.

The court charged the jury. The following parts thereof Scudder excepted:—

"If you find from the evidence that Mr. Scudder, one of the defendants, authorized the drawing of the draft in question, and authorized the clerk, George H. Harbach, to so state to the vice-president of the bank, and that the said draft was discounted by the bank upon the faith of such statement, such conduct on the part of Mr. Scudder may be considered by you as evidence of an implied promise by the defendants to pay the draft; and it is not necessary for that purpose that Mr. Scudder should have expressly sent word to the bank if such statements were made in his hearing and presence, and no objections made to them by him; that is to say, if he stood by and allowed either Leland or Harbach to send such word to the bank without dissenting therefrom. If you find by a fair preponderance of the testimony that Mr. Scudder knew the pork had been delivered to Leland & Harbach at the time the draft was drawn, and acquiesced in the drawing of the draft, and acquiesced in the word sent to the bank that he had authorized it, you may from such facts find an implied promise by the defendants to pay the draft. It was not necessary that Scudder should go to the bank and state that he had authorized the draft, if you are satisfied that he allowed such statement to be made by the messenger.

"It being an admitted fact that the defendants have the proceeds of the pork against which this draft was drawn, such fact may also be considered by you as an additional circumstance tending to show a promise on the part of the defendants to pay the 'draft.

"The real issue in this case is, whether Mr. Scudder authorized the drawing of the draft in question, and expressly or impliedly promised to pay it."

The jury found a verdict in favor of the bank; and the court, overruling a motion for a new trial, rendered judgment. Scudder sued out this writ of error.

Mr. Justice Hunt delivered the opinion of the court.

It is not necessary to examine the question, whether a denial of the motion to set aside the summons can be presented as a ground of error on this hearing. The facts are so clearly against the motion, that the question does not arise.

It does not become necessary to examine the question of pleading, which is so elaborately spread out in the record. The only serious question in the case is presented upon the objection to the admission of evidence and to the charge of the judge.

Upon the merits, the case is this: The plaintiff below sought to recover from the firm of Henry Ames & Co., of St. Louis, Mo., the amount of a bill of exchange, of which the following is a copy; viz. :—

"$8,125.00.   "CHICAGO, July 7, 1871.
 "ᴾay to the order of Union National Bank eight thousand one hundred and twenty-five dollars, value received, and charge to account of   "LELAND & HARBACH.
 "To Messrs. Henry Ames & Co., St. Louis, Mo."

By the direction of Ames & Co., Leland & Harbach had bought for them, on the seventh day of July, 1871, shipped to them at St. Louis, 500 barrels of pork, and gave their check on the Union bank to Hancock, the seller of the same, for $8,000.

Leland & Harbach then drew the bill in question, and sent

the same by their clerk to the Union Bank (the plaintiff below) to be placed to their credit. The bank declined to receive the bill, unless accompanied by the bill of lading or other security. The clerk returned, and reported accordingly to Leland & Harbach. One of the firm then directed the clerk to return to the bank, and say that Mr. Scudder, one of the firm of Ames & Co. (the drawees), was then in Chicago, and had authorized the drawing of the draft; that it was drawn against 500 barrels of pork that day bought by Leland & Harbach for them, and duly shipped to them. The clerk returned to the bank, and made this statement to its vice-president; who thereupon, on the faith of the statement that the bill was authorized by the defendants, discounted the same, and the proceeds were placed to the credit of Leland & Harbach. Out of the proceeds the check given to Hancock for the pork was paid by the bank.

The direction to inform the bank that Mr. Scudder was in Chicago and had authorized the drawing of the draft was made in the presence and in the hearing of Scudder, and without objection by him.

The point was raised in various forms upon the admission of evidence, and by the charge of the judge, whether, upon this state of facts, the firm of Ames & Co., the defendants, were liable to the bank for the amount of the bill. The jury, under the charge of the judge, held them to be liable; and it is from the judgment entered upon that verdict that the present writ of error is brought.

The question is discussed in the appellant's brief, and properly, as if the direction to the clerk had been given by Scudder in person. The jury were authorized to consider the direction in his name, in his presence and hearing, without objection by him, as made by himself.

The objection relied on is, that the transaction amounted at most to a parol promise to accept a bill of exchange then in existence. It is insisted that such a promise does not bind the defendants.

The suit to recover upon the alleged acceptance, or upon the refusal to accept, being in the State of Illinois, and the contract having been made in that State, the judgment is to be given according to the laws of that State. The law of the expected place of performance, should there be a difference, yields to the *lex fori* and the *lex loci contractus*.

In Wheaton on Conflict of Laws, sect. 401, *p*, the rule is thus laid down:—

"Obligations, in respect to the mode of their solemnization, are subject to the rule *locus regit actum;* in respect to their interpretation, to the *lex loci contractus;* in respect to the mode of their performance, to the law of the place of their performance. But the *lex fori* determines when and how such laws, when foreign, are to be adopted, and, in all cases not specified above, supplies the applicatory law."

Miller v. *Tiffany,* 1 Wall. 310; *Chapman* v. *Robertson,* 6 Paige, 634; *Andrews* v. *Pond,* 13 Pet. 78; *Lamesse* v. *Baker,* 3 Wheat. 147; *Adams* v. *Robertson,* 37 Ill. 59; *Ferguson* v. *Fuffe,* 8 C. & F. 121; *Bain* v. *Whitehaven and Furness Junction Ry. Co.,* 3 H. L. Cas. 1; *Scott* v. *Pilkinton,* 15 Abb. Pr. 280; Story, Confl. Laws, 203; 10 Wheat. 383.

The rule is often laid down, that the law of the place of performance governs the contract.

Mr. Parsons, in his "Treatise on Notes and Bills," uses this language: "If a note or bill be made payable in a particular place, it is to be treated as if made there, without reference to the place at which it is written or signed or dated." P. 324.

For the purposes of payment, and the incidents of payment, this is a sound proposition. Thus the bill in question is directed to parties residing in St. Louis, Mo., and contains no statement whether it is payable on time or at sight. It is, in law, a sight draft. Whether a sight draft is payable immediately upon presentation, or whether days of grace are allowed, and to what extent, is differently held in different States. The law of Missouri, where this draft is payable, determines that question in the present instance.

The time, manner, and circumstances of presentation for accpetance or protest, the rate of interest when this is not specified in the bill (*Young* v. *Harris,* 14 B. Mon. 556; *Parry* v. *Ainsworth,* 22 Barb. 118), are points connected with the payment of the bill; and are also instances to illustrate the meaning of the rule, that the place of performance governs the bill.

The same author, however, lays down the rule, that the place of making the contract governs as to the formalities necessary to the validity of the contract. P. 317. Thus, whether a contract shall be in writing, or may be made by parol, is a formality to be determined by the law of the place where it is made. If valid there, the contract is binding, although the law of the place of performance may require the contract to be in writing. *Dacosta* v. *Hatch,* 4 Zab. 319.

So when a note was indorsed in New York, although drawn and made payable in France, the indorsee may recover against the payee and indorser upon a failure to accept, although by the laws of France such suit cannot be maintained until after default in payment. *Aymar* v. *Shelden,* 12 Wend. 439.

So if a note, payable in New York, be given in the State of Illinois for money there lent, reserving ten per cent interest, which is legal in that State, the note is valid, although but seven per cent interest is allowed by the laws of the former State. *Miller* v. *Tiffany,* 1 Wall. 310; *Depeau* v. *Humphry,* 20 How. 1; *Chapman* v. *Robertson,* 6 Paige, 634; *Andrews* v. *Pond,* 13 Pet. 65.

Matters bearing upon the execution, the interpretation, and the validity of a contract are determined by the law of the place where the contract is made. Matters connected with its performance are regulated by the law prevailing at the place of performance. Matters respecting the remedy, such as the bringing of suits, admissibility of evidence, statutes of limitation, depend upon the law of the place where the suit is brought.

A careful examination of the well-considered decisions of this country and of England will sustain these positions.

There is no statute of the State of Illinois that requires an acceptance of a bill of exchange to be in writing, or that prohibits a parol promise to accept a bill of exchange: on the contrary, a parol acceptance and a parol promise to accept are valid in that State, and the decisions of its highest court hold that a parol promise to accept a bill is an acceptance thereof. If this be so, no question of jurisdiction or of conflict of laws arises. The contract to accept was not only made in Illinois, but the bill was then and there actually accepted in Illinois, as perfectly as if Mr. Scudder had written an acceptance across its face, and signed thereto the name of his firm. The contract to accept the bill was not to be performed in Missouri. It had already, by the promise, been performed in Illinois. The contract to pay was, indeed, to be performed in Missouri; but that was a different contract from that of acceptance. *Nelson* v. *First Nat. Bank,* 48 Ill. 39; *Mason* v. *Dousay,* 35 id. 424; *Jones* v. *Bank,* 34 id. 319.

Unless forbidden by statute, it is the rule of law generally, that a promise to accept an existing bill is an acceptance thereof, whether the promise be in writing or by parol. *Wynne* v. *Raikes,* 5 East, 514; *Bank of Ireland* v. *Archer,* 11 M. & W. 383; *How* v. *Loring,* 24 Pick. 254; *Ward* v. *Allen,* 2 Met. 53; *Bank* v. *Wood-*

ruff, 34 Vt. 92; *Spalding* v. *Andrews*, 12 Wright, 411; *Williams* v. *Winans*, 2 Green (N. J.), 309; *Storer* v. *Logan*, 9 Mass. 56; Byles on Bills, sect. 149; *Barney* v. *Withington*, 37 N. Y. 112. See the Illinois cases cited, *supra.*

Says Lord Ellenborough, in the first of these cases, "A promise to accept an existing bill is an acceptance. A promise to pay it *is* also an acceptance. A promise, therefore, to do the one or the other,—i. e., to accept or certainly pay, cannot be less than an acceptance."

In *Williams* v. *Winans*, Hornblower, C. J., says, "The first question is, whether a parol acceptance of a bill will bind the acceptor; and of this there is at this day no room to doubt. The defendant was informed of the sale, and that his son had drawn an order on him for $125; to which he answered, it was all right. He afterwards found the interest partly paid, and the evidence of payment indorsed upon it in the handwriting of the defendant. These circumstances were proper and legal evidence from which the jury might infer an acceptance."

It is a sound principle of morality, which is sustained by well-considered decisions, that one who promises another, either in writing or by parol, that he will accept a particular bill of exchange, and thereby induces him to advance his money upon such bill, in reliance upon his promise, shall be held to make good his promise. The party advances his money upon an original promise, upon a valuable consideration; and the promisor is, upon principle, bound to carry out his undertaking. Whether it shall be held to be an acceptance, or whether he shall be subjected in damages for a breach of his promise to accept, or whether he shall be held to be estopped from impeaching his word, is a matter of form merely. The result in either event is to compel the promisor to pay the amount of the bill with interest. *Townley* v. *Sumdel*, 2 Pet. 170; *Boyce* v. *Edwards*, 4 id. 111; *Goodrich* v. *Gordon*, 15 Johns. 6; *Scott* v. *Pilkinton*, 15 Abb. Pr. 280; *Ontario Bank* v. *Worthington*, 12 Wend. 593; *Bissell* v. *Lewis*, 4 Mich. 450; *Williams* v. *Winans, supra.*

These principles settle the present case against the appellants.

It certainly does not aid their case, that after assuring the bank, through the message of Leland & Harbach, that the draft was drawn against produce that day shipped to the drawees, and that it was drawn by the authority of the firm (while, in fact, the produce was shipped to and received ar ' sold by them), and that the bank in reliance upon this assurance discounted the bill, Mr.

Scudder should at once have telegraphed his firm in St. Louis to delay payment of the draft, and, by a subsequent telegram, should have directed them not to pay it.

The judgment must be affirmed.

PRITCHARD v. NORTON, 1882.

[106 U. S. 124.]

ERROR to the Circuit Court of the United States for the District of Louisiana.

This action was brought by Eliza D. Pritchard, a citizen of Louisiana, executrix of Richard Pritchard, deceased, against Norton, a citizen of New York, in the court below, upon a writing obligatory, of which the following is a copy:—

"STATE OF NEW YORK,
    "County of New York.

"Know all men by these presents, that we, Henry S. McComb, of Wilmington, State of Delaware, and Ex Norton, of the city of New York, State of New York, are held and firmly bound, jointly and severally, unto Richard Pritchard, of New Orleans, his executors, administrators, and assigns, in the sum of fifty-five thousand ($55,000) dollars, lawful money of the United States, for the payment whereof we bind ourselves, our heirs, executors, and administrators firmly by these presents. Sealed with our seals and dated this thirtieth day of June, A. D. eighteen hundred and seventy-four.

"Whereas the aforesaid Richard Pritchard has signed an appeal bond as one of the sureties thereon, jointly and severally, on behalf of the defendant, appellant in the suit of J. P. Harrison, Jr. v. The New Orleans, Jackson, and Great Northern Railroad Co., No. 9261 on the docket of the Seventh District Court for the Parish of Orleans:

"Now, the condition of the above obligation is such that if the aforesaid obligors shall hold harmless and fully indemnify the said Richard Pritchard against all loss or damage arising from his liability as surety on the said appeal bond, then this obligation shall be null and void; otherwise, shall remain in full force and effect.

        "H. S. McComb.   [L. s.]
        "Ex Norton.   [L. s.]"

The appeal bond mentioned in the bond was executed.

A judgment was rendered on that appeal in the Supreme Court of Louisiana, May 30, 1876, against the railroad company, in satisfaction of which Pritchard became liable to pay, and did pay, the amount, to recover which this action was brought against Norton. The condition of this appeal bond was that the company "shall prosecute its said appeal, and shall satisfy whatever judgment may be rendered against it, or that the same shall be satisfied by the proceeds of the sale of its estate, real or personal, if it be cast in the appeal; otherwise that the said Pritchard *et al.*, sureties, shall be liable in its place."

The defendant set up, by way of defence, that the bond sued on was executed and delivered by him to Pritchard in the State of New York, and without any consideration therefor, and that by the laws of that State it was void, by reason thereof.

There was evidence on the trial tending to prove that the appeal bond was not signed by Pritchard at the instance or request of McComb or Norton, and that there was no consideration for their signing and executing the bond of indemnity passing at the time, and that the latter was executed and delivered in New York. There was also put in evidence the following provisions of the Revised Statutes of that State, 2 Rev. Stat. 406:—

"SECT. 77. In every action upon a sealed instrument, and when a set-off is founded upon any sealed instrument, the seal thereof shall only be presumptive evidence of a sufficient consideration, which may be rebutted in the same manner and to the same extent as if the instrument were not sealed.

"SECT. 78. The defence allowed by the last section shall not be made unless the defendant shall have pleaded the same, or shall have given notice thereof at the time of pleading the general issue, or some other plea denying the contract on which the action is brought."

At the request of the defendant the Circuit Court charged the jury that the indemnifying bond, in respect to its validity and the consideration requisite to support it, was to be governed by the law of New York, and not of Louisiana; and that if they believed from the evidence that the appeal bond signed by Richard Pritchard as surety was not signed by him at the instance or request of McComb and Norton, or either of them, and that no consideration passed between Pritchard and McComb and Norton for the signing and execution of the indemnifying bond by them, then that the bond was void for want and absence of any consideration valid in law to sustain it, and no recovery could be had upon it.

The plaintiff requested the court to charge the jury that if they found from the evidence that the consideration for the indemnifying bond was the obligation contracted by Pritchard as surety on the appeal bond, and that the object of the indemnifying bond was to hold harmless and indemnify Pritchard from loss or damage by reason of or growing out of said appeal bond, then that the consideration for said indemnifying bond was good and valid, and is competent to support the action upon the bond for the recovery of any such loss or damage sustained by Pritchard. This request the court refused. Exceptions were duly taken to these rulings, which the plaintiff now assigns for error, there having been a judgment for the defendant, which she seeks to reverse.

MR. JUSTICE MATTHEWS, after stating the case, delivered the opinion of the court.

It is claimed on behalf of the plaintiff that by the law of Louisiana the pre-existing liability of Pritchard as surety for the railroad company would be a valid consideration to support the promise of indemnity, notwithstanding his liability had been incurred without any previous request from the defendant. This claim is not controverted, and is fully supported by the citations from the Civil Code of Louisiana of 1870, art. 1893–1960, and the decisions of the Supreme Court of that State. *Flood* v. *Thomas*, 5 Mart. N. S. (La.) 560; *N. O. Gas Co.* v. *Paulding*, 12 Rob. (La.) 378; *N. O & Carrollton Railroad Co.* v. *Chapman*, 8 La. Ann. 97; *Keane* v. *Goldsmith, Haber & Co.*, 12 id. 560. In the case last mentioned it is said that "the contract is, in its nature, one of personal warranty, recognized by articles 378 and 379 of the Code of Practice." And it was there held that a right of action upon the bond of indemnity accrued to the obligee, when his liability became fixed as surety by a final judgment, without payment on his part, it being the obligation of the defendants upon the bond of indemnity to pay the judgment rendered against him, or to furnish him the money with which to pay it.

The single question presented by the record, therefore, is whether the law of New York or that of Louisiana defines and fixes the rights and obligations of the parties. If the former applies, the judgment of the court below is correct; if the latter, it is erroneous.

The argument in support of the judgment is simple, and may be briefly stated. It is, that New York is the place of the contract, both because it was executed and delivered there, and because no other place of performance being either designated or necessarily implied, it was to be performed there; wherefore the law of New York, as the *lex loci contractus,* in both senses, being the *lex loci celebrationis* and *lex loci solutionis,* must apply to determine not only the form of the contract, but also its validity.

On the other hand, the application of the law of Louisiana may be considered in two aspects: as the *lex fori,* the suit having been brought in a court exercising jurisdiction within its territory and administering its laws; and as the *lex loci solutionis,* the obligation of the bond of indemnity being to place the fund for payment in the hands of the surety, or to repay him the amount of his advance, in the place where he was bound to discharge his own liability.

It will be convenient to consider the applicability of the law of Louisiana, first, as the *lex fori,* and then as the *lex loci solutionis.*

1. The *lex fori.*

The court below, in a cause like the present, in which its jurisdiction depends on the citizenship of the parties, adjudicates their rights precisely as should a tribunal of the State of Louisiana according to her laws; so that, in that sense, there is no question as to what law must be administered. But, in case of contract, the foreign law may, by the act and will of the parties, have become part of their agreement; and, in enforcing this, the law of the forum may find it necessary to give effect to a foreign law, which, without such adoption, would have no force beyond its own territory.

This, upon the principle of comity, for the purpose of promoting and facilitating international intercourse, and within limits fixed by its own public policy, a civilized State is accustomed and considers itself bound to do; but, in doing so, nevertheless adheres to its own system of formal judicial procedure and remedies. And thus the distinction is at once established between the law of the contract, which may be foreign, and the law of the procedure and remedy, which must be domestic and local. In respect to the latter the foreign law is rejected; but how and where to draw the line of precise classification it is not always easy to determine.

The principle is, that whatever relates merely to the remedy and constitutes part of the procedure is determined by the law of the forum, for matters of process must be uniform in the courts of the same country; but whatever goes to the substance of the obligation and affects the rights of the parties, as growing out of the contract itself, or inhering in it or attaching to it, is governed by the law of the contract.

The rule deduced by Mr. Wharton, in his Conflict of Laws, as best harmonizing the authorities and effecting the most judicious result, and which was cited approvingly by Mr. Justice Hunt in *Scudder* v. *Union National Bank,* 91 U. S. 406, is, that "Obligations in respect to the mode of their solemnization are subject to the rule *locus regit actum;* in respect to their interpretation, to the *lex loci contractus;* in respect to their mode of their performance, to the law of the place of their performance. But the *lex fori* determines when and how such laws, when foreign, are to be adopted, and, in all cases not specified above, supplies the applicatory law." This, it will be observed, extends the operation of the *lex fori* beyond the process and remedy, so as to embrace the whole of that residuum which cannot be referred to other laws. And this conclusion is obviously just; for whatever cannot, from the nature of the case, be referred to any other law, must be determined by the tribunal having jurisdiction of the litigation, according to the law of its own locality.

Whether an assignee of a chose in action shall sue in his own name or that of his assignor is a technical question of mere process, and determinable by the law of the forum; but whether the foreign assignment, on which the plaintiff claims is valid at all, or whether it is valid against the defendant, goes to the merits and must be decided by the law in which the case has its legal seat. Wharton, Conflict of Laws, sects. 735, 736. Upon that point Judge Kent, in *Lodge* v. *Phelps,* 1 Johns. (N. Y.) Cas. 139, said: "If the defendant has any defence authorized by the law of Connecticut, let him show it, and he will be heard in one form of action as well as in the other."

It is to be noted, however, as an important circumstance, that the same claim may sometimes be a mere matter of process, and so determinable by the law of the forum, and sometimes a matter of substance going to the merits, and therefore determinable by the law of the contract. That is illustrated in the application of the defence arising upon the Statute of Limitations. In the courts of England and America, that defence is governed by the law of the forum, as being a matter of mere procedure; while in continental Europe the defence of prescription is regarded as going to the substance of the contract, and therfore as governed by the law of the seat of the obligation. "According to the true doctrine," says Savigny, "the local law of the obligation must determine as to the term of prescription, not that of the place of the action; and this rule, which has just been laid down in respect to exceptions in general, is further confirmed, in the case of prescription, by the fact that the various grounds on which it rests stand in connection with the substance of the obligation itself." Private Inter. Law, by Guthrie, 201. In this view Westlake concurs. Private Inter. Law (ed. 1858), sect. 250. He puts it, together with the case of a merger in another cause of action, the occurrence of which will be determined by the law of the former cause, *Bryans* v. *Dunseth*, 1 Mart. N. s. (La.) 412, as equal instances of the liability to termination inherent by the *lex contractus*. But notwithstanding the contrary doctrine of the courts of England and this country, when the Statute of Limitations of a particular country not only bars the right of action, but extinguishes the claim or title itself, *ipso facto*, and declares it a nullity, after the lapse of the prescribed period, and the parties have been resident within the jurisdiction during the whole of that period, so that it has actually and fully operated upon the case, it must be held, as it was considered by Mr. Justice Story, to be an extinguishment of the debt, wherever an attempt might be made to enforce it. Conflict of Laws, sect. 582. That rule, as he says, has in its support the direct authority of this court in *Shelby* v. *Guy*, 11 Wheat. 361–371; its correctness was recognized by Chief Justice Tindal in *Huber* v. *Steiner*, 2 Bing. N. C. 202, 211; and it is spoken of by Lord Brougham in *Don* v. *Lippmann*, 5 Cl. & Fin. 1, 16, as "the excellent distinction taken by Mr. Justice Story." *Walworth* v. *Routh*, 14 La. Ann. 205. The same principle was applied by the Supreme Court of Ohio in the case of *P. C. & St. L. Railway Co.* v. *Hine's Admx.*, 25 Ohio St. 629, where it was held, that under the act which requires compensation for causing death by wrongful act, neglect, or default, and gives a right of action, provided such action shall be commenced within two years after the death of such deceased person, the proviso is a condition qualifying the right of action, and not a mere limitation on the remedy. *Bonte* v. *Taylor*, 24 id. 628.

The principle that what is apparently mere matter of remedy in some circumstances, in others, where it touches the substance of the controversy, becomes matter of right, is familiar in our constitutional jurisprudence in the application of that provision of the Constitution which prohibits the passing by a State of any law impairing the obligation of contracts. For it has been uniformly held that "any law which in its operation amounts to a denial or obstruction of the rights accruing by a contract, though professing to act only on the remedy, is directly obnoxious to the prohibition of the Constitution." *McCracken* v. *Hayward*, 2 How. 608, 612; Cooley, Const. Lim. 285.

Hence it is that a vested right of action is property in the same sense in which tangible things are property, and is equally protected against arbitrary interference. Whether it springs from contract or from the principles of the common law, it is not competent for the legisature to take it away. A vested right to an existing defence is equally protected, saving only those which are based on informalities not affecting substantial rights, which do not touch the substance of the contract and are not based on equity and justice. Cooley, Const. Lim. 362–369.

The general rule, as stated by Story, is that a defence or discharge, good by the law of the place where the contract is made or is to be performed, is to be held of equal validity in every other place where the question may come to be litigated. Conflict of Laws, sect. 331. Thus infancy, if a valid defence by the *lex loci contractus*, will be a valid defence everywhere. *Thompson* v. *Ketcham*, 8 Johns. (N. Y.) 189; *Male* v. *Roberts*, 3 Esp. 163. A tender and refusal, good by the same law, either as a full discharge or as a present fulfilment of the contract, will be respected everywhere. *Warder* v. *Arell*, 2 Wash. (Va.) 282. Payment in paper-money bills, or in other things, if good by the same law, will be deemed a sufficient payment everywhere. 1 Brown, Ch. 376; *Searight* v. *Calbraith*, 4 Dall. 325; *Bartsch* v. *Atwater*, 1 Conn. 409. And, on the other hand, where a payment by negotiable bills or notes is, by the *lex loci*, held to be conditional payment only, it will be so held even in States where such payment under the domestic law would be held absolute. So, if by the law of the place of a contract equitable defences are allowed in favor of the maker of a negotiable note, any subsequent indorsement will not change his rights in regard to the holder. The latter must take it *cum onere*. *Evans* v. *Gray*, 12 Mart. (La.) 475; *Ory* v. *Winter*, 4 Mart. n. s. (La.) 277; *Chartres* v. *Cairnes*, id. 1; Story Conflict of Laws, sect. 332.

On the other hand, the law of the forum determines the form of the action, as whether it shall be assumpsit, covenant, or debt.

Warren v. *Lynch,* 5 Johns. (N. Y.) 239; *Andrews* v. *Herriot,*
4 Cow. (N. Y.) 508; *Trasher* v. *Everhart,* 3 Gill & J. (Md.) 234;
Adams v. *Kers,* 1 Bos. & Pul. 360; *Bank of the United States* v.
Donally, 8 Pet. 361; *Douglas* v. *Oldham,* 6 N. H. 150. In *Le Roy*
v. *Beard,* 8 How. 451, where it was held that assumpsit and not
covenant was the proper form of action brought in New York
upon a covenant executed and to be performed in Wisconsin, and
by its laws sealed as a deed, but which in the former was not
regarded as sealed, it was said by this court, that it was so
decided "without impairing at all the principle, that in deciding
on the obligation of the instrument as a contract, and not the
remedy on it elsewhere, the law of Wisconsin, as the *lex loci contractus,* must govern." It regulates all process, both mesne and
final. *Ogden* v. *Saunders,* 12 Wheat. 213; *Mason* v. *Haile,* id.
370; *Beers* v. *Haughton,* 9 Pet. 329; *Von Hoffman* v. *City of
Quincy,* 4 Wall. 535. It also may admit, as a part of its domestic
procedure, a set-off or compensation of distinct causes of action
between the parties to the suit, though not admissible by the law
of the place of the contract. Story, Conflict of Laws, sect. 574;
Gibbs v. *Howard,* 2 N. H. 296; *Ruggles* v. *Keeler,* 3 Johns. (N.
Y.) 263. But this is not to be confounded, as it was in the case
Second National Bank of Cincinnati v. *Hemingray,* 31 Ohio St.
168, with that of a limited negotiability, by which the right of
set-off between the original parties is preserved as part of the law
of the contract, notwithstanding an assignment. The rules of
evidence are also supplied by the law of the forum. *Wilcox* v.
Hunt, 13 Pet. 378; *Yates* v. *Thomson,* 3 Cl. & Fin. 544; *Bain* v.
Whitehaven, &c. Railway Co., 3 H. of L. Cas. 1; *Don* v. *Lippmann,* 5 Cl. & Fin. 1. In *Yates* v. *Thomson, supra,* it was decided
by the House of Lords that in a suit in a Scotch court, to adjudge
the succession to personalty of a descendent domiciled in England, where it was admitted that the English law governed the
title, nevertheless it was proper to receive in evidence, as against
a will of the decedent, duly probated in England, a second will
which had not been proved there, and was not receivable in English
courts as competent evidence, because such a paper according to
Scottish law was admissible. In *Hoadley* v. *Northern Transportation Co.,* 115 Mass. 304, it was held that if the law of the place,
where a contract signed only by the carrier is made for the carriage of goods, requires evidence other than the mere receipt by
the shipper to show his assent to its terms, and the law of the
place where the suit is brought presumes conclusively such assent

from acceptance without dissent, the question of assent is a question of evidence, and is to be determined by the law of the place where the suit is brought. In a suit in Connecticut against the indorser on a note made and indorsed in New York, it was held that parol evidence of a special agreement, different from that imputed by law, would be received in defence, although by the law of the latter State no agreement different from that which the law implies from a blank indorsement could be proved by parol. *Downer* v. *Cheseborough*, 36 Conn. 39. And upon the same principle it has been held that a contract, valid by the laws of the place where it is made, although not in writing, will not be enforced in the courts of a country where the Statute of Frauds prevails, unless it is put in writing. *Leroux* v. *Brown*, 12 C. B. 801. But where the law of the forum and that of the place of the execution of the contract coincide, it will be enforced, although required to be in writing by the law of the place of performance, as was the case of *Scudder* v. *Union National Bank*, 91 U. S. 406, because the *form* of the contract is regulated by the law of the place of its celebration, and the *evidence* of it by that of the forum.

Williams v. *Haines*, 27 Iowa, 251, was an action upon a note executed in Maryland, and, so far as appears from the report, payable there, where the parties thereto then resided, and which was a sealed instrument, according to the laws of that State, in support of which those laws conclusively presumed a valid consideration. By the laws of Iowa, to such an instrument the want of consideration was allowed to be proved as a defence. It was held by the Supreme Court of that State, in an opinion delivered by Chief Justice Dillion, that the law of Iowa related to the remedy merely, without impairing the obligation of the contract, and the *lex fori*, must govern the case. He said: "Respecting what shall be good defences to actions in this State, its courts must administer its own laws and not those of other States. The common-law rules do not so inhere in the contract as to have the portable quality ascribed to them by the plaintiff's counsel, much less can they operate to override the plain declaration of the legislative will." The point of this decision is incorporated by Mr. Wharton into the text of his Treatise on the Conflict of Laws, sect. 788, and the case itself is referred to in support of it. He deduces the same conclusion from those cases, already referred to, which declare that assumpsit is the only form of action that can be brought upon an instrument which is not under seal, according to the laws of the forum, although by the law of the place where it was executed, or was to be performed, it would be regarded as under seal, in which debt or covenant would lie, on the ground that a plea of want or failure of consideration is recognized as a defence in all actions of assumpsit. Wharton, Conflict of Laws, sect. 747.

If the proposition be sound, its converse is equally so; and the law of a place where a suit may happen to be brought may forbid the impeachment of a contract, for want of a valid consideration, which, by the law of the place of the contract, might be declared invalid on that account.

We cannot, however, accept this conclusion. The question of consideration, whether arising upon the admissibility of evidence or presented as a point in pleading, is not one of procedure and remedy. It goes to the substance of the right itself, and belongs to the constitution of the contract. The difference between the law of Louisiana and that of New York, presented in this case, is radical, and gives rise to the inquiry, what, according to each, are the essential elements of a valid contract, determinable only by the law of its seat; and not that other, what remedy is provided by the law of the place where the suit has been brought to recover for the breach of its obligation.

On this point, what was said in *The Gaetano & Maria*, 7 P. D. 137, is pertinent. In that case the question was whether the English law, which was the law of the forum, or the Italian law, which was the law of the flag, should prevail, as to the validity of a hypothecation of the cargo by the master of a ship. It was claimed that because the matter to be proved was, whether there was a necessity which justified it, it thereby became a matter of procedure, as being a matter of evidence. Lord Justice Brett said: "Now, the manner of proving the facts is matter of evidence, and, to my mind, is matter of procedure, but the facts to be proved are not matters of procedure; they are matters with which the procedure has to deal.

It becomes necessary, therefore, to consider the applicability of the law of Louisiana as—

2. The *lex loci solutionis.*

The phrase *lex loci contractus* is used, in a double sense, to mean, sometimes, the law of the place where a contract is entered into; sometimes, that of the place of its performance. And when it is employed to describe the law of the seat of the obligation, it is, on that account, confusing. The law we are in search of, which is to decide upon the nature, interpretation, and validity of the engagement in question, is that which the parties have, either expressly or presumptively, incorporated into their contract as constituting its obligation. It has never been better described than it was incidentally by Mr. Chief Justice Marshall in *Wayman* v. *Southard*, 10 Wheat. 1, 48, where he defined it as a principle of universal law,—"The principle that in every forum a contract is governed by the law with a view to which it was made." The same idea has been expressed by Lord Mansfield in *Robinson* v. *Bland*, 2 Burr. 1077, 1078. "The law of the place," he said, "can never be the rule where the transaction is entered into with an *express* view to the law of another country, as the rule by which it is to be governed." And in *Lloyd* v. *Guibert*, Law Rep. 1 Q. B. 115, 120, in the Court of Exchequer Chamber, it was said that "It is necessary to consider by what general law the parties intended that the transaction should be governed, or rather, by what general law it is just to presume that they have submitted themselves in the matter." *Le Breton* v. *Miles*, 8 Paige (N. Y.), 261.

It is upon this ground that the presumption rests, that the contract is to be performed at the place where it is made, and to be governed by its laws, there being nothing in its terms, or in the explanatory circumstances of its execution, inconsistent with that intention.

So, Pillimore says: "It is always to be remembered that in obligations it is the will of the contracting parties, and not the law, which fixes the place of fulfilment—whether that place be fixed by *express words* or by *tacit implication*—as the place to the jurisdiction of which the contracting parties elected to submit themselves." 4 Int. Law, 469.

The same author concludes his discussion of the particular topic as follows: "As all the foregoing rules rest upon the presumption that the obligor has voluntarily submitted himself to a particular local law, that presumption may be rebutted, either by an express declaration to the contrary, or by the fact that the obligation is illegal by that particular law, though legal by another. The parties cannot be presumed to have contemplated a law which would defeat their engagements." 4 Int. Law, sect. DCLIV. pp. 470, 471.

This rule, if universally applicable, which perhaps it is not, though founded on the maxim, *ut res magis valeat, quam pereat*, would be decisive of the present controversy, as conclusive of

30

the question of the application of the law of Louisiana, by which alone the undertaking of the obligor can be upheld.

At all events, it is a circumstance, highly persuasive in its character, of the presumed intention of the parties, and entitled to prevail, unless controlled by more express and positive proofs of a contrary intent.

It was expressly referred to as a decisive principle in *Bell* v. *Packard*, 69 Me. 105, although it cannot be regarded as the foundation of the judgment in that case. *Milliken* v. *Pratt*, 125 Mass. 374.

If now we examine the terms of the bond of indemnity, and the situation and relation of the parties, we shall find conclusive corroboration of the presumption, that the obligation was entered into in view of the laws of Louisiana.

The antecedent liability of Pritchard, as surety for the railroad company on the appeal bond, was confessedly contracted in that State, according to its laws, and it was there alone that it could be performed and discharged. Its undertaking was, that Pritchard should, in certain contingencies, satisfy a judgment of its courts. That could be done only within its territory and according to its laws. The condition of the obligation, which is the basis of this action, is, that McComb and Norton, the obligors, shall hold harmless and fully indemnify Pritchard against all loss or damage arising from his liability as surety on the appeal bond. A judgment was, in fact, rendered against him on it in Louisiana. There was but one way in which the obligors in the indemnity bond could perfectly satisfy its warranty. That was, the moment the judgment was rendered against Pritchard on the appeal bond, to come forward in his stead, and, by payment, to extinguish it. He was entitled to demand this before any payment by himself, and to require that the fund should be forthcoming at the place where otherwise he could be required to pay it. Even if it should be thought that Pritchard was bound to pay the judgment recovered against himself, before his right of recourse accrued upon the bond of indemnity, nevertheless he was entitled to be reimbursed the amount of his advance at the same place where he had been required to make it. So that it is clear, beyond any doubt, that the obligation of the indemnity was to be fulfilled in Louisiana, and, consequently, is subject, in all matters affecting its construction and validity, to the law of that locality.

This construction is abundantly sustained by the authority of judicial decisions in similar cases.

In *Irvine* v. *Barret,* 2 Grant's (Pa.) Cas. 73, it was decided that where a security is given in pursuance of a decree of a court of justice, it is to be construed according to the intention of the tribunal which directed its execution, and, in contemplation of law, is to be performed at the place where the court exercises its jurisdiction; and that a bond given in another State, as collateral to such an obligation, is controlled by the same law which controls the principal indebtedness. In the case of *Penobscot & Kennebec Railroad Co.* v. *Bartlett,* 12 Gray (Mass), 244, the Supreme Judicial Court of Massachusetts decided that a contract made in that State to subscribe to shares in the capital stock of a railroad corporation established by the laws of another State, and having their road and treasury there, is a contract to be performed there, and is to be construed by the laws of that State. In *Lanusse* v. *Barker,* 3 Wheat. 101, 146, this court declared that "where a general authority is given to draw bills from a certain place, on account of advances there made, the undertaking is to replace the money at that place."

The case of *Cox* v. *United States,* 6 Pet. 172, was an action upon the official bond of a navy agent. The sureties contended that the United States were bound to divide their action, and take judgment against each surety only for his proportion of the sum due, according to the laws of Louisiana, considering it a contract made there, and to be governed in this respect by the law of that State. The court, however, said: "But admitting the bond to have been signed at New Orleans, it is very clear that the obligations imposed upon the parties thereby looked for its execution to the city of Washington. It is immaterial where the services as navy agent were to be performed by Hawkins. His accountability for non-performance was to be at the seat of government. He was bound to account, and the sureties undertook that he should account for all public moneys received by him, with such officers of the government of the United States as are duly authorized to settle and adjust his accounts. The bond is given with reference to the laws of the United States on that subject. And such accounting is required to be with the Treasury Department at the seat of government; and the navy agent is bound by the very terms of the bond to pay over such sum as may be found due to the United States on such settlement; and such paying over must be to the Treasury Department, or in such manner as shall be directed by the secretary. The bond is, therefore, in every point of view in which it can be considered, a contract to be executed at the city of Washington, and the liability of the parties must be governed by the rules of the common law." This decision was repeated in *Duncan* v. *United States*, 7 Pet. 435.

These cases were relied on by the Supreme Court of New York in *Commonwealth of Kentucky* v. *Bassford*, 6 Hill (N. Y.), 526. That was an action upon a bond executed in New York conditioned for the faithful performance of the duties enjoined by a law of Kentucky authorizing the obligees to sell lottery tickets for the benefit of a college in that State. It was held that the stipulations of the bond were to be performed in Kentucky, and that, as it was valid by the laws of that State, the courts of New York would enforce it, notwithstanding it would be illegal in that State.

Boyle v. *Zacharie*, 6 Pet. 635, is a direct authority upon the point. There Zacharie and Turner were resident merchants at New Orleans, and Boyle at Baltimore. The latter sent his ship to New Orleans, consigned it to Zacharie and Turner, where she arrived, and, having landed her cargo, the latter procured a freight for her to Liverpool. When she was ready to sail she was attached by process of law at the suit of certain creditors of Boyle, and Zacharie and Turner procured her release by becoming security for Boyle on the attachment. Upon information of the facts, Boyle promised to indemnify them for any loss they might sustain on that account. Judgment was rendered against them on the attachment bond, which they were compelled to pay, and to recover the amount so paid they brought suit in the Circuit Court of Maryland against Boyle upon his promise of indemnity. A judgment was rendered by confession in that cause, and a bill in equity was subsequently filed to enjoin further proceedings on it, in the course of which various questions arose, among them, whether the promise of indemnity was a Maryland or Louisiana contract. Mr. Justice Story, delivering the opinion of the court, said: "Such a contract would be understood by all parties to be a contract made in the place where the advance was to be made, and the payment, unless otherwise stipulated, would also be understood to be made there;" "that the contract would clearly refer for its execution to Louisiana.

The very point was also decided by this court in *Bell* v. *Bruen*, 1 How. 169. That was an action upon a guaranty written by the defendant in New York, addressed to the plaintiffs in London, who, at the latter place, had made advances of a credit to Thorn. The operative language of the guaranty was, "that you may consider this, as well as any and every other credit you may open in his favor, as being under my guaranty." The court said: "It was an engagement to be executed in England, and must be construed and have effect according to the laws of that country," citing *Bank of United States* v. *Daniel*, 12 Pet. 54. As the money was advanced in England, the guaranty required that it should be replaced there, and that is the precise nature of the obligation in the present case. Pritchard could only be indemnified against loss and damage on account of his liability on the appeal bond, by having funds placed in his hands in Louisiana wherewith to discharge it, or by being repaid there the amount of his advance. To the same effect is *Woodhull* v. *Wagner*, Baldw. 296.

We do not hesitate, therefore, to decide that the bond of indemnity sued on was entered into with a view to the law of Louisiana as the place for the fulfilment of its obligation; and that the question of its validity, as depending on the character and sufficiency of the consideration, should be determined by the law of Louisiana, and not that of New York. For error in its rulings on this point, consequently, the judgment of the Circuit Court is reversed, with directions to grant a new trial.

New trial ordered.

CHAPTER XIV.

CONTRACTS.—[Continued.]

AKERS v. DEMOND, 1869.

[103 Mass. 318.]

WELLS, J. The defence to this suit is, that the bills of exchange are void for usury, under the laws of New York, where they were first negotiated. The statute of New York, Rev. Sts. part 2, c. 4, tit. 3, § 5, declares such securities void "whereupon or whereby there shall be reserved or taken or secured, or agreed to be reserved or taken," a greater rate of interest than seven per cent. The superior court ruled that, upon the testimony offered, no defence was established; and instructed the jury to return a verdict for the plaintiffs. The testimony is reported for our consideration, so far as admissible and competent, subject to the several objections made thereto by the plaintiffs.

1. Conversations between the drawer and first indorser of the bill are competent, so far as they relate to and form part of the transactions of indorsing and negotiating the paper and disposing of the proceeds.

2. The conversation between Reed and one of the plaintiffs, in regard to the rate of discount charged by them upon the bills, was competent to show that fact. It was no part of any negotiation for an adjustment, although occurring at an interview for that purpose, but was an independent statement of a collateral fact.

3. The refusal of William H. Russell to answer the question, whether certain statements made by him at the time he negotiated the bills to the plaintiffs, and which had been called for by two previous questions, were true or false, is not a ground for rejecting the whole deposition. If the purpose of the inquiry was to prove what the facts were in those particulars, it should have been made by questions directly as to those facts. If the purpose was to show false representations made at that time, it was immaterial to the issue. The question being impertinent, the answer is excusable.

4. We know of no rule of law or of practice which forbids a

second or supplementary deposition of the same witness to be taken, either for the proof of additional facts, or to supply omissions in the answers to the interrogatories of the first commission.

5. The objection that certain interrogatories are leading is an objection to the form merely, and cannot be taken for the first time when the deposition is offered in court.

6. The drawer and indorser are competent witnesses to prove the usury; the plaintiffs not being innocent indorsers, but parties to the usury.

7. For the same reason, the defence is not precluded by the statute of Massachusetts of 1863, c. 242.

The testimony thus held to be admissible and competent tends to prove that the bills in suit were drawn by Reed and indorsed by William H. Russell, the payee, in New York, and accepted by the defendant in Boston, being upon their face addressed to him there. Both the acceptance and the indorsement were for the accommodation of Reed. The possession of collateral security, whether subsequent or at the time, does not change the character of the acceptance or the relations of the parties. *Dowe v. Schutt,* 2 Denio, 621. After the return of the acceptances to Reed, by an arrangement between him and the nominal payee, the latter procured the bills to be discounted by the plaintiffs, at the rate of one and a half per cent. a month. The proceeds of one of the bills were retained by William H. Russell, the payee, as a loan from Reed, and the proceeds of the other handed over by him to Reed.

As the case is now presented, in the absence of controlling testimony on the part of the plaintiffs, the foregoing statement must be taken as the result of the evidence. It shows that the transaction by which the plaintiffs became holders of the bills was the original negotiation of the paper; a loan upon discount, and not a mere sale of the bills. They are therefore open to the defence of usury. This is so clearly shown to be the law of New York, by the decisions of the courts of that state referred to in *Ayer v. Tilden,* 15 Gray, 178, as to require no further citations.

The defendant is entitled to set up the usury, although not paid by himself, and although the loan was not made to him nor on his account. *Van Schaack v. Stafford,* 12 Pick. 565. *Dunscomb v. Bunker,* 2 Met. 8. *Cook v. Littlefield.* 5 Selden, 279. *Clark v. Sisson,* 22 N. Y. 312.

The difficult question in the case arises from the fact that the

paper was made payable in Boston. It is contended that the
contract of the acceptor is to be governed by the laws of the
place where the bills are made payable. The general principle
is, that the law of the place of performance is the law of the
contract. This rule applies to the operation and effect of the
contract, and to the rights and obligations of the parties under
it. But the question of its validity, as affected by the legality
of the consideration, or of the transaction upon which it is
founded, and in which it took its inception as a contract, must
be determined by the law of the state where that transaction
was had. No other law can apply to it. Usury, in a loan
effected elsewhere, is no offence against the laws of Massachusetts. In a suit upon a contract founded on such a loan, the
penalty for usury could not be set up in defence, under statutes
formerly in force in this Commonwealth. Neither can a penalty,
as a partial defence, authorized by the laws of one state, be
applied or made effective in the courts of another state. *Gale* v.
Eastman, 7 Met. 14. Such penal laws can be administered only
in the state where they exist. But when a usurious or other
illegal consideration is declared by the laws of any state to be
incapable of sustaining any valid contract, and all contracts
arising therefrom are declared void, such contracts are not only
void in that state, but void in every state and everywhere. They
never acquire a legal existence. Contracts founded on usurious
transactions in the state of New York are of this character.
Van Schaack v. *Stafford,* 12 Pick. 565. *Dunscomb* v. *Bunker,*
2 Met. 8. The fact that the bills now in suit were accepted in
Boston and were payable there does not exempt them from this
operation of the laws of New York. They were mere "nude
pacts," with no legal validity or force as contracts, until a consideration was paid. The only consideration ever paid was the
usurious loan made by these plaintiffs in New York. That then
was the legal inception of the alleged contracts. *Little* v. *Rogers,*
1 Met. 108. *Cook* v. *Littlefield,* 5 Selden, 279. *Clark* v. *Sisson,*
22 N. Y. 312. *Aeby* v. *Rapelye,* 1 Hill, 1. By the statutes of
New York, that transaction was incapable of furnishing a legal
consideration; and, so far as the bills depend upon that, they
are absolutely void. The original validity of such a contract
must be determined by the law of the state in which it is first
negotiated or delivered as a contract. *Hanrick* v. *Andrews,* 9
Porter, 9. *Andrews* v. *Pond,* 13 Pet. 65. *Miller* v. *Tiffany,* 1
Wallace, 298. *Lee* v. *Selleck,* 33 N. Y. 615.

There is no pretence that a discount of one and a half per cent. a month was justifiable by reason of any added exchange between New York and Boston; nor that it was otherwise than usurious, if any amount of charge upon paper payable elsewhere than in New York would be usurious there. It has often been held, in states where restrictions upon the rate of interest are maintained, that it is not usury to charge upon negotiabl paper whatever is the lawful rate of interest at the place where the paper is payable, although greater than the rate alowable where the negotiation takes place. But if the paper is so made for the purpose of enabling the larger rate to be taken, or the greater rate is received with intent to evade the statutes relating to usury, and not in good faith as the legitimate proceeds of the contract, it is held to be usury. So also, if a greater rate is taken than is allowed by the law of either state, it is usury. Such a rate necessarily implies an intent to disregard the statutes restricting interest. *Andrews* v. *Pond,* 13 Pet. 65. *Miller* v. *Tiffany,* 1 Wallace, 298. The legal rate of interest or discount in Massachusetts is six per cent, *per annum;* and, at the date of the negotiation of these bills, a greater rate than six per cent. was usurious and unlawful.

It follows, from these considerations, that, upon the evidence as it now stands upon the part of the defendant, the transaction, upon which alone the bills in suit must depend for a ʼconsideration to give them validity as contracts, was illegal, and such as, under the laws of New York, renders them utterly void. No action, therefore, can be maintained upon them in the courts of Massachusetts, unless the effect of this evidence be in some way overcome or controlled. The verdict for the plaintiff must be set aside, and a *New trial granted.*

MILLER v. TIFFANY, 1863.

[1 Wall. (U. S.) 298.]

"The general principle in relation to contracts made in one place to be performed in another is well settled. They are to be governed by he law of the place of performance, and if the in terest allowed by the law of the place of performance is higher than that permitted at the place of contract, the parties may stipulate for the higher interest without incurring the penalties of usury." *Andrews* v. *Pond.* 13 Peters, 77, 78; *Curtis et al.* v. *Leavitt,* 15 N. Y. 92; *Berrien* v. *Wright,* 26 Barbour, 213. The converse of this proposition is also well settled. If the rate of interest be higher at the place of the contract than at the place of performance, the parties may lawfully contract in that case also for the higher rate. *Depeau* v. *Humphrey*, 20 How. 1; *Chapman* v. *Robinson*, 6 Paige, 634.

These rules are subject to the qualification, that the parties act in good faith, and that the form of the transaction is not adopted to disguise its real character. The validity of the contract is determined by the law of the place where it is entered into. Whether void or valid there, it is so everywhere. *Andrews* v. *Pond*, 13 Peters, 78; *Mix et al.* v. *The Madison Ins. Co.*, 11 Indiana, 117; *Corcoran & Riggs* v. *Powers et al.*, 6 Ohio State, 19.

FESSENDEN v. TAFT, 1888.

[65 N. H. 39.]

BILL IN EQUITY, to foreclose a mortgage of land in New Hampshire, given to secure a promissory note for $4,000, made in Massachusetts by George Taft, and payable to the plaintiff, both Taft and the plaintiff being at the time residents of Massachusetts. Facts found by a referee. The consideration for the note was in part a prior indebtedness of $2,200 from said Taft to the plaintiff, and it was agreed that the balance of $1,800 should be retained by the plaintiff until the release of an attachment upon the premises made in a suit brought by one Roberts against said Taft. Afterwards, said Roberts having prevailed in the suit, the plaintiff paid him the $1,800, and the attachment was dissolved.

In pursuance of a verbal agreement between said Taft and the plaintiff, interest was reckoned and paid on the note at various rates higher than six per cent. during various periods ending April 28 1883, when the last payment was made. The Massachusetts Public Statutes, *c.* 77, *s.* 3, provide as follows: "When there is no agreement for a different rate, the interest of money shall be at the rate of six dollars upon each one hundred dollars for a year, but it shall be lawful to pay, reserve, or contract for any rate of interest or of discount; but no greater rate than that before mentioned shall be recovered in any action, unless the agreement to pay such greater rate is in writing."

The defendant, James Taft, claims to own one undivided half of the "Jordan lot," which is part of the premises in controversy, together with the barn on the lot. The land was paid for George and James Taft, James paying one-half, but when did not appear.

The barn on the lot was built by the firm of James Taft & Co., which firm was composed of James, George, and Albert Taft, and was sold on the decease of Albert Taft, as personal property, by the surviving partners, and purchased by James Taft, who has since occupied it. The referee finds that it is personal property.

Some evidence was introduced by the defendants to show title in James Taft by adverse possession to one undivided half of the "Jordan lot," and the referee reported certain facts to the court, submitting the question whether upon these facts such title had been acquired.

The plaintiff was allowed to testify to conversations and matters between him and George Taft pertaining to the note and mortgage; and the defendants excepted.

CLARK, J. The note being a Massachusetts contract is governed by the law of Massachusetts. The mortgage, although executed in Massachusetts by citizens of that state, being a conveyance of land in New Hampshire, is controlled by the law of New Hampshire. The consideration of the note being an indebtedness of the maker to the payee of twenty-two hundred dollars, and a promise of the payee to pay to the maker eighteen hundrd dollars when the mortgaged premises were released from attachment was sufficient, and the mortgage is valid by the law of New Hampshire. The amount of the advance, eighteen hundred dollars, the contingency upon which it was to be made, and the obligation of the mortgagee to make it, were definitely agreed upon at the execution and delivery of the note and mortgage, and the agreement was afterwards performed, and the mortgage is not within the New Hampshire statute prohibiting mortgages to secure future advances. *Stearns* v. *Bennett*, 48 N. H. 400; *Abbott* v. *Thompson*, 58 N. H. 256.

The law of Massachusetts allowed the parties to contract for any rate of interest (Mass. St. of 1867, *c.* 56, *s.* 2), and the payments of interest at the rate agreed upon were legal and binding. *Marvin* v. *Mandell*, 125 Mass. 562. It is immatrial that the agreement was not in writing. The statute does not declare such an agreement illegal: it merely declares "that no greater rate of interest than six per centum per annum shall be recovered in any action, except when the agreement to ⁀ay such greater rate of interest is in writing." The question is not whether, under the law of Massachusetts, an oral executory agreement to pay interest at a higher rate than six per cent. can be enforced by action, but whether such agreement is valid when full executed. Money paid as usurious interest is allowed to be recovered back on the theory that the law regards the payment as made under duress (*Albany* v. *Abbott*, 61 N. H. 168); but the general rule is, that payments voluntarily made with a full knowledge of all material facts cannot be recovered back, even though made upon an illegal consideration, which the law would not enforce. *Caldwell* v. *Wentworth*, 14 N. H. 431. In determining the amount due upon the note, the endorsements of interest are to be applied as the parties understood and intended when the payments were made.

The Jordan lot was conveyed to George Taft May 3, 1855, and he held the title when the plaintiff's mortgage was given. James Taft paid one-half of the money for the Jordan property, but it does not appear when he paid it. To establish a resulting trust in his favor, it must appear that the payment was made at the time of the purchase, since the trust results by operation of law from the payment of the money, and a subsequent payment would be ineffectual. *Pritchard* v. *Brown*, 4 N. H. 397; *Pembrook* v. *Allenstown*, 21 N. H. 107; *Francestown* v. *Deering*, 41 N. H. 438; *Bodwell* v. *Nutter*, 63 N. H. 446. No resulting trust is shown, and if the facts were sufficient to establish a trust, it could not be set up to defeat the mortgage of the plaintiff who had no notice of it.

The claim of James Taft to title to an undivided half of the Jordan lot by adverse possession is not sustained. The burden is on him to show title, and the referee does not find that he has acquired any title by adverse possession.

The barn built bv Taft & Co. on the Jordan lot has always been treated as personal estate, and is now the property of James Taft. No legal ground appears for excluding the testimony of the plaintiff as to transactions with George Taft.

The plaintiff is entitled to a decree of foreclosure of the mortgaged premises, excepting therefrom the barn on the Jordan lot, for the amount due on the mortgage note, being the sum of thirty-three hundred dollars, with interest at six per cent from April 28, 1883.

Decree accordingly.

HART v. WILLS, 1879.

[52 Iowa 56.]

DAY, J. The court, we think, erred in holding that the contract upon which the note was executed was to be performed in Missouri, and that the law of Missouri was the *lex loci contractus*. The evidence shows the following state of facts: The note in question was given for money borrowed in equal sums by Uriah Wills and S. Sprague. A. T. Grimes is a surety upon the note. The defendants Wills and Sprague had some conference in Iowa with the plaintiff, Buton Hart, respecting Wm. M. Hart, who lived in Missouri. Subsequently the defendants Sprague and Buton Hart visited Wm. M. Hart in Missouri, where the note in question was signed by Sprague. Wm. M. Hart then gave Buton Hart a package of money to bring to Iowa, and directed him, when the note was executed by the other parties, to pay the money to the defendants. Wills and Grimes signed the note in Decatur county, Iowa, and then the note was delivered and the money was paid over. Under these circumstances the note must be regarded as an Iowa contract, and governed by its laws. In Second Parson's on Notes and Bills, page 327, it is said: "The *lex loci contractus* depends not upon the place where the note or bill is made, drawn, or dated, but upon the place where it is delivered from drawer to drawee, from promissor to payee, from indorser to indorsee. It has been frequently stated that a note is nothing until delivered; and that indorsement is not merely writing, but transferring from the hand of the one party to that of the other." See, also, cases cited in note *z*. It is urged bv appellee that if no place be designated in a note as a place of payment, the law of the place where it is made determines its construction, obligation and place of payment, citing Second Parson's on Notes and Bills, page 333. This is true if the making of a note be regarded as including the delivery, but not otherwise. The appellee further insists that the dating of the note at Princeton, Missouri, designates that place as the place of payment. No authority is cited in support of this position, and we think it is not maintainable. In *Cook* v. *Moffat*, 5 How. 295, notes drawn and dated at Baltimore, but delivered in New York in payment of goods purchased there, were held to be payable in and governed by the laws of New York. In that case GRIER, J., said: "Although the notes purport to have been made in Baltimore, they were de-

livered in New York in payment of goods furnished there, and
of course were payable there, and governed by the laws of that
place." See, also, other authorities cited in Second Parson's on
Notes and Bills, page 327, note *z*. The court erred in holding
that the defence of usury could not be considered. The cause
must be remanded for new trial.

REVERSED.

MAYNARD v. HALL, 1896.

[92 Wis. 565.]

APPEAL from a judgment of the circuit court of La Fay-
ette county: GEO. CLEMENTSON, Circuit Judge. *Reversed.*

This action was brought for the foreclosure of a mortgage
executed by the defendants *Thomas Hall* and *Mary Jane Hall*,
his wife, to the plaintiff, a citizen of Illinois, to secure the payment of a note dated June 9, 1887, for $4,000, executed by
them in Illinois, and payable to the plaintiff or order, on or
before June 9, 1888, at the Bank of Apple River, at Apple River,
Illinois, with interest after date at the rate of eight per cent.
per annum, payable annually, until paid. The answer contests the
right of the plaintiff to recover any more than the principal sum
of $4,000, on the ground that the note and mortgage given to
secure the debt of that amount were usurious under the law of
Illinois in force at the time, which was pleaded and proved at
the trial.

It was found by the court that at the date of the note the
defendant *Thomas Hall* was indebted to the plaintiff in a sum
exceeding $4,000, and to secure that portion of said indebtedness
the promissory note and mortgage in question were executed,
and that it was agreed at the time that the defendant *Hall* should
pay, and the plaintiff should receive, for interest on the said
$4,000, twelve per cent. per annum, eight per cent, whereof was
agreed to be paid by the terms of the said note, and the additional
four per cent., or $160, up to the maturity of the note, one year
after date, was to be and was paid at the time in advance; that
soon after the maturity of the note, it was further agreed that
the defendant *Hall* should pay, and the plaintiff should receive,
twelve per cent. interest upon the said note for the year next
after its maturity,—that is to say, four per cent. per annum, or
$160, in addition to the eight per cent. secured thereby,—which
the defendant *Hall* paid, and the plaintiff then received, in
advance; both payments having been made by checks drawn on

the plaintiff, who was a banker, by the defendant *Hall*, against his account with him, and were thereupon paid and charged accordingly. It was further found that the note and mortgage were Illinois contracts, to be governed by the interest and usury laws of that state existing at the time; and the cases of *First Nat. Bank v. Davis,* 108 Ill. 633, and *Harris v. Bressler,* 119 Ill. 467, and other cases in the supreme and appellate courts of that state, were read in evidence. The court found the amount due on the note and mortgage was the principal sum of $4,000, with interest from June 9, 1888, the time when the note, by its terms, became due, at the rate of six per cent. per annum, and gave judgment of foreclosure accordingly, from which the defendants *Thomas Hall* and *Mary Jane Hall,* his wife, appealed.

PINNEY, J. The only question involved is whether the plaintiff was entitled to recover any money for interest on the note and mortgage. They are Illinois contracts, and governed wholly by the Illinois laws. The judgment to be given, in respect to the questions of usury and interest thereon, is to be such as the courts of that state would give, according to the laws of Illinois. By the Revised Statutes of Illinois of 1881 (ch. 74, secs, 1, 4–6), it is provided, in substance, that the lawful rate of interest shall be six per cent.; that it should be lawful, by written contract, for parties to agree that eight per cent. per annum, or any less sum, should be paid; that no person should, directly or indirectly, accept or receive, in money, goods, etc., or in any other way, any greater sum or greater value for the loan, forbearance, or discount of any money, goods, or thing in action, than above specified, and that "if any person or corporation in this state shall contract to receive a greater rate of interest or discount than eight per cent. upon any contract, verbal or written, such person or corporation shall forfeit the whole of said interest so contracted to be received, and shall be entitled only to recover the principal sum due to such person or corporation; and that all contracts executed after this act shall take effect, which shall provide for interest or compensation at a greater rate than herein specified on account of nonpayment at maturity, shall be deemed usurious, and only the principal sum due thereon shall be recoverable." The above provisions are also made applicable to any written contract, wherever payable, if made in Illinois, or between citizens or corporations of that state and citizens or corporations of any other state, territory, or country, or shall be secured by mortgage or trust deed on lands in such state.

It is difficult to see how there can be any room for doubt of the legislative intent where it is enacted, as in these provisions, that, if any person or corporation shall contract to receive a greater rate of interest or discount than eight per cent., such person or corporation "shall forfeit the whole of said interest so contracted to be received, and shall be entitled *only to recover the principal sum due* to such person or corporation." The latter clause is too clear and decisive to admit of doubt or require construction. The statute is aimed at the evil supposed to grow out of usurious contracts, and it imposes the loss of *all* interest, not only such as might accrue before the maturity of the obligation, but that, as well, which might accrue thereafter. The case of *First Nat. Bank v. Davis*, 108 Ill. 633, relied on by the plaintiff which arose under a statute the same in substance, holds that, where the contract is usurious, after the maturity of the obligation the principal sum will draw the legal rate of interest at six per cent., and that interest at that rate may be recovered thereon. This appears to be directly contrary to the words of the statute. The decision was by a divided court; two of its judges dissenting from this view, and two others of the seven holding that the transaction in question was not usurious. The proposition, therefore, for which the case is cited, could not have had the concurrence, it would seem, of more than three judges,— a minority of the court. In the subsequent case of *Harris v. Bressler*, 119 Ill. 467, 471, where the same question again arose, the case of *First Nat. Bank v. Davis, supra,* was considered, and it was expressly overruled, as to this question, by the unanimous decision of the court, made before the securities in question were executed; and it was held in *Harris v. Bressler, supra,* that in such case no interest, but only the principal sum, could be recovered. Had the plaintiff sued the defendant *Hall* on the note in Illinois, it is manifest that, on the defence made that it was usurious, he could not have recovered any interest, and would have been "entitled only to recover the principal sum due." This view is decisive of the case.

As the defendants have not applied for equitable relief, the equity rule applicable to cases requiring a tender of the principal sum loaned, as a condition of relief, does not apply. The defendants stand on the defensive, and claim only what the statute secures to them.

The provisions of sec. 1692, R. S., that "when any person shall set up the plea of usury in any action instituted against him, such person, to be entitled . . . to the benefit of such plea, shall prove a tender of the principal sum of money or thing loaned to the party entitled to receive the same," is a provision of the usury laws of this state, and relates only to actions upon contracts made usurious by the provision of the statute of this state, and has no application to a case like the present, arising under and governed by the statute against usury of another state.

It follows that the judgment of the circuit court is erroneous as to the sum adjudged due, and must be reversed. The plaintiff cannot have judgment for more than the principal sum of $4,000 and costs.

By the Court.—The judgment of the circuit court is reversed, and the cause is remanded with directions to enter judgment in conformity to the opinion of this court.

LEROUX v. BROWN, 1852.

[74 Eng. Com. Law 800.

ASSUMPSIT. The declaration stated, that, on the 1st of December, 1849, at Calais, in France, to wit, at Westminster, in the county of Middlesex, in consideration that the plaintiff, at the request of the defendant, then agreed with the defendant to enter into the service of the defendant as clerk and agent, and to serve the defendant in that capacity *for one year certain,* at certain wages, to wit, 100*l.* a year, to be paid by the defendant to the plaintiff by equal quarterly payments during his continuance in such service, the defendant then promised the plaintiff to receive him into his said service, and to retain and employ him in his said service, at the wages aforesaid: Averment that the plaintiff, confiding in the promise of the defendant, was then, and from thence continually had been, ready and willing to enter into the service of the defendant as aforesaid, and to serve the defendant, for the wages aforesaid: Breach, that, though the plaintiff afterwards, to wit, on the day and year aforesaid, requested the defendant to receive the plaintiff into the service of the defendant as aforesaid, and to retain and employ him in such service, at the wages aforesaid; yet the defendant, not regarding his promise, did not, nor would, at the time he was so requested as aforesaid, or at any other time, receive the plaintiff into his service as aforesaid, or retain or employ him, at such wages as aforesaid, or in any other way, but wholly neglected and refused so to do; whereby the

31

plaintiff not only lost and was deprived of all the profits and emoluments which might and would otherwise have arisen and accrued to him from entering into the service of the defendant, but also lost and was deprived of the means and opportunity of being retained and employed by and in the service of divers other persons, and remained wholly out of service and unemployed for a long time, to wit, for the year then next following, and was and is otherwise greatly injured, &c.

Pleas,—first, non assumpsit,—secondly, that the plaintiff was not ready and willing to enter into the service of the defendant, and to serve him the defendant, for the wages in the declaration mentioned, in manner and form as in the declaration was alleged, —thirdly, that the plaintiff did not request the defendant to receive him, the plaintiff, into the service of him, the defendant, or to retain or employ him, the plaintiff, in such service, at the wages in the declaration mentioned, in manner and form as the plaintiff had above in the declaration alleged.

Upon each of these pleas issue was joined.

The cause was tried before Talfourd, J., at the second sitting in Middlesex, in Trinity Term last. It appeared that an oral agreement had been entered into at Calais, between the plaintiff and the defendant, under which the latter, who resided in England, contracted to employ the former, who was a British subject resident at Calais, at a salary of 100*l.* per annum, to collect poultry and eggs in that neighborhood, for transmission to the defendant here,—the employment to commence at a future day, and to continue for one year certain.

Evidence was given on the part of the plaintiff to show, that, by the law of France, such an agreement is capable of being enforced, although not in writing.

For the defendant, it was insisted, that, notwithstanding the contract was made in France, when it was sought to enforce it in this country, it must be dealt with according to our law; and, being a contract not to be performed within a year, the statute of frauds, 29 Car. 2, c. 3, s. 4, required it to be in writing.

Under the direction of the learned judge, a verdict was entered for the plaintiff on the first issue,—leave being reserved to the defendant to move to enter a nonsuit or a verdict for him on that issue, if the court should be of opinion that the contract could not be enforced here.

JERVIS, C. J.—I am of opinion that the rule to enter a nonsuit must be made absolute. There is no dispute as to the principles which ought to govern our decision. My Brother Allen admits, that, if the 4th section of the statute of frauds applies, not to the validity of the contract, but only to the procedure, the plaintiff cannot maintain this action, because there is no agreement, nor any memorandum or note thereof, in writing. On the other hand, it is not denied by Mr. Honyman,—who has argued this case in a manner for which the court is much indebted to him,— that, if the 4th section applies to the contract itself, or, as Boulle-nois expresses it, to the *solemnities* of the contract, inasmuch as our law cannot regulate foreign contracts, a contract like this may be enforced here. I am of opinion that the 4th section ap plies not to solemnities of the contract, but to the procedure; and therefore that the contract in question cannot be sued upon here. The contract may be capable of being enforced in the country where it was made: but not in England. Looking at the words of the 4th section of the statute of frauds, and contrasting them with those of the 1st, 3d, and 17th sections, this conclusion seems to me to be enevitable. The words of s. 4 are, "no action shall be brought upon any agreement which is not to be per-formed within the space of one year from the making thereof, unless the agreement upon which such action shall be brought, or some memorandum or note thereof, shall be in writing, and signed by the party to be charged therewith, or some other person thereto by him lawfully authorized." The statute, in this part of it, does not say, that, unless those requisites are complied with, *the contract shall be void,* but merely that *no action shall be brought upon it:* and, as was put with great froce by Mr. Hony-man, the alternative, "unless the agreement, *or* some memoran-dum or note thereof, shall be in writing,"—words which are satisfied if there be any written evidence of a previous agreement, —shows that the statute contemplated that the agreement may be good, though not capable of being enforced if not evidenced by writing. This therefore may be a very good agreement though, for want of a compliance with the requisites of the statute, not enforceable in an English court of justice. This view seems to be supported by the authorities; because, unless we are to infer that the courts thought the agreement itself good, though not made in strict compliance with the statute, they could not con-sistently have held, as was held in the cases referred to by Sir Edward Sugden, that a writing subsequent to the contract, and addressed to a third person, was sufficient evidence of an agree-ment, within the statute. It seems, therefore, that both authority and practice are consistent with the words of the 4th section. The cases of Carrington v. Roots, and Reade v. Lamb, however, have been pressed upon us as being inconsistent with this view. It is sufficient to say that the attention of the learned judges by whom those cases were decided, was not invited to the particular point now in question. What they were considering was, whether, for the purposes of those actions, there was any substantial difference·between the 4th and 17th sections. It must be borne in mind that the meaning of those sections has been the subject of discussion on other occasions. In Crosby v. Wadsworth, 6 East, 602, Lord Ellenborough, speaking of the 4th section, says,— "The statute does not expressly and immediately vacate such contracts, if made by parol: it only precludes the bringing of actions to enforce them." Again, in Laythoarp v. Bryant, 2 N. C. 735, 3 Scott, 238, Tindal, C. J., and Bosanquet, J., say distinctly that the contract is good, and that the statute merely takes away the remedy, where there is no memorandum or note in writing. I therefore think we are correct in holding that the contract in this case is incapable of being enforced by an action in this country, because the 4th section of the 29 Car. 2, c. 3, relates only to the procedure, and not to the right and validity of the contract itself. As to what is said by Boullenois in the passage last cited by Brother Allen, it is to be observed that the learned author is there speaking of what pertains ad vinculum obligationis et solemnitatem, and not with reference to the mode of procedure. Upon these grounds, I am of opinion that this action cannot be maintained, and that the rule to enter a nonsuit must be made absolute.

MAULE, J.—I am of the same opinion. The 4th section of the statute of frauds enacts that "no action shall be brought upon any agreement which is not to be performed within the space of one year from the making thereof, unless the agreement upon which such action shall be brought, or some memorandum or note thereof, shall be in writing, and signed by the party to be charged therewith, or some other person thereto by him lawfully authorized." Now, this is an action brought upon a contract which was not to be performed within the space of one year from the making thereof, and there is no memorandum or note thereof in writing signed by the defendant or any lawfully authorized agent. The case, therefore, plainly falls within the distinct words of the statute. It is said that the 4th section is not applicable to this case, because the contract was made in France. This particular section does not in terms say that no such contract as before stated shall be of any force; it says, *no action shall be brought upon it.* In their literal sense, these words mean that no action shall be brought upon such an agreement in any court in which the British legislature has power to direct what shall and what shall not be done; in terms, therefore, it applies to something which is to take place where the law of England prevails. But we have been pressed with cases which it is said have decided that the words "no action shall be brought" in the 4th section, are equivalent to the words "no contract shall be allowed to be good" which are found in another part of the statute. Suppose it had been so held, as a general and universal proposition, still I apprehend it would not be a legitimate mode of construing the 4th section, to substitute the equivalent words for those actually used. What we have to construe, is, not the equivalent words, but the words we find there. If the substituted words import the same thing, the substitution is unnecessary and idle: and, if those words are susceptible of a different construction from those actually used, that is a reason for dealing with the latter only. It may be, that, for some purposes, the words used in the 4th and 17th sections may be equivalent; but they clearly are not so in the case now before us; for, there is nothing to prevent this contract from being enforced in a French court of law. Dealing with the words of the 4th section as we are bound to deal with all words that are plain and unambiguous, all we say, is, that they prohibit the courts of this country from enforcing a contract made under circumstances like the present,—just as we hold a contract incapable of being enforced, where it appears upon the record to have been made more than six years. It is parcel of the procedure, and not of the formality of the contract. None of the authorities which have been referred to seem to me to be at all at variance with the conclusion at which we have arrived.

TALFORD, J.—I am of the same opinion. The argument of Mr. Honyman seems to me to be quite unanswerable. That drawn from Laythoarp v. Bryant and that class of cases in which it has been held that the 4th section of the statute of frauds is satisfied by a subsequent letter addressed to a third party, containing evidence of the terms of the contract, shows clearly that that section has reference to procedure only, and not to what are called by the jurists the rights and solemnities of the contract. Rule absolute.

EMERY v. BURBANK, 1895.

[163 Mass. 326.]

HOLMES, J.—This is an action on an oral agreement, alleged to have been made in Maine in 1890, by the defendant's testatrix, Mrs. Rumery, to the effect that, if the plaintiff would leave Maine and take care of Mrs. Rumery, the latter would leave the plaintiff all her property at her death, and also would put four thousand dollars into a house which the plaintiff should have. At the trial evidence was introduced tending to prove the agreement as alleged. The presiding justice ruled that the action could not be maintained, and the case is here on exceptions. As we are of opinion that the ruling must be sustained under St. 1888, c. 372, requiring agreements to make wills to be in writing, a fuller statement of the facts is not needful.

There is no doubt of the general principals to be applied. A contract valid where it is made is valid everywhere, but it is not necessarily enforceable everywhere. It may be contrary to the policy of the law of the forum. *Van Reimsdyk* v. *Kane*, 1 Gall. 371, 375. *Greenwood* v. *Curtis*, 6 Mass. 358. *Fant* v. *Miller*, 17 Grat. 47, 62. Or again, if the law of the forum requires a certain mode of proof, the contract, although valid, cannot be enforced in that jurisdiction without the proof required there. This is as true between the States of this Union as it is between Massachusetts and England. *Hoadley* v. *Northern Transportation Co.* 115 Mass. 304, 306. *Pritchard* v. *Norton*, 106 U. S. 124, 134. *Downer* v. *Chesebrough*, 36 Conn. 39. *Kleeman* v. *Collins*, 9 Bush. (Ky.) 460. *Fant* v. *Miller*, 17 Grat. 47. *Hunt* v. *Jones*. 12 R. I. 265, 266. *Yates* v. *Thomson*, 3 Cl. & Fin. 544, 586, 587. *Bain* v. *Whitehaven & Furness Junction Railway*, 3 H. L. Cas. 1, 19. *Leroux* v. *Brown*, 12 C. B. 801. When the law involved is a statute, it is a question of construction whether the law is addressed to the necessary constituent elements, or legality, of the contract on the one hand, or to the evidence by which it shall be proved on the other. In the former case the law affects contracts made within the jurisdiction, wherever sued, and may affect only them. *Drew* v. *Smith*, 59 Maine, 393. In the latter, it applies to all suits within the jurisdiction, wherever the contracts sued upon were made, and again may have no other effect. It is possible, however, that a statute should affect both validity and remedy by express words, and this being so, it is possible that words which in terms speak only of one should carry with them an implication also as to the other. For instance, in a well known English case Maule, J., said, "The fourth section of the statute of frauds entirely applies to procedure." And on this ground it was held that an action could not be maintained upon an oral contract made in France. But he went on "It may be that the words used, operating on contracts made in England, renders them void." *Leroux* v. *Brown*, 12 C. B. 801, 805, 827. We cite the language, not for its particular application, but as a recognition of the possibility which we assert.

The words of the statute before us seem in the first place, and most plainly, to deal with the validity and form of the contract. "No agreement . . . shall be binding, unless such agreement is in writing." If taken literally, they are not satisfied by a written memorandum of the contract; the contract itself must be made in writing. They are limited, too, to agreements made after the passage of the act, a limitation which perhaps would be more likely to be inserted in a law concerning the form of a contract than in one which only changed a rule of evidence. But we are of opinion that the statute ought not to be limited to its operation on the form of contracts made in this State. The generality of the words alone, "no agreement," is not conclusive. But the statute evidently embodies a fundamental policy. The ground, of course, is the prevention of fraud and perjury, which are deemed likely to be practised without this safeguard. The nature of the contract is such that it naturally would be performed or sued upon at the domicil of the promisor. If the policy of Massachusetts makes void an oral contract of this sort made within the State, the same policy forbids that Massachusetts testators should be sued here upon such contracts without written evidence, wherever they are made.

If we are right in our understanding of the policy established by the Legislature, it is our duty to carry it out so far as we can do so without coming into conflict with paramount principles. "If oral evidence were offered which the *lex fori* excluded, such exclusion, being founded on the desire of preventing perjury, might claim to override any contrary rule of the *lex loci contractus*, not only on the ground of its being a question of procedure, but also because of that reservation in favor of any stringent domestic policy which controls all maxims of private international law." Westlake. Priv. Int. Law, (3d ed.) § 208. Wharton, Confl. Laws, (2d ed.) § 766.

In our view, the statute, whatever it expresses, implies a rule

of procedure broad enough to cover this case. It is not necessary to decide exactly how broad the rule may be,—whether, for
instance, if, by some unusual chance, a suit should happen to be
brought here against an ancillary administrator upon a contract
made in another State by one of its inhabitants, the contract
would have to be in writing. The rule extends at least to contracts by Massachusetts testators. It might be possible to treat
the words, "signed by the party whose executor or adminsitrator
is sought to be charged," as meaning "signed by the party whose
executor or administrator is sought to be charged in Massachusetts," and to construe the whole statute as directed only to procedure. Compare *Fant* v. *Miller*, 17 Grat. 47, 72, *et seq.* *Denny*
v. *Williams*, 5 Allen, 1, 3, 9. Upon this question also we express
no opinion. All that we decide is that the statute does apply to a
case like the present.

The law of the testator's domicil is the law of the will. A
contract to make a will means an effectual will, and therefore a
will good by the law of the domicil. In a sense, the place of
performance, as well as the forum for a suit in case of breach, is
the domicil. We do not draw the conclusion that therefore the
validity of all such contracts, wherever sued on, must depend on
the law of the domicil. That would leave many such contracts
in a state of indeterminate validity until the testator's death, as
he may change his domicil so long as he can travel. But the
consideration shows that the final domicil is more concerned in
the policy to be insisted on than any other jurisdiction, and
justifies it in framing its rules accordingly. There would be no
question to be argued if the law were in terms a rule of evidence.
It is equally open for a State to declare, upon the same considerations which dictate a rule of evidence, that a contract must have
certain form if it is to be enforced against its inhabitants in its
courts. Legislation of this kind for contracts which thus necessarily reach into the jurisdiction in their operation hardly goes
as far as statutes dealing with substantive liability which have
been upheld. *Commonwealth* v. *Macloon*, 101 Mass. 1.

If the statute applies, the fact that the plaintiff has furnished
the stipulated consideration will not prevent its application.

Exceptions overruled.

HEATON v. ELDRIDGE, 1897.

[56 Ohio St. 87.]

ERROR to the Circuit Court of Franklin county.

Action was brought by Eliza Heaton against Eldridge & Higgins, in the court of common pleas, on several promissory notes executed by the defendants, amounting in the aggregate to something over two thousand dollars.

The answer set up a counter-claim for damages resulting from the breach of an oral agreement which, it was alleged, had had been entered into by the parties, whereby the plaintiff agreed to employ the defendants as her agents for the sale of cigars of the plaintiff's manufacture, at a stipulated compensation, and for a specified time extending beyond the period of one year. The agreement, it is averred, was made and to be performed in the state of Pennsylvania, where the law did not require contracts of that kind to be in writing, nor a written memorandum thereof to be signed by either party, nor forbid the bringing of an action thereon. The allegations of the answer were specifically denied by reply, and at the trial the plaintiff interposed the statute of frauds of this state to the evidence offered in support of them. The evidence offered to establish the agreement, which consisted of oral testimony only, was excluded from the consideration of the jury; and there being no defense to the notes, judgment was rendered for the plaintiff for the amount due on them. The judgment was reversed by the circuit court, for error in the exclusion of the testimony; the court holding that, as the contract was valid where it was made, our statute was not an obstacle to its enforcement here; and whether that holding is correct is the only question brought before this court.

WILLIAMS, J.—It is provided by section 4199, of the Revised Statutes, that: "No action shall be brought * * * upon any agreement that is not to be performed within the space of one year from the making thereof; unless the agreement upon which such action is brought, or some memorandum or note thereof, is in writing, and signed by the party to be charged therewith, or some person thereunto by him or her lawfully authorized."

There is no doubt that the law of the state or country where a contract is executed and is to be performed, enters into and becomes a part of contract, in the sense that its validity and obligatory effect are to be determined and controlled by that law; and when valid there, the contract will be sustained everywhere, and accorded the interpretation required by the law of the place where made, when the law is properly brought to the attention of the court, unless the contract is against good morals, or contravenes a set tled policy of the state or country in whose tribunals its enforcement is sought. The rule is founded on the presumption that parties contract with reference to the laws to which they are subject at the time, and on the principles of comity prevailing among civilized nations. But it does not extend so far that the remedial system and methods of procedure established by one state or country will yield to those of another, nor that either will recognize or enforce those of the other. Each provides and alters at will its own rules and regulations in the administration of justice, to which those seeking redress in its courts must conform.

So that, the solution of the question presented involves the inquiry whether the provision of the statute above quoted appertains to the remedy on contracts to which it refers, or goes to their validity. We have found no expression on the question by this court, though it has been the subject of repeated adjudications both in England, and in several of the states. This provision of our statute is copied from the 4th section of the English Statute of Frauds; and in the case of *Leroux* v. *Brown*, 12 C. B. (74 Eng. C. L.), 801, where the precise question we have before us arose, it was held, that the section affected the remedy only, and was so applied as to defeat a recovery on a parol contract not to be performed within a year, which was made in France, where it was capable of proof by parol evidence. The case appears to have been thoroughly argued and considered, and the decision has since been adhered to by the English courts, and followed or cited with approbation by many American cases, and generally accepted by text writers, as the established law. *Bain* v. *Whitehaven*, 3 H. L. Cases, 1; *Williams* v. *Wheeler*, 8 C. B. N. S. 316; *Madison* v. *Alderson*, L. R. 8 App. Case, 467, 488; *Pritchard* v. *Norton*, 106 U. S., 127; *Dower* v. *Chesebrough*, 36 Conn., 39; *Townsend* v. *Hargrave*, 118 Mass., 326; *Bird* v. *Monroe*, 66 Me., 337; *Emery* v. *Burbank*, 163 Mass., 326; Wald's Pallock on Contracts, 604-607, and notes. Anson on Contracts, p. 79; Brown on the Statute of Frauds, sections 136, 115*a*; Agnew on Statute of Frauds, 64-66; Wood on Statute of Frauds, section 166; Wharton on Conflict of Laws, section 690. And while the case of *Leroux* v. *Brown* has been criticized, those criticisms have been directed chiefly to the distinction drawn between the 4th and 17th sections of the statute, and the opinion expressed that the language of the latter section was such as to render invalid contracts within its provisions, for which reason it did not, as did section 4, constitute a regulation affecting the remedy. This distinction has not met with general approval, and has been repudiated in some of the latter cases, which hold, that the 17th section relates to the remedy, like section 4, and that the difference in the phraseology of the two sections is not such as to warrant a different interpretation in that respect, but that both sections prescribe rules of evidence which courts, where the remedy is sought, are required to observe. *Townsend* v. *Hargrave,* 118 Mass., 326; *Bird* v. *Monroe,* 66 Me., 337, 343; *Pritchard* v. *Norton,* 106 U. S., 127; *Madison* v. *Alderson,* L. R. 8 App. Cas., 467-488; Brown on the Statute of Frauds, section 136, note.

In Story on Conflict of Laws, section 262, a different view of the question was taken, which has been adopted by some courts; but the decided weight of authority is in accordance with the decision in *Leroux* v. *Brown.* The views of Judge Story were brought to the attention of the court in that case; and, in an edition of his work published after that case was decided, a section was added, in which it is said, that "the statute of frauds is, like the statute of limitations, a matter affecting the remedy merely; and if by the law of the forum no action can be maintained on a particular oral contract, if made in that country, the like rule will obtain as to a contract made elsewhere, although it was valid by the law of the place where made." Story on Conflict of Laws, 7 ed., section 576.

The question being an open one in this state, we are not disinclined to consider it on principle. The principle which must control its decision is the fundamental one that contracts receive their sanction and interpretation from the law of the place where they are made and to be performed; but the remedy upon them must be taken and pursued according to the law of the place where they are sought to be enforced; and a decision of the question will be reached when it is ascertained within which of these rules the statute of frauds finds its appropriate place. The language of the statute under consideration, that no action shall be brought on any agreement therein mentioned, unless it, or "some memorandum or note thereof is in writing and signed by the party to be charged," fairly imports that the agreement precedes the written memorandum, and may exist as a complete and valid agreement, independent of the writing. The memorandum, which is merely the evidence of the contract, may be made and signed after the completion of the agreement, and even a letter from the party to be charged, reciting the terms of the agree ment, is sufficient to satisfy the requirements of the statute; but it cannot be said that the letter constitutes the agreement; that was made when the minds of he parties met with respect to its terms, and the letter furnishes the necessary evidence to prove the agreement in an action for its enforcement. And generally, when parties reduce their contracts to writing, the writing becomes the evidence of the agreement which they had previously entered into; and, having adopted that mode of evidencing their agreement, the parties are not allowed to make proof of it by verbal testimony. This statute, in plain terms, forbids the maintenance of an action in any of the courts of this state, on any agreement which, by its terms, is not to be performed within a year, unless the action is supported by the required written evidence. The evidence by which a contract shall be proved is no part of the contract itself, but its admission or rejection becomes a part of the proceeding on the trial, where its competency and sufficiency must be determined. When the required evidence is lacking, the courts must refuse the enforcement of the contract. And it seems clear, that such a statutory regulation prescribing the mode or measure of proof necessary to maintain an action or defense, pertains to the remedy, and constitutes a part of the procedure of the forum in administering the remedy. The statute contains no exception or limitation on account of the place where the contract was entered into, or to be performed; but denies remedy on any contract of the kind designated by it, wherever made, which can not be established by the evidence required.

That such was the intended scope of the statute is manifest when the purpose of its enactment is considered. Its well known design was, as declared in the English statute of frauds, after which ours, and those of most of the states are patterned, to prevent perjuries and fraudulent practices which were the outgrowth of the general admission of parol testimony to prove almost every kind of contract, and by means of which people were often stripped of their estates, and burdened with liabilities by testimony of alleged conversations and verbal declarations. The opportunities thus afforded for the perpetration of frauds, constituted temptations so strong for the commission of perjuries, that legislation excluding that kind of evidence in a large number of cases became, or was considered a necessity. These mischiefs, to remedy which was the chief aim of the statute, arose from the admission of oral evidence in trials of actions and suits, and in the course of judicial procedure; and obviously, the opportunity and temptation for the commission of frauds and perjuries by admitting parol proof to establish the contracts with which the statute is concerned, are not any the less in cases where the agreement was made in another state or country, than in those where the agreement involved is one made in this state; the mischief is the same in either case, and to allow the former to be so proved, would, that far at least, prevent the accomplishment of the salutary purposes of the statute. The statute is founded on considerations of public policy, and those of a moral nature, and declared a peremptory rule of procedure which the courts of this state are not at liberty to disregard in defference to the laws of any other state or country.

The agreement set up in the defendant's answer could not, according to its terms, be performed within one year from the time it was made. An action upon it could be supported only by evidence which complied with the statutory requirements; and to be available as a counterclaim, which is a cross action, such evidence was indispensable. It was not offered, and the court, we think, properly excluded the parol evidence relied on to prove the agreement. The judgment of the circuit must therefore be reversed, and that of the common pleas affirmed.

Judgment accordingly.

FIRST NAT. BANK v. SHAW, 1902.

[70 Southwestern Rep. 807.]

McALLISTER, J. The only question presented for determination upon this record is the liability of the defendant Mrs. Stella V. Harley upon the following note: "$500.00. Geneva, Ohio, Dec. 3, 1892. Six months after date, value received, we jointly and severally promise to pay to the First National Bank of Geneva, at their banking house, $500.00, interest 8% after maturity. Interest paid to maturity, $17.50. D. H. Harley. Stella V. Harley. M. P. Shaw." Mrs. Harley, in her answer to the bill, avers that she was a married woman at the time said note was executed, and relies on the plea of coverture. She further avers that she and her husband, D. H. Harley, were

residents of and living in the state of Tennessee at the time said
note was executed, and had since continuously lived in this state,
and she denies that the note was an Ohio contract.

The facts found by the court of chancery appeals are, viz.:
First. The note sued on is a renewal note. The original note was
made June 6, 1891. It was renewed December 5, 1891; renewed
again January 4, 1892; and again December 3, 1892; the note
last renewed or made being the one in suit. Second. Previous
to the execution of the first note, and since 1889, Mrs. Harley
was a married woman, living with her husband continuously in
Tennessee. She owned no property in the state of Ohio. Third.
The weight of the proof is, and we so find as a fact, that she
signed all the notes in Tennessee; and it is practically conceded,
and, if not conceded, we find the fact to be, that she signed the
note sued on in Tennessee. Fourth. The original note was negotiated in Geneva, Ohio. The note sued on was received by the
bank at Geneva, Ohio, through the mail, from Chattanooga,
Tenn. Fifth. It is conceded that, under the statute law of Ohio,
married women are liable in that state on their contracts.

It will be preceived that the legal question presented is
whether a married woman, domiciled with her husband in Tennessee, is liable on a note signed by her in this state, but payable
in the state of Ohio. The first question, of course, to be determined, is whether, upon the facts found, this is a Tennessee
or Ohio contract. Says Mr. Tiedeman, in his work on Commercial Paper (page 506): "It is not the law of the place where
the contract was signed or executed, but the law of the place
where the contract was consummated, by delivery or otherwise,
which governs the construction of the contract made in one state,
to be performed in another. Thus notes drawn in one state, and
delivered and payable in another, for purchases made there, are
governed by the law of the latter state, and are considered there
made; for by delivery, only, the act of making is fully consummated." So it was held in Hall v. Cordell, 142 U. S. 116, 12
Sup. Ct. 154, 35 L. Ed. 956: "But where there is nothing to
show that the parties had in view, in respect to the execution of
the contract, any other law than the law of the place of performance, that law must determine the rights of the parties."
Hubble v. Improvement Co., 95 Tenn. 585, 32 S. W. 965. In
2 Pars. Cont. 586, it is said: "So if one in New York orders
goods from Boston, either by carrier whom he points out, or
in the usual course of trade, this would be a completion of the

making of the contract, and it would be a Boston contract, whether he gave no note, or a note payable in Boston, or one without express place of payment." We think it quite plain that the note in suit is an Ohio contract, notwithstanding it was signed by Mrs. Harley in Tennessee, it having been delivered and consummated in Ohio, and is payable in that state, as the place of performance. Armstrong v. Best, 112 N. C. 59, 17 S. E. 14, 25 L. R. A. 188, 34 Am. St. Rep. 473; Milliken v. Pratt, 125 Mass. 374, 28 Am. Rep. 241.

The next inquiry is whether the plea of coverture to a note made in Ohio, valid and enforceable against a married woman in that state, is available in a suit on said note in this state, where such a contract is voidable at the election of the married woman. In Story, Confl. Laws, c. 4, § 103, it is said: "In regard to questions concerning infancy, competency to marry, incapacities incident to coverture, guardianship, and other personal qualities and disabilities, the law of the domicile or birth, or other fixed domicile, is not generally to govern, but the 'lex loci contractus aut actus,' the law of the place where the contract is made or the act done," or, as he elsewhere sums it up, "although foreign jurists generally hold that the law of the domicile ought to govern in regard to the capacity of persons to contract, yet the common law holds a different doctrine, namely, that lex loci contractus is to govern." Story, Confl. Law, §§ 103, 241. Chancellor Kent, while at one time inclined to the doctrine of the civilians, afterwards approved the doctrine which has just been quoted from Mr. Story. 2 Kent, Comm. 233, note, 458, 459, and note. The same doctrine was announced by this court in Pearl v. Hansborough, 9 Humph. 426, in an opinion by Judge Turley. Applying this rule, it was held in Milliken v. Pratt, 125 Mass. 374, 28 Am. Rep. 241 (Mr. Justice Gray delivering the opinion of the court), that a contract of guaranty, signed by a married woman, domiciled with her husband in Massachusetts, and sent by mail to Maine, where it was accepted and acted on, was a contract made in the state of Maine, and, when sued on in the state of Massachusetts, would be determined by the law of Maine. In that case it appeared that by the statutes of Maine, in force at the date of the contract of guaranty, the contracts of a married woman were valid and enforceable as if made by a feme sole, while the law of Massachusetts, as then existing, did not allow her to enter into a contract as surety or for the accommodation of her husband. But it further appeared that since the making of the contract sued

on, and before the bringing of the action, the law of Massachusetts had been changed so as to enable married women to make
such contracts. The court of Massachusetts therefore permitted
a recovery against a married woman on the contract of guaranty
made in Maine. See, also, Bell v. Packard, 69 Me. 105, 31 Am.
Rep. 251. But in Tennessee the contracts of a married woman
are voidable, and will not be enforced against her when there is a
plea of coverture. It would be a strange anomaly to hold that
such a contract made by a married woman in Tennessee would
not be enforced by our courts, while the same contract, if made in
another state, would be valid and enforceable. As stated by Mr.
Justice Gray in Milliken v. Pratt, supra: "As the law of another state can neither operate nor be executed in this state by its
own force, but only by the comity of this state, its operation and
enforcement here may be restricted by positive prohibition of
statute. * * * It is possible, also, that in a state where the
common law prevailed in full force, by which a married woman
was deemed incapable of binding herself by any contract whatever, it might be inferred that such utter incapacity, lasting
throughout the joint lives of husband and wife, must be considered as so fixed by the settled policy of the state for the protection of its own citizens that it could not be held by the courts of
that state to yield to the law of another state in which she might
undertake to contract." While it is true, as contended by counsel
in his very able argument, that the tendency of legislation in
Tennessee is to enlarge the contractual power of married women,
yet such power is very limited and circumscribed, and the settled
policy of this state is to declare nugatory contracts made by her
whenever her plea of coverture is interposed. In Bank v. Walker,
14 Lea, 299, it was held that the lex loci contractus would govern
when not repugnant to the lex fori. The court stated the rule
to be: "Whether we consider the subject-matter under the head
of comity and its rules, or under that of real and person statutes
and its rules, either or both sustain the position that the lex loci
contractus as to relations and property rights will prevail over the
lex fori, unless the enforcement of the former will work an
injury to the subjects of the latter, or is prohibited by the laws
of the latter." It was further said that rights and contracts arising under the laws of a foreign state will not be enforced here,
except under the doctrine of comity of states, and that this doctrine neither requires nor sanctions the enforcement in the courts
of this state of statutory rights and contracts arising under the

laws of a foreign state which are repugnant to the policy and spirit of our laws.

For the reasons indicated, the decree of the court of chancery appeals is affirmed.

BOWLES v. FIELD, 1897.

[78 Fed. Rep. 742.]

BAKER. District Judge. This is a demurrer to a part of the amendment to the bill of complaint which is exhibited here to procure the foreclosure of a mortgage upon real estate situated in the state of Indiana. The larger part of the consideration of the note, which was executed in this state, and which is secured by the mortgage in suit, rests upon certain notes alleged to have been executed by Mrs. Field, in the state of Ohio, as the surety of her husband. The note in suit is for money borrowed by Mrs. Field to pay off the notes executed by her in Ohio as surety of her husband, and also for a certain other sum of money included therein. The validity of the note as to this latter sum of money is not material to the present inquiry.

It is insisted that the notes executed by her as surety in Ohio, and payable there, were void by reason of her coverture, and that the note executed by her for money borrowed to pay them off is pro tanto invalid. It is evident that if the notes executed by her in Ohio as surety for her husband were valid and binding obligations, which, by an action of law, she might have been compelled to pay, in that event she might voluntarily do what she would have been compelled to do,—that is, pay them off; or, if needful, she might lawfully borrow money to make such payment, and execute a valid note to evidence such loan. It is conceded that at the time these notes were executed, to take up which she borrowed money, the law of Ohio gave to a married woman the same power to bind herself by contract as if she were unmarried. It is also admitted that, if she had been a resident of Ohio when these notes were executed, she would have been legally bound to pay them, and that, if she borrowed money in this state to pay off her own valid debts, she would have the power to execute a valid note for the money she borrowed. But it is earnestly contended that, being a resident of Indiana, and having a permanent domicile therein, a note executed by her while transiently in Ohio to a citizen of Ohio is invalid, because, by the law of her domicile, she was prohibited from entering into a contract of suretyship. It is not

32

charged that she went to Ohio, and executed the notes as surety of her husband, for the purpose of evading the law of her domicile.

Whatever may be the views of foreign jurists, it is settled as the general rule, in countries where the common law is prevalent, that the execution, interpretation, and validity of contracts are to be governed by the law of the place where the contract is made. This rule is subject to some exceptions, among which are that the courts of no country or state are under any obligation to enforce contracts which are contrary to good morals, or are violative of its public policy, or are forbidden by its positive law. At common law a married woman was disabled to bind herself to a promissory note either as principal or surety. Her promissory notes were simply void. But long before the feme defendant executed the notes in Ohio as the surety of her husband, all the legal disabilities of married women to make contracts were abrogated, except as otherwise provided, by the legislature of this state. It was provided that a married woman should not enter into any contract of suretyship. It is clear that this limitation on her general power to contract has no extraterritorial force. The law of this state could not prevent a married woman from making a contract elsewhere; and her ability to contract with a citizen of Ohio while she was in that state would be governed by the lex loci contractus.

Judge Story, after a careful review of the authorities, says:

"That in respect to questions of minority or majority, competency or incompetency to marry, incapacities incident to coverture, guardianship, emancipation, and other personal qualities and disabilities, the law of the domicile of birth, or the law of any other acquired and fixed domicile, is not generally to govern, but the lex loci contractus aut actus,—the law of the place where the contract is made or the act is done." Story, Confl. Laws (7th Ed.) § 103.

In Scudder v. Bank, 91 U. S. 406, the supreme court sums up the general principles in these words:

"Matters bearing upon the execution, the interpretation, and the validity of a contract are determined by the law of the place where the contract is made. Matters connected with its performance are regulated by the law prevailing at the place of performance. Matters respecting the remedy, such as bringing of suit, admissibility of evidence, statutes of limitation, depend upon the law of the place where the suit is brought."

In **Pearl v. Hansborough**, 9 Humph. 426, the supreme court of Tennessee said that a contract for the purchase of slaves made by a married woman in that state was void, although she was a citizen of the state of Mississippi, by whose laws such a purchase by her would have been valid.

In **Evans v. Beaver**, 50 Ohio St. 190, 33 N. E. 643, it was held, where a married woman resident in Indiana entered into a contract in that state which was made payable there, that a mortgage duly executed by her upon real estate owned by her in Ohio to secure such contract could not be enforced.

In **Bell v. Packard**, 69 Me. 105, the plaintiff, a resident of Skowhegan, Me., holding an overdue note against Alvin Packard, the husband of the defendant, Harriet A. Packard, then a domiciled resident of Cambridge, Mass., wrote the note in suit at Skowhegan, and inclosed the same in a letter directed to Alvin Packard, at Cambridge, and there received by him, agreeing in the letter to surrender the old note upon the delivery of the new one, signed by him with a good surety. The new note was duly signed by Alvin Packard and the defendant, at Cambridge, and there mailed to, and was received by the plaintiff at Skowhegan. The plaintiff thereupon mailed, at Skowhegan, the old note to Alvin Packard, at Cambridge, who duly received the same. The defendant signed the note as surety of Alvin Packard, her husband, without any consideration received by her, or any benefit to her separate estate. At the time the note was signed, a married woman could not bind herself in such a way in Massachusetts, but she could in Maine. The defendant, Mrs. Packard, being sued in Maine, was held liable.

In **Milliken v. Pratt**, 125 Mass. 374, it was held that a note executed in Maine by a married woman domiciled in and a citizen of Massachusetts, which note a married woman was allowed by the laws of Maine to make, but was not, by the laws of Massachusetts, capable of making, would sustain an action against her in the courts of Massachusetts, although the note was executed by letter sent by her in Massachusetts to the payee in Maine.

See, also, Klinck v. Price, 4 W. Va. 4; Robinson v. Queen, 87 Tenn. 445, 11 S. W. 38; Ruhe v. Buck, 124 Mo. 178, 27 S. W. 412; Baum v. Birchall, 150 Pa. St. 164, 24 Atl. 620; Evans v. Cleary, 125 Pa. St. 204, 17 Atl. 440; Story Confl. Laws, (7th Ed.) §§ 101–103.

There is no statute in this state which prohibits a married woman from executing a note or mortgage to raise money to pay

off a debt for which she is personally liable. The notes executed
by her in Ohio, although as between herself and her husband she
was only surety, were by the lex loci contractus her personal
obligation, and made the debt evidenced thereby, as between herself and the payee of the notes, her personal debt. When she
gave her own individual note as sole maker to take up the old
notes on which she was holden as surety, it became her own primary obligation. The old notes were surrendered to her in consideration of her executing, as sole maker, the note in suit. There
is no statute here which prohibits a married woman from being
sued and held liable upon such a note; and a mortgage on her own
land, if it secures such note, is valid. The demurrer will therefore be overruled, with leave to answer.

LIVERPOOL STEAM CO. v. PHENIX INS. CO., 1888.

[129 U. S. 397.]

MR. JUSTICE GRAY delivered the opinion of the court.

This is an appeal by a steamship company from a decree
rendered against it upon a libel in admiralty, "in a cause of action
arising from breach of contract," brought by an insurance com
pany, claiming to be subrogated to the rights of the owners of
goods shipped on board the Montana, one of the appellant's
steamships, at New York, to be carried to Liverpool, and lost or
damaged by her stranding, because of the negligence of her master and officers, in Holyhead Bay on the coast of Wales, before
reaching her destination.

In behalf of the appellant, it was contended that the loss was
caused by perils of the sea, without any negligence on the part of
master and officers; that the appellant was not a common carrier;
that it was exempt from liability by the terms of the bills of lading; and that the libellant had not been subrogated to the rights
of the owners of the goods.

The question of negligence is fully and satisfactorily discussed in the opinion of the District Court, reported in 17 Fed.
Rep. 377, and in that of the Circuit Court, reported in 22 Blatchford, 372. It is largely, if not wholly, a question of fact, the decision of which by the Circuit Court cannot be reviewed here; and
so far as it can possibly be held to be or to involve a question of
law, it is sufficient to say that the circumstances of the case, as
found by the Circuit Court, clearly warrant, if they do not require a court or jury, charged with the duty of determining issues

of fact, to find that the stranding was owing to the negligence of the officers of the ship.

The contention that the appellant is not a common carrier may also be shortly disposed of.

By the settled law, in the absence of some valid agreement to the contrary, the owner of a general ship, carrying goods for hire, whether employed in internal, in coasting or in foreign com merce, is a common carrier, with the liability of an insurer against all losses, except only such two irresistable causes as the act of God and public enemies. Molloy, bk. 2, c. 2, § 2; Bac. Ab. Car rier, A; *Barclay v. Cuculla y. Gana,* 3 Doug. 389; 2 Kent Com. 598, 599; Story on Bailments, § 501; *The Niagara,* 21 How. 7, 23; *The Lady Pike,* 21 Wall. 1, 14.

In the present case, the Circuit Court has found as facts: "The Montana was an ocean steamer, built of iron, and performed regular service as a common carrier of merchandise and passengers between the ports of Liverpool, England, and New York, in the line commonly known as the Guion Line. By her, and by other ships in that line, the respondent was such common carrier. On March 2, 1880, the Montana left the port of New York, on one of her regular voyages, bound for Liverpool, England, with a full cargo, consisting of about twenty-four hundred tons of merchandise, and with passengers." The bills of lading, annexed to the answer and to the findings of fact, show that the four shipments in question amounted to less than one hundred and thirty tons, or hardly more than one-twentieth part of the whole cargo. It is clear, therefore, upon this record, that the appellant is a common carrier, and liable as such, unless exempted by some clause in the bills of lading.

In each of the bills of lading, the excepted perils, for loss or damage from which it is stipulated that the appellant shall not be responsible, include "barratry of master or mariners," and all perils of the seas, rivers or navigation, described more particularly in one of the bills of lading as "collision, stranding or other peril of the seas, rivers or navigation, of whatever nature or kind soever, and howsoever such collision, stranding or other peril may be caused," and in the other three bills of lading described more generally as any "accidents of the seas, rivers and steam navigation, of whatever nature or kind soever;" and each bill of lading adds, in the following words in the one, and in equivalent words in the others, "whether arising from the negligence, default, or error in judgment of the master, mariners, engineers or others of the crew, or otherwise, howsoever."

If the bills of lading had not contained the clause last quoted, it is quite clear that the other clauses would not have relieved the appellant from liability for the damage to the goods from the stranding of the ship through the negligence of her officers. Collision or stranding is, doubtless, a peril of the seas; and a policy of insurance against perils of the seas covers a loss by stranding or collision, although arising from the negligence of the master or crew, because the insurer assumes to indemnify the assured against losses from particular perils, and the assured does not warrant that his servants shall use due care to avoid them. *General Ins. Co.* v. *Sherwood,* 14 How. 351, 364, 365; *Orient Ins. Co.* v. *Adams,* 123 U. S. 67, 73; *Copeland* v. *New England Ins. Co.,* 2 Met. 432, 448-450. But the ordinary contract of a carrier does involve an obligation on his part to use due care and skill in navigating the vessel and carrying the goods; and, as is everywhere held, an exception, in the bill of lading, of perils of the sea or other specified perils does not excuse him from that obligation, or exempt him from liability for loss or damage from one of those perils, to which the negligence of himself or his servants has contributed. *New Jersey Steam Navigation Co.* v. *Merchants' Bank,* 6 How. 344; *Express Co.* v. *Kountze,* 8 Wall. 341; *Transportation Co.* v. *Downer,* 11 Wall. 129; *Grill* v. *General Iron Screw Co.,* L. R. 1 C. P. 600. and L. R. 3 C. P. 476; *The Xantho,* 12 App. Cas. 503, 510, 515.

We are then brought to the consideration of the principal question in the case, namely, the validity and effect of that clause in each bill of lading by which the appellant undertook to exempt itself from all responsibility for loss or damage by perils of the sea, arising from negligence of the master and crew of the ship.

The question appears to us to be substantially determined by the judgment of this court in *Railroad Co.* v. *Lockwood,* 17 Wall. 357.

That case, indeed, differed in its facts from the case at bar. It was an action brought against a railroad corporation by a drover who, while being carried with his cattle on one of its trains under an agreement which it had required him to sign, and by which he was to pay certain rates for the carriage of the cattle, to pass free himself, and to take the risks of all injuries to himself or to them, was injured by the negligence of the defendant or its servants.

The judgment for the plaintiff, however, was not rested upon the form of the agreement, or upon any difference between railroad corporations and other carriers, or between carriers by land and carriers by sea, or between carriers of passengers and carriers of goods, but upon the broad ground that no public carrier is permitted by law to stipulate for an exemption from the consequences of the negligence of himself or his servants.

The very question there at issue, defined at the beginning of the opinion as "whether a railroad company, carrying passengers for hire, can lawfully stipulate not to be answerable for their own or their servants' negligence in reference to such carriage," was stated a little further on in more general terms as "the question before propounded, namely, whether common carriers may excuse themselves from liability for negligence;" and a negative answer to the question thus stated was a necessary link in the logical chain of conclusions announced at the end of the opinion as constituting the *ratio decidendi.* 17 Wall. 359, 363, 384.

The course of reasoning, supported by elaborate argument and illustration, and by copious references to authorities, by which those conclusions were reached, may be summed up as follows

By the common law of England and America before the Declaration of Independence, recognized by the weight of English authority for half a century afterwards, and upheld by decisions of the highest courts of many States of the Union, common carriers could not stipulate for immunity for their own or their servants' negligence. The English Railway and Canal Traffic Act of 1854, declaring void all notices and conditions made by those classes of common carriers, except such as should be held by the court or judge before whom the case should be tried to be just and reasonable, was substantially a return to the rule of the common law.

The only important modification by the Congress of the United States of the previously existing law on this subject is the act of 1851, to limit the liability of ship-owners, (Act of March 3, 1851, c. 43; 9 Stat. 635; Rev. Stat. §§ 4282-4289,) and that act leaves them liable without limit for their own negligence, and liable to the extent of the ship and freight for the negligence or misconduct of their master and crew.

The employment of a common carrier is a public one, charging him with the duty of accommodating the public in the line of his employment. A common carrier is such by virtue of his occupation, not by virtue of the responsibilities under which he rests.

Even if the extent of these responsibilities is restricted by law or by contract, the nature of his occupation makes him a common carrier still. A common carrier may become a private carrier, or a bailee for hire, when, as a matter of accommodation or special engagement, he undertakes to carry something which it is not his business to carry. But when a carrier has a regularly established business for carrying all or certain articles, and especially if that carrier is a corporation created for the purpose of the carrying trade, and the carriage of the articles is embraced within the scope of its chartered powers, it is a common carrier, and a special contract about its responsibility does not divest it of that character.

The fundamental principle, upon which the law of common carriers was established, was to secure the utmost care and diligence in the performance of their duties. That end was effected in regard to goods, by charging the common carrier as an insurer, and in regard to passengers, by exacting the highest degree of carefulness and diligence. A carrier who stipulates not to be bound to the exercise of care and diligence seeks to put off the essential duties of his employment.

Nor can those duties be waived in respect to his agents or servants, especially where the carrier is an artificial being, incapable of acting except by agents and servants. The law demands of the carrier carefulness and diligence in performing the service; not merely an abstract carefulness and diligence in proprietors and stockholders who take no active part in the business. To admit such a distinction in the law of common carriers, as the business is now carried on, would be subversive of the very object of the law.

The carrier and his customer do not stand upon a footing of equality. The individual customer has no real freedom of choice. He cannot afford to higgle or stand out, and seek redress in the courts. He prefers rather to accept any bill of lading, or to sign any paper, that the carrier presents; and in most cases he has no alternative but to do this, or to abandon his business.

Special contracts between the carrier and the customer, the terms of which are just and reasonable and not contrary to public policy, are upheld; such as those exempting the carrier from responsibility for losses happening from accident, or from dangers of navigation that no human skill or diligence can guard against; or for money or other valuable articles, liable to be stolen or damaged—unless informed of their charatcer or value; or for perishable articles or live animals, when injured without default or negligence of the carrier. But the law does not allow a public carrier to abandon altogether his obligations to the public, and to stipulate for exemptions which are unreasonable and improper, amounting to an abnegation of the essential duties of his employment.

It being against the policy of the law to allow stipulations which will relieve the railroad company from the exercise of care or diligence, or which, in other words, will excuse it for negligence in the performance of its duty, the company remains liable for such negligence.

This analysis of the opinion in *Railroad Co.* v. *Lockwood* shows that it affirms and rests upon the doctrine that an express stipulation by any common carrier for hire, in a contract of carriage, that he shall be exempt from liability for losses caused by the negligence of himself or his servants, is unreasonable and contrary to public policy, and consequently void. And such has always been the understanding of this court, expressed in several cases. *Express Co.* v. *Caldwell*, 21 Wall. 264, 268; *Railroad Co.* v. *Pratt*, 22 Wall. 123, 134; *Bank of Kentucky* v. *Adams Express Co.*, 93 U. S. 174, 183; *Railway Co.* v. *Stevens*, 95 U. S. 655; *Hart* v. *Pennsylvania Railroad*, 112 U. S. 331, 338; *Phoenix Ins. Co.* v. *Erie Transportation Co.*, 117 U. S. 312, 322; *Inman* v. *South Carolina Railway, ante*, 128.

The general doctrine is nowhere stated more explicitly than in *Hart* v. *Pennsylvania Railroad* and *Proenix Ins. Co.* v. *Erie Transportation Co.*, just cited; and there does not appear to us to be anything in the decision or opinion in either of those cases which supports the appellant's position.

In the one case, a contract fairly made between a railroad company and the owner of the goods, and signed by the latter, by which he was to pay a rate of freight based on the condition that the company assumed liability only to the extent of an agreed valuation of the goods, even in case of loss or damage by its negligence, was upheld as just and reasonable, because a proper and lawful mode of securing a due proportion between the amount for which the carrier might be responsible and the compensation which he received, and of protecting himself against extravagant or fanciful valuations—which is quite different from exempting himself from all responsibility whatever for the negligence of himself and his servants.

In the other, the decision was that, as a common carrier

might lawfully obtain from a third person insurance on the goods
carried against loss by the usual perils, though occasioned by
negligence of the carrier's servants, a stipulation in a bill of lading that the carrier, when liable for the loss, should have the benefit of any insurance effected on the goods, was valid as between
the carrier and the shipper, even when the negligence of the carrier's servants was the cause of the loss. Upholding an agreement by which the carrier receives the benefit of any insurance obtained by the shipper from a third person is quite different from
permitting the carrier to compel the shipper to obtain insurance,
or to stand his own insurer, against negligence on the part of the
carrier.

It was argued for the appellant, that the law of New York,
the *lex loci contractus,* was settled by recent decisions of the
Court of Appeals of that state in favor of the right of a carrier
of goods or passengers, by land or water, to stipulate for exemption from all liability for his own negligence. *Mynard* v. *Syracuse Railroad,* 71 N. Y. 180; *Spinetti* v. *Atlas Steamship Co.,* 80
N. Y. 71.

But on this subject, as on any question depending upon mercantile law and not upon local statute or usage, it is well settled
that the courts of the United States are not bound by decisions of
the courts of the State, but will exercise their own judgment,
even when their jurisdiction attaches only by reason of the citizenship of the parties, in an action at law of which the courts of
the State have concurrent jurisdiction, and upon a contract made
and to be performed within the State. *Railroad Co.* v. *Lockwood,* 17 Wall. 357, 368; *Myrick* v. *Michigan Central Railroad,*
107 U. S. 102; *Carpenter* v. *Providence Washington Ins Co.,* 16
Pet. 495, 511; *Swift* v. *Tyson,* 16 Pet. 1; *Railroad Co.* v. *National
Bank,* 102 U. S. 14; *Burgess* v. *Seligman,* 107 U. S. 20, 33; *Smith*
v. *Alabama,* 124 U. S. 365, 478; *Bucher* v. *Cheshire Railroad,* 125
U. S. 555, 583. The decisions of the State courts certainly cannot be allowed any greater weight in the Federal courts when exercising the admiralty and maritime jurisdiction exclusively vested
in them by the Constitution of the United States.

It was also argued in behalf of the appellant, that the validity
and effect of this contract, to be performed pricipally upon the
high seas, should be governed by the general maritime law, and
that by that law such stipulations are valid. To this argument
there are two answers.

First. There is not shown to be any such general maritime

law. The industry of the learned counsel for the appellant has collected articles of codes, decisions of courts and opinions of commentators in France, Italy, Germany, and Holland, tending to show that, by the law administered in those countries, such a stipulation would be valid. But those decisions and opinions do not appear to have been based on general maritime law, but largely, if not wholly, upon provisions or omissions in the codes of the particular country ; and it has been said by many jurists that the law of France, at least, was otherwise. See 2 Pardessus Droit Commercial, no. 542; 4 Goujet & Meyer Dict. Droit Commercial (2d ed.) Voiturier, nos. 1, 81; 2 Troplong Droit Civil, nos. 894, 910, 942, and other books cited in *Peninsular & Oriental Co.* v. *Shand*, 3 Moore P. C. (N. S.) 272, 278, 285, 286; 25 Laurent Droit Civil Français, No. 532; Mellish, L. J., in *Cohen* v. *South-eastern Railway*, 2 Ex. D. 253, 257.

Second. The general maritime law is in force in this country, or in any other, so far only as it has been adopted by the laws or usages thereof; and no rule of the general maritime law (if any exists) concerning the validity of such a stipulation as that now before us has ever been adopted in the United States or in England, or recognized in the admiralty courts of either. *The Lottawanna*, 21 Wall. 558; *The Scotland*, 105 U. S. 24, 29, 33; *The Belgenland*, 114 U. S. 355, 369; *The Harrisburg*, 119, U. S. 199; *The Hamburg*, 2 Moore, P. C. (N. S.) 289, 319; S. C. Brown. & Lush. 253, 272; *Lloyd* v. *Guibert*, L. R. 1 Q. B. 115, 123, 124; *S. C.* 6 B. & S 100, 134, 136; *The Gaetano & Maria*, 7 P. D. 137, 143.

It was argued in this court, as it had been below, that as the contract was to be chiefly performed on board of a British vessel and to be finally completed in Great Britain, and the damage occurred in Great Britain, the case should be determined by the British law, and that by that law the clause exempting the appellant from liability for losses occasioned by the negligence of its servants was valid.

The Circuit Court declined to yield to this argument, upon two grounds: 1st. That as the answer expressly admitted the jurisdiction of the Circuit Court asserted in the libel, and the law of Great Britain had not been set up in the answer nor proved as a fact, the case must be decided according to the law of the Federal courts, as a question of general commercial law. 2d. That there was nothing in the contracts of affreightment to indicate a contracting in view of any other law than the recognized law of such forum in the United States as should have cognizance of suits on the contracts. 22 Blatchford, 397.

The law of Great Britain, since the Declaration of Independence is the law of a foreign country, and, like any other foreign law, is matter of fact, which the courts of this country cannot be presumed to be acquainted with, or to have judicial knowledge of, unless it is pleaded and proved.

The rule that the courts of one country cannot take cognizance of the law of another without plea and proof has been constantly maintained, at law and in equity, in England and America. *Church* v. *Hubbart,* 2 Cranch, 187, 236; *Ennis* v. *Smith,* 14 How. 400, 426, 427; *Dainese* v. *Hale,* 91 U. S. 13, 20, 21; *Pierce* v. *Indseth,* 106 U. S. 546; *Ex parte Cridland,* 3 Ves. & B. 94, 99; *Lloyd* v. *Guibert,* L. R. 1 Q. B. 115, 129; *S. C.* 6 B. & S. 100, 142. In the last case cited, Mr. Justice Willes, delivering judgment in the Exchequer Chamber, said: "In order to preclude all misapprehension, it may be well to add, that a party who relies upon a right or an exemption by foreign law is bound to bring such law properly before the court, and to establish it in proof. Otherwise the court, not being entitled to notice such law without judicial proof, must proceed according to the law of England."

The decision in *Lamar* v. *Micou,* 112 U. S. 452, and 114 U. S. 218, did not in the least qualify this rule, but only applied the settled doctrine that the Circuit Courts of the United States, and this court on appeal from their decisions, take judicial notice of the laws of the several States of the Union as domestic laws; and it has since been adjudged, in accordance with the general rule as to foreign law, that this court, upon writ of error to the highest court of a State, does not take judicial notice of the law of another State, not proved in that court and made part of the record sent up, unless by the local law that court takes judicial notice of it. *Hanley* v. *Donohue,* 116 U. S. 1; *Renaud* v. *Abbott,* 116 U. S. 277, 285.

The rule is as well established in courts of admiralty as in courts of common law or courts of equity. Chief Justice Marshall, delivering judgment in the earliest admiralty appeal in which he took part, said: "That the laws of a foreign nation, designed only for the direction of its own affairs, are not to be noticed by the courts of other countries, unless proved as facts, and that this court, with respect to facts, is limited to the statement made in the court below, cannot be questioned." *Talbot* v.

Seeman, 1 Cranch, 1, 38. And in a recent case in admiralty, Mr. Justice Bradley said: "If a collision should occur in British waters, at least between British ships, and the injured party should seek relief in our courts, we would administer justice according to the British law, so far as the rights and liabilities of the parties were concerned, provided it were shown what that law was. If not shown, we would apply our own law to the case. In the French or Dutch tribunals they would do the same." *The Scotland,* 105 U. S. 24, 29.

So Sir William Scott, in the High Court of Admiralty, said: "Upon all principles of common jurisprudence, foreign law is always to be proved as a fact." *The Louis,* 2 Dodson, 210, 241. To the same effect are the judgments of the Judicial Committee of the Privy Council in *The Prince George,* 4 Moore P. C. 21, and *The Peerless,* 13 Moore P. C. 484. And in a more recent case, cited by the appellant, Sir Robert Phillimore, said: "I have no doubt whatever that those who rely upon the difference between the foreign law and the law of the forum in which the case is brought are bound to establish that difference by competent evidence." *The Duero,* L. R. 2 Ad. & Ec. 393, 397.

It was, therefore, rightly held by the Circuit Court, upon the pleadings and proofs upon which the case had been argued, that the question whether the British law differed from our own was not open.

But it appears by the supplemental record, certified to this court in obedience to a writ of *certiorari,* that after the Circuit Court had delivered its opinion and filed its findings of fact and conclusions of law, and before the entry of a final decree, the appellant moved for leave to amend the answer by averring the existence of the British law and its applicability to this case, and to prove that law; and that the motion was denied by the Circuit Court, because the proposed allegation did not set up any fact unknown to the appellant at the time of filing the original answer, and could not be allowed under the rules of that court. 22 Blatchford, 402-404.

On such a question we should be slow to overrule a decision of the Circuit Court. But we are not prepared to say that if, upon full consideration, justice should appear to require it, we might not do so, and order the case to be remanded to that court with directions to allow the answer to be amended and proof of the foreign law to be introduced. *The Adeline,* 9 Cranch, 244, 284; *The Marianna Flora,* 11 Wheat. 1, 38; *The Charles Morgan,*

115 U. S. 69; *Merchants' Ins. Co.* v. *Allen,* 121 U. S. 67; *The Gazelle,* 128 U. S. 474. And the question of the effect which the law of Great Britain, if duly alleged and proved, should have upon this case has been fully and ably argued.

Under these circumstances, we prefer not to rest our judgment upon technical grounds of pleading or evidence, but, taking the same course as in *Merchants Ins. Co.* v. *Allen,* just cited, proceed to consider the question of the effect of the proof offered, if admitted.

It appears by the cases cited in behalf of the appellant, and is hardly denied by the appellee, that under the existing law of Great Britain, as declared by the latest decisions of her courts, common carriers, by land or sea, except so far as they are controlled by the provisions of the Railway and Canal Traffic Act of 1854, are permitted to exempt themselves by express contract from responsibility for losses occasioned by negligence of their servants. *The Ducro,* L. R. 2 Ad. & Ec. 393; *Taubman* v. *Pacific Co.,* 26 Law Times (N. S.) 704; *Steel* v. *State Line Steamship Co.,* 3 App. Cas. 72; *Manchester &c. Railway* v. *Brown,* 8 App. Cas. 703. It may therefore be assumed that the stipulation now in question, though invalid by our law, would be valid according to the law of Great Britain.

The general rule as to what law should prevail, in case of a conflict of laws concerning a private contract, was concisely and exactly stated before the Declaration of Independence by Lord Mansfield (as reported by Sir William Blackstone, who had been of counsel in the case) as follows: "The general rule, established *ex comitate et jure gentium,* is that the place where the contract is made, and not where the action is brought, is to be considered in expounding and enforcing the contract. But this rule admits of an exception, when the parties (at the time of making the contract) had a view to a different kingdom." *Robinson* v. *Bland,* 1 W. Bl. 234, 256, 258; *S. C.* 2 Bur. 1077, 1078.

The recent decisions by eminent English judges, cited at the bar, so clearly affirm and so strikingly illustrate the rule, as applied to cases more or less resembling the case before us, that a full statement of them will not be inappropriate.

In *Peninsular & Oriental Co.* v. *Shand,* 3 Moore P. C. (N. S.) 272, 290, Lord Justice Turner, delivering judgment in the Privy Council, reversing a decision of the Supreme Court of Mauritius, said, "The general rule is that the law of the country where a contract is made governs as to the nature, the obligation and the interpretation of it. The parties to a contract are either the subjects of the power there ruling, or as temporary residents owe it a temporary allegiance; in either case equally, they must be understood to submit to the law there prevailing, and to agree to its action upon their contract. It is, of course, immaterial that such agreement is not expressed in terms; it is equally an agreement, in fact, presumed *de jure,* and a foreign court interpreting or enforcing it on any contrary rule defeats the intention of the parties, as well as neglects to observe the recognized comity of nations."

It was accordingly held, that the law of England, and not the French law in force at Mauritius, governed the validity and construction of a contract made in an English port between an English company and an English subject to carry him hence by way of Alexandria and Suez to Mauritius, and containing a stipulation that the company should not be liable for loss of passengers' baggage, which the court in Mauritius had held to be invalid by the French law. 3 Moore P. C. (N. S.) 278.

Lord Justice Turner observed, that it was a satisfaction to find that the Court of Cassation in France had pronounced a judgment to the same effect, under precisely similar circumstances, in the case of a French officer taking passage at Hong Kong, an English possession, for Marseilles in France, under a like contract, on a ship of the same company, which was wrecked in the Red Sea, owing to the negligence of her master and crew. *Julien* v. *Peninsular & Oriental Co.,* imperfectly stated in 3 Moore P. C. (N. S.) 282, note, and fully reported in 75 Journal du Palais (1864) 225.

The case of *Lloyd* v. *Guibert,* 6 B. & S. 100; *S. C. L. R.* 1. Q. B. 115; decided in the Queen's Bench before, and in the Exchequer Chamber after, the decision in the Privy Council just referred to, presented this peculiar state of facts: A French ship owned by Frenchmen was chartered by the master, in pursuance of his general authority as such, in a Danish West India island, to a British subject, who knew her to be French, for a voyage from St. Marc in Hayti to Havre, London or Liverpool, at the charterer's option, and he shipped a cargo from St. Marc to Liverpool. On the voyage, the ship sustained damage from a storm which compelled her to put into a Portuguese port. There the master lawfully borrowed money on bottomry, and repaired the ship, and she carried her cargo safe to Liverpool. The bondholder proceeded in an English Court of Admiralty against the ship, freight and cargo, which being insufficient to satisfy the bond, he brought an action at law to recover the deficiency against the owners of the ship; and they abandoned the ship and freight in such a manner as by the French law absolved them from liability. It was held that the French law governed the case, and therefore the plaintiff could not recover.

It thus appears that in that case the question of the intent of the parties was complicated with that of the lawful authority of the master; and the decision in the Queen's Bench was put wholly upon the ground that the extent of his authority to bind the ship, the freight or the owners was limited by the law of the home port of the ship, of which her flag was sufficient notice. 6 B. & S. 100. That decision was in accordance with an earlier one of Mr. Justice Story, in *Pope* v. *Nickerson*, 3 Story, 465; as well as with later ones in the Privy Council, on appeal from the High Court of Admiralty, in which the validity of a bottomry bond has been determined by the law prevailing at the home port of the ship, and not by the law of the port where the bond was given. *The Karnak*, L. R. 2 P. C. 505, 512; *The Gaetano & Maria*, 7 P. D. 137. See also *The Woodland*, 7 Benedict, 110, 118; 14 Blatchford, 499, 503, and 104 U. S. 180.

The judgment in the Exchequer Chamber in *Lloyd* v. *Guibert* was put upon somewhat broader ground. Mr. Justice Willes, in delivering that judgment, said: "It is generally agreed that the law of the place where the contract is made is *prima facie* that which the parties intended, or ought to be presumed to have adopted as the footing upon which they dealt, and that such law ought therefore to prevail in the absence of circumstances indicating a different intention, as, for instance, that the contract is to be entirely performed elsewhere, or that the subject matter is immovable property situated in another country, and so forth; which latter, though sometimes treated as distinct rules, appear more properly to be classed as exceptions to the more general one, by reason of the circumstances indicating an intention to be bound by a law different from that of the place where the contract is made; which intention is inferred from the subject matter and from the surrounding circumstances, so far as they are relevant to construe and determine the character of the contract." L. R. 1 Q. B. 122, 123; 6 B. & S. 133.

It was accordingly held, conformably to the judgment in *Peninsular & Oriental Co.* v. *Shand*, above cited, that the law of England, as the law of the place of final performance or port of discharge, did not govern the case, because it was "manifest that what was to be done at Liverpool was but a small portion of the entire service to be rendered, and that the character of the contract cannot be determined thereby," although as to the mode of delivery the usages of Liverpool would govern. L. R. 1 Q. B. 125, 126; 6 B. & S. 137. It was then observed that the law of Portugal, in force where the bottomry bond was given, could not affect the case; that the law of Hayti had not been mentioned or relied upon in argument; and that "in favor of the law of Denmark, there is the cardinal fact that the contract was made in Danish territory, and further, that the first act done towards performance was weighing anchor in a Danish port:" and it was finally, upon a view of all the circumstances of the case, decided that the law of France, to which the ship and her owners belonged, must govern the question at issue.

The decision was, in substance, that the presumption that the contract should be governed by the law of Denmark, in force where it was made, was not overcome in favor of the law of England, by the fact that the voyage was to an English port and the charterer an Englishman, nor in favor of the law of Portugal by the fact that the bottomry bond was given in a Portuguese port; but that the ordinary presumption was overcome by the consideration that French owners and an English charterer, making a charter party in the French language of a French ship, in a port where both were foreigners, to be performed partly there by weighing anchor for the port of loading, (a place where both parties would also be foreigners,) partly at that port by taking the cargo on board, principally on the high seas, and partly by final delivery in the port of discharge, must have intended to look to the law of France as governing the question of the liability of the owner beyond the value of the ship and freight.

In two later cases, in each of which the judgment of the Queen's Bench Division was affirmed by the Court of Appeal, the law of the place where the contract was made was held to govern, notwithstanding some of the facts strongly pointed towards the application of another law; in the one case, to the law of the ship's flag; and in the other, to the law of the port where that part of the contract was to be performed, for the nonperformance of which the suit was brought.

In the first case, a bill of lading, issued in England in the English language to an English subject, by a company described therein as an English company and in fact registered both in

33

England and in Holland, for goods shipped at Singapore, an English port, to be carried to a port in Java, a Dutch possession, in a vessel with a Dutch name, registered in Holland, commanded by a Dutch master and carrying the Dutch flag, in order to obtain the privilege of trading with Java, was held to be governed by the law of England, and not by that of Holland, in determining the validity and construction of a clause exempting the company from liability for negligence of master and crew; and Lords Justices Brett and Lindley both considered it immaterial whether the ship was regarded as English or Dutch. *Chartered Bank of India* v. *Netherlands Steam Navigation Co.*, 9 Q. B. D. 118, and 10 Q. B. D. 521, 529, 536, 540, 544.

As Lord Justice Lindley observed: "This conclusion is not at all at variance with *Lloyd* v. *Guibert,* but rather in accordance with it. It is true that in that case the law of the flag prevailed; but the intention of the parties was admitted to be the crucial test; and the law of the ship's flag was considered as the law intended by the parties to govern their contract, as there really was no other law which they could reasonably be supposed to have contemplated. The plaintiff there was English, the defendant French; the *lex loci contractus* was Danish; the ship was French; her master was French, and the contract was in the French language. The voyage was from Hayti to Liverpool. The facts here are entirely different, and so is the inference to be deduced from them. The *lex loci contractus* was here English, and ought to prevail unless there is some good ground to the contrary. So far from there being such ground, the inference is very strong that the parties really intended to contract with reference to English law." 10 Q. B. D. 540.

In the remaining English case, a contract made in London between two English mercantile houses, by which one agreed to sell to the other 20,000 tons of Algerian esparto, to be shipped by a French company at an Algerian port on board vessels furnished by the purchasers at London, and to be paid for by them in London on arrival, was held to be an English contract, governed by English law; notwithstanding that the shipment of the goods in Algiers had been prevented by *vis major,* which, by the law of France in force there, excused the seller from performing the contract. *Jacobs* v. *Credit Lyonnais,* 12 Q. B. D. 589.

The result was reached by applying the general rule, expressed by Denman, J., in these words: 'The general rule is, that where a contract is made in England between merchants carrying on business here, as this is, but to be performed elsewhere, the construction of the contract, and all its incidents, are to be governed by the law of the country where the contract is made, unless there is something to show that the intention of the parties was that the law of the country where the contract is to be performed should prevail;" and summed up by the Court of Appeals, consisting of Brett, M. R., and Bowen, L. J., as follows: "The broad rule is that the law of a country where a contract is made presumably governs the nature, the obligation and the interpretation of it, unless the contrary appears to be the express intention of the parties." 12 Q. B. D. 596, 597, 600.

This court has not heretofore had occasion to consider by what law contracts like those now before us should be expounded. But it has often affirmed and acted on the general rule, that contracts are to be governed, as to their nature, their validity and their interpretation, by the law of the place where they were made, unless the contracting parties clearly appear to have had some other law in view. *Cox* v. *United States,* 6 Pet. 172; *Scudder* v. *Union Bank,* 91 U. S. 406; *Pritchard* v. *Norton,* 106 U. S. 124; *Lamar* v. *Micou,* 114 U. S. 218; *Watts* v. *Camors,* 115 U. S. 353, 362.

The opinion in *Watts* v. *Camors,* just cited, may require a word or two of explanation. It was there contested whether, in a charter party made at New Orleans between an English owner and an American charterer of an English ship for a voyage from New Orleans to a port on the continent of Europe, a clause regulating the amount payable in case of any breach of the contract was to be considered as liquidating the damages, or as a penalty only. Such was the question of which the court said that if it depended upon the intent of the parties, and consequently upon the law which they must be presumed to have had in view, they "must be presumed to look to the general maritime law of the two countries, and not to the local law of the State in which the contract is signed." The choice there was not between the American law and the English law, but between the statutes and decisions of the State of Louisiana, and a rule of the maritime law common to the United States and England.

Some reliance was placed by the appellant upon the following observations of Mr. Justice Story, sitting in the Circuit Court:

"If a contract is to be performed, partly in one country and partly in another country, it admits of a double aspect, nay, it has a double operation, and is, as to the particular parts, to be inter-

preted distinctively; that is, according to the laws of the country
where the particular parts are to be performed or executed. This
would be clearly seen in the case of a bill of lading of goods, deliverable in portions or parts at ports in different countries. Indeed, in cases of contracts of affreightment and shipment, it must
often happen that the contract looks to different portions of it to
be performed in different countries; some portions at the home
port, some at the foreign port, and some at the return port."
"The goods here were deliverable in Philadelphia; and what
would be an effectual delivery thereof, in the sense of the law,
(which is sometimes a nice question,) would, beyond question,
be settled by the law of Pennsylvania. But to what extent the
owners of the schooner are liable to the shippers for a non-fulfil-
ment of a contract of shipment of the master—whether they in-
cur an absolute or a limited liability, must depend upon the nature
and extent of the authority which the owners gave him, and this
is to be measured by the law of Massachusetts," where the ship
and her owners belonged. *Pope* v. *Nickerson*, 3 Story, 465, 484,
485.

But in that case the last point stated was the only one in
judgment, and the previous remarks evidently had regard to such
distinct obligations included in the contract of affreightment as
are to be performed in a particular port—for instance, what would
be an effectual delivery, so as to terminate the liability of the carrier, which, in the absence of express stipulation on that subject,
is ordinarily governed by the law or usage of the port of discharge. *Robertson* v. *Jackson*, 2 C. B. 412; *Lloyd* v. *Guibert*, L.
R. 1 Q. B. 115, 126; *S. C.* 6 B. & S. 100, 137.

In *Morgan* v. *New Orleans &c. Railroad*, 2 Woods, 244, a
contract made in New York, by a person residing there, with a
railroad corporation having its principal office there but deriving
its powers from the laws of other states, for the conveyance of
interests in railroads and steamboat lines, the delivery of property
and the building of a railroad in those states, and which, there
fore, might be performed partly in New York, and must be per
formed partly in the other states, was held by Mr. Justice Bradley, so far as concerned the right of one party to have the con
tract rescinded on account of nonperformance by the other party,
to be governed by the law of New York, and not by either of the
diverse laws of the other states in which parts of the contract
were to be performed.

In *Hale* v. *New Jersey Steam Navigation Co.*, 15 Conn. 538,

546, goods were shipped at New York for Providence in Rhode Island or Boston in Massachusetts, on a steamboat employed in the business of transportation between New York and Providence; and an exemption, claimed by the carrier under a public notice, was disallowed by the Supreme Court of Connecticut, because by the then law of New York the liability of a common carrier could not be limited by such a notice. Chief Justice Williams, delivering judgment, said: "The question is, by what law is this contract to be governed. The rule upon that subject is well settled, and has been often recognized by this court, that contracts are to be construed according to the laws of the state where made, unless it is presumed from their tenor that they were entered into with a view to the laws of some other state. There is nothing in this case, either from the location of the parties or the nature of the contract, which shows that they could have had any other law in view than that of the place where it was made. Indeed, as the goods were shipped to be transported to Boston or Providence, there would be the most entire uncertainty what was to be the law of the case if any other rule was to prevail. We have, therefore, no doubt that the law of New York, as to the duties and obligations of common carriers, is to be the law of the case."

In *Dyke* v. *Erie Railway*, 45 N. Y. 113, 117, a passenger travelling upon a ticket by which a railroad corporation, established in New York, and whose road extended from one place to another in that state, passing through the States of Pennsylvania and New Jersey by their permission, agreed to carry him from one to another place in New York, was injured in Pennsylvania, by the law of which the damages in actions against railroads for personal injury were limited to $3000. The Court of Appeals of New York held that the law of Pennsylvania had no application to the case; and Mr. Justice Allen, delivering the opinion, referred to the case of *Peninsular & Oriental Co.* v. *Shand*, before cited, as analogous in principle, and said: "The contract was single and the performance one continuous act. The defendant did not undertake for one specific act in part performance, in one state, and another specific and distinct act in another of the states named, as to which the parties could be presumed to have had in view the laws and usages of distinct places. Whatever was done in Pennsylvania was a part of the single act of transportation from Attica or Waverly, in the State of New York, to the city of New York, and in performance of an obligation assumed and undertaken in this state, and which was indivisible. The obligation was created here, and by force of the laws of this state, and force and effect must be given to it in conformity to the laws of New York. The performance was to commence in New York, and to be fully completed in the same state, but liable to breach, partial or entire, in the States of Pennsylvania and New Jersey, through which the road of the defendant passed; but whether the contract was broken, and if broken the consequences of the breach, should be determined by the laws of this state. It cannot be assumed that the parties intended to subject the contract to the laws of the other states, or that their rights and liabilities should be qualified or varied by any diversities that might exist between the laws of those states and the *lex loci contractus.*"

In *McDaniel* v. *Chicago & Northwestern Railway,* 24 Iowa, 412, 417, cattle transported by a railroad company from a place in Iowa to a place in Illinois, under a special contract made in Iowa, containing a stipulation that the company should be exempt from liability for any damage, unless resulting from collision or derailing of trains, were injured in Illinois by the negligence of the company's servants; and the Supreme Court of Iowa, Chief Justice Dillon presiding, held the case to be governed by the law of Iowa, which permitted no common carrier to exempt himself from the liability which would exist in the absence of the contract. The court said: "The contract being entire and indivisible, made in Iowa, and to be partly performed here, it must, as to its validity, nature, obligation and interpretation, be governed by our law. And by our law, so far as it seeks to change the common law, it is wholly nugatory and inoperative. The rights of the parties, then, are to be determined under the common law, the same as if no such contract had been made."

So in *Pennsylvania Co.* v. *Fairchild,* 69 Illinois, 260, where a railroad company received in Indiana goods consigned to Leavenworth, in Kansas, and carried them to Chicago in Illinois, and there delivered them to another railroad company, in whose custody they were destroyed by fire, the Supreme Court of Illinois held that the case must be governed by the law of Indiana, by which the first company was not liable for the loss of the goods after they passed into the custody of the next carrier in the line of transit.

The other cases in the courts of the several states, cited at the bar, afford no certain or satisfactory guide. Two cases, held not to be governed by a statute of Pennsylvania providing that no railroad corporation should be liable for a loss of passenger's baggage beyond $300, unless the excess in value was disclosed and paid for, were decided (whether rightly or not we need not consider) without much reference to authority, and upon their peculiar circumstances—the one case, on the ground that a contract by a New Jersey corporation to carry a passenger and his baggage from a wharf in Philadelphia across the Delaware River, in which the States of Pennsylvania and New Jersey had equal rights of navigation and passage, and thence through the State of New Jersey to Atlantic City, was a contract to be performed in New Jersey and governed by the law of that state; *Brown* v. *Camden & Atlantic Railroad*, 83 Penn. St. 316; and the other case, on the ground that the baggage, received at a town in Pennsylvania to be carried to New York city, having been lost after its arrival by negligence on the part of the railroad company, the contract, so far as it concerned the delivery, was to be governed by the law of New York. *Curtis* v. *Delaware & Lackawanna Railroad*, 74 N. Y. 116. The suggestion in *Barter* v. *Wheeler*, 49 N. H. 9, 29, that the question, whether the liability of a railroad corporation for goods transported through parts of two states was that of a common carrier or of a forwarder only, should be governed by the law of the state in which the loss happened, was not necessary to the decision, and appears to be based on a strained inference from the observations of Mr. Justice Story in *Pope* v. *Nickerson*, above cited. In a later case, the Supreme Court of New Hampshire reserved an expression of opinion upon a like question. *Gray* v. *Jackson*, 51 N. H. 9, 39.

This review of the principal cases demonstrates that according to the great preponderance, if not the uniform concurrence, of authority, the general rule, that the nature, the obligation and the interpretation of a contract are to be governed by the law of the place where it is made, unless the parties at the time of making it have some other law in view, requires a contract of affreightment, made in one country between citizens or residents thereof, and the performance of which begins there, to be governed by the law of that country, unless the parties, when entering into the contract, clearly manifest a mutual intention that it shall be governed by the law of some other country.

There does not appear to us to be anything in either of the bills of lading in the present case, tending to show that the contracting parties looked to the law of England, or to any other law than that of the place where the contract was made.

The bill of lading for the bacon and hams was made and dated at New York, and signed by the ship's agent there. It acknowledges that the goods have been shipped "in and upon the steamship called Montana, now lying in the port of New York and bound for the port of Liverpool," and are to be delivered at Liverpool. It contains no indication that the owners of the steamship are English, or that their principal place of business is in England, rather than in this country. On the contrary, the only description of the line of steamships, or of the place of business of their owners, is in a memorandum in the margin, as follows: "Guion Line. United States Mail Steamers. New York: 29 Broadway. Liverpool: 11 Rumford St." No distinction is made between the places of business at New York and at Liverpool, except that the former is named first. The reservation of liberty, in case of an interruption of the voyage, "to tranship the goods by any other steamer," would permit transhipment into a vessel of any other line, English or American. And general average is to be computed, not by any local law or usage, but "according to York-Antwerp rules," which are the rules drawn up in 1864 at York in England, and adopted in 1877 at Antwerp in Belgium, at international conferences of representatives of the more important mercantile associations of the United States, as well as of the maritime countries of Europe. Lowndes on General Average (3d ed.) Appendix Q.

The contract being made at New York, the ship-owner having a place of business there, and the shipper being an American, both parties must be presumed to have submitted themselves to the law there prevailing, and to have agreed to its action upon their contract. The contract is a single one, and its principal object, the transportation of the goods, is one continuous act, to begin in the port of New York, to be chiefly performed on the high seas, and to end at the port of Liverpool. The facts that the goods are to be delivered at Liverpool, and the freight and primage, therefore, payable there in sterling currency, do not make the contract an English contract, or refer to the English law the question of the liability of the carrier for the negligence of the master and crew in the course of the voyage. *Peninsular & Oriental Co.* v. *Shand, Lloyd* v. *Guibert,* and *Chartered Bank of India* v. *Netherlands Steam Navigation Co.,* before cited.

There is even less ground for holding the three bills of lading of the cotton to be English contracts. Each of them is made and dated at Nashville, an inland city, and is a through bill of lading, over the Louisville and Nashville Railroad and its connections, and by the Williams and Guion Steamship Company, from Nashville to Liverpool; and the whole freight from Nashville to Liverpool is to be "at the rate of fifty-four pence sterling per 100 lbs. gross weight." It is stipulated that the liability of the Louisville and Nashville Railroad and its connections as common carriers "terminates on delivery of the goods or property to the steamship company at New York, when the liability of the steamship commences, and not before;" and that "the property shall be transported from the port of New York to the port of Liverpool by the said steamship company, with liberty to ship by any other steamship or steamship line." And in the margin is this significant reference to a provision of the statute of the United States, applicable to the ocean transportation only: "ATTENTION OF SHIPPERS IS CALLAD TO THE ACT OF CONGRESS OF 1851: 'Any person or persons shipping oil of vitrol, unslacked lime, inflammable matches [or] gunpowder, in a ship or vessel taking cargo for divers persons on freight, without delivering *at the time of shipment* a note in writing, expressing the nature and character of such merchandise, to the master, mate or officer, or person in charge of the loading of the ship or vessel, shall forfeit to the *United States One Thousand Dollars.*'" Act of March 3, 1851, c. 43, § 7; 9 Stat. 636; Rev. Stat. § 4288.

It was argued that as each bill of lading, drawn up and signed by the carrier and assented to by the shipper, contained a stipulation that the carrier should not be liable for losses by perils of the sea arising from the negligence of its servants, both parties must be presumed to have intended to be bound by that stipulation, and must therefore, the stipulation being void by our law and valid by the law of England, have intended that their contract should be governed by the English law; and one passage in the judgment in *Peninsular & Oriental Co.* v. *Shand* gives some color to the argument. 3 Moore P. C. (N. S.) 291. But the facts of the two cases are quite different in this respect. In that case, effect was given to the law of England, where the contract was made; and both parties were English, and must be held to have known the law of their own country. In this case, the contract was made in this country, between parties one residing and the other doing business here; and the law of England is a foreign law, which the American shipper is not presumed to know. Both parties or either of them may have supposed the stipulation to be valid; or both or either may have known that by our law, as declared by this court, it was void. In either aspect, there is no ground for inferring that the shipper, at least, had any intention, for the purpose of securing its validity, to be governed by a foreign law, which he is not shown, and cannot be presumed, to have had any knowledge of.

Our conclusion on the principal question in the case may be summed up thus: Each of the bills of lading is an American and not an English contract, and, so far as concerns the obligation to carry the goods in safety, is to be governed by the American law, and not by the law, municipal or maritime, of any other country. By our law, as declared by this court, the stipulation by which the appellant undertook to exempt itself from liability for the negligence of its servants is contrary to public policy and therefore void; and the loss of the goods was a breach of the contract, for which the shipper might maintain a suit against the carrier. This being so, the fact that the place where the vessel went ashore, in consequence of the negligence of the master and officers in the prosecution of the voyage, was upon the coast of Great Britain, is quite immaterial.

This conclusion is in accordance with the decision of Judge Brown in the District Court of the United States for the Southern District of New York in *The Brantford City,* 29 Fed. Rep. 373, which appears to us to proceed upon more satisfactory grounds than the opposing decision of Mr. Justice Chitty, sitting alone in the Chancery Division, made since this case was argued, and, so far as we are informed, not reported in the Law Reports, nor affirmed or considered by any of the higher courts of Great Britain. *In re Missouri Steamship Co.,* 58 Law Times (N. S.) 377.

The present case does not require us to determine what effect the courts of the United States should give to this contract, if it had expressly provided that any question arising under it should be governed by the law of England.

The question of the subrogation of the libellant to the rights of the shippers against the carrier presents no serious difficulty.

From the very nature of the contract of insurance as a con tract of indemnity, the insurer, upon paying to the assured the amount of a loss, total or partial, of the goods insured, becomes, without any formal assignment, or any express stipulation to that effect in the policy, subrogated in a corresponding amount to the assured's right of action against the carrier or other person re-sponsible for the loss; and in a court of admiralty may assert in his own name that right of the shipper. *The Potomac,* 105 U. S. 630, 634; *Phoenix Ins. Co.* v. *Erie Transportation Co.,* 117 U. S. 312, 321.

In the present case, the libellant, before the filing of the libel, paid to each of the shippers the greater part of his insurance, and thereby became entitled to recover so much, at least, from the carrier. The rest of the insurance money was paid by the libellant before the argument in the District Court, and that amount might have been claimed by amendment, if not under the original libel. *The Charles Morgan,* 115 U. S. 69, 75; *The Gazelle,* 128 U. S. 474. The question of the right of the libellant to recover to the whole extent of the insurance so paid was litigated and included in the decree in the District Court, and in the Circuit Court on appeal; and no objection was made in either of those courts, or at the argument in this court, to any insufficiency of the libel in this particular.

The appellant does, however, object that the decree should not include the amount of the loss on the cotton shipped under through bills of lading from Nashville to Liverpool. This objection is grounded on a clause in those bills of lading, which is not found in the bill of lading of the bacon and hams shipped at New York; and on the ajudication in *Phoenix Ins. Co.* v. *Erie Transportation Co.,* 117 U. S. 312, that a stipulation in a bill of lading, that a carrier, when liable for a loss of the goods, shall have the benefit of any insurance that may have been effected upon them, is valid as between the carrier and the shipper, and therefore limits the right of an insurer of the goods, upon paying to the shipper the amount of a loss by stranding, occasioned by the negligence of the carrier's servants, to recover over against the carrier.

But it behooves a carrier setting up such a defence to show clearly that the insurance on the goods is one which by the terms of his contract he is entitled to the benefit of. *Inman* v. *South Carolina Railway, ante,* 128. The through bills of lading of the cotton are signed by an agent of the railroad companies and the steamship company, "severally, but not jointly," and contain, in separate columns, two entirely distinct sets of "terms and conditions," the first relating exclusively to the land carriage by the railroads and their connections, and the second to the ocean transportation by the steamship. The clause relied on, providing that in case of any loss or damage of the goods, whereby any legal liability shall be incurred, that company only shall be held answerable in whose actual custody the goods are at the time, and the carrier so liable shall have the full benefit of any insurance that may have been effected upon or on account of said goods," is inserted in the midst of the terms and conditions defining the liability of the railroad companies, and is omitted in those defining the liability of the steamship company, plainly signifying an intention that this clause should not apply to the latter. It is quite clear, therefore, that the appellant has no right to claim the benefit of any insurance on the goods. See *Railroad Co.* v. *Androscoggin Mills,* 22 Wall. 594, 602.

The result of these considerations is that the decree of the Circuit Court is in all respects correct and must be

'*Affirmed.*

BURNETT v. PA. RY. CO., 1896.

[176 Pa. St. 45.]

OPINION BY MR. JUSTICE FELL, May 28, 1896:

The refusal of the court to charge that "as the contract for transportation was made in New Jersey it will be enforced in this state as in that, and as the defendant was released from responsibility by the free pass the verdict must be for the defendant," raises the only question to be considered. The plaintiff was employed by the defendant as a flagman at Trenton, N. J. He applied for and was granted free transportation for himself, his wife and daughter to Elmira, N. Y. He received two passes—one from Trenton to Philadelphia, the terms of which do not appear in evidence; the other an employee's trip pass from Philadelphia to Elmira, by the terms of which he assumed all risks of accident. He was injured at Harrisburg, Pa., through the admitted negligence of the defendant's employees.

It was proved at the trial that under the laws of New Jersey the contract by which the plaintiff in consideration of free transportation assumed the risk of accident was valid, and that in that state he could not recover; and it is conceded that in Pennsylvania the decisions are otherwise, and that such a contract will not relieve a common carrier from responsibility for negligence: Goldey v. Penna. R. R. Co., 30 Pa. 242; Penna. R. R. Co. v. Henderson, 51 Pa. 315; Penna. R. R. Co. v. Butler, 57 Pa. 335; Buffalo, Pittsburg & Western R. R. Co. v. O'Hara, 12 W. N. C. 473. The question then is: By the laws of which state is the responsibility of the defendant to be determined?

The defendant is a corporation of the state of Pennsylvania. The injury occurred in the operation of its road in this state.

The passes, although issued and delivered in New Jersey, were for transportation from the station in Trenton directly across the Delaware river into this state. The service was to be rendered here: this was the place of performance.

Generally as to its formalities and its interpretation, obligation and effect, a contract is governed by the laws of the place where it is made, and if it is valid there it is valid everywhere; but when it is made in one state or country to be performed in another state or country its validity and effect are to be determined by the laws of the place of performance. It is to be presumed that parties enter into a contract with reference to the laws of the place of performance, and unless it appears that the intention was otherwise those laws determine the mode of fulfillment and obligation and the measure of liability for its breach: Daniel on Negotiable Instruments, 658; Byles on Bills, 586; 2 Kent's Commentaries, 620; Wharton on the Conflict of Laws, sec. 401; Story on the Conflict of Laws, sec. 280; Scudder v. Union National Bank, 91 U. S. 406; Brown v. C. & A. R. R. Co., 83 Pa. 316; Waverly Bank v. Hall, 150 Pa. 466. The decision in Brown v. C. & A. R. R. Co. (supra) seems to be conclusive of this case. In that case a ticket was issued in Philadelphia by a New Jersey corporation operating a railroad in that state, and the plaintiff's trunk was delivered to the defendant in Philadelphia, and it did not appear where it had been lost. The liability being admitted, the question was whether the laws of Pennsylvania limiting the amount of liability applied. It was held that as the service was to be rendered by a New Jersey corporation in New Jersey the laws of the place of performance controlled. It was said in the opinion by SHARSWOOD, J.: "The negligence of which the defendants are presumed to have been guilty was in the course of the exercise of their franchises as a New Jersey corporation, and the extent of their liability is therefore to be determined by the laws of that state."

The judgment is affirmed.

CHAPTER XV

TORTS.

MACHADO v. FONTES, 1897.

[2 L. R. Q. B. D. 231.]

Appeal from Kennedy, J., at chambers.

The plaintiff brought this action to recover damages from the defendant for an alleged libel upon the plaintiff contained in a pamphlet in the Portugese language alleged to have been published by the defendant in Brazil.

The defendant delivered a statement of defence (in which, amongst other defences, he denied the alleged libel), and he afterwards took out a summons for leave to amend his defence by adding the following plea: "Further the defendant will contend that if (contrary to the defendant's contention) the said pamphlet has been published in Brazil, by the Brazilian law the publication of the said pamphlet in Brazil cannot be the ground of legal proceedings against the defendant in Brazil in which damages can be recovered, or (alternatively) cannot be the ground of legal proceedings against the defendant in Brazil in which the plaintiff can recover general damages for any injury to his credit, character, or feelings."

The summons came before Kennedy, J., in chambers, who allowed the plea to be added, but expressed some doubt as to the propriety of so doing, and gave leave to plaintiff to bring the present appeal.

Lopes, L. J. I am of opinion that this appeal ought to be allowed. [The Lord Justice then referred to the facts, and, after reading the plea, continued:]

Now that plea, as it stands, appears to me merely to go to the remedy. It says, in effect, that in this case no action in which damages could be recovered would lie in Brazil, and, assuming that any damages could be recovered in Brazil, they would be special damages only. Mr. Walton contends that that is not the meaning of the plea; that the plea is intended to raise a larger question than that, and to say that libel cannot be made the subject of any civil proceedings at all in Brazil, but is only the subject-matter of criminal proceedings; and, for the purposes of what I am about to say, I will assume that to be so.

Now the principle applicable in the present case appears to me to be this: where the words have been published outside the jurisdiction, then, in order to maintain an action here on the ground of a tort committed outside the jurisdiction, the act complained of must be wrongful—I use the word "wrongful" deliberately—both by the law of this country and also by the law of the country where it was committed; and the first thing we have to consider is whether those conditions are complied with.

In the case of Phillips *v.* Evre, L. R. 6 Q. B. 1, Willes, J., lays down very distinctly what the requisites are in order to found such an action. He says this (at p. 28): "As a general rule, in order to found a suit in England for a wrong alleged to have been committed abroad, two conditions must be fulfilled: First, the wrong must be of such a character that it would have been actionable if committed in England. . . . Secondly, the act must not have been justifiable by the law of the place where it was done." Then in The M. Moxham, 1 P. D. 107, James, L. J., in the course of his judgment, uses these words (at p. 111): "It is settled that if by the law of the foreign country the act is lawful or is excusable, or even if it has been legitimized by a subsequent act of the Legislature, then this court will take into consideration that state of the law,—that is to say, if by the law of the foreign country a particular person is justified, or is excused, or has been justified or excused for the thing done, he will not be answerable here."

Both those cases seem to me to go this length: that, in order to constitute a good defence to an action brought in this country in respect of an act done in a foreign country, the act relied on must be one which is innocent in the country where it was committed. In the present case there can be no doubt that the action lies, for it complies with both of the requirements which are laid down by Willes, J. The act was committed abroad, and was actionable here, and not justifiable by the law of the place where it was committed. Both those conditions are complied with; and, therefore, the publication in Brazil is actionable here.

It then follows, directly, the right of action is established in this country, that the ordinary incidents of that action and the appropriate remedies ensue.

Therefore, in this case, in my opinion, damages would flow from the wrong committed just as they would in any action brought in respect of a libel published in this country.

It is contended that it would be much better that this question should not be decided at the present time, but that a commission should go to Brazil, and that the Brazilian law should be inquired into. If our view is correct, it seems to me that that would be a great waste of time and money, because, having regard to the authorities I have mentioned, this plea is absolutely bad, and ought to be struck out.

RIGBY, L. J. I am of the same opinion. I do not propose to decide this case on any technical consideration as to what may be the precise meaning of the allegation that is proposed to be introduced into the defence; I give it the widest possible construction it can reasonably bear; and I will assume it to involve that no action for damages, or even no civil action at all, can be maintained in Brazil in respect of a libel published there. But it does not follow from that that the libel is not actionable in this country under the present conditions, and having regard to the fact that the plaintiff and defendant are here.

Willes, J., in Phillips, v. Eyre, was laying down a rule which he expressed without the slightest modification, and without the slightest doubt as to its correctness; and when you consider the care with which the learned judge prepared the propositions that he was about to enunciate, I cannot doubt that the change from "actionable" in the first branch of the rule to "justifiable" in the second branch of it was deliberate. The first requisite is that the wrong must be of such a character that it would be actionable in England. It was long ago settled that an action will lie by a plaintiff here against a defendant here, upon a transaction in a place outside this country. But though such action may be brought here, it does not follow that it will succeed here, for, when it is committed in a foreign country, it may turn out to be a perfectly innocent act according to the law of that country; and if the act is shown by the law of that country to be an innocent act, we pay such respect to the law of other countries that we will not allow an action to be brought upon it here. The innocency of the act in the foreign country is an answer to the action. That is what is meant when it is said that the act must be "justifiable" by the law of the place where it was done.

It is not really a matter of any importance what the nature of the remedy for a wrong in a foreign country may be.

The remedy must be according to the law of the country which entertains the action. Of course, the plea means that no action can be brought in this country in respect of the libel (if any) in Brazil. But I think the rule is clear. It was very carefully laid down by Willes, J., in Phillips *v.* Eyre; and in the case of The M. Moxham, all the learned judges of the Court of Appeal in their judgments laid down the law without hesitation and in a uniform manner: and first one judge and then another gave, in different language but exactly to the same purport and effect, the rule enunciated by Willes, J. So that if authority were wanting there is a decision clearly binding upon us, although I think the principle is sufficient to decide the case.

I think there is no doubt at all that an action for a libel published abroad is maintainable here, unless it can be shown to be justified or excused in the country where it was published. James, L. J., states, in The M. Moxham, what the settled law is. Mellish, L. J., is quite as clear upon that point as James, L. J., in laying down the general rule; and Baggallay, L. J., also takes the same view. We start, then, from this: that the act in question is *prima facie* actionable here, and the only thing we have to do is to see whether there is any peremptory bar to our jurisdiction arising from the fact that the act we are dealing with is authorized, or innocent or excusable, in the country where it was committed. If we cannot see that, we must act according to our own rules in the damages (if any) which we may choose to give. Here we cannot see it, and this appeal must be allowed with costs.

Appeal allowed.

DENNICK v. RY. CO., 1880.

[103 U. S. 11.]

ERROR to the Circuit Court of the United States for the Northern District of New York.

MILLER, J. It is understood that the decision of the court below rested solely upon the proposition that the liability in a civil action for damages which, under the statute of New Jersey, is imposed upon a party, by whose wrongful act, neglect, or default death ensues, can be enforced by no one but an administrator, or other personal representative of the deceased, appointed by the authority of that State. And the soundness or unsoundness of this proposition is what we are called upon to decide.

It must be taken as established by the record that the accident by which the plaintiff's husband came to his death occurred in New Jersey, under circumstances which brought the defendant within the provisions of the first section of the act making the company liable for damages, notwithstanding the death.

It can scarcely be contended that the act belongs to the class

34

of criminal laws which can only be enforced by the courts of the State where the offence was committed, for it is, though a statutory remedy, a civil action to recover damages for a civil injury.

It is indeed a right dependent solely on the statute of the State; but when the act is done for which the law says the person shall be liable, and the action by which the remedy is to be enforced is a personal and not a real action, and is of that character which the law recognizes as transitory and not local, we cannot see why the defendant may not be held liable in any court to whose jurisdiction he can be subjected by personal process or by voluntary appearance, as was the case here.

It is difficult to undestand how the nature of the remedy, or the jurisdiction of the courts to enforce it, is in any manner dependent on the question whether it is a statutory right or a common law right.

Wherever, by either the common law or the statute law of a State, a right of action has become fixed and a legal liability incurred, that liability may be enforced and the right of action pursued in any court which has jurisdiction of such matters and can obtain jurisdiction of the parties.

The action in the present case is in the nature of trespass to the person, always held to be transitory, and the venue immaterial. The local court in New York and the Circuit Court of the United States for the Northern District were competent to try such a case when the parties were properly before it. Mostyn v. Fabrigas, 1 Cowp. 161; Rafael v. Verelst, 2 W. Bl. 983, 1055; McKenna v. Fisk, 1 How. 241. We do not see how the fact that it was a statutory right can vary the principle. A party legally liable in New Jersey cannot escape that liability by going to New York. If the liability to pay monev was fixed by the law of the State where the transaction occurred, is it to be said it can be enforced nowhere else because it depended upon statute law and not upon common law? It would be a very dangerous doctrine to establish that in all cases where the several States have substituted the statute for the common law, the liability can be enforced in no other State but that where the statute was enacted and the transaction occurred. The common law never prevailed in Louisiana, and the rights and remedies of her citizens depend upon her civil code. Can these rights be enforced or the wrongs of her citizens be redressed in no other State of the Union? The contrary has been held in many cases. See Ex parte Van Riper, 20 Wend. (N. Y.) 614; Lowry v. Inman, 46 N. Y. 119; Pickering *v.* Fisk, 6 Vt. 102; Railroad *v.* Sprayberry, 8 Bax. (Tenn.) 341; Great Western Railway Co. *v.* Miller, 19 Mich. 305.

But it is said that, conceding that the statute of the State of New Jersey established the liability of the defendant and gave a remedy, the right of action is limited to a personal representative appointed in that State and amenable to its jurisdiction.

The statute does not say this in terms: "Every such action shall be brought by and in the names of the personal representatives of such deceased person." It may be admitted that for the purpose of this case the words "personal representatives" mean the administrator.

The plaintiff is, then, the only personal representative of the deceased in existence, and the construction thus given the statute is, that such a suit shall *not* be brought by her. This is in direct contradiction of the words of the statute. The advocates of this view interpolate into the statute what is not there, by holding that the personal representative must be one residing in the State or appointed by its authority. The statute says the amount recovered shall be for the exclusive benefit of the widow and next of kin. Why not add here, also, by construction, "if they reside in the State of New Jersey"?

It is obvious that nothing in the language of the statute requires such a construction. Indeed, by inference, it is opposed to it. The first section makes the liability of the corporation or person absolute where the death arises from their negligence. Who shall say that it depends on the appointment of an administrator within the State?

The second section relates to the remedy, and declares who shall receive the damages when recovered. These are the widow and next of kin. Thus far the statute declares under what circumstances a defendant shall be liable for damages, and to whom they shall be paid. In this there is no ambiguity. But fearing that there might be a question as to the proper person to sue, the act removes any doubt by designating the personal representative. The plaintiff here is that representative. Why can she not sustain the action? Let it be remembered that this is not a case of an administrator, appointed in one State, suing in that character in the courts of another State, without any authority from the latter. It is the general rue that this cannot be done.

The suit here was brought by the administratrix in a court of the State which had appointed her, and of course no such objection could be made.

If, then, the defendant was liable to be sued in the courts of
the State of New York on this cause of action, and the suit could
only be brought by such personal representative of the deceased,
and if the plaintiff is the personal representative, whom the courts
of that State are bound to recognize, on what principle can her
right to maintain the action be denied.

So far as any reason has been given for such a proposition,
it seems to be this: that the foreign administrator is not responsible to the courts of New Jersey, and cannot be compelled tó distribute the amount received in accordance with the New Jersey
statute.

But the courts of New York are as capable of enforcing the
rights of the widow and next of kin as the courts of New Jersey.
And as the court which renders the judgment for damages in
favor of the administratrix can only do so by virtue of the New
Jersey statute, so any court having control of her can compel
distribution of the amount received in the manner prescribed by
that statute.

Again: it is said that, by virtue of her appointment in New
York, the administratrix can only act upon or administer that
which was of the estate of the deceased in his lifetime. There
can be no doubt that much that comes to the hands of administrators or executors must go directly to heirs or devisees, and is not
subject to sale or distribution in any other mode, such as specific
property devised to individuals, or the amount which by the legislation of most of the States is set apart to the family of the deceased, all of which can be enforced in the courts; and no reason
is perceived why the specific direction of the law on this subject
may not invest the administrator with the right to receive or
recover by suit, and impose on him the duty of distributing under
that law. There can be no doubt that an administrator, clothed
with the apparent right to receive or recover by suit property or
money, may be compelled to deliver or pay it over to some one
who establishes a better right thereto, or that what he so recovers
is held in trust for some one not claiming under him or under the
will. And so here. The statute of New Jersey says the personal
representative shall recover, and the recovery shall be for the
benefit of the widow and next of kin. It would be a reproach to
the laws of New York to say that when the money recovered in
such an action as this came to the hands of the administratrix, her
courts could not compel distribution as the law directs.

It is to be said, however, that a statute of New York, just like the New Jersey law, provides for bringing the action by the personal representative, and for distribution to the same parties, and that an administrator appointed under the law of that State would be held to have recovered to the same uses, and subject to the remedies in his fiduciary character which both statutes prescribe.

We are aware that Woodward ?" Michigan Southern & Northern Indiana Railroad Co. (10 Ohio St. 121) asserts a different doctrine, and that it has been followed by Richardson *v.* New York Central Railroad Co., 98 Mass. 85, and McCarthy *v.* Chicago, Rock Island, & Pacific Railroad Co., 18 Kan. 46. The reasons which support that view we have endeavored to show are not sound. These cases are opposed by the latest decision on the subject in the Court of Appeals of New York, in the case of Leonard, Administrator, *v.* The Columbia Steam Navigation Co., not yet reported, but of which we have been furnished with a certified copy.

The right to recover for an injury to the person, resulting in death, is of very recent origin, and depends wholly upon statutes of the different States. The questions growing out of these statutes are new, and many of them unsettled. Each State court will construe its own statute on the subject, and differences are to be expected. In the absence of any controlling authority or general concurrence of decision, this court must decide for itself the question now for the first time presented to it, and with every respect for the courts which have held otherwise, we think that sound principle clearly authorizes the administrator in cases like this to maintain the action.

Judgment reversed with directions to award a new trial.

DAVIS v. NEW YORK RY., 1887.

[143 Mass. 301.]

DEVENS, J. The defendant is a railroad corporation, operating a railroad through Massachusetts and Connecticut, as a continuous line, by virtue of the St. of 1873, *c.* 289, and exists as a corporation by the laws of each of these States. This action is brought by the plaintiff, as administrator of the estate of Mrs. Ruth L. Brown, for alleged injury to her, which finally resulted in her death, by reason of the carelessness of the defendant and that of its servants, while she was being conveyed as a passenger over its railroad in Connecticut, the intestate being herself at the time in the exercise of due care.

The law of the State of Connecticut has been properly determined as a fact by the judge presiding at the trial, and his finding in regard to it is conclusive. *Ames* v. *McCamber*, 124 Mass. 85, 91. From this it appears "that, by the common law in Connecticut, an action for personal injuries does not survive to the admininstrator of the person injured; that there is no statute or law in Connecticut by virtue of which a common law action for personal injuries is revived, or made to survive to an administrator of the person injured." The facts, as they are alleged, "do not constitute a cause of action under the laws of the State of Connecticut by the administrator in behalf of the intestate's estate, and this action could not be maintained in that State, if duly brought by an administrator there." The administrator may there maintain, upon these facts, a special action, penal in its nature, created by the statutes of Connecticut, by which the damages recoverable are limited to not more than $5000, and under which the damages recovered do not become assets of the estate, but are recovered in behalf of certain persons not thus entitled to the same according to the laws of distribution, and are to be paid over in specified proportions to them.

The plaintiff does not contend that he may maintain this action as the special one provided by the statute of Connecticut, nor under the laws of that State. *Richardson* v. *New York Central Railroad*, 98 Mass. 85. We are aware that the correctness of this decision has been called in question by the Supreme Court of the United States in *Dennick* v. *Railroad*, 103 U. S. 11; but it is unnecessary to reconsider our own decision, as the plaintiff seeks only to maintain his action under our statute, which provides that, in case of damage to the person, the action shall survive, and may thus be prosecuted by an administrator. Pub. Sts. *c.* 165, § 1. *Hollenbeck* v. *Berkshire Railroad*, 9 Cush. 478. The inquiry is therefore presented, whether a cause of action at common law, which dies with the person in the State where it accrued, not having been made there to survive by any statute, will survive under and by virtue of the statutes of survivorship of another state, so that, if jurisdiction is there obtained over the person or property of the defendant, judgment may properly be rendered against him or his property. That our statute would furnish a remedy, where the cause of action was one recognized by the law of this State as the foundation of an action at common law, although it accrued without the State, it being there recognized as existing, and not discharged or extinguished, will be conceded.

It must certainly be the right of each State to determine by its laws under what circumstances an injury to the person will afford a cause of action. If this is not so, a person who is not a citizen of the State, or who resorts to another State for his remedy, if jurisdiction can be obtained, may subject the defendant in an action of tort to entirely different rules and liabilities from those which would control the controversy were it carried on where the injury occurred; and, as by the law of Massachusetts it is required that a person injured while travelling upon a railroad must prove, not only the negligence of the defendant, but also that he himself was in the exercise of due care, and as jurisdiction may be obtained by an attachment of property of the defendant in another State, the plaintiff might relieve himself of the necessity of proving his own due care, if, by the law of the State to which he may resort, such proof is not required, and thus put upon the railroad company a higher responsibility than is imposed by the State in which it was performing its business. In a similar way, if a traveller upon a steam or horse railroad could not recover in this State for an injury done by carelessness in transporting him, because he was travelling upon Sunday, in violation of the laws of the State, he might, unless the law prescribed in this State is to govern, recover in any State where laws forbidding travelling on Sunday did not exist, if jurisdiction could there be obtained over the defendant or its property. Where an injury occurs in another State, which would be the foundation of an action at common law, and it is known that the general law of that state is the common law, it may be inferred that the transaction is governed by its rules as here applied, in the absence of evidence to the contrary; but, when it is shown to be otherwise, the law of the State where the injury occurs is to be regarded. It is a general principle, that, in order to maintain an action of tort founded upon an injury to person and property, the act which is the cause of the injury and the foundation of the action must at least be actionable by the law of the place where it is done, if not also by that of the place in which redress is sought. *Le Forest* v. *Tolman*, 117 Mass. 109, and cases cited. It must be for the State of Connecticut to prescribe when, and under what circumstances, a cause of action shall arise against a corporation which operates a railway within its limits, by reason of an

act done bv it. It may provide that, for an injury done by its
carelessness, there shall be no cause of action on behalf of the
injured party, but punishment by indictment only, or it may give
to such injured person a cause of action, and for the same injury
make the corporation responsible, by indictment or other proceeding, for a fine or damages which shall go to the State, to relatives of the injured party, or to any other persons named. *Commonwealth* v. *Metropolitan Railroad,* 107 Mass. 236.

The intestate did, by the common law of Connecticut, have a
right of action during her lifetime, but for this has been substituted in that State, she having deceased, the penal action created
by the statute.

It is the contention of the plaintiff, that the cause of action
may be held to survive by virtue of our statute, notwithstanding
no cause of action now exists in Connecticut. Pub. Sts. *c.* 165, § 1.
That the special action in Connecticut can now be maintained is
not controverted. If, therefore, this contention of the plaintiff is
correct, the defendant continues liable for its act or neglect in
Connecticut by the law of Massachusetts, while it is also liable
by reason of the penalty imposed upon it by the law of Connecticut as a substitute for its original liability, such penalty being still
capable of enforcement. The design of our statutes of survivorship is primarily to provide for survival of those actions of tort
the causes of which occur in this State. If similar statutes
existed in another State, where the original cause of action
accrued, it would not be difficult to hold that our own applied to
such causes, upon the same principle by which we hold that the
intestate herself might originally have brought her action here.
When no such cause of action now exists in the State where the
injury occurred, it is not easy to see how it can exist here,
especially when, in such State. another cause of action, growing
out of the same facts, has been substituted for it. This would be
to subject the defendant to two liabilities, one existing by the law
of the State in which jurisdiction over person or property was
obtained, but in which the accident did not occur; and the other
imposed by the law of the State where it did occur, and where the
defendant had its residence; while in either State the liability
there imposed would be the only one to which the defendant could
by its law be subjected.

It may be suggested that the law of Connecticut, in failing to
provide that an action for a personal injury shall survive to the
administrator, has, negatively, only the same effect as a statute

of limitations, which operates merely to take away the remedy of a plaintiff, while his cause of action still exists.

By the ancient common law, as it existed before the St. of 4 Edw. III. *c. 7*, which was adopted and practised on in this State before the Constitution, 6 Dane Abr. 607, no action *ex delicto* survived to the personal representative, the maxim *Actio personalis moritur cum persona* being of universal application. *Wilbur v. Gilmore*, 21 Pick. 250. Subsequently to that statute, which was liberally construed, an action for a tort, by which the personal property of one was injured or destroyed, survived to his administrator, such tort being an injury to the property which otherwise would have descended to him. But the theory that a personal injury to an individual was limited to him only, that no one else suffered thereby, and that therefore by his decease the cause of action itself ceased to exist, continued.

While the action for personal injury is spoken of as surviving, as there previously was no responsibility to the estate, the statute creates a new cause of action. It imposes a new liability, and does not merely remove a bar to a remedy such as is interposed by the statute of limitations, which, if withdrawn by the repeal of the statute, would allow an action to be maintained for the original cause. What the new liability shall be, by what conditions it shall be controlled, and whether the original liability shall be destroyed, must be determined by the law of the State where the injury occurs, unless the legislation of other States is to have extra-territorial force, and govern transactions beyond their limits. We perceive no intention to invest it with such force, even if it were possible so to do.

By the decease of the intestate, the cause of action at common law which she once had in Connecticut has there ceased to exist. It is for that State to determine what provision, by action or indictment, if any, shall be made in order to indemnify the estate of the intestate, or her relatives, or to punish the party causing the injury to her. Our statute, permitting the survival of similar actions in this State, does not therefore apply.

The question considered in the case at bar was fully and ably discussed in *Needham v. Grand Trunk Railway*, 38 Vt. 294, and the same result reached as that at which we have arrived. To the same effect also is *State v. Pittsburgh & Connellsville Railroad*, 45 Md. 41.

The plaintiff, in his argument, attaches importance to the St. of 1873, *c.* 289, by virtue of which the defendant's railroad is operated in the several States through which it runs as a continuous line; but the fact that it is a corporation by the law of Massachusetts as well as by that of Connecticut cannot make its liabilities different or greater in this State on account of transactions occurring entirely in Connecticut; nor are the rights of the plaintiff greater because his intestate, who was injured in this transaction, was a citizen of this Commonwealth. *Whitford* v. *Panama Railroad,* 23 N. Y. 465, 472. *Richardson* v. *New York Central Railroad, ubi supra.*

The ruling that the action could be maintained was therefore erroneous.   *Exceptions sustained.*

HIGGINS v. CENTRAL RY., 1892.

[155 Mass. 176.]

TORT, by the administrator of the estate of James Higgins, for causing his death. The writ was dated June 28, 1891, and the officer's return thereon disclosed an attachment of certain cars belonging to the defendant found in the possession of another railroad company at Northampton in this Commonwealth. The declaration alleges that the intestate was domiciled in Springfield in the county of Hampden in this Commonwealth; that the plaintiff was duly appointed the administrator of his estate by the judge of probate of that county, on February 11, 1891; that the defendant owned and operated a railroad extending from a point in the State of Connecticut into the State of New York; that on October 24, 1890, the intestate, while employed by the defendant as a freight brakeman and engaged in the discharge of his duty as such and in the exercise of due care, was instantly killed in a collision which occurred through the defendant's negligence; and that "thereby an action has accrued to the plaintiff, as administrator as aforesaid, to recover damages not exceeding five thousand dollars, by virtue of sections 1008 and 1009 of the General Statutes of the said State of Connecticut, and he claims damages, as administrator aforesaid, under said laws and statutes." The defendant demurred, for the reason, among others, that "the plaintiff cannot maintain an action in this Commonwealth under or by reason of sections 1008 and 1009 of the General Statutes of the State of Connecticut."

The Superior Court sustained the demurrer; and the plaintiff appealed to this court.

BARKER, J. The plaintiff's intestate was domiciled in Massachusetts, where the plaintiff was appointed administrator. This being the principal administration, the plaintiff succeeded as well to every right of action of the deceased which survived as to his other personal property. Upon the question whether such an administrator takes a right of action by succession from his intestate, it is immaterial that the right arose under the statute of a foreign State; rather than under the common law or the statutes of this State; just as the fact that the intestate's chattels or merchandise had been acquired or were held under the statutes of a foreign State, rather than under the law of his domicil, is immaterial upon the question whether such merchandise or chattels pass to the administrator.

Such an administrator is entitled to the aid of our courts, if they have jurisdiction of the necessary parties, in collecting and reducing into money the property which he takes by succession, whether goods, chattels, or choses in action.

Suits brought to enforce rights of action which the deceased had, and which survive and passed from him to his administrator, differ essentially from those which this court refused to entertain in *Richardson* v. *New York Central Railroad*, 98 Mass. 85, and in *Davis* v. *New York & New England Railroad*, 143 Mass. 301. In Richardson's case an administrator appointed here sought to enforce in our courts a cause of action which his intestate never had, which had not passed to the administrator by succession, and which the statutes of another State had caused to spring up at the death of the intestate, and had provided might be brought by and in the names of his personal representatives, for the exclusive benefit of his widow and next of kin. In Davis's case the intestate had a right of action in his lifetime by the common law of the State of Connecticut, where he was injured; but by the law of Connecticut his right of action did not survive, and was extinguished at his death, while a penal action created by statute was substituted for it in that State.

In the present case the plaintiff's intestate is alleged to have been instantly killed in Connecticut, by the defendant's negligence. It is conceded that the statute of that State makes the defendant liable to pay damages for the injury which caused his death. Can his administrator sue here to recover such damages? The Connecticut statute places in one category "all actions for injury to the person, whether the same do or do not instantaneously or otherwise result in death, and all actions "to the reputation, or to the property, and actions to recover damages for injury to the person of the wife, child, or servant of any person," and provides that all shall survive to the executor or administrator. Gen. Sts. of Conn. of 1888, § 1008. One evident purpose of this statute was to give to actions for injuries resulting in instantaneous death the same incidents as actions which survive have. It is grouped with actions which survive for other injuries to the person, and for injuries to reputation and to property, and all are said to survive. The putting in operation of the negligent or unlawful forces which cause an instantaneous death is a wrong to the person killed, which, by more or less of appreciable time, precedes his death. If the law of the country where such a wrong is committed gives to the person killed a right of action, and provides that it shall survive to his administrator, there is no difficulty in considering that the deceased had that right of action at the instant when he was *vivus et mortuus,* and that by express provisions of law it is made to survive and to pass to his administrator. This the statute referred to has plainly attempted to do. As was held in *Davis* v. *New York & New England Railroad, ubi supra,* it is the right of each State "to determine by its laws under what circumstances an injury to the person will afford a cause of action." Viewing this statute of Connecticut as a whole, it plainly puts such causes of action as the present upon the footing of personal actions which survive, and which are everywhere considered transitory; that is, they go with the person who has the right of action where he goes, and are enforceable in any forum according to its rules of procedure. If they survive, such actions, like other personal estate, are considered to have *situs* in the place of domicil, and to pass to the administrator there appointed. Viewing the causes of action with which the Connecticut statute deals in connection with the one now sued on, our own statutes of survivorship are similar. There is, therefore, nothing in the nature of the cause of action as so far developed to prevent our courts from entertaining it upon principles generally recognized.

Assuming that the cause of action is one not existing at the common law, but created by the statute of another State, we have seen that it is transitory, and that it survives and passes from the deceased to his administrator. When an action is brought upon it here, the plaintiff is not met by any difficulty upon these points. Whether our courts will entertain it depends upon the general principles which are to be applied in determining the question whether actions founded upon the laws of other States shall be heard here. These principles require that, in cases of other than penal actions, the foreign law, if not contrary to our public policy, or to abstract justice or pure morals, or calculated to injure the State or its citizens, shall be recognized and enforced here, if we have jurisdiction of all necessary parties, and if we can see that, consistently with our own forms of procedure and law of trials, we can do substantial justice between the parties. If the foreign law is a penal statute, or if it offends our own policy, or is repugnant to justice or to good morals, or is calculated to injure this State or its citizens, or if we have not jurisdiction of parties who must be brought in to enable us to give a satisfactory remedy, or if under our forms of procedure an action here cannot give a substantial remedy, we are at liberty to decline jurisdiction. *Blanchard* v. *Russell,* 13 Mass. 1, 6. *Prentiss* v. *Savage,* 13 Mass. 20, 24. *Ingraham* v. *Geyer,* 13 Mass. 146. *Tappan* v. *Poor,* 15 Mass. 419. *Zipcey* v. *Thompson,* 1 Gray, 243, 245. *Erickson* v. *Nesmith,* 15 Gray, 221, and 4 Allen, 233, 236. *Halsey* v. *McLean,* 12 Allen, 438, 443. *New Haven Horse Nail Co.* v. *Linden Spring Co.* 142 Mass. 349, 353. *Bank of North America* v. *Rindge,* 154 Mass. 203.

Applying these rules, we find no sufficient reason for declining to entertain the present action. Our own statutes have, in several instances, changed the policy of the common law, so as to allow damages for death occasioned by negligence. Pub. Sts. c. 52, § 17; c. 73, § 6, c. 112, § 212. St. 1883, c. 243. St. 1887, c. 270, § 2. The right created by the Connecticut statute is in terms a right to recover "just damages." Gen. Sts. of Conn. of 1888, § 1009. Neither the fact that the statute creating it limits the amount of the recovery to a sum not exceeding five thousand dollars, nor that the damages are to be distributed to the husband, widow, heirs, or next of kin, makes it a penal action. The effect of such provisions as to the distribution of the damages is to say that they shall not be assets for the payment of debts, and shall not pass by the will of the deceased, but shall be applied to the compensation of the persons who are presumed to have suffered the most by the death of the person injured. Such a right is not unjust, nor contrary to good morals, nor calculated to injure the State or its citizens. Our courts have jurisdiction of the necessary parties. Looking at the statute creating the right of action as a part of the sytem of law in force in Connecticut, and considering that, if the action is to be prosecuted here, our rules of law regulating procedure, and fixing the elements which are to enter into the assessment of the damages, must govern the trial, it is probable that the result will not be exactly the same as if the remedy had been pursued in Connecticut. But we see no such difficulty as to lead us to suppose that injustice may be done to the defendant, and none which ought to make us decline jurisdiction, if the plaintiff elects to sue here.

The statutes which create and limit the right of action are found in the provisions regulating civil actions in the courts of Connecticut, and are part of its general system of law. By "the costs and expenses of suit," which, under § 1009, are to be deducted from the damages before they are distributed, were intended costs of suit allowed under Connecticut laws, and the expenses of the suit exclusive of such costs, these expenses, including those of trials not resulting in a verdict, are a constituent element of the "just damages" under the Connecticut system. The same system allows exemplary and vindictive damages. *Noyes* v. *Ward*, 19 Conn. 250. *Beecher* v. *Derby Bridge & Ferry Co.* 24 Conn. 491, 497. *Murphy* v. *New York & New Haven Railroad*, 29 Conn. 496, 499. If, in the action prosecuted here, neither the expenses of the suit nor exemplary nor vindictive damages can be recovered, that fact is no hardship upon the defendant. There is no reason why the plaintiff may not be allowed to waive those elements of damage, by bringing his action in a forum where they cannot be allowed. It is also a part of the Connecticut system, that, upon the default of a defendant in such actions, the plaintiff has no right to have his damages assessed by a jury, and in practice the assessment is uniformly made by the court alone. Gen. Sts. of Conn. of 1888, § 1106. *Raymond* v. *Danbury & Norwalk Railroad*, 43 Conn. 596, 598. Upon such assessment in Connecticut, the defendant, to reduce the damages to a nominal sum, may show contributory negligence, or any matter which, if pleaded and proved in bar, would have defeated the action. *Daily* v. *New York & New Haven Railroad*, 32 Conn. 356. *Carey* v. *Day*, 36 Conn. 152. But even if it appeared that the motive for bringing an action here was to insure an assessment of the damages by a jury, we cannot perceive in that a valid reason for declining to take jurisdiction.

It is to be noticed that, while the statute upon which the plaintiff founds his claim makes the cause of action one which accrued to the plaintiff's intestate in his lifetime, and provides that it shall survive and pass to his administrator, it does not say in terms that the damages shall or shall not be assets of the intestate estate, but provides that they shall be distributed in a way which may or may not be different from the disposition to be made under our law of the assets of the deceased to be administered. As this intestate was domiciled in Massachusetts, we are not to be taken as now deciding how any damages which the plaintiff may recover are to be here administered.

Demurrer overruled.

HERRICK v. MINNEAPOLIS & ST. LOUIS RY., 1883.

[31 Minn. 11.]

MITCHELL, J. The defendant owned and operated a line of railroad from Albert Lea, in this state, to Fort Dodge, in the state of Iowa. The plaintiff entered the service of defendant, in Iowa, as brakeman on one of its trains, to be operated wholly in that state. While coupling cars on his train in the discharge of his duty in that state, plaintiff was injured through the negligence of the engineer in charge of the train, under such circumstances as to give him a right of action under a statute of Iowa, which makes every corporation operating a railway in that state liable for all damages sustained by any person, including employes of such corporation, in consequence of the neglect of agents, or by mismanagement of the engineers or other employes of such corporation, when such wrongs are in any manner connected with the use or operation of any railway on or about which they shall be employed. Code of Iowa, 1873, tit. 10, c. 5, § 1307. This action was brought to recover damages for the personal injury thus sustained in that state. The court below dismissed the action, on the ground that the right of action thus accruing under the statute of Iowa could only be enforced in that state. The correctness of this ruling is the only question involved in this appeal.

The general rule is that actions for personal torts are transitory in their nature, and may be brought wherever the wrongdoer may be found, and jurisdiction of his person can be obtained. As to torts which give a right of action at common law, this rule has never been questioned, and we do not see why the transitory character of the action, or the jurisdiction of the courts of another state to entertain it, can in any manner be affected by the question whether the right of action is statutory or common-law. In actions *ex contractu* there is no such distinction, and there is no good reason why any different rule should be applied in actions *ex delicto*. Whenever, by either common law or statute, a right of action has become fixed and a legal liability incurred, that liability, if the action be transitory, may be enforced, and the right of action pursued, in the courts of any state which can obtain jurisdiction of the defendant, provided it is not against the public policy of the laws of the state where it is sought to be enforced. Of course, statutes that are criminal or penal in their nature will only be enforced in the state which enacted them; but the statute under which this action is brought is neither, being purely one for the reparation of a civil injury.

The statute of another state has, of course, no extraterritorial force, but rights acquired under it will always, in comity, be enforced, if not against the public policy of the laws of the former. In such cases the law of the place where the right was acquired, or the liability was incurred, will govern as to the *right of action;* while all that pertains merely to the *remedy* will be controlled by the law of the state where the action is brought. And we think the principle is the same, whether the right of action be *ex contractu or ex delicto.*

The defendant admits the general rule to be as thus stated, but contends that as to statutory actions like the present, it is subject to the qualification that, to sustain the action, the law of the forum and the law of the place where the right of action accrued must concur in holding that the act done gives a right of action. We admit that some text-writers—notably, Rorer on Inter-State Law—seem to lay down this rule, but the authorities cited generally fail to sustain it. We have examined all the numerous cases cited on this point by defendant, and we find only one which, in our opinion, sustains him, while several are really against him. Most of the cases thus cited belong to one or the other of the two following classes: *First,* cases which hold that statutes giving a right of action for injuries causing the death of another, having no extraterritorial operation, only apply to injuries inflicted in the State which enacted the statute, and not to injuries inflicted or acts done in another state. Such is the case of *Whitford* v. *Panama R. Co.*, 23 N. Y. 465. This undoubtedly is the settled law, but it does not touch the present case. The *second* class consists of cases which hold that where the statute gives such a right of action to the personal representatives of the deceased, it can only be maintained by an administrator or executor appointed and acting under the laws of the state which enacted the statute, taking the ground that this right of action is not a right of property which passes to the estate, but is for

the benefit of the family or next of kin of the deceased, and therefore the statute contemplates the exercise of the power and the
execution of the trust only by a personal representative appointed
under domestic laws. To this class belong the cases of *Richardson* v. *N. Y. Central R. Co.*, 98 Mass. 85, and *Woodward* v.
Michigan, etc., R. Co., 10 Ohio St. 121. Some courts refuse to
adopt this rule. But this question is not involved in the present
case.

A few cases appear to lay some stress upon the fact that the
statutes of both states were similar, but rather as evidence of the
fact that the statute of the state giving the right of action is not
contrary to the policy of the laws of the state where the action is
brought. Such is the case of *Chicago, etc., R. Co.* v. *Doyle*, 8
Am. & Eng. R. Cases, 171, in which, after saying that the action
may be asserted because of the coincidence of the statutes of the
two states, the court add: "And, independently of this, because a
right of action created by the statute of another state, of a transitory nature, may be enforced here when it does not conflict with
the public policy of this state to permit its enforcement; and our
statute is evidence that our policy is favorable to such rights of
action instead of being inimical to them." But it by no means
follows that, because the statute of one state differs from the law
of another state, therefore it would be held contrary to the policy
of the laws of the latter state. Every day our courts are enforcing
rights under foreign contracts where the *lex loci contractus* and
the *lex fori* are altogether different, and yet we construe these
contracts and enforce rights under them according to their force
and effect under the laws of the state where made. To justify a
court in refusing to enforce a right of action which accrued under
the law of another state, because against the policy of our laws,
it must appear that it is against good morals or natural justice,
or that, for some other such reason, the enforcement of it would
be prejudicial to the general interests of our own citizens. If
the state of Iowa sees fit to impose this liability upon those operating railroads within her bounds, and to make it a condition of the
employment of those who enter their service, we see nothing in
such a law repugnant either to good morals or natural justice, or
prejudicial to the interests of our own citizens.

The only case which goes to the length of holding that this
action cannot be maintained, is that of *Anderson* v. *Milwaukee &
St. P. Ry. Co.*, 37 Wis. 321, which, on the facts, is on all-fours
with the present case, and in which the court holds that such an

35

action will only lie in the state of Iowa, which enacted the statute. But with due deference to that court, and especially to the eminent jurist who delivered the opinion in that case, we think they entirely failed to distinguish between the *right of action*, which was created by the statute of Iowa and must be governed by it, and the *form of the remedy*, which is always governed by the law of the forum, whether the action be *ex contractu* or *ex delicto*. It is elementary that the remedy is governed by the law of the forum, and this is all that is held by any case cited by the court in support of their opinion.

The case of *Bettys v. Milwaukee & St. P. Ry. Co.*, 37 Wis. 323, was an action brought under an Iowa statute to recover *double* damages for cattle killed in Iowa. This case was probably correctly decided upon the second ground stated in the opinion, viz., that the statute was *penal*, and therefore could only be enforced in the state which enacted it.

The following cases, we think, support our conclusion that this action may be maintained, although we have no such statute in this state: *Dennick v. Railroad Co.*, 103 U. S. 11; *Leonard v. Steam Nav. Co.*, 84 N. Y. 48; *Chicago, etc, R. Co. v. Doyle, supra; Nashville & C. R. Co. v. Sprayberry*, 8 Baxt. (Tenn.) 341. See, also, *Selma, etc., R. Co. v. Lacy*, 43 Ga. 461, and *S. C.*, 49 Ga. 106.

2. The defendant further contends that the statute of Iowa is in violation of the fourteenth amendment to the constitution of the United States, which declares that "no state shall deny to any person within its jurisdiction the equal protection of the laws." The ground for this contention consists in the fact that the law does not apply to all persons, but only to railroad companies, thus imposing on them a liability not imposed on others. There is great danger that some of the provisions of this fourteenth amendment will be attempted to be applied to cases for which it was never designed. In view of the history surrounding its adoption, we doubt whether it was ever intended to apply to cases like the present. But, even if it was, we find nothing in this statute repugnant to its provisions. The provision of the constitutional amendment referred to does not surround the citizen with any protection additional to those before given under the constitutions of the states. It was not in the power of the states, before the adoption of this amendment, to deprive citizens of the United States of the equal protection of the laws; the only change produced by making this constitutional principle a part of the

federal constitution is to make the supreme court of the United States the final arbiter oi cases in which a violation of this principle by state law is complained of. If a state, in view of the peculiar nature of the service upon railroads, and the danger inci dent to it, shall, as a matter of state policy, require these corpora tions, which are creatures of its statutes, to assume the risk of injuries to their servants resulting from the negligence of fellow servants also in their employ, we think they have a right to do so. Statutes imposing special duties and liabilities upon railroad companies are to be found on the statute-books of almost every state, and, if general in their application to all such corporations, they are valid. *McAunich* v. *Mississippi & M. Ry. Co.*, 20 Iowa, 338; *Johnson* v. *Chicago, M. & St. P. Ry. Co.*, 29 Minn. 425.

Order reversed.

INTESTATE SUCCESSION.

LAWRENCE v. KITTERIDGE, 1852.

[21 Conn. 576.]

1. Law of Domicil of an Intestate at Time of Death Determines Distribution of Personal Property.

2. Law of Place where Real Estate is Situated Determines Descent of Real Estate.

THIS was an appeal from two decrees of the court of probate for the district of Norfolk; one passed on the 29th day of September, 1851, and the other on the 20th day of October, 1851. The former directed, that the remainder of the estate of Cephas Pettibone, deceased, situate in the district of Norfolk, after payment of the debts and charges against that estate in this state, should be transmitted to the administrator on such estate in the state of Vermont, there to be distributed according to the laws of that state, and not according to the laws of this state. By the latter decree, in the settlement of the administration account, the sum of forty-one dollars, thirty-one cents, was allowed against said estate to Michael F. Mills, Esq.

At the hearing before the superior court, February term, 1852, the following facts were found.

In relation to the first decree appealed from, Cephas Pettibone, the settlement of whose estate was in question, died intestate, leaving no children, nor the representatives of any children, but a brother of the whole blood, Augustus Pettibone, Esq., late of Norfolk, since deceased, and several brothers and sisters of the half blood, residing in Vermont, or elsewhere, out of the jurisdiction of this state. At the time of Cephas Pettibone's decease, he was an inhabitant of, and had his domicil in, the state of Vermont. All his personal estate consisted of a debt of about one thousand dollars, due from the estate of said Augustus Pettibone, who, at the time of his death, and for many years before, resided in this state. Original administration on the estate of Cephas Pettibone was granted in Vermont, and was in progress, when an ancillary administration was granted in this state, and the first decree appealed from, was passed. At this time, there were no unsatisfied debts due from the estate, here or in Vermont; and nothing to complete the settlement of the estate, remained to be done, except the distribution thereof.

As to the last decree, it was found, that at the death of the intestate, there was justly due from his estate to Michael F. Mills, Esq., the sum of forty-one dollars, thirty-five cents; and it was agreed between him and W. C. Kitteridge, the administrator in Vermont, that the latter should become personally responsible for the debt, and gave said Mills a receipt in discharge of his claim against the estate; which was done. The object of this arrangement was, to enable the administrator to settle his administration account.

E. Grove Lawrence, the appellant, is the devisee, and one of the heirs at law, of said Augustus Pettibone, the brother of the whole blood of the intestate, and is thus interested in the distribution of the estate in question.

The case was reserved for the advice of this court as to what judgment should be rendered thereon.

CHURCH, Ch. J. The first decree of the court of probate appealed from, was predicated upon facts essentially as follows, *viz.*, Cephas Pettibone, the intestate, at the time of his death, was an inhabitant of, and had his domicil in, the state of Vermont, and was possessed of an estate there; and there was due to him here, from a citizen of this state, a debt of about one thousand dollars. Original administration upon his estate was granted in the state of Vermont, and was in progress, when an ancillary administration was granted in this state. When the decree appealed from was made, there were no unsatisfied debts due from the estate, here or in Vermont, and nothing but a distribution of the estate remained to be done.

The intestate died, leaving brothers and sisters of the whole and half blood; all, excepting the late Augustus Pettibone, Esq., of Norfolk, who was a brother of the whole blood, residing in Vermont, or elsewhere, out of this state; and he had no other heirs at law. By the laws of Vermont, the brothers and sisters of an intestate of the whole and half blood are entitled equally to the estate, under the statute of distribution.

Upon the foregoing state of facts, the court of probate for the district of Norfolk was of opinion, that the personal estate of Cephas Pettibone—the chose in action of one thousand dollars—should be distributed according to the laws of the state of Vermont; and that this could better be done, and without injury to any citizen of this state, by transmitting the money to the administrator there, and to the jurisdiction of the court of principal administration, than to order a distribution of it here. And therefore, the decree appealed from, was made.

The Appellant, who is the representative of Augustus Pettibone, the brother of the whole blood residing in the district of Norfolk, objects to this decree, and appeals from it. He claims, that the assets or money in the hands of the administrator here, should have been distributed here, and according to the laws of this state, which prefer a brother or sister of the whole blood to one of the half blood.

1. We had supposed, that the law of the country of the domicil of an intestate governed and regulated the distribution of his personal estate; and that this was a principle of international law, long ago recognized by jurists in all enlightened governments, and especially recognized by this court, in the recent case of *Holcomb* v. *Phelps,* 16 Conn. R. 127, 133, in which we say, that, "It certainly is now a settled principle of international law, that personal property shall be subject to that law which governs the person of the owner, and that the distribution of and succession to personal property, wherever situated, is to be governed by the laws of that country where the owner or intestate had his domicil at the time of his death." Sto. Confl. Laws, 403, *in notis,* §§ 480, 465. 2 Kent's Com. Lect. 37. 2 Kaine's Prin. Eq. 312, 826. *Potter* v. *Brown,* 5 East, 124. *Balfour* v. *Scott,* 6 Bro. Parl. Cas. 550. (Toml. ed.) *Bempbe* v. *Johnstone,* 2 Ves. 198. *Pepon* v. *Pepon,* Amb. 25, 415. *Guier* v. *O'Daniel,* 7 Binn. 349, *in notis. Harvey* v. *Richards,* 1 Mason, 381.

It is not necessary that we should now examine the reasons, whether of public policy or legal propriety, which have led the tribunals of civilized nations to relax from antiquated notions on this subject; some of these are well considered, by Judge Story, in the case of *Harvey* v. *Richards,* 1 Mason, 381, and by Chancellor Kent, in his Commentaries, vol. 2, Lect. 37.

It is true, that it is in the power of every sovereignty, and within the constitutional powers of the states of this Union, to repudiate this salutary doctrine, in its application to themselves, or to modify it, for what they may suppose to be the protection of their own citizens; but without some peculiar necessity, it cannot be supposed, that any well regulated government will do it. It was claimed in argument, in this case, that this had been done in this state, and by the provision of the 49th section of our statute for the settlement of estates, (Stat. 357.) by declaring, that when there are no children, &c. of an intestate, his "real and personal estate shall be set off equally to the brothers and sisters of the whole blood." But it was not the purpose of this provision to disregard the universal and salutary doctrine of the law to which we have referred, but only to regulate the descent and distribution of the estate of our own citizens. This provision of our statute is not peculiar to ourselves; a similar one, we presume, may be found in the codes of other states; at least, imperative enactments exist in every state, directing the distribution of estates; but none of them are intended to repeal the law of the domicil, in its effect upon the personal estate of the owner. The controversy, in the case of *Holcomb* v. *Phelps,* arose under the same section of our law as does the one now under consideration, and the result of that case must settle this question, if it be one.

There are cases, in which the law of the domicil has been modified or restrained, in its full operation, for what courts have supposed to be the proper protection of the rights of the citizens of their own states; but these are generally confined to cases in which creditors are, in some way interested under insolvent proceedings, assignments, or bankrupt laws, and never, we believe, are extended to mere cases of distribution, as here claimed. Sto. Conf. L. 277, § 337.

The views of the court of probate in regard to the operating law of distribution, in this case, were correct; and the remaining question, in this part of the case, is whether the decree which followed, directing the money in the hands of the administrator here, to be transmitted to the proper jurisdiction in Vermont, for distribution, should be reversed; or whether the court here, should, by its own decree, have made distribution according to the laws of Vermont?

There was but one estate to be settled; and this was, in legal view, attached to the person of the owner, at the time of his death, so far as it was personal. There were two administrations; one original and principal in Vermont; the other ancillary and subordinate, in this state. *Perkins* v. *Stone,* 18 Conn. R. 270. Sto. Conf. L. 423.

The creditors of this estate, and all persons having claims upon it, in this state and in Vermont, were satisfied, and nothing remained to be done, but in the distribution of it among those who, by the laws of the state of Vermont, were entitled to it. Why were two distributions of this one estate necessary? Without special reasons requiring a different course, there would seem to be a propriety, that the consummating act in the settlement, should have been done, by the tribunal exercising the principal jurisdiction, and that the money accidentally and temporarily in this state, should be transmitted thither, for that purpose. Otherwise, there might have been conflicting decrees, and the courts of the different jurisdictions, upon varying proofs, might have found different persons entitled to take as distributees. The law of Vermont was the governing law, and known to the courts of that state, as a matter of *certainty;* but here, to be ascertained only by proofs, as a matter of *fact.*

There are cases in which the courts of the ancillary administration have retained the assets, and distributed them according to the law of the domicil; and others, in which they have been transmitted to the principal and original jurisdiction for final action. *Harvey* v. *Richards,* 1 Mason, 391. *Richards* v. *Dutch,* 8 Mass. R. 506. *Dawes* v. *Boylston,* 9 Mass. R. 355.

We do not think it to be a legal consequence, because distribution should be made according to the law of the domicil, that the assets should be transmitted for distribution; the courts of the ancillary jurisdiction may distribute them. *Stevens* v. *Gaylord,* 11 Mass. R. 256. *Dawes* v. *Heath &* al. 3 Pick. 128. *Bruce* v. *Bruce,* 2 Bos. & Pull. 229. *Balfour* v. *Scott,* 6 Bro. Parl. Cas. 550. *Hog* v. *Lashley,* Id. 577. *Drummond* v. *Drummond,* Id. 601. *Somerville* v. *Somerville,* 16 Ves. 791.

But it seems now to be settled, that the power of the court granting the ancillary administration is a discretionary one, and should depend for its exercise upon the circumstances and equity of each case. This is a salutary principle, and can work no harm; but in its application, the citizens of the state of the ancillary administration and their rights, are not alone to be regarded, but also the rights of all interested. *Harvey* v. *Richards*, I Mason, 381. *Dawes* v. *Head*, 3 Pick. 128. *Topham* v. *Chapman*, I Rep. Const. Court, S. C. 292. 2 Kent's Com. Lect. 37. Sto. Conf. L. 424

We see no good reason to be dissatisfied with the application of this principle and the exercise of this discretion, by the court of probate, in the decree appealed from. The original administration was granted, by a court in a sister state near by; and within one or two days' reach of the appellant, who represents the only person interested in the estate here! All the other interested parties—and there were several of them—resided in the state of Vermont, or elsewhere, where they could, with equal convenience, protect their interests, and receive their portions of the distributed estate, as if the distribution had been made by the court of probate for the district of Norfolk. A greater inconvenience and expense has been avoided, by the transmission of the money to Vermont for final distribution, than if it had been retained here. And still we do not say, that we would, even under the circumstances of this case, have reversed an order of distribution, if made by the court of probate here.

2. The objection to the allowance of forty-one dollars to the administrator, for payment of a debt due from the estate to Michael F. Mills, Esq., and the appeal from the order making that allowance, is frivolous.

The estate owed the debt, and the administrator has satisfied it, by substituting his own private responsibility, which the creditor has received as payment in full.

The superior court is advised, that the orders and decrees of the court of probate should be affirmed.

TESTAMENTARY SUCCESSION.

MOULTRIE v. HUNT, 1861.

[23 N. Y. 394.]

1. Validity of Will of Personal Property.
2. Formalities, Capacity, and Interpretation of Will of Personal Property.
3. Validity of Will of Real Estate.
4. Formalities, Capacity, and Interpretation of Will of Real Estate.

APPEAL from the Supreme Court. Application was made in April, 1856, to the Surrogate of the county of New York, for the issuing of a commission to take proofs of the execution in Charleston, South Carolina, of an alleged will of Benjamin F. Hunt, who, it was averred in the petition, had died in the city of New York, having his residence and leaving his personal property there. The commission was issued; and the evidence taken under it established the fact that Mr. Hunt, in August, 1849, being then a citizen of South Carolina, executed under his hand and seal an instrument purporting to be a will of real and personal estate. It was attested at his request by three witnesses, but Mr. Hunt did not state to the witnesses the nature of the paper which he requested them to attest. The Surrogate made a decree admitting the will to probate. which, on appeal by one of the next of kin, was affirmed by the Supreme Court at general term in the first district, and an appeal was thereupon taken to this court.

DENIO, J. One of the requisites to a valid will of real or personal property, according to the Revised Statutes, is, that the testator should, at the time of subscribing it, or at the time of acknowledging it. declare, in the presence of at least two attesting witnesses, that it is his last will and testament. (2 R. S., p. 63, § 40.) The will which the Surrogate of New York admitted to probate, by the order under review, was defectively executed in this particular—the only statement which the alleged testator made to the witnesses being that it was his signature and seal which was affixed to it. It was correctly assumed by the Surrogate in his opinion, and by the Supreme Court in pronouncing its judgment of affirmance, that the instrument could not be sustained as a will under the provision. of the Revised Statutes, but that, if it could be upheld at all, it must be as a will executed in another State, according to the law prevailing there; and, upon that view, it was established by both these tribunals as a valid testament. In point of fact the instrument was drawn, signed and attested at Charleston, in South Carolina, where such a declaration of the testator to the witnesses, as has been 'mentioned, is not required to constitute a valid execution of a will. Mr. Hunt, the alleged testator, resided at that time in Charleston; but, some time before his death, he removed to the city of New York, and he continued to reside in that city from that time until his death. The will was validly executed, according to the laws of South Carolina.

Although the language of our statute, to which reference has been made, includes, in its generality, all testamentary dispositions, it is, nevertheless, true, that wills, duly executed and taking effect in other States and countries according to the laws in force there, are recognized in our courts as valid acts, so far as concerns the disposition of personal property. (*Parsons* v. *Lyman*, 20 N. Y., 103.)   This is according to the law of international comity. Every country enacts such laws as it sees fit as to the disposition of personal property by its own citizens, either *inter vivos* or testamentary; but these laws are of no inherent obligation in any other country.   Still, all civilized nations agree, as a general rule, to recognize titles to movable property created in other states or countries in pursuance of the laws existing there, and by parties domiciled in such states or countries.   This law of comity is parcel of the municipal law of the respective countries in which it is recognized, the evidence of which, in the absence of domestic legislation or judicial decisions, is frequently sought in the treatises of writers on international law, and in certain commentaries upon the civil law which treat more or less copiously upon subjects of this nature.

If the alleged testator in the present case had continued to be an inhabitant of South Carolina until his death, we should, according to this principle, have regarded the will as a valid instrument, and it would have been the duty of our probate courts to have granted letters testamentary to the executors named in it. The statute contemplates such a case when it provides for the proving of such wills upon a commission to be issued by the Chancellor, and for granting letters upon a will admitted to probate in another State. (2 R. S., p. 67, §§ 68, 69.) These provisions do not profess to define under what circumstances a will made in a foreign jurisdiction, not in conformity with our laws, shall be valid. It only assumes that such wills may exist, and provides for their proof.

The question in the present case is, whether, inasmuch as the testator changed his domicil after the instrument was signed and attested, and was, at the time of his death, a resident citizen of this State, he can, within the sense of the law of comity, be said to have made his will in South Carolina. The paper which was signed at Charleston had no effect upon the testator's property while he remained in that State, or during his lifetime. It is of the essence of a will that, until the testator's death, it is ambulatory and revocable. No rights of property or powers over property, were conferred upon any one by the execution of this instrument; nor were the estate, interest or rights of the testator in his property in any way abridged or qualified by that act. The transaction was, in its nature, inchoate and provisional. It prescribed the rules by which his succession should be governed, provided he did not change his determination in his lifetime. I think sufficient consideration was not given to this peculiarity of testamentary dispositions, in the view which the learned Surrogate took of the case. According to his opinion, a will, when signed and attested in conformity with the law of the testator's domicil, is a "consummate and perfect transaction." In one sense it is, no doubt, a finished affair; but I think it is no more consummate than a bond would be which the obligor had prepared for use by signing and sealing, but had kept in his own possession for future use. The cases, I concede, are not entirely parallel; for a will, if not revoked, takes effect by the death of the testator, which must inevitably happen at some time, without the performance of any other act on his part, or the will of any other party; while the uttering of a written obligation, intended to operate *inter vivos*, requires a further volition of the party to be bound, and the intervention of another party to accept a delivery, to give it vitality. But, until one or the other of these circumstances—namely, the death, in the case of a will, or the delivery, where the instrument is an obligation—occur, the instrument is of no legal significancy. In the case of a will it requires the death of the party, and in that of a bond a delivery of the instrument, to indue it with any legal operation or effect. The existence of a will, duly executed and attested, at one period during a testator's lifetime, is a circumstance of no legal importance. He must die leaving such a will, or the case is one of intestacy. (*Betts* v. *Jackson*, 6 Wend., 173–181.) The provisions of a will

made before the enactment of the Revised Statutes, and in entire
conformity with the law as it then existed, but which took effect
by the death of the testator afterwards, were held to be annulled
by certain enactments of these Statutes respecting future estates,
notwithstanding the saving contained in the repealing act, to the
effect that the repeal of any statutory provision shall not affect
any act done, &c., previous to the time of the repeal. (*De Peyster*
v. *Clendining*, 8 Paige, 295; 2 R. S., p. 779, § 5; *Bishop* v. *Bishop*,
4 Hill, 138.) The Chancellor declared that the trusts and provisions of the will must depend upon the law as it was when it
took effect by the death of the testator; and the Supreme Court
affirmed that doctrine. There is no distinction, in principle, between general acts bearing upon testamentary provisions, like the
statute of uses and trusts, and particular directions regarding
the formalities to be observed in authenticating the instrument;
and I do not doubt that all the wills executed under the former
law, and which failed to conform to the new one, where the
testator survived the enactment of the Revised Statutes, would
have been avoided, but for the saving in the 70th section, by
which the new statute was not to impair the validity of the execution of a will made before it took effect. (2 R. S., p. 68.) If, as
has been suggested, a will was a consummated and perfect transaction before the death of the testator, no change in the law
subsequently made would affect it—the rule being, that what has
been validly done and perfected respecting private rights under
an existing statute is not affected by a repeal of the law. (*Reg.*
v. *The Inhabitants of Denton*, 14 Eng. L. Eq., 124, per Lord
CAMPBELL, Ch. J.)

If then a will legally executed under a law of this State,
would be avoided by a subsequent change made in the law, before
the testator's death, which should require different or additional
formalities, it would seem that we could not give effect to one
duly made in a foreign state or country, but which failed to conform to the laws of this State, where, at the time of its taking
effect by the testator's death, he was no longer subject to the
foreign law, but was fully under the influence of our own legal
institutions. The question in each case is, whether there has
been an act done and perfected under the law governing the
transaction. If there has been, a subsequent change of residence
would not impair the validity of the act. We should be bound
to recognize it by the law of comity, just as we would recognize
and give validity to a bond reserving eight per cent interest.

executed in a State where that rate is allowed, or a transfer of property which was required to be under seal, but which had in fact been executed by adding a scroll to the signer's name in a State where that stood for a seal or the like. An act done in another State, in order to create rights which our courts ought to enforce on the ground of comity, must be of such a character that if done in this State, in conformity with our laws, it could not be constitutionally impaired by subsequent legislation. An executed transfer of property, real or personal, is a contract within the protection of the Constitution of the United States, and it creates rights of property which our own Constitution guarantees against legislative confiscation. Yet I presume no one would suppose that a law prescribing new qualifications to the right of devising or bequeathing real or personal property, or new regulations as to the manner of doing it, and making the law applicable in terms to all cases where wills had not already taken effect by the death of the testator, would be constitutionally abjectionable.

I am of opinion that a will has never been considered, and that it is not by the law of this State, or the law of England, a perfected transaction, so as to create rights which the courts can recognize or enforce, until it has become operative by the death of the testator. As to all such acts which remain thus inchoate, they are in the nature of unexecuted intentions. The author of them may change his mind, or the State may determine that it is inexpedient to allow them to take effect, and require them to be done in another manner. If the law-making power may do this by an act operating upon wills already executed, in this State, it would seem reasonable that a general act, like the statute of wills, contained in the Revised Statutes, would apply itself to all wills thereafter to take effect by the death of the testator in this State, wherever they might be made; and that the law of comity, which has been spoken of, would not operate to give validity to a will executed in another State, but which had no legal effect there until after the testator, by coming to reside here, had fully subjected himself to our laws; nor then, until his testamentary act had taken effect by his death.

It may be that this conclusion would not, in all cases, conform to the expectations of testators. It is quite possible that a person coming here from another State, who had executed his will before his removal, according to the law of his former residence, might rely upon the validity of that act; and would die intestate, contrary to his intention, in consequence of our laws exacting additional formalities with which he was unacquainted. But it may be also that a well-informed man, coming here under the same circumstances, would omit to republish, according to our laws, his will, made at his former domicil, because he had concluded not to give legal effect, in this jurisdiction, to the views as to the disposition of his property which he entertained when it was executed. The only practical rule is, that every one must be supposed to know the law under which he lives, and conform his acts to it. This is the rule of law upon all other subjects, and I do not see any reason why it should not be in respect to the execution of wills.

In looking for precedents and juridical opinions upon such a question, we ought, before searching elsewhere, to resort to those of the country from which we derive our legal system, and to those furnished by the courts and jurists of our own country. It is only after we have exhausted these sources of instruction, without success, that we can profitably seek for light in the works of the jurists of the continent of Europe.

The principle adopted by the Surrogate is that, as to the formal requirements in the execution of a will, the law of the country where it was in fact signed and attested is to govern, provided the testator was then domiciled in such country, though he may have afterwards changed his domicile, and have been at his death a domiciled resident of a country whose laws required different formalities. Upon an attentive examination of the cases which have been adjudged in the English and American courts, I do not find anything to countenance this doctrine; but much authority, of quite a different tendency. The result of the cases, I think, is, that the jurisdiction in which the instrument was signed and attested, is of no consequence, but that its validity must be determined according to the domicil of the testator at the time of his death. Thus, in *Grattan* v. *Appleton* (3 Story's R., 755), the alleged testamentary papers were signed in Boston, where the assets were, and the testator died there, but he was domiciled in the British province of New Brunswick. The provincial statute required two attesting witnesses, but the alleged will was unattested. The court declared the papers invalid, Judge STORY stating the rule to be firmly established, that the law of the testator's domicil was to govern in relation to his personal property, though the will might have been executed in another state or country where a different rule prevailed. The

Judge referred, approvingly, to *Desesbats* v. *Berquier* (1 Bin., 336), decided as long ago as 1808. That was the case of a will executed in St. Domingo by a person domiciled there, and sought to be enforced in Pennsylvania, where the effects of the deceased were. It appeared not to have been executed according to the laws of St. Domingo, though it was conceded that it would have been a good will if executed by a citizen of Pennsylvania. The alleged will was held to be invalid. In the opinion delivered by Chief Justice TILGHMAN, the cases in the English ecclesiastical courts, and the authorities of the writers on the laws of nations, were carefully examined. It was declared to be settled, that the succession to the personal estate of an intestate was to be regulated according to the law of the country in which he was a domiciliated inhabitant at the time of his death, and that the same rule prevailed with respect to last wills. I have referred to these cases from respectable courts in the United States, because their judgments are more familiar to the bar than the reports of the spiritual courts in England. But these decisions are fully sustained by a series of well considered judgments of these courts. (*De Bonneval* v. *De Bonneval*, 1 Curt, 856; *Curling* v. *Thornton*, 2 Addams, 6; *Stanley* v. *Bernes*, 3 Hag., 373; *Countess Ferraris* v. *Hertford*, 3 Curt, 468.) It was for a time attempted to qualify the doctrine, in cases where the testator was a British subject who had taken up his residence and actual domicil in a foreign country, by the principle that it was legally impossible for one to abjure the country of his birth, and that therefore such a person could not change his domicil; but the judgment of the High Court of Delegates, in *Stanley* v. *Bernes*, finally put the question at rest. In that case an Englishman, domiciled in Portugal and resident in the Portuguese Island of Maderia, made a will and four codicils, all of which were executed according to the Portuguese law, except the last two codicils, and they were all executed so as to be valid wills by the law of England, if it governed the case. Letters were granted upon the will and two first codicils, but the other codicils were finally pronounced against. The Reporter's note expresses the result in these words: "If a testator (though a British subject) be domiciled abroad, he must conform, in his testamentary acts, to the formalities required by the *lex domicilii.*" See, also, *Somerville* v. *Somerville*, 5 Ves., 750; and *Price* v. *Dewhurst*, 8 Simons, 279, in the English Court of Chancery.)

It is true that none of these decisions present the case of a change of domicil, after the signing and attesting of a will. They are, notwithstanding, fully in point, if I have taken a correct view of the nature and effect of a will during the lifetime of the testator. But the remarks of judges in deciding the cases, and the understanding of the Reporters clearly show, that it is the domicil of the testator at the time of his death, which is to be considered in seeking for the law which is to determine the validity of the will. Thus, in *De Bonneval* v. *De Bonneval,* the question was upon the validity of the will executed in England, of a French nobleman who emigrated in 1792, and died in England in 1836. Sir HERBERT JENNER states it to have been settled by the case of *Stanley* v. *Bernes,* that the law of the place of the domicil, and not the *lex loci rei sitæ* governed "the distribution of, and succession, to personal property in *testacy* or intestacy." The Reporters' note is, that the validity of a will "is to be determined by the law of the country where the deceased was domiciled *at his death.*"

Nothing is more clear than that it is the law of the country where the deceased was domiciled at the time of his death, which is to regulate the succession of his personalty in the case of intestacy. Judge STORY says, that the universal doctrines were recognized by the common law, is, that the succession to personal property, *cb intestato,* is governed exclusively by the law of the actual domicil of the intestate at the time of his death. (Conf. Laws, § 481.) It would be plainly absurd to fix upon any prior domicil in another country. The one which attaches to him at the instant when the devolution of property takes place, is manifestly the only one which can have anything to do with the question. Sir RICHARD PEPPER ARDEN, Master of the Rolls, declared, in *Somerville* v. *Somerville,* that the rule was that the succession to the personal estate of an intestate was to be regulated by the law of the country in which he was domiciled at the time of his death, without any regard whatever to the place of nativity, or the place where his actual death happened, or the local situation of his effects.

Now, if the legal rules which prevail in the country where the deceased was domiciled at his death, are those which are to be resorted to in case of an intestacy, it would seem reasonable that the laws of the same country ought to determine whether in a given case there is an intestacy or not, and such we have seen was the view of Chief Justice TILGHMAN. Sir LANCELOT SHADWELL, Vice-Chancellor, in *Price* v. *Dewhurst,* also expressed the same view. He said, "I apprehend that it is now clearly established by a great variety of cases which it is not necessary to go through in detail, that the rule of law is this: that when a person dies intestate, his personal estate is to be administered according to the law of the country in which he was domiciled at the time of his death, whether he was a British subject or not; *and the question whether he died intestate or not must be determined by the law of the same country."* The method of arriving at a determination in the present case, according to this rule, is, to compare the evidence of the execution of his will with the requirements of the Revised Statutes. Such a comparison would show that the deceased did not leave a valid will, and consequently that he died intestate.

Being perfectly convinced that according to the principles of the common law, touching the nature of last wills, and according to the result of the cases in England and in this country which have been referred to, the will under consideration cannot be sustained, I have not thought it profitable to spend time in collecting the sense of the foreign jurists, many of whose opinions have been referred to and copiously extracted in the able opinion of the learned Surrogate, if I had convenient access to the necessary books, which is not the case. I understand it to be conceded that there is a diversity of opinion upon the point under consideration among these writers; but it is said that the authors who assert the doctrine on which I have been insisting, are not those of the highest character, and that their opinions have been criticised with success by M. Felix, himself a systematic writer of reputation on the conflict of laws. Judge STORY, however, who has wrought in this mine of learning with a degree of intelligence and industry which has excited the admiration of English and American judges, has come to a different conclusion. His language is, "but it may be asked, what will be the effect of a change of domicil after a will or testament is made, of personal or movable property, if it is valid by the law of the place where the party was domiciled when it was made, and not valid by the law of his domicil at the time of his death? The terms in which the general rule is laid down would seem sufficiently to establish the principle that in such a case the will and testament is void; for it is the law of his actual domicil at the time of his death, and not the law of his domicil at the time of his making his will and testament of personal property which is to govern." (§ 473.) He then quotes at length the language of John Voet to the same

36

general effect. It must, however, be admitted that the examples
put by that author, and quoted by Judge STORY, relate to testamentary capacity as determined by age, and to the legal ability
of the legatees to take, and not to the form of executing the
instrument. And the Surrogate has shown, by an extract from
the same author, that a will executed in one country according
to the solemnities there required, is not to be broken solely by a
change of domicil to a place whose laws demand other solemnities.
Of the other jurists quoted by the Surrogate, several of them
lay down rules diametrically opposite to those which confessedly
prevail in this country and in England. Thus, Tollier, a writer
on the civil law of France, declares that the form of testaments
does not depend upon the law of the domicil of the testator, but
upon the place where the instrument is in fact executed; and
Felix, Malin and Pothier are quoted as laying down the same
principle. But nothing is more clear, upon the English and
American cases, than that the place of executing the will, if it is
different from the testator's domicil, has nothing to do with determining the proper form of executing and attesting. In the case
referred to from Story's Reports, the will was executed in Boston,
but was held to be invalid because it was not attested as required
by a provincial statute of New Brunswick, which was the place
of the testator's domicil. If the present appeal was to be determined according to the civil law, I should desire to examine the
authorities more fully than I have been able to do; but considering it to depend upon the law as administered in the English
and American courts, and that according to the judgment of these
tribunals it is the law of the domicil of the testator at the time
of his death that is to govern, and not that of the place where the
paper happened to be signed and attested, where that is different
from his domicil at the time of his decease, I cannot doubt that
the Surrogate and Supreme Court fell into an error in establishing
the will.

I have not overlooked an argument which has been addressed
to us, based upon certain amendments of the Revised Statutes,
contained in chapter 320 of the act of 1830. The revised code
of the State, as originally enacted, had omitted to make provision
for the proving of wills, where the attesting witnesses resided
out of the State, and their attendance here could not be procured. The Surrogates' Courts, to which they committed the
proof of wills of real and personal estates, being tribunals of
special jurisdiction, and having no common law powers like the

Supreme Court, could not issue a commission in such cases, and hence there might often be a failure of justice. It might happen, in various ways, that the witnesses to a will would reside out of the jurisdiction of this State. If the will were executed here by a resident citizen, in the usual manner, the witnesses might change their residence and live in some other state or country, when it came to be proved; or it might be executed out of the State according to the forms prescribed by our statute of wills, by a resident of this State who was temporarily abroad. In either case the will would be perfectly valid, though the Surrogate having jurisdiction would be unable to admit it to probate for want of power to cause the testimony to be taken and returned. To remedy this inconvenience, five new sections were introduced, in 1830, by way of amendment, to the title of the Revised Statutes, respecting the proof of wills, numbered from 63 to 67, inclusive. The provision which they make is limited to the case of "a will duly executed according to the laws of this State, where the witnesses to the same reside out of the jurisdiction of this State;" and in regard to such wills, it is enacted, that they may be proved by means of a commission issued by the Chancellor upon the application of any person interested; and detailed directions are given respecting the return of the proof, the allowance of the will and the record of it in the office of the Surrogate having jurisdiction.

But, thus far, the proof of a will made in a foreign jurisdiction, according to the laws of such jurisdiction, and taking effect there by the death of the testator, was left unprovided for. Such wills are perfectly valid as to personal assets in this State, as was shown in *Parsons* v. *Lyman*. We recognize the foreign will, according to the comity of nations, just as we do the rules of distribution and of inheritance of another country when operating upon a domiciled citizen of such country who has died there, leaving assets in this State. Then, as to the proof of such wills, the section following those just mentioned provides for the case in these words: "Wills of personal estate, duly executed by persons residing out of the State, according to the laws of the state or country in which the same were made, may be proved under a commission to be issue by the Chancellor, and when so proved may be established and transmitted to the Surrogate having jurisdiction," &c. (§ 68.) The remainder of the section provides for the case of such a foreign will which has been proved in the foreign jurisdiction. Letters testamentary are to be issued in such cases upon the production of an authenticated copy of the will. It is clearly enough implied, perhaps, by the language of this section, that the will, to be proved and established under its provisions, and which is allowed to be executed, as to assets in this State, must be a legal will according to the law of the testator's domicil in which it was executed; but, for abundant caution, a section is added to the effect that "no will of personal estate, made out of this State, by a person not being a citizen of this State, shall be admitted to probate under either of the preceding provisions unless such will shall have been executed according to the laws of the state or country in which the same was made." (§ 69.) Chancellor WALWORTH appears to have understood the words, "a citizen of this State," as used in this section, to refer to political allegiance; and, "in the matter of Roberts' will," he held that the will then in question, executed in the island of Cuba, and which had been proved under a commission, and had been shown to be executed according to the laws of Spain, was a legal will, though the testator was a resident of this State at the time of his death. But he put the decision on the ground that the testator was a foreigner, and not a citizen, though domiciled here, and upon a verbal construction of the 69th section. But Mr. Hunt, the alleged testator in the will now in question, was not only domiciled here, but he was, at his death, a citizen of this State, and, consequently, the section, as interpreted by the Chancellor, has no application to the case. He, however, fully admitted the rule of law to be as I have stated it, in cases not within the influence of the 69th section. "The provision of the Revised Statutes requiring wills of personal property to be executed in the presence of two witnesses," he says, "does not apply to wills executed out of this State by persons domiciled in the state or country where the will is made, and who *continue* to be thus domiciled at the time the will takes effect by death." "As the testator resided in this State at the time of his death, in 1837, this will would be valid according to the law of the testator's domicil *when the will took effect by death*, if he had been a citizen at that time. But, as he was a foreigner, and there is no evidence that he was ever naturalized here, the amendments of the Revised Statutes of 1830, under which the present proceedings are instituted, expressly prohibit the admitting of the will to probate by a decree of this court, unless it was also duly executed according to the laws of the country where it was actually made." But for this case, I should have been of the opinion that the words, "a citizen of this

State," as used in the 69th section, did not refer to political allegiance, but were used in the sense of a demiciled inhabitant of this State. The meaning of the section would then be, that, if a person, other than a domiciled inhabitant of this State, makes his will out of the State, it must be executed according to the laws of the state or country where made. or it cannot be admitted to probate here, according to the preceding provisions of the act. The Chancellor seems to me to have taken the same view of the statute when passing upon the execution of the will of Catherine Roberts. (8 Paige, 519.) He says: "The statute, in express terms, authorizes a will of personalty executed out of the State, *by a person not domiciled here,* to be admitted to probate, provided it is duly executed according to the laws of the state or country where the same was made; and prohibits all other foreign wills from being admitted to probate, under the special provisions incorporated into the statutes of April, 1830." The words, "a person not domiciled here," are used in the paraphrase as the equivalent of "a person not being a citizen of this State:" and I think that rendering is perfectly correct. The provisions of the act do not, in my opinion, suggest any distinction between the place where a will is actually signed and attested and that in which it takes effect by the death of the testator. They are intended to provide simply for the case of the will of a person domiciled out of the State which it is desired to prove here; and the statutory mandate is, in effect, that it shall not be established here unless it was executed according to the requirements of the foreign law.

The will under immediate consideration was not, we think, legally executed; and the determination of the Surrogate and of the Supreme Court, which gave it effect, must be reversed.

FORD v. FORD, 1887.

[70 Wis. 19.]

1. The validity of every devise or disposition of real estate by will must be governed by the law of the place where the land is situated, and this includes not only the form and mode of the execution of the will, but also the lawful power and authority of the testator to make such disposition. Story, Confl. Laws, § 474, and note; 2 Greenl. Ev. § 670; 1 Redf. Wills, 398, subd. 8; *Robertson v. Pickrell*, 109 U. S. 608; *White v. Howard*, 46 N. Y. 144. The importance of this proposition in considering the validity of a will covering lands in so many different states will be appreciated by all.

2. On the contrary although not as well defined, nor as extensively enforced, yet the authorities clearly support the prop-osition that the validity of a bequest or disposition of personal property by last will and testament must be governed by the law of the testator's domicile at the time of his death, and this includes not only the form and mode of the execution of the will, but also the lawful power and authority of the testator to make such disposition; and especially is this true where, as here, the testator's domicile at the time of making his will continues to be the same until the time of his death. Story, Confl. Laws, §§ 467, 468; *Stewart v. McMartin*, 5 Barb. 438; *Moultrie v. Hunt*, 23 N. Y. 394; *Nat v. Coons*, 10 Mo. 543; *Desesbats v. Berquier*, 1 Bin. 336; *S. C.* 2 Am. Dec. 448; *Somerville v. Somerville*, 5 Ves. Jr. 750, 786; *Anstruther v. Chalmer*, 2 Sim. 1; *Price v. Dewhurst*, 8 Sim. 279; *S. C.* on appeal, 4 Mylne & C. 76; *Enohin v. Wylie*, 8 Jur. (N. S.), 897; *S. C.* 10 H. L. Cas. 1; *Crispin v. Doglioni*, 8 J. U. R. (M. S.) 633; *S. C.* on appeal, L. R. 1 H. L. App. Cas. 301; *Eames v. Hacon*, L. R. 16 Ch. Div. 407; *S. C.* on appeal, L. R. 18 Ch. Div. 347. This is not shaken by the criticism of Lord WESTBURY'S opinion in *Enohin v. Wylie*, *supra*, by the Earl of SELBORNE, L. C., in *Ewing v. Ewing*, L. R. 9 App. Cas. 39.

3. The same rule, as to the law of the testator's domicile, governs in the interpretation or construction of wills. Story, Confl. Laws, §§ 479a–479c; *Van Steenwyck v. Washburn*, 59 Wis. 510. In the words of Mr. Justice STORY: "The language of wills is not of universal interpretation, having the same precise import in all countries and under all circumstances. They are supposed to speak the sense of the testator according to the received laws or usages of the country where he is domiciled, by a sort of tacit reference, unless there is something in the language which repels or controls such a conclusion." *Harrison v. Nixon*, 9 Pet. 504; *Trotter v. Trotter*, 4 Bligh (N. S.), 502; *Enohin v. Wylie, supra; Chamberlain v. Napier*, L. R. 15 Ch. Div. 614. The general rule is the same respecting real estate, when-ever the object is merely to ascertain the meaning and intent of the testator from the language employed in the will. *Ibid.;* 2 Greenl. Ev. § 671.[23]

---

[23]"If testator changes domicil before death, law of domicil at time will was made determines interpretation. *Atkinson v. Staigg, 13 R. I. 725.* A will is to be construed according to the law of the place of his domicil in which it is made. *Ford v. Ford, 80 Mich. 42.*
In the case of *Despard v. Churchill, 53 N. Y. 192,* the Court said:

The testator had his domicil in the state of California. He made his will there. No question is made but that it is in all of its provisions valid by the law of that state. It, however, by its terms, disposes of certain property in this state and by provisions which are invalid here, inasmuch as they run counter to our statute law. The statute law here referred to embodies the *policy* of this state in relation to perpetuities and accumulations. As this sovereignty will not uphold a devise or bequest by one of its citizens in contravention of that policy, it will not give its direct aid to sustain, enforce or administer here such a devise or bequest made by a citizen of another sovereignty.

In *Edgerly v. Bush, 81 N. Y. 199,* the Court held: The exercise of comity in admitting or restraining the application of the laws of another country must rest in sound judicial discretion, dictated by the circumstances of the case.

EXECUTION OF POWER IN WILL.

COTTING v. DE SARTIGES, 1892.

[17 R. I. 668, 16 L. R. A. 367.]

BILL IN EQUITY for instructions and for the administration of a trust.

Newport, March 28 1892. STINESS, J. The complainant, trustee under the will of Mary M. Bourne, late of Newport, deceased, brings this bill, practically a bill for instructions, for the distribution of the trust fund, and the case is submitted on bill, answer, and proofs. The will was dated September 30, 1879, and admitted to probate in Newport January 16, 1882. The testatrix bequeathed one-sixth of her residuary estate to the complainant in trust for the benefit of her grandson, Charles Allen Thorndike Rice, during his life, and upon his decease to transfer and pay over the same to his issue, if he should leave any, as he should appoint "by will, or instrument in the nature thereof, executed in the presence of three or more witnesses; and if he leaves no issue, to and among such persons, and upon such uses and trusts, as he shall so appoint;" and in default of such appointment and issue, to and among those who should then be her heirs at law.

The grandson died in New York, May 16, 1889, without issue; leaving a will executed in England, September 17, 1881, which was duly probated in New York, where he was domiciled at his death. The will did not specifically dispose of the trust fund, which was subject to Mr. Rice's appointment, nor make any mention of it. The complainant is both trustee under the will of

Mrs. Bourne and executor of the will of Mr. Rice. In the latter capacity he claims the right to receive and distribute the fund, as one which passes by appointment to the legatees under Rice's will. On the other hand, the heirs of Mrs. Bourne contend that there is a default of appointment, and so, under the will, the fund goes to them. The issue now raised, therefore, is whether there has been an execution of the power by the general residuary clause of Mr. Rice's will. Upon this issue our first inquiry must be, by what law the execution of the power is to be determined. It is admitted that both in England, where the will was executed, and in New York, where the donee of the power was domiciled, there are statutory provisions to the effect that a general devise or bequest will include property over which the testator has power of appointment, and will operate as an execution of such power, unless an intention not to execute the power shall appear by the will. If, therefore, the question is to be determined by the law of either England or New York, the power has been executed. Clearly the mere accident that Mr. Rice's will was executed in England, while he was temporarily there awaiting a steamer, cannot control its operation by impressing upon it the law of the place where it was made. It was neither the domicile of the testator, nor the *situs* of the property, nor the *forum* where the question comes for determination. *Caulfield* v. *Sullivan*, 85 N. Y. 153. The property in dispute being personal property, which, strictly speaking, has no *situs*, the question must be decided by the law either of New York, the domicile of the donee of the power, or of this State, the domicile of the donor. The will is a Rhode Island will; it disposes of property belonging to a resident of Rhode Island; the trustee under the will is, in effect, a Rhode Island trustee, and jurisdiction over the trustee and the fund is here. The fund in question belonged to Mrs. Bourne, and never belonged to Mr. Rice. True, he had the income from it for life, and power to dispose of it at death; practically the dominion of an owner, and yet it was not his.

The fund, then, being a Rhode Island fund, disposable under a Rhode Island will, it follows, naturally and necessarily, that the fact of its disposition must be determined by Rhode Island law.

The question is not what intent is to be imputed to the will of Mr. Rice, but what intent is to be imputed to the will of Mrs. Bourne. She authorized a disposition of her property by an appointment, and it is under her will that the question arises whether an appointment has been made. Her will is to be adjudged by the law of her domicile. So far as assumptions of intent may be made, it is to be presumed she intended the appointment to be made according to the law of her domicile, and not by the law of New York or England, or any other place where the donee of the power might happen to live. It is not the fact of Mrs. Bourne's ownership of the property which points to the law of this State as the criterion, but the fact that her will is the controlling instrument in the disposition of the property. Precisely this question arose in *Sewell v. Wilmer*, 132 Mass. 131, where Judge Gray remarked that the question is singularly free of direct authority. In that case a Massachusetts testator gave to his daughter a power of appointment of certain property. The daughter lived in Maryland, where she died, leaving a will devising all her property to her husband, but making no mention of the power. In Massachusetts this was an execution of the power, but in Maryland it was not; and the question arose which law should govern. It was held that the will of the father was the controlling instrument, and hence that the law of his domicile was to apply. The same decision was made in *Bingham's Appeal*, 64 Pa. St. 345, which is cited in *Sewall v. Wilmer* with approval. In England, also, it has been held that the validity of the execution of a power is to be determined by the law of the domicile of the donor of the power. *Tatnall v. Haukey*, 2 Moore P. C. 342; *In re Alexander*, 6 Jur. N. S. 354.

The principle on which these cases proceed is that to which we have already alluded, viz., that the appointer is merely the instrument by whom the original testator designates the beneficiary, and the appointee takes under the original will, and not from the donee of the power. The law of the domicile of the original testator is, therefore, the appropriate test of an execution of a power. The case of *D'Huart v. Harkness*, 34 Beav. 324, 328, apparently holds the contrary, but, we think, only apparently. In that case property was held under an English will, with power of appointment, by will, in a woman domiciled in France. She died, leaving a holograph which was valid as a will in France, but not in England. Under the Wills Act it was admitted to probate in England as a foreign will, which gave it all the validity of an English will. The probate in England was held to be conclusive that it was a good will according to English law, and being a will it executed the power. The case was really decided by the law of England. While there are numerous decisions upon the geneial rule that a will is to be governed by the law of the testator's domicile, such decisions are not to be confounded with the present question : Which testator is the one to be considered in the case of a testamentary power? We know of no case which applies the law of the domicile of the donee of the power without reference to that of the donor. For these reasons we think the law of the domicile of the doner of the power should control, and hence that the law of Rhode Island must goven in this case.

What is the law of Rhode Island relating to the execution of a power? In *Phillips* v. *Brown*, 16 R. I. 279, the general rule of construction, laid down by Kent, both as to deeds and wills, that if an interest and a power coexist in the same person, an act done without reference to the power will be applied to the interest and not to the power, was examined and followed. The same rule was also followed in *Grundy* v. *Hadfield*, 16 R. I. 579, and in *Brown* v. *Phillips*, 16 R. I. 612. In *Matteson* v. *Goddard*, ante, p. 299, it was held that a general residuary clause in a will did not execute a subsequently created power of appointment. While those cases are not decisive of this one, the reasoning upon which they rest is equally applicable, viz., where nothing appears to show an intent to execute a power, the court cannot infer an intent to do so. This was the almost uniform rule prior to the adoption of statutes upon this subject. In New York and in England it was thought that the rule often defeated the intention of testators who probably intended to dispose of everything they had power to dispose of; and so acts were passed which carried property, over which one had a power of appointment, by a general gift of his own property, unless an intention not to execute the power appeared. We do not see that the reason upon which such statutes are based is conclusive. It is equally open to conjecture that one who means to execute a power will signify in some way an intention to do so. If a computation could be made, it would doubtless appear that, in the execution of powers, a large majority of wills make proper reference to the power. The statute gives an arbitrary direction, against which, it seems to us, the reason is stronger than for it. The rule already recognized in this State is as applicable to wills as to deeds, and in our opinion it should be so applied. The same rule is laid down in *Mines* v. *Gambrill*, 71 Md. 30; *Hollister* v. *Shaw*, 46 Conn. 248; *Funk* v. *Eggleston*, 92 Ill. 515; *Bilderbach* v. *Boyce*, 14 S. Car. 528, and cases cited in our previous opinions. The same rule also pervailed in England, New York, and Pennsylvania prior to the passage of statutes. In Massachusetts alone was a contrary rule adopted by the court. The law, therefore, has been practically uniform except as it has been changed by statutes. It is urged that these statutes show a tendency of opinion which the court should follow by adopting the rule of the statutes. The opportunity to make law is alluring, but it tempts beyond the judicial path. As our province is to declare law rather than to make it, we deem it our duty to adhere to the rule which is commended to us by reason and precedent, until, as elsewhere, it shall be changed by legislative authority. If such a rule be the wiser one, the legislature can enact it; but outside of a statute it is hard to see upon what ground a court can decree an intention to execute a power when in fact no such intention is in any way evinced. Applying to this case, then, the rule that, to support an execution of a power, something must appear to show an intent to execute it, we come to the inquiry whether such an intent appears. To solve this we must look to the will itself and not to extrinsic facts, except as they enter into and give color to the will. In the will there is no reference to the power, but it is urged that an intention to execute the power is to be inferred from its contents and the circumstances of its execution. It is claimed that Rice's relations with his grandmother were so intimate as to raise a presumption that he knew the contents of her will, especially in view of the fact that his bequests exceeded the amount of his own estate. Rice's will was made at Liverpool pursuant to a suggestion from the complainant that, owing to the will of his grandmother, he ought not to cross the ocean without making his will. He received $625,000 outright under his grandmother's will, beside the income of one sixth of the residuary estate for life, with the power of appointment. If he knew of this power, it is most natural that he would in some way have referred to it. If he knew the amount absolutely bequeathed to him, or expected a large bequest, it would account for all the legacies in his will. After he knew of the power of appointment he did not change his will. Perhaps his mind so dwelt upon the legacy of $625,000 that he gave no thought to a possible appointment of one fifth of that amount in the residuary clause; or perhaps, after hearing of the power, he intended some time to make a disposition of it. But, however it was, he gave no sign as to the power. The fact that at the time of his death his estate was somewhat less than his bequests is not significant; for evidently he was not a close financier, and gave little heed to the depreciation of his estate. The deficiency, however, is not so marked as to raise a presumption in favor of the execution of the power, even if we could properly look to that fact for that purpose. This and several other interesting legal questions have been raised and ably presented, upon the point of intention, but we do not deem it necessary to pass upon them, inasmuch as we do not find from the facts any sufficient or satisfactory evidence of an intention to execute the power. We therefore decide that the fund in question did not so pass by appointment under the will of Mr. Rice, and therefore belongs to the heirs of Mrs. Bourne according to the terms of her will.   *Decree accordingly.*[29]

---

[29]See *Bullerdick v. Wright, 148 Ind. 477, 47 N. E. 931; Meeker v. Breintnall, 38 N. J. Eq. 345; Hassam v. Hazen, 156 Mass. 93, 30 N. E. 469; Kimball v. Bible Society, 65 N. H. 139, 23 Atl. Rep. 83; In re Price, 1 Chan. Rep. 442 (1900); In re D'Estes Settlement, 1 Ch. Rep. 898 (1903); Lane v. Lane, 55 Atl. Rep. 184 (1903).*

CHAPTER XVI.

PROCEDURE.

[Dicey Conflict of Laws, Chap. 31.*]

1. Procedure.
2. Pleading Foreign Laws.
3. Judicial Notice and Proof of Foreign Laws.
4. Presumption as to Foreign Law.

All matter of procedure are governed wholly by the local or territorial law of the country to which a Court wherein an action is brought or other legal proceeding is taken belongs (*lex fori*).

In this Digest the term "procedure" is to be taken in its widest sense, and includes (*inter alia*)—

(1) remedies and process;
(2) evidence;
(3) limitation of an action or other proceeding;
(4) set-off or counter-claim.

COMMENT.

The principle that procedure is governed by the *lex fori* is of general application and universally admitted, but the Courts of any country can apply it only to proceedings which take place in, or at any rate under the law of, that country. In a body of Rules, therefore, such as those contained in this Digest, which state the principles enforced by an English Court, the maxim that procedure is governed by the *lex fori* means in effect that it is governed by the ordinary law of England, without any reference to any foreign law whatever. The maxim is in fact a negative rule; it lays down that the High Court, in common, it may be added, with every other English Court, pursues its ordinary practice and adheres to its ordinary methods of investigation whatever be the character of the parties, or the nature of the cause which is brought before it.

"A person," it has been said, "suing in this country, must take "the law as he finds it; he cannot, by virtue of any regulation in "his own country, enjoy greater advantages than other suitors

---

*This chapter is inserted by permission of the American Publisher of "Dicey on the Conflict of Laws."

"here, and he ought not therefore to be deprived of any superior
"advantage which the law of this country may confer. He is to
"have the same rights which all the subjects of this kingdom are
"entitled to," and the foreign defendant, it may be added, is to
have the advantages, if any, which the form of procedure in this
country gives to every defendant.

Whilst, however, it is certain that all matters which concern
procedure are in an English Court governed by the law of England, it is equally clear that everything which goes to the substance
of a party's rights and does not concern procedure is governed by
the law appropriate to the case.

"The law on this point is well settled in this country, where
"this distinction is properly taken, that whatever relates to the
"remedy to be enforced must be determined by the *lex fori*,—the
"law of the country to the tribunals of which the appeal is made,"
but that whatever relates to the rights of the parties must be determined by the proper law of the contract or other transaction
on which their rights depend.

Our Rule is clear and well established. The difficulty of its
application to a given case lies in discriminating between matters
which belong to *procedure* and matters which affect the *substantive rights* of the parties. In the determination of this question
two considerations must be borne in mind:—

First. English lawyers give the widest possible extension to
the meaning of the term "procedure." The expression, as interpreted by our judges, includes all legal remedies, and everything
connected with the enforcement of a right. It covers, therefore,
the whole field of practice; it includes the whole law of evidence,
as well as every rule in respect of the limitation of an action or of
any other legal proceeding for the enforcement of a right, and
hence it further includes the methods, *e. g.*, seizure of goods or
arrest of person, by which a judgment may be enforced.

Secondly. Any rule of law which solely affects, not the *enforcement* of a right but the *nature* of the right itself, does not
come under the head of procedure. Thus, if the law which governs, *e. g.*, the making of a contract, renders the contract absolutely void, this is not a matter of procedure, for it affects the
rights of the parties to the contract, and not the remedy for the
enforcement of such rights.

Hence any rule limiting the time within which an action may
be brought, any *limitation* in th strict sense of that word, is a matter of procedure governed wholly by the *lex fori*. But a rule

which after the lapse of a certain time extinguishes a right of action—a rule of *prescription* in the strict sense of that word—is not a matter of procedure, but a matter which touches a person's substantive rights, and is therefore governed, not by the *lex fori,* but by the law, whatever it may be, which governs the right in question. Thus if, in an action for a debt incurred in France, the defence is raised that the action is barred under French law by lapse of time, or that for want of some formality an action could not be brought for the debt in a French Court, the validity of the defence depends upon the real nature of the French law relied upon. If that law merely takes away the plaintiff's *remedy,* it has no effect in England. If, on the other hand, the French law extinguishes the plaintiff's *right* to be paid the debt, it affords a complete defence to an action in England.

To this it must be added that an English statutory enactment, which affects both a person's rights and the method of its enforcement, establishes a rule of procedure and therefore applies to an action in respect of a right acquired under foreign law. Hence the 4th Section of the Statute of Frauds, and the 4th Section of the Sale of Goods Act, 1893, which, whether affecting rights or not, certainly affect procedure, apply to actions on contracts made in a foreign country and governed by foreign law. Whence the conclusion follows that a contract though made abroad, which does not satisfy the provisions of the 4th section of the Statute of Frauds, or of the Sale of Goods Act, 1893, respectively, cannot be enforced in England.

With regard to the Illustrations to this Rule it must always be borne in mind that, as we are dealing with proceedings before an English Court, the *lex fori* is the same thing as the law of England.

ILLUSTRATIONS.

(*1*) *Remedies and Process.*

1. *A* brings an action against *X* to obtain specific performance of a contract made between *A* and *X* in and subject to the law of a foreign country. The contract is one of which *A* might, according to the law of that country (*lex loci contractus*), obtain specific performance, but it is not one for which specfic perform ance can be granted according to the law of England (*lex fori*). *A* cannot maintain an action for specifi performance.

2. *A* brings an action against *X* for breach of a contract

made with X in Scotland as a member of a Scotch firm. According to the law of Scotland (*lex loci contractus*), A could not maintain an action against X until he had sued the firm, which he has not done. According to the law of England (*lex fori*), the right to bring an action against the member of a firm does not depend upon the firm having been first sued. A can maintain an action against X.

3. A, a Portuguese, at a time when arrest of a debtor on mesne process is allowable under the law of England (*lex fori*), but is not allowable under the law of Portugal (*lex loci contractus*), brings an action against X, a Portuguese, for a debt contracted in Portugal. A has a right to arrest X.

4. A in Spain sells X goods of the value of £50. The contract is made by word of mouth, and there is no memorandum of it in writing. The contract is valid and enforceable according to Spanish law (*lex loci contractus*). A contract of this description is, under the Sale of Goods Act, 1893, s. 4 (*lex fori*), not enforceable by action. A cannot maintain an action against X for refusal to accept the goods.

(2) Evidence.

5. A brings an action against X to recover a debt incurred by X in and under the law of a foreign country (*lex loci contractus*). A tenders evidence of the debt which is admissible by the law of the foreign country, but is inadmissible by the law of England (*lex fori*). The evidence is inadmissible.

6. A brings an action against X, an Englishman, for breach of a promise of marriage made by X to A, a German woman, at Constantinople. A has not such corroborative evidence as is required by 32 & 33 Vict. cap. 68, s. 2 (*lex fori*). A cannot prove the promise or maintain the action.

7. A, a Frenchman, makes a contract in France with X, an Englishman, to serve him in France from a future date for a year certain. The contract is made by word of mouth, and there is no memorandum of it in writing. It is a contract valid by the law of France (*lex loci contractus*), for the breach of which an action might be brought in a French Court, but under the 4th section of the Statute of Frauds no action can be brought on such an agreement unless there is a memorandum thereof in writing. The enactment applies to procedure. A cannot maintain an action in England against X for breach of the contract.

'3) *Limitation.*

8. *X* contracts a debt to *A* in Scotland. The recovery of the debt is not barred by lapse of time, according to Scotch law (*lex loci contractus*), but it is barred by the English Limitation Act, 1623, 21 Jac. I. cap. 16 (*lex fori*). *A* cannot maintain an action against *X*.

9. *X* incurs a debt to *A* in France. The recovery of such a debt is barred by the French law of limitation (*lex loci contractus*), but is not barred by any English Statute of Limitation. *A* can maintain an action for the debt against *X*.

10. *A* in a Manx Court brings an action against *X* for a debt incurred by *X* to *A* in the Isle of Man. The action, not being brought within three years from the time when the cause of action arose, is barred by Manx law, and judgment is on that account given in favor of *X*. *A* then, within six years from the time when the debt is incurred, brings an action against *X* in England. This action is not barred by the English Limitation Act, 1623 (*lex fori*). *A* can maintain his action against *X*.

11. *X*, under a bond made in India, is bound to repay *A* £100. Specialty debts have, under the law of India (*lex loci contractus*), no higher legal value than simple contract debts, and under that law the remedy for both is barred by the lapse of three years. The period of limitation for actions on specialty debts is, under the law of England,—3 & 4 Will. IV. cap. 42, s. 3, (*lex fori*),—twenty years. *A*, ten years after the execution of the bond, brings an action in England upon it against *X*. *A* can maintain the action.

(4) *Set-off.*

12. *X* in 1855 contracts in Prussia with *A* for the carriage by *A* of goods by sea from Memel to London. *A* brings an action against *X* for the freight, and *X* under Prussian law (*lex loci contractus*), claims to set off money, due to him by way of damages from *A*, which could not at that date be made, according to the rules of English procedure (*lex fori*), the subject either of a set-off or a counter-claim. *X* is not allowed to set off, against the money due to *A*, the damages due from *A* to *X*.

Lex Fori not Applicable.

13. *A* brings an action on a contract made by word of mouth between *X* and *A* in and under the law of a foreign country. It is a kind of contract which under the law of England (*lex fori*)

is valid though not made in writing, but under the law of the foreign country (*lex loci contractus*) is void if not made in writing. *A* cannot maintain this action, *i. e.*, the validity of the contract is governed in England, not by the *lex fori*, but by the *lex loci contractus*.

14. *A* brings an action against *X* for breach of a contract made in a foreign country. It is proved that under the law of that country (*lex loci contractus*) the contract for want of a stamp is uninforceable. If the want of the stamp merely deprives *A* of his remedy in the foreign country, then he can maintain an action in England for breach of the contract, *i. e.*, the want of the stamp merely affects procedure which is governed by the *lex fori*. If the want of a stamp makes the contract void *ab inito*, then *A* cannot maintain an action in England, *i. e.*, the want of a stamp affects a matter of right and is governed by the *lex loci contractus*.

15. *X* commits an assault upon *A* in Jamaica. For some time after the assault is committed, *A* might, had *X* been in England, have maintained an action for it there against *X*. Before *X* returns to England the legislature of Jamaica passes an Act whereby *X* is in respect of the assault acquitted and indemnified against the Queen and all other persons, and the assault is declared to be lawful. *X* then returns to England, and *A* brings an action against *X* for the assault. *A* cannot maintain the action, *i. e.*, the character of the act done by *X*, or *A*'s right to treat it as a wrong, is governed, not by the *lex fori*, but by the *lex loci delicti commissi*.[30]

[30]**Procedure.**—A person suing in this country must take the law as he finds it; he cannot, by virtue of any regulation in his own country, enjoy greater advantages than other suitors here, and he ought not therefore to be deprived of any superior advantage which the law of this country may confer. *De La Vega v. Vianna, 1 Barn. & Adolph., 284 (1830); Atwater v. Townsend, 4 Conn. 47; Smith v. Spinolla, 2 Johns. 198.*

Remedies are governed by the law of the forum. A confession of judgment pertains to the remedy. A party seeking to enforce here a contract made in another state must do so in accordance with the laws of this state. Parties cannot by contract made in another state engraft upon our procedure here remedies which our laws do not authorize. *Hamilton v. Schoenberger, 47 Iowa 385 (1877).*

The law of the remedy is no part of the contract. All questions as to forms or methods, or conduct or process or remedy, statutes of limitations, statute of frauds, set-offs, and exemptions are all governed by the law of the place where suit is brought. *Mineral Point Ry. Co. v. Barron, 83 Ill. 365 (1876); Hoadley v. Transportation Co., 115 Mass. 304.* For a discussion as to the law that shall control in case of a statute of limitations, see *Townsend v. Jemison, 9 How. 407 (1849).*

Questions of evidence, such as whether a witness is competent or not, whether a writing is required or not, whether a stamp is necessary, and questions of damages or interest, all those are determined by the law of the forum. *Bain v. Whitehaven, 3 H. L. C. 1.*

1. If a contract be entered into in one place to be performed in another, and the rate of interest differ in the two countries, the parties may stipulate for the rate of interest of either country, and thus by their own express contract, determine with reference to the law of which country that incident of the contract shall be decided. 2. If the contract, so entered into, stipulate for interest generally, it shall be the rate of interest of the place of payment, unless it appear the parties intended to contract with reference to the law of the other place. 3. If the contract be so entered into, for money, payable at a place on a day certain, and no interest be stipulated, and payment be delayed, interest, by way of damages, shall be allowed according to the law of the place of payment where the money may be supposed to have been required by the creditor for use, and where he might be supposed to have borrowed money to supply the deficiency thus occurring, and to have paid the rate of interest of that country. *3 Kent 116; Peck v. Mayo, 14 Vt. 33; Ayer v. Tilden, 15 Gray 178; Meyer v. Estes, 164 Mass. 457.*

An agreement to pay an additional percentage as costs for collection of the note may be enforced where the note was executed, but the courts of another state or country are not bound to do so. The effect of such an agreement was to provide for an increase of costs which must depend upon the law of the forum, and if in the nature of a penalty, may not be enforced at all. *Commercial Bank v. Davidson, 18 Oregon 57 (1889).*

Pleading Foreign Laws.—Foreign laws must be specially pleaded unless the rule is changed by statute. If the foreign law is immaterial or a mere matter of evidence it need not be pleaded. Under this rule, the States of the Union are foreign to one another. *Raynham v. Canton, 3 Pick. 293; Thomson-Houston Electric Co. v. Palmer. 52 Minn. 174, 53 N. W. Rep. 1137; Thatcher v. Morris, 11 N. Y. 437; Liverpool Steam Co. v. Ins. Co., 129 U. S. 397; Kelley v. Kelley, 161 Mass. 111; In re Capper's Will, 85 Iowa 82.*

Judicial Notice and Proof of Foreign Laws.—Foreign Laws, like other facts, must be proved, unless established by presumptions. The state courts do not take judicial notice of the laws of sister states or of foreign countries. The federal courts in enforcing state laws within their territorial jurisdiction, take judicial notice of them. The Supreme Court of the United States, in hearing appeals from federal courts, takes judicial notice of the laws of the states, but in hearing a case from a state court it takes judicial notice of the laws of the state from which the case comes and that is all. *Kline v. Baker, 99 Mass. 253; Liverpool Steam Co. v. Ins. Co., 120 U. S. 397; Hanley v. Donaghue, 116 U. S. 1, 277.* In speaking of the proof of foreign law, the court, in the case of *Finney v. Guy, 189 U. S. 335 (1903),* said: "Although the law of a foreign jurisdiction may be proved as a fact, yet the evidence of a witness stating what the law of a foreign jurisdiction is, founded upon the terms of a statute, and the decisions of the courts thereon as to its meaning and effect, is really a matter of opinion, although proved as a fact, and courts are not concluded thereby from themselves consulting and construing the statutes and decisions which have been themselves proved, or from deducing a result from their own examination of them that may differ from that of a witness upon the same matter."

In *Owings v. Hull, 9 Pet. (U. S.) 607 (1835),* Judge Story said: "We are of opinion that the circuit court was bound to take judicial notice of the laws of Louisiana. The circuit courts of the United States are created by congress, not for the purpose of administering the local law of a single state alone, but to administer the laws of all the states in the

Union in cases to which they respectfully apply. The judicial power conferred on the general government by the constitution extends to many cases arising under the laws of the different states. And this court is called upon, in the exercise of its appellate jurisdiction, constantly to take notice of and administer the jurisprudence of all the states. That jurisprudence is, then, in no just sense, a foreign jurisprudence, to be proved, in the courts of the United States, by the ordinary modes of proof by which the laws of a foreign country are to be established; but it is to be judicially taken notice of in the same manner as the laws of the United States are taken notice of by these courts."

Statutory law is proved by producing the statute itself, or such a copy of it as is approved by the law of the forum. The judicial decisions are not usually received to prove the statute law, but such decisions may be received to determine the proper construction of the foreign law. *Kenny v. Clarkson, 1 Johns, Rep. 385; Emery v. Berry, 28 N. H. 473, 61 Am. Dec. 622; Tenant v. Tenant, 110 Pa. St. 478, 1 Atl. 532; Gilchrist v. Oil Co., 21 W. Va. 115, 45 Am. Rep. 555; Jessup v. Carnegie, 80 N. Y. 441, 36 Am. Rep. 643; Bucher v. Ry. Co., 125 U. S. 555; Van Matre v. Sankey, 148 Ill. 356, 23 L. R. A. 665.*

The common law or unwritten law of a country is to be proved by the best evidence. It may be proved by the testimony of judges or lawyers of the foreign state, or it may be proved by the official reports of cases. *Hall v. Costello, 48 N. H. 176; Loring v. Thorndike, 5 Allen 257; Ganer v. Lanesborough, 11 Cl. & F. 124; Gardner v. Lewis, 7 Gill 378; Ufford v. Spaulding, 156 Mass. 65; Alexander v. Pa. Co., 48 Ohio St. 623, 30 N. E. 69; Kelley v. Kelley, 161 Mass. 111.*

Presumption as to Foreign Law.—In the absence of any evidence to the contrary, it is presumed that the law of a foreign country is like our own, providing that the law in this country is not statute law. This presumption exists as between states or countries whose system is based upon the common law. This presumption cannot be used to ascertain the law of a foreign country whose laws are founded upon some other system, such for instance, as the civil law. *Com. v. Graham, 157 Mass. 73; Buchanan v. Hubbard, 119 Ind. 187, 21 N. E. 538; Thorn v. Weatherly, 50 Ark. 37; Mohr v. Meisen, 47 Minn. 228; Flagg v. Baldwin, 38 N. J. Eq. 219, 48 Am. Rep. 308; Knapp v. Knapp, 55 N. W. Rep. 353; Houghtailing v. Ball, 19 Mo. 84, 59 Am. Dec. 331.*

FINIS.

INDEX

ALIENS:
 liability of, for crimes committed on high seas, 16-53.
 status may be determined by commercial domicil, 82-88.
 friends and enemies, 124, 125.
 rights of, 124, 125.
 where they may sue, 126-149.

ALIEN ENEMIES:
 may be ascertained by commercial domicil, 82-88, 124.

ALIMONY:
 what jurisdiction is necessary in case of, 184-200.

ALLEGIANCE:
 distinguished from domicil, 58-79.
 defined, 106-126.

AMBASSADORS:
 privileges of, 47.

ANIMUS MANENDI:
 in domicil, 56.

APPEARANCE:
 as a part of procedure, 573-580.

APPOINTMENT:
 of executors and receivers, 215-229.
 power of, in a will, 567-572.

APPRENTICE:
 domicil of, 96.

ASSAULT:
 committed on high seas, 16-53.

ASSIGNEE:
 in bankruptcy, 200-214.

ASSIGNMENT:
 of a vessel on the high seas, 52.
 in bankruptcy, 200-214.
 of personal property, 362-379.

ATTACHMENT
 of a debt, 254-261.

BANKRUPTCY:
 title of foreign assigns in, 204, 214.
 statutory assignment in, 204, 210, 211, 214.
 voluntary assignment in, 204, 214.
 when foreign assignees may sue, 204, 206, 209.
 jurisdiction necessary in cases of, 211, 213.
 discharge of debt in case of, 213, 214.
 administration in, 214.

38

MARRIAGE SETTLEMENTS:
   extra-territorial effect of, 352-361.

MARRIED WOMEN:
   domicil of, 89-95.
   when married woman may choose domicil, 89-95, 184-200.
   property rights of, 352-361.
   power to contract, 493.

MATRIMONIAL DOMICIL: 184-200.
   determines property rights, 352-361.

MINORS:
   domicil of, 95, 96.
   cannot change domicil, 95, 96.
   emancipation gives capacity to choose domicil, 95, 96.
   capacity of determined by what law, 262-265.

MORTGAGES:
   of personal property, 400.
   of real estate, 401.

MOVABLES:
   alienation of, in uncivilized countries, 104.
   action in case of injury to, 126-149.
   assignment of, in case of bankruptcy, 200-214.
   control of executors, administrators, trustees, and receivers, over, 215-229.
   jurisdiction of, in cases of attachment or garnishment, 254-261.
   extra-territorial transfers of, 362-379.
   conditional sales of, 380, 386, 392.
   mortgages of, 400.
   gifts of, 397.
   distribution of, where no will, 547-553.
   validity of will of, 553-567.

NATIONS:
   territorial jurisdiction of, 16-53.

NATIONALITY·
   is not determined by domicil, 57, 58.
   in United States, 106-125.

NATURALIZATION:
   citizens by, 106-125.
   who may become citizens by, 123, 124.
   who may provide for, in United States, 106-125.
   methods of, 106-125.
   conditions of, 124.

NEUTRALS:
   commercial domicil may determine status of, 82-88.

SOLDIERS:
    domicil of, 96.
SOVEREIGNTY:
    of states, 169-184.
STAMP LAWS:
    extra-territorial effect of, 573-580.
STATE:
    territorial jurisdiction of, 16-53, 169-184.
    bankrupt or insolvency laws, effect of, 200-214.
    power of to exclude corporations, 265-282.
    what constitutes doing business in, 281.
STATUS:
    of children is determined by domicil of parents, 64.
    political and civil explained, 72.
    what each kind of status determines, 72.
STATUTES:
    extra-territorial effect if penal, 150-168.
STATUTES OF DESCENT:
    law of, in case of real estate, 547-553.
STATUTES OF DISTRIBUTION
    what law governs in personal property, 547-553.
STATUTE OF FRAUDS·
    effect of, on contracts, 481, et. seq.
    as procedure, 573-580.
STATUTE OF LIMITATIONS:
    as procedure, 573-580.
STUDENTS:
    domicil of, 96.
    right to vote, 96.
SUCCESSION
    to movable property, is governed by what law, 100.
    intestate, law of domicil determines distribution of personality, 547-552.
    intestate, law of place where real estate is situated governs, 547-552.
    to real estate by will, 553-567.
    to personal property by will, 553-567.
SUCCESSION DUTY:
    is governed by the law of what place, 98-101.
TAXES:
    domicil as a basis for, 98-101.
    on personal property, what law governs, 99-101.
    on real estate, what law governs, 99-101.
    succession, governed by what law, 98-101.

Floyd R. Mechem, Professor of Law in the University of Chicago. Second Edition. $2.00.

Agency—Mechem on Agency. A treatise by Floyd R. Mechem. $4.00 net.

American Law—Andrews' American Law. Second Edition by J. D. Andrews. 2 vols. $12.00. Same, 1 vol. ed., $5.00 net.

Bailments and Carriers—Goddard's Outlines, by Edwin C. Goddard, Professor of Law in the University of Michigan. $2.50 net.

Bailments and Carriers—Van Zile, by Philip T. Van Zile, Dean Detroit College of Law. Second Ed. $5.00.

Bankruptcy—Bays. A handbook on Debtor, Creditor and Bankruptcy, by A. W. Bays. $1.50.

Banks and Banking. A handbook by A. W. Bays. $1.50.

Blackstone's Commentaries—Cooley. 4th Edition Commentaries on the Laws of England by William Blackstone, with a translation of all foreign words and phrases appearing in the text and very full and copious notes by Thomas M. Cooley. Fourth Edition by J. D. Andrews. 2 volumes $9.00 net. Same, 3rd Edition $6.00 net.

Business Methods and Finance—By George L. Corlis, Dean Benton College of Law.

Carriers—Hutchinson. The Law of Carriers. Second Ed. by Floyd R. Mechem. $4.00.

Code Pleading—Phillips. Principles of Pleadings in Actions under the Codes of Civil Procedure by G. L. Phillips. $4.00 net.

Commercial Law—Bays. American Commercial Law Series. 9 vols. $12.00. Separately per volume $1.50.

Commercial Law—Corlis. By George L. Corlis, Dean Benton College of Law. 1 volume.

Common Law Pleading—Andrews' Stephen's Pleadings. By Henry John Stephen. Second Edition by J. D. Andrews. $3.50 net.

Contracts—Anson. Second American Edition, by Jerome C. Knowlton, Professor of Law in the University of Michigan. $3.50 net.

Contracts—Bays. A handbook, by A. W. Bays. $1.50.

Contracts—Hammon. The General Principles of Contracts, by Louis L. Hammon. $5.00 net.

Contracts—Willis. A treatise by Hugh E. Willis, Professor of Law, University of Minnesota Law School. $2.00 net.

Corporations—Municipal—Elliott. Second Edition, by John E. Macy, Professor in Boston University Law School. $4.00 net.

Corporations—Bays. A handbook by A. W. Bays. $1.50.

Corporations—Marshall—[Private]. A treatise. Second Edition by William L. Marshall and William L. Clark. $4.00 net.

Corporations—Abbott—[Public]. A treatise by Howard S. Abbott. 1 volume $4.00.

Criminal Law—Clark & Marshall—Crimes. Second Edition by Herschell B. Lazell. $5.00 net.

Criminal Law and Procedure Outlines—Washburn. By Emery Washburn. Third Ed. by M. D. Ewell. $2.50 net.

Damages—Willis. A concise treatise by Hugh E. Willis, Professor of Law, University of Minnesota. $2.00 net.

Dictionary—Cyclopedic Law Dictionary—Words, Phrases, Maxims, Definitions, Translations Thumb Index. 1 large volume $6.00.

Dictionary—Kinney's Dictionary and Glossary. $4.00.

Evidence—Hammon. A treatise mon. $5.00 net.

Evidence—Hughes. An illus Thomas W. Hughes, Profes University of Illinois. $4.00

Evidence—Kennedy. A pract Richard Lee Kennedy. $2.0(

Evidence—Reynolds Theory of iam Reynolds. $3.00 net.

Evidence—Reynolds on Eviden and Cross Examination, Law

Insurance—Bays. A handbook,

Insurance—Kerr. $5.00.

International Law—Bordwell's W. P. Bordwell, Professor of Missouri. $3.50 net.

International Law—Taylor. of, by Hannis Taylor. $5.5(

Jurisprudence—Pattee. The Law, by W. S. Pattee, Dea University of Minnesota. $

Legal Ethics—Warvelle. A fessional conduct by George

Negotiable Instruments—Bays Alfred W. Bays. $1.50.

Negotiable Instruments—B Bunker, Professor of Law Michigan Law School. $3.5(

Negotiable Instruments—Ogde of the Indiana Law School.

Negotiable Instruments—Selov by Wm. H. Oppenheimer.

Partnership—Bays. A handbook

Partnership—Mechem. By Second edition, $2.50 net.

Partnership—Shumaker. By Second edition. $3.00 net.

Personal Property—Childs, by sometime Professor of La College of Law. $4.00 net.

Quizzers—Walsh. Students Q bers. Paper, each 50 cents

Real Property—Bays. A h Bays. $1.50.

Real Property—Tiffany, by 2 volumes. $10.00. Student's edition [2 volume

Real Property—Warvelle. E W. Warvelle. Second editi

Roman Law—Sandar's Justin American Ed. by W. E.

**Sales—A handbook by Alfre

Suretyship—Spencer. A tre and Guaranty, by Edward Marquette Univ., College of

Torts—Cooley. A new Law John Lewis. $5.00 net.

Torts—Cooley's Elements, by $3.50 net.

Trusts—Pound, by Roscoe Pou

STANDARD LAW SCHOOL CASE BO

dministration and Government—Goodnow's Cases on Government and A
tion, by Frank J. Goodnow, Eaton Professor of Administrative Law and
Science in Columbia University. 1 volume $2.50 net.

gency—Mechem's Cases on the Law of Agency, by Floyd R. Mechem, P
Law in the University of Chicago. 1 volume $3.00 net.

erican Administrative Law—Goodnow's Cases on American Administr
Including Public Officers and Extraordinary Legal Remedies, by Fran
now. 1 volume $6.00 net.

ppellate Practice—Sunderland's Cases on Appellate Practice, by Edson
land, Professor in the University of Michigan Law School. $4.50 net.

ailments and Carriers—Goddard's Cases on Bailments and Carriers, by
Goddard, Professor of Law in the University of Michigan. 1 volume

ode Pleading—Hinton's Cases Code Pleading Under Modern Codes, by
Hinton, Professor of Law, University of Missouri. 1 volume $4.00 ne

ode Pleading—Sunderland's Cases on Code Pleading, by Edson R. S
Professor in the University of Michigan Law School. $4.50 net.

ommercial Law—Bays' Cases on Commercial Law (in preparation).

ommon Law Pleading—Shipp and Daish's Cases on Common Law Plead
Richard Shipp and John B. Daish. 1 volume $2.50 net.

ommon Law Pleading—Sunderland's Cases on Common Law Pleading, by
Sunderland, Professor in the University of Michigan Law School. $4.

onflict of Laws, Cases. See International Law.

onstitutional Law—Boyd's Cases on American Constitutional Law, by C.
Second edition by C. E. Boyd $3.00 net.

riminal Law, Knowlton's Cases on Criminal Law, by Jerome C. Knowl
shall Professor of Law in the University of Michigan. 1 volume $3.00

riminal Procedure—Sunderland's Cases on Criminal Procedure, by Edso
derland, Professor of Law in the University of Michigan Law School.

amages—Russell's Cases, by Isaac Franklin Russell, Professor of Law in
University Law School. 1 volume $4.00 net.

omestic Relations—Holbrook's Cases, by Evans Holbrook, Professor of L
University of Michigan. (In Preparation.)

quity Pleading and Practice—Rush's Cases, by G. Fred Rush. $2.50.

quity Pleading and Practice—Sunderland's Cases on Equity Pleading and
by Edson R. Sunderland, Professor in the University of Michigan La
$4.50 net.

quity Pleading and Practice—Thompson's Cases on Equity Pleading and
by Bradley M. Thompson, Professor of Law in University of Michigan.

vidence—Sunderland's Cases on Evidence. By Edson R. Sunderland, Pr
the University of Michigan Law School. $4.50 net.

xtraordinary Legal Remedies—Goodnow's Cases on Officers, including
nary Legal Remedies, by Frank J. Goodnow of the Law Department of
University. 1 volume $5.00 net.

ternational Law—Dwyer's Cases Private International Law, second ed.,
W. Dwyer, of the Law Department, University of Michigan. $4.00 net.

egotiable Instruments, Bunker's Cases on Negotiable Instruments, by
Bunker, Professor of Law in the University of Michigan. 1 volume $4.

fficers—Goodnow's Cases on Law of Officers, including Extraordinary L
dies, by Frank J. Goodnow, of the Law Department of Columbia Uni
volume $5.00 net.

artnership—Mechem's Cases on Partnership, by Floyd R. Mechem. Seco
by Frank L. Sage, Professor of Law in the University of Michigan. 1 vol.

artnership—Enlarged Edition, Mechem's Cases, same as above with a
Supplement. 1 volume, third edition, $4.50 net.

rocedure—Sunderland's Cases on Procedure, 7 volumes $4.50 each (in pre

roperty—Rood's Cases on Property. Second Edition b J b

CPSIA information can be obtained at www.ICGtesting.com
Printed in the USA
BVOW02s1100230915

419332BV00025B/321/P

9 781330 042847